Studies from the Scriptures

A SURVEY OF THE OLD TESTAMENT

the Bible Jesus Used

John Stevenson

Redeemer Publishing

Scripture quotations taken from the New American Standard Bible®,
Copyright © 1960, 1962, 1963, 1968, 1971, 1972, 1973,
1975, 1977 by The Lockman Foundation
Used by permission (www.Lockman.org)

To My Brothers
David and Dennis

TABLE OF CONTENTS

Other books by John Stevenson:

Doctrines of the Bible: *Outlines in Systematic Theology*
Facing the Flames: *A Fire Fighter's Meditations on the
    Spiritual Life*
Genesis: *The Book of Beginnings, Genesis 1-22*
Joshua, Judges, and Ruth: *Victory, Defeat, and Hope in an
    Age of Heroes*
The Historical Books of the Old Testament: *One God, One
    People, One Land*
Ecclesiastes: *A Spiritual Journey*
Preaching from the Minor Prophets
Mark: *The Servant who Came to Save*
Luke: *In the Footsteps of the Savior*
Romans: *The Radical Righteousness of God*
First Corinthians: *Striving for Unity*
Galatians: *Our Freedom in Christ*
Ephesians: *The Wealth and Walk of the Christian*
Hebrews: *The Supremacy of the Savior*
James: *A Faith that Works*

A special and heartfelt thanks to
Lou Ellen Hardy
for her priceless work in
proofreading, questioning,
and suggesting

INTRODUCTION

The Bible of Jesus, Paul, the other apostles, and of the entire early church was the Old Testament Scriptures. This is not to discount the moving of the Holy Spirit or the value of the New Testament, but all of the writers of that New Testament assumed a prior knowledge of the Old Testament. It was their Bible. One of the reasons that a great deal of the church is immature today in its development is because of a weak understanding of the Old Testament. By ignoring the Old Testament, people have sought to build their theology on an inadequate foundation.

WHY STUDY THE OLD TESTAMENT?

If the truth be known, most of us are much better acquainted with the New Testament than we are with the Old Testament. For one thing, the New Testament is a lot smaller than the Old Testament. If you open your Bible to Matthew 1 and look to see what is left (not counting any index or maps), then you will quickly see that the majority of the Bible is within the Old Testament.

But is it necessary? Couldn't we get along quite nicely if we all merely hold to the New Testament? I want to suggest several reasons why a study of the Old Testament is important:

1.   The Old Testament is Foundational.

Do you want to know where it all started? You have to go to the Old Testament. Doctrines such as sin and salvation, man and his mandates, the kingdom and the Christ all find their foundational teachings in the Old Testament.

The Old Testament was the Bible that Jesus used. The writers of the New Testament regularly assumed that their readers were familiar with its message. So often a person begins to read the Bible for himself and where does he begin? The book of Revelation! He is immediately set upon with images and symbols of all sorts of things. Lions and lambs and witnesses and seals and trumpets and altars and beasts abound. Every single one of these images finds its origin in the Old Testament. It is assumed that the reader has this key to unlock the meaning of these symbols. Without that key, the book of Revelation is not a revelation at all.

2.   The Old Testament is Practical.

This might not seem so obvious when you first turn to the Old Testament. After all, the people of the Old Testament are far removed from us today. They lived in a different culture and in a different age. Yet there are some commonalities that we share.

- God has not changed. He is still the same God yesterday and today and forever (Hebrews 13:8).
- People have not changed. We go through the same sorts of struggles, temptations, doubts, and fears that they faced in the Old Testament.
- Truth has not changed. The things that applied in that day still apply today.

3.   The Old Testament Presents Christ.

Jesus illustrated this point on the road to Emmaus. He was with two of his disciples following the resurrection and they did not recognize Him. It is one of the heights of irony that these two disciples began to tell Jesus about Jesus. They told of His life and His ministry and His betrayal and arrest. They told of His death and His burial and His... well, they stopped at His burial. That was for them the end of the story. But it is here that Jesus stepped in.

> *And He said to them, "O foolish men and slow of heart to believe in all that the prophets have spoken! 26 Was it not necessary for the Christ to suffer these things and to enter into His glory?" 27 And beginning with Moses and with all the prophets, He explained to them the things concerning Himself in all the Scriptures. (Luke 24:25-27).*

Notice that Jesus pointed out to these blinded disciples that He was to be found in Moses and with all the prophets. Of His coming, He says in verse 25 that all the prophets have spoken.

- Not some of the prophets.
- Not a couple of verses here or there.
- All of the prophets.

If it is true that all of the prophets spoke of him, then it seems a reasonable deduction that we could turn to the writings of any of the prophets and we could find where they have spoken of Jesus.

4.   The Old Testament was Written for Us.

> *For whatever was written in earlier times was written for our instruction, that through perseverance and the encouragement of the Scriptures we might have hope (Romans 15:4).*

> *Now these things happened to them as an example, and they were written for our instruction, upon whom the ends of the ages have come. (1 Corinthians 10:11).*

When we study the Old Testament, we ought to recognize that there is a message that is being given on several levels. For example, when we read the creation account of Genesis 1, we see God interacting with creation.

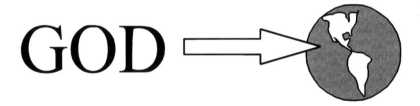

At the same time, we also ought to see another interaction taking place between Moses as the human author of this book and the original recipients of this writing, the Israelites in the wilderness. He has a particular purpose in mind that is specific to his audience and he writes so that they will learn some lessons that are significant to their own circumstances.

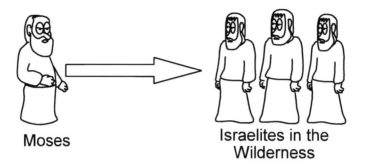

As we read the events of Genesis 1 while standing in the sandals of Moses and the Israelites who have just come out of Egypt, we shall see certain things come to light that we might not otherwise notice.

- The God who creates light and darkness is the same God who brought darkness over Egypt during the plagues.

- The God who separates the waters from the waters on the second day of creation is the same God who separated the waters of the Red Sea to deliver the Israelites from Pharaoh.

- The God who created the sun and the moon and the stars is the Creator of those things that were worshiped back in Egypt.

- While back in Egypt the various gods were worshiped in the form of all sorts of beasts and birds and creeping things, it is the God of Creation who first brought all of these into being.

- It is not only the Pharaoh of Egypt, but all men who are made in the image of God and this extends to both male and female.

When the Israelites in the wilderness are disheartened and discouraged and they think back to the gardens of Egypt and the food that was available there, they will be reminded that God has a better garden and that the same God who made Eden has promised them a land that is flowing with milk and honey.

Finally, when we have seen the message of the original narrative and then have seen it through the eyes of the original author and recipients, we will be ready to also see that there is a message here for us.

THE CANON OF THE OLD TESTAMENT

The Greek architects had an instrument that they used to measure various distances as they were designing and constructing a building. It was a straight rod with marks set into its side, much like our modern rulers.

- It had to be unbendable.
- It had to be dependable as to its straightness.

It was called a καυων (*kanon*). From this came the idea of a body of truth or a rule of faith. The same term is used by Paul in the New Testament when he says: *Peace and mercy to all who follow this **rule**, even to the Israel of God (Galatians 6:16, NIV).* This same word came to be used by Christians to describe those books which set the rule and standard of faith.

When we talk about canonizing someone, we speak of recognizing their authority. The Roman Catholic Church uses this term to confer sainthood. When the church speaks of "canon law" it refers to the infallible criteria by how things are to be measured. When we speak of the Canon of Scripture, we are speaking of that collection of writings which constitute the authoritative and final norm or standard of faith and practice. This means that we think of the Word of God as the measuring stick for our beliefs and for our lives. We use it to check our doctrine and our daily lifestyle.

Canonicity is the process by which the books of the Bible were gathered and collected so that they came to be regarded as the standard and norm for Christians. This means that canonicity refers to the church's recognition of the authority of the inspired writings. An important distinction must be made in that canonicity does not make a book into the word of God. Rather, canonicity is the process of recognizing that a book is the word of God.

THE BOOKS OF THE OLD TESTAMENT

The Old Testament which we have is made up of 39 books. The Hebrews numbered these as only 22 books -- they counted all of the Minor Prophets as a single book and, where we have 1st Samuel and 2nd Samuel and others like this, they counted each of these as a single book. In the same way, some books such as Ezra and Nehemiah were counted as a single book. These 22 books were divided in the Hebrew Bible into three groups:

Division	Books
Torah (Law)	Genesis, Exodus, Leviticus, Numbers, Deuteronomy
Navi'im (Prophets)	Former Prophets: Joshua, Judges-Ruth, Samuel, Kings
	Latter Prophets: Isaiah, Jeremiah-Lamentations, Ezekiel, The Twelve Minor Prophets
Kethuvim (Writings)	Psalms, Job, Proverbs, Song of Solomon, Ecclesiastes, Esther, Daniel, Ezra-Nehemiah, Chronicles

Jesus made reference to this same threefold division of the Old Testament in Luke 24:44 when he said, "Everything must be fulfilled that is written about me in the Law of Moses, the Prophets and the Psalms." Because the Psalms were the first book of the Writings, they were used as a title for the entire collection. We Christians hold to the same books that are found within the Hebrew Bible, but we have traditionally placed them into a different order.

1.   The Pentateuch (same as the Hebrew Torah).

2.   The Historical Books: Joshua through Esther.

3.   The Writings / Poetical Books: Job, Psalms, Proverbs, Ecclesiastes, Song of Solomon.

4.   The Prophetic Book (Major and Minor Prophets).

It should be noted that there is a similarity of this arrangement to the New Testament:

	Old Testament	New Testament
Foundations for belief	Law	Gospels
Histories	Historical Books	Acts
Writings	Poetical Books	Epistles
Prophecy	Prophets	Revelation

THE APOCRYPHA

After all of the books that make up our Old Testament had been written, a second collection of books began to emerge. It became known as the "Apocrypha," meaning "hidden away." The books of the Apocrypha were never accepted by the Jews as having been a part of their Scriptures.

Josephus, the Jewish general-turned scholar, wrote a rebuttal to anti-Jewish propaganda in the latter part of the first century. In this writing, Josephus describes the Hebrew canon of scripture that was recognized by the Jews of his day.

> For we have not an innumerable multitude of books among us, disagreeing from and contradicting one another [as the Greeks have], but only twenty-two books, which contain the records of all the past times; which are justly believed to be divine... (Contra Apion 1:8).

The same 39 books that we have in our Bible were condensed into the 22 books of the Hebrew Bible. For example, they consolidated a single book of Samuel and of Kings and of Chronicles. The Minor Prophets were grouped together into a single book called the Twelve.

Notice that even in that day Josephus recognized that the various books of the Bible did not contradict each other. He goes on to group the books of the Scriptures into the three common divisions which we have described.

> ...and of them, five belong to Moses, which contain his laws and the traditions of the origin of mankind till his death... The prophets, who were after Moses, wrote down what was done in their times in thirteen books. The remaining four books contain hymns to God and precepts for the conduct of human life. (Contra Apion 1:8).

Josephus puts the number of books in the Hebrew Bible at 22 and divides them into the following categories:

(a)   Moses (Torah).
(b)   The Prophets (Nevi'im).
(c)   Hymns & Precepts (Ketuvim).

The words of Josephus are important because they give us a point of view that is unbiased by Christianity. Specifically, he says that the Apocrypha did not have the same recognized authority because "there has not been an exact succession of prophets" since the time that the writing of the Scriptures ended.

According to Josephus, the test of authority for the Scriptures was that they were written by one who was recognized as a prophet. Who did the recognizing? The previous prophets! But then, a day came when the last of the prophets had spoken. It was the prophet Malachi. He foretold that the Lord would come and that just prior to His coming He would be announced by Elijah. But that is not all. Notice what Josephus has to say about the Apocrypha.

> It is true, our history has been written since Artaxerxes, very peculiarly, but has not been esteemed of the like authority with the former by our forefathers, because there has not been an exact succession of prophets since that time. (Contra Apion 1:8).

Josephus tells us that the Jews rejected the Apocrypha because it had not been penned by a prophet and because there had been no unbroken line of prophets who spoke and who wrote the words of God.

THE TRANSMISSION OF THE OLD TESTAMENT

Since inspiration, by its very definition, extends only to the original manuscripts of the Bible, and since none of the original manuscripts are in existence today, how can we rely on the accuracy of our modern Hebrew Old Testament? The answer to this question is found in the science of Textual Criticism.

Textual criticism is scholarly work with available manuscripts aimed at the recovery within the limits of possibility of the original text. We do not have the original papyri that Moses used to write the Torah. All we have are copies of copies of copies, etc. Textual criticism involves carefully examining and comparing those copies to find out what is the original text. This has been a very difficult study with regards to the Old Testament. The areas of study fall into four major categories:

1.   The Masoretic Texts.

The Masoretes were a group of Hebrew scholars who worked at preserving the Scriptures and the traditions of the Jews (the word means "tradition"). There were initially two groups:

(1)   The Eastern Masoretes were located in Mesopotamia.
(2)   The Western Masoretes began in Tiberias.

The Western Masoretes eventually gained in prominence and it is the result of their work that survives today. The Masoretes developed a system of vowel-points, but there was initial resistance to this among certain Jewish groups who felt that this was a sacrilegious adding to the Word of God.

2.   The Septuagint Family.

This is the Greek translation of the Hebrew Scriptures, created in 250 B.C. in Alexandria, Egypt. The problem with the Septuagint was that it made no attempt to be a word-for-word translation. It was, instead, a "Dynamic Equivalent," much as is the New International Version. There were also wide variations within different copies of the Septuagint.

3.   The Samaritan Pentateuch.

The Samaritan Pentateuch differs from the Masoretic Text in about 6000 instances (most of these are mere differences in spelling). One interesting difference is seen in Exodus 20:17 where an eleventh commandment is inserted - to build a sanctuary upon Mount Gerizim. In about 1900 of these instances, the Samaritan Pentateuch agrees with the Septuagint against the Masoretic Text.

4.   Dead Sea Scrolls.

The discovery of the Dead Sea scrolls had a profound impact upon Old Testament Textual Criticism. On the one hand, there was evidence that the Masoretic Scrolls were very accurate in their rendition of the Hebrew Bible. At the same time, it was discovered that there were some Hebrew manuscripts which seemed to follow the Septuagint reading. This indicates that perhaps some of the differences in the Masoretic Text versus the Septuagint are not just translational but point to differences in copying transmission.

HIGHER CRITICISM AND THE DOCUMENTARY HYPOTHESIS

When we speak of Higher Criticism, that is to be understood in contrast to Lower Criticism. Lower Criticism involves the study of the text itself, trying to determine what was the original text from a study of the various copies in our possession. By contrast, Higher Criticism looks at how the text came to be written in the first place, noting the historical circumstances behind the writing to determine what role these circumstances might have played.

> LOWER CRITICISM is the science of determining the historical background and grammar of the original text.
> HIGHER CRITICISM often involves a presupposition against the authenticity of the Bible.

From the very beginning the Christian church has believed the Scriptures to be true. Both Protestants and the Roman Catholic Church were unified in holding to this position. It was not until the Enlightenment – the modern rationalistic movement beginning in the 1780's – that this began to change.

1. Jean Astruc.

Astruc was a French professor of medicine. He wrote a book in 1753 entitled *Conjectures Concerning the Original Memoranda* which it Appears Moses Used to Compose the Book of Genesis. He suggested that when Moses wrote the book of Genesis, he used two source documents. He reasoned that this accounted for the two different names for God found there.

> Astruc held that Moses wrote from various sources. But later critics maintained that Moses could not even write. Now we know that Egyptian scribes could write in both hieroglyphs and in cuneiform.

Yahweh pointed to the "J Document."
Elohim came from the "E Document."

There was no proof for this theory. Astruc's view was based only upon supposition. His followers went on to say that the entire

Pentateuch was to be divided up in this same way.

2.   Geddes (1800).

Geddes was a Scottish Roman Catholic priest who held that there was a mass of fragments (not actual documents) that were pieced together by a redactor 500 years after the death of Moses.

3.   Heinrich Ewald (1830).

Ewald held that the first six books of the Bible had originally been written by a single Elohist author, but that a later parallel document arose which used the name "Jehovah." A later editor is said to have taken excerpts from the J Document and inserted them into the E Document.

Ewald later changed his theory to say that there had been five different editors, the last one in the days of King Uzziah. He also held that the book of Deuteronomy was an independent work added about 500 B.C. This became known as the D Document.

4.   Karl H. Graf.

In the 1860's, Graf suggested that the J Document had been written first, placing the order of JEDP.

5.   Julius Wellhausen (1878).

Wellhausen took Graf's revised documentary hypothesis and popularized it, putting it into evolutionary terms that had become popular through the influence of Charles Darwin.

- The earliest parts of the Pentateuch came from the J Document (850 B.C.) and the E Document (750 B.C.).
- Deuteronomy was written in Josiah's day and incorporated into the J Document.
- The priestly legislation in the E Document was the work of Ezra and is referred to as the P Document.

It has been said that you can put three higher critics into a room, wait an hour, and you will have sixteen opinions. It was not long before new theories expanded upon the themes introduced by Graf and Wellhausen. It was suggested that a later editor brought together all of the conglomeration of documents by about 200 B.C. to form the Pentateuch which we have today. Why was it considered to be necessary to place the writing of the Bible so late in history? Because it was recognized that the Bible contains a great deal of prophecy and an embarrassing amount of it was fulfilled in historic times. Those who had adopted the position that there is no such thing as future prophecy were forced to come up with theories to explain those prophecies away and so it was insisted that they had been written after the events they had foretold.

Wellhausen's view swept across Europe, England and America. All "learned" people concluded that Moses did not write the Pentateuch. As liberals came to the pulpits, they did not preach against the Bible; they merely ignored the Bible, preaching a message of the fatherhood of God and the brotherhood of man. All of this was in spite of the fact that not one single scrap of objective evidence existed for the history of any source document.

J Document	God seen as Israel's national god, judging all men in righteousness according to their deeds.
E Document	God is seen in theological terms, revealing himself only through dreams, visions, or angels. God seen as the transcendental one, separated by a great gulf from all of his creatures.
P Document	The focus is upon man's activities to please God.

Since that time, the JEDP Theory has fallen into some disrepute. In 1979, Jewish archaeologist Gabriel Barkay was excavating some graves south of the Hinnon Valley. One grave contained an amulet around a skeleton's neck. Inside the amulet was a tiny scroll containing the Aaronic benediction of Numbers 6. This find was dated at the time of Jeremiah, before the P Document is supposed to have been written.

Dr. K. A. Kitchen points out that the use of several different names to indicate both people as well as deities was a common practice in the ancient world, yet no one ever thinks of assigning redactors to various ancient inscriptions. In the same poem, Baal can be called Baal, Aliyn Baal, Dagan's Son, or Rider of Clouds.

Wellhausen did not base his theory upon archaeological finds. There was no archaeology to speak of in that day. Instead,

Wellhausen based his views upon Hegel's prevailing philosophy. This was an ideological theory instead of one based upon facts. Wellhausen lived in a day of high anti-Semitism and anti-Catholicism and his theory reflected an obvious bias.

In answer to Wellhausen and the advocates of the JEDP theory, the following points can be presented:

- Moses was qualified to write the book of Genesis.

    It was argued by Wellhausen and his supporters that Moses could not have written the Pentateuch because writing was unknown at that early date and that Moses would have been an illiterate nomad. Today we know this is far from the truth. We have examples of writing that can be dated far earlier than Moses.

    Moses was scholastically qualified to write Genesis, having been trained in the wisdom of the Egyptians (Acts 7:22). He was prepared to understand any and all of the available records, manuscripts, and oral traditions that might have been at his disposal.

    It was claimed by Wellhausen that Moses could not have written the Pentateuch because writing was unknown that early in either the Sinai or Canaan. Since that time, finds at Amarna, Nuzi, Ras Shamra and Mari have demonstrated that Semitic languages akin to Hebrew were already being written long before Moses.

    It is true that we have found almost no papyrus documents in Palestine aside from the caves around the Dead Sea. There is a reason for this. Papyrus does not survive for long periods of time in moist climates. Only in the hot, dry climates of Egypt and around the shores of the Dead Sea have these materials survived the ravages of time and weather.

- The Style of Genesis reflects an Egyptian influence.

    The author of Genesis has a very definite insight and knowledge of the history, customs, and culture of Egypt. Furthermore, the Pentateuch contains more Egyptian loan words than any other of the books of the Bible.

- The unity of the book of Genesis reflects a single author.

    Professor Gary A. Rendsburg, chairman of the Department of Jewish Studies at Rutgers University in New Brunswick, New Jersey, makes the following observation:

> ...there is much more uniformity and much less fragmentation in the book of Genesis than generally assumed. The standard division of Genesis into J, E, and P strands should be discarded. This method of source criticism is a method of an earlier age, predominantly of the 19th century. If new approaches to the text, such as literary criticism of the type advanced here, deem the Documentary Hypothesis unreasonable and invalid, then source critics will have to rethink earlier conclusions and start anew (1986:105).

The actual books of the Pentateuch often contain large paralleled outlines and chiasms that only fit if they are a unified whole rather than a conglomeration of isolated parts. For example, the entire life of Abraham is presented in a chiastic format showing that it is a unified whole.

Furthermore, there is a complete absence of Persian loan words in the Pentateuch. We would expect the complete opposite from a work that was completed after the Babylonian Captivity and during the Persian period.

• Although the differences in the divine names was the starting point for higher criticism, these are no longer considered to be especially significant by the higher critics. It is now understood that there were good reasons for variations in keeping with the message of the book.

Genesis 1	Genesis 2
Formulaic: Names and dates.	A story teller style.
God is transcendent.	God is imminent and anthropomorphic.
P Document.	J Document.

This was originally thought to set the pattern for the J and the P Documents in the rest of the book of Genesis. What was ignored in all of this analysis was the tendency of Hebrew authors to write using parallelisms. Such a style is found all throughout both Old and New Testaments. This kind of parallelism is an intrinsic part of all ancient writing. By the same token, changes of topic often call for a corresponding change of style.

- The New Testament attributes the various portions of the Pentateuch to Moses without regard to the various names that are used.

In conclusion, we must stress that there is a complete lack of any objective evidence for the existence of any of the supposed source documents. The Documentary Hypothesis remains a hypothesis without documents.

THE WORLD OF THE OLD TESTAMENT

The world of the Old Testament is the world of the Fertile Crescent. This area of relative fertility extends in a giant arc from the Persian Gulf to the Nile River. Joining these two great river valleys is a narrow land bridge known alternately as Palestine, Israel or Canaan. This land bridge effectively joins three continents together. It is not without reason that the Israelites considered the land of Israel to be at the center of the world. Two of the world's earliest centers of civilization grew up on either side of this land bridge.

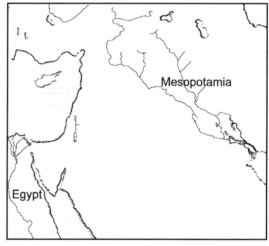

- Mesopotamia: The name comes from the later Greek and means "land between the two rivers." It was known to the Jews as Aram Nahara'im — "Aram of the two rivers."

This area saw the rise of cities and civilization a thousand years before Abraham appeared on the scene. Archaeologists have uncovered evidence and even written records of kings and kingdoms and conquests that paint a rich and vivid picture of life in this time.

- Egypt

The Land of Egypt was the land of the Nile. Although Egypt today has some very specific longitudinal boundaries, the Egypt of the ancient world was located along the Nile. Civilization grew up early along the Nile and reached a high level of sophistication. By the time that Abraham came to Egypt, the Pyramids were already a thousand years old.

The lands of Mesopotamia and Egypt make for an interesting contrast as the two centers of early civilization:

Mesopotamia	Egypt
The flooding of the Euphrates and Tigris was irregular and destructive.	The flooding of the Nile was both predictable and beneficial.
No natural borders to keep out invaders.	Bounded by natural borders of desert and sea.
Ruled by a large succession of rulers of differing nationalities.	Most of Egypt's history saw a dynastic succession of domestic rulers.
People tended to have a pessimistic outlook on life.	Literature demonstrates a cheerful outlook on life.
The gods of Mesopotamia were cold and cruel and could not be trusted.	The gods of Egypt were considered to be good and benevolent.

Very early in the history of Mesopotamia we see the construction of ziggurats — large temple towers that are built at the center of each metropolis. These were places of worship and usually contained various sorts of astrological symbols. By contrast, Egypt was known for its pyramids. Although the shape of the ziggurat and the pyramid are somewhat similar, they represent two

Ziggurat

17

greatly diverse ideas.

Ziggurat	Pyramid
Served as a temple	Served as a tomb
Located at the center of the city	Located along the west bank of the Nile
Contained a stairway to the top	Contained a burial place at the center
Constructed of bricks	Constructed of stone

The origin of the ziggurat is commonly thought to be reflected in the account of the Tower of Babel where men determined to build a tower to the heavens.

THE LAND OF CANAAN

The land of Canaan acts as a narrow land bridge between Mesopotamia and the continent of Africa. This is a relatively small area of land, no larger in area than the state of Maryland. The name Palestine takes its name from the ancient name *Peleset*, meaning "land of the Philistines."

1.   The Topography of Canaan.

Canaan is one of the most diverse lands in the world. Within its small area, one can find snow capped mountains, fertile plains, steaming deserts and lush forests. It is home both to sparkling waterways full of fish as well as the most desolate body of water in the world.

a.   The Coastal Plain.

The coastline of Canaan is devoid of any natural harbors from Tyre all the way down to Egypt. The plain itself is generally low, fertile and open. It is broken only once where the Mount Carmel Promontory juts out into the Mediterranean.

b.   The Central Mountain Range.

A long ridge of mountains runs parallel to the Coastal Plain from the Mountains of Lebanon all the way down to the tip of the Sinai Peninsula. The lowest point of this ridge is 1500 feet and many of its segments rise to twice that height. This Central Spine is a natural impediment to east west travel. At some places it consists of up to five parallel ridges, each separated by deep valleys. This Mountain Range is broken only once by the long Valley of Jezreel, also known by the more popular name of Armageddon.

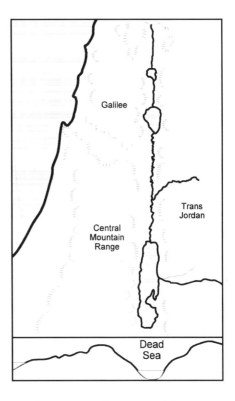

c.   The Jordan River Valley.

This valley is a part of the Afro Arabian Rift Valley, one of the longest and the deepest fissures in the world, following a geological fault line from the Amanus Mountains of southeastern Turkey through Syria, Lebanon and Israel, down the Gulf of Aqaba and then running the entire length of the Red Sea to Ethiopia and then continuing southward to become a part of the Great African Rift Valley.

The Jordan River finds its major source in the melting snows of Mount Hermon which towers 9,200 feet above sea level. Hundreds of small streams cascade down to flow into Lake Hula. In Abram's day, Lake Hula was a shallow marsh. Since the formation of the nation of Israel in 1948, the lake has been drained for farmland. This has created an ecological imbalance in the Sea of Galilee. The swamp used to act as a natural filter, straining out any impurities from the waters which flowed southward into the Sea of Galilee.

The Sea of Galilee rests in the crater of an extinct volcano which, in ages past, spewed out its lava over the Golan Heights to the east. The Sea is 600 feet below sea level and is surrounded on all sides by steep hills.

From the Sea of Galilee, the Jordan River runs south down the sunken rift. This narrow valley used to be a fertile forest full of wildlife, including lions and boar. The name Jordan derives from a verb meaning "to descend." It flows downhill in its long, meandering course until it reached the Dead Sea.

The shore of the Dead Sea is the lowest point on the surface of the earth, lying 1300 feet below sea level. The salt level of this sea is six times that of the ocean and, as a result, no fish can live in its waters.

d.   The Transjordan Plateau.

Rising up sharply from the Jordan Valley is a high, fertile tableland between 30 to 80 miles in width and stretching from Damascus to the Gulf of Aqaba. The northern regions of this tableland are well watered and fertile. To the east of this plateau, the land gives way to the impassible Desert of Arabia.

2.   Valleys and Rivers of Canaan.

We have already mentioned the Jordan River and its river valley as the primary river of Canaan. Most of the other rivers and valleys flow east and west and intersect with the Jordan.

The Jezreel Valley is the one major break in the Central Mountain Range as it moves from Lebanon to the Negev, the desert in the south. This wide valley provides some of the richest farming lands in all of Canaan. There are three rivers that run into the Jordan from the east. They formed boundaries for those lands.

• The Yarmuk River is the northernmost of these rivers. It serves today as the boundary between the modern countries of Syria and Jordan. In Old Testament times it was the boundary between Bashan to the north and Gilead to the south.

- The Jabbok River

  The Hebrew word "Jabbok" means "to wrestle" and it was on the bank of this river that Jacob had his famous wrestling match with an angel.

- The Arnon River

  The Arnon has formed a very deep wadi (canyon) over the years and this became the traditional northern boarder for the land of Moab.

3.   The Climate of Canaan.

In Egypt, the chief deities were the sun and the Nile River. The most important deity of the Canaanites was Baal, the storm god of wind and rain. It never needed to rain in Egypt or Mesopotamia, since their river systems were fed by mountains hundreds of miles away. Canaan, on the other hand, had no great rivers and depended heavily upon the regular rainfall to feed the small mountain streams which irrigated the land. The chief deity of the Canaanites was Baal, the god of rain and thunder.

The "Early Rains" begin in October and the rainy season continues through until the "Latter Rains" of April and May. The heaviest rainfall comes during the winter months. There is not a drop of rain from June to September.

The topography of the country is broken enough to provide some striking local variations in temperature. In summer along the Coastal Plains, the winds tend to hold down temperatures from reaching oppressive levels. Further inland, where the wind has lost its affect, the temperatures can rise to stifling degrees.

In the winter months along the Coastal Plain the climate is mild and frost is virtually unknown, due to the incoming wind of the Mediterranean Sea. As one travels up into the mountains, temperatures decrease markedly with height. The winter months in the mountain region produce a long lying snow cover.

4. Major Routes of Travel.

There were two major north-south highways that ran through Canaan.

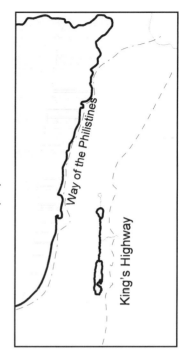

*   The King's Highway came south from Damascus and ran along the eastern bank of the Jordan River and made its way south all the way to the Gulf of Aqaba. Because of the difficulty of traversing some of the deeper river canyons, it followed a path about 25 miles to the east of the Jordan River.

*   The Way of the Sea (also known as the Way of the Philistines) cut through Galilee, passing by the ancient city of Megiddo and then along the Mediterranean as it made its way to Egypt. This pass became renown for the many battles that have been fought here and gives rise to the symbolism of the book of Revelation that speaks of the final conflict between good and evil.

*   There was also a route that forded the Jordan River near Jericho and which ran across the central mountain range to link up to the Way of the Philistines. This would be the route that the Israelites would take to enter the land in the days of Joshua.

THE HISTORICAL BACKDROP OF THE OLD TESTAMENT

1. The Early Bronze Age (3300-2000 B.C.).

Very early in human history we see the rise of advanced civilizations in both Mesopotamia and Egypt. There are roads and kingdoms and cities and peoples and tribes throughout this entire region, but the highest degree of civilization tends to congregate around these two river valleys.

It is at the close of this period that we see Abraham leaving his home in Ur of the Chaldees and following the line of the Fertile Crescent to come to the land of Canaan.

2.   The Middle Bronze Age (2000-1350 B.C.).

This is the era of the Patriarchs. Egypt sees the rise and fall of the Middle Kingdom while in Mesopotamia, the fall of the Sumerian culture gives rise to the Amorites, the Kassites and other invading Semitic groups. It is during this time of great upheaval that the little band of Israelites move down into Egypt in the days of Jacob and Joseph.

Israel is not the only group to migrate to Egypt during this period. Another Semitic people known to us as the Hyksos also invade Egypt and even rule for a time over that land, establishing their own dynasty before being driven off.

Although there is some disagreement among scholars as to the date of the Exodus, for the purposes of our class I will be using the traditional date according to the Masoretic Text, placing it at around 1440 B.C. and therefore still within the Middle Bronze Age.

3.   The Late Bronze Age (1350-1200 B.C.).

This is the period of the Judges. The Israelites are in the land, not as a united nation, but as a divided group of tribes with little or no unity.

4.   Iron Age (1200 B.C.).

Although there were limited uses of iron prior to this period, it is at about 1200 B.C. that the secret of smelting iron begins to make itself known among the more advanced cultures of the ancient world. For the first two hundred years of this era it would be a carefully guarded secret just as atomic and nuclear weapons were a carefully guarded secret during the 20th century.

In Judges we read of how the Israelites were forced to contend with the iron chariots of their enemies (Judges 1:19, 4:3; 4:13). Even in the days of King Saul, the Philistines kept their monopoly over the secret of iron working.

> *Now no blacksmith could be found in all the land of Israel, for the Philistines said, "Lest the Hebrews make swords or spears." 20 So all Israel went down to the Philistines, each to sharpen his plowshare, his mattock, his axe, and his hoe. 21 And the charge was two-thirds of a shekel for the plowshares, the mattocks, the forks, and the axes, and to fix the hoes. (1 Samuel 13:19-21).*

This monopoly prevented the Israelites from owning modern weapons and gave rise to the battle cry, "Beat your plowshares into swords, and your pruning hooks into spears" (Joel 3:10).

The beginning of the iron age also sees a migration of a group known to us as the "sea peoples." They attempt to invade Egypt and are repulsed by Rameses III. A portion of this group is thought to have settled along the coastlands of southern Palestine. These people were known as the Peleset. We know them as the Philistines.

5.   The United Monarchy.

It was only under the leadership of Saul, David, and Solomon that the 12 tribes of Israel joined to become a single nation. Prior to the coming of these kings, the tribes had been divided and sometimes even in conflict with one another.

The period from 1200-800 B.C. is analogous to the Dark Ages of the Medieval Period. The superpowers in Egypt and Mesopotamia waned and it was during this time that David and Solomon were able to exert considerable influence over the Levant.

6.   The Divided Kingdom.

The Kingdom of Israel did not survive long after the death of Solomon. Within a short time it divided into two separate kingdoms.

*   The Southern Kingdom of Judah
*   The Northern Kingdom of Israel (also known as Ephraim)

These two kingdoms were in competition with one another and even occasionally fought one another on the battlefield. In the southern kingdom there were a series of revivals where the people sometimes would turn back to the Lord. In the northern kingdom, there were no such spiritual revivals.

7.   Assyria and the Fall of the Northern Kingdom of Israel.

The Northern Kingdom of Israel fell to the Assyrians in 721 B.C. Most of the inhabitants of the land were taken away into captivity and resettled east of Mesopotamia. Other conquered peoples were resettled in the land that had been vacated and these peoples intermarried with the surviving Israelites of the land. It is from these descendants that we have the Samaritans of New Testament times.

8.   Judah and Babylon.

The Assyrian Empire eventually fell into a state of decline as her surrounding enemies collaborated together to bring about her downfall. A coalition of Babylon and Media eventually succeeded in destroying the capital city of Nineveh in 612 B.C. These forces were led by a young Chaldean prince known to us as Nebuchadnezzar.

The Southern Kingdom of Judah now found itself between the two superpowers of Babylon and Egypt. Jerusalem eventually fell to the Babylonian King Nebuchadnezzar. He brought about three successive deportations, at the end of which Jerusalem was destroyed and the Temple was burned to the ground in 586 B.C.

9.   The Babylonian Captivity.

While Jeremiah and Ezekiel relate the successive deportations and the events that were taking place in Judah, the book of Daniel tells us of events that took place in Babylon during the captivity.

10.   Post Exilic Israel.

Ezra and Nehemiah tell of the return of the Jews from captivity and of the rebuilding of the Temple (Ezra) and of the walls of Jerusalem (Nehemiah). The events of the book of Esther take place in far-off Persia during this period.

GENESIS
The Book of Beginnings

The word "genesis" is synonymous with beginnings. When we speak of the genesis of a thing, we are referring to its origins. The book of Genesis is a book of beginnings. It relates a number of beginnings:

- The beginning of the heavens and the earth.
- The beginning of mankind.
- The beginning of marriage and family.
- The beginning of sin and death.
- The beginning of the nations.
- The beginning of the people of Israel.

Genesis is foundational to the Bible. Every major theme within the Bible finds its origins in Genesis. Indeed, the rest of the Bible would be incomprehensible without the doctrinal foundation which is set down in this first book.

THE TITLE AND OUTLINE OF THE BOOK

1.   The Hebrew Title.

The Old Testament, including Genesis, was originally written in Hebrew. The Hebrews commonly took the first line of a book and made that the title. Thus they called this book בְּרֵאשִׁית (*BeRishyth*), "In the beginning."

2.   The Greek Title.

Our title "Genesis" is taken from the Septuagint, the Greek translation of the original Hebrew Bible — Γενεσις (*Genesis*) — it means "beginnings." That is a good title for this book. In the Septuagint, the phrase Βιβλος Γενεσις (*Biblos Genesis*) is found nine different times. Each time it is translated: *"These are the generations of..."*

The book of Genesis has its own internal outline which is based upon the repetition of this same Hebrew phrase *elleh toledoth* ("these are the generations").

"THESE ARE THE GENERATIONS OF..."		
Formula	**Contents**	**Location**
In the beginning God...	Creation	1:1 - 2:3
1. This is the account of the heaven and the earth	Creation	2:4 - 4:26
2. This is the written account of Adam's Line	Genealogy: Seth to Noah	5:1 - 6:8
3. This is the account of Noah	Flood & Covenant	6:9 - 9:29
4. This is the account of Shem, Ham & Japheth	Table of Nations & Babel	10:1 - 11:9
5. This is the account of Shem	Genealogy: Shem to Abraham	11:10-26
6. This is the account of Terah	Story of Abraham	11:27 - 25:11
7. This is the account of Abraham's son Ishmael	Genealogy of Ishmael	25:12-18
8. This is the account of Abraham's son Isaac	Transition of blessing from Isaac to Jacob	25:19 - 35:29
9. This is the account of Esau	Genealogy of Esau	36:1-43
10. This is the account of Jacob	Joseph & Israel in Egypt	37:1 - 50:26

Notice that there is a symmetrical pattern which finds Abraham at its center. The entire first half of the book moves toward Abraham and the entire latter part of the book flows from his life and from the covenant promises that are given to him.

Adam →	Abraham	← Israel in Egypt
Genesis 2:4 - 11:26		Genesis 11:27 - 50:26
5 *Toledoth* from Adam to Abraham		5 *Toledoth* from Abraham to Israel

Thus, the person of Abraham stands at the center and as the pivotal point of the book of Genesis. He is the father of the nation through whom all of the world is to be blessed. He stands in contrast to Adam through whom all the world was cursed.

The first 11 chapters of Genesis form a prologue to the rest of the Pentateuch. This prologue is worded in cosmic terms, taking in all of mankind and all of the world.

GENESIS 1-11	GENESIS 12-50
Events predominant • Creation • The Fall into sin • The Flood • The Tower of Babel	Persons predominant • Abraham • Isaac • Jacob • Joseph
The Race as a Whole	The Family of Abraham
Over 2000 years	*250 years*

The New Testament counterpart to Genesis is the book of Revelation. What is introduced in the book of Genesis finds its conclusion in Revelation.

Genesis	**Revelation**
Creation of the heavens and earth.	A new heaven and a new earth.
The Tree of Life in the Garden.	The Tree of Life in the New Jerusalem.
A river runs through the Garden.	A river runs through the New Jerusalem.
The first marriage: Adam and Eve.	The last marriage: The last Adam to the church.

The beginning of the career of Satan.	The end of Satan's career: The Lake of Fire.
Death enters.	Death is destroyed.
Man lost privileges because of sin.	Man regains privileges because of Christ's payment for sin.
Beginning of sorrow, pain, and death.	Christ wipes away all tears.
The first murder.	No more death.
The beginning of Babylon.	Babylon destroyed.

Throughout Genesis we see God's blessings and provision for man and man's failure to appropriate that grace. Ironically, this is illustrated by comparing the first and last verses of the book.

| Genesis begins with God | *In the beginning God created...* |
| Genesis ends with a corpse | *...in a coffin in Egypt* |

But this does not mean that Genesis is a book without hope, for even in recording the death and burial of Joseph in Egypt, there is a continuing promise of a redemption to come.

AN OVERVIEW OF THE CREATION ACCOUNT

1.	The Similarity to the Babylonian Creation Account.

	Scholars have made much of the fact that other creation accounts in other cultures predate Moses and the Israelites in the wilderness. Of particular interest is one such account known as the Enuma Elish found in Mesopotamia.

	It was customary in the very earliest written history to name a book or a scroll after the first word or phrase found in body of the work. The Enuma Elish ("When on high") draws its title from the first sentence of its narrative.

When on high the heaven had not been named, firm ground below had not been named...

The text was found written on seven tablets, but this has no bearing on the seven days of the Genesis account. If the tablets had been larger then there would only have been six. The narrative tells the story of how mankind was created as a chance result of a war between the gods.

This account is only superficially related to the Genesis account. Since the initial discovery of the seven tablets, other copies have been found relating the same story but on ten tablets. There is a real difference between the Genesis account and the creation accounts of other pagan religions. In other ancient religious systems, the natural world was seen as a manifestation of all of the deities - the sun, moon, stars, oceans, storms. The cosmos always had the status of deity. The Bible is unique in that the cosmos is merely creation. Only God is God.

2.   The Nature of the Two Creation Accounts.

A reading of Genesis 1-2 will show immediately that we have two separate and distinct accounts of creation that can be compared and contrasted.

GENESIS 1	GENESIS 2
The heavens and the earth are created in six days.	Creation of the man and the woman (no time element mentioned).
Shows man in his cosmic setting.	Shows man as central to God's purpose.
A panoramic view of creation as a whole.	A detailed view of one particular aspect of creation.
Centers on God creating the heavens and the earth.	Centers on man as the crowning of God's creation.

Rather than contradicting, these two accounts are complimentary. Indeed, this method of first giving a panoramic view and then coming back to focus on important details is found all through Genesis. For example, in the account of Jacob and Esau, Esau's story comes first, but it is Jacob's which is more fully developed and which holds the place of higher importance to the theme of the book.

THEORIES OF CREATION

1.   Supernatural versus Evolutionary.

The Supernaturalist says that creation occurred in a way that is completely foreign to anything that may be observed today. The creation account indicates that God has completed his creative work (Genesis 2:1-3).

On the other hand, there are Christians who believe that God may have acted through evolutionary means to bring about creation. It is true that God often works through what we think of as "natural processes." They are in reality His regular and faithful workings.

2.   A superficial appearance of history.

The description that we have of God's creative work seems to imply creation with an appearance of age. This is vividly seen in the creation of man. On the day that Adam was created, how old was he? He was one day old! But the Scriptures seem to describe him as a full-grown man rather than as a baby. The implication is that he was created with an appearance of age.

The same is seen of animals and plant life. We do not read that God created seedlings, but rather that He created trees yielding fruit that had within them seeds for perpetuating further growth (Genesis 1:12). When we were children, we used to discuss what came first, the chicken or the egg. The Biblical answer is that God created egg-laying chickens who looked and acted every bit like those who had been hatched and had grown to adulthood.

3.   The Gap Theory.

This view places a great chronological gap between Genesis 1:1 and 1:2 during which the earth was destroyed and then recreated. According to this theory, millions of years ago God created a perfect heaven and earth. This universe continued in a perfect state until Satan rebelled by desiring to become like God (Isaiah 14:12-17). Because of Satan's fall, sin entered the universe. As a result, the earth became *"formless and void"* until a global ice age swept over the earth as light and heat were removed. The six days which follow refer to the **reconstruction** of the earth.

Support for the Theory	Objections to the Theory
The verb *hayeta* in Genesis 1:2 can be translated "became" so that we could read that "the earth **became** without form and void."	The normal rendering of *hayeta* is "was" and indicates a state of being. To translate it differently would mandate that several factors take place that are not present in this verse.
The words *tohu wabohu* ("formless and void") are said to refer to a destruction which took place after God's original creation. In Jeremiah 4:23 and Isaiah 34:11 these words describe a destruction.	The words *tohu wabohu* ("formless and void") need not describe destruction. They can just as easily describe an unconstructed state.
Isaiah 45:18 says that God did not create the earth void (*tohu*) while Genesis 1:2 says that the earth was now void. It is reasoned that the earth must have come to be in this manner after its original creation.	Isaiah 45:18 simply tells us that God's intention for the earth in its completed form was that it would not be *tohu*, but rather that it might be inhabited. The prophet is simply stating the purpose of creation.
The darkness which characterized the formless and void condition is indicative of evil.	Darkness does not always indicate evil. Both light and darkness existed upon the finished earth and it was still said to be good.

As a technical footnote, it should be added that there are two situations in which the verb היה (*hayah*) can be translated as "became" rather than "was."

- It can be used to describe the resulting state of being with a word that is preceded by the preposition ל or כ. Thus Genesis 2:7 describes how man became a living soul (לְנֶפֶשׁ חַיָּה). In the same way, Genesis 3:22 has God saying that "the man has become like one of us (הָיָה כְּאַחַד מִמֶּנּוּ)."

- It can be connected to a verse in a causal consecutive chain where a causal relationship exists between the two words so that the present state of being exists because of the action of the previous verb. An example of this is seen in Genesis 25:27 where "the boys grew up and Esau became (וַיְהִי) a skillful hunter" (Esau becoming a skillful hunter depended upon the boys growing up).

Neither of these two situations take place in this verse. It can therefore be seen that the Gap Theory does not fit the grammar of the Hebrew text.

4.   The Day/Age Theory.

This view says that the six days of creation are not to be taken as literal days but rather are symbolic for long periods of time.

Support for the Theory	Objections to the Theory
The word "day" is sometimes used in the Scriptures to describe a period of time longer than a 24 hour period ("the day of the Lord").	The word "day" does not normally refer to an extended period of time when it appears with a modifier (1st day, 2nd day, etc).
2 Peter 3:8 states that with the Lord one day is as a thousand years.	These days are clearly defined in Genesis 1:5 when God calls the light day and the darkness night.
The sun and the moon are not created until the 4th day. This indicates that the previous days are not literal.	The very purpose of the sun was to rule over the day while the moon was to rule over the night.

The observation that the word "day" (Hebrew יוֹם, *yom*) does not normally refer to an extended period of time when it appears with a modifier (1st day, 2nd day, etc) is not without exception. For example, Hosea 6:2 speaks of the actions of the Lord toward the nation of Israel and says:

He will revive us after two days;
He will raise us up on the third day
That we may live before Him.

Expositors have traditionally taken this to refer, not to literal periods of 24 hours, but to extended periods of time. It should be noted that this view that the days of creation were other than a literal and unbroken period of a week was held by theologians long before the advent of modern evolutionary theory. Origen, Augustine and Aquinas were among some of the early theologians who suggested that the days of Genesis were not necessarily limited to a 24 hour day.

5.   The Non-Sequential Theory/Framework Theory.

This view says that the first two chapters of Genesis are not meant to teach us anything about the chronological order of creation and that we should only learn general lessons from these chapters. The creation week is seen merely as a literary device, a framework in which a number of very important messages are held. [1] Thus, the chronological sequence is merely to be regarded as the packaging in which the real message is wrapped. The problem with this view is that the Bible often contains similar literary devices even when it is obvious that the writer intended his readers to understand they were reading a historical narrative. For example, the entire life of Abraham can be demonstrated to follow a chiastic parallel. This in no way suggests that the life of Abraham was to be considered only packaging for a deeper spiritual truth.

> "Bringing a question of chronological order to Genesis 1 is like bringing a question of meteorology to Psalm 139."

On the other hand, there are times when we read a historical narrative that is juxtaposed with a descriptive account filled with poetic imagery. One example of this is seen in the account of Deborah and

---

[1] See Ridderbos, *Is there a Conflict between Genesis 1 and Natural Science"* and Meredith Kline, *The Genesis Debate.*

the Israelites battling the Canaanites as recorded in Judges 4. The chapter which follows contains the song of Deborah and tells the same story, albeit in figurative language. It has been suggested that Genesis 1 bears the same relationship to Genesis 2 as that which is seen in those two chapters of Judges. Genesis 1 tells the story by way of the figure of days while Genesis 2 tells the specifics of the story.

6.   The Literal Interpretation.

If we read the passage naturally, we seem to see a literal six-day period of creation since the entire idea of a "day" and a "night" is defined within the passage where *"God called the light DAY..."* For this reason, this has been the accepted interpretation from both Jewish and Christian scholars throughout most of history.

Most of the other interpretations of Genesis have as their motivating force the desire to bring the teachings of this chapter into line with popular geological and evolutionary theory. This is not a bad thing if those modern theories can be demonstrated to be correct. We have done similar works of interpretation when we take

> An obvious exception to the influence of modern science to various views of Genesis 1 would be that held by Augustine who pointed to an interpretation other than six literal days of the absence of the sun and moon.

archaeological discoveries into account and use them to help us to understand and to interpret the Scriptures.

For example, when Isaiah 11:12 speaks of the Lord gathering His people *"from the four corners of the earth,"* we utilize our understanding of geography to interpret this as a figure of speech rather that to insist that planet earth has literal corners.

Bruce Waltke and Cathi Fredricks point out that *general revelation in creation, as well as the special revelation of Scripture, is also the voice of God. We live in a "universe," and all truth speaks with one voice.*[2] If this is the case, then we do not need to fear listening to the discoveries of geologists when they give evidence for the age of the earth.

---

[2] Genesis. Grand Rapids, MI: Zondervan, 2001. Page 77.

STRUCTURAL PATTERN OF GENESIS 1

The six days of creative work are topical in nature. This does not rule out a literal interpretation, but the topical nature should also be realized. The outline for this structure can be seen in Genesis 1:2 where the earth was described as being unformed and unfilled. The first three days involve forming the earth while the second three days involve filling the earth.

Unformed		Unfilled	
DAY 1:	Light.	**DAY 4:**	Light-givers (Sun, moon & stars).
DAY 2:	Water & sky divided.	**DAY 5:**	Fish and birds.
DAY 3:	Land & Vegetation	**DAY 6**:	Land animals & man.

The Jews delighted in this sort of parallelism. It was akin to poetry. This observation has led some to suggest that we are not meant to take the teachings of this chapter with a rigid literalness but rather as a poetic passage teaching us that God is indeed the creator of all things. On the other hand, we shall see that the entire book of Genesis is rich in parallelism, even those sections in which all agree are to be taken as historical in nature.

THE CREATION OF MAN

The first chapter of Genesis builds us to a crescendo that culminates in the creation of man.

1.   The Divine Plan.

> *Then God said, "Let Us make man in Our image, according to Our likeness; and let them rule over the fish of the sea and over the birds of the sky and over the cattle and over all the earth, and over every creeping thing that creeps on the earth."*
> *And God created man in His own image, in the image of God He created him; male and female He created them. (Genesis 1:26-27).*

The creative work of God reaches a crescendo when it reaches the creation of man.

a.   The Plurality of the Planner.

Notice the use of the plural pronoun ("Let **us** make man in **our** image"). The Jews held this to be a conversation that the Lord was having with the angels. However, the fulfillment of the plan in verse 27 does not say that God created man in the image of God and the angels. Indeed, angels are nowhere mentioned in the first half of the book of Genesis.

This may be a foreshadowing of the doctrine of the Trinity. This is the view suggested by the Epistle of Barnabas. On the other hand, it may also be a literary device known as a "plural of majesty" or a "plural of deliberation." This same sort of plural usage will be seen in Genesis 3:22 and 11:7.

Several other uses of the plural of majesty in the Bible can be suggested:

- Ezra 4:18 - Xerxes writes, *"The document which you sent to US has been translated and read before me."* The context in verses 11-13 shows that the document in question was sent to the king alone.

- 2 Chronicles 10:9 might be a plural of majesty - *"What counsel do you give that WE may answer this people..."*

- Isaiah 6:8 goes back and forth between the singular and the plural: *Also I heard the voice of the Lord, saying, "Whom shall I send, and who will go for us?" Then said I, "Here am I; send me."*

It is notable that the New Testament writers never pointed to this usage as evidence for the deity of Jesus. They did point to Psalm 110 on several occasions.

b.   In the Image of God.

In what way was man created in the image and likeness of God? Some have suggested that it is in the area of free will.

Others have tried to see in this statement a tri-unity within man - that he is body, soul and spirit (as a reflection of the Trinitarian God). Still another view postulates that God has a body. But none of these views is supported by the context of Genesis. The context suggests only one way - the area of rulership. This is seen in the very next verse.

> *And God blessed them; and God said to them, "Be fruitful and multiply, and fill the earth, and subdue it; and **rule** over the fish of the sea and over the birds of the sky, and over every living thing that moves on the earth." (Genesis 1:28).*

As God was sovereign over all that He had created, so now man was placed into a position of relative sovereignty over all that was upon the earth.

c.   There Are Two Separate Words for Man.

- אדם (*adam*) is the generic word for "man" or "mankind." Notice that Adam's name was "Man." This name points to his origins. The related word אדמה (*admah*) is the Hebrew word for "ground." Genesis 1:27 indicates that אדם refers to both the man and the woman.

- איש (*ish*) indicates man as a male, in contrast to אשה (*ishah*) referring to "woman."

d.   The Purpose of the Creation Account.

We must remember that the creation account does not stand alone. It is a part of the larger book of Genesis, which is itself a part of the larger work of the Torah. Therefore, the purpose of this account must be seen in terms of the covenant people of Israel who had come out of Egypt.

Genesis 1	The Israelite Experience
Light and darkness are made by God on Day 1	They had seen God bring light and darkness over Egypt

A division of the waters on Day 2	They had passed through the Red Sea
The sun and moon and stars created on Day 4	The Egyptians worshiped the sun and moon and stars and had seen the sun darkened in Egypt.
Man is created in the image of God	Only the Pharaoh was thought to be in the image of God
Man is told to rule over the earth	Only the Pharaoh had the right of rulership
Man is placed into a beautiful garden	Israelites are tempted to return to the meats of Egypt, but Canaan is to be seen as the new promised Eden.

In Egypt the images of birds and beasts had been used to represent the various gods. But in Genesis 1 we see man made in the image of God and told to rule over birds and beasts. This analogy continues in Genesis 2 where man is placed into a garden. This garden in Eden is seen in contrast to false gardens like Egypt and Sodom and Gomorrah (they are described as being "like" Egypt in Genesis 13:10). The Nile was the River of Egypt, but the Garden of Eden was a much richer garden because it had four rivers flowing out of it.

What is the point of all this? It is to show the Israelites that their God was no mere tribal god. He was the Creator of all the universe and He provided for His people that which is better than what they experienced in Egypt. Furthermore, it is not merely the pharaoh or the king who is created in the image of God, but all mankind that shares the divine image. It is because of this high calling that all mankind is given the ordinance of rulership.

2.   An Ordinance of Rulership.

> *God blessed them; and God said to them, "Be*

fruitful and multiply, and fill the earth, and subdue it;
and rule over the fish of the sea and over the birds of
the sky and over every living thing that moves on the
earth." (Genesis 1:28).

Man is given both the privilege and the responsibility of rulership over all life on planet earth. There is a sense in which he is to be God's representative on the planet.

a.   This is what it means for man to have been created in the image of God. He is in God's place, the place of rulership, with respect to the rest of life on this planet.

b.   Mankind was given the position of federal headship over the earth. It is because of this that man's fall was able to impact all of the rest of creation. When man fell into sin, the rest of creation followed suit because it was under man's dominion.

c.   If mankind has been given the position of stewardship over the rest of creation, then it stands to reason that the Christian has an obligation toward the faithful stewardship of that with which he has been entrusted. The Christian has a basis for ecology that goes far beyond the pragmatic. He has been entrusted with the care of God's creation. He is to act toward the rest of creation with the same grace and favor that God has shown him, for he is the representative of the divine to the rest of creation.

Man's rulership over the animal kingdom flies in the face of the paganism of the ancient world that called for men to bow down before the images of various animals.

3.   A Declaration of Goodness.

God saw all that He had made, and behold, it was
very good. And there was evening and there was
morning, the sixth day. (Genesis 1:31).

The sixth day concludes, not merely with a declaration of goodness, but with the statement that is was *very good*. This summary statement is not given until mankind has been created. This is going to stand in contrast to the events that shall take place in Genesis 3 when the Lord looks at the entry of sin into the world. This tells us something about the world in which we live. It exists today in an unnatural state. The world was not created in a fallen condition. It was created to be very good. The entrance of sin into the world brought about an unnatural state that is quite different from the way in which it was originally created.

It is in the work of Jesus Christ that we see the promise of a new heavens and a new earth. The redemption of the cross involves not only a redemption with regard to personal salvation, but also a redemption of planet earth.

GENESIS 2 - THE SECOND ACCOUNT OF CREATION

Genesis 1 is given in parallel symmetry with the first three days of creation serving as a parallel to the latter three days. In Genesis 2 we find a different sort of symmetrical arrangement. It is known as a chiasm and the various points of the parallel find their pivot at the center of the passage. In this case, the pivotal point is the warning against eating of the forbidden fruit.

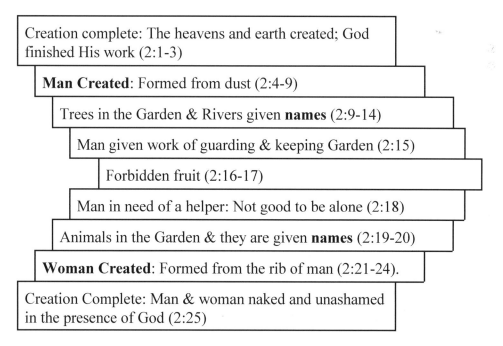

Creation complete: The heavens and earth created; God finished His work (2:1-3)

Man Created: Formed from dust (2:4-9)

Trees in the Garden & Rivers given **names** (2:9-14)

Man given work of guarding & keeping Garden (2:15)

Forbidden fruit (2:16-17)

Man in need of a helper: Not good to be alone (2:18)

Animals in the Garden & they are given **names** (2:19-20)

Woman Created: Formed from the rib of man (2:21-24).

Creation Complete: Man & woman naked and unashamed in the presence of God (2:25)

As we approach Genesis 2, it seems at first as though we are dealing with a totally separate account of creation. In an initial reading of this chapter, we note that it contains several references to God's creation that are already described in chapter 1. Because of this, some have wondered whether the two passages were not written by two different authors. However closer observation will show that these two chapters form a unit. Neither account is able to stand complete in itself.

The relationship between Genesis 1 and Genesis 2 is easily understood when we consider the literary structure of the entire book of Genesis. At first, the less important things are dealt with in a rapid survey. Then the things that are deemed more important to the theme of the book are studied and developed more fully. For example, in the account of Jacob and Esau, it is Esau's story that comes first. But it is Jacob's story that is more fully developed and which holds the place of higher importance to the overall theme of the book. The same is true of these first two chapters of Genesis. This will be seen as we take the two chapters and contrast them.

Genesis 1	Genesis 2
Gives a brief outline of God's creation	Tells us in detail of the creation of man
Sets out the order of creation	Sets out the purpose of creation
Shows man in his cosmic setting	Shows man as the central theme of the book
Gives us a panoramic view of creation as a whole	Gives us a detailed view of one particular aspect of creation
Centers on God creating the heavens and the earth	Centers on man, the crowning of God's creation

From this we can see that the two chapters are complimentary. Each contains unique material that is necessary in understanding who God is and what He has done for us.

THE FALL INTO SIN

The narrative of the temptation and the fall into sin is foundational to the rest of the Bible. If the Bible is a book of Redemption, then the origin of that redemptive message is found in this chapter. The very last words of

Genesis 2 record that the man and woman were naked but were not ashamed. This introduces a motif which follows through chapter 3 and into chapter 4.

Genesis 2	They were not ashamed
Genesis 3	"I was ashamed and I hid myself"
Genesis 4	Adam knew his wife

Thus, while there is the fall in chapter 3, there is also a promise of future restoration through the "seed of the woman." The first prophecy of a coming Messiah was not made to either the man or the woman, but to the serpent.

> *"And I will put enmity between you and the woman, and between your seed and her seed; He shall bruise you on the head, and you shall bruise Him on the heel." (Genesis 3:15).*

This verse provides the theme of the rest of Genesis. This will be a book about two seeds. The first will be the seed of the serpent; the second will be the seed of the woman. We can well understand that the "seed of the serpent" is not speaking of a race of literal snakes. There is a spiritual seed in view. Likewise, the "seed of the woman" has both spiritual as well as physical ramifications.

The Seed of the Serpent	The Seed of the Woman
Points ultimately to Satan	Points ultimately to Jesus Christ
He receives a wound to the head -- this is a fatal wound.	He receives a wound to the heel -- painful but not lasting.
He was fatally bruised for all eternity.	He was temporarily bruised while on the cross.

Though this ultimately points to Satan and to Jesus Christ, this is also the story of the entire human race. All people are in either one of two groups. They are following one of two seeds. The seed of the serpent is Satan. He is the way of rebellion against God. He is the voice of independence. The seed of the woman is Jesus. He is the One whose "heel" was crushed by Satan.

But He was pierced through for our transgressions, He was crushed for our iniquities; the chastening for our well-being fell upon Him, and by His scourging we are healed.

All of us like sheep have gone astray, each of us has turned to his own way; but the Lord has caused the iniquity of us all to fall on Him. (Isaiah 53:5-6).

When Jesus died upon the cross, it was no mere human death that He died. His death was special. It was special because it also involved a spiritual death. He was judged by God as if He were a guilty sinner. Our sins were laid upon Him.

God initially created all life to reproduce after its kind. But man rebelled and sinned against God. And so, a promise was given. It was a promise of two seeds. The first seed was to be the seed of the serpent. It was the seed of rebellion and of sin. It was made up of all who walked in the way of Adam in turning against God. But there is also a second seed promised. It is the seed of the woman. This second seed is set over against the first seed. The two seeds are at war with one another. And God has decreed that the second seed shall ultimately win.

From our vantage point, we know that this second seed is ultimately fulfilled in Jesus Christ, the One who was bruised for our iniquities as He crushed underfoot the Serpent's Head.

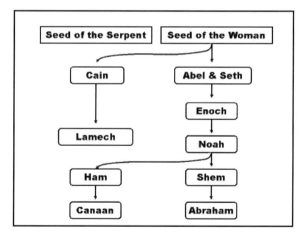

The rest of Genesis is the story of these two seeds. First we read of Cain and Abel. Although they are brothers descended from the same father and mother, Cain shows himself to be of the spiritual seed of the serpent by murdering his brother. But God replaces murdered Abel with Seth.

We see the genealogy of each. Cain's seed leads us to Lamech, a man who is willing not only to murder a man, but to compose a song in which he boasts of his deed. Seth's seed leads us to Enoch who walks with God, and from there to Noah who is spared the destruction of the Flood.

But the story does not stop there. Noah has three sons. And one of them performs an evil deed which demonstrates that he is of the spiritual seed of the serpent. He and his descendants through Canaan are cursed (the impact of this was not missed on the Israelites to whom Moses wrote the book of Genesis). Noah's other son, Shem, is given the promise of blessing.

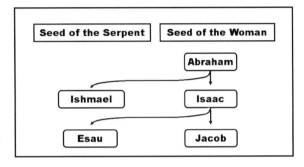

The Babel Rebellion is an account of men trying to make a *SHEM* for themselves (*Shem* is the Hebrew word for "name"). They are dispersed among the nations. But one is called out to be a blessing to the nations. His name is Abraham. He has two sons. One is seen to be the seed of the serpent - he is cast out. The other is of the spiritual seed of God. He is Isaac.

Isaac also has two sons. They are twins, but one is of the spiritual seed of the serpent. Esau does not hold the blessings of God in high esteem. Jacob, on the other hand, shows himself to be of the seed of the woman.

Jacob has twelve sons. Only one of them shows from the outset that he is of the seed of the woman. The others are rebellious. Two of them murder the inhabitants of a town. Another is involved in a sexual scandal. They sell their younger brother into slavery. But the Lord uses this to His own ends and all of the brothers are redeemed in Egypt; they all receive the promises of God.

As Moses writes the book of Genesis, the children of Israel are in the wilderness. And the question before them is this - which seed are they to be? Will they follow in the footsteps of the serpent? Or will they show themselves to be of the seed of the Lord? Genesis will be a book about a line of children. Thus, a key word in Genesis will be "generations."

- The Hebrew word for "generations" is *toledoth.*
- It is taken from the root word *yalad*, *"to give birth."*

Each new generation will determine which seed it is. Will it continue in the covenant relation to God and show itself to be a part of the promised seed? Or will it turn from God to join and be a part of the seed of the serpent? Thus, the "big idea" in Genesis is the idea of the "covenant generation." The word covenant is used throughout this book and it is here that we shall see the Lord and Abraham enter into a very formal covenant in Genesis 12, 15 and 17.

THE FLOOD NARRATIVE

The Flood Narrative brings to a close one segment of the book of Genesis and introduces a new segment. There is an interesting contrast to be seen in the first six chapters of Genesis with the second of the six chapters of this book as we move from creation/fall history to the flood/nations history:

Genesis 1-5	Genesis 6-11
Creation History	Noahic History
Adam's sons (4:1-16)	Noah's sons (9:18-29)
Technological Development of Mankind (4.17-26)	Ethnic Development of Mankind (10:1-32)
Ten Generations from Adam to Noah (5:1-32)	Ten Generations from Noah to Terah (11:10-26)

There is a chiastic parallel that makes up the flood narrative. These elements can be viewed as the rising and falling actions within the story.

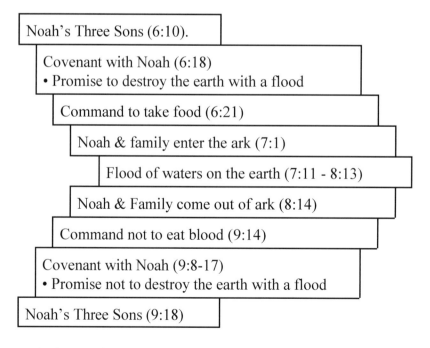

Noah's Three Sons (6:10).

Covenant with Noah (6:18)
• Promise to destroy the earth with a flood

Command to take food (6:21)

Noah & family enter the ark (7:1)

Flood of waters on the earth (7:11 - 8:13)

Noah & Family come out of ark (8:14)

Command not to eat blood (9:14)

Covenant with Noah (9:8-17)
• Promise not to destroy the earth with a flood

Noah's Three Sons (9:18)

The instructions of the building of the ark are detailed and exact. This is striking because at the end of the book of Exodus we have another detailed set of building instructions. In that case, it is the tabernacle that is the subject of the instructions. We are meant to see these in parallel. There is a sense in which the ark was to Noah and his family what the tabernacle would be to Moses and the children of Israel. Each was a picture of Christ. Each had as its focus salvation from the judgment of God. In the case of the ark, it would be the vehicle for saving Noah and his family from the flood. In the case of the tabernacle, it was the vehicle for covenant worship on the part of those who had passed through the "flood" of the Red Sea.

1.   The Word "Ark."

The Hebrew word is *Tebah* (תֵּבַת). This same word is used in Exodus 2:3-5 to refer to the ark that the mother of Moses used to hide her child. *Tebah* is thought to be an Egyptian loan-word to describe a box. There are four different "arks" mentioned in Scripture.

> The ark here is different from *'aron*, (אָרוֹן) which is used to describe the ark of the covenant.

- Noah's ark - *Tebah* (תֵּבַת).
- The coffin in which the bones of Joseph were placed - *Aron* (אָרוֹן).
- The ark into which the infant Moses was placed - *Tebah* (תֵּבַת).
- The Ark of the covenant - *Aron* (אָרוֹן).

Each of these was a symbol of judgment; each carried a reference to death. But each was a place of peace and safety in the midst of a hostile environment.

2.   The Size of the Ark.

The dimensions of the ark are given in cubits. A cubit was the distance from a man's elbow to the tip of his fingers - generally about 18 inches.[3] There was also a royal cubit which was a few inches longer (kings suffered from the same malady known to Texans, they liked to be thought of as bigger than everyone else). Assuming the standard cubit, we are left with the following dimensions:

---

[3] This is called "a cubit of a man in Deuteronomy 3:11.

	Cubits	Feet
Length	300	450
Width	50	75
Height	30	45

It has often been noted that these are the dimensions of an ocean-going barge, the size of which would have been sufficient to carry a large selection of animals.

3.   The Building Materials: *Make for yourself an ark of gopher wood (6:14).*

The ark was to be made of *atsey-gopher* (עֲצֵי־גֹפֶר). Our English text reads "gopher wood." Rather than a translation, this is actually a transliteration. The word *gopher* (גֹפֶר) is a hapaxlegomena — it is not used elsewhere in the Bible. This makes it difficult to determine what type of wood it is. It has been suggested that this is a textual error, but there is no textual evidence for this. It is more likely that this is either an Akkadian or a Sumerian loan word.

Noah was also told to *cover it inside and outside with pitch* (6:14). This literally reads "*cover* it within and without in *covering.*" The word for "cover" is *kaphar* (כָּפַר). It is the same word which describes the act of atonement. Indeed, we still use the same word today when we speak of the Jewish Festival of Yom Kippur.

4.   The Nature of the Flood.

> *In the six hundredth year of Noah's life, in the second month, on the seventeenth day of the month, on the same day all the fountains of the great deep burst open, and the floodgates of the sky were opened. (Genesis 7:11).*

It is evident from the chronological formula given that we are meant to understand this as an actual historical event. But what is the nature of this event? Was this a world-wide flood or was it merely limited to the geographical area of Mesopotamia?

a.   Arguments for a Universal Flood.

- The depth of the flood. Genesis 7:19-20 says that *all* the high mountains which were under *all* the heavens were covered by the waters of the flood. The peak of Mount Ararat extends to an elevation of around 17,000 feet. If only this one single peak was covered, then most of the world would also be covered.

- The duration of the flood. The flood is said to have lasted 371 days, a little over a year. Local floods do not last this long.

- The need for the ark. If the flood was to be merely confined to a certain isolated area, it would not have necessitated Noah spending all that time and effort in building the ark. He could have moved to high ground.

- The testimony of the Apostle Peter: *...the world at that time was destroyed, being flooded with water. 7 But the present heavens and earth by His word are being reserved for fire, kept for the day of judgment and destruction of ungodly men. (2 Peter 3:6-7).* Peter's words imply a total destruction of the enter world.

b.   Arguments for a Local Flood.

- The Hebrew word which is translated "the world" throughout the flood narrative (*HaAretz*) can be translated "the land." A few examples will suffice:

    "The LAND of Nod" (Genesis 4:16).
    "In the LAND of Shinar" (Genesis 10:10).
    "Out of that LAND went forth Asshur" (Genesis 10:11).
    "Go forth from your COUNTRY, and from your relatives and from your father's house, to the LAND which I will show you..." (Genesis 12:1).
    "And in you all the families of the EARTH shall be blessed" (Genesis 12:3).

    Each of these instances uses the same basic word. It can

refer to the entire world, or it can merely refer to a certain area of land. By the same token, when the Bible says that the world was covered by water, we need not take this to refer to the entire planet earth. It could merely be a reference to that land area.

- Universalist terms can be used in a limited sense. The Scriptures sometimes use terms like "all" and "every" in a way which is understood to be a limited sense. We need not go very far to prove this point. Note the following verses:

  The man called his wife's name Eve, because she was the mother of ALL living (Genesis 3:20).

Was Eve the mother of all life? Or merely the mother of all human life? If we are to understand her to be the mother only of human life, then we must agree that this universal term is used in a limited sense.

  "Of EVERY living thing of ALL flesh, you shall bring two of every kind into the ark..." (Genesis 6:19).

Most people who advocate a universal flood do not take this command to refer to ocean animals (no goldfish bowls on the ark). Thus even the universalist understands that there are times when universal language is used in a limited sense. Therefore when we read of every living thing being destroyed in the flood, we can understand it to refer to the living land animals in that particular area, not necessarily to a flood which covered the entire planet.

- Where did the water go?

Mount Everest rises over 5 miles above sea level. There are many other mountains in the world which are over the 3 mile height. For flood waters to completely cover the earth would mandate that either the mountains were not there (thus they would have to be very recent in origin) or else that water came from some supernatural source and then went away again. Another possibility would be that the ocean beds somehow sank to collect the excess water.

It is interesting to note that sediment deposits have been found underneath the Sumerian ruins at Ur, at Fara, and at Kish. However, these flood deposits would seem to be extremely local in nature and not significant enough even to account for the Genesis account as a local flood.

Recent theories have arisen from scientific studies in and around the Black Sea that suggest a large inundation cause, at least in part, by the overflow of the waters of the Mediterranean into what is today the Black Sea. Though such theories might be appealing, we ought to be careful not to come too quickly to a conclusion in attempting to reconcile various scientific theories with the Bible.

5.   Summary of Arguments for a Universal / Local Flood.

UNIVERSAL FLOOD	LOCAL FLOOD
The Biblical account says that the waters covered the whole earth.	The word *aretz* is often used to describe a local area.
The Biblical language goes out of its way to use language of totality.	The account is given from the viewpoint of the narrator; from his perspective the destruction is total.
The size of the ark indicates that this was no local flood.	The size of the ark is not related to the extent of the flood.
The purpose of the ark was punishment of world-wide sin. In a local flood some could have escaped.	God could have made certain all flesh was destroyed without flooding the entire globe.
There are world-wide traces of a flood.	The evidence is scattered and sometimes seemingly inconsistent.

The promise of no future floods (Gen. 9:15) is not true if this is only a local flood.	The promise is for no flood to "destroy all flesh."

As various theories are considered regarding the cause and extent of the flood, we must point out that the Bible does not deny cause and effect. Indeed, it is because of the "natural laws" that God has instituted that we have come to expect such causes and effects in our world.

On the other hand, we do not believe that cause and effect operate apart from and independently of divine intervention. The atheist states that everything is explained only by the material universe and he makes a leap of faith to deny that any spiritual force is at work in history. By contrast, we know that God works in history and that He acts in the lives of men. He is the Master Cause of all things and He intervenes in history, both through His divine power and also through the agency of cause and effect and those means that we normally think of as "natural causes."

6.   The Place of the Ark: *And in the seventh month, on the seventeenth day of the month, the ark rested upon the mountains of Ararat (Genesis 8:4).*

We are not told that Ararat was the name of the mountain on which the ark landed. Instead, it is the name of the country in which the mountains were located. This land is mentioned in 2 Kings 19:37 and Isaiah 37:38 where the assassins of Sennacherib escaped to the land of Ararat. This evidently refers to a portion of the land of Armenia. Its ancient name among the Assyrians was *Urartu.*

This is the land from which both the Tigris and the Euphrates Rivers find their headwaters. It is a mountainous region and has a particularly high peak that boasts the name of Ararat, but our Biblical text does not say the ark landed on this peak.

There have been a number of expeditions to Mount Ararat to search for the ark, but none have produced any documented evidence of an ark. Various claims continue to be unsubstantiated. What happened to the ark? It is unlikely that a vessel made of wood thus exposed to the elements would be preserved over thousands of years. On a lighter note, the manifest of animals would have included at least two termites.

THE TOWER OF BABEL

It is no accident that the land of Mesopotamia contains the ruins of a number of ziggurats — large temple towers which served as the religious centers of the city-states where they were located. Not only is there confirmation of this account in the existence of such towers, but even the mode of their construction is described. There is a special mention of the specific building materials.

Instead of stone...	They used brick
Instead of mortar...	They used tar

Why is this significant? Remember that this is written to the Israelites who have just come out of Egypt. They have spent their lives making bricks in Egypt. When they reach Mount Sinai and are given the Law, they are ordered to build an altar to the Lord. But that altar will not be made of bricks.

> *"You shall make an altar of earth for Me, and you shall sacrifice on it your burnt offerings and your peace offerings, your sheep and your oxen; in every place where I cause your name to be remembered, I will come to you and bless you. 25 And if you make an altar of stone for Me, you shall not build it of cut stones, for if you wield your tool on it, you will profane it." (Exodus 20:24-25).*

The altar was not to be a monument to men's architecture, but rather a monument to the Lord. By contrast, the Tower of Babel was to be a monument to the makers — they were seeking self-glory. The tower was to be their symbol of unity and strength. In short, it was a symbol of their rebellion against God.

1.   The tower was to have its top oriented toward heaven — בַּשָּׁמַיִם

וְרֹאשׁוֹ (*weRoshu baShamayim*) — literally, "and its head in the heavens." Some have suggested the initial idea of a "flood-proof tower." More likely is the idea that it was a tower which was dedicated to astrology and the worship of the heavens. The Sumerian name for Babylon was Esagila, meaning "the structure with the upraised head."

2. There was also a cult of egotism at work. This is seen in the continued use of the personal pronoun: *And they said to one another, "Come, let **us** make bricks and burn them thoroughly." And they used brick for stone, and they used tar for mortar. And they said, "Come, let **us** build for **ourselves** a city, and a tower whose top will reach into heaven, and let **us** make for **ourselves** a name; lest **we** be scattered abroad over the face of the whole earth."* (Genesis 11:3-4).

Notice that a part of this plan was to make a name (שֵׁם – *shem*) for themselves. Was this in reaction to the promises which had been made to *Shem* (שֵׁם)? It would seem that the plans described here in the building of the city and the tower were the acts of deliberate rebellion against the decree of the Lord. We fall into this same sort of rebellion when we set out to build our own kingdoms instead of seeking the Lord and His kingdom. You are building a kingdom. The only question is what is the nature of that kingdom and for whom are you building?

> *And the Lord came down to see the city and the tower which the sons of men had built. 6 And the Lord said, "Behold, they are one people, and they all have the same language. And this is what they began to do, and now nothing which they purpose to do will be impossible for them. 7 Come, let Us go down and there confuse their language, that they may not understand one another's speech." (Genesis 11:5-7).*

As men had gathered and counseled together over their plans, so we have a picture of the Lord holding a divine council to determine the fate of mankind.

> *So the Lord scattered them abroad from there over the face of the whole earth, and they stopped building the city. (Genesis 11:8).*

We should not take this to mean that every dialect and language spoken today was immediately changed into its present form. The growth of languages has been a slow, on going process. On the other hand, there are a number of specific language groups that are recognized as being separate and distinct from one another.

- Indo European corresponds roughly with the descendants of Japheth.
- Semitic languages tend to be spoken by the descendants of Shem.
- Hamitic languages are spoken by a number of widely scattered groups.

> *Therefore its name was called Babel, because there the Lord confused the language of the whole earth; and from there the Lord scattered them abroad over the face of the whole earth. (Genesis 11:9).*

There is a play on words used here. It was of a kind that delighted the Jewish mind. The name of the city is given as Babel. The Akkadian name for Babylon (Babelu) means "Gate of God." The verb "confuse" is *babal*.

In a very real sense, what happened at Babel was a curse. The nations were scattered through this confusion of languages. But the cursing will be turned to blessing in the next chapter when God calls one man, Abram, and promises to make him a blessing to all the nations.

This promise would be fulfilled in Jesus Christ. Within a few days of Christ's ascension into heaven, the curse of confusion would be seen to be overturned in a dramatic way by the Pentecost Incident when Jews from all over the world would hear God's Word proclaimed in all of the Gentile languages. Furthermore, there is coming a day when every tongue shall confess that Jesus Christ is Lord (Philippians 2:11).

THE PATRIARCHS

There is a certain similarity of style in the lives of the first three Patriarchs (Abraham, Isaac, Jacob).

1.   Each is given a series of promises by God which include the following:

- A Seed.
- A Land.
- A Blessing.
- Blessing to the Nations.

2.   Each live as aliens in the land of Canaan, wandering among the inhabitants of the land.

3.   Each had wives who experienced barrenness before giving birth to the promised sons.

- Sarah (11:20; 15:2-3; 16:1).
- Rebekah (25:21).
- Rachel & Leah (29:31; 30:9; 30:17; 30:22).

4.   Each had to deal with rivalry among his sons.

THE CALL TO ABRAHAM

> Now the LORD said to Abram, "Go forth from your country, And from your relatives And from your father's house, To the land which I will show you; 2 and I will make you a great nation, And I will bless you, And make your name great; And so you shall be a blessing; 3 and I will bless those who bless you, And the one who curses you I will curse. And in you all the families of the earth shall be blessed." (Genesis 12:1-3).

Throughout the first part of the book of Genesis, there is a pattern seen concerning the judgments of God. After God pronounces a judgment upon sin, He follows that judgment by offering a way of escape and salvation from that judgment.

JUDGMENT	WAY OF SALVATION
Adam & Eve cast out of Garden of Eden.	Promise of redemption through seed of the Woman.

Cain banished from the presence of God for murdering his brother.	God places a mark on Cain so that no one will take vengeance
Flood brought upon the earth.	Eight souls saved in Ark.
Confusion of languages and nations dispersed.	Abraham to be a blessing to the nations.

- When God cast Adam and Eve out of the Garden of Eden, He also gave them the first promise of redemption through the Seed of the Woman.

- When God banished Cain from His presence after he had murdered Abel, He set a mark upon Cain to protect him from anyone who might be seeking revenge.

- When the Lord brought a flood upon the earth to destroy all life, He allowed eight people to be saved within the ark.

- When God confused the languages at the Tower of Babel, He doomed the world to an existence of misunderstanding, strife, and confusion. We have seen the account of this judgment in chapter 11. Then, at the end of chapter 11, we have the introduction to one particular individual whom God chooses to bless. His name is Abram. It will be through Abram that all of the nations in the world will be blessed, just as they have previously been judged at Babel.

We normally think of the first promises of the land being given to Abraham. But the idea of a land that was given is found first here in Genesis 2 where the first man was given the first land. It was a paradise. This means that the promise of a land that was given to Abraham is a promise of a redeemed land. It is a promise of a return to a new paradise.

ABRAM AND LOT

Early in the Abram narrative, we are told of God's promise to Abram regarding a seed. God promises to make of him a great nation. The problem with this promise is that Sarai, Abram's wife, is barren. She has never been able to have children and now they are both advanced in years.

However, Abram is accompanied by his nephew, Lot. It might have been presumed that the promise of a seed would be fulfilled through Lot who was of close relations to Abram. However, they have not been in the land for very long before friction begins to arise between the shepherds of Abram and the shepherds of Lot. They ultimately part company and it becomes evident that Lot will not be the source of the promised seed.

GENESIS 15: THE COVENANT CEREMONY

While each of these chapters in the life of Abram contain promises, it is chapter 15 that is the most striking because here God and Abram play out the traditional covenant ceremony that was commonly used between two people who were entering into a covenant. When the Israelites in the wilderness read this chapter, they say to themselves, "I get it!" Unless we understand the cultural background of these events, it usually goes right over our heads, especially the part about the cutting up of the animals and the smoking oven and the burning torch.

The Israelite who was reading this book at the feet of Moses in the wilderness would have considered the first 11 chapters to be merely introductory material that set the stage for the central portion of the book - and in a sense he would have been correct. There are only 11 chapters dealing with such great events as the creation, the fall, the flood and the Tower of Babel. The lion's share of the book deals with Abraham, Isaac, Jacob and his sons.

Indeed, a good way to read through this book is to ask yourself in each chapter, "What would this have meant to Moses as he wrote it and what would it have meant to the Israelites in the wilderness for whom it was initially written?" They had been prisoners in Egypt where false gods were worshiped, so they needed to know that Jehovah was not just another part of the pantheon, but rather that He was the creator of heaven and earth. But this great and majestic God of heaven did not remain only transcendent, He also came near to enter into a covenant with mankind.

> So He said to him, "Bring Me a three year old heifer, and a three year old female goat, and a three year old ram, and a turtledove, and a young pigeon." 10 Then he brought all these to Him and cut them in two, and laid each half opposite the other; but he did not cut the birds. (Genesis 15:9-10).

These were the preparations one typically understood in order to enter into a binding covenant. The making of this sort of covenant involved several animals being sacrificed. The animals would be cut into two parts and then placed in parallel with a pathway between the pieces. Then when the parties who were entering into the covenant were ready to go through the covenant ceremony, they would walk between the

> When Jesus went to the cross, it was to pay the penalty of our broken covenant. Even though He was without sin, He was treated as though He were a covenant breaker so that we might be treated as though we had kept the covenant. The New Testament alludes to this when it describes how Christ "became a curse for us" (Galatians 3:13).

pieces of the animals as they verbally stated the terms of the covenant. The idea behind the ceremony was that they were binding themselves by oath to the fate of the slain animals that, if they broke their word, they might suffer the same fate. They were saying in effect, "If I break the terms of this covenant, then may I similarly be torn apart and die."

> *And it came about when the sun had set, that it was very dark, and behold, there appeared a smoking oven and a flaming torch which passed between these pieces. (Genesis 15:17).*

When the time comes for the parties to pass between the pieces of the animals, Abraham is unable to do so. He has fallen asleep with a "deep sleep" and we do not read of him passing between the pieces. Instead, we read of an apparition described as a smoking oven and a flaming torch. It is this which passes between the pieces.

This is evidently a manifestation of the presence of the Lord. But why is the description given in such a manner? What is the significance of a smoking oven and a flaming torch? To answer this question, we must remember who is the human author of this account and who are his recipients. It is Moses who writes these words and he writes them to the Israelites who are in the wilderness. The first thing they see each morning when they look out their tent is a cloud over the tabernacle. The last thing they see before they go to bed at night is a pillar of fire. A smoking oven and a flaming torch! God is describing Himself in the very terms with which they are familiar.

The entire Abraham narrative contains a chiastic pattern in which there are a number of parallels given. Notice that there are two different occasions when:

- Abraham sojourns with a foreign king.
- He falls into the lie of saying regarding Sarah, "She is my sister."
- There are negotiations concerning Lot and Lot is rescued.

Promises given
- Abram called to leave his family
- Promise of Seed (12:1-3)

Travels in the land
- Abram journeys (12:4-9)
- Sojourn in Egypt, "She is my sister" (12.10-20)

Lot and Abram
- Lot and Abram negotiate over land (13).
- Abram rescues Lot and people of Sodom (14)

God's covenant ceremony with Abram and promise of the Land (15)

Hagar and Ishmael (16)

God's covenant naming of Abraham and promise of Seed (17)

Lot and Abraham
- Abraham negotiates with God over Lot and Sodom (18).
- Angels rescue Lot as Sodom is destroyed (19)

Travels in the land
- Abraham journeys southward (20:1)
- Sojourn in Gerar, "She is my sister" (20.1-18)

Promises fulfilled
- Isaac born; Hagar and Ishmael sent out from covenant family (21)
- Abraham's Test: Blessing of Seed (22:1-19)

The "bookends" of the story are the promise that is given to Abraham at the outset of the narrative and the fulfillment and ultimate test of faith Abraham faces at the end of the narrative.

THE ISAAC NARRATIVE

1.   His Name.

Isaac's name means "laughter." He was given this name because, when the Lord gave a promise to Abraham and Sarah that she would become pregnant and they would have a son, their first response was to laugh (Abraham laughed in Genesis 17:17 and Sarah laughed in Genesis 18:12). It was the Lord who had the last laugh as He delivered this son of promise.

2.   The Offering of Isaac.

The great test of Abraham's life was when he was told by God to take Isaac, his promised son, and to sacrifice him to the Lord.

> *Now it came about after these things, that God tested Abraham, and said to him, "Abraham!" And he said, "Here I am."*
> *2 And He said, "Take now your son, your only son, whom you love, Isaac, and go to the land of Moriah; and offer him there as a burnt offering on one of the mountains of which I will tell you." (Genesis 22:1-2).*

Abraham responds in obedience, taking Isaac with him to a mountain in the area of Moriah. Where is the land of Moriah? The Bible gives the answer.

> *Then Solomon began to build the house of the Lord in Jerusalem on Mount Moriah, where the Lord had appeared to his father David, at the place that David had prepared, on the threshing floor of Ornan the Jebusite. (2 Chronicles 3:1).*

The place where Abraham was sent to sacrifice his son was the same place where the Temple would one day be constructed. It was on the site of today's Dome of the Rock in Jerusalem.

> *Then they came to the place of which God had told him; and Abraham built the altar there, and arranged the wood, and bound his son Isaac, and laid him on the altar on top of the wood. 10 And Abraham stretched out his hand, and took the knife to slay his son. (Genesis 22:9-10).*

Abraham and Isaac finally arrive on the scene and go about the work of preparing for the sacrifice. The altar is built. The wood is arranged. The passage is strangely quiet about Isaac's response as he is taken and bound and placed upon the altar.

- Did Isaac protest?
- Did Abraham offer any explanation?
- Were there tears?

We are not told. The reason that we are not told is because that is not the "big idea" of the narrative. We are not meant to come here and look at Abraham's noble sacrifice or Isaac's submissiveness to his father. Those points are valid, but if you come here and see only those things, then you have missed the bigger idea of the passage. You are meant to come here and see God's substitute.

> *But the angel of the Lord called to him from heaven, and said, "Abraham, Abraham!" And he said, "Here I am." 12 And he said, "Do not stretch out your hand against the lad, and do nothing to him; for now I know that you fear God, since you have not withheld your son, your only son, from Me." (Genesis 22:11-12).*

Abraham has passed the test of faithfulness. Notice what is said -- you have not withheld your son, your only son, from Me. This is not a denial of the existence of Ishmael, but it is to say that Isaac was the special son; the son of promise. Because Abraham has not withheld the sacrifice of his son, his only son, God knows that Abraham fears , honors, and loves Him.

The good news is that what God has called us to do, He has also done Himself. God has not withheld His Son -- His only Son -- from us. And because God has passed the faithfulness test, we can trust in Him and we can trust in His love.

THE JACOB NARRATIVE

1.   His Name.

        Jacob's name has a special meaning that is drawn both from the circumstances of his birth and also from the character he displayed in his early life. Jacob was a twin. When the two brothers were born, the second born son was holding onto the heel of the first born. This was considered to be a significant omen and this child was named Jacob, meaning "heel grabber." This was an idiom for a con artist; someone who is out to "trip you up." We have a similar idiom today when we speak of "pulling someone's leg."

2.   The Birthright.

        Jacob's role as a heel grabber is seen in his dealings with his older brother. The first such indication is when Esau, the outdoors man to Jacob's stay-at-home approach to life, came in from the fields to find Jacob with a tasty pot of stew. We are not told whether or not Jacob had craftily planned the incident or whether he happened to be in the right place at the right time with the right temptation. The result was the same in any case -- Esau was persuaded to sell his birthright for a pot of stew. No used car salesman ever made such a deal.

3.   The Blessing.

        The heel-grabbing came to full fruition when their father, Isaac, determined to give to Esau the family blessing. While Esau was away, Jacob was coaxed by his mother to don a disguise that would fool his aged and blind father into thinking he was Esau. By means of this deception, he was able to steal the family blessing.
        For Esau, this was the last straw. As far as he was concerned, Jacob had swindled him for the last time. He swore revenge and Jacob was forced to leave his home, fleeing from the wrath of Esau, never to see his beloved mother again.

4.   Jacob's Ladder.

        It was while he was on the run, that Jacob had his first significant encounter with God.

        And Jacob departed from Beersheba and went toward Haran. 11 And he came to a certain place, and spent the night there, because the sun had set; and he took one of the stones of the place and put it under his head, and lay down in that place (Genesis 28:10-11).

The dream involved a vision of a ladder. This seems odd because there is no mention earlier in Genesis of a ladder. The word used here for ladder is *sullam*. It is a hapaxlegomenon. It is only used this one time in the Old Testament. It seems to come from the more common verb, selah, to lift up. It has been suggested that the same word would have been used to indicate a stairway, perhaps pointing to the ziggurats of Mesopotamia, but there are more definite words for stairway (*ma'alah* would be the normal word for "stairway").

This picture of the angels of God ascending and descending is found in only one other place in the Bible. It is John 1:51 when Jesus speaks to Nathanael.

> *And He said to him, "Truly, truly, I say to you, you shall see the heavens opened, and the angels of God ascending and descending on the Son of Man." (John 1:51).*

In the words of Jesus, there is no mention of the ladder. The angels are ascending and descending on the Son of Man. He is the ladder. Thus, if the ladder represents God's presence upon earth, then Jesus is seen as the One who is "God with us."

5.   Sojourn in Haran.

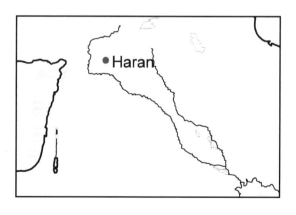

When Jacob arrives in Haran, he meets up with his Uncle Laban. He also meets up with Uncle Laban's two daughters and he falls head over heels in love with the younger one. Her name is Rachael. Apparently, Rachael was visually breathtaking. The Bible tells us that she was beautiful of form and face (Genesis 29:17). By contrast, we read that Leah's eyes were weak (29:17). I don't think it is speaking of her lack of 20/20 vision or that she needed glasses. Rather, this seems to be a euphemism for someone who is an "eye sore."

It has been said that the reason most women would rather have beauty than brains is because most guys can see better than they can think. That was the situation in Jacob's case. He fell in love with Rachael on the spot and did not give Leah another look. He entered into marital negotiations with her father to obtain her hand in marriage.

Jacob was penniless in a day and an age when a woman would be entitled to a dowry. And so, he agreed to work for his Uncle Laban for a period of seven years. Those seven years seemed to him but a few days because of his love for her (Genesis 29:20).

When the time came for the marriage, the father of the bride held a wedding party. Weddings in that day involved a celebration that make our weddings tame by comparison. We are accustomed to the wedding ceremony followed by a reception. In that day, the reception could last from several days up to a week. There was singing, there was celebration, there was honeymooning, and when the next morning came, Jacob awoke to find his new bride. There was only one problem. It was the wrong bride. It was the one whose eyes were weak. It was Leah.

Jacob the trickster had been tricked. Jacob the heel-grabber had been tripped up. Laban had slipped in the wrong daughter in the makings of this three-way romantic triangle. And so, Jacob agrees to work for another seven years in order to obtain his beloved Rachael. And then, in later years, he continues to work for Laban for a percentage of the increase of the crops.

As we read of Jacob's life during these years, we find ourselves wondering what God is doing in his life. We read of his growing prosperity and we are not quite sure if it is God that is blessing him or if his success is the result of his own conniving and scheming. We read of no ladders from heaven. We see no altars being built. There are no messages from the Almighty. It is almost as though heaven has grown silent.

The years pass and Jacob and his growing family finally turn their steps toward home. Jacob has lived the life of a nomad for over 20 years and now he is coming home. There is only one problem. Esau is back home and the matter between them in unresolved.

6.   Esau Incident.

It is while Jacob is returning to Canaan and wrestling with his upcoming reunion with Esau that he finds himself in the middle of the night wrestling with an unknown opponent.

Then Jacob was left alone, and a man wrestled

with him until daybreak. (Genesis 32:24).

The name of the River where this all took place is the River Jabbok. The word Jabbok means "to wrestle." It seems as though Jacob was alone with himself and then suddenly he was no longer alone and he was wrestling with an unknown figure in the night. What began as a physical struggle seemed to take on epic proportions as it continued throughout the entire night. It must have seemed endless to Jacob, but he would not quit. This was the story of his life. He had come into this world as the heel-grabber, grasping for what he could get. All his life had been a struggle and a striving and a wrestling. With his father; with his brother; with his Uncle Laban. But the real struggle had always been with this one with whom he now grappled – this unknown adversary in the night.

> *And when he saw that he had not prevailed against him, he touched the socket of his thigh; so the socket of Jacob's thigh was dislocated while he wrestled with him. 26 Then he said, "Let me go, for the dawn is breaking." But he said, "I will not let you go unless you bless me." (Genesis 32:25-26).*

Jacob's victory is not one of strength, but of desperation. It is a struggle of faith. He holds on to the angel and refuses to let go. The One to whom he holds is not bound by Jacob's strength, but by Jacob's faith. Jacob wants what he has always wanted -- the blessing of God. He holds to the One who can give the blessing. He holds to the One who is the blessing. Jacob's victory was not one of power. Rather, it was a victory of grace. He was given that for which he was undeserving to be given and which he was powerless to take.

> *So he said to him, "What is your name?" And he said, "Jacob." 28 And he said, "Your name shall no longer be Jacob, but Israel; for you have striven with God and with men and have prevailed." (Genesis 22:27-28).*

Jacob's name is changed. No longer will he be Jacob the heel-grabber; Jacob the con-artist. From this time on, he shall be known as Israel because he has *ISRA*-ed with EL, that is, he has striven with God.

This incident can be seen as the climactic event in the Jacob narrative as the events come full circle from the beginning of that narrative. At the beginning, Jacob is named "heel-grabber;" now at the end of the narrative, he is given his new name of Israel.

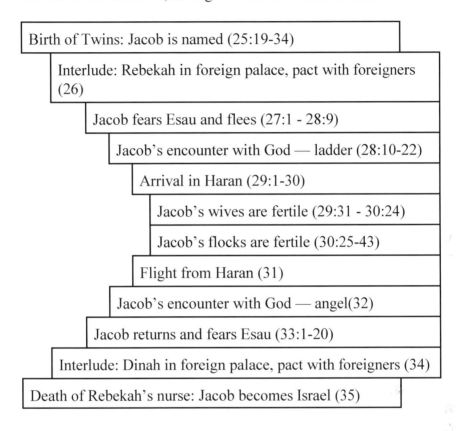

Birth of Twins: Jacob is named (25:19-34)

Interlude: Rebekah in foreign palace, pact with foreigners (26)

Jacob fears Esau and flees (27:1 - 28:9)

Jacob's encounter with God — ladder (28:10-22)

Arrival in Haran (29:1-30)

Jacob's wives are fertile (29:31 - 30:24)

Jacob's flocks are fertile (30:25-43)

Flight from Haran (31)

Jacob's encounter with God — angel(32)

Jacob returns and fears Esau (33:1-20)

Interlude: Dinah in foreign palace, pact with foreigners (34)

Death of Rebekah's nurse: Jacob becomes Israel (35)

THE JOSEPH NARRATIVE

Genesis sets forth a contrast between Joseph and Judah, the fourth son of Jacob who eventually received the leadership of the Israelites.

Judah	Joseph
Went to a foreigner of his own will.	Taken to Egypt against his will.
Sexual immorality: went in to his daughter-in-law (38:12-18).	Sexual morality: resisted seduction (39:6-12)
Left his seal & his cord.	Left his garment.
Accuser (38:24).	Falsely accused (39:13-20).

Judgment of God (38:6-10).	Blessing of God (39:20-23).
True accusation of a woman (38:25).	False accusation of a woman (39:13-20).

Moses is contrasting the moral character of Judah as the head of his tribe with the moral character of Joseph as the head of Ephraim and Manasseh. Why is this important for the Israelites in the Wilderness to know? Because it explains why Joseph's tribes receive a double portion, both here in the Wilderness and when they enter the

> These chapters serve as a warning to the rest of Israel not to follow in the footsteps of their ancestors as they see Joseph's tribes receive the double portion.

promised land. Jacob demonstrated that Joseph was his favorite son and heir to the double portion inheritance by awarding him a "coat with sleeves." This was the sign of one who was to be the leader of the clan.

1.   Sold into Egypt.

The hatred of the brothers had its climax in a murderous plot which ended only when Joseph had been sold to some passing slavers. Joseph found himself being sold to an official of Egypt. Meanwhile, the Midianites sold him in Egypt to Potiphar, Pharaoh's officer, the captain of the bodyguard. (Genesis 37:36).

The word translated "officer" is *seriys* and is usually translated "eunuch." The problem with this is that eunuchs were not married men and Potiphar clearly had a wife. However *seriys* seems to be an Akkadian loan-word which went through a change of meaning between the first and second millennia.

- In the 2nd millennia is described a court official.
- By the 1st millennia it had come to mean a eunuch.

2.   Egypt in the Days of Joseph.

> The pyramids were already ancient monuments when Joseph came to Egypt.

Joseph entered Egypt in the days of the Middle Kingdom. Egypt during this period was ruled by a strong, centralized government. The pharaohs of this period had their power held somewhat in check by the individual governors.

Mines in the Sinai and in Ethiopia brought precious metals to the courts of the pharaoh and a line of military fortresses were established around the borders of Egypt to protect from outside invaders. Just prior to Joseph entering Egypt, the capital was moved from Thebes to a place near the Delta. This meant the pharaoh would have had more opportunity to interact with visitors coming to Egypt from the Levant.

3.   Joseph's Imprisonment.

For a time, Joseph prospered in the house of Potiphar. This time of prosperity was brought to a close in the attempted seduction by Potiphar's wife. When Joseph rebuffed her, she falsely accused him of attempted rape.

> Joseph's coat had gotten him into slavery in Egypt in the first place. Now it is again his garment which gets him into trouble.

Joseph was taken and thrown into the royal prison where political prisoners were held. It was there that he befriended the pharaoh's butler. This friendship, along with a God given gift of interpreting dreams, would result in Joseph's promotion to the Court of Pharaoh.

4.   Joseph's Exaltation.

In a single day, Joseph found himself propelled up to the position of Viceroy over all Egypt, second only to the Pharaoh. Joseph's economic plan called for him to store up grain and food supplies for a coming time of famine. When that time came, Joseph was able to heighten the Pharaoh's political hold over the nobility and the landowners of Egypt by allowing the people to sell all of their lands to him in return for food.

So Joseph bought all the land of Egypt for Pharaoh, for every Egyptian sold his field, because the famine was severe upon them. Thus the land became Pharaoh's.

And as for the people, he removed them to the cities from one end of Egypt's border to the other.

Only the land of the priests he did not buy, for the priests had an allotment from Pharaoh, and they lived off the allotment which Pharaoh gave them. Therefore, they did not sell their land. (Genesis 47:20

22).

From this time on, Egypt became a virtual feudal state with the Pharaoh owning the land and allowing the people to work it and keep 80% of the profit.

5.   Israel's Entrance into Egypt.

After several dramatic encounters with his brothers, Joseph invited the entire clan to move into Egypt. The immediate reason for Israel's entrance into Egypt was because of the famine; but there were some underlying reasons. God's plan and purpose for Israel was to maintain a pure people, set apart for the purpose of loving and serving Yahweh as their God, eventually spreading His name throughout all the earth. When we examine the Patriarchs with this concept in mind, we are able to note a startling contrast among them.

a.   Altars and Worship.

Abraham, Isaac and Jacob each would move to a new place within the land and build an altar there, proclaiming the name of the Lord.

b.   A Sense of Purpose.

Each of these Patriarchs had a sense of purpose, a sense of destiny because of the promises that God had given. The altars were symbolic of that purpose in the land.

c.   Unity.

Because of that distinctive purpose, they also had a sense of unity that there would be no division between the worshipers of Yahweh. Thus, when strife arose between the servants of Abraham and the servants of Lot, a peaceful means was found to co exist.

d.   Racial and Religious Purity.

Their sense of unity led them to a realization of the need for separation from the Canaanites in whose midst they were dwelling. This unity was a part of the purpose of God that they would be a distinct and separate people from the nations around them. Thus, when it came time for Isaac to take a wife, Abraham took great pains to make certain that it would not be a Canaanite woman: *And Abraham said to his servant, the oldest of the household, who had charge of all that he owned, "Please place your hand under my thigh. 3 And I will make you swear by the Lord, the God of heaven and the God of earth, that **you shall not take a wife for my son from the daughters of the Canaanites**, among whom I live." (Genesis 24:2 3).*

In the same way, Jacob was sent to Haran with the express purpose of finding a wife from his own people: *So Isaac called Jacob and blessed him and charged him, and said to him, "You shall not take a wife from the daughters of Canaan. 2 Arise, go to Paddan aram, to the house of Bethuel your mother's father; and from there take to yourself a wife from the daughters of Laban your mother's brother." (Genesis 28:1-2).*

Abraham, Isaac and Jacob each followed these principles. However, when you come to the sons of Israel, you find a very big generation gap. They built no altars and are never said to proclaim the name of Yahweh. They show no sense of purpose. They seem only interested in filling their own fleshly desires. They have absolutely no concern for the unity among their family. Quite the contrary, they are motivated by jealousy and strife. This is best demonstrated when they sell their own brother into slavery. They recognize no need for separation from the Canaanites. Instead, we see them intermarrying with the people of Canaan and going off to live with them. This manifests itself in a number of ways.

(1)   Lack of chastity in Dinah.

(2)   Simeon & Levi murder the population of an entire city.

(3)   Reuben sleeps with his father's concubine.

(4)   Judah has a child by his own daughter in law.

Only in Joseph do we find anyone within that generation who demonstrates a sense of unity, purpose, and faith. Therefore, God moves in history to bring the Israelites out of Canaan and into Egypt.

Why Egypt? Aside from the obvious fact that Egypt was the breadbasket of the world and could support and feed the growing embryo of the nation that would one day be Israel, there was a very significant reason for Egypt to be the host mother of Israel.

The Canaanites followed a policy of integration. They were constantly seeking to intermarry and form family alliances with those around them (Genesis 19:14, 26:10; 26:34; 27:46; 34:8-10). This would have resulted in the breakdown and the absorption of the Jewish nation before it had even begun.

The Egyptians, on the other hand, were extremely strict segregationalists (Genesis 43:32; 46:34). Thus the Israelites in Egypt would have no choice but to remain a pure, undefiled, and separated nation as God prepared them in Egypt. Four hundred years later, God would lead them out of Egypt and into the land that He had prepared for them.

All these died in faith, without receiving the promises, but having seen them and having welcomed them from a distance, and having confessed that they were strangers and exiles on the earth. (Hebrews 11:13).

A PATTERN OF YOUNGER AND OLDER

Throughout the book of Genesis, there is a continuing pattern in which the younger is chosen over the older. That is not the way things were supposed to happen in the ancient world. The inheritance in the ancient world was always supposed to go to the older. But instead we see…

- Abel chosen over Cain
- Isaac chosen over Ishmael
- Jacob chosen over Esau
- Judah and Joseph chosen over Reuben

- Ephraim chosen over Manasseh

When the book of Hebrews want to describe the one act of faith for which Jacob is known, we do not find a reference to his working for Rachael for seven years or of his wrestling with an angel or of his love for Joseph. Instead, we find the reference to his blessing Ephraim over Manasseh.

> *By faith Jacob, as he was dying, blessed each of the sons of Joseph, and worshiped, leaning on the top of his staff. (Hebrews 11:21).*

Joseph brought his two sons to grandfather Jacob to be blessed by him. Joseph carefully arranged for the oldest to be by Jacob's right hand and for the young to be by Jacob's left hand. The right hand was the hand of honor and signified the greater portion. When Jacob went to give the blessing, he crossed his hands so that his right hand was upon the head of the younger while his left hand was upon the head of the older. Joseph wasn't pleased at all, but Jacob remained adamant.

What is the point? It is that now, at the end of his life, Jacob demonstrated that he finally understood that God doesn't choose the way the world chooses. God doesn't choose the one who is exalted or proud. God loves to choose the weak to confound the strong. He loves to choose the foolish to confound the wise. He loves to take that which the world despises and to lift him up to the position of first place so that God will receive the glory and honor.

EXODUS
The Book of Redemption

The theme of Exodus is *Redemption*. The Exodus from Egypt was the redemptive event of the Old Testament. It is not stating the matter too strongly to say that what the cross is to the New Testament, the Exodus Event was to the Old Testament.

| Old Testament | ↔ | New Testament |
| THE EXODUS | | THE CROSS |

This redemption theme involved three parts and these three sections will form a working outline of the book:

- The deliverance from Egypt.
- The establishing of the Covenant of Law.
- The regulations for worship as the means for approaching God.

There are some interesting similarities and parallels in Exodus with Genesis:

Genesis	Exodus
Begins with all of humanity in view	Begins with all of the Israelites in view
Eventually focuses upon one man - Abraham and his family	Eventually focuses upon one man - Moses and his family
Abraham has two siblings: Nahor & Haran	Moses has two siblings: Aaron & Miriam
Called to leave and travel to a foreign land	Forced to leave and flee to Midian

The big idea in the book of Exodus is the presence of the Lord. This is seen in the third chapter where He reveals Himself as the "I AM" and sends Moses to deliver the people that they may come and be with the Lord. This involves taking them out of Egypt, calling them to holiness, and the construction of the tabernacle. The climax of the narrative is when the presence of the Lord comes and resides in the tabernacle so that the Lord can be with His people.

Just as Genesis was organized around ten sets of generations, so also there are a number of groups of tens in Exodus: 10 plagues on the Egyptians, 10 commandments, 10 items to be built.

DELIVERANCE				WORSHIP	
Preparation of the Deliverer	Pharaoh & Plagues	Through the Red Sea	Provision in the Wilderness	The Giving of the Law	Regulations for the Tabernacle
Israel in Egypt		Enroute to the Sinai		Israel at the Sinai	
Ten Plagues		Ten Commandments		Ten Items	
1 - 6	7 - 12	13 - 15	15 - 18	19 - 24	25 - 40

There is a movement within this book as God takes His people from their slavery and brings them to the place where they can worship Him in freedom.

The Israelites are enslaved in Egypt	⇨	The Covenant People worshiping their God in Sinai

While the message in Genesis is hope in Yahweh, the message (ie. 'Big Idea') in Exodus would seem to be the presence of Yahweh, revolving around the revelation of His name and its etymology in the Hebrew, "I Am." Each transition centers on one aspect of what His presence meant for the Israelites: deliverance from bondage through the plagues, call to holiness through the commandments, and guidance through the building of the Tabernacle. The climactic action is when the glory of the Lord come and fills the Tabernacle with His presence. That same presence that guided the Israelites in all their travels in the wilderness now comes and dwells among His people.

PLACE OF WRITING

There is evidence to indicate that the Mosaic History was not a single unified work. Genesis ends with the death of Joseph. But then Exodus recaps the Joseph story in Exodus 1:1-7. A further example is seen in the period of time which is covered in Exodus.

> *And the sons of Israel ate the manna **forty years**, until they came to the border of the land of Canaan. (Exodus 16:35).*

Either Moses is writing this at the end of their Wilderness Wanderings or else Joshua takes up the prophetic mantle (under the direction of the Holy Spirit) and edits this book following the death of his mentor. On the other hand, there is a certain continuity between Genesis and Exodus. This is why Exodus starts with a ו ("and").

DATING THE EXODUS

Perhaps the key chronological question of the Old Testament is the dating of the Exodus. Two major views have been set forth.

- The Early Date: 1446 B.C.

  This date is taken from 1 Kings 6:1 which designates a span of 480 years from the Exodus to the dedication of Solomon's Temple, an occurrence which has been established at 966 B.C.

- The Late Date: About 1270 B.C.

  This date is based upon the Septuagint reading of Exodus 12:40. The Massoretic text reads:

  > *Now the time that the sons of Israel lived in Egypt was four hundred and thirty years. (Exodus 12:40).*

  When we read the Greek Septuagint, we find the addition of the words και ἐν γή Χανααν:

  > *Now the time that the sons of Israel lived in the land of Egypt **and in the land of Canaan** was four hundred and thirty years. (Exodus 12:40 LXX).*

This view sees the period from Abraham's entrance into the land of Canaan to the Exodus as being a period of 400 years.

The following chart provides a summary of the various arguments that are used to support each date:

THE EARLY DATE (15TH CENTURY)	THE LATE DATE (13TH CENTURY)
The reigning Pharaoh would have been Amenhotep II of the 18th Dynasty.	The Pharaoh of the Exodus would have been either Rameses II or Merenptah.
1 Kings 6:1 designates 480 from the Exodus to the dedication of Solomon's Temple (966 B.C.).	The 480 years is made up of 12 generations (12x40=480). In reality a generation was only about 25 years.
In Judges 11:26 Jephthah says that 300 years had passed from his day since the entrance into Canaan.	Jephthah's remark was a generalization and was not meant to be taken literally.

Historical and archaeological factors to be considered in the establishing of the date of the exodus event:

1.   In Exodus 1:11 the Israelites are said to have been involved in the building of the city of Rameses. There are several possibilities here:

   • The name Rameses was used prior to the 13th century and could have been given to this city at that time.

   • Even according to this account, the city was being built prior to the birth of Moses and therefore 80 years before the Exodus as well as before the reign of Rameses II. Therefore we cannot make too much of the fact of the name of the city.

> The fact that there is no mention of either Moses or the Exodus from Egypt in any of the extant inscriptions should not surprise us. The Egyptians did not record their own defeats and would have carefully edited anything in the way of the exodus event. A similar sort of denial was seen in the 2003 American invasion of Iraq when the Iraqi minister of propaganda stood before the newsmen and announced that the American forces had all been defeated in the desert. Two minutes later, the American tanks rolled down the same street where he stood.

- It is possible that this city was later named after Rameses II and that our Biblical Text was "modernized" by later scribes. This takes place frequently within the Pentateuch.

2. The Merenptah Stela (dated at about 1220 B.C.) mentions Israel by name as one of the recognized people-groups in Canaan. This would mandate that Israel had to have entered the land at a considerably earlier date.

3. The Amarna Tablets contain letters written from cities in Canaan to the pharaoh of Egypt. They tell of an upheaval caused by invading "Habiru." It is disputed as to whether this is a reference to the Israelite Hebrews as the term Habiru seems to be used of a wider group than merely the Israelites. On the other hand, the Bible itself uses the term in a wider sense and thus describes Abram as a "Hebrew" in Genesis 14:13, indicating that it was a recognized designation for a particular people group long before it came to be associated with the Israelites.

THE EARLY CAREER OF MOSES

Although born as the third child to a poor Hebrew family, a social outcast and condemned from birth, God preserved Moses through a magnificent sequence of events to become the son of Pharaoh's daughter.

1. Birth and Infancy.

Moses was born in troubled times. The pharaoh of Egypt had issued a decree that all newborn Hebrew males were to be killed. Moses was hidden at first by his parents and then placed in a box of reeds and set to drift on the Nile River. There he was found by one of the daughters of the Pharaoh who had come down to bathe. There is a touch of irony here in that the order of the Pharaoh had been that the Hebrew children were to be thrown into the Nile. The mother of Moses obeys the letter of the law and placed him into the Nile, albeit in a place of safety. She carefully places him into a wicker basket that had been covered with tar and pitch. The description of this basket it meant to remind the reader of that with which he is already familiar from a reading of the book of Genesis. It calls to mind the story of Noah and the Flood.

Noah	Moses
Ordered to build an ark (תֵּבַת)	His mother gets a basket (תֵּבַת)
It will protect Noah and his family and the animals from the destruction of the flood.	It will protect Moses from the destruction mandated by the pharaoh's orders.
Noah is delivered from the waters of the flood.	Moses is delivered from the waters of the Nile.

Note the word "basket." The Hebrew text refers to it as a *tebath* (תֵּבַת — ark). This is the same word that is used for Noah's Ark. This is the only other usage of the word in the entire Bible. What does this basket have in common with Noah's ark?

- They save lives
- They are meant to float
- They are covered with pitch

One is very big and the other is very small. Moses assumes that you will make the connection with the previous *tebah*. What other phrases or words from the first part of Exodus are reminiscent of the book of Genesis?

- She saw that he was good (2:2).
- God saw that it was good (seen all throughout Genesis 1).
- They multiplied and the land was filled with them (Ex 1:7).
- Multiply and fill the earth (Genesis 1:28).

Moses is bringing forth the language of Genesis. Why? Because he wishes to give a creation motif. Instead of the creation of the earth, now we are seeing the creation of the nation of Israel. This is the story of a birth of a nation. Thus it is

> The same sort of motif is seen in the birth of Jesus.
> - The king tries to put him to death.
> - Other children are killed in the process.
> - He is hidden from the king.
> - He is taken to Egypt.
> - He becomes the savior of the nation.

appropriate to use creation language. He is telling you that the two most important events in his world are the creation of the world and the creation of the nation of Israel.

We no longer live in a literary world, so we are not used to picking up literary details. Today we are more used to movies. People watch the same movie over and over and often pick up the tiny details. In the ancient world, those who listened to the same passage would pick up these tiny details in the repeated readings.

The baby Moses is placed into the carefully constructed basket and placed *among the reeds by the bank of the Nile*. He is not merely cast adrift, but is placed in the midst of protective reeds that will keep the basket from drifting. There is in this simple narrative a touch of humorous irony. The edict of the pharaoh was that all newborn Hebrew males were to be thrown into the Nile and this baby has been placed into the Nile in keeping with that edict. The baby is even given a babysitter in the person of his older sister.

We know from later in the book of Exodus that her name is Miriam, but it is not given here. I want to suggest there is a specific reason for this omission. Similarly, when our passage opened, we were told about the parents of Moses, but we were not given their names. They are named later in Exodus, but their names are absent here. There is instead an air of anonymity to the entire story. The content of the story is that the parents are trying to be secretive. In doing so, the story takes on the mode of secrecy so as to take the reader into the same sort of anonymity.

As the story unfolds, Moses is adopted by the daughter of Pharaoh and given the name Moses, which means "one drawn out." As a pagan Nile worshiper, she perhaps attributed this infant to a gift from the Nile River.

2. Education.

There is only one verse in all of the Bible which even mentions the education of Moses in Egypt. *"And Moses was educated in all the learning of the Egyptians, and he was a man of power in words and deeds." (Acts 7:22).* It would seem from this that Moses was given the finest education available in what was at that time the most advanced nation on earth. This would have included math, astronomy, engineering, literature and military science. His teachers had all of the learning of the engineers who designed the pyramids and the sphinx. Notice that the fame of Moses was both "in words and deeds."

Josephus, the Jewish historian who lived in the days of the New Testament, tells a story of an invasion of Ethiopian tribes to the south which threatened to overwhelm the land of Egypt. According to Josephus, it was Moses who led the armies of Egypt southward to meet the Ethiopian hordes, driving them back to their own lands.

3.   The Decision of Moses.

> *"But when he was approaching the age of forty, it entered his mind to visit his brethren, the sons of Israel." (Acts 7:23).*

The children of Israel had settled in the area of Goshen, located on the eastern side of the Delta region of Egypt. They lived here in their own villages because the Egyptians did not hold to integration. To the contrary, they were perhaps the most bigoted segregationists in all of history.

Though he had been raised as an Egyptian, there came a day when Moses decided to visit the people of Israel. I think that it was at this time that Moses began to learn of the God of Abraham, Isaac and Jacob. He heard the promises that had been given to these people. And, having heard this message, Moses made a decision.

> *By faith Moses, when he had grown up, refused to be called the son of Pharaoh's daughter; 25 choosing rather to endure ill-treatment with the people of God, than to enjoy the passing pleasures of sin; 26 considering the reproach of Christ greater riches than the treasures of Egypt; for he was looking to the reward." (Hebrews 11:24-26).*

Moses made a decision to reject his Egyptian heritage. This man was "the son of Pharaoh's daughter" and possibly the crown prince of Egypt. And yet, he gave it all up. And for what? To be identified with a group of slaves without homes or possessions, a people who had nothing but a promise.

4.   The Murder.

It was some time after this that another event took place in the life of Moses that was to become a turning point in his life.

Now it came about in those days, when Moses had grown up, that he went out to his brethren and looked on their hard labors; and he saw an Egyptian beating a Hebrew, one of his brethren. 12 So he looked this way and that, and when he saw there was no one around, he struck down the Egyptian and hid him in the sand. (Exodus 2:11-12).

Moses had already made one decision. He had already decided to throw in his lot with the Israelites. Now, he comes upon an injustice. An Egyptian is beating a Hebrew. Moses makes another decision. He decides to stop the injustice - permanently.

"And he supposed that his brethren understood that God was granting them deliverance through him; but they did not understand." (Acts 7:25).

Somehow Moses had come to recognize that God was going to use him in delivering the Israelites. He had heard the promises to Abraham, Isaac, and Jacob that the people of Israel would be delivered from Egypt. He recognized that God had chosen him and protected him. And so, he figures that this is as good a time as any to begin the work of deliverance.

Do you see what he was doing? He was trying to do God's work in his own way. He was very sincere. But he was sincerely wrong. Being sincere is never a substitute for righteousness. It is true that God is going to use Moses to deliver the people of Israel. But it will not be by Moses's strength or power or wisdom that this will be accomplished.

5.   Flight to Midian.

Moses had thrown in his lot with the hated Israelites and no longer had the throne of Egypt to protect him. If the traditional early chronology is correct, then this murder took place near the end of the reign of Hatshepset as Thutmoses III was soon coming to the throne. Already as vice-regent under his stepmother, he may have posed a threat to the life of Moses. The Biblical account specifically states that "when Pharaoh heard of this matter, he tried to kill Moses" (Exodus 2:15). Eugene Merrill makes the following observation:

That the pharaoh himself took note of what would otherwise have been a relatively minor incident suggests that this particular pharaoh had more than casual interest in ridding himself of Moses (1987:62).

It is possible that Thutmoses III saw Moses as a potential rival to the throne and therefore sought to use this opportunity to be rid of him? It would not be until after the death of Thutmoses III that Moses would feel free to return to Egypt (Exodus 2:23).

Moses was forced to flee Egypt. He sought refuge in Midian, the wilderness lands to the east of the Gulf of Aqaba. The Anastasi Papyri are made up of official reports from the Egyptian border authorities and demonstrate the tight control which they held over the Egyptian border.

- Anastasi III records the daily border crossings of immigrants during the reign of Pharaoh Mernptah.
- Anastasi VI records the passage of an entire tribe from Edom into Egypt during a drought.
- Anastasi V describes the escape of two slaves from the royal palace at Pi-Rameses. The Egyptian commander of the boarder writes the following: *In life, prosperity, health! In the favor of Amon-Re, King of the gods, and of the ka of the King of Upper and Lower Egypt... I was sent forth... at the time of evening, following after these two slaves... When I reached the fortress, they told me that the scouts had come from the desert, saying that they had passed the walled place north of the Migdol of Seti Merne-Ptah* (BAR Jan/Feb 1999).

Though these date after the 18th Dynasty, they reflect the control over the boarders of Egypt in Biblical times.

MOSES VERSUS PHARAOH

Then the Lord said to Moses, "See, I make you as God to Pharaoh, and your brother Aaron shall be your prophet." (Exodus 7:1).

Exodus presents a contest between the God of Israel versus the gods of Egypt and a contest between Moses versus Pharaoh.

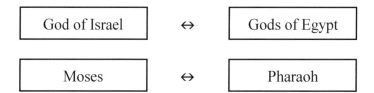

For Moses to meet with Pharaoh, it must follow that Moses is on the same level with Pharaoh. How was Pharaoh viewed in ancient Egypt? He was viewed as a god. There was a hierarchy of position in the ancient world. The highest position was that of a god. Next was that of a prophet. Then came the priest. Finally came all of the other people. There is a sense in which both Aaron and Moses are commissioned to act the part of a higher office than is their own.

- Moses the prophet acts the part of God to Aaron and to Pharaoh.
- Aaron the priest acts the part of a prophet.

> *"Moreover, he shall speak for you to the people; and it shall come about that he shall be as a mouth for you, and you shall be as God to him." (Exodus 4:16).*

Moses gets a temporary promotion along with Aaron. Moses will act in the place of God to Aaron and Aaron will act in the place of prophet. In this way, God challenges Pharaoh on his own turf. "You think that your gods and magicians can accomplish all of these terrific miracles. I will accomplish them before your eyes and show you that I am God rather than Pharaoh or the false gods of Egypt."

THE PLAGUES

The plagues were God's judging hand against those who had enslaved and were persecuting His people. It has been suggested that many (if not all) of these plagues were directed against the false gods of Egypt.

- The Nile was worshiped.
- Heqt, the god of resurrection, took the form of a frog.
- Hathor, the mother-goddess, took the form of a cow. Bulls were also held sacred.
- Nut was the sky goddess.
- Isis was the goddess of life.

- Seth was the protector of crops.
- The sun was worshiped as the symbol of several different gods.
- The pharaoh was worshiped as a god.

Notice that there is an increase in severity in the progression of the plagues. They begin with discomfort and move on to suffering, followed by destruction and finally death. The first nine plagues can be arranged into three groups of three plagues each.

PLAGUES	EFFECTS	INITIATOR
1-3	Loathsome.	Inflicted by hand of Aaron using the rod.
4-6	Painful.	Inflicted by the hand of the Lord.
7-9	Destructive beyond anything ever before experienced in Egypt.	Inflicted by the hand of Moses.

The first three plagues were upon all of the inhabitants of Egypt. By contrast, the last six plagues fall only upon the Egyptians and do not directly affect the Israelites.

1.   The plagues were an attack upon the gods of Egypt. The religion of Egypt was animistic in that they worshiped the sun, the moon, and the Nile as well as holding a vast variety of animals and insects to be representative of their various deities.

2.   There is an escalation of power seen in contrast with the growing inability of the Egyptian priesthood. When the conflict between Moses and the gods of Egypt begins, the priests of Egypt are able to manifest a certain degree of power.

- The magicians were able to turn their staffs into serpents (Exodus 7:11).
- The magicians were able to turn water into blood (Exodus 7:22).
- The magicians brought about more frogs (Exodus 8:7).

The turning point comes in   Exodus 8:18 when the Egyptian

magicians failed to bring about more gnats. We finally see them in Exodus 9:11 where they cannot face Moses because they are covered with boils.

3. The Exodus from Egypt took place at a time in history when Egypt was at its pinnacle of strength. It was a superpower. The lesson is that the God we worship is very powerful.

4. Throughout all of these plagues, we see a continuing hardening of Pharaoh's heart. This brings up a question. Who hardened Pharaoh's heart?

- God hardened Pharaoh's heart (Exodus 4:21; 7:3; 9:12; 10:1, 20, 27; 11:10; 14:4, 8, 17).

- Pharaoh hardened his own heart (Exodus 8:15, 32; 9:34).

Which is correct? They both are. There was a synergistic action taking place within Pharaoh. Both the Lord as well as Pharaoh himself were involved in the process. It is not as though Pharaoh wished to release the people but was being prevented by God's work in his life. Pharaoh had already set himself against God. In the same way, there are times when God "greases the tracks" in the direction you have chosen to go.

THE CROSSING OF THE RED SEA

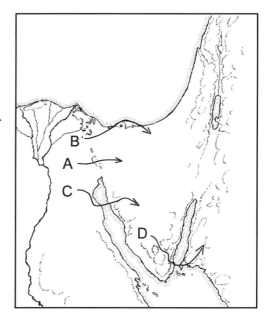

The crossing of the Red Sea was, by all accounts, a momentous event. It marked the destruction of the army of Pharaoh and it also marked the liberation of the Israelites from Egypt.

1. The Place of the Crossing. Several theories have been advanced as to where the crossing of the Red Sea took place and as to the

nature of that crossing.

a.   The Lakes East of the Delta.

        Much ado has been made about the fact that the Hebrew
        Scriptures have the Israelites crossing the *Yam Suph* (literally,
        "Sea of Reeds"). It is argued that this must refer to one of the
        marshy lakes that lay between the Red Sea and the
        Mediterranean. This view is often made to say that these lakes
        were very shallow and that the Israelites were able to wade
        across while the heavy chariots of the Egyptians became stuck
        in the soft mush of the marsh.

b.   The Gulf of Elath.

        Another view identifies the Yam Suph as the Gulf of Elath,
        located to the northeast of the Nile Delta. There is a narrow
        strip of land that curves out into the Mediterranean. The
        problem with this view is that the Bible expressly says that
        Israel did not take the route known as "the way of the
        Philistines" (Exodus 13:17).

c.   The Red Sea.

        The Bible continues to speak of the Yam Suph in a way that
        is an obvious reference to the Red Sea. In 1 Kings 9:26,
        Solomon is said to have built a fleet of ships on the shore of
        the Yam Suph. It is unlikely that these ships were located in
        some desert marshes or any other small body of water.

d.   The Gulf of Aqaba.

        This view has the Israelites going through the Sinai Desert
        and then crossing the relatively narrow area on the south end
        of the Gulf of Aqaba. This portion of the gulf has something
        of an underwater land bridge and is only about 150 feet deep
        as opposed to the 1000 foot depth on either side.

        The problem with this view is that the Israelites would not
        have had enough time to leave Migdol at the border of Egypt,
        avoid the way of the Philistines, and then arrive at the Gulf of
        Aqaba, cross that portion of the Red Sea, and then spend

another three days in the wilderness of Shur, camping at Elam and then leaving there to go to the wilderness of Sin in the allotted time.

Gordon Franz points out why we can know that Mount Sinai was outside the Land of Midian: *In Exodus 18, Moses and the Israelites are camped at "the Mountain of God" (Mt. Sinai) when Jethro, Moses' father-in-law, visits them. Verse 27 says, "Then Moses let his father-in-law depart [from Mt. Sinai], and he went his way to his own land [Midian]."* [4]

2.   The Means of Parting the Waters.

When the Bible describes the actual parting of the waters of the Red Sea, there are several interesting factors which are mentioned.

> *Then Moses stretched out his hand over the sea; and the Lord swept the sea back by a strong east wind all night, and turned the sea into dry land, so the waters were divided.*
> *And the sons of Israel went through the midst of the sea on the dry land, and the waters were like a wall to them, on their right hand and on their left. (Exodus 14:21-22).*

Notice that the parting of the water was directly caused by the "strong east wind." The prevailing winds in that area are normally from the west. An east wind comes off the desert and brings heavy dust. In this case, it must have been a very localized wind to drive back the waters at the precise place that Israel could cross.

Although the waters were parted on the "right hand and on their left," we must not infer that the path through the sea was a narrow hall as has been portrayed in modern movies. The indication is that the entire tribe of Israel numbering many hundreds of thousands passed through in the space of a single night. If this is so, then the parting of the sea might well have been up to a mile wide so that all could make the crossing.

---

[4] Paper presented at the ETS / NEAS meeting Thursday, November 15, 2001.

3.   The Destruction of Pharaoh's army.

The chariot corps of Egypt took off through the Red Sea in pursuit of Israel. Here, they ran into trouble.

> *And He caused their chariot wheels to swerve, and He made them drive with difficulty... (Exodus 14:25a).*

A traffic jam took place on the sea bottom. Before they could retreat, the sea returned to its normal state, covering chariot and soldier alike so that all were lost.

THE MOSAIC COVENANT

With the escape of the Israelites into the Sinai Wilderness, the first step in the formation of the nation was completed. Next, the Lord moves to give the Israelites a constitution which will bind them together and unify them as a nation. Upon arrival at Mount Sinai, the Lord entered into a constitutional covenant with Israel. There were five parts to this covenant.

1.   The Preamble.

Just as the Constitution of the United States of America has a Preamble which states the purpose of that Constitution, so in Exodus 19:5-6 we have the Preamble to the Israelite Constitution designed by God.

> *"Now then, if you will indeed obey My voice and keep My covenant, then you shall be My own possession among all the peoples, for all the earth is Mine; 6 and you shall be to Me a kingdom of priests and a holy nation." These are the words that you shall speak to the sons of Israel." (Exodus 19:5-6).*

In these verses, we see God's purpose and plan for the nation of Israel. It was a threefold plan.

- • A Possession.

First, Israel is to be a possession belonging to the Lord. She will be valued above the other nations of the earth, even though they all belong to the Lord.

- A Kingdom of Priests.

Secondly, Israel is to be a kingdom of priests. A priest is one who acts as an intermediary between man and God. The way of access to the Lord will now be through the sons of Israel. There will be no access to God apart from the priesthood of God's special nation.

- A Holy Nation.

Finally, Israel will be a nation completely set apart from the other nations of the world as a holy nation to the Lord.

It is toward these three goals that all of the commands in the Mosaic Law are directed. These three goals are ultimately fulfilled in Jesus Christ and in His church. All of these qualities are ascribed both to Jesus and to His body, the united assembly of covenant believers.

2.   The Decalogue.

When we speak of the Decalogue, we are referring to the Ten Commandments given in Exodus 20:1-17. They express the eternal, moral, and righteous will of God.

(1)   No other gods: Israel was to be set apart from the other nations of the world in that she was to be monotheistic, worshiping only the one true God.

(2)   No idols: The language of this passage does not necessarily forbid statues or paintings as long as they are not objects of worship.

(3)   God's name: It is declared sinful to use the name of Yahweh irresponsibly or in profane speech.

(4)   The Sabbath: The keeping of the Sabbath was the sign of the Mosaic Covenant (Exodus 31:13-17).

Covenant	Sign
Noahic Covenant	The rainbow
Abrahamic Covenant	Circumcision
New Covenant	Lord's Supper and baptism

By working six days and resting on the seventh, Israel gave outward symbolic indication that she had entered into a covenant relationship with the Creator who had originally worked six days and rested on the seventh.

(5) Respect for parents: This command contains with it a promise; a prolonged life as the reward for obedience.

(6) No murder: This is in the pi'el stem in the Hebrew, giving what would normally refer to killing the intensive significance of murder. This is a command that protects the individual's right to life.

(7) No adultery: This command protects the individual's marriage and family.

(8) No stealing: This command protects the individual's personal property.

(9) No false witness: This command protects the individual's reputation. It is also a call for truth.

(10) No coveting: All of the previous commands deal with outward actions. This one deal with an inward attitude.

The first four commandments deal with Israel's relationship with Yahweh and give reasons for each command. These first four commands are completely unique to this constitution. No other society in the ancient world recognized laws similar to these since it was unthinkable to have only one God.

The last six commandments deal with principles of morality in man's relationship to other men. These are laws common to any society which recognizes basic establishment principles. This is why no explanation of them is necessary.

3.   The Judgments.

The Judgments (*Mishpatim*) were the laws which governed the social laws of Israel (Exodus 21-24). They were case laws which further developed the Decalogue. Each one begins with an "if" clause ("If you do this, then you will do that...").

4.   The Tabernacle and the Ark of the Covenant.

The Tabernacle was an elaborate tent which served as a portable temple for the Lord. It had an outer court where sacrifices could be offered, and the tent itself which was further divided into the Holy Place and the Holy of Holies. At the center of this innermost sanctum was the Ark of the Covenant.

The Ark was a wooden box overlaid with gold and having a solid gold cover known as the Mercy Seat. This Mercy Seat symbolized the throne of the King. The Shekinah glory of Yahweh would reside upon the mercy seat. The Ark was kept in the Holy of Holies within the Tabernacle. Therefore, the Tabernacle was the capital of the King. It was the center of government as well as the center of religion.

The Tabernacle pictures the person of Jesus who became flesh and "tabernacled" among us. It pictures our great High Priest who entered heaven itself with His own blood. And it pictures the One who is the Sinless Lamb of God who was offered to bear the sins of the world.

The building of the Tabernacle, its completion, and God's entrance into it provides the climax to which the entire book of Exodus has been building. This movement is seen in the following overview:

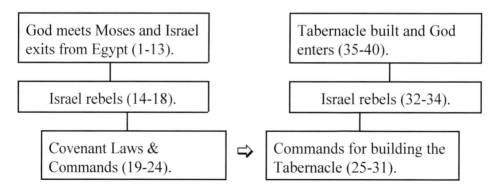

LEVITICUS
The Book of Worship

*You shall consecrate yourselves therefore and be holy,
for I am the Lord your God. 8 And you shall keep My statutes
and practice them; I am the Lord who sanctifies you.
(Leviticus 20:7-8).*

ABOUT THE BOOK OF LEVITICUS

1.   The Name of the Book.

     a.   Hebrew Name: The names of the first five books of Moses
           are taken from the first words which open the book. In this
           case, the opening word is *wa-ayiqra*, "and he called."

     b.   Greek Name: The Greek Septuagint uses the title *Leuitikon*,
           meaning "that which pertains to the Levites." This title was
           given because so much of the book deals with the ministry of
           the priesthood which descended from the tribe of Levi.

2.   Theme of Leviticus.

The book of Leviticus is a book about the rituals of Worship and
holiness. In this, it is a continuation of the Law which is set forth in
Exodus.

Exodus ends with the construction of the Tabernacle.		Leviticus tell us about the worship which takes place within that Tabernacle.

*Then the Lord called to Moses and spoke to
him from the tent of meeting... (Leviticus 1:1).*

Exodus ends with the glory of the Lord moving into the Tabernacle.
Leviticus picks up with the presence of the Lord calling out to Moses
from inside the Tabernacle. Leviticus teaches God's people how they
are to approach Him and live pleasing in His sight. Its central

93

command is to "be holy."

> *"...You shall be holy, for I the Lord your God am holy" (Leviticus 19:2).*

GENESIS	EXODUS	LEVITICUS
Origins of the Nation	Deliverance of the Nation	Life of the Nation
Theocracy Born	Theocracy Established	

Genesis begins with creation - it depicts the rise of God's people. Exodus begins in bondage - it tells of the redemption from Egypt. Leviticus begins in sacrifice - it sets forth the ritual of worship.

3.　　Structure of the Book. Leviticus is written in the form of a large chiasm - a parallel. A chiasm usually is used to bring emphasis to that which takes place at its pivotal point.

Appointed Offerings (1-7).
Laws of the Priests (8-10)
Laws of Purity (11-15).
Day of Atonement (16).
Laws of Holiness (17-20).
Laws of the Priests (21-22).
Appointed Times (23-25).
• Penalties for Disobedience (26)
• Making vows before the Lord (27)

The last two chapters dealing with the penalties for disobedience (chapter 26) and with the making of vows before the Lord (chapter 27) have been described as an appendix; something that was added on at the end of the book because there was no better place for it to go. But this is not the case. Rather than seeing them as a parenthetical appendix, I believe them to be the climactic portion of the book.

They describe what is to take place if the people do not pursue a course of holiness. As such, these chapters form the "so what?" of the book. They deliver the punch line. They tell us what God's response will be if they fail to follow the path of holiness.

Furthermore, the remainder of the Old Testament is the story of how these warnings were fulfilled in the history of the nation of Israel. It will be virtually impossible to read and to understand the prophets without understanding that the warnings they issued to the people in their day were a virtual repeating of the warnings of these two chapters.

LAWS OF OFFERINGS (LEVITICUS 1-7)

There are five specific types of offerings outlined in Leviticus.

Offering	Purpose	God's Portion	Priest's Portion	Symbolism
Burnt Offering (1:1-17).	Worship toward God.	All that is burned.	Skins (7:8).	Christ was offered up for us.
Grain Offering (2:1-16).	Described as a soothing aroma to the Lord.	All except when it is first fruits.	Remainder (6:16-18).	Jesus is the Bread of Life.
Peace Offering (3:1-17).		All that is burned.	Breast & right shoulder (7:31-32).	Jesus has a ministry of reconciliation to bring us back to God.
Sin Offering (4:1-5:13).	Sacrifice for Sin.	Fat burned outside the camp.	Only eaten by the priest if it has not entered the Tabernacle (6:30).	Sin is not permitted into the presence of God. But Jesus died "outside the camp" (Hebrews 13:11-13).
Guilt Offering (5:14-6:7).		Fat, kidneys & liver.	Eaten by males in priest's family.	Sin requires death.

In all cases, animal sacrifices were to be spotless and without blemish. Furthermore, it was always an animal which had been domesticated and raised by men. Wild animals were never used as offerings.

1.   The Burnt Offering.

The word used to describe the "burnt offering" is עֹלָה (*olah*) and is taken from the root verb meaning, "to go up" or "ascend." It is an offering of ascension. This referred to the fact that the entire offering was burned and "ascended to God."

a.   It was the foundational offering which allowed men to come into the presence of the Lord. For this reason, Leviticus 1:3 says that a man makes this offering *"that he may be accepted before the Lord"* and verse 4 adds that *"it may be accepted for him to make atonement on his behalf."*

b.   A life was offered upon the altar.

c.   It was to be completely burnt upon the altar. This showed that man's duty to God was not in the mere giving up of a portion, but in the entire surrender of all.

d.   Depending upon the financial status of the one making the offering, it could be comprised of a bull, a lamb, or a dove.

2.   The Grain Offering.

a.   It did not involve the taking of a life. Instead, it was made up of flour, oil, and incense.

It looked to the time at creation when God had given to man *"every plant yielding seed that is on the surface of the earth, and every tree which has fruit yielding seed"* (Genesis 1:29).

b.   This is a picture of the One who became our "Bread of Life" and who was anointed with the "Oil" of the Holy Spirit.

c.   Honey was forbidden; instead frankincense was used.

This is because honey would eventually turn sour (leaven was also forbidden); but frankincense received its highest degree of fragrance after it had been burned.

    d.   It was to be seasoned with salt - the picture of preservation (2:13).

3.   Peace Offering.

Everyone ate a portion of the peace offering (Offerer, the Lord, the priest, even the priest's children). In the Burnt Offering and the Grain Offering, the Lord and the Priest had a portion, but not the one making the offering. This signified communion with God. When you sit at a table and eat with someone, it signifies that you are at peace with him. Christ has become our peace offering. In Him both God and man find common food. It is noteworthy that the Peace Offering was generally accompanied by a libation of wine - bread and wine at the table of the Lord.

4.   Sin Offering.

    a.   The first three offerings were offered as acts of worship. This offering is made for atonement for sin.

    b.   The first three offerings were burnt upon the altar in the compound of the Tabernacle. This offering is burnt on the bare earth outside the camp. This is a picture of Jesus who was crucified outside of Jerusalem.

> *Therefore Jesus also, that He might sanctify the people though His own blood, suffered outside the gate. (Hebrews 13:12).*

5.   Guilt Offering.

This offering is the only one which is not described as a soothing aroma (even the Sin Offering is so described in Leviticus 4:31).

This offering is closely aligned to the sin offering; and yet there are a few subtle differences.

    a.   While the sins which call for the Sin Offering are only mentioned in a general sense, there are a number of specific offenses which mandate a Guilt Offering.

b.   A part of the Guilt Offering includes a financial recompense to the party that was wronged (6:5). Thus, the Guilt Offering included the principle of restitution.

LAWS OF THE PRIESTS (LEVITICUS 8-10)

Chapters 6-7 have a gradual shift to the part of the priesthood in the various offerings and this in turn brings us to the Laws of the Priests.

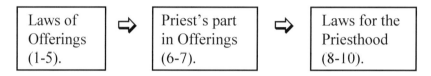

| Laws of Offerings (1-5). | ⇨ | Priest's part in Offerings (6-7). | ⇨ | Laws for the Priesthood (8-10). |

1.   The Anointing of the Priest.

> *Moses then took the anointing oil and anointed the tabernacle and all that was in it, and consecrated them.*
> *And he sprinkled some of it on the altar seven times and anointed the altar and all its utensils, and the basin and its stand, to consecrate them.*
> *Then he poured some of the anointing oil on Aaron's head and anointed him, to consecrate him. (Leviticus 8:10-12).*

There were only three groups of people who were commonly anointed in the Old Testament.

- Priests.
- Prophets.
- Kings.

Jesus filled each of these positions. And because He did, He is *HaMeshiah* - the "anointed One."

2.   Made Holy.

After having been cleansed and anointed, Aaron and his sons were required to stay at the door of the Tabernacle for seven days (8:35). They were being set apart for the work of the Lord. They were holy and this meant that they must be separate and distinct from the rest of the people. On the eighth day, another sacrifice was made and Aaron blessed the people.

> *Then Aaron lifted up his hands toward the people and blessed them, and he stepped down after making the sin offering and the burnt offering and the peace offerings.*
> *And Moses and Aaron went into the tent of meeting. When they came out and blessed the people, THE GLORY OF THE LORD APPEARED to all the people.*
> *Then fire came out from before the Lord and consumed the burnt offering and the portions of fat on the altar; and when all the people saw it, they shouted and fell on their faces. (Leviticus 9:22-24).*

3.   The Sin of Aaron's Sons (10:1-5).

The offering had been consumed by the supernatural fire of God (9:24). The sons of Aaron took it upon themselves to use a "strange fire" upon the altar - that is, a fire which was different from the flame which the Lord had sent. The result was that fire came out from the presence of the Lord in the Tabernacle and killed them. There are several lessons.

- We learn that God must be worshiped as He ordains that He is to be worshiped. We call this the regulative principle.

- We learn that obedience is better than sacrifice (1 Samuel 15:22). This obedience extends to the rituals which God has ordained.

- The presence of God can be either a curse or a blessing. The same fire which warmed the Israelites by night could also be used for judgment against those who sinned. While Jesus will be Judge when He sits "as a smelter and purifier of sliver" (Malachi 3:3; 4:1), He will also be the "Sun of Righteousness... with healing in His wings" (Malachi 4:2).

- It is possible to do the right thing in the wrong way. It is not that these sons of Aaron were trying to do evil. They seem to have been acting on good motives. They were seeking to worship the Lord. Like Uzzah (2 Samuel 6:7) they try to do a service for the Lord, but they do it improperly.

LAWS OF PURITY (LEVITICUS 11-15)

This section begins with a general chapter on unclean foods (both animals and water). It has been noted that many of these dietary requirements had value with regard to the kinds of diseases which could be caught. However, the purpose given for these laws was that God's people might be holy (11:44).

Uncleanliness was not limited to that which could be eaten or drunk. There were other aspects of ceremonial uncleanliness which were maintained within a person's body.

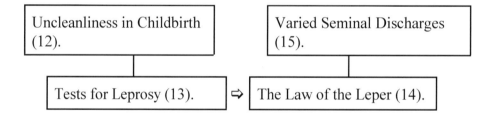

Uncleanliness in Childbirth (12).		Varied Seminal Discharges (15).
Tests for Leprosy (13).	⇨	The Law of the Leper (14).

THE DAY OF ATONEMENT (LEVITICUS 16)

Occupying a central place in the book of Leviticus is the most holy day of the year, *Yom Kippur*, the Day of Atonement.

1.   This Service was Performed by the High Priest Alone.

        The Tabernacle was to be emptied of all other inhabitants upon this day. The High Priest would be completely alone as he performed those parts of the ritual which took place within the Tabernacle. This was a picture of Jesus who was forsaken by all when He became the covering for our sins (Psalm 22:1).

2.   This Service Involved Passing within the Veil.

The priests were required to minister within the Tabernacle each morning and each evening. But the one thing they were never permitted to do in any of their ministry was to pass beyond the veil which separated the Holy Place from the Holy of Holies.

> *And the Lord said to Moses, "Tell your brother Aaron that he shall not enter at any time into the holy place inside the veil, before the mercy seat which is on the ark, lest he die; for I will appear in the cloud over the mercy seat." (Leviticus 16:2).*

The one exception to this rule took place on the Day of Atonement. On this day (and only on this day), the High Priest was permitted to pass beyond the veil into the very presence of God.

3.   The Clothing of the High Priest.

On this special day, the High Priest would be clothed in simple linen. The breastplate and the tunic and the gold and the blue and the scarlet would all be put aside. It was a picture of the Messiah who would lay aside His glory (Philippians 2:7).

4.   Offering for the High Priest.

Before he could act as mediator between God and the people, the High Priest first had to offer up a bull as an atonement for his own sins and for those of his family.

5.   The Two Goats.

Two goats were then to be taken and presented before the Lord. Lots would be cast.

> *And Aaron shall cast lots for the two goats, one lot for the Lord, and the other lot for the scapegoat.*
> *Then Aaron shall offer the goat on which the lot for the Lord fell, and make it a sin offering.*
> *But the goat on which the lot for the scapegoat fell shall be presented alive before the Lord, to make atonement upon it, to send it into the wilderness as the scapegoat. (Leviticus 16:8-10).*

Two goats were brought before the presence of the Lord. There was nothing to distinguish them apart. Lots were cast. These lots would determine which goat would live and which would die. The goat on whom the lot fell was killed and used as a sin offering. The other goat is referred to as the "scapegoat."

The phrase translated "for the scapegoat" is the Hebrew לַעֲזָאזֵל *(LaAzazel)*. This is a compound word made up of the joining of two Hebrew words. The problem is that there are several different Hebrew words that can fit.

- עַז *(Az)* is the Aramaic word for a "goat," though it is normally used to refer to a female goat. This same word can also refer to "power" or "strength" or even to "ferocity."

- אָזַל *(Azel)* is the verb, "to go."

Thus, this would refer either to the "goat of sending away" or else to "the sending forth of ferocity," thus depicting the wrath of God being sent out of the camp. Aaron was to take this goat and place both his hands upon it as he confessed all of the sins of Israel (for most sacrifices he only placed one hand upon the animal).

> *Then Aaron shall lay both his hands on the head of the live goat, and confess over it all the iniquities of the sons of Israel, and all their transgressions in regard to all their sins; and he shall lay them on the head of the goat and send it away into the wilderness by the hand of a man who stands in readiness. (Leviticus 16:21).*

The sins of the nation would be identified with the goat. And then the goat would be led away into the wilderness, signifying that the sins of the people had been carried away. The language used here is later repeated to speak of how the Lord would lay upon Messiah the sins of us all (Isaiah 53:6).

The writer of the Epistle to the Hebrews sets forth a series of contrasts and comparisons between the ritual sacrifices of the Day of Atonement and the work of Christ upon the cross.

The Old Covenant	The New Covenant
Therefore it was necessary for the copies of the things in the heavens to be cleansed with these (9:23).	But the heavenly things themselves with better sacrifices than these (9:23).
For Christ did not enter a holy place made with hands, a mere copy of the true one (9:24).	But into heaven itself, now to appear in the presence of God for us (9:24).
Nor was it that He should offer Himself often, as the high priest enters the holy place year by year with blood not his own, otherwise, He would have needed to suffer often since the foundation of the world (9:25-26).	But now once at the consummation of the ages He has been manifested to put away sin by the sacrifice of Himself (9:26).
And inasmuch as it is appointed for men to die once and after this comes judgment (9:27).	So Christ also, having been offered once to bear the sins of many, shall appear a second time for salvation without reference to sin, to those who eagerly await Him (9:28).

The rituals of the Day of Atonement were to be repeated each year. For over a thousand years, this drama was acted out, first within the Tabernacle, and later within the Temple. The ritual found its fulfillment on a spring day in the first century A.D. The Romans had set aside three crosses. Three thieves were destined to hang upon those crosses. They had been apprehended, judged, and found to be guilty. They were placed under the sentence of death. But one of those thieves missed his appointment. He never went to the cross. His name was Barabbas. Another man went to the cross in his place. Jesus died upon the cross of Barabbas and Barabbas was set free. We have been set free, too. And it was not because we were any more deserving. It was a gift of grace.

LAWS OF HOLINESS (LEVITICUS 17-20)

These laws were designed to make the people of God different than the rest of the peoples of the world.

1.   Laws of Blood (Leviticus 17).

There was a definite injunction against eating or drinking blood. The reason for this was because blood symbolized life.

> *For the life of the flesh is in the blood, and I have given it to you on the altar to make atonement for your souls; for it is the blood by reason of the life that makes atonement. (Leviticus 17:11).*

2.   Laws of Sexual Morality (Leviticus 18).

The Ten Commandments had forbidden adultery. Now the Law goes on to specify the various forms of sexual immorality which are forbidden in that general law.

3.   General Laws (Leviticus 19-20).

The general laws follow a varied pattern of subjects as we move from law to law.

BE HOLY
Sabbaths, Idols, & Sacrifices (19:3-8).
Fields & the Needy (19:9-10).
Dealing with Neighbors (19:11-18).
Statutes & Sacrifices (19:19-22).
Fields & Fruit (19:23-25).
Avoid occult practices (19:26-31).
Honor the Aged (19:32).
Dealing with strangers & neighbors (19:33-37).
Avoid occult practices (20:1-6).
BE HOLY
Honor your parents (20:9).
Laws of sexual morality (20:10-21).
BE HOLY

As can be seen from the above chart, the main theme of this section (if not of the entire book) is to be holy (19:2; 20:7; 20:26). There is an important principle here. The foundation for all true morality rests upon the existence of a holy God. These laws included the treatment of one's neighbor.

> *You shall not oppress your neighbor, nor rob*
> *him. The wages of a hired man are not to remain with*
> *you all night until morning. (Leviticus 19:13).*

One of the commands given to this section is to "love your neighbor as yourself" (19:18). We normally think of this command as having come from Jesus, but it had its origins in the Old Testament.

> Verse 28 gives a warning against allowing tattoos or marks on the body.

This command is also extended to strangers and aliens who reside among the Israelites.

> *The stranger who resides with you shall be to*
> *you as the native among you, and you shall love him*
> *as yourself; for you were aliens in the land of Egypt:*
> *I am the Lord your God. (Exodus 19:34).*

LAWS OF THE PRIESTS (LEVITICUS 21-22)

The priests had a great privilege. They were permitted to serve in the Tabernacle and to partake of the holy things. With that increased privilege came increased responsibility.

- The ordinary Israelite could touch his parent's corpse at the funeral. The priest could not do this (21:1-4).
- The ordinary Israelite could marry whomever he chose. The priest could not (21:7).
- An immoral Israelite was punished, but a member of a priest's family who committed an immoral act was burned with fire (21:9).

There is a principle here. For every liberty there is a corresponding responsibility. For every privilege there is a corresponding duty. This has an application today when we realize that all believers are priests (1 Peter 2:9). We have the privilege of entering into the Holy Place (Hebrews 10:19-22). But with that great privilege comes a great responsibility. It is the responsibility to be holy.

APPOINTED TIMES (LEVITICUS 23-25)

1.   The Seven Convocations.

The Book of Leviticus started with the setting forth of five types of offerings. Now as we near its close, we have set forth for us seven appointed convocations.

    a.   The Weekly Sabbath (23:3).

> Weeks were sometimes called sabbaths (Lev 23:15; Deut 16:9).

The Sabbath serves as the foundation for all other memorials. It is foundational because it was established at Creation.

        (1)   The day was counted as beginning at sunset (23:32).

        (2)   The Jews observed a lunar month of 28 days each.

        The first day of the month could not be determined until the appearance of the new moon (after sunset), although by the time of David the Jews had learned to calculate the day of the new moon (1 Samuel 20:5).

        (3)   The Jewish year consisted of 12 lunar months (354 days, 8 hours, 45 minutes, 38 seconds).

        (4)   An extra month was added to the year periodically to keep the year in conformity with the solar year (four times every 11 years).

        If no adjustment had been made, the Feasts would have made a complete cycle of the seasons once every 34 years. This was not possible among a people who were geared to an agricultural economy.

        Thus, a second month of Adhar was added whenever the 12th month ended more than 4 weeks before the Spring Equinox.

        (5)   The Jews also observed a civil year which began in

the seventh month of the religious year (Exodus 23:16; 34:22). The Year of Jubilee began in the seventh month of the ritual year (Leviticus 25:8-10).

b.   The Passover (23:5).

The Passover is only mentioned briefly, since it had been fully described in Exodus. Notice that the Passover was to be held on the 14th day of the month. The Jews followed a lunar calendar. Their month would begin with the New Moon. This means that the 14th day of the month would be the time of the Full Moon.

Some have wondered if the darkness of the sun at the death of Christ could have been caused by a solar eclipse. But this could not be the case, for it took place in the season of Passover - the time of the Full Moon.

c.   The Feast of Unleavened Bread (23:6-14).

The day following the Passover was to begin a week of feasting. For this entire week, God's people were to eat unleavened bread. On each day an offering was to be presented to the Lord. Once the Israelites were in the Land, they would further celebrate this feast by bringing a sheaf of the firstfruits of their harvest. It was to be brought before the priest at the Tabernacle.

On the first day of the week, he would take the sheaf and wave it before the Lord. Accompanying the sheaf would be the offering of a lamb and a grain offering with a libation of wine.

- The First Day of the Week.
- The Firstfruit sheaf.
- A sacrificed lamb.
- Flour mixed with oil.
- Wine.

This was a picture of the Resurrection of Christ. He is our Firstfruits. His resurrection is a promise of our resurrection which is to follow. Because of that, we have a continuing observance. It is an observance of bread and wine. It remembers the Sacrificed Lamb. And it looks forward to the day when the Firstfruits will be joined by the rest of the Harvest.

d.   The New Grain Offering - Pentecost (23:15-21).

The next observance was to take place 50 days after the first Sabbath of the Week of Unleavened Bread. It would also take place on the First Day of the Week. Several offerings were to be made on this day.

(1)   A Grain Offering of two loaves of bread - but these loaves were to be baked with leaven.

(2)   A Burnt Offering of...

- Seven lambs of the first year.
- A bull.
- Two rams.

(3)   A Sin Offering of a male goat.

(4)   A Peace Offering of two male lambs.

It was upon the celebration of this day following the death and resurrection of Christ that the Holy Spirit was given.

e.   The Blowing of Trumpets (23:24-25).

The Fall Festivals were initiated with a blowing of trumpets. This Festival fell on the first day of the month (the day of the New Moon). Today the Jews celebrate Rosh HaShanah on this date (the New Year).

f.   The Day of Atonement (23:26-32).

We have already seen the Day of Atonement at length in Leviticus 16. This was the day on which the High Priest would enter into the Holy of Holies to make atonement for the nation. It was different from all of the other Festival Times in that this was a day of fasting and a day when you were to "humble your souls" (23:27).

g.   The Feast of Booths (23:33-44).

This was the last of the Festivals (Purim and Hanukkah would be added much later). For an entire week, the people were to live in Booths. They were to "camp out." The weather in Palestine was suited to this at this time of the year. The heat of summer had passed and the "early rains" were still a month away.

2.   Ordinances of Light & Bread (24:1-9).

a.   The Lord commands oil to be brought for a continual light on the Lampstand.

b.   Twelve cakes of bread are to be set upon the Table within the Tabernacle. Pure frankincense is to be sprinkled upon these loaves.

The priests were to eat these loaves of bread within the Temple as a part of their duty of worship before the Lord.

3.   The Holiness of God's Name (24:10-23).

> *Now the son of an Israelite woman, whose father was an Egyptian, went out among the sons of Israel; and the Israelite woman's son and a man of Israel struggled with each other in the camp.*
> *And the son of the Israelite woman blasphemed the Name and cursed. So they brought him to Moses... (Leviticus 24:10-11a).*

The trouble started with a mixed marriage (this was later forbidden in Deuteronomy 7:3-4 and Nehemiah 13:25). This was not to be the last time that the "Mixed Multitude" would be the cause of trouble in the Camp (Numbers 11).

An altercation took place between this young man and an Israelite. The source of the altercation is not important. What is important is that it resulted in the sin of blasphemy against the name of the Lord. This sin called for the death of the guilty. It was the responsibility of the entire congregation to carry out the sentence so that no one person would be the executioner.

4.   Sabbatical Year & Jubilee (25).

Just as the Israelites were to rest each seventh day, so also, they were to observe every seventh year (there are also instances where they were to observe the seventh week and the seventh month). The seventh cycle of sabbatical years was to be a most special year. On the Day of Atonement (the 7th month) of the 7th cycle of sabbatical years, the Year of Jubilee was to be ushered in.

> *You shall thus consecrate the fiftieth year and proclaim a release through the land to all its inhabitants. It shall be a jubilee for you, and each of you shall return to his own property, and each of you shall return to his family. (Leviticus 25:10).*

This was to be a time of great rejoicing. The fasting of the Day of Atonement was over. Sins had been proclaimed forgiven. Now there was to be a time of rest. It was to last an entire year. In addition to the rest, all debts were to be wiped out. Slaves were to be freed. All land was to revert to its original owners.

> *The land, moreover, shall not be sold permanently; for the land is Mine; for you are but aliens and sojourners with Me. (Leviticus 25:23).*

Notice the principle of divine ownership. The land did not belong to the people. It was the Lord's land.

BLESSINGS AND CURSINGS (LEVITICUS 26)

The Lord sets forth the results of both discipline and obedience. Obedience brings blessing. Disobedience brings cursing. The result of this obedience would be that Israel would enjoy the blessings of the covenant relationship.

> *I will also walk among you and be your God, and you shall be My people. (Leviticus 26:12).*

We have the same promise of blessing today. Paul quotes this passage in his second epistle to the Corinthians.

> *Or what agreement has the temple of God with idols?*
> *For we are the temple of the living God; just as God said, "I*
> *will dwell in them and walk among them; and I will be their*
> *God, and they shall be My people." (2 Corinthians 6:16).*

This has been the message of Leviticus. It is the big "so what" of the entire book. It has been the message that God is going to dwell with Israel. He will be their God and they will be His people. This covenant relationship continues even today. It is a relationship which is found in the church. We have entered into the promise that was initially given to Israel.

NUMBERS
The Book of Wanderings

The Lord bless you, and keep you;
The Lord make His face to shine on you, and be gracious to
you;
The Lord lift up His countenance on you, and give you peace.
(Numbers 6:24-26).

What do you think of when I speak of the book of Numbers? A lot of boring genealogy? The taking of a census? A book for tax accountants and mathematicians? It sounds about as exciting as falling off a log. And yet, this is an exciting book. It is a book of successes and a book of failures. It is a book of endurance under testings. It is a book which teaches us lessons for wisdom for our journey in the wilderness.

INTRODUCTION TO NUMBERS

1.   Title of the Book.

Our English Title "Numbers" is translated from the title found in the Greek Septuagint.

        a.   The Greek Title: *Arithmoi* ("Numbers"). The book received this name from the two numberings which took place within its pages. And yet, there is a lot more in this book than the mere recording of a census. There are 36 chapters in this book. Each census takes up only one chapter.

        b.   The Hebrew Title: *BaMidbar* ("In the Wilderness"). This original title for the book is taken from the first verse of the first chapter.

> *Then the Lord spoke to Moses in the*
> *wilderness of Sinai... (Numbers 1:1).*

This is an appropriate title. Numbers is the book that tells us what happened during the 40 years of wandering in the wilderness.

2.   Place in the Pentateuch.

Each of the Five Books of Moses had a special meaning to the people who were living in that day.

BOOKS	LESSONS TO BE LEARNED
Genesis	Sets forth Israel's relation with the Covenant God, both as Creator of the universe, as well as the God of Abraham, Isaac, and Jacob.
Exodus	Relates the narrative of how God redeemed His people from their slavery in Egypt. He is pictured as entering into a covenant with His people whom He has purchased as His priced possession.
Leviticus	Deals with the question of how men are to approach the Covenant God. It outlines the sacrifices and the forms of worship.
Numbers	Since there is very little historical narrative in Leviticus, it takes up the historical narrative where Exodus ended.

Numbers is written at the close of the Wilderness Wanderings. That tells us something about the recipients of this book. They were not the same generation which had left Egypt. They are a new generation. The old generation has died in the wilderness. Moses now challenges the new generation to fulfill the covenant made by their fathers, and not to fall in the way that their fathers fell. There is a lesson here. It is that there is always a need to teach the old truths to the new generation.

3.   Contrast with Leviticus.

Leviticus	Numbers
The believer's worship.	The believer's work.

Purity.	Pilgrimage.
Our spiritual position.	Our spiritual progress.
Ceremony in the sanctuary.	History in the wilderness.

4.   Outline of the Book of Numbers.

1:1 10:10	10:11 14:45	15:1 21:41	22:1 36:13
MOUNT SINAI	**FROM SINAI TO KADESH**	**KADESH TO MOAB**	**THE PLAINS OF MOAB**
Preparation for the Journey	The Test	Wilderness Wanderings	End of the Journey
The Old Generation			The New Generation
Several Weeks	38 Years		Several Months
Mt Sinai	*Mt Hor*		*Mt Nebo*

5.   Occasion for Writing.

The book of Numbers is written on the plains of Moab at the close of the Wilderness Wanderings. It covers both the history and the reason for those wanderings. The book begins with the numbering of the people of God as they are called to His service. The standard of holiness for that service is outlined in the following chapters.

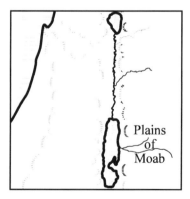

The people of God failed in that service and, as a result, were condemned to die in the wilderness. Now a new generation has arisen. They are also numbered. They are also called to the service of the Lord. They will also be tested. And they will also be given a standard of holiness. This book is written to prepare this second generation of Israelites for that service. The first generation has failed and died. What will the second generation do?

PREPARATIONS FOR THE JOURNEY (NUMBERS 1-10)

The Preparations for the Journey	
The Camp as a whole (1:1 - 4:49).	Individual preparations (5:1 - 10:10).

Then the Lord spoke to Moses in the wilderness of Sinai, in the tent of meeting, on the first day of the second month, in the second year after they had come out of the land of Egypt (Numbers 1:1).

Exodus 40:17 tells us that the Tabernacle was completed on the first month of the second year following the Exodus from Egypt. This means that the Laws which make up the book of Leviticus were given within the space of that first month.

A month has now passed since the glory of the Lord descended upon the Tabernacle. It is now time to continue the journey. But first, the Lord instructs Moses to number the people.

1.   The Numbering of the People (Numbers 1-4).

The fighting men of Israel who were over the age of 20 were numbered at over 600,000 (Numbers 1:45-46). If this number is correct, then it would mean that the nation itself must have numbered upwards of 2 million.

Why did God command this census to take place? And why is it recorded in the pages of the Bible? Is this merely to give us a bit of mathematical trivia? No. I think that there are several reasons for this numbering.

a.   This numbering serves as a call to arms for the holy army of God. In the past, the Israelites have been enslaved in Egypt. From this time forth, they shall be numbered as the people of God.

b.   This numbering is a call to service. In Exodus we have the account of the redemption of Israel. Leviticus tells us how those redeemed are to worship the Lord. In Numbers, we see

115

those redeemed who have been motivated through worship now called to serve the Lord. Here is the principle. Redemption and worship should always motivate us to service.

c.   God is a God of order. In serving God, everything needs to be done decently and in order (1 Corinthians 14:40).

Chapter 3 begins with the familiar formula: "These are the records of the generations of Aaron and Moses" (3:1). This introduces a special blessing which was to be enjoyed by the tribe of Levi.

> *Again the Lord spoke to Moses, saying,* 12 *"Now, behold, I have taken the Levites from among the sons of Israel instead of every first-born, the first issue of the womb among the sons of Israel. So the Levites shall be Mine.* 13 *For all the first-born are Mine; on the day that I struck down all the first-born in the land of Egypt, I sanctified to Myself all the first-born in Israel, from man to beast. They shall be Mine; I am the Lord." (Numbers 3:11-13).*

Due to the plague of the first-born in Egypt, all firstborn males are the legal property of the Lord. However, He takes as a substitute the priestly tribe of Levi. Because Levi holds this special position, a special census is taken of all of the members of the tribe of Levi in chapter 4.

2.   Purgings and Presentations (Numbers 5-9).

5:1	Purgings	The Unclean
5:5	for God	The Immoral
6:1	Presentations	Nazarite Vows
7:1	to God	Offerings from Leaders
7:89	God's Presence in the Voice & at the Lampstand.	
8:5	Purging	Cleansing of Levites
9:1	Presentation	Cleansing at Passover

9:15	God's Presence in the Cloud and announced by Trumpets.

a.   Chapter 5 gives regulations concerning purity within the camp. It deals with the problems of leprosy, theft, and sexual unfaithfulness.

b.   Chapter 6 deals with the guidelines of the Nazarite vow. The word "Nazarite" is taken from the Hebrew root *nazar*, meaning "to separate." It is a vow of separation. This chapter closes with a special blessing for Israel.

> *The Lord bless you, and keep you;*
> *The Lord make His face shine on you,*
> *And be gracious to you;*
> *The Lord lift up His countenance on you,*
> *And give you peace. (Numbers 6:24-26).*

In 1979, a small silver scroll was excavated from a tomb on the outskirts of Jerusalem. The scroll had been rolled up and made into a tiny cylindrical amulet. When it was unrolled, it was found to contain this same priestly benediction. The scroll has been dated to the 7th century B.C. and is our oldest copy of Scripture.

c.   Chapter 7 describes the actual worship that took place after the Tabernacle was erected. This worship began with the leaders of the tribes and clans of Israel coming to worship and to dedicate the altar. It culminates with Moses hearing the voice of the Lord within the Tabernacle.

> *Now when Moses went into the tent of meeting to speak with Him, he heard the voice speaking to him from above the mercy seat that was on the ark of the testimony, from between the two cherubim, so He spoke to him. (Numbers 7:89).*

Throughout the Psalms, the Lord is known as the "One who sits between the cherubim." This was the throne of the Lord. We have found many ancient wall paintings of Egyptian thrones from this era. It is very common to see the pharaoh pictured sitting upon a throne which had as its two armrests the images of two four-legged winged creatures.

d. Numbers 8:1-4 repeats the description of the lamps and the lampstand which stood within the Tabernacle. This lampstand was fashioned into the shape of a tree and the lamps were in the form of flowers.

e. The remainder of chapter 8 deals with the ceremonial cleansing of the Levites as the people of this tribe were set apart for service unto the Lord.

> *For every first-born among the sons of Israel is Mine, among the men and among the animals; on the day that I struck down all the first-born in the land of Egypt I sanctified them for Myself.* 18 *But I have taken the Levites instead of every first-born among the sons of Israel. (Numbers 8:17-18).*

The basis of Levite service looked back to the time of the first Passover when all first-born in the land of Egypt were under the sentence of death. Rather than take the first-born of the Israelites, the Lord chose the tribe of Levi to be His select priesthood.

f. In Number 9:1-14 the Israelites are called to celebrate the Passover, marking the first anniversary of the Exodus from Egypt. The next Passover that they will celebrate will be in the Promised Land.

g. The rest of the chapter describes the Lord's leadership of the nation through the cloud and the fire. This leadership was further facilitated through the use of two silver trumpets (10:1-10).

THE FAILURE AT KADESH (NUMBERS 10-14)

The Israelites receive their marching orders from the Lord and they are led from Sinai to the Wilderness of Paran. This area lies to the northwest of the Gulf of Elath and is composed of a high plateau ranging from 3900 to 5290 feet above sea level.

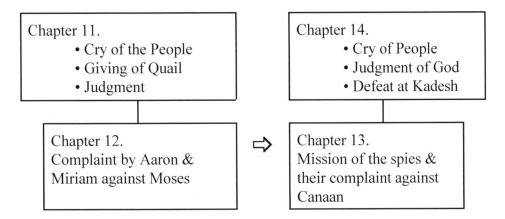

This section of the book of Numbers records the repeated failure of the Israelites to believe the provisions of the Lord. Some of these failures were public while others were private.

1.   Crying & Quail (Numbers 11).

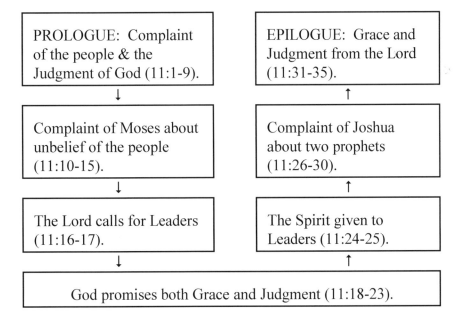

This chapter begins with a brief prologue which describes an initial judgment from God. It is a judgment of fire *(berah)*. And so, the Israelites call the name of the place "Taberah." However, the

Israelites continued to complain. This time, the complaint took on a new form. It was a complaint over the same menu. For a year, the Lord had provided them with manna to eat. And now, they begin to suffer from the problem of selective memory.

> *"We remember the fish which we used to eat free in Egypt, the cucumbers and the melons and the leeks and the onions and the garlic, 7 but now our appetite is gone. There is nothing to look at except this manna." (Numbers 11:6-7).*

They remembered the food of Egypt but they forgot their past slavery. They remembered the free fish, but they forgot that they themselves had not been free. Sin is like that. When we are tempted, it is because we have forgotten the consequences of our sins. Sin always carries baggage with it. Remember the baggage!

Moses takes these complaints and all that they imply, both against his own leadership as well as the rebellion against God, before the Lord. The Lord responds both in grace and in judgment.

a.   Grace.

The grace response is seen in the provision of the Holy Spirit for the leaders of the nation. No more will the Holy Spirit speak only through Moses. From now on there will be others who are also filled with the Spirit. It is interesting that two of these leaders receive the Spirit in a manner which is not consistent with the others.

> *But two men had remained in the camp; the name of one was Eldad and the name of the other Medad. And the Spirit rested upon them (now they were among those who had been registered, but had not gone out to the tent), and they prophesied in the camp.*
>
> *So a young man ran and told Moses and said, "Eldad and Medad are prophesying in the camp."*
>
> *Then Joshua the son of Nun, the attendant of Moses from his youth, answered and said, "Moses, my lord, restrain them."*
>
> *But Moses said to him, "Are you*

jealous for my sake? Would that all the Lord's people were prophets, that the Lord would put His Spirit upon them!" (Numbers 11:26-29).

We can learn an important lesson from this episode. It is that the Lord does not always bestow His gifts in the nice, neat ways that our theology prefers. Joshua was not aware of this. His theology said that the Spirit

> He who today forbids what God allows will tomorrow allow what God forbids.

is only bestowed at the Tabernacle. And when he saw two men who received the Spirit outside the Tabernacle, he did not like it. Moses was not troubled by this. He realized that God is bigger than the Tabernacle. God does not always fit into our theological boxes.

It is interesting that the desire of Moses was that all men prophecy. This desire was later stated in the form of a prophecy by the prophet Joel.

> *And it will come about after this that I will pour out My Spirit on all mankind; and your sons and daughters will prophesy, your old men will dream dreams, your young men will see visions. 29 And even on the male and female servants I will pour out My Spirit in those days." (Joel 2:28-29).*

This prophecy was fulfilled at the Pentecost Incident in Acts 2. It was at that time that the Spirit was poured out in an indiscriminate manner.

The grace of God is further seen in the provision of a great flock of quail. It is grace heaped up and overflowing.

b.   Judgment.

It is only after the people have seen the grace of God both in the giving of His Spirit and in the sending of the quail that judgment falls.

121

Why does it fall now? It falls because there has been no repentance. There is a lesson here. It is a lesson about the patience of God.

2.   Complaint Against Moses (Numbers 12).

A complaint is now brought against Moses by those who are the closest to him - his brother and sister. The complaint regard his taking of a Cushite woman as his wife.

> *Then Miriam and Aaron spoke against Moses because of the Cushite woman whom he had married (for he had married a Cushite woman); 2 and they said, "Has the Lord indeed spoken only through Moses? Has He not spoken through us as well?" And the Lord heard it. (Numbers 12:1-2).*

While there seems to be perhaps an undercurrent of jealousy and sibling rivalry (they may have had a difficult time accepting their "little brother's" leadership), the spark which set this event off was the marriage of Moses to a Gentile. In the midst of this family feud, the Lord intervenes and calls Aaron and Miriam to account.

> *Then the Lord came down in a pillar of cloud and stood at the doorway of the tent, and He called Aaron and Miriam. When they had both come forward, 6 He said, "Hear now My words:*
> *If there is a prophet among you,*
> *I, the Lord shall make Myself known to him in a vision.*
> *I shall speak with him in a dream.*
> *Not so, with My servant Moses,*
> *He is faithful in all My household;*
> *With him I speak mouth to mouth,*
> *Even openly, and not in dark sayings,*
> *And he beholds the form of the Lord.*
> *Why then were you not afraid to speak against My servant, against Moses?"*
> *(Numbers 12:5-8).*

The Septuagint translates the phrase *peh al peh* (פֶּה אֶל־פֶּה – literally "mouth to mouth") as "face to face." The context shows this the be the idea behind the phrase. There is a sense in which we have experienced this kind of communication in the person of Jesus Christ. He brought God face to face with men.

In 1 Corinthians 13:10, Paul quotes the Septuagint version of this passage. He is speaking amidst the contrast of the partial that we know today versus that perfect that we shall one day know.

> *For we know in part, and we prophecy in part; 10 but when the perfect comes, the partial will be done away.*
>
> *When I was a child, I used to speak as a child, think as a child, reason as a child; when I became a man, I did away with childish things.*
>
> *For now we see in a mirror dimly, but then **face to face**; now I know in part, but then I shall know fully just as I also have been fully known. (1 Corinthians 13:9-12).*

To what does "the perfect" refer? It is the face-to-face communication with God that Moses experienced. Those who met Jesus had such an experience. But Paul does not speak of the "perfect" as having already come. He describes it as still future. What is the "perfect"? It is the state of perfect communication with God. It is that which we shall experience when we finally see Him face to face.

3.   The Spies (Numbers 13).

Why were spies sent into Canaan? Up to this time, the Lord Himself had led the people. Why was there a need for spies? Deuteronomy 1:22-23 give us a clue.

> *"Then all of you approached me and said, 'Let us send men before us, that they may search out the land for us, and bring back to us word of the way by which we should go up, and the cities which we shall enter.'*
>
> *"And the thing pleased me and I took twelve of your men, one man for each tribe." (Deuteronomy 1:22-23).*

The impetus for the plan to send in spies came from the

people. On the other hand, the Lord did affirm the plan. And so, representatives from each of the twelve tribes of Israel were selected to spy out the land. Of the twelve who went out...

- Ten came back with a majority report.
- Two came back with a minority report.

Perhaps there is a lesson here. It is that the majority is not always right.

> *"There also we saw the Nephalim (the sons of Anak are part of the Nephalim); and we became like grasshoppers in our own sight, and so we were in their sight." (Numbers 13:33).*

The interesting thing about this fear is that there was a corresponding fear of the Israelites on the part of the Canaanites. When Israel finally does enter the Promised Land, it is to find that the Canaanites had heard of the power of the Lord and were frightened by it (Joshua 2:9-11). Why did the spies fall prey to the "grasshopper complex?" Dr. Erwin Lutzer lists several reasons:

a.   Negative thinking.

The spies saw more reasons why they couldn't do it than why they could. Caleb saw all of the same things, but he also saw that the Lord was on their side.

b.   They exaggerated the situation ("we are like grasshoppers"). Unbelief has a way of exaggerating the situation. The enemy was big, but not that big.

c.   Their desire to return to Egypt (14:2-3).

They preferred to be enslaved to the bondage of Egypt than to take a chance with the Lord.

4.   Rebellion and Judgment (Numbers 14).

The reaction to the people to the report of the spies was one of unbelief and rebellion against the Lord.

a.   They grumble against Moses and Aaron (14:2).

b.   They state their preference to have died in the wilderness (14:2). Be careful what you wish for - you might get it.

c.   They determine to choose for themselves another leader who will take them back to Egypt (14:4).

When Joshua and Caleb attempt to warn the people, they find themselves facing execution by stoning. Into this situation, the Lord appears in the Tabernacle and passes judgment upon the rebellious nation.

> *"Your children, however, whom you said would become a prey - I will bring them in, and they shall know the land which you have rejected.*
> *"But as for you, your corpses shall fall in this wilderness. 33 And your sons shall be shepherds for forty years in the wilderness, and they shall suffer for your unfaithfulness, until your corpses lie in the wilderness.*
> *"According to the number of days which you spied out the land, forty days, for every day you shall bear your guilt a year, even forty years, and you shall know My opposition." (Numbers 14:31-34).*

The judgment was to be one of death. The entire generation would die in the wilderness.

- Only adults - those who had joined in the rebellion - were included in the judgment (14:29).

- God did not condemn the righteous with the guilty - Caleb and Joshua were spared.

- Their children for whom they feared were the very ones who would eventually receive the land.

- On the other hand, these children would suffer with their parents the next 38 years wandering in the wilderness.

Instead of submitting to the judgment of God, the people further rebelled against God by trying to invade the land on their own. They were defeated and driven back.

THE WILDERNESS WANDERINGS (NUMBERS 15-21)

1.   Laws for a Future Land (15).

Even though the present generation was to die in the wilderness, there were instructions to be given for future generations (it helps us to remember that the audience to whom Moses is writing is that next generation). These laws deal with...

- Various offerings.
- Penalties for disobedience.

What follows is a situation in which a man was found in flagrant violation of the stated Law of God. He was gathering wood on the Sabbath. The penalty was death. Why? Because he had "despised the word of the Lord and broken His commandment" (Numbers 15:31).

2.   The Korah Rebellion (16).

The rebellion against the authority of Moses came from members of his own tribe - the Tribe of Levi. It revolved around a man named Korah.

> *And they assembled together against Moses and Aaron, and said to them, "You have gone far enough, for all the congregation are holy, every one of them, and the Lord is in their midst; so why do you exalt yourselves above the assembly of the Lord." (Numbers 16:3).*

Now, let me ask you a question. Was this a true claim? Wasn't it true that all of Israel was holy and that the Lord was in the midst of all? Yes, it was. But it was also true that the Lord had appointed leaders over the people.

It was God who had appointed Moses. Therefore this was not merely a rebellion against Moses. It was also a rebellion against God. This sin of Korah was that of wanting to reject God's ordained leaders.

There is a lesson for us to learn. It is a lesson of leadership.

The fact that the church is a royal priesthood does not mean that there is not God-ordained leadership within the church. Korah denied that leadership. His claim was that Moses had no right to be leader since all of the Israelites were God's chosen people. Moses called for the people to separate themselves from Korah, warning that the judgment of God was about to fall in a way that it had not previously done.

> *Then it came about as he finished speaking all these words, that the ground that was under them split open; 32 and the earth opened its mouth and swallowed them up, and their households, and all the men who belonged to Korah, with their possessions.*
>
> *So they and all that belonged to them went down alive to Sheol; and the earth closed over them, and they perished from the midst of the assembly. (Numbers 16:31-33).*

> *Fire also came forth from the Lord and consumed the two hundred and fifty men who were offering the incense. (Numbers 16:35).*

Jude 11 speaks of those within the Christian church who have "perished in the rebellion of Korah." The implication is that it is possible today to sin in the same way that Korah sinned. What type of sin is this? It is the sin of rebellion from God-ordained authority. It is a sin which can be committed both within and without the church.

3.   The Staff of Aaron (17).

Korah's rebellion had brought the leadership of Moses and Aaron into question. Now the Lord sets out to document the priesthood of Aaron through a special sign.

> *Then the Lord spoke to Moses, saying, 2 "Speak to the sons of Israel, and get from them a rod for each father's household: twelve rods, from all their leaders according to their fathers' households. You shall write each name on his rod, 3 and write Aaron's name on the rod of Levi; for there is one rod for the head of each of their fathers' households." (Numbers 17:1-3).*

127

These rods were taken and placed within the Tabernacle. The next day, one of the rods had sprouted with leaves and had borne fruit - ripe almonds. It was the rod of Aaron. It was to be kept in the Tabernacle from this date hence and it would serve as the sign and the seal of Aaron's priesthood.

4.   Levitical Duties (18-19).

The next two chapters deal with the duties and responsibilities of Aaron and his priestly descendants.

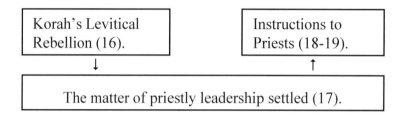

5.   The Failure at Meribah (Numbers 20:1-13).

The most common testing which the Israelites faced in the Wilderness as the lack of food and water - especially water.

> *And there was no water for the congregation; and they assembled themselves against Moses and Aaron. (Numbers 20:2).*

The people had faced this test before. When they had first come into the Wilderness, they had been without water and the Lord had Moses strike a rock and a river of water had gushed forth (Exodus 17:1-7). Now they are facing the same test. And once again, they begin to complain and to murmur against the Lord.

> *Then Moses and Aaron came in from the presence of the assembly to the doorway of the tent of meeting, and fell on their faces. Then the glory of the Lord appeared to them;*
> *And the Lord spoke to Moses, saying, 8 "Take the rod; and you and your brother Aaron assemble the congregation and speak to the rock before their eyes, that it may yield its water. You shall thus bring forth water for them out of the rock and let the*

congregation and their beasts drink." (Numbers 20:6-8).

The instructions of the Lord are very explicit. Moses is to go and speak to the rock. On the previous occasion, Moses was to strike the rock with the rod. Why is he merely to speak to it now? Evidently, this is a test of Moses' obedience.

But I think that there may be another reason as well. The rock is a type of Christ (1 Corinthians 10:4). It is from Him that we receive rivers of living water. And we receive those waters because He was struck on our behalf. But He was only struck once. His sacrifice was once and for all. He does not have to be sacrificed repeatedly. To approach Him now, we need only speak to Him in prayer. Moses failed the test. He failed to obey the command of the Lord.

> *Then Moses lifted up his hand and struck the rock twice with his rod; and water came forth abundantly, and the congregation and their beasts drank.*
>
> *But the Lord said to Moses and Aaron, "Because you have not believed Me, to treat Me as holy in the sight of the sons of Israel, therefore you shall not bring this assembly into the land which I have given them." (Numbers 20:11-12).*

Because of this failure, neither Moses or Aaron would be permitted to actually enter the Promised Land.

6.   Detour at Edom (Numbers 20:14-21).

As the Israelites approach the boarders of the land of Edom, Moses sends messengers asking for permission to cross through this territory. This permission is refused. Because of this, the Israelites

> Edom was made up of the descendants of Esau, the brother of Jacob.

would be forced to make a 175 mile detour around the southern boarder of Edom's territory (Numbers 21:4).

7.   Death of Aaron (Numbers 20:22-29).

As they come to Mount Hor, Aaron dies and the vestments of

the high priest are bestowed upon his son, Eleazer. From this time forward, the position of high priest will descend from father to son.

8.   Conquest of Arad (Numbers 21:1-3).

Although the Israelites had stopped short of going to war with Edom, they had no such hesitation when it came to fighting with the Canaanite neighbor of Arad. The cities of Arad were taken and destroyed.

9.   The Incident of the Fiery Serpents (Numbers 21:4-9).

Once again, the Israelites faced the tests of a lack of food and water. Once again, they failed the test by speaking against Moses and against the Lord. This time, judgment came in the form of "fiery serpents."

> *And the Lord sent fiery serpents among the people and they bit the people, so that many people of Israel died. (Numbers 21:6).*

There were dead and dying throughout the camp of Israel. People with poison in their veins now came to Moses for healing. That healing was brought in the form of the image of a serpent.

> *Then the Lord said to Moses, "Make a fiery serpent, and set it on a standard; and it shall come about that everyone who is bitten, when he looks at it, he shall live."*
> *And Moses made a bronze serpent and set it on the standard; and it came about, that if a serpent bit any man, when he looked to the bronze serpent, he lived. (Numbers 21:8-9).*

The way of healing was in the bronze image of a serpent lifted up on a standard. By simply looking at this image, a person could be healed. Jesus likened that instance to the salvation which He brings when a person simply looks to Him in faith (John 3:14).

10.   Further Travels (Numbers 21:10-20). These travels brought the Israelites to a point northeast of the Dead Sea.

11.   Conquest of Sihon, King of the Amorites (Numbers 21:21-32).

         Coming north along the route known as the King's Highway, Moses sends a message to the Amorite King Sihon requesting the right of passage through his territory. This permission was refused and met with an attack. Israel emerged victorious and thus took possession of the lands of the Amorites from the Arnon River in the south to the Jabbok River in the north. It should be noted that Israel avoided any military conflicts with the cities of Edom, Moab and Ammon during this period.

12.   Conquest of Og, King of Bashan (Numbers 21:33-35).

         The land of Bashan lay to the north of the Jabbok River and to the east of the Sea of Galilee. These lands also fell to the Israelites, giving them all of the lands of the Transjordan.

MOAB & THE END OF THE JOURNEY (NUMBERS 22-36)

The conquest of the Amorites and Bashan gave the territories immediately to the east of the Jordan River into the hands of Israel, but there were still the Moabites, the Ammonites, and the Edomites with which to be reckoned.

1.   Balaam and Balak (Numbers 22-24).

         The demise of the Amorites must have filled the people of nearby Moab with alarm. Balak, king of Moab, knows that he cannot defeat Israel in battle. And so, he seeks the help of the supernatural.

> *So he sent messengers to Balaam the son of Beor, at Pethor, which is near the River, in the land of the sons of his people, to call him, saying, "Behold, a people came out of Egypt; behold, they cover the surface of the land, and they are living opposite me.*
> *"Now, therefore, please come, curse this people for me since they are too mighty for me; perhaps I may be able to defeat them and drive them out of the land. For I know that he whom you bless is*

131

blessed, and he whom you curse is cursed." (Numbers 22:5-6).

Balak engages the services of Balaam, a prophet-for-profit (2 Peter 2:15-16). The Lord comes to Balaam and warns him that He has blessed Israel and that he will not be permitted to curse them.

> Joshua 24:9-10 indicates that Balaam had sought the Lord to curse Israel.

Balaam travels to the land of Moab and meets with Balak, encountering an angel from the Lord and making an ass of himself on the way.

After a lengthy ceremony involving seven altars and the sacrificing of seven bulls and seven rams, Balaam pronounces a blessing upon the people of Israel. Balak is mortified. He asks that Balaam reconsider and that perhaps at least he can pronounce a neutral prophecy that at least will not be so much in favor of Israel (23:25). When Balaam refuses, Balak suggests that they go to another place and engage in the same sacrificial ceremony, thinking that the place would make a difference in the prophecy (23:27). Each time, the Lord indicates that Israel is His chosen and blessed people.

2.   Apostasy in the Camp (Numbers 25).

While living in the land of Moab, the Israelites begin to worship false gods and enter into the immoral practices of their neighbors. The tide is turned with a liberal use of capital punishment.

3.   The Second Census (Numbers 26 - 27:11).

A second census is taken of all of the Israelite men of 20 years old and upward. This sets forth the fact of the new generation. As the old generation of God's people failed to enter the land, now the new generation will be challenged to succeed.

The fact that only men of fighting age are numbered demonstrates that we are to think of this numbering as one of a holy army. It is a call to arms. They are the army of God. And they are to pick up the banner which fell with the first army in the wilderness.

4.   Joshua as Successor. (Numbers 27:12-23).

Joshua, the servant of Moses, is chosen to replace him as the leader of Israel. He goes through an ordination ceremony.

5.   Ordinances (Numbers 28-30).

Ceremonial observances of various feasts (28-29).

Laws regarding the making of vows (30).

6.   Judgment against Midian (Numbers 31).

God orders the Israelites to destroy the Midianites for their part in the previous apostasy of Israel. Balaam is one of those who is put to death. The reason for this is because it had been Balaam's plan to lead the Israelites astray through compromising their purity (31:16).

7.   Settlement of Reuben, Gad, and Manasseh (Numbers 32).

As the Israelites arrived in the land of Moab, the tribes of Reuben, Gad and half of Manasseh looked at this land and they said to themselves, "This sure is a lot better than the wilderness." And so, they sent representatives to Moses and they asked for this land as their inheritance. In doing so, they were settling for second-best. It was to cost them early.

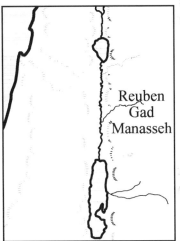

a.   It was not flowing with milk and honey. It was better than the wilderness, but it was not as good as the Promised Land.

b.   They were to serve as a buffer between Israel and the other nations of the world. Every time the Edomites or Moabites or Ammonites got mad, they would attack these three tribes first.

c.   They had to go into the Promised Land and fight for possession of land that would not be theirs. While they were there, they would see first-hand what they had given up.

If there is a lesson here, it is this: when it comes to the blessings of God, don't settle for second-best. They missed out on the fulness of God's promise because of what they saw in the immediate rather than trusting upon the goodness of the Lord.

8.   Review and Remembrance (Numbers 33).

The entire Wilderness Journey is reviewed during this chapter in a panorama that takes the original readers from their past to their future.

Concluding Tasks			
Present		Past	Future
Disposal of the Midianites (31).	Disposition of the request of three Tribes (32).	Rehearsal of the Journey (33:1-49).	Anticipation of the Conquest (33:50 -36:13).

9.   Preparation for Entering the Land (Numbers 34-36). Commands are given in preparation of going into the Promised Land.

LESSONS FROM THE WILDERNESS

Have you ever had a wilderness experience? It was a time when everything seemed to dry up - a time when God took you and put you on the shelf. It happened to me with drastic suddenness on my 30th birthday. I had been serving within a small church when suddenly, through no fault of my own, the situation changed and I found myself removed from the teaching ministry. For the next two and a half years, my wife and I were without a church home. During that time, I did very little teaching.

Now, I want you to know that there is nothing harder for a Bible teacher to do than to keep quiet. But God wanted to teach me something during that period. I couldn't hear Him at first, but He was shouting to me in that silence.

God speaks to us in the wilderness. I have learned a lot about God in Bible College and in seminary. I have learned a lot about Him in the church and in Bible Studies. But I learned the most about Him in the wilderness. Are you in the wilderness right now? There are some lessons that you can learn in the wilderness.

1.   The Lesson of the Faithfulness of the Lord.

Throughout the book of Numbers, we are constantly impressed with the unfaithfulness of Israel in contrast to the faithfulness of the Lord. God is faithful, even when we are faithless.

2.   The Lesson of the Cost of Disobedience.

The book of Numbers begins on a very positive note. The people are headed for the Promised Land. They have on their side the God who defeated Egypt, the greatest military power on earth. But there is also great failure within this book. Paul gives us a short commentary on this book within his epistle to the Corinthians.

> *For I do not want you to be unaware, brethren, that our fathers were all under the cloud, and all passed through the sea; 2 and all were baptized into Moses in the cloud and in the sea; 3 and all ate the same spiritual food; 4 and all drank the same spiritual drink, for they were drinking from a spiritual rock which followed them; and the rock was Christ.*
> *Nevertheless, with most of them God was not well-pleased; for they were laid low in the wilderness. (1 Corinthians 10:1-5).*

Notice the repeated use of the word "all." **All** were under the cloud. **All** passed through the sea. **All** ate the same spiritual food. **All** drank the same spiritual drink. They all started the journey. But they didn't all finish. Most of them died in the wilderness. Why? Because of disobedience.

> *Now these things happened as examples for us, that we should not crave evil things, as they also craved.*
> *And do not be idolaters, as some of them were; as it is written, "The people sat down to eat and drink, and stood up to play."*
> *Nor let us act immorally, as some of them did, and twenty-three thousand fell in one day.*
> *Nor let us try the Lord, as some of them did, and were destroyed by the serpents.*
> *Nor grumble, as some of them did, and were destroyed by the destroyer. (1 Corinthians 10:6-10).*

The fact that Israel fell is a warning to us. It is possible for us to fall in each one of these areas. It is possible for us to be tempted in these areas and to fall into sin.

You see, this illustration of Israel in the wilderness is not just a sad story. It is not just for out intellectual enjoyment. It is to teach us something. It is to teach us how we ought to live. It is not just for Sunday morning. We need to take it to work with us on Monday and keep it through the week.

Why is this so important? Because temptation is going to come on Monday and on Tuesday and throughout the rest of the week. It is important that we understand its consequences. It will only be then that we will be able to use God's provision against its lure.

Israel is a type of the Christian. The Exodus from Egypt is a picture of the salvation of the Christian. Just as all of Israel were under the cloud, so we have all come under God's protection. Just as all of Israel passed through the sea, so we have all passed from the bondage of sin to freedom in Christ. Just as all of Israel was baptized into Moses, so we have all been baptized into Christ. Just as all of Israel ate the same spiritual food, so we have all been made partakers of the body of Christ. Just as Moses struck the rock and all of Israel drank from it, so also Christ died for us and we have all partaken of His death.

The goal of the Christian life is to win the race, to enter into the Promised Land. But some are disqualified. Some do not enter in. The reason for this is sin.

A lot of books and leaflets have been written on what is wrong with the church today. We are told that if only we will have more programs, greater giving, more powerful preaching, motivated missions, better body life, or updated Sunday school programs, that all of the problems of the church will be solved. But one thing is usually neglected - the presence of sin.

> *Now these things happened to them as an example, and they were written for our instruction, upon whom the ends of the ages have come. (1 Corinthians 10:11).*

This tells me something about the Old Testament. It was written for my benefit. It was written for my instruction. It contains lessons that I need to learn.

There is a teaching that is going around today that says that the Old Testament is not for the Christian today - that it was written to a previous dispensation who lived before Christ and that it has nothing of practical value for the Christian in the 21st Century. Not true! All of the Scriptures are inspired by God. All of the Scriptures are profitable to me in the areas of doctrine and of reproof and of instruction in how to be righteous.

Therefore, let him who thinks he stands take heed lest he fall. 13 No temptation has overtaken you, but such as it common to man; and God is faithful, who will not allow you to be tempted beyond what you are able, but with the temptation will provide the way of escape also, that you may be able to endure it. (1 Corinthians 10:12-13).

Though you are warned against being over-confident, this does not mean that you should have an attitude of defeatism. You have a strong word of encouragement. It is that God has made provision for you in your hour of temptation. He will never take you into a tunnel that does not have a light at the end of it. And He will never take you into the wilderness without being with you through it.

DEUTERONOMY
The Second Giving of the Law

There are 80 references to the book of Deuteronomy in the New Testament. It is quoted in 17 out of the 27 books in the New Testament. Deuteronomy ranks with Genesis, Psalms and Isaiah as the four most quoted Old Testament books in the New Testament. It was from Deuteronomy that Jesus quoted when He was being tempted by Satan in the wilderness.

THE TITLE OF THE BOOK

1. Hebrew Title: אלה הדברים (*Eleh HaDevarim*). The Hebrew title for the book is taken from the very first phrase of Deuteronomy 1:1 - "These are the words..." This is significant. In the ancient world, a king's word was considered to be law. Thus, when Moses spoke the words of Israel's King, he was speaking law.

    > While Deuteronomy is known as the "Words," Jesus is known as the Word.

2. Greek Title: Our English title is taken from the title found in the Greek Septuagint. It is a compound word, coming from two Greek words.

    - Δυο (*duo*) means "two" or "second."
    - Νομος (*nomos*) is the Greek word for "law."

    Deuteronomy, then, means "second law." This isn't really a very good title, for Deuteronomy doesn't give a second law. Rather, it explains and expounds upon the first law that was given at Sinai.

    As we go through the book of Deuteronomy, we will see very little chronological movement. Nearly the entire book takes place within a single month's time. Likewise, there is no geographic movement. This is in stark contrast to the book of Numbers which records all of the wilderness wanderings. The entire book of Deuteronomy takes place upon the plains of Moab.

PURPOSE OF THE BOOK

We have already pointed out the word "Deuteronomy" means "second law" but that it is really the second giving of the first law. The fact that the law was being given again is significant. It means that God is the God of second chances.

The Israelites had broken God's law in the wilderness. They had rebelled against the Lord. God said, "Go into the land," and they retorted, "We won't do it!" They refused to trust in Him. They broke the terms of their covenant with Him. As a result, they were condemned to die in the wilderness.

That could easily have been the end of the nation of Israel. God was under no further obligation to these people. The descendants of Abraham could have passed into extinction and God would have been just and righteous in making it happen.

But instead, God responded in grace. He allowed for a new generation. And with this new generation, He again makes His covenant. Again there will be a relationship established between God and men. Again there will be a people of God.

Is this significant to you today? Absolutely! If there had been no covenant people, there would be no Messiah. Without a Messiah, there would be no salvation and you would still be in your sins. Without the book of Deuteronomy, you would not be saved.

THEME OF DEUTERONOMY

There are really two themes running throughout this book. The first leads to the second.

1.   The Love of God for His People. The book starts on this note. It shows how God has loved and cared for His people whom He had chosen.

2.   Our Obedience toward God. If we really love God, how do we show that love? It is through obeying Him. Jesus said, "If you love Me, keep My commandments."

OUTLINE OF DEUTERONOMY

Deuteronomy consists of several sermons from Moses. They are all given at the close of his life. Meredith Kline notes that these sermons are arranged in a structure that is similar to the order of ancient suzerain treaties. The suzerain would be the victor of the treaty; he was the "big king." The vassal would be the loser; he would be the "lesser king." The covenant treaty would outline their future relationship and would follow a certain structure:

1.   Preamble (1:1-4).

        The Suzerain (the king) identifies himself as the author of the proposed covenant in such a way as to inspire fear and awe in his vassal. In the case of the Hittite treaty, it looked like this:

> *The regulations which the great prince of Hatti, Hattusiles, the powerful, the son of Mursilis, the great prince of Hatti, the powerful, the son of Suppululiumas, the great prince of Hatti, the powerful.*

        In the Mosaic Covenant, Yahweh identifies Himself and shows His relationship to Israel's genealogy, Abraham, Isaac and Jacob. He also shows His greatness in conquering Israel s enemies (Exodus 20:1; Deuteronomy 1:1-5).

2.   Historical Prologue (1:5 - 4:49).

        The Suzerain describes in detail the previous relationship between himself and his vassal. A great emphasis is placed upon the deeds of kindness of the Suzerain toward his vassal so that the vassal finds himself obligated to be loyal to his Suzerain.
        In the Mosaic Covenant, the Lord recalls how He has brought Israel out of Egypt and how, in spite of her constant rebellion, He has fought for Israel and protected her, caring for her in the wilderness. He goes on to show how He still intends to give her the land of Canaan for a possession (Exodus 20:2; Deuteronomy 1:6; 3:29).

3.   Stipulations (5:1 - 26:19).

        These are obligations which are imposed by the suzerain and accepted by the vassal. They usually include the following demands.

- The Suzerain prohibits foreign relationships outside his own empire.
- The Suzerain prohibits oppression by one of his vassals over another.
- The vassal must aid the Suzerain in any military endeavor in which he partakes.
- The vassal is not to take in any refugees from other countries.
- The vassal must appear before the Suzerain once a year.
- Controversies between vassals must be settled by the Suzerain.

Each of these stipulations finds its counterpart in the Mosaic Covenant (Deuteronomy 4-26). The terms of God's covenant are that His people should live lives that are holy and set apart unto Him. These commands are set forth in great detail, beginning with the original Ten Commandments and then expanding upon them with case law and further explanations.

A provision is made for the deposit of a copy of the covenant in the vassal's sanctuary or temple. In a normal suzerain treaty, each king would take his copy of the treaty back to his own nation and keep it within the temple of his city. But God gives both copies of the treaty to Moses because God is going to reside with His people. He is the suzerain who resides with His vassals.

Since the treaty was so involved with the witness of deities, it was regarded as a religious object and therefore was kept in the temple. There was also a provision made for the public reading of the covenant terms to the people (Deuteronomy 10:1-5; 31:9-13).

4.   Blessing, Curses, and Ratification of the Covenant (27:1 - 30:20).

The treaty was not merely a legal document to be enforced by the Suzerain. It was a religious document. It was the gods who had served as witnesses who were to punish the vassal if he broke the treaty. Curses were invoked upon the vassal and were to become activated if he broke the treaty. Blessings were invoked upon him if he was faithful to the terms of the covenant.

In the Mosaic Covenant, the order of the curses and blessings are reversed. Blessings are first described and then the cursings (Leviticus 26:3-33; Deuteronomy 28:1-68).

5.   Succession (31:1 - 34:12).

There would be a stated plan for passing the terms of the covenant on to future generations so that it would not automatically end with the passing away of one of the two kings.

1:1	Preamble		Remembrance of the Past	Introduction
1:5	Historical Prologue	Rehearsal of the Journey		Sinai to Kadesh
2:1				Kadesh to Moab
4:1		Spiritual Applications		Don't Forget the Covenant!
5:1	Stipulations	The Ten Commands	Commands for the Present	The Ten Words
12:1		Related Commands		Ceremonial Righteousness
17:1				Governmental Righteousness
21:15				Practical Righteousness
26:1			Options for the Future	"When you enter the land..."
27:1	Blessings & Cursings	Prophetic		• Curses • Blessings • Covenant
31:1	Succession	Personal	Parting words of Moses	• Charge • Song • Benediction • Departure

When we come to Deuteronomy 32, we have this entire outline repeated in summary form as we are taken through a covenant lawsuit that specifies the times Israel has been guilty of breaking the covenant.

INTERPRETING THE BOOK OF DEUTERONOMY

How are we to interpret this book? What are we to do with its message? Will the study of this book help me in how I live my life this week? Is it relevant to my needs?

1.   Historical Interpretation.

    This view sees Deuteronomy as a mildly interesting history lesson but with no direct application for today.

2.   Directly Applicable.

    This view goes to the other extreme of applying the laws and ordinances of Deuteronomy directly for today for complete implementation within any given country or society.

3.   Typology.

    This view sees Deuteronomy as containing pictures and types and shadows of Jesus. This is very easy with the sacrificial system. It is not so easy with some of the commands and ordinances.

4.   The Reformed View.

    The Reformers taught that the Law has three possible uses for Christians today.

    a.   *Civicus Usus*: This is the use which keeps you from doing something that you should not be doing. Have you ever noticed what happens when you are driving on the highway and you spot a police car? You immediately check to see if you are within the confines of the law. The law was designed to keep you from sin.

    b.   *Pedagogious Usus*: This is the use of the law which convicts you of your sin and which turns you to Christ as you realize that, apart from Him, you have no hope.

    c.   *Didacticus* Usus: The law is used to teach us about the righteousness of God. God is absolutely righteous, and the

Law shows us what that righteousness involves.

DEUTERONOMY COMPARED TO OTHER BOOKS OF THE BIBLE

1. Compared to the other four books of Moses.

Preparation for the Building of God's Kingdom	
Genesis	Foundational truths for the kingdom
Exodus	Inauguration of the kingdom at Sinai
Leviticus	Spiritual organization of the kingdom
Numbers	Political organization of the kingdom
Deuteronomy	Recapitulation of the Preparation of the kingdom

Portrait of...	Man	God	Activity
Genesis	Ruin	Creator	Selection
Exodus	Redemption	Power	Salvation
Leviticus	Renewal	Holiness	Sanctification
Numbers	Rebellion	Judge	Service
Deuteronomy	Renaissance	Faithful	Survey

2. Contrasted to the other four books of Moses.

Genesis to Numbers	Deuteronomy
The human story.	The spiritual significance.
Outward facts.	Inward spirit.
Course of Israel's history.	Philosophy of Israel's history.
Divine performances.	Divine principles.

JOSHUA
The Book of the Conquest

The book of Joshua heads the Nabi'im - the collection of books known as "the Prophets." These books cover the period of Israel's history from the entrance into the promised land to the Babylonian Exile. Joshua is the bridge which brings the people of God from the Wilderness wanderings into the land.

Pentateuch (Israel in the Wilderness)	Joshua	Prophets (Israel in the Land)

THE SCOPE OF THE BOOK

The book of Joshua takes up where Deuteronomy leaves off with the Israelites about to enter the promised land.

Deuteronomy	Joshua
Israelites in the Wilderness.	Israelites entering into the Promised Land.
A vision for faith.	A venture of faith.
Israel promised an inheritance.	Israel takes possession of its inheritance.
Faith in principle.	Faith in action.
Possibility.	Realization.

Deuteronomy ends with the death of Moses. The book of Joshua will end with the death of Joshua. As the book of Joshua opens, Moses has just died. Before his death, he had laid his hands upon Joshua who was to be the new leader. This book can be divided into two parts.

1.   The first part details the actual taking of the land.

2.   The second part deals with the distribution of that land to the various tribes of Israel.

Joshua - The Book of the Conquest			
1:1 - 5:15	6:1 - 12:24	13:1 - 22:9	22:10 - 24:33
Preparations to take the Land	Conquest of the Land	Distribution of the Land	Living in the Land
Remembrance	Action	Inheritance	Remembrance
Initial Appeal	In the Land		Closing Appeal

This book is actually arranged in the format of a large chiastic parallel. Thus, it can be seen that this book begins and ends with a focus upon the Covenant of the Lord with His people.

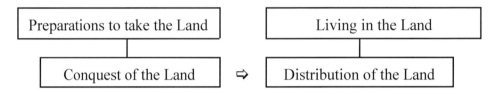

This is the message of the book of Joshua. It is that God has been faithful to keep His promises regarding a land and an inheritance for His people. Because God has been faithful in the keeping of His covenant relationship, so also the people of Israel are to be faithful in keeping the terms of the covenant.

AUTHORSHIP OF THE BOOK

The author of the book is not specifically identified within the book, although there is the occasional use of the plural pronoun ("we"), indicating his identification with the Israelites coming into the land.

> *For the sons of Israel walked forty years in the wilderness, until all the nation, that is, the men of war who came out of Egypt, perished because they did not listen to the*

voice of the Lord, to whom the Lord had sworn that He would not let them see the land which the Lord had sworn to their fathers to give US, a land flowing with milk and honey. (Joshua 5:6).

This could be an editorial "us" and does not automatically mandate that the writer had been in the wilderness (verse 1 of the same chapter has a similar plural pronoun, but only in certain Hebrew manuscripts).

1.   Likewise, there is an indication that Rahab was still living at the time of the writing of this book (Joshua 6:25).

2.   The Talmud states that this book was written by Joshua himself, that Eleazar wrote the section detailing Joshua's death and that Phinehas added the verses telling of Eleazar's death.

3.   However, there are several other events about which Joshua could not have written, since they took place after his death.

   • Caleb's conquest of Hebron (Joshua 15:13-14 with Judges 1:1, 10, 20).
   • Othniel's capture of Debir (Joshua 15:15-19 with Judges 1:1; 1:11-15).
   • The migration of Dan to Leshem (Joshua 19:47 with Judges 17:18 indicates that this was a time when idolatry was permitted; this did not take place until after the death of Joshua - Joshua 24:31).
   • The town of Zephath had its name changed to Hormah in the days of the Judges (Joshua 12:14; 15:30 with Judges 1:16-17).

4.   There are also certain factors which indicate later editorial additions to the book. On several occasions we are given the modern equivalents for older names of places (Joshua 15:9,49,54).

Joshua 6:24 makes reference to "silver and gold and vessels of bronze and iron" that were saved for the "House of the Lord." This phrasing has been taken to indicate that Joshua was written after the building of the Temple. However, it is possible that the *Beyth-Yahweh* is merely used to describe the "dwelling-place of the Lord."

An example of this type of usage is seen in instances where Abraham describe his house (Genesis 14:14; 15:2-3; 17:12-13) and in Exodus 23:19 soon after the construction of the Tabernacle.

The book also gives an evaluation of the elders who outlived Joshua.

> *And Israel served the Lord all the days of Joshua and all the days of the elders who survived Joshua, and had known all the deeds of the Lord which He had done for Israel. (Joshua 24:31).*

5. The book of Joshua also makes reference to other written documents in the book of Jasher (10:13) and of a written description of the land which Joshua ordered to be written (18:9).

JOSHUA AS THE SECOND MOSES

The book of Joshua seems to contain a number of deliberate parallels that are meant to make us see Joshua as the successor to Moses. The following parallel is pointed out by Dale Allison (1997:27).

Moses	Joshua
Sends spies into the land (Numbers 13)	Sends spies into the land (Joshua 2)
The song of the Sea: "All the inhabitants of Canaan have melted away, terror and dread fall upon them" (Exodus 15).	Rahab says: "The fear of you has fallen upon us and... all the inhabitants of the land melt away before you" (Joshua 2).
Israel celebrates the Passover and shortly afterward eats manna (Exodus 12).	Israel celebrates the Passover and afterward the manna dries up (Joshua 5:10-13).
Moses has a vision and is told: "Put off your shoes from your feet, for the place on which you are standing is holy ground (Exodus 3:5).	Joshua has a vision and is told: "Put off your shoes from your feet, for the place on which you are standing is holy ground (Joshua 5:15).
When Moses, with the staff of God, holds up his hands, the battle goes to Israel (Exodus 17).	When Joshua stretches out his hand with his sword, the victory goes to Israel (Joshua 8).

Moses delivers a farewell speech that includes a reference to his old age (Deut 31:2), promises future victory over people of the land (31:3-5), calls for obedience to the Torah (31:12-13, and sets forth the alternative of serving God or other gods and the consequent blessings and curses (30:15-20).	Joshua delivers a farewell speech that includes a reference to his old age (Josh 23:2), promises future victory over people of the land (23:4-5), calls for obedience to the Torah (23:6), and sets forth the alternative of serving God or other gods and the consequent blessings and curses (23:6-16).
Moses mediates a covenant; the people say: "All that the Lord has spoken we will do, and we will be obedient" (Ex 24:7).	Joshua mediates a covenant; the people say: "The Lord our God we will serve, Him we will obey" (Joshua 24:24).

THE CHARGE TO JOSHUA (JOSHUA 1)

"Be strong and courageous, for you shall give this people possession of the land which I swore to their fathers to give them." (Joshua 1:6).

Four times in this chapter, Joshua is told to "be strong and courageous." But that is not all. Before Moses died, he told Joshua twice to "be strong and courageous" (Deuteronomy 31:6-7). And again, when the Lord commissioned Joshua, He told him to "be strong and courageous" (Deuteronomy 31:23).

And now, in this opening chapter of Joshua, the Lord tells him three times to "be strong and courageous" (1:6,7,9) and then the people of Israel respond by charging Joshua to "be strong and courageous" (1:18). When this sort of repetition takes place in the Scriptures, one can be certain that there is a reason for it.

1.   Why is this repeated so many times? It is because Joshua was going to need strength and courage.

        a.   First, God told Joshua to be strong and courageous because he would have to take the land (1:6).

                The good news is that God had given Him the land; the bad

news was that He gave it to someone else first. Joshua was facing a land of walled cities. And to make matters worse, he had no siege engines.

b.   Secondly, God told Joshua to be strong and courageous because he would have to obey God's law (1:7). It takes courage to obey God when everybody else isn't. It takes even more courage to obey God as a leader and to condemn sin when public opinion says it's okay.

c.   Thirdly, God told Joshua to be strong and courageous because the Lord would be with him (1:9). A leader has to fake it, even when he doesn't feel it. Inside, the leader is often scared to death. But it helps a leader to know that he is not alone.

Joshua was called to conquer a land. We have been called to conquer the world. Our calling is to make disciples of every nation. Our weapons are different, for we do not fight against flesh and blood. But the need for strength and courage is no less.

2.   Second Best.

In the midst of this charge to Joshua, there is also a charge and a call to the two and a half tribes which had chosen lands on the east bank of the Jordan to be their inheritance.

> *And to the Reubenites and to the Gadites and to the half-tribe of Manasseh, Joshua said, "Remember the word which Moses the servant of the Lord commanded you, saying, `The Lord your God gives you rest, and will give you this land.' Your wives, your little ones, and your cattle shall remain in the land which Moses gave you beyond the Jordan, but you shall cross before your brothers in battle array, all your valiant warriors, and shall help them, until the Lord gives your brothers rest, as He gives you, and they also possess the land which the Lord your God is giving them. Then you shall return to your own land, and possess that which Moses the servant of the Lord gave you beyond the Jordan toward the sunrise." (Joshua 1:12-15).*

This is the story of the two and a half tribes who took God's second best. In Numbers 32, these tribes looked at the land to the west of the Jordan River and they said to themselves, "This sure is a lot better than the wilderness." And so, they sent representatives to Moses and asked for this land as their inheritance. This was God's second best. It was to cost them dearly.

a.   First, it was not flowing with milk and honey.
       It was better than the wilderness, but it was not as good as the promised land.

b.   Secondly, they were to serve as a buffer state between Israel and the other nations of the world. This meant that every time the Moabites, the Ammonites, the Edomites, the Assyrians, or the Babylonians got mad, they first attacked these two and a half tribes.

c.   Third, they had to go into the promised land and fight for land that would not be theirs. While they were there, they would see what they had given up.

I have seen far too many girls who married the first guy who came along and who, in doing so, got God's second best. Don't take second best. And don't BE second best.

SPYING OUT THE LAND (JOSHUA 2)

1.   Rahab: *Then Joshua the son of Nun sent two men as spies secretly from Shittim, saying, "Go, view the land, especially Jericho." So they went and came into the house of a harlot whose name was Rahab, and lodged there. (Joshua 2:1).*

       A lot of Christians have trouble accepting the fact that there is a prostitute in the Bible. Not only that, but in the New Testament she is praised.

              By faith Rahab the harlot did not perish along with those who were disobedient, after she had welcomed the spies in peace. (Hebrews 11:31).

Not only is she praised, her name is found in the genealogy of Jesus (Matthew 1:5). She is said to be the mother of Boaz and the wife of Salmon.

Some commentaries have tried to suggest that Rahab was only an innkeeper. But that isn't true. This woman was a prostitute. She was an *ishih zonah* - a woman of harlotry. There is a lesson here. It is that the church is not a gathering for good people. The church is a hospital for sinners. We say we believe that, but our actions often show that we don't. We become proud of our own righteousness.

2.   Rahab's Deception.

> *And the king of Jericho sent word to Rahab, saying, "Bring out the men who have come to you, who have entered your house, for they have come to search out all the land."*
>
> *But the woman had taken the two men and hidden them, and she said, "Yes, the men came to me, but I did not know where they were from. And it came about when it was time to shut the gate, at dark, that the men went out; I do not know where the men went. Pursue them quickly, for you will overtake them."*
>
> *But she had brought them up to the roof and hidden them in the stalks of flax which she had laid in order on the roof. (Joshua 2:3-6).*

Rahab lied through her teeth. And yet, she is praised in the New Testament and held up as an example of faith. How can we reconcile this? Rahab is never commended for her lying. She is commended for her faithfulness. The heros (and heroines) of the Bible are real people who had real problems just like you and me. They are not stained-glass saints. They are real people.

David is described as a man after God's own heart. He was the greatest king of Israel. His reign was considered the golden age. He wrote beautiful songs of worship to the Lord. There are a lot of good things that the Bible tells us about David. But the Bible never commends him for his affair with Bathsheba.

Peter was a great apostle. He stood up for the faith and was imprisoned for preaching the gospel. Jesus gave to him the keys of the kingdom. But the Bible never praises Peter for denying Jesus.

We live in a fallen world. That means that sometimes decisions are grey. Sometimes it is not a decision between good and bad. Sometimes it is a decision between two bad things. Sometimes you have to decide which is the best between two evils.

This does not mean that I believe in situational ethics. The Bible does not teach that the end justifies the means. Wrong is still wrong. But it does teach that I live in a fallen world. Sometimes I may have to choose between what is bad and what is worse. However, it is important when making such a grey decision to never call it anything less than sin.

3.   Rahab's Reason.

> *Now before they lay down, she came up to them on the roof, and said to the men, "I know that the Lord has given you the land, and that the terror of you has fallen on us, and that all the inhabitants of the land have melted away before you.*
>
> *"For we have heard how the Lord dried up the water of the Red Sea before you when you came out of Egypt, and what you did to the two kings of the Amorites who were beyond the Jordan, to Sihon and Og, whom you utterly destroyed.*
>
> *"And when we heard it, our hearts melted and no courage remained in any man any longer because of you; for the Lord your God, He is God in heaven above and on earth beneath." (Joshua 2:8-11).*

The Exodus from Egypt had taken place 40 years earlier. But it had not been forgotten. It was still the topic of discussion in Canaan. They recognized that the God of Israel had devastated the greatest and most powerful nation on earth. Rahab had come to believe in the God who divided the Red Sea and who preserved the Israelites in the wilderness. And so, she seeks to join herself to the covenant community. She asks for salvation both for herself and for her family.

4.   The Scarlet Cord.

> *And the men said to her, "We shall be free from this oath to you which you have made us swear, unless, when we come into the land, you tie this cord of scarlet thread in the window through which you let us down, and gather to yourself into the house your*

father and your mother and your brothers and all your father's household." (Joshua 2:17-18).

The very rope that provided a way of escape for the two spies would also be the sign of salvation for Rahab and her family. It enabled the spies to escape from Jericho and it would enable Rahab and her family to escape the destruction of Jericho.

Matthew tells us that Rahab was a part of Jesus' genealogy, presumably through Joseph, which was His claim to the throne of David. Also a part of that genealogy was a Canaanite woman named Tamar. When she gave birth to twins, the midwives tied a scarlet thread to the hand of the firstborn. It was this same firstborn whose descendants later went on to sit on the throne of Israel.

The use of this cord also has strong similarities with the covenental sign of Passover, that of the blood on Israelite houses on the night of the slaughter of the firstborn in Egypt (Exodus 12:7, 13, 22-23).

There is a scarlet cord running from Genesis to Revelation. It is the picture of the shed blood of the Messiah of Israel. Archaeologists tell us that as far back as we can go in human history, man has always felt that something ought to be sacrificed as a substitute and as an appeasement for sin. It is rooted in all of society. God has given a universal consciousness of the need for a sacrifice. It all comes to focus upon a hill called Golgotha where a Jewish rabbi was nailed between two crossbeams.

5.   The Report of the Spies.

And they said to Joshua, "Surely the Lord has given all the land into our hands, and all the inhabitants of the land, moreover, have melted away before us." (Joshua 2:24).

Joshua had picked his spies carefully. He had learned from his previous experience. Forty years earlier, twelve spies had been sent into to land of Canaan. Only two had returned with a positive report. This time, only two spies are sent. I can't help but wonder if ten others were interviewed and told, "Don't call us, we'll call you."

The land of Canaan had not changed. The people were not any shorter. The walls of the cities were not any lower. But these spies knew that they could win. Sometimes we need to be told that we can win. We look at our situation and it seems to be hopeless.

That is when we need a word of encouragement. That is when we need to be told that we can win.

INCIDENT AT THE JORDAN (JOSHUA 3-4)

As we come to these two chapters, there is a hermeneutical rule of which we need to be aware. It is that the amount of space devoted to a subject is indicative of the importance that God has given to that subject.

You will notice that the writer of Joshua gives two chapters to the crossing of the Jordan. He does this because God sees that particular act as very important to His redemptive program. The writer could have covered this in four sentences. He could have said...

They came to the Jordan.
It was flooded.
God stopped the waters.
They crossed over.

But He did not do this. We should not do it either. You can apply this rule to the entire Bible. The importance of a passage can be determined by the amount of space given over to it. This provides an important caution to believers. It is that you need to be careful not to major in the minors.

There is a corollary to this. The amount of time you devote in your life will give evidence to the subjects that you think are important. How much time do you spend with your family? How about time in the Word? How much do you pray?

1.   Following the Ark.

> *And it came about at the end of three days that the officers went through the midst of the camp; and they commanded the people, saying, "When you see the ark of the covenant of the Lord your God with the Levitical priests carrying it, then you shall set out from your place and go after it.*
>
> *However, there shall be between you and it a distance of about 2,000 cubits by measure. Do not come near it, that you may know the way by which you shall go, for you have not passed this way before." (Joshua 3:2-4).*

The ark of the covenant is mentioned a number of times in this chapter. The Hebrew word for "ark" is *'aron*. It is the same word which describes the coffin into which the body of Joseph was placed (Genesis 50:26). It describes a box or a chest. In modern Hebrew, it is used to refer to a closet.

The ark was a wooden box overlaid with gold. It was the symbolic representation of the presence of God among His people. Inside the ark were the tablets of the Law. The ark was covered with a top of pure gold. It was known as the "mercy seat." This was the throne of God.

As the Israelites prepare to enter into the land, it will be the ark which leads them. For the past 40 years, they have followed the presence of God in a pillar of fire and a column of smoke through the wilderness. Now they will continue to follow the presence of God. But now it will be in the form of the ark.

They are instructed to keep a distance of about 1000 yards from the ark. There is to be no familiarity with it. It is to be considered holy and set apart from the ordinary. We would have been making little arks and selling them as souvenirs. We might have been tempted to place the ark in a fence and set out television cameras around it and charged an admission to come and see it.

If there is a danger in American Christianity, it is that we tend to forget that we worship the God of the universe. He is not Santa Claus. He is not sweet. He is not a genie in a bottle that you rub and get three wishes. He is not a sweet little old man who is slightly hard of hearing. He is God.

2.   The Preparation of Consecration.

> *Then Joshua said to the people, "Consecrate yourselves, for tomorrow the Lord will do wonders among you." (Joshua 3:5).*

The phrase "consecrate yourselves" is translated from *hithkadashu* - the Hithpa'el imperative of *kadash*, to make holy. The Israelites were called to be holy - set apart to God. They were cut out from the rest of the world and separated to be a special people. They ate different food. They wore different clothes. They worshiped a different God. We are called to be different. We have been sanctified - set apart to God.

3.   The Stopping of the Waters..

So it came about when the people set out from their tents to cross the Jordan with the priests carrying the ark of the covenant before the people, and when those who carried the ark were dipped in the edge of the water (for the Jordan overflows all its banks all the days of harvest), that the waters which were flowing down from above stood and rose up in one heap, a great distance away at Adam, the city that is beside Zarethan; and those which were flowing down toward the sea of the Arabah, the Salt Sea, were completely cut off. So the people crossed opposite Jericho. (Joshua 3:14-16).

Notice that the passage does not say that the waters were parted, but that the upstream waters stopped flowing (the downstream waters continued on their way, leaving dry land). What is more, the location at which the waters stopped is the city of Adam. This city was located 16 miles upstream, near the point where the Jabbok flows into the Jordan. At this point, there are high clay banks reaching some 40 feet over the river. This area is subject to landslides. It was reported by Albright that during an earthquake in 1927, these banks collapsed, damming the river for a period of nearly 24 hours.

4.   Memorial Stones.

"Then Joshua set up twelve stones in the middle of the Jordan at the place where the feet of the priests who carried the ark of the covenant were standing, and they are there to this day." (Joshua 4:9).

As the Israelites crossed through the dry riverbed of the Jordan, Joshua had two groups of stones set up. They were memorial stones. They were to be a constant reminder of the power of God which was able to stop the waters of the Jordan so that they could

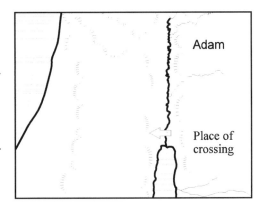

cross over.

Remembering is important. Nostalgia can be good. It is good to remember God and His faithfulness. We need reminders. The Lord's Supper is such a reminder. The real danger in Christianity is that we forget. That is how we fall into sin. Every time a Jew walked past that stack of rocks, he would be reminded of the power and the goodness of God.

There were actually two stacks of rocks. The first group is seen in verse 8. They are twelve stones taken from the riverbed and placed outside the river.

> The NIV translates this differently in order to suggest that there was only a single stack of rocks. However, if the stones in Joshua 4:8 were meant to be understood as the same stones as those mentioned in Joshua 4:9, then we would have expected to see the article with the word "stones." Instead the syntax suggests that verse 9 is disjunctive, indicating a contrast with verse 8.

But there is also a second group. This group is seen here in verse 9. This group is also composed of twelve stones. But they are not placed outside the river. They are placed "in the middle of the Jordan." It seems like a funny place to place memorial stones, doesn't it? After all, who is going to see them at the bottom of the river?

Let me suggest that, in the same way that the first group was to remind the Israelites of the faithfulness and the power of God, so also this second group of stones would also be a reminder to the Israelites.

But when would they see this second group? Only in the dry season when the level of the river lowered. During the dry season, when the crops were in danger of dying and the people were praying for the coming rains, these stones in the middle of the river would become visible. They would be a reminder that God is faithful - even in the dry season.

5.   The Crossing: *...and the people hurried and crossed (Joshua 4:10b).*

Notice that the people went across quickly. Why quickly? Why did they hurry? I think that it was because they were afraid. These people had grown up in the desert and I don't think they knew how to swim. They were afraid to cross the Jordan. But they crossed anyway. It is okay to be afraid to cross the Jordan. But it is not okay to stay on the wrong side.

6.   The Results of the Crossing.

>   *Now it came about when all the kings of the*
>   *Amorites who were beyond the Jordan to the west,*
>   *and all the kings of the Canaanites who were by the*
>   *sea, heard how the Lord had dried up the waters of*
>   *the Jordan before the sons of Israel until they had*
>   *crossed, that their hearts melted, and there was no*
>   *spirit in them any longer, because of the sons of*
>   *Israel. (Joshua 5:1).*

When the Israelites saw the miracle of the Jordan River, they were impressed. They thought that the reason God had done this was so that they could cross over. That was one reason. But there was also another. It was so that the other nations would see the miracle and they would fear the Lord. Do you see the application of this? We are some of the nations who have heard of that miracle. We should fear the Lord as a result.

CIRCUMCISION & PASSOVER (JOSHUA 5)

1.   Circumcision.

>   *At that time the Lord said to Joshua, "Make*
>   *for yourselves flint knives and circumcise again the*
>   *sons of Israel the second time." (Joshua 5:2).*

The covenant sign of circumcision had been given to Abraham. When the Israelites had come out of Egypt in the Exodus, they had reintroduced this covenant sign. But there is now a new generation. And they had not partaken in the sign of the covenant. They are called to do so now. This was a sign of their faith (Romans 4:11).

This event put the army of Israel in a vulnerable position for several days. And to make matters worse, they were right under the shadow of Jericho. But when you are obeying the commands of the Lord, it is okay to be vulnerable.

2.   The Passover.

> *While the sons of Israel camped at Gilgal, they observed the Passover on the evening of the fourteenth day of the month on the desert plains of Jericho. (Joshua 5:10).*

God's army had taken the sign of the covenant (circumcision) and now ate at the Lord's Table (Passover). These preparations were necessary for them to go forth and to conquer the land.

The church today has a similar preparation to undergo. We must take the sign of the covenant (baptism) and eat at the Lord's Table before we can take the sword of the Spirit forth to conquer the nations.

3.   The Manna Removed.

> *And the manna ceased on the day after they had eaten some of the produce of the land, so that the sons of Israel no longer had manna, but they ate some of the yield of the land of Canaan during that year. (Joshua 5:12).*

When the people moved into the promised land, were circumcised, and partook of the Passover, the manna stopped. There is a principle here. God helps those who can't help themselves. God also helps those who can help themselves, but He helps them in a different way. When I was a new believer, everything just seemed to fall into my lap. I would walk up to someone and ask, "Do you want to meet Jesus?" and they would answer, "Yes, will you tell me how?" I didn't know anything about apologetics. I wasn't particularly good at explaining my faith. But that was okay because God could use me where I was.

But I want you to know that it isn't as easy as it used to be. Nowadays God sends me the agnostic and the hardened atheist. Why? Because He knows that I can handle it.

4.   Confrontation with an Angel.

> *Now it came about when Joshua was by Jericho, that he lifted up his eyes and looked, and behold, a man was standing opposite him with his sword drawn in his hand, and Joshua went to him and said to him, "Are you for us or for our adversaries?"*

(Joshua 5:13).

Joshua issues a challenge to this unknown warrior. It is in the form of a question: "Whose side are you on?" Joshua knew that it is impossible to remain neutral in God's battles. You always choose sides. And even if you try to remain neutral, the truth is that you have chosen a side.

> *And he said, "No, rather I indeed come now as captain of the host of the Lord." And Joshua fell on his face to the earth, and bowed down, and said to him, "What has my lord to say to his servant?" (Joshua 5:14).*

The captain of God's army does not say that he is on Joshua's side. Rather it is Joshua who is on His side. Here is the principle. The battle is the Lord's. It is His conflict. We are merely soldiers under His command.

THE CAMPAIGN AGAINST JERICHO

1.   The City of Jericho.

        As the Jordan River nears the Dead Sea, the river valley widens to a width of about 10 miles. On the western edge of this wide valley lies the ancient city of Jericho.

        The site of the Old Testament city is a mound rising up 50 feet above the surrounding bedrock of the southern Jordan valley (Jericho is 825 feet below sea level). It is located about 10 miles to the NNW of the mouth of the Dead Sea and directly west of fords which make it possible to cross the Jordan except during the rainy season.

        There is a natural spring known as Ain es-Sultan which originally attracted settlers to this site. This oasis gave the city its nickname, "City of Palm Trees."

The city was fairly small (only 6 acres), but held a strategic position at the hub of four major roads radiating outward to Bethel, Jerusalem, Hebron, and eastward to the fords across the Jordan.

2.   Instructions to March around the City.

The first battle within the Promised Land is one which the Lord Himself would fight, completely apart from the strength of the Israelites. The instructions given to Joshua were limited to marching orders. I can't help but to think that the Israelites might have been tempted to think they were a bit foolish for merely marching around the city each day and then going home. But they obeyed the word of the Lord. This is what obedience is all about. Obeying even when you do not see the reason for it.

3.   The Falling of Jericho's Walls.

> *So the people shouted, and priests blew the trumpets, and it came about, when the people heard the sound of the trumpet, that the people shouted with a great shout and the wall fell down flat, so that the people went up into the city, every man straight ahead, and they took the city. (Joshua 6:20).*

No siege engines were needed to take this city. This is a good thing because siege machines were largely unknown at this time in history. The Lord brought the walls down. Some have speculated that an earthquake was involved (the area is prone to earthquakes). But the passage does not mention any such additional phenomenon. It merely says that the walls fell.

This was no small breach in the wall. These walls fell in such a way so that every Israelite warrior surrounding the city could go straight into the city.

4.   The Destruction of the City.

> *And they burned the city with fire, and all that was in it. Only the silver and gold and articles of bronze and iron, they put into the treasury of the house of the Lord. (Joshua 6:24).*

How could a good God do such terrible things to the city of Jericho? Our sensitivities are offended by this account. What is the answer? We must be very careful in judging a different culture by 20th century standards. Life was harsh in those days. The standards were different. There are several fallacies which we have bought into and which need to be dispelled.

a. There is a noble primitive savage and we shouldn't try to destroy their culture.

Margaret Mead was an anthropologist who wrote about the nobility of the savages of New Guinea. She described them as wonderful, gentle people without guilt or harshness. But this has since been revealed to be completely false. The primitive aborigines were brutal and harsh.

The culture of Jericho was equally harsh. They would murder their children in religious orgies by throwing their screaming bodies into flames of fire. They were a plague on the landscape.

b. God is sweet, kind, and gentle and will always forgive every misdeed.

We are idolaters. We think of a god of our own making and we put him up on a shelf and take him down to worship him once in a while. Spiro Agnew once said, "The vice president is like adding maternity benefits to social security - it's there but you don't need it." We look at God that way. He is there but we don't need Him. And that is blasphemy.

c. Sin is only a manifestation of our humanness. It means very little to God and therefore should not mean very much to us.

God had given a prophecy of the judgment of the Amorites in Genesis 15:15-16. He said that judgment would be a long time coming because "the iniquity of the Amorites was not yet full." God waited until the badness of the people of Canaan had reached its maximum limits.

d. Sin is your own business. It doesn't affect others.

God told His people to destroy everything in the land because He knew that if they didn't, it wouldn't be long before they were infected with the same sin. Sin is a cancer. It spreads.

THE CAMPAIGN AGAINST AI

If Jericho was a great victory for the Israelites, then Ai marked their first defeat under Joshua's command. The chapter is given in a chiastic format.

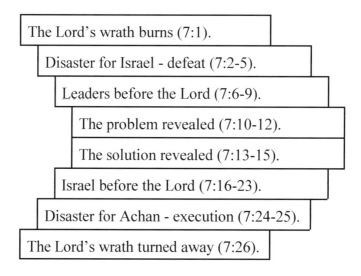

The Lord's wrath burns (7:1).

Disaster for Israel - defeat (7:2-5).

Leaders before the Lord (7:6-9).

The problem revealed (7:10-12).

The solution revealed (7:13-15).

Israel before the Lord (7:16-23).

Disaster for Achan - execution (7:24-25).

The Lord's wrath turned away (7:26).

1.   The Sin of Achan.

> *But the sons of Israel acted unfaithfully in regard to the things under the ban, for Achan, the son of Carmi, the son of Zabdi, the son of Zerah, from the tribe of Judah, took some of the things under the ban, therefore the anger of the Lord burned against the sons of Israel. (Joshua 7:1).*

God had said that everything in Jericho was to be burned as a sacrifice to Him. Nothing was to be taken from it. The entire city was to be a first fruit offering to Him. But Achan decided to take some of the valuables for himself. Verse 21 says that he took an ornate Babylonian robe along with some silver and gold. By doing so, Achan was transferring his allegiance and his love from Israel to Jericho - from God to gold.

Notice that the passage says that "the anger of the Lord burned against the sons of Israel." The stolen treasures were supposed to be burned as a sacrifice to the Lord. And when the sacrifice was withheld, that "burning anger" which would have been appeased in the sacrifice was now directed toward the people of Israel. This is a picture of Jesus. He is the perfect sacrifice who has appeased the anger of God (we call this doctrine "propitiation"). Without the sacrifice of Jesus, we are left to face God's anger.

There is a lesson here. It is a dangerous thing to rob God. Achan was killed for it. And so were Ananias and Saphira in the New Testament. In both cases, their sin was an attempt to rob the Lord and then to hide their sin and lie about it.

2.   The City of Ai.

The city of Ai is always found in the Hebrew with the definite article, "the heap" or "the ruin." Joshua 7:2 indicates that Ai was "east of Bethel."

> The modern site of Et Tell is generally thought to be the location of the ancient city of Ai (about two miles from Bethel).

3.   Israel's Defeat at Ai.

Ai was so small that it was not considered to be worth the mobilization of the entire force of the Israelites. The spies who went in and observed it advised that only a token force of 2000 to 3000 men would be needed to take the city.

> *And the men of Ai struck down about thirty-six of their men, and pursued them from the gate as far as Shebarim, and struck them down on the descent, so the hearts of the people melted and became as water. (Joshua 7:5).*

The battle at Ai goes the exact opposite of what had taken place at Jericho. At Jericho, everything had gone completely right. At Ai, everything goes completely wrong. Why did the Israelites suffer such a setback? A number of reasons have been offered.:

- It has been pointed out that there is no mention of prayer prior to the attack on Ai.
- Furthermore, it is obvious that the Israelites exhibited an overconfidence.

But the real reason for the defeat has nothing to do with these two surface reasons. The real reason is because God's command had been ignored and there was sin in the camp. A little sin goes a long way.

3. The Prayer of Joshua.

> *And Joshua said, "Alas, O Lord God, why did You ever bring this people over the Jordan, only to deliver us into the hand of the Amorites to destroy us? If only we had been willing to dwell beyond the Jordan!" (Joshua 7:7).*

These words sound familiar. The Israelites had said the same thing to Moses by the edge of the Red Sea. This time, it is Joshua who is saying it. He was discouraged (remember all those times he had been warned to be strong and courageous?). Joshua complains to God. There is nothing wrong with such a prayer. It is one thing to complain to God; it is quite another to complain about God. Joshua goes to the Lord with his complaints and the Lord answers his prayer.

> *So the Lord said to Joshua, "Rise up! Why is it that you have fallen on your face? Israel has sinned, and they have also transgressed My covenant which I commanded them. And they have even taken some of the things under the ban and have both stolen and deceived. Moreover, they have also put them among their own things." (Joshua 7:10-11).*

Notice the corporate nature of sin. God doesn't single out Achan. He considers the enter nation to be guilty. Here is the principle. Your sin affects others. There is no such thing as a solitary sin. This is why church discipline is so important. Sin is a cancer that infects the entire body. It must be cut out.

4. The Execution of Justice.

Armed with this information, Joshua used a system of casting lots to determine the guilty party. In this instance, the lot fell upon Achan and a search of his tent revealed the stolen goods.

> *And Joshua said, "Why have you troubled us? The Lord will trouble you this day." And all Israel stoned them*

with stones; and they burned them with fire after they had stoned them with stones. (Joshua 7:25).

This punishment seems unduly harsh. This man and his family are put to death for stealing a few tidbits. The problem is that we have an inadequate view of justice.

- A total of 36 men had just died for Achan's sin.
- His family had participated in his crime (he buried the items in their midst).
- Achan had ample time to confess and to seek the Lord's forgiveness. He was standing quietly by, hoping that someone else would be punished for his sin. When they started throwing stones, Achan and his family would have been up there throwing stones, too.

Here is the principle. In the midst of the battle, you cannot afford the luxury of leniency. Treason is bad at any time. But it is worse when you are fighting for your life. We are fighting for eternal life.

And they raised over him a great heap of stones that stands to this day, and the Lord turned from the fierceness of His anger. Therefore the name of that place has been called the valley of Achor to this day. (Joshua 7:26).

There is a play on words here. The phrase in verse 25, "Why have you troubled us?" is literally "why have you *ACHORED* us?" He goes on to say the "the Lord will trouble you this day (*ACHOR*). And so, the valley was given the name, the Valley of Trouble (*ACHOR*). This valley is mentioned in a prophecy given by the prophet Hosea. It is a prophecy of hope.

"Then I will give her vineyards from there,
And the valley of Achor as a door of hope.
And she will sing there as in the days of her youth,
As in the day when she came up from the land of Egypt."
(Hosea 2:15).

God is talking about the same place. He promises to make the Valley of Achor a Valley of Hope. There is a lesson here. It is that there is no sin that is so horrible that God cannot take it and make it into a Valley of Hope.

5.   Second Campaign at Ai.

> *Now the Lord said to Joshua, "Do not fear or be dismayed. Take all the people of war with you and arise, go up to Ai; see, I have given into your hand the king of Ai, his people, his city, and his land." (Joshua 8:1).*

We are given more details on the military strategy of the taking of Ai than any other battle in Canaan. Joshua's plans are careful and detailed. There is a reason for this. It is because Joshua knew that it is always harder to reclaim lost ground. Once you have been defeated, it is always harder to win that victory.

When I was a lot younger, I used to be able to do handstands on a high bar. One of the most impressive parts was a dismount in which I would bring my legs over the bar and then fall backwards, swinging out and doing a flip in the air before landing on my feet. I was doing this on a tree one day when I overcompensated and landed flat on my back. It was a rather high tree and I hit hard enough to knock the wind out of me. It hurt and it hurt badly. I want you to know that I was never able to do that flip again. I would get ready for it and then I would freeze. Why? Because it is always harder to reclaim lost ground.

> Most archaeologists identify Ai with the modern site of Et-Tel, about two miles southeast of Bethel. There is a problem with this identification. Et-Tel was uninhabited from 2200 to 1200 B.C. Furthermore, in the early Bronze Age when Et-Tel was inhabited, it was a city covering 27 acres with a stone wall 25 feet wide and 30 feet high. This does not match the description given by the spies that this was a town of only a few men. When the spies had checked it out, they had suggested that Joshua only send in a few troops (Joshua 7:3). I am forced to conclude that the site of Ai is still unknown.

Even now, Joshua didn't really need 30,000 men to take Ai. He could have taken himself and two toddlers and it would have been enough. But in Joshua 8:1, the Lord tells him, "Take all the people of war with you." Why? Because it is always harder to reclaim lost ground.

> *So Joshua rose with all the people of war to go up to Ai; and Joshua chose 30,000 men, valiant warriors, and sent*

them out at night.

And he commanded them, saying, "See, you are to ambush the city from behind it. Do not go very far from the city, but all of you be ready. Then I and all the people who are with me will approach the city. And it will come about when they come out to meet us as at the first, that we will flee before them.

"And they will come out after us until we have drawn them away from the city, for they will say, `They are fleeing from before us as at the first.' So we will flee before them.

"And you shall rise from your ambush and take possession of the city, for the Lord your God will deliver it into your hand." (Joshua 8:3-7).

The taking of Ai was to be through a carefully laid trap. It would involve a pretended rout in which the enemy would be tricked into pursuit while a much larger force would come in from behind and take the undefended city. Yet with all of these elaborate plans, it is the Lord who is going to deliver Ai into the hand of Israel.

With the power of God, even the great city of Jericho could be taken. Without the power of God, not even the little town of Ai could be taken.

6.   Altar at Ebal.

> *Then Joshua built an altar to the Lord, the God of Israel, in Mount Ebal" (Joshua 8:30).*

We would think that this is a bad time for prayer of revival. They were involved in a major military campaign. They are surrounded by enemies. But this really is the best time.

a.   The necessity for definition.

> *...Moses the servant of the Lord had commanded the sons of Israel... (Joshua 8:31).*

The great danger of the church is that, as we become involved in our society, that we become like our society. God tells His people that they are different. He gives them a new identity.

You are not like the world. Go down to Shechem and you will find an altar there. It will remind you of who you are.

b. The necessity of remembering.

Have your noticed how many times Joshua has said, "These stones are here to this day" (4:9; 4:21-22; 7:25; 8:29)? In each case, the stones were there to remind you of what God had done. God knows that we will forget unless there are reminders. That is why we have the Lord's Supper. It is a reminder to us of what God has done.

c. The necessity of rededication.

The 2nd Law of Thermodynamics says that things run down. This takes place in every area of life. It works in life itself. You get older and your body begins to break down. If you have owned a car, then you know that things run down. Cars break down. Commitments run down, too. You will always tend to take the point of least resistance as your commitment runs down. You cannot run your spiritual engine on yesterday's gasoline.

d. The necessity of reaffirmation.

We need to constantly reaffirm the truths that we hold. In a society which bombards us with all sorts of ungodly thinking, we need to tell ourselves and remind ourselves what we believe.

e. The necessity of emotion.

Sometimes we neglect the emotional content of our faith. But God created emotions. We are to worship the Lord with our heart as well as with our mind. Christianity is not merely an intellectual exercise. If you have never been excited about God, then you probably have never met Him.

The Mountains of Ebal and Gerizim faced one another. Between them lay an ancient well which had been excavated by Jacob - it was known as Jacob's Well. It would be here that Jesus would one day spend an afternoon talking to a Samaritan woman.

And all Israel with their elders and officers and their judges were standing on both sides of the ark before the Levitical priests who carried the ark of the covenant of the Lord, the stranger as well as the native. Half of them stood in front of Mount Gerizim and half of them in front of Mount Ebal, just as Moses the servant of the Lord had given command at first to bless the people of Israel. (Joshua 8:33).

This was a solemn memorial. Half of the people standing on Mount Gerizim. Half of them standing on Mount Ebal. One side reading the blessings of the covenant. The other side reading the curses of the covenant (see the instructions given in Deuteronomy 27:11-14).

THE CAMPAIGN AGAINST THE KINGS OF THE SOUTH

1.   The Deception of the Gibeonites.

The city of Gibeon was the next in line from Ai and Bethel. It would be the next to fall if the Israelites continued their westward march. And so, the people of Gibeon came up with a plan. They determined to deceive the Israelites.

They had several of their ambassadors dress up in their oldest clothes and they gathered some moldy bread and they set out for the Israelite camp, all of five miles away. When they arrived, they told a yarn about how their clothes and the food had been new at the outset of their journey and, on this basis, they negotiated a peace treaty with Israel. Joshua and the people were properly suspicious and they went on to conduct a proper and careful investigation.

- *"Perhaps you are living within our land; how then shall we make a covenant with you?"* (9:7).
- *"Who are you, and where do you come from?"* (9:8).

They asked all the right questions. That is not the problem. The problem is that the Israelites, for their part, *"did not ask for the counsel of the Lord"* (Joshua 9:14). They did not utilize the heavenly resources. They figured that they could handle this one on their own.

The problem is a lack of faith. Here is the question. Do you only ask of God as a means of last resort? Or do you go to God as a means of first resort? This sin is the sin of independence from God. When they found out how they had been deceived, the Israelites were in something of a quandary as to what to do.

> *And the sons of Israel did not strike them because the leaders of the congregation had sworn to them by the Lord the God of Israel. And the whole congregation grumbled against the leaders.*
> *But all the leaders said to the whole congregation, "We have sworn to them by the Lord, the God of Israel, and now we cannot touch them. 20 This we will do to them, even let them live, lest wrath be upon us for the oath which we swore to them."*
> *(Joshua 9:18-20).*

There are those who were in favor of ignoring the oath and attacking the Gibeonites. But the leadership prevails. This cannot be done because it would involve breaking an oath that had been made in the name of the Lord. It would involve bringing dishonor upon the name of the Lord.

Do you hold the honor of God in such high esteem that you are willing to suffer loss rather than to see His name dishonored by your actions? You should. There is a lesson here. It is that there are times when Christians are called to live with the results of their folly. Israel made a poor decision and now Israel would have to live with those results.

There are Christians today who have made bad decisions. Perhaps it was in entering into a marriage with an unbeliever. That is one of the worst possible decisions one can make. But if you have done this, you are called to remain in that marriage as long as you are able. You are called to be a faithful and loving marriage partner and to make every attempt to make that marriage work. What is at stake in your marriage is nothing less than the honor of God.

In the case of the Gibeonites, it was determined that the oath would be honored and that they would become servants of Israel.

> *But Joshua made them that day hewers of wood and drawers of water for the congregation and for the altar of the Lord, to this day, in the place which He would choose. (Joshua 9:27).*

2.   The Battle of Gibeon.

It was not long before this new treaty between Gibeon and Israel brought a swift retaliation from the kings of southern Canaan.

> *Now it came about when Adoni-zedek king of Jerusalem heard that Joshua had captured Ai, and had utterly destroyed it (just as he had done to Jericho and its king, so he had done to Ai and its king), and that the inhabitants of Gideon had made peace with Israel and were within their land, that he feared greatly, because Gibeon was a great city, like one of the royal cities, and because it was greater than Ai, and all its men were mighty. (Joshua 10:1-2).*

The kings of the south determine to make an example of Gibeon for having entered into an alliance with the Israelites. The cities of Gibeon sent messengers to Joshua, asking that they honor their covenant and come to their aid. Joshua responds by making a forced all-night march and attacking this federation.

> *And it came about as they fled from before Israel, while they were at the descent of Beth-horon, that the Lord threw large stones from heaven on them, as far as Azekah, and they died; there were more who died from the hailstones than those whom the sons of Israel killed with the sword. (Joshua 10:11).*

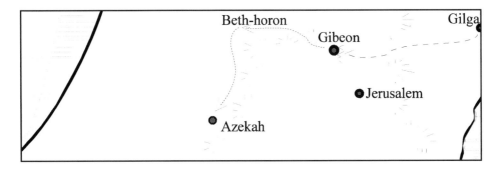

This Amorite League was thrown into a panic by the unexpected appearance of the Israelites in their rear and they fled westward down the pass of Beth-horon before turning southward. As they retreated, they were confronted with an even more terrifying enemy - great stones falling from the sky.

- These stones were *Min-HaShamaim* - "from heaven."
- They were thrown by Yahweh.
- This phenomenon took place "as far as Azekah."
- These stones caused a great loss of life upon the enemies of Israel. We are not told whether any Israelites were killed by the falling stones.

However, later in the same verse there is a slightly different phrase. It is translated "hailstones." The question is whether the "large stones" mentioned in the first part of the verse are the same as the "stones of hail" described at the end of the verse.

> *Then Joshua spoke to the Lord in the day*
> *when the Lord delivered up the Amorites before the*
> *sons of Israel, and he said in the sight of Israel,*
> *"O sun, stand still at Gibeon,*
> *And O moon in the valley of Aijalon."*
> *So the sun stood still, and the moon stopped,*
> *Until the nation avenged themselves of their*
> *enemies.*
> *Is it not written in the book of Jashar? And the sun stopped*
> *in the middle of the sky, and did not hasten to go down for*
> *about a whole day. (Joshua 10:12-13).*

There have been several different interpretations offered for this passage.

a.   Poetical Interpretation: Both the command and its fulfillment are seen as poetical language consisting in an appeal for renewed strength and vigor for the warriors of Israel.

- The command to "stand still" is the Hebrew Qal Imperative of *damas*. It can mean both "be still" or "be silent."

- The fact that the moon is also called to stand still is seen as an indication of the poetical nature of the passage. The moon would have been no help in providing light if the sun remained in the sky.

   On the other hand, if the sun literally set leaving only the light of the moon, then the call for the moon's light to assist them would make sense.

- An alternate poetic interpretation is that Joshua was calling for the sun to be still in shining so brightly. This interpretation says that the last thing Joshua wanted was more sunlight - rather, he was seeking relief from the heat of the day. Joshua's prayer was answered by an icy hailstorm which both cooled the attackers and destroyed many of the enemy.

> Some have suggested that this is descriptive of a solar eclipse, but we are able to plot which solar eclipses were visible in Palestine and none of them fit the date of Joshua.

An obvious problem with this interpretation is that the moon is also said to have stayed. There would be no reason for this since the moon gives off no heat.

b. Literal Interpretation: The passage explains the words of Joshua by saying that "the sun stopped in the middle of the sky, and did not hasten to go down for about a whole day." The phrase "the sun stopped" can carry the idea of standing still.

Furthermore, the passage goes on to explain its terms by describing how that the sun "did not hasten to go down for about a whole day" (literally, "did not hurry to go for a complete day").

If we adopt the literal interpretation, then we are still left with another question: Is this a localized phenomenon, or was it caused by a stopping of the rotation of the entire planet?

- A localized phenomenon could have been caused by refraction of the light of the sun and the moon (a mirage) in which they appeared to be out of their regular phases.

- The other way for this miracle to have taken place would have been for the earth to stop its movement. Considering that the earth rotates at a speed of about 1000 miles per hour at the equator, this would have caused massive earthquakes and seismic disturbances of epic proportions.

Such a phenomenon would have resulted in a long afternoon, a long evening, a long night, depending upon what part of the world the observer stood.

No matter which interpretation we choose, it should be recognized that this was seen as an unprecedented miracle.

> *And there was no day like that before it or after it, when the Lord listened to the voice of a man; for the Lord fought for Israel. (Joshua 10:14).*

You cannot believe the Bible without also believing in miracles. Many people want to take the miracles out of the Bible.

a.   Whether one believes in miracles or does not believe in miracles has absolutely nothing to do with whether or not miracles are true.

Philosophers have said that the supernatural cannot take place. And so, they have tried to define miracles out of existence.

But that doesn't make miracles go away. Reality has nothing to do with public opinion.

b.   To deny miracles is to deny the Bible.

There is a great debate on the date of the book of Daniel. The critics want to date it in the 2nd century B.C. Why? Because it clearly predicts things that did not happen until the 2nd century B.C. They have already decided that there is no such thing as predictive prophecy. Since Daniel records prophecy and since there is no such thing as prophecy, then Daniel could not have written this prophecy and it must have been written after the fact.

Question: Do you live a supernatural life? If you woke up one morning to find that God had left, how would it affect your life? What is it in your life that can only be explained in the terms of the supernatural?

God intervenes in history. You look at your present situation and you ask, "Why doesn't He intervene now?"

(1)   God intervenes when a great promise has been made. God has given promises and He will move heaven and earth to fulfill those promises. God is very concerned about His good name. He does not want His name blemished by an unfulfilled promise.

(2)   God intervenes when great faith is present. Remember the story of David and Goliath? The people said, "He is too big to hit." And David replied, "He is too big to miss." Jesus spoke about mountain-moving faith. If you believe, then nothing is impossible.

> *And it came about when they brought these kings out to Joshua, that Joshua called for all the men of Israel, and said to the chiefs of the men of war who had gone with him, "Come near, put your feet on the necks of these kings." So they came near and put their feet on their necks. (Joshua 10:24).*

This was done to increase the faith of the people. It was a public presentation that God was stronger than the kings of Canaan. Here is the lesson - it is that God is bigger than your problems.

(3)   God intervenes when a great cause is attempted. He gears the degree of His intervention to the degree of your commitment.

(4)   God intervenes when a great emphasis is needed.

> *And Joshua captured all these kings and their lands at one time,*

177

*because the Lord, the God of Israel,
fought for Israel. (Joshua 10:42).*

Notice why Joshua won. It was because the Lord was on his side. God is doing something with Joshua which will teach us something about God for the next 3000 years. The point is that God does supernatural miracles for HIS benefit, not for yours.

(5)   God intervenes when a great grace is manifested.

> *"The Lord did not set His love on you nor chose you because you were more in number than any of the peoples, for you were the fewest of all peoples." (Deuteronomy 7:7).*

God didn't choose Israel because they were so wonderful. He chose Israel because He is so wonderful. It was grace. The same is true of us.

THE CAMPAIGN AGAINST THE KINGS OF THE NORTH

1.   The Northern Alliance.

Just as the Amorite Kings of the south had formed an alliance, so also the kings in the area of Galilee formed an alliance. The leader of this coalition is said to have been Jabin, king of Hazor. This is not too surprising. Hazor was the largest city in all of Canaan. It had massive ramparts of beaten earth and a heavily protected wall surrounded by a deep ditch.

To make matters worse, the Northern Federation was able to field horse-drawn chariots. These were light chariots with spoked wheels and had an incredible mobility. They were to ancient warfare what the armored tank was to modern warfare.

2.   The Battle of Merom.

So Joshua and all the people of war with him

came upon them suddenly by the waters of Merom,
and attacked them.

    And the Lord delivered them into the hand of
Israel, so that they defeated them, and pursued them
as far as Great Sidon and Misrephoth-maim and the
valley of Mizpeh to the east; and they struck them
until no survivor was left to them. (Joshua 11:7-8).

Merom was centrally located among the cities of the Northern Federation. Its disadvantage lay in the fact that this was an area of rolling hills and thick forests, thus negating the strength and mobility of their chariot corps.

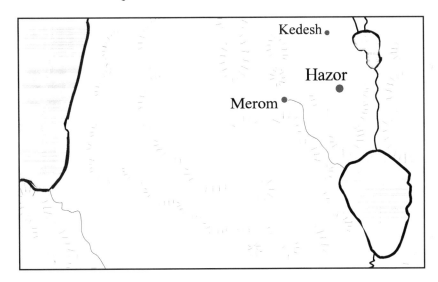

    It seems likely that they had intended to use this area only as a rendezvous for their combined forces (Joshua 11:7 indicates that this was a surprise attack).

3.   Destruction of the Chariot Corps.

    And Joshua did to them as the Lord had told
him; he hamstrung their horses, and burned their
chariots with fire. (Joshua 11:9).

    God ordered Joshua to destroy the best military weapons he had ever seen. Joshua was a general. When he saw these weapons, his mouth started watering. He said to himself, "Boy, if I had a few hundred of those chariots and horses, there isn't anything I wouldn't be able to do." But God told him to destroy the chariots and to render the horses useless. This goes against all human logic.

There is a principle here. If you have chariots and horses, you begin to depend upon chariots and horses instead of depending upon the Lord. If you have only God, then you will depend upon God.

> *"You shall not make for yourself an idol, or any likeness of what is in heaven above or on the earth beneath or in the water under the earth.*
>
> *You shall not worship them or serve them; for I, the Lord your God, am a jealous God, visiting the iniquity of the father on the children, and on the third and the fourth generation of those who hate Me, but showing lovingkindness to thousands, to those who love Me and keep My commandments." (Deuteronomy 5:8-10).*

Every god that you have that isn't God, He will destroy. God wants to be your God. If you put anything else in first place, He will destroy it.

4.   Joshua's Obedience.

> *Just as the Lord had commanded Moses his servant, so Moses commanded Joshua, and so Joshua did; he left nothing undone of all that the Lord commanded Moses. (Joshua 11:15).*

Joshua is a study in submission. He was successful because he did it God's way. He made it a point to do all of the Lord's commands and to leave nothing undone. Even though he was now the leader of Israel he took the commands that had been handed down from Moses and acted upon them.

> *Remember those who led you, who spoke the word of God to you; and concerning the result of their conduct, imitate their faith. (Hebrews 11:7).*

We are to submit to God's authority. He has set authorities over us: family, church, government.

5.   Summary.

Joshua waged war a long time with all these kings. (Joshua 11:18).

It took a long time. Why didn't God wipe them out immediately? He could have, but He didn't. There is a principle here. It takes a long time to win a war. Cults promise a quick way. They promise instant answers. But there are no instant answers in the Christian life.

SUMMARY OF THE CONQUEST OF CANAAN

If we are not careful, we will fall into the trap of thinking that the conquest of the land took place within a very brief period of time. However, a closer look reveals that only a few key battles are recorded and that the conquest of Canaan took many years.

1.   Even at the death of Joshua, there would remain a number of areas still to be taken. These strongholds of defense would include the following:

- The territories of the Philistines (Joshua 13:1-13 with Judges 3:1-3).

- Megiddo and the other cities of the Valley of Jezreel (Joshua 17:11 with Judges 1:27).

- Dor, Gezer, and other cities along the Coastal Plain (Joshua 13:4; 16:10; 17:11; Judges 1:27; 1:29).

- Jerusalem (Joshua 15:63; Judges 1:21).

It has been noted that the Israelites had difficulties conquering the cities of the lowlands - possibly due to the fact that these cities often had both high ramparts and iron chariots.

2.   There is no record of Egyptian interference, even though Egypt was still one of the leading world powers of the day. The Amarna Tablets bear witness of the lack of action taken by Egypt toward the threat of

the Habiru. [5]

THE DISTRIBUTION OF THE LAND

As can be seen from this chart, the major portion of this section deals with the Distribution of the Land to the various tribes of Israel.

The Distribution of the Land			
13:1	Introduction	Special Allotments	East of the Jordan
13:8	Two & a half Tribes		
14:1	Caleb	Major Allotments to the nine Tribes	West of the Jordan
15:1	Judah		
16:1	The Sons of Joseph		
18:1	Remaining 7 Tribes		
20:1	Cities of Refuge	Special Provisions	Both Sides of the Jordan
21:1	Levi		
21:43	Summary Statement		

Reading through much of this portion of Joshua is a bit like reading through the telephone book. You don't know the names and they don't mean a lot to you. But it would be different if you took an old personal address book and had a walk down "memory lane." This would be full of old friends and would likely bring back many fond memories.

These chapters would have meant a lot more to the original recipients of the book of Joshua. After all, they were living in the land that was portioned out. It was their inheritance and their possession.

We also have an inheritance. It is not a physical inheritance, but one reserved in heaven for us.

The Spirit Himself bears witness with our spirit that
we are children of God, and if children, heirs also, heirs of

---

[5] Among the inscriptions of the Amarna Tablets are a number of letters from the king of Jerusalem to Amenhotep III asking for help against invaders known as the Habiru. At one point, this letter says: *The Habiru are plundering all the lands of the king. If no troops come in this very year, then all the lands of the king are lost.* (King of Jerusalem).

God and fellow heirs with Christ, if indeed we suffer with Him in order that we may also be glorified with Him. (Romans 8:16-17).

1.   Special Allotments (Joshua 13-14)

We have already seen the story of the 2 ½ Tribes which chose for themselves the lands on the east bank of the Jordan and therefore took second best. Because of their impatience, they had fought for a land that they could not now inherit. As a result, there would develop something of a schism between those Israelites living on the west bank and those living on the east bank.

The next special allotment is given to Caleb. He comes to Joshua and asks: *"Now then, give me this hill country about which the Lord spoke on that day, for you heard on that day that Anakim were there, with great fortified cities; perhaps the Lord will be with me, and I shall drive them out as the Lord has spoken." (Joshua 14:12).*

If I had been Caleb, I might have said, "Joshua, I'm not as young as I used to be. Why don't you give me a little peaceful place where I can live quietly?" But Caleb didn't feel the need to do that. Caleb had a big God. How big is your God? Perhaps the reason He only does a little is because you think so little of Him.

Caleb didn't have the best pedigree. His relatives had come into the Israelite community through the back door. He was the descendant of one of the sons of Judah and Tamar. He was part Canaanite. But he was given a portion from among the Jews.

"And now behold, the Lord has let me live, just as He spoke, these forty-five years, from the time that the Lord spoke this word to Moses, when Israel walked in the wilderness; and now behold, I am eighty-five years old today.

I am still as strong today as I was in the day Moses sent me; as my strength was then, so my strength is now, for war and for going out and coming in." (Joshua 14:10-11).

> Caleb was a man who realized that everything he got was from God. A turtle on a gatepost realizes that he didn't get there by himself.

Notice to what it is that Caleb attributes his long life. Not in the eating of health food. Not a regular program of exercise. Not good luck - or good genes. It is the promise of the Lord that has kept Caleb healthy and going strong.

> *Every good thing bestowed and every perfect gift is from above, coming down from the Father of lights, with whom there is no variation, or shifting shadow. (James 1:17).*

There is a saying that the Scots are a race of self-made men, thereby relieving the Almighty of a terrible responsibility. But the truth is that there are no self made men. God makes all men and, in the best of our accomplishments, we can give Him the credit.

2.   Complaint from the Tribes of Joseph (Joshua 17).

One of the promises that was initially given to Abraham regarded an inheritance of the land of Canaan. In Genesis 13:14-15, the Lord had Abram look to the north and the south and the east and the west and told him that all those lands on which he could lay his eyes would be given to his descendants. In these chapters of Joshua we read of the fulfillment of that promise.

When we come to chapter 17, we see a complaint from the tribes that were descended from Joseph:

> *Then the sons of Joseph spoke to Joshua, saying, "Why have you given me only one lot and one portion for an inheritance, since I am a numerous people whom the Lord has thus far blessed?"*
>
> *And Joshua said to them, "If you are a numerous people, go up to the forest and clear a place for yourself there in the land of the Perizzites and of the Rephaim, since the hill country of Ephraim is too narrow for you."*
>
> *And the sons of Joseph said, "The hill country is not enough for us, and all the Canaanites who live in the valley have chariots of iron, both those who are in Beth-shaen and its towns, and those who are in the valley of Jezreel."*
>
> *And Joshua spoke to the house of Joseph, to Ephraim and Manasseh, saying, "You are a numerous people and have great power; you shall not have one*

lot only, but the hill country shall be yours. For though it is a forest, you shall clear it, and to its farthest borders it shall be yours; for you shall drive out the Canaanites, even though they have chariots of iron, and though they are strong." (Joshua 17:14-18).

The double tribe of Joseph brought a complaint to Joshua. It was that their inheritance was too small. I cannot help but wonder whether they thought they would get special privileges because Joshua was from Ephraim - one of the tribes of Joseph.

Complaint #1: The land is too small.	Answer: Clear the forests from the hill country.
Complaint #2: There is still not enough land and the Canaanites have iron chariots.	Answer: You are a numerous and a powerful people - use your numbers and your power to drive out the Canaanites.

A lot of Christians are like these two tribes. They complain that they have not been given enough.

- Enough money.
- Enough good looks.
- Enough ability.

What they often need to do is to use the gifts and abilities and resources that they have been given.

3.   Shiloh.

Then the whole congregation of the sons of Israel assembled themselves at Shiloh, and set up the tent of meeting there; and the land was subdued before them. (Joshua 18:1).

> Shiloh was the site of an ancient Canaanite town dating to the time of Abraham. It had been deserted for several hundred years by the time of the Israelite conquest.

We are not told why Shiloh was chosen as the site for the

185

Tabernacle. Perhaps it was because this was a central location for all the tribes of Israel. Another possibility is that it was considered to be uncontaminated by pagan religion due to its having been deserted for such a long time. This was to be the center of worship until the time of Samuel.

4.   A Survey of the Land.

> *Then the men arose and went, and Joshua commanded those who went to describe the land, saying, "Go and walk through the land and describe it, and return to me; then I will cast lots for you here before the Lord in Shiloh.*
> *So the men went and passed through the land, and described it by cities in seven divisions in a book; and they came to Joshua to the camp at Shiloh.*
> *And Joshua cast lots for them in Shiloh before the Lord, and there Joshua divided the land to the sons of Israel according to their divisions. (Joshua 18:8-10).*

The Israelites had no maps or drawings of the land. This made it rather difficult to divide the land among the various tribes. And so, before such a distribution could be made, Joshua ordered that three men be commissioned from each tribe who would do the work of a surveyor, traveling through the land and writing out a detailed description. It was also their job to divide the land into seven distinct parcels (two and a half tribes already had their land on the east bank of the Jordan). They would try to be as even as possible, since it was not known which parcel their own tribe would inherit.

When the job was completed, these descriptions were brought back to Joshua and he cast lots before the Lord. The implication was that the Lord was making the decision as to where each tribe would live.

> *The lot is cast into the lap,*
> *But its every decision is from the Lord. (Proverbs 16:33).*

There is an ongoing principle from this passage. It is not that we cast lots to decide where we are going to live, but it is that the Lord is still in control over where men live. He has determined our times and the boundaries of our habitation (Acts 17:26).

5.   A Portion Given to Joshua.

> *When they finished apportioning the land for inheritance by its borders, the sons of Israel gave an inheritance in their midst to Joshua the son of Nun. 50 In accordance with the command of the Lord they gave him the city for which he asked, Timnath-serah in the hill country of Ephraim. So he built the city and settled in it. (Joshua 19:49-50).*

This section concludes with the inheritance that is awarded to Joshua. There is an interesting pattern that can be seen that begins and ends with Caleb and Joshua. It is made up of all of the portions that were given to the tribes on the west side of the Jordan.

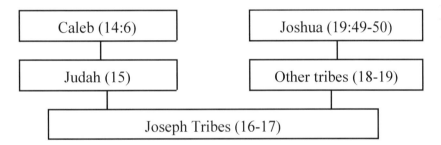

6.   Cities of Refuge.

> *Then the Lord spoke to Joshua, saying, "Speak to the sons of Israel, saying, `Designate the cities of refuge, of which I spoke to you through Moses, that the manslayer who kills any person unintentionally, without premeditation, may flee there, and they shall become your refuge from the avenger of blood.'"' (Joshua 20:1-3).*

The concept of the Cities of Refuge had been set forth in Numbers 35:6-34. Such a concept was needed to keep the peace in the absence of a police force. It was to be implemented in the case of manslaughter - when a man had been killed either by accident or in an unpremeditated altercation. In such a case, it would often be the inclination the friends and family of the deceased to see that justice was done. But to stop blood feuds from starting, six cities were designated as places of refuge. These were cities belonging to the tribe of Levi. No vengeance was to be taken within these cities.

Cities West of the Jordan	Cities East of the Jordan
Kedesh	Bezer
Shechem	Ramoth
Hebron	Golan

These cities were distributed throughout the length of Canaan. A person who had caused the death of another could flee here until a trial could be arranged.

> *"And he shall dwell in that city until he stands before the congregation for judgment..." (Joshua 20:6a).*

The cities of refuge pointed to the value of human life as having been made in the image of God.

- The life of the slayer was spared until the case could be heard.
- The city of refuge became a virtual prison for the one who had taken a life.

Verse 6 tells us that the party who was guilty of unintentional manslaughter was a prisoner in the city of refuge until the death of the high priest. After that time, no vengeance could be taken against him. By the same token it is through the death of Jesus Christ, our high priest, that we are set free from our imprisonment.

7.   An Offending Altar.

> *And the sons of Reuben and the sons of Gad and the half-tribe of Manasseh returned home and departed from the sons of Israel at Shiloh which is in the land of Canaan, to go to the land of Gilead, to the land of their possession which they had possessed, according to the command of the Lord through Moses. (Joshua 22:9).*

These are the two and a half tribes who had opted for second-best. They had asked for their inheritance to be the lands on the east side of the Jordan River. They were granted their request on the

188

condition that they first cross over and fight alongside the rest of Israel to take the land of Canaan. But now the fighting is finished. And so, they are permitted to return home.

> *And when they came to the region of the Jordan which is in the land of Canaan, the sons of Reuben and the sons of Gad and the half-tribe of Manasseh built an altar there by the Jordan, a large altar in appearance. (Joshua 22:10).*

When news of the construction of this altar reaches the other tribes of Israel, they jump to the conclusion that these two and a half tribes have apostatized. After all, the only proper place to build an altar is at the tabernacle - and there is only one tabernacle.

Therefore the Israelites prepare themselves for war against the two and a half tribes. But before they march, they send Phinehas, the son of Eleazar, the high priest along with a representative from each of the ten tribes.

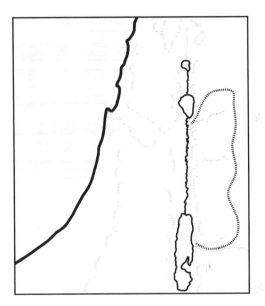

When they meet, the leaders of the two and a half tribes explain that the altar which they have constructed is not an altar for burnt offerings or for sacrifice, but rather a mound of memorial stones. It is to remind the Israelites who live in Canaan that there are people of the covenant who do not live in the land of Canaan but that they are no less children of the covenant.

Instead of intending to divide the nation, this altar was to be a symbol of their unity. There is a lesson here. All too often, we tend to judge people's actions in the worst possible light. The better part of wisdom is that we make certain of all the facts before passing judgment. We are called to be righteous in our judgments and that demands a care toward both accuracy and grace.

COVENANT RATIFICATION & CHARGE

22:1	23:1	24:1
An Offending Altar	Joshua's Final Charge	
	To the Elders	To the People
People to People	Leader to Leaders	Leader to People
Take Care not to Offend Others	Be Certain to Warn Others	Be Faithful to Challenge Others

Joshua 24 describes the renewal of the covenant. It was to take place at Shechem, the place where Jacob had first purchased a portion of land (Genesis 33:18-19). This was the first place where Abraham had built an altar to the Lord (Genesis 12:6-7).

> *Then Joshua gathered all the tribes of Israel to Shechem, and called for the elders of Israel and for their heads and their judges and their officers; and they presented themselves before God. (Joshua 24:1).*

This chapter follows the five-fold outline for a covenant (this same outline is the one we saw for the entire book of Deuteronomy).

- The Suzerain is Identified (24:2).
- The Historical Record of the past relationship between the Suzerain and His vassal subjects (24:2-13).
- The Stipulations which the Suzerain imposes upon His vassals (24:14-15).
- The warning of cursing for disobedience (24:19-20). The normal form called for both blessing in the case of obedience as well as cursing in the case of disobedience.
- Witnesses are set forth - the people themselves serve as witnesses against themselves (24:21-24).

But that is not all. A memorial stone is set up which is to also serve as a witness of the covenant (24:26-27).

> *So Joshua made a covenant with the people that day, and made for them a statute and an ordinance in Shechem.*

(Joshua 24:25).

The terms of this covenant were put in writing. Literally, the Hebrew says that "Joshua **cut** a covenant..." This may have involved the sacrificing of an animal.

> *And Joshua wrote these words in the book of the law of God; and he took a large stone and set it up there under the oak that was by the sanctuary of the Lord.*
> *And Joshua said to all the people, "Behold, this stone shall be for a witness against us, for it has heard all the words of the Lord which He spoke to us; thus it shall be for a witness against you, lest you deny your God." (Joshua 24:26-27).*

Joshua set up a large stone near the tabernacle. It was to be a memorial-stone and would serve as a witness of the covenant. It is reminiscent of the time that Jesus was entering the Temple in Jerusalem to the praises of the people. When the Jewish authorities heard these praises, they objected. Jesus replied, "If these become silent, the stones will cry out!" (Luke 19:40).

24:29	24:32	24:33
Death of Joshua	Burial of Joseph	Death of Eleazar
Buried in the Hill Country of Ephraim	Buried at Shechem (inheritance of Joseph's sons)	Buried in the Hill Country of Ephraim

There is a sense in which the narrative begun in Genesis comes to a final completion here at the end of Joshua. Genesis ends with a promise that the bones of Joseph will be returned to the Promised Land. Joshua closes with the fulfillment of that promise.

JUDGES
The Age of Heroes

The book of Judges is a book of action. It contains great deeds as well as great failures. It is a book of both victory and defeat. Often graphic in its contents, it is not a book for the squeamish.

THE TITLE OF THE BOOK

Both the title found in the Greek Septuagint as well as our common English title of this book are taken from the Hebrew Title.

- Greek: *Kritai.*
- Hebrew: *Shophatim* from the Hebrew root *shaphat*, "to judge."

The Shophatim had more than mere judicial roles. They also served as military leaders in times of crisis. They were men whom God would raise up to lead His people in those difficult times.

The book of Judges forms the bridge between the Conquest of the Land under Joshua and the establishment of the Monarchy under Saul, David and Solomon. Prior to the book of Judges, we read of the nation of Israel being led by the Lord through the mediatorial ministries of Moses and Joshua.

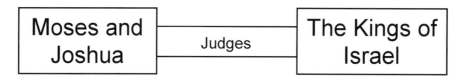

After the book of Judges, we shall see kings appointed to rule God's people. During this transitional period, Israel was led by a varied group of "Judges." This was a dark period of Israel's history. It was a period of failure and of lawlessness.

THE SCOPE OF THE BOOK

The book of Judges takes up where Joshua leaves off, with the death of Joshua as the Israelites have taken residence in the promised land.

Joshua	Judges
A story mostly of Victory	A story mostly of Defeat
One man is prominent	A number of men and women are presented
Israel's Faith	Israel's Apostasy
Israel taking a stand for God	Israel turning away from God
Freedom	Servitude
The sin of the Canaanites is judged	The sin of the Israelites is judged

The narrative of Judges takes place over a period of over 300 years. It is a period when the Israelites are making the transition from having been a nomadic nation freshly escaped from Egypt to the status of a new nation, firmly established in their own land. This book can be divided into three parts.

1.   Introduction - a Faltering Conquest (1:1 - 2:4).

        The first two chapters form an introduction to the book, setting forth what are to be the overall themes and patterns of this period of Israel's history.

2.   Cycles of Apostasy (2:5 - 16:31).

        The central chapters set forth the history of the judges in a series of cycles of apostasy, repentance, and deliverance.

3.   Anarchy under the Levites (17:1 - 21:25).

        The last five chapters form an appendix which portray the darkest days of the period of the Judges.

Judges - The Book of Heroes		
1:1	3:1	17:1
The Pattern of Failure Established	The Career of the Judges • Othniel • Deborah • Gideon • Jephthah • Samson	The Pattern of Sin Illustrated in two parallel accounts of Heinous Sins.
The entire period is presented in summary form	Chronological accountings of the period	Non-chronological accounts which characterized the period

DATE OF WRITING

We are not told either who is the writer or when this book is written. But there are several factors which indicate that it was written early in the Israelite monarchy.

1.   The Jebusites are said to live in Jerusalem "to this day" (Judges 1:21). Since the city was taken by the Israelites early in David's reign, this is an indication that the book was written before the fall of Jerusalem to David.

2.   Sidon is described as the chief city of Phoenicia (Judges 18:28). However, by the reign of Solomon, Tyre had become their chief city.

3.   Conversely, there is evidence to show that it was written after Saul had become king.

        Four times, the author contrasts the political situation in the days of the Judges with that of his own day, saying, *"In those days Israel had no king"* (Judges 17:6; 18:1; 19:1; 21:25). The way in which the phrase is used seems to indicate that a monarchy was still viewed as something positive. It has been argued that this points to a time of writing before the Divided Kingdom and before either Judah or Israel had seen any ungodly kings.

4.   Judges 18:30 refers to "the captivity of the land."

> *And the sons of Dan set up for themselves the graven image; and Jonathan, the son of Gershom, the son of Manasseh, he and his sons were priests to the tribe of the Danites until the day of the captivity of the land. (Joshua 18:30).*

The most obvious interpretation is that this refers to either the Babylonian or Assyrian Captivity. This phrase would have been added either after Samaria had fallen to Assyria (this was the beginning of the captivity of that portion of the land) or after Jerusalem had fallen to Nebuchadnezzar.

Does this mean that the book could not have been penned until after the fall of Samaria in 721 B.C.? Not necessarily. It is entirely possible that this chronological note could have been changed and "updated" by a later editor. Nevertheless, these factors point to the possibility of a gap between the events described in the book of Judges and the recording of those events within this book.

1400	1043	931	721	586	
Joshua	Period of the Judges	Saul, David & Solomon	Period of the Divided Monarchy	Samaria into Captivity	Judah taken in Babylonian Captivity
		Possible Periods of the Writing of the book of Judges			

On the other hand, Jewish and early church traditions point to Samuel as the author of the book of Judges. While there is no definite internal evidence that this is the case, it is certainly a possibility.

PURPOSE OF THE BOOK

1.   The book of Judges illustrates the disastrous effects of compromise.

The Israelites had been told to take the land and to completely wipe out all of the inhabitants. Because they did not obey this command, they were seduced into worshiping the false gods of the people of the land, always with catastrophic consequences.

2.   The book of Judges is written as an apologetic for Israel's monarchy. It shows Israel's need for a king.

Especially in the latter part of the book, we are treated to a series of spectacles of the results of Israel's apostasy and then reminded that "in those days Israel had no king" (Judges 17:6; 18:1; 19:1; 21:25).

- Without a king the tribes faltered in their conquest of the land.
- The office of judge was only able to bring sporadic relief from the cycles of apostasy.
- The priests and Levites failed to provide social or religious stability in the absence of a king.

There is also a strong anti-Benjamite slant to the closing chapters of the book, indicating that it was written after David had come to power.

THE CYCLICAL NATURE OF JUDGES

The first two chapters of Judges set the stage for the remainder of the book. They present a pattern, both of victorious conquest as well as of crushing defeat.

1:1	**A Partial**	Judah & Simeon - Success!	
1:12		Othniel & Caleb	
1:17	**Conquest**	Judah & Simeon - Failure!	
1:22		House of Joseph - Success!	
1:27		Manasseh Ephraim Zebulun Asher Naphtali Dan	Failure

2:1	**A Pattern**	Angel of the Lord - A Promise of Judgment
2:6	**for Failure**	Death of Joshua & the Coming of the Next Generation
2:11		Cycles of... Rebellion Retribution Repentance Redemption Restoration

> *Now it came about after the death of Joshua that the sons of Israel inquired of the Lord, saying, "Who shall go up first for us against the Canaanites, to fight against them?" (Judges 1:1).*

It has been suggested that the phrase, "Now it came about after the death of Joshua," is to be regarded as a title heading for the whole book, especially in light of the fact that Joshua is seen alive in chapter 2. But such an interpretation is not necessary. Chapter 2 can easily be seen to be a flashback as the author steps back to view the entire period of the Judges, beginning with the career of Joshua. This chapter sets forth the pattern of the central part of the Book of Judges. It is a cyclical pattern.

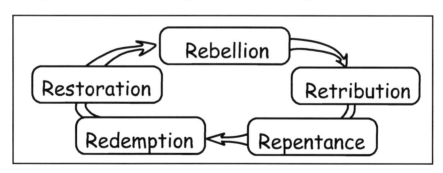

1.   The Coming of the New Generation.

> *And that generation also were gathered to their fathers; and there arose another generation after them who did not know the Lord, nor yet the work which He had done for Israel. (Judges 2:10).*

The generation which came out of the Wilderness and which took the promised land committed itself to follow the Lord. But this had little impact upon the next generation as they did not make the same decision to follow the Lord that their parents had made. They departed from the ways of the Lord. Why? Was it because there was no training in the home? Perhaps. After all, Proverbs 22:6 says to "train up a child in the way he should go, even when he is old he will not depart from it." But such training is no guarantee of spirituality on the part of the children. And the spiritual walk of parents is not automatically passed on to children.

There is a principle here. It is that the spirituality of one generation is no guarantee of spirituality in the next generation. The most that parents can do is to train up their children in the way in which they ought to go. But those children must develop their own relationship with the Lord. This is not to downplay the importance of training up children in the way of the Lord. We are responsible for the upbringing of tomorrow's church. The church has always been only a generation away from extinction. Its only chance is always the new generation.

2.   The Rebellion of Idolatry.

> *Then the sons of Israel did evil in the sight of the Lord, and served the Baals, and they forsook the Lord, the God of their fathers, who had brought them out of the land of Egypt, and followed other gods from among the gods of the peoples who were around them, and bowed themselves down to them; thus they provoked the Lord to anger. (Judges 2:11-12).*

Their sin was the fundamental sin which underlies all other sins. It was the sin of idolatry. They "served the Baals." Here is the principle. You will always serve something. Either you will become a servant of the Lord, or else you will serve another god. It might be a god of your own making.

- Money.
- Power.
- Popularity.

Whatever it is, it involves idolatry. This does not necessarily mean that the Israelites completely abandoned the outward worship of the Lord. It is possible that they continued to give lip service at the tabernacle. But they also began to worship the Baalim and the Ashtaroth (Judges 2:13).

This mixture of true religion and false is known as "syncretism." It is a smorgasbord type of religion, combining some true and some false. Satan is a master of this type of counterfeit. He presents himself as an angel of light. He mixes truth with lies and the result is poison (like mixing a teaspoon of arsenic into a full cup of coffee).

The modern term for syncretism is "pluralism." It is the idea that our culture should be a mixture of many religious ideas and that they all have equal value. Pluralism includes the idea that there is no such thing as absolute truth.

3.   Retribution - The Judgment of God.

> *And the anger of the Lord burned against Israel, and He gave them into the hands of plunderers who plundered them; and He sold them into the hands of their enemies around them, so that they could no longer stand before their enemies.*
>
> *Wherever they went, the hand of the Lord was against them for evil, as the Lord had spoken and as the Lord has sworn to them, so they were severely distressed. (Judges 2:14-15).*

When we read this, we are inclined to think of God as a fierce and a terrible Judge who is angry with those who have transgressed His law. And so we should. He IS described in these terms. But He is also a God of grace. And in the midst of this judgment, there is a message of grace. You see, the enemies which God raised up were not only designed to judge Israel - they were also designed to drive Israel back to the Lord.

There is another reason that God raised up these enemies. It is seen in Judges 3:1-2. It is so that "the generations of the sons of Israel might be taught war" (Judges 3:2). This seems to refer to the fact that the military capabilities of the Israelites were honed by their having to fight their enemies.

Many years ago I was involved in the martial arts. There is a lesson I learned there. It is that shadow boxing has limited value. There comes a time when you have to go out and spar against an actual opponent. The same is true of being a Christian witness. You can take dozens of classes and attend a host of seminars on personal evangelism. But you won't really learn how to share your faith until you go out and do it.

4.   Redemption - The Lord Raised up Judges.

> *Then the Lord raised up judges who delivered them from the hands of those who plundered them. (Judges 2:16).*

The word "judge" is the Hebrew word *shaphat*. When used as a verb, it usually carries the idea of the passing of some type of verdict and its resulting sentence. And yet, there is evidence that the judges of Israel did more than merely hear legal cases.

The related Akkadian word *shapitu* carried the idea of an "officer." The Phoenician *shuphetim* described the "regents" and the Carthaginian *suphetes* were the "chief magistrates." Hence, it seems that the judges of Israel served as leaders to the nation. This leadership involved two aspects:

- A part of this leadership involved the hearing of legal cases.

- Another part of this leadership sometimes involved military action - delivering the people of God from their oppressors..

- A third feature of the judge's ministry seems to have been that of a teacher and a prophet. This is seen in verse 17.

> *And yet they did not listen to their judges, for they played the harlot after other gods and bowed themselves down to them. They turned aside quickly from the way in which their fathers had walked in obeying the commandments of the Lord; they did not do as their fathers. (Judges 2:17).*

The fact that not listening to their judge is equated with turning to other gods indicates that one of the ministries of the judge was to call people to worship the Lord.

The Central section of the book of Judges (chapters 3-17) focuses upon the varied ministries of the Judges. Some of these judges are mentioned only in passing. Only a few are described in detail.

OPPRESSOR	JUDGE	TRIBE	SCRIPTURE
Mesopotamia	Othniel	Judah	Judges 3:8
Moabites	Ehud	Benjamin	Judges 3:9-30
Philistines	Shamgar	-	Judges 3:31
Canaanites	Deborah	Ephraim	Judges 4-5
Midianites	Gideon	Manasseh	Judges 6-8
Abimelech	-	Manasseh	Judges 9
	Tola	Ephraim	Judges 10:1-2
	Jair	Gilead	Judges 10:3-6
Ammonites	Jephthah	Gilead	Judges 10:10-12:7
	Ibzan	Judah	Judges 12:8-10
	Elon	Zebulun	Judges 12:11-12
	Abdon	Ephraim	Judges 12:13-15
Philistines	Samson	Dan	Judges 13-16

It should not be assumed that this is necessarily a chronologically progressive account. There seem to be places where the ministry of the judges had a certain amount of overlap.

EHUD

1.   The Oppression of Moab.

>   *Now the sons of Israel again did evil in the sight of the Lord. So the Lord strengthened Eglon the king of Moab against Israel, because they had done evil in the sight of the Lord.*
>   *And he gathered to himself the sons of Ammon and Amalek; and he went and defeated Israel, and they possessed the city of the palm trees.*
>   *And the sons of Israel served Eglon the king of*

Moab eighteen years. (Judges 3:12-14).

The Moabites and the Ammonites were descendants of Lot. The Israelites had in the past deliberately avoided military conflict with Moab and Ammon for this reason. But this did not stop these two kingdoms from invading Israel. Eglon, the king of Moab, formed an alliance in order to invade Israel. It involved three kingdoms:

a. Moab.

The kingdom of Moab was located on the eastern shore of the Dead Sea between the Zered and the Arnon Rivers.

b. Ammon.

The Ammonites lived to the north east of Moab. In past years, they had been pushed eastward off their homeland along the eastern bank of the Jordan by the Amorites. Their new home was located to the east of the Amorites on the border of the desert and east of the headwaters of the Jabbok River. Their capital city, Rabbath-ammon, 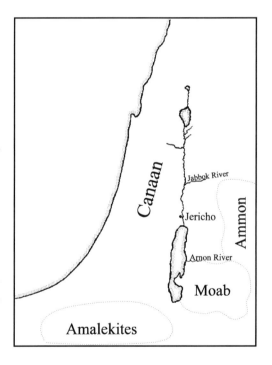 still stands today as the capital city of Jordan. It is known simply as Ammon.

c. Amalekites.

The Amalekites lived in the Negev to the south of Canaan. They were descendants of Esau and were initially one of the desert tribes of Edom.

The "city of the palm trees" is a designation for Jericho (Deuteronomy 34:3). Though the city had been destroyed by Joshua and remained uninhabited, the site remained an important one due to its control of the important trade route through the center of Canaan.

The site of the Old Testament city is a mound rising up 50 feet above the surrounding bedrock of the southern Jordan valley (Jericho is 825 feet below sea level). It is located about 10 miles to the NNW of the mouth of the Dead Sea and directly west of fords which make it possible to cross the Jordan except during the rainy season.

There is a natural spring known as Ain es-Sultan which originally attracted settlers to this site. This oasis gave the city its nickname, "City of Palm Trees." The site held a strategic position at the hub of four major roads radiating outward to Gerizim, Jerusalem, Hebron, and westward to the fords across the Jordan.

2.   Ehud the Man.

Judges 3:15-26 tells the story of Ehud and his premeditated murder of Eglon, king of Moab (perhaps "assassination" is a better word). Ehud is the hero of the story. It was the Lord who raised him up to be a deliverer for the Israelites (3:15). This act would serve as an impetus for an uprising against Moab.

> *But when the sons of Israel cried to the Lord, the Lord raised up a deliverer for them, Ehud the son of Gera, the Benjamite, a left-handed man. And the sons of Israel sent tribute by him to Eglon the king of Moab. (Judges 3:15).*

Ehud was a "left-handed man," literally, "a man bound in his right hand." There is a play on words here. He was a "left handed man" but he was also a Benjamite, a "son of the right hand." The fact that Ehud was left-handed was significant.

In that culture, a left-handed man was considered something of a social misfit. The right hand was normally the social hand (we still speak of extending the "right hand of fellowship"). The left hand was used solely for matters of personal hygiene. It was considered the unclean hand. That is why in matters of judgment, the condemned would be placed at the left hand of the king (remember this the next time you look at the judgment of the sheep and the goats and see what happens to those whom Christ places at His left hand). And yet, it was this social misfit that God chose to deliver the

Israelites from their oppressors. There is a lesson here. It is that God uses the unusable. Even Jesus was described as "the stone that the builders rejected."

3.	The Assassination of Eglon.

> *And Ehud made himself a sword which had two edges, a cubit in length; and he bound it on his right thigh under his cloak.*
>
> *And he presented the tribute to Eglon king of Moab. Now Eglon was a very fat man.*
>
> *And it came about when he had finished presenting the tribute, that he sent away the people who had carried the tribute.*
>
> *But he himself turned back from the idols which were at Gilead, and said, "I have a secret message for you, O king." And he said, "Keep silence." And all who attended him left him.*
>
> *And Ehud came to him while he was sitting alone in his cool roof chamber, And Ehud said, "I have a message from God for you." And he arose from his seat.*
>
> *And Ehud stretched out his left hand, took the sword from his right thigh, and thrust it into his belly.*
>
> *The handle also went in after the blade, and the fat closed over the blade, for he did not draw the sword out of his belly; and the refuse came out.*
>
> *Then Ehud went out into the vestibule and shut the doors of the roof chamber behind him, and locked them. (Judges 3:16-23).*

The very thing that made him a social outcast was utilized by Ehud in carrying out his execution of the king.

Ehud makes his escape while the servants wait outside the king's room, thinking that he is merely taking

> It is not only mentioned that Eglon was fat (3:17), but we are given graphic details of his fat closing in over the handle of the assassin's blade (3:22). Furthermore, we are given a glimpse of the embarrassment of the servants as we view their thoughts of their master (3:24-25).

his time in matters of personal hygiene ("he is only relieving himself in the cool room" - 3:24).

4.   Military Deliverance.

> *Now Ehud escaped while they were delaying, and he passed by the idols and escaped to Seirah.*
>
> *And it came about when he had arrived, that he blew the trumpet in the hill country of Ephraim; and the sons of Israel went down with him from the hill country, and he was in front of them.*
>
> *And he said to them, "Pursue them, for the Lord has given your enemies the Moabites into your hands," So they went down after him and seized the fords of the Jordan opposite Moab, and did not allow anyone to cross.*
>
> *And they struck down at that time about ten thousand Moabites, all robust and valiant men; and no one escaped.*
>
> *So Moab was subdued that day under the hand of Israel. And the land was undisturbed for eighty years. (Judges 3:26-30).*

Ehud did not stop with the assassination of the Moabite king. In this, he was not like the Israelites who had taken the land but who had failed to take the opportunity to completely drive out the Canaanites. He escaped only to rally the Israelites. While he had previously gone against the enemy alone, now he walked at their head.

Perhaps there is a principle of leadership to be found here. It is that if you will do the right thing when you are alone, then when you are not alone, others will follow. Ehud's military strategy was as cunning as his assassination ploy had been. He first

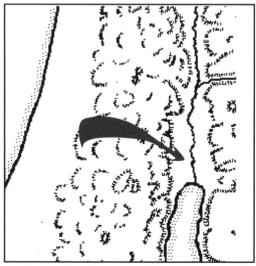

They seized the fords of the Jordan opposite Moab

marched to the fords of the Jordan on the east side of Jericho, captured these, and thereby cut off the retreat of the enemy. By doing so, he denied them any attempt to rally and return. The period of peace that ensued was 80 years - the longest of any period during the days of the judges.

DEBORAH

> *Then the sons of Israel again did evil in the sight of the Lord, after Ehud died.*
>
> *And the Lord sold them into the hand of Jabin king of Canaan, who reigned in Hazor; and the commander of his army was Sisera, who lived in Harosheth-hagoyim.*
>
> *And the sons of Israel cried to the Lord; for he had nine hundred iron chariots, and he oppressed the sons of Israel severely for twenty years. (Judges 4:1-3).*

Ancient Hazor has been identified with Tell el-Qeday. It is located nine miles north of the Sea of Galilee. The site is made up of an oval-shaped tell of about 25 acres and a much larger plateau covering an area of 175 acres. This made Hazor one of the largest cities in Canaan. What made Hazor so formidable was the fact that it boasted a chariot corps numbering 900 chariots. It must be remembered that chariots were to the ancient world what the armored tank has been to the modern world.

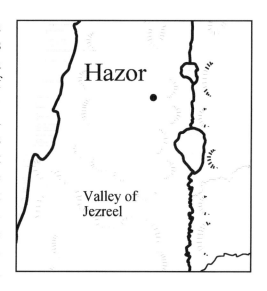

> *Now Deborah, a prophetess, the wife of Lappidoth, was judging Israel at that time.*
>
> *And she used to sit under the palm tree of Deborah between Ramah and Bethel in the hill country of Ephraim; and the sons of Israel came up to her for judgment. (Judges 4:4-5).*

Throughout most of antiquity, women had a fairly low standing in society. And yet, this woman was known as a prophetess and a judge. She was a housewife and a mother (Judges 5:7 mentions that she was a mother in Israel). But that did not stop the Lord from speaking through her.

Here is the principle. Women are not excluded from ministry. I am not advocating that women should hold offices within the church (though Deborah certainly did hold an exalted office in the nation of Israel). But I am saying that women have an important ministry within the church.

> *Now she sent and summoned Barak, the son of Abinoam from Kedesh-naphtali, and said to him, "Behold, the Lord, the God of Israel, has commanded, 'Go and march to Mount Tabor, and take with you ten thousand men from the sons of Naphtali and from the sons of Zebulun, 7 and I will draw out to you Sisera, the commander of Jabin's army, with his chariots and his many troops to the river Kishon; and I will give him into your hand.'"*
>
> *Then Barak said to her, "If you will go with me, then I will go; but if you will not go with me, I will not go." (Judges 4:6-8).*

Barak said that he would go, but only on one condition. He would only go if Deborah would come along. Barak believed that the Lord was with Deborah. He wasn't so certain that the Lord was with him. And so, he wanted to bring someone along who would guarantee the presence of the Lord. By insisting that Deborah come, Barak was showing true faith. But he was also showing weak faith.

> *And she said, "I will surely go with you; nevertheless, the honor shall not be yours on the journey that you are about to take, for the Lord will sell Sisera into the hands of a woman." Then Deborah arose and went with Barak to Kedesh. (Judges 4:9).*

If I gave a quiz in the average Sunday school class, quite a few would recognize the name of Deborah. But not that many would remember the name of Barak.

As the battle commenced, the forces of Sisera consisted of a large chariot corps mobilized "from Harosheth-hagoyim to the river Kishon" (Judges 4:13). We know the location of the river Kishon. It is a fairly small stream that runs in a northwesterly direction along the southern part of the Valley of Jezreel, emptying out into the Mediterranean just north of Mount Carmel.

What is interesting is the other place-name mentioned. It is *Harosheth-hagoyim*. As near as I can make out, it seems to mean "the cutting of the nations." The key city of this valley, although not mentioned in this text, is the ancient walled city of Megiddo. It is from this that we get the Hebrew "Armageddon" (*Har-Megiddo* - "Mount of Megiddo" - the problem being is that Megiddo is not on a mountain, it is a hill on the edge of a valley).

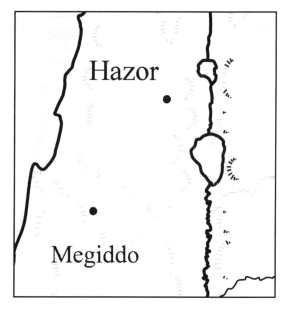

In the historical account of the passage, we read that "the Lord routed Sisera and all his chariots and all his army" (4:15). The passage makes it quite clear that the instrument which the Lord used to accomplish this was Barak and the Israelites.

Judges 5 follows up the battle with a song of victory. In this song, Deborah says that "the torrent of Kishon swept them away" (5:21) - seemingly a reference to the Kishon River overflowing its banks, although whether this is simply poetic imagery or whether it actually happened in the course of the battle is difficult to tell. As I read this account, I am struck by the "coincidence" of its echoing repetition in the book of Revelation.

- The kings of the nations (*Ha-Goyim*) are described as being gathered together to the place known as Har-Megiddo (Armageddon).
- It is the Lord who goes and fights for His people.
- There is a "torrent" in Judges while Revelation describes blood "to the horse's bridle."

This was the original battle of Armageddon.

> *The kings came and fought;*
> *Then fought the kings of Canaan*
> *At Taanach near the waters of Megiddo;*
> *They took no plunder in silver. (Judges 5:19).*

This battle was to become the pattern for the victory of the Lord against the powers of darkness. The church (the new Deborah) is still called to a battle.

And the good news is that the Lord still promises the victory.

> *And the Lord routed Sisera and all his chariots and all his army, with the edge of the sword before Barak; and Sisera alighted from his chariot and fled away on foot. (Judges 4:15).*

How did Barak and his 10,000 under-equipped foot soldiers manage to defeat a chariot corps of 900 war chariots? This was like having a bunch of Indians defeat a modern mechanized armor division. And what is more, they did it in open terrain. They were on the valley of Megiddo. This was perfect territory for chariot warfare. The Israelites had no right to win.

But God was bigger than Sisera's chariot corps. In her song of victory, Deborah says that "the earth quaked, the heavens also dripped, even the clouds dripped water" (Judges 5:4). Furthermore, she says that "the torrent of Kishon swept them away, the ancient torrent, the torrent of Kishon" (Judges 5:21 - this torrent of Kishon is also mentioned in Psalm 83:9).

If this is not merely figurative language, then it is possible that the Lord brought about a rainstorm and a flooding of the Kishon River to turn the valley floor into mud, thereby immobilizing Sisera's chariot force. The Israelites were unaffected by this adverse weather and attacked their enemies, routing them.

As Sisera flees on foot, he will come into contact with another woman who will be used of the Lord. It is noteworthy that this woman was married to a man who had rejected the Lord.

> *Now Heber the Kenite had separated himself from the Kenites, from the sons of Hobab the father-in-law of Moses, and had pitched his tent as far away as the oak in Zaanannim, which is near Kedesh. (Judges 4:11).*

Heber had come from a distinguished family. He was a descendant of the father-in-law of Moses. But he had long since disassociated himself from his fellow Israelites. Instead of living with them, he had parted from their company and had pitched his tent in the area of Kedesh Naphtali on the southwest shore of the Sea of Galilee. He had also made an alliance with the Canaanite city of Hazor and the enemies of the people of God.

> *Now Sisera fled away on foot to the tent of Jael the wife of Heber the Kenite, for there was peace between Jabin the king of Hazor and the house of Heber the Kenite. (Judges 4:17).*

This man had made peace at a time where there ought to have been no peace. He made peace with the enemies of Israel. Is there a lesson here? Perhaps it is that there are certain alliances into which we ought not enter. Though I believe in the unity of the church, there are certain people with whom we should not be united.

Apparently, the wife of Heber understood this principle. When Sisera sought refuge within her tent, she at first acquiesced, feeding him and hiding him under a rug within her tent.

> **Discussion Question:** Did Jael do wrong by offering hospitality and then murdering her guest?

> *But Jael, Heber's wife, took a tent peg and seized a hammer in her hand, and went secretly to him and drove the peg into his temple, and it went through into the ground; for he was sound asleep and exhausted. So he died. (Judges 4:21).*

In such a way, the prophecy was fulfilled. It was by the hand of a woman that Sisera met his end. As Deborah describes the slaying of Sisera (5:23-27), there is a picture of the spiritual war that was introduced in Genesis 3:15.

Genesis 3:15	Deborah's Song
The woman.	"Most blessed of women is Jael"
The wife of Adam who had fallen into sin.	"The wife of Heber the Kenite"
He shall bruise you on the head.	"She struck Sisera, she smashed his head; and she shattered and pierced his temple"

As a result of this victory, there are 40 years of peace in the land (Judges 5:31). It is a peace that is broken again by invaders.

GIDEON

Gideon's story is a lesson of what God can do with a man who will simply say, "Yes," to God. The interesting thing about him is that he initially seems to have been inclined to say, "No." It wasn't that he was a fearless man. Indeed, there are several evidences that he dealt with real fear. It was that he overcame that fear to obey the Lord.

Only a fool is without fear. The Bible speaks of the fear of the Lord being the beginning of wisdom. The brave man is one who faces his fear and does what needs doing in spite of that fear. Here is the point. You are to be afraid of that which is worthy of your fear. And in the long run, only God is worthy of your fear.

> *"And do not fear those who kill the body, but are*
> *unable to kill the soul; but rather fear Him who is able to*
> *destroy both soul and body in hell." (Matthew 10:28).*

There is One whom you ought to fear. The Lord is truly worthy of our fear, for only He has power over both body and soul.

6:1	Gideon's Call		Oppression at the hands of Midian
6:7			A Prophet
6:11			Angel of the Lord
6:25	Gideon's Commitment		Pull down Altar to Baal
6:33			Call to Arms
6:36			Laying out the Fleece
7:1	Gideon's Conquest		Reduction of his Forces
7:9			Spying out the Enemy
7:15			Sharing the Strategy
7:19			The Battle
7:24		Ephraim	Their Involvement
8:1			Their Contention
8:4	Gideon's Conquest		Rejection by Succoth & Penuel
8:10			Victory at Karkor
8:13			Accounting at Succoth & Penuel
8:18			Death of Zebah & Zalmunna
8:22	Gideon's Culpability		Offer of Kingship

8:24		The Ephod at Ophrah
8:29		Many wives
8:31		Abimelech

1.   Oppression at the hands of Midian.

> *Then the sons of Israel did what was evil in*
> *the sight of the Lord; and the Lord gave them into the*
> *hands of Midian seven years. (Judges 6:1).*

The Midianites were descendants of Abraham and Keturah (Genesis 25:1-4). They settled in the lands of Arabia to the east of the Gulf of Aqabah where they adopted a nomadic lifestyle.

In Judges 3:8 and 4:2 we read that the Lord sold the Israelites into the hands of their enemies. This time He gave them away. This period lasted for seven years. For seven years, the Midianites made successive raids into Canaan. They always came at the time of the harvest. They would wait until the Israelites had done all the work of planting and cultivating, and then they would swarm over the land, taking the crops at will. Their invasion of the land at such a time was likened unto a plague of locusts (Judges 6:5).

2.   Gideon's Call.

> *Then the angel of the Lord came and sat under*
> *the oak that was in Ophrah, which belonged to Joash*
> *the Abiezrite as his son Gideon was beating out wheat*
> *in the wine press in order to save it from the*
> *Midianites. (Judges 6:11).*

In verses 11 and 12 He is called the "angel of the Lord." When we come to verse 14 He is simply called "the Lord." This should not confuse us. The angel of the Lord always represents the very presence and message of God.

Gideon wasn't expecting such an angelic visitor. He was expecting Midianites. That is why he was beating wheat in a place where you didn't normally beat wheat. He was in hiding.

> *And the angel of the Lord appeared to him and*

212

said to him, "The Lord is with you, O valiant warrior." (Judges 6:12).

Gideon didn't look much like a valiant warrior. He looked more like the "before" picture on a "before & after" poster. He was here in hiding doing "woman's work" (the grinding of grain was considered to be the work of women - Exodus 11:5). But God declared him to be a "valiant warrior." That is what God does with us, too. He justifies us. He declares us to be righteous, not because we are righteous, but because of the righteousness of Jesus Christ which has been reckoned to us. He says, "I have declared you to be righteous - now be righteous."

3. Gideon's Requests for a Sign.

Gideon didn't make only one request for a sign. He made three such requests (though he acted in faith and obedience prior to making the last two requests).

Request #1	"Show me a sign" (Fire springs from the rock and consumes the offering).	Judges 6:17-22
Request #2	Let dew be on the fleece while the ground remains dry.	Judges 6:36-38
Request #3	Let the fleece be dry while dew is on the ground.	Judges 6:39-40

Was Gideon wrong to ask for a sign? It should be noted that the reason he asked for a sign was to make certain that he had not misunderstood the Word of the Lord (Judges 6:36). The first sign involved Gideon preparing an offering of meat, bread, and broth and bringing it to the angel of the Lord. These were placed on a rock.

> *Then the angel of the Lord put out the end of the staff that was in his hand and touched the meat and the unleavened bread, and fire sprang up from the rock and consumed the meat and the unleavened bread. Then the angel of the Lord vanished from his sight. (Judges 6:21).*

I cannot help but wonder if the charred surface of that rock was to serve as a constant reminder that the Lord had been there. Indeed, Gideon chose to immortalize that place by building an altar there.

> *Then Gideon built an altar there to the Lord*
> *and named it The Lord is Peace. To this day it is still*
> *in Ophrah of the Abiezites. (Judges 6:24).*

If I had been there, I might have named it "the place of the burning rock." But I wasn't. Perhaps Gideon realized something that is all too easily missed. He named it, "The Lord is Peace." He understood that the fact that a sacrifice had been accepted by God was a sign of peace between God and men.

4.   Gideon Destroys the Altar of Baal.

> *Now the same night it came about that the*
> *Lord said to him, "Take your father's bull and a*
> *second bull seven years old, and pull down the altar*
> *of Baal which belongs to your father, and cut down*
> *the Asherah that is beside it; 26 and build an altar to*
> *the Lord your God on the top of this stronghold in an*
> *orderly manner, and take a second bull and offer a*
> *burnt offering with the wood of the Asherah which*
> *you shall cut down." (Judges 6:25-26).*

Baal was the storm god of the Canaanites. The word "Baal" means "lord" or "master." It is used in modern Hebrew to describe a "husband." Baal was the god who was said to produce rain which was so necessary to the raising of crops and cattle. He was also the god of reproduction and produce. The Israelites had begun to worship this false god. As a sign of their worship, they had built an altar to Baal.

> *Then Gideon took ten men of his servants and*
> *did as the Lord had spoken to him; and it came about,*
> *because he was too afraid of his father's household*
> *and the men of the city to do it by day, that he did it by*
> *night. (Judges 6:27).*

The tearing down of this altar was no simple affair. A Baal altar found at Megiddo measured 26 feet across and 4 feet high. It was made of stones cemented together with dried mud. Next to it would be an "Asherah" - a fertility symbol.

So loyal were the Israelites to the worship of Baal that Gideon feared to destroy the altar by day. The account goes on to show that his fear was not misplaced, for the Israelites respond by demanding his death and it is only when his father intercedes for him that he is allowed to live.

> *Then the men of the city said to Joash, "Bring out your son, that he may die, for he has torn down the altar of Baal, and indeed, he has cut down the Asherah which was beside it."*
>
> *But Joash said to all who stood against him, "Will you contend for Baal, or will you deliver him? Whoever will plead for him shall be put to death by morning. If he is a god, let him contend for himself, because someone has torn down his altar."*
>
> *Therefore on that day he named him Jerubbaal, that is to say, "Let Baal contend against him," because he had torn down his altar. (Judges 6:30-32).*

There is a play on words here. Gideon is given the nickname "Jerubbaal" because it was suggested by his father that they should "let Baal contend against him" (literally, "let Baal *jerub* him").

5.   The Reduction of Gideon's Forces.

> *Then Jerubbaal (that is, Gideon) and all the people who were with him, rose early and camped beside the spring of Harod; and the camp of Midian was on the north side of them by the hill of Moreh in the valley (Judges 7:1).*

The last chapter mentioned that the Midianites had a camel corps (Judges 6:5). These would have been the desert version of cavalry and, as such, would be more suited to warfare on the open plains as opposed to mountain terrain.

With this in mind, they had moved their forces into the Valley of Jezreel and had encamped near the village of Endor on the north side of the Hill of Moreh. Gideon and his forces encamped to the south of the Midianites with only the ridge of Moreh separating the two forces. It was a time of tension with battle in the air. And

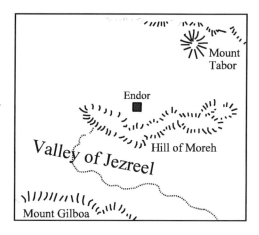

it was now that the Lord instructed Gideon to whittle down his forces. When we get to Judges 8:10, we shall see that the entire force of the Midianites numbered 135,000 men. The Israelites at the outset were outnumbered nearly four to one.

32,000 men	*"Whoever is afraid and trembling, let him depart"*	22,000 leave
10,000 men	*"Separate everyone who laps like a dog"*	9,700 sent home
300 men	*"I will deliver you with the 300 men."*	

It is not that these 300 were so great. It is that God is very big. It isn't the size of the army that counts; it's the size of the God in the army.

6.   The Battle.

> *And he divided the 300 men into three companies, and he put trumpets and empty pitchers into the hands of all of them, with torches inside the pitchers.*
> *And he said to them, "Look at me, and do likewise. And behold, when I come to the outskirts of the camp, do as I do. 18 When I and all who are with me blow the trumpet, then you also blow the trumpets all around the camp, and say, `For the Lord and for Gideon.'" (Judges 7:16-18).*

This isn't much of a battle strategy. In one hand they would hold a trumpet. In the other hand they would hold a pitcher and a torch. What's wrong with this picture? They had no weapons! But that is okay, because the Lord would be their sword.

> *And when they blew 300 trumpets, the Lord set the sword of one against the other even throughout the whole army; and the army fled as far as Beth-shittah toward Zererah, as far as the edge of Abel-melolah, by Tabbath. (Judges 7:22).*

The attack was set for the "middle watch." This was in the dead of night when the camp would be filled with slumber. Suddenly there was a clattering of shattered pottery and 300 swirling lights around the camp.

The battle quickly turned into a rout. The army of the Midianites fled back the way they had come. As they retreated, the other tribes of Israel were called to join in.

Lessons Learned
1. God's battles can be won by the few as well as by the many.
2. The quality of the soldier is more important than the quantity.

> *Then Gideon and the 300 men who were with him came to the Jordan and crossed over, weary yet pursuing. (Judges 8:4).*

Gideon knew that victory would not be complete without destroying the military might of the Midianites. With this in mind, he began a chase of the Midianites that was to take him 150 miles.

> *And he said to the men of Succoth, "Please give loaves of bread to the people who are following me, for they are weary, and I am pursuing Zebah and Zalmunna, the kings of Midian."*
>
> *The leaders of Succoth said, "Are the hands of Zebah and Zalmunna already in your hands, that we should give bread to your army.?"*
>
> *And Gideon said, "All right, when the Lord has given Zebah and Zalmunna into my hands, then I will thrash your bodies with the thorns of the*

wilderness and with briars." (Judges 8:5-7).

As we read a bit further, we find that Gideon received this same repulse from the town of Penuel. These were Israelite towns. They were inhabited by those two and a half tribes which had elected to remain on the east bank of the Jordan River.

Succoth	Declined to assist Gideon through the sharing of provisions.	*"I will thrash your bodies with thorns & briars"*
Penuel		*"I will tear down this tower"*

Do you see what has happened? The men of Succoth and Penuel are no longer identifying themselves with the covenant people of God. They want to "play it safe." They have not yet chosen sides in the conflict.

I wonder if there are not those today who are similar. "Fence-sitters" in the cause of Christ. Not against the Lord, but not with Him, either. The Lord allows no such "fence-sitting."

> *"He who is not with Me is against Me; and he who does not gather with Me scatters." (Matthew 12:30).*

We are involved in a great spiritual war. The weapons of our warfare are not spears or arrows - or even torches and pots. They are spiritual weapons. But the battle is no less real. And you are called to choose sides. If you are not on a side, then you have already chosen.

7.   Offer of Kingship.

> *Then the men of Israel said to Gideon, "Rule over us, both you and your son, also your son's son, for you have delivered us from the hand of Midian."*
> *But Gideon said to them, "I will not rule over you, nor shall my son rule over you; the Lord shall rule over you." (Judges 8:22-23).*

Gideon did not let his victory go to his head. In this he is to be commended. He was offered the position of a king and he instead gave the glory and the credit of his victory to the Lord. Yet he does make a request from the spoils of the victory.

8. The Ephod at Ophrah.

> *Yet Gideon said to them, "I would request of you, that each of you give me an earring from his spoil." For they had gold earrings, because they were Ishmaelites. (Judges 8:24).*

The people agree to this request and a total of 1700 shekels (about 42 pounds) of gold along with other ornaments are gathered and given to Gideon.

> *And Gideon made it into an ephod, and placed it in his city, Ophrah, and all Israel played the harlot with it there, so that it became a snare to Gideon and his household. (Judges 8:27).*

An "Ephod" was an apron-looking garment. It was worn by the high priest. It was the badge of priesthood (Judges 17:5). It was held in place by a waistband and associated with the Urim and Thummim which were kept within a breastplate.

What caused Gideon to do such a thing? Was it pride? Or the sudden wealth that was awarded him? He had faced the hoards of Midian and won. He faced the temptation of sudden wealth and lost. We often do not realize what a snare prosperity can be. The epistle of James warns us of the snare of riches. The point can be made that whatever you own owns you.

ABIMELECH

Gideon's closing years were a time of great prosperity. A part of this prosperity was in the fact that he had no less than seventy sons. One of these sons was by a concubine from Shechem. His name was Abimelech, meaning "My father the king." Often when a ruler dies, his son succeeds him. But what happens when that ruler has seventy sons? The answer is - Trouble!

Following the death of his father, Abimelech goes to Shechem and raises support to build for himself a throne and to establish himself as king. They supply him with funds by which he hires a band of "worthless and reckless fellows" - bad and wanton men. Seventy pieces of silver are used to hire these men who help to murder seventy brothers.

> *Then he went to his father's house at Ophrah, and killed his brothers the sons of Jerubbaal, seventy men, on one stone. But Jotham the youngest son of Jerubbaal was left, for he hid himself.*
> *And all the men of Shechem and all Beth-millo assembled together, and they went and made Abimelech king, by the oak of the pillar which was at Shechem. (Judges 9:5-6).*

There is an interesting play on words as the men of Shechem "made king Abimelech as king" (literally, "they *meleched* Abimelech"). Shechem was a Canaanite city. It had been there in the days of Jacob (see Genesis 34 for the story of Dinah and the people of Shechem). They were used to the idea of a king and were especially prone to accept a man whose mother came from their city. Thus, the advent of Abimelech was as an anti-Israelite king.

Jotham, the youngest and only surviving son of Gideon, goes to Mount Gerizim and pronounces a curse upon the city of Shechem. It begins with a parable in which the trees embark upon a quest for a king. Nobler trees such as the olive and the fig and even the vine refuse such a position. But the bramble bush agrees.

> *"And the bramble said to the trees, `If in truth you are anointing me as king over you, come and take refuge in my shade; but if not, may fire come out from the bramble and consume the cedars of Lebanon.'" (Judges 9:15).*

The picture is obvious. The more noble trees such as the olive and the fig tree represent the past leaders of Israel, Moses and Joshua and the judges

> There is a motif established here of a false anointed one.

who had refused to take the mantle as king, but who instead had recognized that the Lord was the true king of Israel. Finally the bramble bush had accepted the title, even though the bramble has no shade by which it is able to shade the mighty cedars. He is likening the bramble bush to Abimelech and to the men of Shechem who had accepted him as king and who had put to death all of the other sons of Gideon.

Shechem lies on the saddle ridge between the twin peaks of Gerizim and Ebal. This is significant as these were the two mountains upon which

Joshua had all of the Israelites stand and recite the blessings and the cursings of the law. It is here that Jotham pronounces a curse upon those who had recognized the kingship of Abimelech and who therefore endorsed his murderous actions:

> "...let fire come out from Abimelech and consume the men of Shechem and Beth-millo; and let fire come out from the men of Shechem and Beth-millo, and consume Abimelech." (Judges 9:20).

The rest of this chapter deals with the fulfillment of this curse. Following a three year reign, *God sent an evil spirit between Abimelech and the men of Shechem" (Judges 9:23)*. Abimelech captures a rebellious Shechem and burns its tower fortress to the ground, sowing the city with salt. This is possibly related to the concept of a "covenant of salt." The idea was that salt would preclude anything from growing in that location in the future. Abimelech then goes on to attack Thebez. This is another city within the realm of Manasseh and located some 6 miles to the northeast of Shechem. It is here that Abimelech is killed.

> So Abimelech came to the tower and fought against it, and approached the entrance of the tower to burn it with fire.
> But a certain woman threw an upper millstone on Abimelech's head, crushing his skull.
> Then he called quickly to the young man, his armor bearer, and said to him, "Draw your sword and kill me, lest it be said of me, `A woman slew him.'" So the young man pierced him through, and he died. (Judges 9:52-54).

Abimelech's death is an ignoble one - he is killed by a lowly weapon (the millstone) and at the hands of a woman. This is reminiscent of the death of Sisera.

Sisera	Killed by a woman	Tent peg through the head
Abimelech		A millstone crushed his head

This motif of the crushed head of the enemy of God harkens back to the prophecy of the seed of the serpent from Genesis 3:15. It is a continuation of that motif. Once again we see the enemy of God being crushed by the seed of the woman.

JEPHTHAH

> *Then the sons of Israel again did evil in the sight of the Lord, served the Baals and the Ashtaroth, the gods of Aram, the gods of Sidon, the gods of Moab, the gods of the sons of Ammon, and the gods of the Philistines; thus they forsook the Lord and did not serve Him.*
>
> *And the anger of the Lord burned against Israel, and He sold them into the hands of the Philistines, and into the hands of the sons of Ammmon. (Judges 10:6-7).*

Once again the Israelites turned away from the Lord and indulged in the pagan practices of the nations around them. This time, judgment came from two separate directions.

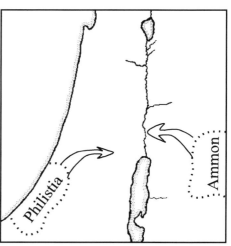

- ♦ The Philistines.

  These were a group of warriors known as the "Sea Peoples." They had attempted an invasion of Egypt and had only barely been repulsed in the days of Rameses III. They had subsequently founded five cities on the seacoast area of southwestern Canaan.

- ♦ The Ammonites.

  These were the descendants of Lot through his incestuous relationship with his daughter. They were located to the southeast of Gilead.

It is the second of these two groups that is of foremost interest in this passage. The Philistines become a major concern as we examine Samson. Thus, Jephthah will be to the eastern tribes what Samson will be to the tribes of the west.

> *Now Jephthah the Gileadite was a valiant warrior, but he was the son of a harlot. And Gilead was the father of Jephthah.*

> *And Gilead's wife bore him sons; and when his wife's sons grew up, they drove Jephthah out and said to him, "You shall not have an inheritance in our father's house, for you are the son of another woman."*
>
> *So Jephthah fled from his brothers and lived in the land of Tob; and worthless fellows gathered themselves about Jephthah, and they went out with him. (Judges 11:1-3).*

Jephthah was illegitimate. As such, he was a social outcast and was stripped of any rights to inheritance. This was no fault of his own. He was being persecuted for the sins of his parents. Those who speak of sexual sins as merely "a matter between consenting adults" normally forget the repercussions that such activities have upon the children.

Jephthah was forced to live in exile in "the land of Tob." This was the area to the southeast of the Sea of Galilee that would later be known as the Decapolis. Here he became the leader of a group who are described as "worthless fellows" - "empty men"). The same term was used of the men who followed Abimelech (Judges 9:4).

> *And it happened when the sons of Ammon fought against Israel that the elders of Gilead went to get Jephthah from the land of Tob; 6 and they said to Jephthah, "Come and be our chief that we may fight against the sons of Ammon." (Judges 11:5-6).*

It must have taken a great deal for the elders of Gilead to swallow their pride and come to Jephthah. They ask that he come and be their "chief." In verse 11 they make him "head and chief" over them . It is interesting that Jephthah makes the elders repeat the promise before he finally accepts their offer. Before seeking a military resolve, Jephthah sends messengers to the king of the Ammonites in an attempt to negotiate a peaceful resolve. Several arguments are given.

- Israel took only the land of the Amorites and then only after being attacked when they sought safe passage through that land (Judges 11:15-22).
- It was the Lord who drove out the Amorites, something that Chemosh, the god of the Ammonites had failed to do (Judges 11:23-24).
- This land had now been the uncontested property of the Israelites for the past 300 years (Judges 11:26).

> *Now the Spirit of the Lord came upon Jephthah, so*
> *that he passed through Gilead and Manasseh; then he passed*
> *through Mizpah of Gilead, and from Mispah of Gilead he*
> *went on to the sons of Ammon. (Judges 11:29).*

This is only the second time up to this point that it had been said of one of the judges that *"the Spirit of the Lord came upon"* him. It is an indication that Jephthah was trusting in the Lord for this victory. Indeed, Hebrews 11:32 lists Jephthah as one of those who *"by faith conquered kingdoms, performed acts of righteousness, obtained promises, shut the mouths of lions, quenched the power of fire, escaped the edge of the sword, from weakness were made strong, became mighty in war, put foreign armies to flight"* (Hebrews 11:33-34).

> *So Jephthah crossed over to the sons of Ammon to*
> *fight against them; and the Lord gave them into his hand.*
> *And he struck them with a very great slaughter from*
> *Aroer to the entrance of Minnith, twenty cities, and as far as*
> *Abel-keramim. So the sons of Ammon were subdued before*
> *the sons of Israel. (Judges 11:32-33).*

We are not told the specific strategy used, only that it was the Lord who gave the victory. The result was not only that the Ammonites were pushed back into their own land, but that the entire line of fortresses which divided the lands of Israel from those of Ammon now fell to the Israelites.

Prior to the battle, Jephthah made a vow to the Lord that if he was victorious then upon his return *"whatever comes out of the doors of my house to meet me when I return in peace from the sons of Ammon, it shall be the Lord's, and I will offer it up as a burnt offering"* (Judges 11:31). Upon his victorious return, the first one to come out of the door of his house was his daughter. He responds in sorrow.

> *And it came about when he saw her, that he tore his*
> *clothes and said, "Alas, my daughter! You have brought me*
> *very low, and you are among those who trouble me; for I*
> *have given my word to the Lord, and I cannot take it back."*
> *(Judges 11:35).*

She asks for a two month respite to mourn "because of my virginity" (Judges 11:37).

> *And it came about at the end of two months that she*

*returned to her father, who did to her according to the vow
which he had made; and she had no relations with a man.
Thus it became a custom in Israel, 40 that the daughters of
Israel went yearly to commemorate the daughter of Jephthah
the Gileadite four days in the year. (Judges 11:39-40).*

This passage has led to some difficult questions since the natural reading seems to indicate that Jephthah engaged in human sacrifice, putting his own daughter to death in order to fulfill his foolish vow. There are two possibilities:

- Jephthah did not actually have her put to death, but only sacrificed her in the sense of wholly dedicating her to the service of the Lord.
- Jephthah actually performed a human sacrifice, putting his daughter to death as a sacrifice to God.

Evidences have been offered for both of these interpretations.

Dedicated to God	Human Sacrifice
Being a Judge, Jephthah must have been God-fearing and so would not have violated the Law	The promise of a simple animal sacrifice would hardly be a convincing vow in this situation
The Spirit of the Lord comes on Jephthah and he is mentioned in Hebrews 11 as being one of faith	This does not take place while the Spirit of the Lord is on him and he is not commended for this action
Daughter bewails her virginity and Judges 11:29 makes comment that "she knew not a man"	The burnt offering involves death in all 286 Old Testament occurrences
Exodus 38:8 and 1 Samuel 2:22 speak of women in service of the Tabernacle	If it was a frequent practice for women to serve in the Tabernacle, then why would this be a case for mourning?

Human sacrifice would have been clearly understood as a violation of God's Law; public opinion would have disallowed it	Human sacrifice was viewed as a last ditch effort in battle (2 Kings 3:27).
Leviticus 27:1-8 allows for redemption of humans vowed for sacrifice	There is little evidence of Jephthah's knowledge of the Law

Deuteronomy 12:31 warns that the Israelites were not to engage in the pagan practices of the Canaanites, *"for every abominable act which the Lord hates they have done for their gods; for they even burn their sons and daughters in the fire to their gods."* On the other hand, we read in 1 Samuel of how Saul sought to put his own son, Jonathan, to death in fulfillment of a similar vow (1 Samuel 14:44-45).

Discussion Question: Obviously, a man in ancient Israel who swore an oath to the Lord was duty-bound to keep it (Numbers 30:2; Deuteronomy 23:21-23). But God's Law also forbids human sacrifice via the Sixth Commandment against killing. Are we obligated to keep oaths, even if it leads to the breaking of the Law? Or does an oath which leads to the breaking of the Law automatically render itself null and void, leaving us free to disregard the oath?

Matthew 14:1-12 presents another such case of a foolishly given oath. It is the story of Herod Antipas who gave a carte blanche oath to Salome and as a result murdered John the Baptist.

In Matthew 21:28-32 Jesus told a parable of two sons who were asked to go and work in their father's vineyard. The first refused and then changed his mind. He was commended, even though he acted contrary to what he said he would do, because he acted in keeping with his father's will.

SAMSON

Samson is a study in paradoxes. As such, he is not an exemplary example. He is a man of great physical strength, but of great moral weakness. He is heroic in his victories as well as in his defeats.

> *Now the sons of Israel again did evil in the sight of the Lord, so that the Lord gave them into the hands of the*

Philistines forty years. (Judges 13:1).

We have already made mention of the advent of the five cities of the Philistines upon the shores of southwest Canaan.

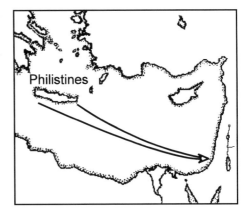

- Their name: The word "Philistine" is not a Hebrew or even a Semitic word. It seems to be Indo-European in origin. It is from this name that we derive the term "Palestine."

- Their origins: Genesis 10:14 identifies the tribal origins of the Philistines as a Hamitic people coming from the Casluhim (See also Jer. 47:4; Amos 9:7; Deut. 2:23 and 1 Chron. 1:12). The most plausible theory is that these were related either to the Minoans of Crete or to the Mycenaeans of early Greece. Egyptian records speak of an invading group of "Sea Peoples" who were barely repulsed by Rameses III in 1188 B.C. It is probable that the Philistines were among these Sea Peoples.

- Their cities: With the exception of Ekron, the five major cities of the Philistines were all originally Canaanite cities which were taken over by the Philistines. From their position on the coast, they controlled the major trade route into Egypt.

  (1) Ashkelon was the only city to have its own harbor and so it was the major seaport for the Philistines. Letters from Ashkelon appear among the Amarna Tablets in Egypt.

  > The Scallion Onion derives its name from Ashkelon.

  (2) Gaza was located 3 miles inland from the coast of the Mediterranean. The city was situated on a hight hill 100 feet above the surrounding plain. It boasted 15 fresh water wells.

  (3) Ashdod was originally inhabited by the Anakim. The city boasted a temple to their god Dagon. It would be here that the Philistines would bring the captured Ark in the days of Samuel.

(4)   Ekron is the only city to have been built by the Philistines and not merely taken over.

(5)   Gath (means "Winepress") was the home of the Anakim, a race of giants, one of whom was Goliath. As there were several towns by the name of Gath, the exact location of this city has not yet been determined.

These five cities lie within the area that today is known as the Gaza Strip. When we read of the Philistines, we should remember that we are not speaking of a group who were culturally backwards. To the contrary, they represented the educated culture of the day. They possessed the secret of smelting iron ore and they possessed cities that engaged in trade across the Mediterranean.

1.   Promise of Samson's Birth.

The parents of Samson were of the tribe of Dan. The woman of this marriage was barren. This was the worst possible condition that anyone in the ancient world could face. In a day when there was no social security, it meant that there would be no one to care for them in their old age.

a.   Agent of the promise.

Judges 13:3 says that "the angel of the Lord" appeared to the wife of Manoah and promised that a son would be born who would begin to deliver Israel (reminiscent of the "seed motif"). In verse 6 we read her description of him. She calls him "a man of God" whose appearance "was like the appearance of the angel of God." When Manoah requests the name of the angel, he is asked, *"Why do you ask my name, seeing it is **wonderful**?" (Judges 13:18).* The noun form of this word is seen in Isaiah 9:6 where we read that the name of the Promised Son shall be called "**wonderful** Counselor."

b.   Instructions and a promise.

"For behold, you shall conceive and give birth to a son, and no razor shall come upon his head, for the boy shall be a Nazarite to God from the womb; and he shall begin to deliver Israel from the hands of the

Philistines." (Judges 13:5).

The requirements of the Nazarite Vow had been set forth in Numbers 6:2-8. It was a "vow of dedication." Indeed, the word "Nazarite" comes from the Hebrew word *nazar*, "to separate." Samson was to be separated unto God from the womb. While those who partook of the Nazarite Vow generally only did so for a limited time, Samson was to be a permanent Nazarite.

c.   The repetition of the announcement.

There is a literary device that is used in this passage in which details of the announcement of the angel is given to the wife and then she relates that same announcement to her husband, yet some of the details are different. As the reader, you are supposed to read these two announcements and you are supposed to note the differences. This same literary device is seen in Genesis 3 when the woman relates the instructions of God regarding the eating of the forbidden fruit to the serpent and then adds the injunction, "Neither shall you touch it." In this case, the woman relates both more and less than was originally told to her from the angel.

Her Addition	Her Omission
She adds a reference to "the day of his death" (13:7).	She fails to mention that he would be a deliverer (13:5).

These two aspects are going to be connected in the Samson narrative. It is in Samson's death that he will do his greatest work of deliverance. In this, he is a type of another who also did His greatest work of salvation in His death.

2.   Birth and Early Life.

Then the woman gave birth to a son and named him Samson; and the child grew up and the Lord blessed him.
And the Spirit of the Lord began to stir him in

Mahanch-Dan, between Zorah and Eshtaol. (Judges 13:24-25).

The name "Samson" seems to be taken from the Hebrew word *shemesh*, "sun." Perhaps this was because he was born only a few miles away from Beth-Shemesh ("House of the Sun"). As such, it was a Canaanite name, for they worshiped the sun.

At some point in his life, the Spirit of God "began to stir" within Samson. Perhaps this stirring was with reference to his great strength. We should not necessarily think of Samson as a great muscleman. Rather, he seems to have been an ordinary man gifted with extraordinary strength.

3.   His Desire for a Philistine Woman.

> *Then Samson went down to Timnah and saw a woman in Timnah, one of the daughters of the Philistines. (Judges 14:1).*

Samson lived in a cross-cultural community. The Sorek Valley hosted both Israelite, Canaanite and Philistine towns.

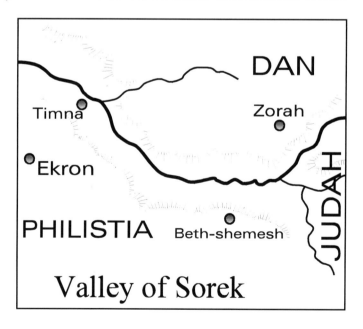

As Samson came of marital age, his eye fell upon a Philistine woman. In verse 3 he says to his father, *"Get her for me, for she looks good to me."* Again in verse 7 we read that *"she looked good*

to Samson." In both these cases, the Hebrew says literally, "She is right in my eyes." This is a refrain which we will see throughout the closing chapters of the book of Judges when *"every man did what was right in his own eyes"* (Judges 17:6; 21:25).

Samson was a He-Man with a "she-weakness." He had a tendency toward lust that was to conquer him. But the real point of this story is how God used Samson in spite of his failures. It is a story of the sovereignty of God.

Judges 14:4 says that all of his troubled relationships were *"of the Lord, for He was seeking an occasion against the Philistines."* The judges had two different types of ministry. Some were called to judge. Others were called to deliver Israel from her enemies (the best of the judges did both, like Deborah). This brings up a question. Why is the name of Samson mentioned in Heb 11:32 as an example of a man of faith? It certainly is not because Samson was faithful to God. He broke every one of the requirements of the Nazarite Vow. He wasn't faithful, but he did believe God and he called upon the Lord (Judges 16:28). He was not afraid to ask God for big things, even when he knew that he did not deserve them.

Perhaps we can learn something from this. I know that I do not deserve to expect a positive answer from God when I pray. If Samson teaches me anything, he teaches me about the grace of God and that God answers the prayer of faith, even when the one who offers it is a sinful, fallen, and marred person.

4.   The Wedding Incident.

Wedding feasts were no short affair. They customarily lasted as long as a week (14:17). The groom would throw a great party to which he would invite all of his friends. Since the wedding was taking place in a Philistine town, it was a group of Philistines who came to attend the feast.

Normally, custom mandated that the wedding feast be at the house of the groom. But this was not the case here. Instead of this Philistine girl associating herself with the people of God, Samson was associating himself with the Philistines. In the midst of the feast, Samson proposes a riddle and a very expensive wager.

> *So he said to them, "Out of the eater came something to eat, and out of the strong came something sweet." (Judges 14:14).*

After three days, the Philistine guests have not discovered the answer, so they threaten his bride with death and with the destruction of her father's home. She, in turn, solicites the answer from Samson and betrays him.

> *Then the Spirit of the Lord came upon him mightily, and he went down to Ashkelon and killed thirty of them and took their spoil, and gave the changes of clothes to those who told the riddle. And his anger burned, and he went up to his father's house. (Judges 14:19).*

Samson's attack on the Philistines was motivated, not from spiritual reasons, but merely of revenge. Revenge is one of the most natural human responses. And also one of the most destructive.

> *Never take your own revenge, beloved, but leave room for the wrath of God, for it is written, "Vengeance is Mine, I will repay," says the Lord. (Romans 12:19).*

The lesson will be illustrated in the case of Samson as his conflict with the Philistines escalates to the point where he is ultimately defeated. Remember that the Lord was using his strength in spite of his impure motivations. This is the first of several escalating conflicts with the Philistines.

Verse	Incident	Number Killed
14:19	Samson kills men of Ashkelon to take their clothes in payment	30 men
15:5	Samson burns farmlands of Philistines	Unknown
15:8	Samson strikes with a great slaughter	Unknown
15:15	Samson breaks ropes that bind him and fights with the jawbone of an ass	1000 men

| 16:30 | Samson pushes down the house of Dagon, killing all within | More than he had killed in his life |

5.   In the Time of Wheat Harvest - An Escalating Vengeance.

The anger of his vengeance temporarily cooled, Samson returns to take his wife, only to find that she has been given to another man. Samson takes this as a further insult and takes up a career as an arsonist, burning up a great number of the fields of the Philistines. The Philistines respond by burning the home of his would-be bride and her father. They die in the flames, she suffering the very death she had sought to avoid in initially betraying Samson. The escalation continues as Samson *"struck them ruthlessly with a great slaughter"* (Judges 15:8). Following this, Samson escapes to a refuge in a cave near the town of Etam (a mere 2 miles from Bethlehem) in the territory of Judah.

6.   The Lehi Incident - the Jawbone of an Ass.

Samson's actions had already brought retribution upon his bride and father-in-law. Now the Philistines invade the territory of Judah, putting pressure upon the Israelites to turn Samson over to them. They agree and Samson is bound and made a captive of the Philistines.

> *When he came to Lehi, the Philistines shouted as they met him. And the Spirit of the Lord came upon him mightily so that the ropes that were on his arms were as flax that is burned with fire, and his bonds dropped from his hands.*
> *And he found a fresh jawbone of a donkey, so he reached out and took it and killed a thousand men with it. (Judges 15:14-15).*

The name "Lehi" means "jawbone." It seems likely that it was given this designation following this event. This was Samson's greatest victory to date. It can only be attributed to the working of God through him. When the killing was completed, Samson became aware of a great thirst. He asks the Lord for water and the Lord answers his prayer, making water to come from the "hollow place."

Throughout this section, we have seen an escalating conflict between Samson and the Philistines. We have already been told that the Lord was bringing this about.

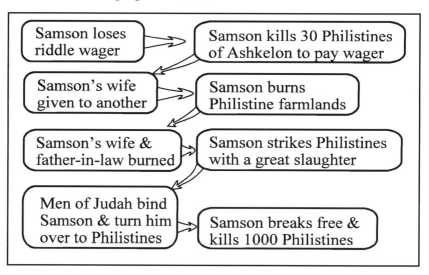

7.   The Gates of Gaza.

>   *Now Samson went to Gaza and saw a harlot there, and went in to her.*
>   *When it was told to the Gazites, saying, "Samson has come here," they surrounded the place and lay in wait for him all night at the gate of the city. And they kept silent all night, saying, "Let us wait until the morning light, then we will kill him."*
>   *Now Samson lay until midnight, and at midnight he arose and took hold of the doors of the city gate and the two posts and pulled them up along with the bars; then he put them on his shoulders and carried them up to the top of the mountain which is opposite Hebron. (Judges 16:1-3).*

This is the second time a woman became the source of trouble for Samson. Perhaps as many as 20 years had passed since his last encounter with the Philistines (Judges 15:20).

While they lie in wait for him, he literally breaks out of the city, carrying the city gates with him. This had a special significance in the ancient world. A city was considered to be no stronger than its gates. To have the gates carried off was the height of humiliation for this city.

Hebron is located nearly 40 miles to the east of Gaza.

Furthermore, it is uphill all the way, rising to a height of 3000 feet above sea level. Apparently, Samson took these gates there as a trophy of the strength of the God of Israel.

8.   Samson and Delilah.

> *After this it came about that he loved a woman*
> *in the valley of Sorek, whose name was Delilah.*
> *(Judges 16:4).*

Though Delilah is not described as a Philistine, her name does not seem to be Semitic in origin and so it is likely that she was a Philistine. The lords of the Philistines offer her a large bribe if she will discover the secret of Samson's great strength. Samson is at first evasive, telling her lie after lie. But ultimately he relents. Delilah is quick to make use of this information and, while he is sleeping, she has his head shaved.

> *Then the Philistines seized him and gouged*
> *out his eyes; and they brought him down to Gaza and*
> *bound him with bronze chains, and he was a grinder*
> *in the prison*
> *However, the hair of his head began to grow*
> *again after it was shaved off. (Judges 16:21-22).*

The gouging of the eyes of a hated prisoner was common in the ancient world. It assured him a fate of servitude. He is brought to Gaza, the city which he had humiliated by carrying away the gates. Thrown into prison, he is assigned the duty of grinding mill by hand (the large animal-powered mills were not yet in use).

9.   Samson's Death.

> *Now the lords of the Philistines assembled to*
> *offer a great sacrifice to Dagon their god, and to*
> *rejoice, for they said, "Our god has given Samson our*
> *enemy into our hands." (Judges 16:23).*

Dagon was the god of the Philistines. Though the name is similar to *dag*, the Hebrew word for "fish," more recent archaeological studies have identified Dagon as a Canaanite deity which had been borrowed by the Philistines. In Ugaritic literature he is the father of Baal. Dagon was the god of **grain**. Perhaps this was why Samson had been given the task of grinding grain in the prison. They attributed this victory, not to Samson's disobedience, but to the power of their own god. In the midst of their celebration, they have Samson brought out for their amusement. In the midst of this entertainment, Samson prays one last time to the Lord.

> *Then Samson called to the Lord and said, "O Lord God, please remember me and please strengthen me just this time, O God, that I may at once be avenged of the Philistines for my two eyes."*
>
> *And Samson grasped the two middle pillars on which the house rested, and braced himself against them, the one with his right hand and the other with his left.*
>
> *And Samson said, "Let me die with the Philistines!" And he bent with all his might so that the house fell on the lords and all the people who were in it. So the dead whom he killed at his death were more than those whom he killed in his life. (Judges 16:28-30).*

Samson's last act was one which was designed both to avenge his treatment at the hands of the Philistines as well as to deliver a blow against the false god that was being proclaimed in place of the Lord. His is the story of a man with great strength and great weakness. In one sense, it is a tragedy, for his personal life was his undoing. In another sense, the Lord took this tragic life and brought about a victory for the people of God. What made the difference? How can we see Samson as the victor instead of Samson the blind suicide bomber? It is by recognizing that, in spite of all his failings, Samson had faith. It is for this reason he is listed in Hebrews 11 in that great hall of faith. He bears witness to us that God is able to take a sinful man and through such a tool do great things.

It is interesting to note the parallels as well as the contrasts between Samson and Jesus Christ. Both exhibited an impossible birth, both were deliverers, each was betrayed by a loved one, and each did his greatest work in his death. On the other hand, one came on the scene with his physical strength, the other was known for his gentleness. One was about revenge while the other was about forgiveness.

The story of Samson is the story of the Lord battling with the

Philistines, the arch enemies of Israel. It ends with the death of both Samson as well as the Philistines and this anticipates the rise of a king in Israel who will finish the work of defeating the Philistines. David will be that king who accomplishes this victory. Yet we cannot help but be reminded of the Greater Son of David who defeats the enemies of the Lord through His own death. It is a reminder of the redemptive story that ties together all the stories of the Bible.

WHEN THERE WAS NO KING IN ISRAEL

The entire book of Judges can be arranged in a large parallel known as a Chiasm. It begins with a two-part prologue. It ends with a two-part epilogue. In the middle are all of the stories of the Judges.

The Prologue established that the book of Judges would be primarily a story of great defeat. Though there would be heroes and times of victory, these would never last. As we come to the last two narratives, this theme of spiritual defeat comes to the forefront.

Prologue in Two Parts (1:1–2:5)

Othniel Narrative (3:7-11)

Ehud Narrative (3:12–31)
- Judge is a social outcast
- Deals with oppressors on the east bank of the Jordan

Deborah-Barak Narrative (4:1–5:31)
- Woman slays enemy of God with a blow to the head

Gideon Narrative (6:1–8:32)

Abimelech Narrative (8:33–10:5)
- Woman slays enemy of God with a blow to the head

Jephthah Narrative (10:6–12:15)
- Judge is a social outcast
- Deals with oppressors on the east bank of the Jordan

Samson Narrative (13:1–16:31)

Epilogue in Two Parts (17:1–21:25)

The Epilogue follows a similar pattern to the Prologue in that it is plainly divided into two separate stories. The first story concerns the Tribe of Dan. The second story deals with the Tribe of Benjamin.

- Neither story speaks of Baal worship. Where there is sin involving worship, it involves worshiping the Lord in an improper way.
- The closing refrain for both of these stories is that "in those days there was no king in Israel" (17:6; 18:1; 19:1; 21:25). This describes a period of anarchy when men were doing what was right in their own eyes.
- Both of these narratives seem to take place early in the period of the Judges. This means the sins which these narratives illustrate would grow in severity as time passed.

The first narrative will tell the story of how the tribe of Dan relocated from their original inheritance near the land of the Philistines to the northernmost part of Israel on the slopes of Mount Hermon at the headwaters of the Jordan River. You will remember that Samson was from the tribe of Dan and his story is in close proximity to the land of the Philistines, so this story is set in the period after the Samson narrative.

Now there was a man of the hill country of Ephraim whose name was Micah. (Judges 17:1).

With this verse, we are introduced to an even darker section of what has already been a dark period of the history of Israel. This is a portrayal of a man who had drifted away from the Lord. The story begins with a theft of silver. Micah is the guilty party and he returns the stolen silver to his mother, not because of any feelings of remorse, but because she has put a curse on it. He is doing the right thing for the wrong reason. As a result, she rewards him by giving a portion of it back to him in order *"to make a graven image and a molten image"* (17:3).

And the man Micah had a shrine and he made an ephod and household idols and consecrated one of his sons that he might become his priest. (Judges 17:5).

This man had further disobeyed the law by making his own place of worship. It is described as a shrine, literally, a "house of gods." He had filled it with *teraphim* - small household idols which were common among the Canaanites. Finally, he had disregarded the Levitical priesthood and had appointed one of his own sons to be a priest.

This is the picture of a man who is seeking to approach God on his own terms. It is a religion of superstition. It is noteworthy that archaeological finds from this period attest to the pluralism of the Jews and how quick they were to adopt the pagan practices of the Canaanites whom they had displaced.

> *In those days there was no king in Israel; every man did what was right in his own eyes. (Judges 17:6).*

This is the first of four times that we will be told that "there was no king in Israel." From the context of these statements, it is evident that not even the Lord was considered to be the king. This was a period of anarchy.

> *Now there was a young man from Bethlehem in Judah, of the family of Judah, who was a Levite, and he was staying there. (Judges 17:7).*

Bethlehem was not one of the cities which had been set aside for the Levites. This means that this man had either rejected or had denied his inheritance from the Lord.

> *Then the man departed from the city, from Bethlehem in Judah, to stay wherever he might find a place; and as he made his journey, he came to the hill country of Ephraim to the house of Micah. (Judges 17:8).*

This man was an opportunist, out for the best possible deal. He didn't care for the city to which he had been assigned, so he set out to find a better place. Levites were not to be opportunistic. They were to be the Lord's. But this man was only interested in profit. And when he was offered wages, room and board to serve as a priest in Micah's shrine, he agreed.

> *So Micah consecrated the Levite, and the young man became his priest and lived in the house of Micah. (Judges 17:12).*

Levites were not qualified to serve as priests. Only a descendant of Aaron could be a priest. And such a priest could only conduct his priestly duties at the Tabernacle. This did not stop Micah from using this Levite as his own family priest.

> *Then Micah said, "Now I know that the Lord will*

prosper me, seeing I have a Levite as priest." (Judges 17:13).

Again, we can see that Micah was trying to approach the Lord on his own terms. He felt that the Lord might bless him simply because he had hired a Levite as priest. It's a little like the person who thinks that he is acceptable to God simply because his parents were Christians or because he is affiliated with a certain denomination.

It was a sin to worship the Lord in the wrong way. God was very clear in stating that they were to worship in the place which He had chosen (Deuteronomy 12:11; 16:7). There is a lesson here. It is that it is possible to do the right thing in the wrong way. It is not merely the results which count and the ends do not always justify the means.

> *In those days there was no king in Israel; and in those days the tribe of the Danites was seeking an inheritance for themselves to live in, for until that day an inheritance had not been allotted to them as a possession among the tribes of Israel. (Judges 18:1).*

When the land was divided among the twelve tribes of Israel, Dan received the hills and lowlands to the west of Jerusalem (Joshua 19:40-48). However, it was one thing to be awarded that land, it was another thing to take possession of it.

The first chapter of Judges relates how *"the Amorites forced the sons of Dan into the hill country"* and *"did not allow them to come down to the valleys"* (Judges 1:34). Because of this situation, the people of Dan determined to look for another place to live. Do you see what they are doing? They are rejecting the inheritance which was given to them by God and seeking another inheritance - one that will be more easily obtained. In doing so, they are seeking for that which "is right in their own eyes."

> *So the sons of Dan sent from their family five men out of their whole number, valiant men from Zorah and Eshtaol, to spy out the land and to search it; and they said to them, "Go, search the land." And they came to the hill country of Ephraim, to the house of Micah, and lodged there. (Judges 18:2).*

In their quest for a homeland, they send out a group of five representatives to find a place where they can live. These five find lodging with Micah and, while they are there, ask the Levite-turned-priest to inquire of the Lord as to whether they shall be prosperous.

And the priest said to them, "Go in peace; your way in which you are going has the Lord's approval." (Judges 18:6).

This priest proclaims the Lord's sanctions upon the actions of the Danites. This brings up a question. Was this man speaking from the Lord? Was he speaking truly? We do not know. The passage does not say either way.

The Danite scouts continue their northward journey, coming at last to the city of Laish, located just south of Mount Hermon close to one of the tributaries of the Jordan River. The mound of the site rises today 75 feet above the surrounding grassland. They choose this site to be the new homeland of the tribe of Dan.

Then from the family of the Danites, from Zorah and from Eshtaol, six hundred men armed with weapons of war set out. (Judges 18:11).

When this 600-man force comes to the home of Micah, they help themselves to his idols, images, and the priestly garments. When the priest challenges them, they offer him a position as priest over their tribe and he accepts. Micah challenges their actions, but to no avail.

Then they took what Micah had made and the priest who had belonged to him, and came to Laish, to a people quiet and secure, and struck them with the edge of the sword, and they burned the city with fire.

And there was no one to deliver them, because it was far from Sidon and they had no dealings with anyone, and it was in the valley which is near Beth-roab. And they rebuilt the city and lived in it.

And they called the name of the city Dan, after the name of Dan their father who was born in Israel; however, the name of the city formerly was Laish. (Judges 18:27-29).

Laish was an ancient city. Gates from this city dating back to Abraham's day have now been excavated in the area of Dan (see photo). This city was taken by the tribe of Dan and became their new home. The city of Dan was to become the northern boundary of the nation of Israel. But if they thought that this was to be the best of all possible locations, they were mistaken. Dan was located midway between Sidon and Tyre on the seacoast and Damascus on the edge of the Syrian Desert. When the king of Damascus went to war against Israel, the first city that he would attack would be Dan (1 Kings 15:20).

The closing section of the book of Judges, related in chapters 19-21, is perhaps the darkest ever described in the pages of the Bible.

Archaeological excavation of the gate of Laish

1.   Setting for the Story.

> *Now it came about in those days, when there was no king in Israel, that there was a certain Levite staying in the remote part of the hill country of Ephraim, who took a concubine for himself from Bethlehem in Judah. (Judges 19:1).*

Once again we see the locations of Ephraim and Bethlehem as the backdrop to the story. Once again there is a Levite involved. And once again, one of the Tribes of Israel is seen in the role of a "villain."

Judges 17 - 18	**Judges 19 - 21**
Micah lived in the hill country of Ephraim	The Levite lived in the hill country of Ephraim
The Levite was from Bethlehem.	His concubine's father lived in Bethlehem.
The Tribe of Dan are the "villains."	The Tribe of Benjamin are the "villains."

2.   Journey to Bethlehem.

The Levite of this story has a concubine who "played the harlot," ending up at her father's home in Bethlehem. He goes to fetch her and ends up staying in the home of his father-in-law for several days. Finally, getting a late start, he leaves with his servant and concubine and begin the journey home.

Their route takes them past the Jebusite city of Jerusalem, but they determine to bypass this city because it is a Canaanite city. They continue on until they come to Gibeah, a city of Benjamin (19:14).

The name "Gibeah" is Hebrew for "hill." Archaeological finds show the site of this small city to have been only three miles north of Jerusalem. It would be from this city that Saul would come.

It seems ironic that, having avoided Jerusalem because of its pagan inhabitants, this Levite and his concubine should be rewarded with such an inhospitable attitude from those of Gibeah. Such an attitude is even more striking when we remember that King Saul will come from the town of Gibeah (1 Samuel 10:26).

And they turned aside there in order to enter and lodge in Gibeah. When they entered, they sat down in the open square of the city, for no one took them into his house to spend the night. (Judges 19:15).

Gibeah was not all that big of a city. It did have a fortress with four corner towers and an open square in the middle. Perhaps this is where the Levite and his party prepared to spend the night. However, at this time, an "old man" from the hill country of Ephraim who had been temporarily working and living in Gibeah came in from the fields and invited the party to lodge at his house.

3.   The Attack of the "Worthless

Fellows."

> *While they were making merry, behold, the men of the city; certain worthless fellows, surrounded the house, pounding the door; and they spoke to the owner of the house, the old man, saying, "Bring out the man who came into your house that we may have relations with him."*
>
> *Then the man, the owner of the house, went out to them and said to them, "No, my fellows, please do not act so wickedly; since this man has come into my house, do not commit this act of folly.*
>
> *"Here is my virgin daughter and his concubine. Please let me bring them out that you may ravish them and do to them whatever you wish. But do not commit such an act of folly against this man." (Judges 19:22-24).*

The description of them as "worthless fellows" is literally "men who were sons of Belial." This is a figure of speech and it is not necessary to view "Belial" as a proper name. This is markedly similar to the incident with Lot and the two angels in the city of Sodom (Genesis 19:4-8). In that instance, there were angelic visitors to the city of Sodom who found refuge with Lot. In the middle of the night, men of Sodom surrounded his house in an endeavor to sexually abuse his visitors. Now it is happening again, not in Sodom, but in an Israelite city.

Genesis 19:4-8	Judges 19:22-24
Takes place in Sodom, a Canaanite city of the Jordan Valley	Takes place in Gibeah, an Israelite city in the hill country
Two angels staying with Lot, an outsider who is currently living in the city	Levite and his party stay with a man of Ephraim who is currently living in the city
In both cases, the men of the city come to the house where the visitors are staying and demand that they be turned over to them to be sexually abused.	

Lot attempts negotiations by offering his two virgin daughters.	Old man attempts negotiations by offering his virgin daughter and the Levite's concubine.
The angels intercede and strike the men of Sodom with blindness.	Levite sacrifices his concubine to save himself.

It is noteworthy that both of these stories reflect the devalued estate of women as it existed in the ancient world. The Bible is not herein condoning such a devaluation. It is merely accurately reporting it. This tells me something about the Bible. The Bible does not look at mankind through rose-colored glasses. It presents real people as they commit real sins.

4.   A Grisly Message.

> *When he entered his house, he took a knife and laid hold of his concubine and cut her in twelve pieces, limb by limb, and sent her throughout the territory of Israel.*
>
> *And it came about that all who saw it said, "Nothing like this has ever happened or been seen from the day when the sons of Israel came up from the land of Egypt to this day. Consider it, take counsel and speak up!" (Judges 19:29-30).*

The cutting up of the body of the woman would find its parallel in the actions of King Saul when he cut seven oxen into pieces and sent them throughout the territory of Israel as a call to arms (1 Samuel 11:7). That would serve as an echo of this event.

Call to Arms in Judges 19	**Call to Arms in 1 Samuel 15**
The slain body of the concubine is cut into twelve pieces and sent to the tribes of Israel.	Saul takes his own oxen and cuts them into twelve pieces and sends them to the tribes of Israel

The reason for the call was because of the great sin committed by the men of Gibeah.	The reason for the call was to gather Israel to save Jabesh-Gilead from the great subjugation of the Ammonites.
Benjamin takes a stand against the other tribes of Israel and is all but destroyed.	Benjamin leads the other tribes of Israel and brings salvation to Jabesh-Gilead.

As a result of this call to arms, representatives of all twelve tribes gather together at Mizpah. It must have been a huge force.

5.   The Gathering at Mizpah.

> *Then all the sons of Israel from Dan to Beersheba, including the land of Gilead, came out, and the congregation assembled as one man to the Lord at Mizpah. (Judges 20:1).*

The word "Mizpah" appears each time with the definite article and means "the watchtower." The exact location of this place is unknown. Apparently, it was located near Shiloh where the Tabernacle and the Ark of the Covenant were kept. It seems to have remained as the place of meeting for the Tribes of Israel from the time of Samuel to the days of the Maccabees (1 Samuel 7:5-12; 10:17; 2 Kings 25:23; 1 Maccabees 3:46).

When the story of the incident is related, the tribes of Israel determine to punish the town of Gibeah. But the people of Benjamin disagree and they even go so far as to go to war against the other tribes over this issue.

6.   War with Benjamin.

> *And the sons of Benjamin gathered from the cities to Gibeah, to go out to battle against the sons of Israel. (Judges 20:14).*

In the ensuing battle, Benjamin is victorious and 22,000 men of the tribe of Judah are slain. After weeping and praying before the Lord, the Israelites ask the Lord if they should go up again. The Lord says to go up. They do and this time they lose 18,000 men.

They go and weep before the Lord again and fast and pray for an entire day, offering sacrifices to the Lord. They ask again whether they should go up against Benjamin. Again, the Lord says to go up. This time, they formulate an ambush, pretending to retreat and drawing the people of Benjamin away from the city of Gibeah while a hidden force enters the city and sets it to the torch.

> *But when the cloud began to rise from the city in a column of smoke, Benjamin looked behind them; and behold, the whole city was going up in smoke to heaven.*
> *Then the men of Israel turned, and the men of Benjamin were terrified; for they saw that disaster was close to them. (Judges 20:40-41).*

As the battle became a rout, a total of 25,000 of the tribe of Benjamin were destroyed. This brings up a question. Why did the Israelites lose the initial two battles? Why did they have to lose 40,000 men before gaining the victory? We are not told. We are told of no sin on their behalf. We read of no lack of faith. We are left with no reason at all.

There is an important lesson here. It is that you can do all the things you are supposed to and still experience failure for no obvious reason. Remember the example of Job? We can see the reason for the tragic events in his life, but he was not privy to these reasons. Here is the lesson. Just because bad things happen for no apparent reason does not mean that there is no reason. Just because things go wrong when I am doing everything right is no excuse to stop doing right.

7.   The Survivors of Benjamin.

Those of the tribe of Benjamin who survived the war with Israel numbered a scant 600 men (Judges 20:47). This raised a problem.

> *Now the men of Israel had sworn in Mizpah, saying, "None of us shall give his daughter to Benjamin in marriage." (Judges 21:1).*

The oath against Benjamin was an oath to cut off Benjamin from intermarriage with the rest of the tribes of Israel. And to make matters worse, the Israelites had destroyed all of the Benjamite cities and had either killed or taken captive all of the women of those cities.

In the months that followed, the Israelites pondered their options. They could not go back on their oath to the Lord. They were unwilling to allow the tribe of Benjamin to become extinct. And so, they came up with a twofold plan.

Plan #1: Operation Jabesh-gilead	This city was punished for not participating in the military action against Benjamin. All are put to the sword except 400 virgins who are given in marriage to the men of Benjamin.
Plan #2: Operation Shiloh	Benjamites are allowed to "kidnap" wives from the Daughters of Shiloh who come down to dance at the festival.

We noted at the outset that these two narratives, the first story concerning the Tribe of Dan, and now this second story dealing with the Tribe of Benjamin are set when "in those days there was no king in Israel" (17:6; 18:1; 19:1; 21:25). They both have their beginning in the town of Bethlehem, the town from which King David will ultimately emerge. There is a reason for this. It is to suggest that the answer to the grievous situation in Israel in the days of the Judges was to be found in a king who would come from Bethlehem. From our vantage point in history, we can see that the real answer to the problem faced by Israel was to come from David's Greater Son who was to be born in Bethlehem.

RUTH
The Romance of Redemption

The story is told of how Dr. Samuel Johnson, the famous 18th century writer, once took a copy of the book of Ruth and read it before a London gathering of free-thinkers and philosophers, presenting it as if it were of modern composition. Thinking it was of recent creation, they were resounding and unanimous in their praise of the manuscript. It was only then that Dr. Johnson informed them that it was taken from a book which they had rejected - the Bible.

In the Hebrew Bible, the book of Ruth does not appear after Judges. Instead, it is found in the Writings as one of the five Megiloth ("Scrolls"), each of which was read at one of the feasts of the nation of Israel.

Megiloth Scrolls	
Song of Solomon	Passover
Ruth	Pentecost
Lamentations	9th of Ab (Anniversary of Jerusalem's destruction)
Ecclesiastes	Feast of Tabernacles
Esther	Purim

In the modern Hebrew Bible, Ruth stands between the Song of Solomon and Lamentations, with sorrow on one side and rejoicing on the other. The fact that Ruth is read on Pentecost is perhaps suggestive to the Christian. Pentecost suggests the birthday of the church and when we look at the story of Ruth, we see a love story that reminds us of our relationship with Christ.

In the Septuagint, as well as in the Latin Vulgate and the Talmud, the book of Ruth follows Judges. There is a reason for this. Ruth seems to be closely associated with the last several chapters of the book of Judges. In Josephus' accounting of the books of the Hebrew Scriptures, Ruth is deemed as a part of the book of Judges.

Judges 17 - 21		Ruth
Says four times that *"there was no king in Israel."*		Begins with the words, *"when the judges governed..."*
Levite from Bethlehem	Concubine from Bethlehem	Naomi and her family were from Bethlehem
A Spiritual Desert		An Oasis amidst the Desert
Depicts the need of a King		Presents the lineage of the King

Although there is an association with the Judges, Ruth does not share any of the great and momentous deeds, the clamor of battle, or the spiritual failings which are so prevalent in that book. If Judges is a book of failure, then Ruth is a book of quiet victory.

DATE OF WRITING

There seems to have been a significant passage of time between the events which the book of Ruth describes and the recording of those events.

1.   The story is said to take place "in the days when the judges governed" (Ruth 1:1). This indicates that it was written in a time when the judges were no longer governing.

2.   Ruth 4:7 speaks of a custom "in former times in Israel" which was evidently no longer in practice at the time of writing.

3.   The fact that David is mentioned at the end of Ruth indicates that it was written after he had become King in Israel. The fact that Solomon is not mentioned indicates that Solomon had not yet come to the throne.

OUTLINE OF RUTH

The story of Ruth is presented in a chiastic format. It begins "when the judges governed." It ends with the genealogy of the reigning King.

Naomi's Bitterness (1:1-22)

Ruth discovers a potential Kinsman Redeemer (2:1-23)

Boaz agrees to be a Kinsman Redeemer (3:1-18)

Boaz acquires right to be a Kinsman Redeemer (4:1-12)

Naomi's Blessing (4:13-21)

PURPOSE OF THE BOOK

1. Ruth is a book about loyalty and love. The heroine of the story is Ruth and it is her loyalty to her mother-in-law as well as to the Lord which is featured.

2. The book also has something to say regarding the missionary ministry which Israel was to have to the world. Ruth, a Moabitess, became the recipient of special blessings as she came to believe in the God of Naomi. This book teaches us that God is no respecter of persons.

    > The word "love" is completely absent from the book of Ruth, though it is a story of love on several levels.

3. The book elevates the role of godly women in the overall redemptive plan of God. This is one of two books in the Bible that is named after a woman. There is an interesting contrast between Ruth and Esther.

Ruth	Esther
A Gentile girl who married an Israelite.	An Israelite girl who married a Gentile.
"Built the house of Israel"	Saved the people of Israel
Her descendant was David, the King of Israel.	She was married to the King of Persia.
Rural setting.	A Royal Palace.

4. This book also highlights the genealogy of King David and shows the

reversal of the curse which had been laid on the people of Moab.

> *"No Ammonite or Moabite shall enter the assembly of the Lord; none of their descendants, even to the tenth generation, shall ever enter the assembly of the Lord" (Deuteronomy 23:3).*

There was a ten-generation curse placed upon the people of Moab and Ammon during the days of Moses because of their inhospitality toward Israel. There is no record of a Moabite or an Ammonite being accepted into the assembly of God's people for the next ten generations after Moses. But this changes with Ruth. She not only enters the assembly of God's people, but she is also included in the royal line of David. Indeed, she is mentioned in the Messianic line of Matthew 1.

SETTING FOR THE STORY (RUTH 1:1-4)

> *Now it came about in the days when the judges governed, that there was a famine in the land. And a certain man of Bethlehem in Judah went to sojourn in the land of Moab with his wife and his two sons. (Ruth 1:1).*

The story begins "in the days when the judges judged." This connects us directly back to the book of Judges. This was the period when, as we were reminded four

> Of the 85 verses within the book of Ruth, there are only 8 that do NOT begin with the ו conjunctive ("and").

times in the closing chapters of the book of Judges, "there was no king in Israel." Just as the last two stories of the book of Judges took place in or around Bethlehem, so this story will be set in Bethlehem. In doing so, these narratives anticipate the king who will come from the tiny village of Bethlehem. They show to us a need for such a king.

At the same time, the book of Ruth is different from the last two narratives of the book of Judges. They are dark and somber, the story of Ruth begins in a time of difficulty, but its end is full of hope. This is by design.

Have you ever notice how, when you visit a jewelry store, the salesperson will often place the jewelry upon a black velvet background. They do that for a reason. It is because the gems stand out all the more brightly when placed against a black backdrop. The book of Ruth is like that. Its backdrop against the dark days of the Judges makes it shine all the more brightly. It is a book of hope and it calls us to hope for better times ahead that are brought by a once and future king.

1.   A Famine in the Land.

What this meant for an agricultural economy is difficult for us to comprehend. A famine involved complete financial devastation and could lead ultimately to starvation. What is ironic is that there was a famine in a place named and known for its bread; the place known as Bethlehem.

2.   Bethlehem in Judah.

The name "Bethlehem" is a compound of two words meaning "House of Bread." The small town is located on the spur of an east-west ridge 4 miles to the south of Jerusalem. It is surrounded on three sides by lush, fertile farmlands. It is bad enough when famine strikes. But when famine strikes the "House of Bread" then things can become desperate. This was the problem which arose. There was no bread in the House of Bread.

Modern Bethlehem

As our story opens, the land is beset with a famine. It impacts the land and it impacts a family that was living in the tiny village of Bethlehem. The beginning of this story serves to remind us that, out of the worst kind of circumstances, God is able to weave something

253

wonderful. Ruth is a lesson that you should not judge the circumstances until the last chapter is over. Indeed, this book would be a book of tragedy were it not for the last chapter.

3.   The Land of Moab.

Moab was located to the east of the Dead Sea, its northern boarder being the Arnon River and its southern boarder being the Zered Wadi. Rising up from the Dead Sea, 1300 feet below sea level, the land rises up to a large plateau.

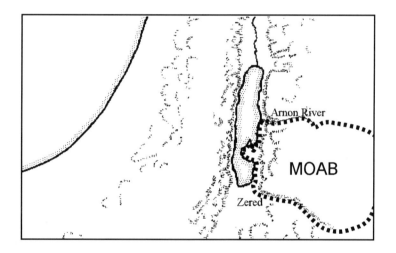

The Moabites were the descendants of Lot through his incestuous relations with his daughter. Moab had refused the Israelites permission to pass through their land in the days of Moses. During the days of the Judges, the Moabites had invaded the territory of Israel until being driven out by Ehud. Moab was now considered to be an accursed nation.

> *"No Ammonite or Moabite shall enter the assembly of the Lord; none of their descendants, even to the tenth generation, shall ever enter the assembly of the Lord, 4 because they did not meet you with food and water on the way when you came out of Egypt, and because they hired against you Balaam the son of Beor from Pethor of Mesopotamia, to curse you."*
> *(Deuteronomy 23:3-4).*

We have already become well acquainted with the people of Moab in our study of the book of Judges. It was by the sword of Ehud that the king of Moab had been slain after he had afflicted the Israelites for eighteen years. When an Israelite thought of Moab, he thought of a dangerous enemy. Now the nation of accursed people becomes a haven for this Hebrew man and his family. The cursing will be ultimately turned into blessing.

There is a lesson here. It is that God can use anyone. He loves to confuse the orthodox by using the kind of people we wouldn't use. He brings a Messiah out of Nazareth, a King out of Bethlehem, disciples from a fishing boat, and the Son of God from a rough-hewn cross.

> The Mishnah (Yevamot 8:3) restricted this prohibition to males based on a reading that is somewhat obscured in translation: *"Lo yavo Ammoni"* "An Ammonite shall not come". In Hebrew, Ammoni is male, the female is "Ammonit". Now, of course, in Hebrew the male gender is supposed to include the female when the intent is to include both. The scriptural justification for this ruling was not only that Boaz married Ruth, but that Rehoboam, the son of Solomon, was the son of an Ammonite woman.
>
> The restriction was completely abolished (Berakhot 28a), reportedly in the first century, on the basis that "Sennacherib has long since mixed up all the nations" so that the contemporary inhabitants of the lands of Moab and Ammon could not be said to be descended from the Moabites and Ammonites of the Bible.

3.   Departure from the Land.

> *And the name of the man was Elimelech, and the name of his wife, Naomi; and the names of his two sons were Mahlon and Chilion, Ephrathites of Bethlehem in Judah. Now they entered the land of Moab and remained there. (Ruth 1:2).*

If there were newspapers published at that time they would have taken no notice of this family of four as they made their way to Moab. They would have reported on the latest events on the national scene. Their stories would have been on the famine, or on the prospects for another raid by the Amorites. But in God's economy, the story of Ruth is the real story.

> *Then Elimelech, Naomi's husband, died; and*

she was left with her two sons.
And they took for themselves Moabite women as wives; the name of the one was Orpah and the name of the other Ruth. And they lived there about ten years. (Ruth 1:2-4).

Elimelech means "God is King" and stands in contrast to the kingly name Abimelech "My father is King." And yet, when things got tough, this man had departed from the inherited land of his king and went to find a home in Moab.

Were things worse for Elimelech and his family than they were for the other inhabitants of Bethlehem who stayed behind? We do not know. There were evidently some who chose not to leave, but to remain in Bethlehem. We do know that neither Elimelech nor his sons ever saw their homeland again. After Elimelech had died, his two sons found for themselves wives among the Moabites, something that was forbidden in the Law (Deuteronomy 7:1-3; 23:3).

The book of Ruth neither commends nor condemns the actions of Elimelech and his sons. The point is not whether they sinned. The point is what God brought about in the midst of tragedy. Here is the lesson. You can't call a tragedy a tragedy until the entire story is known and the entire story is never known this side of heaven.

> Trying to blame the tragedy that takes place in this book on the actions of Elimelech is akin to the actions of the three friends of Job.

NAOMI'S BITTERNESS (RUTH 1:5-18)

1:3 1:5	1:6 1:18
Three Funerals	Three Decisions
Death of Elimelech Death of Mahlon and Chilion	Naomi decides to return Orpah elects to stay in Moab Ruth determines to follow Naomi

1.   The Death of Naomi's Sons.

Then both Mahlon and Chilion also died; and

the woman was bereft of her two children and her husband. (Ruth 1:5).

There are few things more tragic than a widow. One of them is a widow who has also lost her children. That was not a day of social security or life insurance. Such a state would leave Naomi unprotected in a harsh world.

2.   A Yearning for Home: *Then she arose with her daughters-in-law that she might return from the land of Moab, for she had heard in the land of Moab that the Lord had visited His people in giving them food. (Ruth 1:6).*

Naomi determines to return home to Bethlehem. Why? Because there is food there. And perhaps for another reason as well - because the "Lord had visited His people."

3.   Naomi's Care for her Daughters-in-Law.

> But Naomi said, "Return, my daughters. Why should you go with me? Have I yet sons in my womb, that they may be your husbands?
> "Return, my daughters! Go, for I am too old to have a husband. If I said I have hope, if I should even have a husband tonight and also bear sons, 13 would you therefore wait until they were grown? Would you therefore refrain from marrying? No, my daughters; for it is harder for me than for you, for the hand of the Lord has gone forth against me." (Ruth 1:11-13).

This retort of Naomi is Hebraic humor. It is not the humor of the light comedian. It is a grim humor. She is saying, "I have nothing more to offer you." Under the Levitical Law, a widow who had borne no children was to be given to the surviving brother of the deceased so that she might through such a union bear heirs to the estate of the deceased. But in this case there were no surviving brothers. And Naomi says, "There aren't any on the way."

4.   Ruth's Commitment.

Orpah finally is convinced to return to her people. She leaves and we do not hear from her again. Ruth determines otherwise.

> *But Ruth said, "Do not urge me to leave you or turn back from following you; for where you go, I will go, and where you lodge, I will lodge. Your people shall be my people, and your God, my God.*
>
> *"Where you die, I will die, and there I will be buried. Thus may the Lord do to me, and worse, if anything but death parts you and me." (Ruth 1:16-17).*

This is a solemn oath. It is a commitment of loyalty, not only to Naomi, but to the Lord. Are you loyal to your friends, even when they are wrong? I don't mean being a "yes-man." I do mean continuing to look out for their best interests.

British Prime Minister Lord Melbourne criticized the newspaper for their lack of support of his government. They wrote back, "We always support you when you are right." He replied, "I don't need your support when I'm right. I need it when I am wrong." There is enough wrong in the midst of us to go for a long way. We need to be loyal to one another, even when we are wrong.

5.   Naomi's Return.

> *So they both went until they came to Bethlehem. And it came about when they had come to Bethlehem, that all the city was stirred because of them, and the women said, "Is this Naomi?"*
>
> *And she said to them, "Do not call me Naomi; call me Mara, for the Almighty has dealt very bitterly with me.*
>
> *"I went out full, but the Lord has brought me back empty. Why do you call me Naomi, since the Lord has witnessed against me and the Almighty has afflicted me?" (Ruth 1:19-21).*

There is a play on words here. The name "Naomi" seems to carry the idea of "sweet" or "pleasant." It is used in the Proverbs where we read...

> *Stolen water is sweet;*
> *And bread eaten in secret is **pleasant** (Proverbs 9:17).*

Naomi had been known as the one who was *pleasant*. But now she insists that she be known as "Mara," meaning "bitter." It seems as though Naomi had kept everything bottled up back in Moab. But now she is back home. Home is where you can let it all out. She is bitter and her bitterness is directed against God.

6.   Barley Harvest.

> *So Naomi returned, and with her Ruth the Moabitess, her daughter-in-law, who returned from the land of Moab. And they came to Bethlehem at the beginning of barley harvest. (Ruth 1:22).*

We tend to think in terms of a harvest taking place in the fall. But in Palestine, the first harvest began in the spring. There was even a feast to commemorate this harvest. It was known as the Feast of the Firstfruits. Indeed, the book of Ruth came to be associated with this particular feast. It is into this setting that we read of the return of Naomi and Ruth. Even though Ruth had never been to Bethlehem, it is still described as a "return."

IN THE FIELDS OF BOAZ (RUTH 2)

The first chapter of Ruth reads a lot like the first chapter of Job. Everything that could go wrong did go wrong. There was a famine and Naomi lost her home and then her husband died and then her two sons died. She lost everything except her daughter-in-law.

Chapter One	Chapter Two
Begins with a Famine	Begins in the Season of Harvest
In Moab	In Bethlehem
The Shadow of Death	The Specter of New Life

With this chapter comes relief. This is a chapter of hope as it opens by introducing Boaz.

> *Now Naomi had a kinsman of her husband, a man of great wealth of the family of Elimelech, whose name was*

Boaz. (Ruth 2:1).

Boaz was "a man mighty of wealth." He also happened to be a relative of the deceased Elimelech. Here we see the "accident" of God's providence. Things don't happen just by chance. They happen because there is a divine design. Accidents do happen, but they are not just accidents, for they are a part of God's providence.

> *And Ruth the Moabitess said to Naomi, "Please let me go to the field and glean among the ears of grain after one in whose sight I may find favor." And she said to her, "Go, my daughter."*
> *So she departed and went and gleaned in the field after the reapers; and she happened to come to the portion of the field belonging to Boaz, who was of the family of Elimelech. (Ruth 2:2-3).*

Notice that Ruth is called "Ruth the Moabitess." This title shall be used a total of five times throughout this book. It is a constant reminder that she was a cultural outsider. Ruth's request was considered acceptable among the poor of Israel. The Law actually provided for the poor to enter a field on the heels of the reapers.

> *"When you reap the harvest of your land, moreover, you shall not reap to the very corners of your field, nor gather the gleaning of your harvest; you are to leave them for the needy and the alien. I am the Lord your God." (Leviticus 23:22).*

This was the Israelite version of social security. The Law mandated that the leavings of the field reapers were to be left behind for the poor and the alien to take. Ruth fit into both of these categories. She had no other means of caring for herself and Naomi.

The significant point of the story is that she happened to pick the field which belonged to Boaz. The Hebrew says that she "chanced a chance" or "her chance chanced." There is a lesson here. It is that chance is not blind - its path is directed under the eyes of the Lord. God is not only concerned with kings and princes and great battles. He is also concerned with the mundane and the everyday happenstance. They are all within the realm of His plan.

Boaz arrives and sees Ruth working in the fields. We can tell from his statements that he is immediately interested in her.

| Come and eat (2:14). |
| Help yourself to the water jars (2:9). |
| Stay here and do not go to the other fields (2:8). |
| Who is she? (2:5). |

By the time we get to verse 11, we find that Boaz has done some detailed investigation of Ruth. He has asked around about her. He is taken by what he has heard. In verse 8, he refers to her as "my daughter," indicating that he was considerably older than she.

> *Then she fell on her face, bowing to the ground and said to him, "Why have I found favor in your sight that you should take notice of me, since I am a foreigner?"*
>
> *And Boaz answered and said to her, "All that you have done for your mother-in-law after the death of your husband has been fully reported to me, and how you left your father and your mother and the land of your birth, and came to a people that you did not previously know." (Ruth 2:10-11).*

There is a play on words here which does not come through in our English translation. Ruth says, *"Why have I found favor in your sight that you should **take notice** of me (לְהַכִּירֵנִי - LeHakkiyreni), since I am a **foreigner** (נָכְרִיָּה - Nakkriyah - foreigner, one who is conspicuous or noticeable)?"*

Ruth is cognizant of the special attention which is being accorded her. She knows that she is a foreigner. And to make matters worse, she is from Moab. Moab has been an enemy of Israel. There is nothing in the Law that says Boaz has to go to the lengths which he has gone. Her question is a legitimate one. The words of Boaz to Ruth are strikingly similar to that which the Lord spoke to Abraham.

Genesis 12:1	**Ruth 2:11**
Now the Lord said to Abram...	All that you have done has been reported to me...

Go forth
     from your country
     And from your relatives
     And from your father's
     house,
	How you left
	     your father and
	     mother
	     and the land of your
	     birth,

To the land which I will show you.	And came to a people that you did not previously know

While Ruth is not a physical descendant of Abraham, she shows herself to be a spiritual descendant of him by demonstrating the faith of Abraham. And so, Boaz pronounces the Lord's blessing upon Ruth.

> *"May the Lord reward your work, and your wages be full from the Lord, the God of Israel, under whose wings you have come to seek refuge." (Ruth 2:12).*

In this blessing, Ruth is said to be seeking refuge under the wings of the Lord. This will be echoed in the following chapter when Ruth comes to Boaz to seek shelter under his wings.

ON THE THRESHING FLOOR (RUTH 3)

In this chapter the plot thickens. While the meeting of Chapter 2 was by chance, the meeting which shall take place in Chapter 3 is contrived.

Chapter Two	Chapter Three
In the Fields	On the Threshing Floor
At the beginning of the Harvest	At the end of the Harvest
Ruth's Service	Ruth's Request

We are not told how much time passed between the events of chapter 2 and the events of chapter 3. It could have been a number of days or even weeks.

Then Naomi her mother-in-law said to her, "My

daughter, shall I not seek security for you, that it may be well with you?

"And now is not Boaz our kinsman, with whose maids you were? Behold, he winnows barley at the threshing floor tonight.

"Wash yourself therefore, and anoint yourself and put on your best clothes, and go down to the threshing floor; but do not make yourself known to the man until he has finished eating and drinking.

"And it shall be when he lies down, that you shall notice the place where he lies, and you shall go and uncover his feet and lie down; then he will tell you what to do." (Ruth 3:1-4).

Naomi's question, *"My daughter, shall I not seek security* (Hebrew is "rest") *for you"* points to the fact that the lot of a widow was a difficult one. Gleaning was at best a haphazard livelihood. Therefore, Naomi wishes something better for her daughter-in-law.

Naomi instructs Ruth as to her preparations; she is to look her best. Her best clothes would be none too fancy. But it appears they were able to afford a little perfume, as the word "anoint" indicates. Naomi gives Ruth some very practical and down-to-earth advice.

- Wash yourself.
- Put on your best clothes.
- Anoint yourself (use perfume).
- Wait until the work is done and he has finished eating and drinking.

It seems that Naomi has already picked out Boaz as the future husband for Ruth. We are not told whether or not she was aware of the fact that there is a nearer kinsman (identified in chapter 4). This may have been an issue of ignorance. Or it may have been that she knew that this man was already married and was therefore not the best choice (Ruth 4:6).

After the sheaves of grain were collected, they would be placed in a large pile and then beaten with stones and spikes to separate the husks of grain from the straw on which it grew. Then a winnowing fork would be used to throw the grain into the air. The wind would carry away the lighter chaff while the heavier grain would fall to the ground.

Threshing was often down in late afternoon and evening, when a wind might arise to separate chaff from grain. The threshing floors of Palestine were found in an high, open, outdoor area which had been stamped down to make the ground hard.

When Boaz had eaten and drunk and his heart was merry, he went to lie down at the end of the heap of grain; and she came secretly, and uncovered his feet, and lay down. (Ruth 3:7).

At harvest time people would camp out. As the owner of the land, Boaz would have had a place to himself, with his servants sleeping at other places in the vicinity. Ruth waits until Boaz is sound asleep and then she comes to him.

And it happened in the middle of the night that the man was startled and bent forward; and behold, a woman was lying at his feet.

And he said, "Who are you?" And she answered, "I am Ruth, your maid. So spread your covering over your maid, for you are a close relative." (Ruth 3:8-9).

Boaz was startled by something, so he turned, or bent over, and saw Ruth lying at his feet. In reply to Boaz' question, Ruth identifies herself as a maidservant, again taking a lowly position. Ruth uses a very expressive metaphor here in asking him to spread his covering over her. The word "covering" (כָּנָף) here is the same word which is used in Ruth 2:12 where we read, *"May the Lord reward your work, and your wages be full from the Lord, the God of Israel, under whose WINGS you have come to seek refuge."* The term can describe both a "wing" as well as the edge of a garment.

> "A man shall not take his father's wife so that he shall not uncover his father's SKIRT." (Deuteronomy 22:30).

She calls Boaz a "close relative" (גֹּאֵל, *go'el*). This makes her request a formal one, and she is looking to him to resolve the legal question of redemption. Keil and Delitzsch say that the word "covering" (rendered "skirt" in the KJV) refers to the corner of the blanket which Boaz had over him. A man and wife sleeping together would share this blanket. The act of covering Ruth with part of the blanket would have been symbolic of a proposal of marriage. This is seen In Ezekiel 16:8 where the Lord describes His own actions toward Israel: *"Then I passed by you and saw you, and behold, you were at the time for love; so I spread My skirt over you and covered your nakedness. I also swore to you and entered into a covenant with you so that you became Mine," declares the Lord God.*

However, we are not told that Boaz took this action of covering Ruth with his robe. There was a legal question to be resolved before Boaz could marry Ruth. But Boaz does begin the process here which eventually leads to their marriage.

> *Then he said, "May you be blessed of the Lord, my daughter. You have shown your last kindness to be better than the first by not going after young men, whether poor or rich." (Ruth 3:10).*

Boaz's reply is immediate and positive. He thinks that Ruth has shown more kindness now than when she first came to the fields. The earlier kindness he describes was shown by Ruth in not leaving Naomi and in gleaning to provide for their needs. To this Ruth has now added a further evidence of her regard for family relationships.

Ruth has not followed natural inclinations but has shown a responsible attitude to the family in looking to her Go'el for marriage. Boaz knows that she could have married some other eligible young man in Bethlehem; but she did not let these types of personal inclinations rule her. This seems to indicate that Boaz was not a young man. There was likely a significant age difference between them. This is reinforced as he refers to her in verse 11 as "my daughter."

> *"And now, my daughter, do not fear. I will do for you whatever you ask, for all my people in the city know that you are a woman of excellence. (Ruth 3:11).*

The word translated "city" is literally "gate." As we shall see in the next chapter, the city gates was the usual place of public assembly, the place for business, judgment, and for receiving news.

Ruth is described as a "woman of excellence." The term is nearly identical to the description of Boaz in Ruth 2:1 as a "man of wealth." It is also used in Proverbs 31:10 to describe an "excellent wife." This description would seem to preclude the possibility that there was anything immoral going on between Ruth and Boaz.

> *"And now it is true that I am a close relative; however, there is a relative closer than I.*
> *"Remain this night, and when morning comes, if he will redeem you, good; let him redeem you. But if he does not wish to redeem you, then I will redeem you, as the Lord lives. Lie down until morning." (Ruth 3:12-13).*

Boaz affirms that he certainly is a kinsman; but he goes on to point out that there was a man nearer of kin then he. Ruth may have been unaware of the complexities of the family relationships and the legal implications.

Boaz binds his word with an oath. Indeed, this was the strongest possible oath: *"As the Lord lives."* To break such an oath would be to break the third commandment and thus take the name of the Lord in vain.

> *So she lay at his feet until the morning and rose before one could recognize another; and he said, "Let it not be known that the woman came to the floor." (Ruth 3:14).*

The phrase, *"before one could recognize another"* was an idiom used to describe the time before dawn. Though they had done nothing immoral during the night, Boaz takes steps to protect Ruth's reputation.

> Mishnah, Yeb. 2:8 states if a man was suspected of having intercourse with a Gentile woman he could not perform levirate marriage with her.

REDEEMED! (RUTH 4:1-12)

Chapter 2	Chapter 3	Chapter 4
In the Fields	The Threshing Floor	In the Gate
Boaz Sees	Boaz Loves	Boaz Marries

According to the Law of Moses, is was the Lord who was the actual owner of the land which He had given to His people for an inheritance. The Israelites merely had the use of the land which the Lord had given. They were stewards of God's land. Because of this, the existing possessor of the a portion of land could not part with it or sell it, but it was to remain in his family forever.

When anyone was obliged to sell his land, such as by reason of poverty, it was the duty of the nearest relation to redeem it. Even if it should not be redeemed, it would automatically come back in the next Year of Jubilee to its original owner (Leviticus 25:10-28). Therefore, no actual sale took place in our sense of the word. A sale was actually just a lease, or the sale of the yearly produce of the land until the Year of Jubilee.

The custom of Levirate marriage, or the marriage of a brother-in-law, actually predated the Mosaic Law (Genesis 38), but was also sanctioned by the Law (Deuteronomy 25:5-6). If an Israelite who had been married died without children, it was the duty of his brother to marry the widow, his sister-in-law, that he might establish his brother's name in Israel by begetting a son who should take the name of the deceased brother, that the name should not become extinct in Israel.

This son was then the legal heir of the landed property of the deceased uncle. The Law imposed this obligation upon the living brother, but it allowed him to renounce the obligation if he would take on himself the disgrace connected with such a refusal.

Early Israel had no police force. When a person was assaulted, robbed or murdered, it fell to the nearest kinsman to bring the criminal to justice and to protect the lives and property of relatives. This obligation was called "redeeming", and the man who was responsible for fulfilling this duty was known as a "redeemer" (Hebrew: *go-el*). The job of redeemer would fall to full brothers first, then to uncles who were the father's brothers, then to full cousins, and finally to the other blood relatives of the family (Leviticus 25:48). There were four requirements for the redeemer.

(1)   The redeemer must be a near kinsman.
(2)   The redeemer must be able to pay the redemption price.
(3)   The redeemer must be willing to redeem.
(4)   The redeemer must be free from that which caused the need for redemption - he must be free himself.

Jesus fulfilled all four of these requirements for the human race. He became a man and so is the kinsman of the human race. He was able to pay the price by virtue of being the sinless Son of God. He was willing to redeem. And he was free of the sin which bound us.

The nation of Israel as a whole required a Redeemer to redeem the lands which had been taken over by foreign powers, so they looked to Jehovah to become their *go-el*.

> *Now Boaz went up to the gate; and sat down there, and, behold, the close relative of whom Boaz spoke was passing by, so he said, "Turn aside, friend, sit down here." And he turned aside and sat down. (Ruth 4:1).*

The gate of a town or village played a large part in the cities of Judah in these times. Excavations reveal that cities in Palestine were very closely built, with no large open spaces like the Roman forum or the Greek agora. There was some space at the gate for people to gather and do business, and the gate was the center of city life. By coming to the gate, Boaz was in the right place to conduct legal business.

And he took ten men of the elders of the city, and said,
"Sit down here. So they sat down. (Ruth 4:2).

The idea here was to gather a sort of jury to hear the transaction and exercise some kind of judicial function. Elders had far-reaching powers. In this case, the matter was relatively minor, and the elders really had little to do or decide. But any transaction that was witnessed by the elders, and attested to by them, was of absolute validity.

> In later times, ten men were required for a synagogue service, and some commentators suggest that ten was a quorum.

Then he said to the closest relative, "Naomi, who has
come back from the land of Moab, has to sell the piece of land
which belonged to our brother Elimelech.
"So I thought to inform you, saying, 'Buy it before
those who are sitting here, and before the elders of my
people. If you will redeem it, redeem it; but if not, tell me that
I may know; for there is no one but you to redeem it, and I am
after you.'" And he said, "I will redeem it." (Ruth 4:3-4).

Boaz addresses the kinsman and informs him that Elimelech, who was related to both of them, owned some land near Bethlehem, and that the land had to be redeemed in Naomi's favor.

The title to the land would have stayed with Elimelech's family, and such a purchase would have been equivalent to a lease. To redeem the land at this time would have required a payment to the occupant for the balance of his lease. Upon Elimelech's death, the ownership of the land would have passed to his sons.

> The phrase, *"I thought to inform you"* in verse 4 is the Hebrew idiom, *"I said I will uncover your ear."*

Further, you shall speak to the sons of Israel, saying,
"If a man dies and has no son, then you shall transfer his
inheritance to his daughter.
"And if he has no daughter, then you shall give his
inheritance to his brothers.
"And if he has no brothers, then you shall give his
inheritance to his father's brothers.
"And if his father has no brothers, then you shall give
his inheritance to his nearest relative in his own family, and
he shall possess it; and it shall be a statutory ordinance to the

sons of Israel, just as the Lord commanded Moses."
(Numbers 27:8-11).

This passage shows very clearly the sequence of inheritance: first, sons; then, daughters; then, brothers; then, uncles; then, the next nearest kinsman. The widow is not mentioned in the line of inheritance!

On the other hand, it seems from this passage in Ruth that Naomi had legal rights to the land and could realize some money from it. But Ruth was the widow of Mahlon and would have had similar rights.

Verse 4 makes it clear that the kinsman is the nearer relative and Boaz is the next in line. The kinsman is quite ready to buy the land and is prepared to come up with the money. However, Boaz brings up a slight complication.

> *Then Boaz said, "On the day you buy the field from the hand of Naomi, you must also acquire Ruth the Moabitess, the widow of the deceased, in order to raise up the name of the deceased on his inheritance." (Ruth 4:5).*

The problem was that the ownership of the land was bound up with the requirement of a Levirate marriage. To take the land, one must also take Ruth.

> *And the closest relative said, "I cannot redeem it for myself, lest I jeopardize my own inheritance. Redeem it for yourself; you may have my right of redemption, for I cannot redeem it." (Ruth 4:6).*

The fact that marriage with Ruth must accompany the redemption of the field changed the whole picture for the kinsman. It is not clear what prevented the kinsman from fulfilling his obligation. He was ready to buy the field, so the money was not an issue. But he could not marry Ruth. There are several possible reasons for this:

a.   One possibility is that he did not want to marry a Moabite woman. That would have been understandable, and it probably would not have been held against him.

b.   Another reason is that paying for the land and taking on the responsibility for caring for Ruth and Naomi would have involved a considerable expense. He would pay for the land, but the land would stay with Naomi's family. So his own family would suffer the loss of some of their own inheritance.

c.   It is also possible that the kinsman may already have been married and not wanted to have a second wife. He might have been smart enough to know that his wife wouldn't be happy with him bringing home a new wife - and a foreigner at that.

d.   The reason that the kinsman gave for not wishing to marry Ruth was because he felt that such a marriage might jeopardize his own inheritance (4:6). He was eager to preserve his own lineage. And in doing so, he missed the opportunity to be a part of an eternal lineage.

Whatever the reason, the kinsman was emphatic about it, even repeating his statement so there would be no doubt.

> *Now this was the custom in former times in Israel concerning redemption and the exchange of land to confirm any matter; a man removed his sandal and gave it to another; and this was the manner of attestation in Israel.*
> *So the closest relative said to Boaz, "Buy it for yourself." And he removed his sandal. (Ruth 4:7-8).*

The author of Ruth describes this as a "custom in former times." This indicates that this ritual was no longer practiced in his day. Keil and Delitszch suggest that the custom arose from the fact that fixed property was taken possession of by treading upon the soil, and thus, taking off the shoe and handing it to another was a symbol of the transfer of a possession or right of ownership.

> *"Every place on which the sole of your foot shall tread shall be yours..." (Deuteronomy 11:24).*

In this case, there was only a symbolic transfer of the rights to purchase a property, not a transfer of the land itself. The act of handing over the shoe to Boaz was undoubtedly designed to indicate visually to the elders that a formal agreement had been reached.

> *Then Boaz said to the elders, and all the people, "You are witnesses today that I have bought from the hand of Naomi all that belonged to Elimelech and all that belonged to Chilion and Mahlon.*
> *"Moreover I have acquired Ruth the Moabitess, the widow of Mahlon, to be my wife in order to raise up the name of the deceased on his inheritance, so that the name of the*

deceased may not be cut off from his brothers or from the court of his birth place; you are witnesses today." (Ruth 4:9-10).

Here Boaz begins his speech to the elders and people. They listen in an official capacity as leaders of the city and as legal witnesses before the "court." Boaz says he will *"raise up the name of the deceased on his inheritance"* that is, he will provide a son who will carry on the name of the deceased. Then he states the same proposition in the negative, *"that the name of the deceased may not be cut off from his brothers or from the court of his birth place."*

> If a mere man could love an outcast, redeem her and bring her into fellowship with himself, how much more is God able to love all the outcasts of the world, redeem them, and bring them into fellowship with Himself.

The man who was a closer kinsman rejected Ruth because he wished to protect his own family inheritance. But Boaz, by willing to give up his own family genealogy for that of this outcast Moabitess ends up becoming a part of the most fabulous genealogy in history -- that of the Messiah. We never again hear from this other man. We do not even know his name. But the name of Boaz is repeated again and again, even in the pages of the New Testament.

Boaz concludes by reminding his hearers that they are all witnesses. Indeed, they came to be witnesses of what seemed to be a relatively unimportant proceeding, but which, from our perspective, turns out to be one of the building blocks of God's plan of redemption through the ages.

> *So Boaz took Ruth, and she became his wife; and he went in to her. And the Lord enabled her to conceive, and she gave birth to a son. (Ruth 4:13).*

The Lord "enabled her to conceive." Though she had previously been married, that marriage had not been blessed with children. Ruth had hitherto been barren.

> *Then the women said to Naomi, "Blessed is the Lord who has not left you without a redeemer today, and may his name become famous in Israel.*
>
> *"May he also be to you a restorer of life and a sustainer of your old age; for your daughter-in-law, who loves you and is better to you than seven sons, has given birth*

to him."

Then Naomi took the child and laid him in her lap, and because his nurse.

And the neighbor women gave him a name, saying "A son has been born to Naomi." So they named him Obed. He is the father of Jesse, the father of David. (Ruth 4:14-17).

The last spoken words in the book of Ruth come from the lips of these women. They were the same women who saw Naomi's return to Bethlehem when she insisted that she no longer be called Naomi ("sweet") but rather Mara ("bitter"). While the book of Ruth opens with Naomi's bitterness, it now closes with Naomi's blessedness. She was blessed because she finally had a grandchild. This child would be reckoned as Mahlon's.

Chapter 1	Chapter 4
The women see Naomi's bitterness.	The women see Naomi's blessedness
Naomi loses her children.	Naomi gains a child in the child of Ruth and Boaz.

It is because of this that Naomi is said to have a Redeemer. Note that the redeemer is not Boaz. The redeemer is the child which had been born. It is the birth of this child that would take away Naomi's reproach of childlessness. It is this child who would take care of her in her old age. And it is this child of whom it is said, *"May his name become famous* (יִקָּרֵא - "be called") *in Israel."*

Do you see the point? It is through the birth of a baby born in Bethlehem that Naomi is going to find her redemption. This baby has a name which shall be proclaimed both in Israel and throughout the world. For whoever calls upon this name shall be saved.

The story of Ruth and Naomi presents to us a paradigm for looking at the nation of Israel. Like Naomi, the nation of Israel was going to be removed from the land of promise as she goes as a captive in the Assyrian and Babylonian Captivities. Like Naomi, she will return to the land, but in a state of bitterness and of struggle and of sorrow over the loss of past glories. Like Naomi, she will eventually find redemption in the birth of a baby in Bethlehem.

Israel	**Naomi**
Taken from the land in the Assyrian and Babylonian Captivities	Taken from the land to Moab where her husband and sons die
Returns to the land, but in a lesser state of glory	Returns to the land in poverty
Finds her eventual redemption in the birth of Jesus in Bethlehem	Finds her redemption in the birth of a baby in Bethlehem

A genealogy is, to say the least of it, a curious way to end a book. The author does not tell us why he has done this, and we are left to guess.

> *Now these are the generations of Perez: to Perez was born Hezron, 19 and to Hezron was born Ram, and to Ram, Amminadab, 20 and to Amminadab was born Nahshon, and to Nahshon, Salmon, 21 and to Salmon was born Boaz, and to Boaz, Obed, 22 and to Obed was born Jesse, and to Jesse, David. (Ruth 4:18-22).*

Note the way the genealogy begins. *"Now these are the generations of Perez."* It is the same formula which is found throughout Genesis. There are ten names mentioned. The unimportant names are left off to preserve this number. That is how many names we see in the genealogy from Adam to Noah and that is how many names we see in the genealogy from Noah to Abraham. Those were carefully stylized genealogies and this is also a carefully stylized genealogy.

Through the book in all its artless simplicity there runs the note that God is supreme. He watches over people like Naomi and Ruth and Boaz and directs their paths. He never forgets His saving purposes. The child of the marriage of Boaz and Ruth was to lead in due course to the great King David, the man after God's own heart, the man in whom God's purpose was worked out.

These events in Moab and Bethlehem played their part in leading up to the birth of David. But that is not all. David is not an end unto himself. He is merely the forerunner of the Messiah. He is the king whose ultimate Son was the King of kings and Lord of lords.

Here is the point. God's hand is over all history. God works out His purpose, generation after generation. Limited as we are to one lifetime, each of us sees so little of what happens. But we need to realize that God is working out salvation, even among little people like Ruth and Boaz and such a little out-of-the-way place as Bethlehem.

Bethlehem was a nowhere place. These were unknown people. But they gave rise to a king. It was a backward country town that saw some people who were faithful in the midst of hard times. As a result, they saw a baby in a manger and angels and awe-struck shepherds.

1ⁿᵈ & 2ⁿᵈ SAMUEL
The Rise of Kings

While the spotlight of the Judges often shown on very ordinary men, that of 1st and 2nd Samuel focuses upon those who are prophet, priest, and king. These three offices are those which are held by Christ. He is the supreme prophet and priest and king. This means that as we read through the books of 1st and 2nd Samuel, we will find ourselves continually reflecting upon how these books foreshadow the person of Jesus.

THE TITLE OF THE BOOK

The books which we know as First and Second Samuel were originally written as a single book. There is no break between these two in the Masoretic Text. How did it become divided? The scroll of Samuel was probably too large and too cumbersome to be handled as a single scroll, so it was divided into two parts.

1.   The Hebrew Title: Samuel.

        The Hebrew Title is named after the first major character to appear in the book. This is misleading, since Samuel dies in the middle of 1st Samuel and is not mentioned at all in 2nd Samuel. On the other hand, Samuel served as the king-maker for both of the kings whose careers are presented in this book.

2.   The Greek Title.

        The Septuagint groups the books of Samuel with those of Kings and refers to them collectively as "the Books of Kingdoms." Thus, the Septuagint has 1st, 2nd, 3rd, and 4th Kingdoms.

3.   The Latin Title.

        Jerome's Latin Vulgate borrowed the title from the Septuagint and modified it to read *Libri Regum* - "Books of Kings."

The books of Samuel introduce us to the Kings of Israel. This also marks the unification of the Kingdom of Israel following the period of disunity under the Judges.

Israel United			Israel Divided	Judah Alone	Exile	Return
Saul	David	Solomon				
40 Years	40 Years	40 Years	210 Years	135 Years		
			Assyrian Captivity 721 B.C.	Babylonian Captivity 586 B.C.		
1 & 2 Samuel			1 & 2 Kings; 1 & 2 Chronicles		Ezekiel Daniel	Ezra Nehemiah

THE SCOPE OF THE BOOK

The books of Samuel take up where Judges leaves off. The tribes of Israel are living in the land, but are beginning to lose their national unity. There is no king in Israel and each man is doing what is right in his own eyes.

The books of 1st & 2nd Samuel take us through the establishment of the monarchy of Israel via the careers of three men: Samuel, Saul, and David.

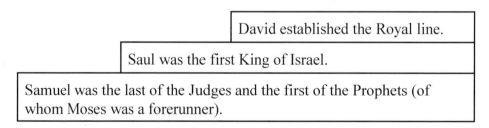

David established the Royal line.

Saul was the first King of Israel.

Samuel was the last of the Judges and the first of the Prophets (of whom Moses was a forerunner).

We are reminded that these two books were first written as a single unit when we note that they begin and end with a song. These songs serve as bookends for the 1st and 2nd Samuel narrative.

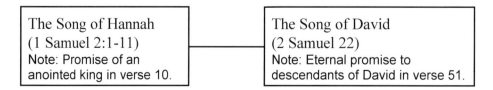

The Song of Hannah (1 Samuel 2:1-11) Note: Promise of an anointed king in verse 10.	The Song of David (2 Samuel 22) Note: Eternal promise to descendants of David in verse 51.

The first song looks forward to a future king. The second looks to God's promise of an eternal kingship and is ultimately fulfilled in Jesus. The books of 1st and 2nd Samuel can be outlined as follows:

1st Samuel			2nd Samuel	
1 - 7	8 - 15	16 - 31	1 - 10	11 - 24
The Rise and Fall of Saul			**The Rise and Fall of David**	
Samuel	Saul reigns	David runs	David reigns	David's troubles

DATE OF WRITING

We are not told either who is the writer or when this book is written. As a part of Second Samuel, it seems evident that it was written after the death of David. It is noteworthy to see how often we read of something taking place "until this day," indicating that some considerable time has passed between the event and its written presentation.

1 Samuel 5:5	*Therefore neither the priests of Dagon nor all who enter Dagon's house tread on the threshold of Dagon in Ashdod **to this day**."*
1 Samuel 6:18	*"...the large stone on which they set the ark of the Lord is a witness **to this day** in the field of Joshua the Beth-shemite."*
1 Samuel 27:6	*"...therefore Ziklag has belonged to the kings of Judah **to this day**."*
1 Samuel 30:25	*"And so it has been from that day forward, that he made it a statute and an ordinance for Israel **to this day**."*
2 Samuel 4:3	*"...the Beerothites fled to Gittaim, and have been aliens there **until this day**"*

The mention of *"kings of Judah"* in 1 Samuel 27:6 might imply that the division between Judah and Israel had already taken place at the time of this writing. It is also noteworthy that these instances seem to lessen during the

277

reign of King David, possibly indicating that the events described therein were that much closer to the writing of this book.

The Babylonian Talmud states that *"Samuel wrote the book that bears his name"* (Baba Bathra 14b), later clarifying this to refer to those chapters which take place before Samuel's death (Samuel dies in 1 Samuel 25:1). If this is the case, then a later writer would have used the account penned by Samuel as he penned the books.

1.   As the books of 1 & 2 Samuel were written as a complete unit, they had to have been written after the reign of King David.

2.   After the Division of Israel.

      1 Samuel 27:6 describes the city of Ziklag as belonging "to the kings of Judah to this day." This seems to indicate that the account is written after the division of the Kingdom. In the same way, 1 Samuel 18:16 speaks of how "all Israel and Judah loved David."

3.   The fact that the books of 1 &2 Samuel contain less Aramaisms than are found in the books of Kings might indicate that it was written at an earlier period.

4.   Written Prior to the Babylonian Captivity.

      The quote from 1 Samuel 27:6 (mentioned above) indicates that these books were written at a time when the Kings of Judah were still reigning.

Saul	David	Solomon	Israel Divided	Judah Alone	Exile
			Assyrian Captivity 721 B.C.	Babylonian Captivity 586 B.C.	
Period of Narrative			Written during this period		

PURPOSE OF THE BOOK

The two institutions of the Monarchy and the Prophetic Order come to light within the books of Samuel. Indeed, the man Samuel gives rise to both of these. He will be the last Judge of Israel. He will also serve as an acting priest, following in the stead of Eli's wicked sons, as well as king-maker of Israel's first two kings.

1.   To Define the Monarchy of Israel as it related to the Rule of God over the nation. These books show the need of a king and both the wrong motives as well as the right motives in desiring a king. It has been said that Saul was a king after the heart of the people while David was a king after God's own heart.

2.   To Legitimize the Reign of King David. It has been suggested that the two books of Samuel set forth an apologetic for the Kingship of the House and Lineage of David.

   a.   The failure of the nation under Eli shows the need of a king.

   b.   The sin of Saul and the later actions of his descendants show that the Lord has rejected Saul as king and set the House of David in his place.

   This does not mean that David is presented through rose-colored glasses. His sin with Bathsheba and his murder of Uriah are presented in open view and with no justification of his sin. However, the death of David is not described in this book (it is not seen until 1 Kings). We have noted that 1 & 2 Samuel gives internal evidence of being written well after David's reign, yet his death is not considered to be germane to the message of the book. This is because this is not primarily a biography of either Saul or David but rather a history of the Kingdom of God and its development during the reigns of these first two kings.

3.   To Emphasize the Importance of Following the Lord and Obeying His Statutes.

   The books of Samuel relate both the triumphs and the tragedies of Saul and David as they were obedient to the Lord and as they were disobedient.

   Saul's obedience leads to victory. His disobedience leads to defeat and the loss of the nation. David's obedience leads to victory and a throne. His disobedience leads to murder and revolt within his own family. In both cases, we learn that it is not enough to begin well. The race goes to the one who runs and who keeps on running well.

Both Saul and David had good beginnings. But sin entered in and brought tragic consequences.

Here is the point. The Kingdom of God grows and develops in spite of our sins. The question is not whether the Kingdom is going to grow. The question rather is whether we are going to be a part of that Kingdom or whether we are going to be cut off and cast aside.

4.   To Teach the Grace of God.

Especially in the case of David, we are witness to a wonderful picture of the mercy of God. Though he suffers greatly from the consequences of his sin, David is forgiven his sin and continues to trust in the Lord. From his experiences, we learn that failure can be overcome through repentance and faith.

RISE OF SAMUEL (1 SAMUEL 1-3)

As the book opens, Samuel is not yet born. Eli is the high priest over the nation. There is no king. Neither is there mention of any judge, although this was the period when the judges judged over Israel. And yet, the book opens, not with kings or judges or national occurrences, but with a family. In this, it is similar to the book of Ruth.

1.   The Prayer of Hannah.

This story is set in the days of the judges. It was a troubled time and this is a troubled family. We could even call it a dysfunctional family.

> *Now there was a certain man from Ramathaim-zophim from the hill country of Ephraim, and his name was Elkanah the son of Jeroham, the son of Elihu, the son of Tohu, the son of Zuph, an Ephraimite.*
> *And he had two wives: the name of the one was Hannah and the name of the other Peninnah; and Peninnah had children, but Hannah had no children. (1 Samuel 1:1-2).*

This story begins with a family. They live in the hill country of Ephraim, the land that would later be known as Samaria. Ramathaim means "two heights" (dual). Its singular form is "Ramah." 1 Chronicles 6 lists Samuel's ancestors as coming from the Kohathite branch of the tribe of Levi, though not from the priestly line of Aaron. Thus, when his father is called an "Ephraimite" it is an indication of where he lived, not his tribal origins. The Levites had no tribal inheritance of their own. The Lord was their inheritance. And so, they could be found residing in the lands of all 12 tribes. There is an interesting parallel in this opening description of this man with the opening of the Samson account in the book of Judges.

Judges 13:2	1 Samuel 1:1-2
And there was a certain man of Zorah, of the family of the Danites	*Now there was a certain man from Ramathaim-zophim from the hill country of Ephraim*
whose name was Manoah...	*and his name was Elkanah*
...and his wife was barren and had borne no children.	*...but Hannah had no children.*

In both cases, a child is given to the barren wife and this child is dedicated to the Lord for a special purpose. In both cases, the sign of this vow would be that the hair of the child would not be cut.

In verse 6 we read that Hannah's barrenness was a source of contention between the two wives. Actually, it was probably the fact that there were two wives that brought about this contention. And Hannah's barrenness was regularly used to demean her.

2. Worship in Shiloh.

> *Now this man would go up from his city yearly to worship and to sacrifice to the Lord of hosts in Shiloh. And the two sons of Eli, Hophni and Phinehas were priests to the Lord there. (1 Samuel 1:3).*

Shiloh was a city in the hill country of Ephraim to the north of Bethel (20 miles north of Jerusalem). Shiloh had been the place of worship in Canaan since the days of Joshua (Joshua 18:1). The Tabernacle and the Ark of the Covenant were located here. It was here that the regular sacrifices were made. And it was Elkanah's regular practice to come here once a year to lead his family in worship. Unfortunately, the attitudes within his family were anything but worshipful. Instead, there was friction in the family. Contention on the way to church. Nagging in the narthex. The very thing that was supposed to reflect the unity of God's people became instead a source of bickering, frustration, and tears.

Elkanah would give a double portion to Hannah which would make Peninnah jealous and then Peninnah would provoke Hannah about her barrenness and Hannah would cry to Elkanah. When Hannah goes to Elkanah with her tears, he tries to comfort her, asking, *"Am I not better to you than ten sons?"* (1:8 — note that he echoes the blessing given to Naomi in Ruth 4:15).

3.   Hannah's Prayer.

Hannah comes to the tabernacle (described here as the "temple of the Lord") with her prayer and her tears.

Her Request	*Give Thy maidservant a son*
Her Vow	*I will give him to the Lord all the days of his life*

The Lord answers her prayer and she subsequently has a son whom she names "Samuel." The name "Samuel" can either mean "name of God" or "God who hears." He was given this name because she had asked of the Lord and He had heard her prayer. But when we come to chapter 3, we shall see Samuel hearing the voice of God. There is an interesting contrast and comparison to be seen between Samuel and Jesus.

Samuel	Jesus
He was born to take away his mother's shame.	He was born to take our shame upon Himself.

He was a prophet.	He was the ultimate prophet.
He was a king maker.	He is the King of kings.

4. Dedicated to the Lord.

> *Now when she had weaned him, she took him up with her, with a three-year-old bull and one ephah of flour and a jug of wine, and brought him to the house of the Lord in Shiloh, although the child was young. (1 Samuel 1:24).*

It was common in Biblical times for breast-feeding to take place until the child was two or three years of age (2 Maccabees 7:27 describes a mother who had nursed her son until the age of three).

Though the child was still very young, Hannah brings him to the place of worship in Shiloh to dedicate him to the service of the Lord.

5. Samuel and the Sinful Sons of Eli.

There is a continuing contrast between the person of Samuel versus the sons of Eli. In chapter 1 (1:16), Eli had accused Hannah of being "a worthless woman" (בַּת־בְּלִיָּעַל - a daughter of belial). 1 Samuel 2:12 says that *"the sons of Eli were worthless men"* (בְּנֵי בְלִיָּעַל - sons of belial). The term "belial" is a compound which seems to indicate "without profit, worthless." The second chapter of 1 Samuel continues this contrast. It is a contrast between the sinful sons of Eli versus young Samuel who was *"growing in stature and in favor both with the Lord and with men"* (2:26).

The Sons of Eli	Samuel
Bullied the worshipers, despising the offering of the Lord (2:12-17).	Ministering to the Lord wearing a linen Ephod supplied annually by his mother (2:18-19).

Seducing female worshipers who had come to the tabernacle (2:22).	Elkanah and Hannah blessed and given more children (2:20-21).
Reproved by Eli for their sinful activities (2:22-25).	Growing in stature and in favor both with the Lord and with men (2:26).

Things come to a head when a man of God comes to Eli and prophesies how his house will come to an end because of the wickedness of his sons (1 Samuel 2:27-31). Both Eli and his sons will be judged. His sons will be judged for their sins, and Eli will be judged for participating in the fruits of their sins. He had "grown fat" on the offerings which should have gone to the Lord. And he had done so without rebuking them (3:13).

	Verse	Fulfillment
2:34	*"This will be the sign to you... Hophni and Phinehas: on the same day both of them shall die."*	*And the ark of God was taken; and the two sons of Eli, Hophni and Phinehas, died (1 Samuel 4:11).*
2:35	*"I will raise up for Myself a faithful priest... I will build him an enduring house, and he will walk before My anointed always"*	Samuel & his Descendants (1 Chronicles 6:23; 6:33). Zadok & his Descendants (1 Chronicles 29:22). The ultimate fulfillment is Christ who became our High Priest.

Notice the contrast. It is the same contrast which always divides humanity. It is the contrast between those who are faithful to the Lord and those who reject the word of

> The last descendant of Phinehas will be the priest Abiathar who will seek to crown Adonijah as king instead of Solomon (1 Kings 1:7).

the Lord. Even though Hophni and Phinehas are physical descendants of Aaron, their priesthood becomes a false and a rejected priesthood. And even though Samuel is not of the right pedigree to be a proper priest, he is the one whom God will choose.

The theme begun in Genesis 3:15 continues here in this passage. Hophni and Phinehas have shown themselves to be followers of the Serpent. They shall be replaced by Samuel, the promised seed of the woman. The lesson of this passage applies to more than priests and prophets and Bible teachers. The New Testament teaches that all believers are part of a royal priesthood (1 Peter 2:9). The question is to what priesthood you belong.

	Chapter 1	Chapter 2	Chapter 3
Failure	Penniah sinks to obscurity	Eli & Sons condemned	Eli's line is to end
Victory	Hannah has Samuel	Samuel grows great before the Lord before men	Replaced by an enduring house

The prophecy of the demise of the sons of Eli is followed by a similar revelation that is given to the young Samuel. This is prefaced by the observation that *word from the Lord was rare in those days, visions were infrequent* (1 Samuel 3:1). This reminds us that the Old Testament was not an era when God was constantly speaking through His prophets. Knowing this will help us to understand that there are periods of history when prophecy is not to be found.

As Eli and Samuel lay sleeping, the Lord called to Samuel (3:4). Samuel had never before heard the voice of the Lord. And so, it is only natural that he assumed that Eli was calling to him. This happened three times. After the third time, Eli realized that there was no one else in the Tabernacle and that the Lord was calling Samuel.

This is a wonderful picture of God coming quietly to His Tabernacle. He came to where the ark was. He did this ultimately in the person of Jesus. The incarnation took place when God "tabernacled" with men.

> *Thus Samuel grew and the Lord was with him and let none of his words fail. 20 And all Israel from Dan even to Beersheba knew that Samuel was confirmed as a prophet of the Lord. (1 Samuel 3:19-20).*

Samuel will be ultimately seen as prophet, priest, and king-maker. His ministry was recognized the entire length of the land. As such, he is the bridge that spans the last of the judges to take us to the period of the kings.

THE ARK OF THE LORD

The entire book of Samuel consists of contrasting "ups and downs." In chapters 4-7, those changing fortunes focus primarily upon the Ark of the Covenant. As goes the ark, so will go the fortunes of the people surrounding the ark.

	Chapters 1-3	Chapters 4-6	Chapter 6-7
Failure	Eli's Line ↘	Ark Lost ↘	People of Beth-shemesh struck down ↘
Victory	Samuel ↗	Ark Returned ↗	Philistines struck down ↗

1.   Defeat at the hands of the Philistines.

> *Thus the word of Samuel came to all Israel. Now Israel went out to meet the Philistines in battle and camped beside Ebenezer while the Philistines camped in Aphek.*
> *And the Philistines drew up in battle array to meet Israel. When the battle spread, Israel was defeated before the Philistines who killed about four thousand men on the battlefield. (1 Samuel 4:1-2).*

For years there had been discord between the Philistines in the lowlands and the Israelites who lived in the hills. Indeed, the reason that the Israelites lived in the hills is because the Philistines had iron chariots and this gave them greater mobility in the lowlands and made them masters of the coastal areas (Judges 1:19). But now, for the first time, the Israelites fight a pitched battle against the Philistines. The result is disastrous.

1 Samuel 4:1 tells us that this battle took place at Ebenezer. It was at this time that this place received that name. The name "Ebenezer" (אֶבֶן הָעֵזֶר) is a compound made up of the joining of two words.

- אֶבֶן (*eben*) is the word for "stone."

- עֵזֶר (*ezer*) is the word, "help."

It therefore means "the stone of help." Unfortunately, there was no help for the people of Israel on that day. The Israelites suffered a great defeat, losing 4,000 men on the battlefield.

> *So the people sent to Shiloh and from there*
> *they carried the ark of the covenant of the Lord of*
> *hosts who sits above the cherubim; and the two sons*
> *of Eli, Hophni and Phinehas, were there with the ark*
> *of the covenant of God. (1 Samuel 4:3-4).*

In light of their defeat, the Israelites determine to bring the ark of the covenant with them into their next battle against the Philistines. They are thinking of it as a good like charm. The second battle is another defeat for Israel.

First Battle of Ebenezer	4,000 Israelites killed
Second Battle of Ebenezer	30,000 Israelites killed The ark is taken Hophni & Phinehas are killed

When Eli hears the news that the ark has been taken, he falls backward off his seat, breaks his neck and dies *"for he was old and heavy"* (4:18).

2. The Ark in the Land of the Philistines.

Chapter 5 records the travels of the ark of the covenant after it had fallen into the hands of the Philistines.

Verse	City	Occurrences
5:1	Ashdod	Idol of Dagon is found on its face. The next day, it is again on its face, this time with head and hands removed. People broke out with tumors.
5:8	Gath	A very great confusion and the men of the city smitten with tumors.

5:10	Ekron	A very great confusion. The men who did not die were smitten with a physical affliction.

The ark was considered to be the throne of God. God was described as *"the Lord of hosts who sits above the cherubim"* (4:4). Since the God of Israel was invisible, His presence could only be determined by the place where He would sit.

"Dagon" (דָּגוֹן) was the god of the Philistines. Though the name is similar to דָּג (*dag*), the Hebrew word for "fish," more recent archaeological studies have identified Dagon as a Canaanite deity which had

> We are struck by the superstition of both Israel and the Philistines in their dealings with the Ark. But we are often guilty of similar superstitions when we play our own pseudo-spiritual games in an attempt to manipulate the Almighty.

been borrowed by the Philistines. In Ugaritic literature he is the father of Baal. Dagon was the god of **grain** (דָּגָן, *dagan*). The significance of the idol being found face down before the ark of the Lord is obvious. And when, the following day, the people found the idol again face down and this time with its head and hands removed, it is an obvious indication that Yahweh had defeated Dagon in battle and had removed these battle trophies, much the same way that David would later remove the head of Goliath.

In 1 Samuel 5:6 we read that the inhabitants of Ashdod were afflicted with "tumors." The Hebrew term (עֳפָלִים, *ephalim*) refers to a "swelling" and can indeed refer to a tumor or a boil or a physical swelling. Aren Maeir has suggested that this is a reference to male sexual disfunction, noting that it is specifically the males who were so afflicted in 1 Samuel 5:9 and that examples of small vial-shaped vessels have been discovered that seem to represent uncircumcised, non-erect phalluses. This is significant because 1 Samuel 6:4 describes the Philistines fashioning golden *ephalim* to send as an offering. [1]

No matter how we understand these *ephalim*, a motif is introduced in this chapter. It is the motif of the hand of the Lord. Though the term is used as early as the book of Exodus, it is not

---

[1] *Did Captured Ark Afflict Philistines with E.D.?*, Biblical Archaeology Review, May-June 2008.

commonplace until we get to this chapter.

5:6	*"Now the **hand** of the Lord was heavy on the Ashdodites..."*
5:7	*"...His **hand** is severe on us and on Dagon our god."*
5:9	*"...the **hand** of the Lord was against the city..."*
5:11	*"...the **hand** of God was very heavy there."*
6:3	*"...it shall be known why His **hand** is not removed from you."*
6:5	*"...perhaps He will ease His **hand** from you, your gods, and your land."*
6:9	*"...His **hand** that struck us..."*
7:13	*"And the **hand** of the Lord was against the Philistines all the days of Samuel."*

There are several lessons that we learn from this chapter.

- God wins, even when those who claim His name do not win. The defeat of the Israelites did not constitute a defeat for the Lord.
- Idolatry is not exclusively an Old Testament sin. There are other forms of idolatry besides bowing down to a graven image. 1 John 5:21 warns to guard yourselves from idols.
- In Colossians 3:5, Paul is listing a number of sins and when he comes to greed, he states that it *amounts to idolatry.* If there is something for which Americans are known, it is their greed and materialism. This verse teaches that this is nothing less than a modern form of idolatry.

3.   The Ark Returns to Israel.

After seven months of passing the ark from city to city, the Philistines determine to send it back home to the land of the Israelites. They do so, sending it back with an offering of five golden tumors and five golden mice (hoping that this would take away the plagues of tumors). They place these along with the ark onto a cart pulled by two cows.

> *And the cows took the straight way in the direction of Beth-shemesh; and they went along the highway, lowing as they went, and did not turn aside to the right or to the left. And the lords of the Philistines followed them to the border of Beth-shemesh.*
>
> *Now the people of Beth-shemesh were reaping their wheat harvest in the valley, and they raised their eyes and saw the ark and were glad to see it.*
>
> *And the cart came into the field of Joshua the Beth-shemite and stood there where there was a large stone; and they split the wood of the cart and offered the cows as a burnt offering to the Lord. (1 Samuel 6:12-14).*

Beth-shemesh is located on the east end of the Sorek Valley, near to where Samson had lived. Its name means "house of the sun." It had been allotted in the days of Joshua to the priests (Joshua 21:16).

These people, working out in their fields, look up to see a strange procession. A pair of oxen pulling a cart on which rests the throne of God. And behind them come five kings and all of their retainers. It was as though the Lord were leading all of the enemies of Israel in a triumphant parade. The people of Beth-shemesh respond in worship, taking apart the cart on which the ark was transported and using both the wood and the oxen as a sacrifice to the Lord.

> *And He struck down some of the men of Beth-shemesh because they had looked into the ark of the Lord. He struck down all the people, 50,070 men, and the people mourned because the Lord had struck down the people with a great slaughter. (1 Samuel 6:19).*

The Philistines had suffered because of the presence of the ark in their cities, but the Israelites were no less immune to the results of a careless treatment of the ark. It is not as though they were ignorant of the importance of the ark. These were Levites. They would have been familiar with the requirements of the Law. They would have known that, in the days in the Wilderness, only the sons of Aaron had been permitted to handle the ark - that even they did not presume to look within the ark, but reverently covered it with a veil each time they were required to move it (Numbers 4:5-20).

There is a lesson here. It is dangerous to trifle with the Lord. He is very big and very powerful and we must never think that we have a handle on Him. Sometimes we get to thinking that God is a Presbyterian. Or a Republican. Or a Charismatic. And we think that we have placed Him into our nice, neat package. And suddenly, He does something like this and we find ourselves with a proper awe of the Lord.

The number translated as 50,070 men reads differently in the Hebrew text (70 men, 50,000 men). Aside from the fact that there were not this many men in the town of Beth-shemesh, the construction of the Hebrew suggests that this reading might be the result of a textual error, even though this is not apparent from either the Massoretic text or from the Septuagint.

4.   The Ark in Kiriath-jearim.

> *And the men of Kiriath-jearim came and took the ark of the Lord and brought it into the house of Abinadab on the hill, and consecrated Eleazar his son to keep the ark of the Lord.*
>
> *And it came about from the day that the ark remained at Kiriath-jearim that the time was long, for it was twenty years; and all the house of Israel lamented after the Lord. (1 Samuel 7:1-2).*

Demoralized by the death of their men, the people of Beth-shemesh sent the ark 10 miles up the road to the town of Kiriath-jearim (only 8 miles from Jerusalem). It is placed into the keeping of Abinadab and his son Eleazar. The ark will remain there until being brought to Jerusalem in the days of David.

This was a period of lamentation. The people of Israel *"lamented after the Lord."* Why? Because their place of worship had been destroyed and their God was in a state of banishment.

5.   Victory Returns to Israel.

> *Then Samuel spoke to all the house of Israel, saying, "if you return to the Lord with all your heart, remove the foreign gods and the Ashtaroth from among you and direct your hearts to the Lord and serve Him alone; and He will deliver you from the*

hand of the Philistines."
So the sons of Israel removed the Baals and
the Ashtaroth and served the Lord alone. (1 Samuel
7:3-4).

It was not only the priests and spiritual leaders of the nation who had been in sin. The Israelites had begun to engage in idol-worship. Samuel calls for repentance. This repentance is threefold:

- Remove the foreign gods.
- Direct your hearts to the Lord.
- Serve Him alone.

Notice that they were not merely called to serve the Lord. They were called to serve God alone. They are to serve Him and are to serve no other. Jesus pointed out this principle when He said that *"no one can serve two masters; for either he will hate the one and love the other, or he will hold to one and despise the other"* (Matthew 6:24).

Now when the Philistines heard that the sons
of Israel had gathered to Mizpah, the lords of the
Philistines went up against Israel. And when the sons
of Israel heard it, they were afraid of the Philistines.
Then the sons of Israel said to Samuel, "Do
not cease to cry to the Lord our God for us, that He
may save us from the hand of the Philistines." (1
Samuel 7:7-8).

What was it that caused the Philistines to attack Israel at this particular time? It was because they heard that the Israelites had gathered at Mizpah. Perhaps they viewed this gathering as a military threat.

Samuel views this as a spiritual battle. He does not outwardly prepare the men for battle. He doesn't beat any plowshares into swords. He doesn't suggest an armament plan or devise a strategy. Instead, he performs an act of worship.

Now Samuel was offering up the burnt
offering, and the Philistines drew near to battle
against Israel. But the Lord thundered with a great
thunder on that day against the Philistines and

*confused them, so that they were routed before Israel.
And the men of Israel went out of Mizpah and
pursued the Philistines, and struck them down as far
as below Beth-car. (1 Samuel 7:10-11).*

The Lord wins the battle and He does so in a way that is reminiscent of the days of Joshua. You remember the story. Joshua was fighting an alliance of five kings and he called upon the sun and the moon to stand still and they obeyed him. The Lord sent great hailstones against the enemies of Israel which killed more than were killed in the fighting. The Israelites pursued their enemies down the descent of Beth-horon.

Now it happens again. An alliance of five kings. A prayer to the Lord. An answer from the skies and a victory in which the Israelites pursue their enemies down the valley (This is the same valley in which lies Beth-car).

If I had been there prior to the battle, I might have been tempted to say, "Hey guys, I know that God used to do this sort of thing, but times have changed. That was a long time ago in another age and God doesn't do that sort of thing anymore." The lesson here is that we dare not underestimate the power of God.

*Then Samuel took a stone and set it as far as
below Beth-car and Shen, and named it Ebenezer,
saying, "Thus far the Lord has helped us." (1 Samuel
7:12).*

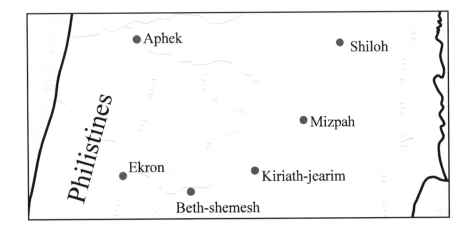

This does not seem to be the same Ebenezer as the one mentioned in chapter 4:1 and 5:1. That first Ebenezer was located near Aphek (4:1). This Ebenezer is between Mizpah and Shen. That first Ebenezer was a place of defeat. This second Ebenezer is a stone of victory. And so, Samuel establishes it as a memorial.

THE RISE OF KING SAUL

From the days in the wilderness, God had told the Israelites that one day they would have a king (Deuteronomy 17:14-17). And yet, it had been understood up to this point that GOD was their king. When the Israelites had offered the kingship to Gideon, he had refused, insisting that *"the Lord shall rule over you"* (Judges 8:23). That changes as we come to this chapter. For the first time, there will be a legitimate king over Israel.

Chapter 8	Chapter 9	Chapter 10	Chapter 11	Chapter 12
A King Requested	A King Chosen		King Goes Forth	Kingdom Admonished
The People request a king	Saul comes to Samuel	Saul Anointed	Saul's call to arms	Samuel's call to commitment

The need for a king is introduced as we look at the character of the two sons of Samuel.

> *And it came about when Samuel was old that he appointed his sons judges over Israel.*
> *Now the name of his first-born was Joel, and the name of his second, Abijah; they were judging in Beersheba.*
> *His sons, however, did not walk in his ways, but turned aside after dishonest gain and took bribes and perverted justice. (1 Samuel 8:1-3).*

Chapter 7 ends on a positive note. The Lord has delivered the Israelites from the Philistine threat and Israel repossesses all of the disputed holdings from Ekron to Gath (7:14). But over the course of years, Samuel grew older and was succeeded by his two sons. Their judging was

It is questionable whether it was proper for Samuel to appoint his sons as judges in the first place. The office of judge was an appointment from the Lord and was not passed from father to son.

characterized by dishonesty and corruption. They followed after a perversion of justice. There is a parallel here between Samuel and Eli. They both judged Israel. They both had two sons. Their sons acted wickedly and were rejected. Perhaps Samuel had learned his parenting skills from Eli. The good news is that he does not seem to have been partaking in their sinful behavior the way in which Eli did. Because his sons were not fit to succeed him, the Israelites perceived a need for a king.

> *Then all the elders of Israel gathered together and came to Samuel at Ramah; 5 and they said to him, "Behold, you have grown old, and your sons do not walk in your ways. Now appoint a king for us to judge us like all the nations." (1 Samuel 8:4-5).*

In verse 1, Samuel had **appointed** his sons to be judges over Israel. Now the elders ask Samuel to **appoint** a king to judge them. There are several things which ought to be mentioned in defense of Israel's request for a king:

- The request was initiated because of the ungodly successors to Samuel. In verse 20 they shall add that they are seeking one who would fight their battles.
- Instead of seeking a king on their own, they sought the right man from the spokesman of the Lord.
- God had told the Israelites that one day they would have a king (Deuteronomy 17:14-17).

Nevertheless, their request was perceived as a rejection, not only of Samuel and his sons, but even of the Lord who tells Samuel that *"they have not rejected you, but they have rejected Me from being king over them"* (8:7). One of the problems with a king was that many of the surrounding nations considered their kings to be gods. The Lord issues a warning of what it will mean for the Israelites to have a king to reign over them.

- He will draft your sons into his military (8:11).
- He will conscript people to do his plowing and harvesting and to manufacture his weapons of war (8:12).
- He will take your daughters for household duties (8:13).
- He will take your lands and vineyards and groves and give them to his retainers (8:14).
- He will tax the produce of your land (8:15).
- He will take your servants and animals (8:16).
- He will take you (8:17).

They have come and asked the Lord for a king. Before it is all over, they will come and ask God to take their king back (8:18). The lesson here is that you be careful for what you pray. You might get it.

The scene suddenly shifts to a young man named Saul. He is described as one of valiant heritage and of personal distinction.

> "...a choice and handsome man, and there was not a more handsome person than he among the sons of Israel, from his shoulders and up he was taller than any of the people." (1 Samuel 9:2).

The word translated "handsome" is טוֹב (*tov*, "good"). We would say that he was "a fine figure of a man." He was a man's man, literally head and shoulders above the rest of his countrymen. And that is not all, he seems to have initially been a capable leader and one who was willing to follow the Lord. Unfortunately, he does not stay that way. The career of Saul is set forth in three acts, each of which consists of several parallel scenes.

	Act 1	**Act 2**	**Act 3**
Scene 1	Saul meets Samuel and is anointed by him (9-10)	Saul meets Samuel and is condemned by him (15).	Saul meets Samuel and his death is foretold (28).
Scene 2	Success in battle with the help of God (11).	Success in battle with the help of David (17-18).	Failure in battle and suicide (31).
Scene 3	Saul's failure before Samuel and Jonathan (13-14).	Saul's failure before David (19-26).	

1.   Saul's Anointing.

Saul comes on the scene, not seeking a kingdom or a throne, but looking for some lost donkeys. As they are about to give up on their quest, Saul's servant suggests that they go and inquire from the local Seer about the missing donkeys. They discuss this plan. Saul is reluctant because they have no gift to give to the Seer. But the servant has a quarter of a shekel of silver. This was not a coin, for coinage would not be invented until the 7th century B.C. This was a weight.

Meanwhile, the Lord had revealed to Samuel that a man was coming from the tribe of Benjamin who would be anointed as the deliverer of the Israelites. Thus, when Saul arrives at the gate of the city, he is met by Samuel who informs him that the donkeys have been found and then proceeds to invite him as the guest of honor to a special dinner.

> *Then Samuel took the flask of oil, poured it on his head, kissed him and said, "Has not the Lord anointed you a ruler over His inheritance?" (1 Samuel 10:1).*

What was the significance of anointing someone with oil? It was a sign of sanctification - of setting apart for a special purpose. It was also a sign of the Spirit of God. Isaiah would later write:

> *The Spirit of the Lord God is upon me,*
> *Because the Lord has anointed me*
> *To bring good news to the afflicted... (Isaiah 61:1a).*

Saul is given three signs which are to serve as witnesses that this anointing is truly from God.

Sign #1	Two men inform him that the donkeys have been found.
Sign #2	Three men on their way to worship the Lord give him two loaves of bread.
Sign #3	Saul meets a group of prophets and the Spirit of God comes upon him and he prophesies.

The third of these signs is particularly striking and has been the subject of considerable speculation.

> *When they came to the hill there, behold, a group of prophets met him; and the Spirit of God came upon him mightily, so that he prophesied among them.*
> *And it came about, when all who knew him previously saw that he prophesied now with the*

prophets, that the people said to one another, "What has happened to the son of Kish? Is Saul also among the prophets?"

And a man there answered and said, "Now, who is their father?" Therefore it became a proverb: "Is Saul also among the prophets?" (1 Samuel 10:10-12).

This mysterious experience would be repeated later in Saul's life (see 1 Samuel 19:20-24). What was this experience and why did it take place.? It was a manifestation of the filling of the Holy Spirit. It took place as a confirmation that Saul was to be the next king of Israel.

Does this mean that the filling of the Spirit must always be accompanied with such a sign? Not at all. Here it is accompanied by prophesying. In Acts 2 it is accompanied by tongues and flames of fire. In Exodus 28:3 and 31:3 is was accompanied by skilled workmanship on the part of the designers of the tabernacle. In Judges 15:14 it resulted in Samson's great strength. In Acts 4:8 is was accompanied by a holy boldness.

What is the point? It is that God does not always have to do things the same way. We should be careful when building doctrines based on historical passages.

2.   Saul's Public Selection as King.

> *Thereafter Samuel called the people together to the Lord at Mizpah (1 Samuel 10:17).*

The name "Mizpah" means "watchtower" -- literally, "place of watching." There were several Mizpahs throughout the land. This Mizpah was likely the place where the Lord had last delivered the Israelites from the attack of the Philistines (1 Samuel 7:5-11). It had since become one of the regular points along Samuel's traveling circuit (1 Samuel 7:16).

> *Thus Samuel brought all the tribes of Israel near, and the tribe of Benjamin was taken by lot.*
> *Then he brought the tribe of Benjamin near by its families, and the Matrite family was taken. And Saul the son of Kish was taken; but when they looked for him, he could not be found.*

> *Therefore he inquired further of the Lord,*
> *"Has the man come here yet?" So the Lord said,*
> *"Behold, he is hiding himself by the baggage."*
>
> *So they ran and took him from there, and when*
> *he stood among the people, he was taller than any of*
> *the people from his shoulders upward.*
>
> *And Samuel said to all the people, "Do you*
> *see him whom the Lord has chosen? Surely there is*
> *no one like him among all the people." So all the*
> *people shouted and said, "Long live the king!" (1*
> *Samuel 10:20-24).*

There is a touch of irony here. When we first saw Saul, he was being sent to look for missing donkeys. Now it is Saul who is missing and the people go looking for him. They find him hiding by the baggage.

Remember, being a king was not something for which Saul had been seeking. He had come on the scene seeking nothing but a pair of lost donkeys. Now that he is chosen, he is still reluctant to take up the mantle of kingship.

There will come a time when that mantle of kingship will be taken away from Saul and he will be equally reluctant to give it up. We shall find it much easier to take things up and to give things up as we realize that those things are given and taken by the Lord. Anything coming into your life comes via a nail-scarred hand. Anything that is taken away is taken by that same hand.

3.   Saul's Mixed Reception.

> *And Saul also went to his house at Gibeah;*
> *and the valiant men whose hearts God had touched*
> *went with him.*
>
> *But certain worthless men said, "How can this*
> *one deliver us?" And they despised him and did not*
> *bring him any present. But he kept silent. (1 Samuel*
> *10:26-27).*

What happened after Saul had been proclaimed the first king of Israel? Did he move into the royal palace? He did not. There was no royal palace into which he could move. And so, when the celebration was over, there was nothing else for him to do but to return home. When next we see him, he will be at the south end of a northbound team of oxen.

Israel at this time was nothing more than a scattered and disunited collection of tribes. This was not a unified nation. You couldn't even get them to agree on what to eat for lunch. And they also did not agree that Saul should be their new king, no matter what Samuel had told them. But this changed dramatically when Saul led the Israelites to victory in battle.

4.   Saul's Victory against the Ammonites.

> *Now Nahash the Ammonite came up and besieged Jabesh-gilead; and all the men of Jabesh said to Nahash, "Make a covenant with us and we will serve you."*
>
> *But Nahash the Ammonite said to them, "I will make it with you on this condition, that I will gouge out the right eye of every one of you, thus I will make it a reproach on all Israel."*
>
> *And the elders of Jabesh said to him, "Let us alone for seven days, that we may send messengers throughout the territory of Israel. Then, if there is no one to deliver us, we will come out to you." (1 Samuel 11:1-3).*

There was bad blood between the Ammonites and the Israelites. The Ammonites were descendants of Lot through his incestuous relationship with one of his daughters (the name Ammon means "my father"). They occupied the territory north of the Arnon River and east of the Dead Sea. They had joined Moab in invading Israel and taking Jericho in the days of Ehud (Judges 3:12-13). They had also warred with Israel in the days of Jephthah and had been defeated by him, losing a number of their border cities to him (Judges 10-11).

Now they were back. The city which they were now attacking was Jabesh-gilead. By strange coincidence, this is the same city which had been destroyed by the Israelites for not joining in the punitive attack against the tribe of Benjamin following the incident at Gibeah in which a Levite's concubine was raped and then dismembered (Judges 19-21).

The city had since been rebuilt and was again inhabited. It is now being attacked, not by Israel, but by Ammon. And because of her past history, it seems doubtful that anyone will come to her aid.

Except for a man from the tribe of Benjamin - Saul's tribe. And specifically, a man of Gibeah - Saul's city.[2]

Judges 19-21	1 Samuel 11
Takes place when Israel had no king.	Becomes the confirming event of Saul's kingship.
Gibeah becomes a city destined to be destroyed for her sins.	Gibeah becomes the city from which salvation goes forth.
Jabesh-gilead refuses to join in Israel's call for punishment against wicked Gibeah.	Jabesh-gilead is besieged and asks for help from Israel.
Benjamin becomes the object of attack.	Benjamin becomes the leader in this holy war.

Then the Spirit of God came upon Saul mightily when he heard these words, and he became very angry.

And he took a yoke of oxen and cut them in pieces, and sent them throughout the territory of Israel by the hand of messengers, saying, "Whoever does not come out after Saul and after Samuel, so shall it be done to his oxen." Then the dread of the Lord fell on the people, and they came out as one man.

And he numbered them in Bezek; and the sons of Israel were 300,000, and the men of Judah 30,000. (1 Samuel 11:6-8).

---

[2] Scroll 4QSam[a] of the Dead Sea Scrolls contains the following additional paragraph by way of explanation:

"Nahash king of the Ammonites sorely oppressed the Gadites and the Reubenites, and he gouged out all their right eyes and struck terror and dread in Israel. Not a man was left among the Israelites beyond Jordan whose right eye was not gouged out by Nahash king of the Ammonites, except for seven thousand men who fled from the Ammonites and entered Jabesh Gilead." (4QSam[a]).

Just as the Israelites had been called to arms against Gibeah by the cutting up of the body of the murdered concubine, so this

> It is possible that the term אֶלֶף ("thousand") is to be understood in a more general sense as a military unit.

time two oxen are cut up and their pieces sent throughout the land as a call to arms. Gibeah which was formerly in need of the heavy hand of punishment has now become the rallying point of salvation for God's people.

And it happened the next morning that Saul put the people in three companies; and they came into the midst of the camp at the morning watch, and struck down the Ammonites until the heat of the day. And it came about that those who survived were scattered, so that no two of them were left together. (1 Samuel 11:11).

Having assembled at the town of Bezek on the mountains of Gilboa, Saul and his force cross the Jordan River and attack the Ammonites just before sunrise. The result is an overwhelming victory.

It is noteworthy that it would be at this same locale on the mountains of

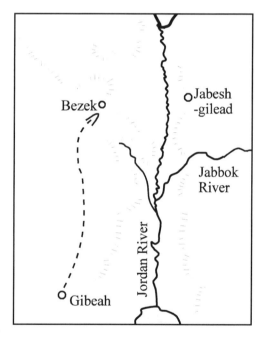

Gilboa that Saul would eventually fight his last battle. And when his body is mutilated and hung up on the wall of the city of Beth-shan, it will be men of Jabesh-gilead who will rescue the body and give it a proper burial.

Flushed with their victory, the people call for the death of those who had originally refused to follow Saul as king. Saul refuses, requiring leniency, pointing out that it is the Lord who has accomplished deliverance.

5.   Saul's Coronation at Gilgal.

> *Then Samuel said to the people, "Come and let us go to Gilgal and renew the kingdom there."*
> *So all the people went to Gilgal, and there they made Saul king before the Lord in Gilgal. There they also offered sacrifices of peace offerings before the Lord; and there Saul and all the men of Israel rejoiced greatly. (1 Samuel 11:14-15).*

Gilgal was located on the western bank of the Jordan River. It was here that Joshua and the Israelites first camped after crossing the Jordan River. They had built a monument here of 12 memorial stones. And it was here that the Israelites had renewed the covenant, circumcising all of the men in the camp. Gilgal will be the scene both of Saul's coronation, his rebuke, and his ultimate rejection as king.

THE FALL OF KING SAUL

Saul is the story of a great beginning. But the spiritual life is not limited to beginnings. It is not a sprint. It is, instead, a marathon. Saul had made an excellent beginning. This young man who had come on the scene looking for lost donkeys had instead found himself as the redeemer of Israel and her first king. The tragedy of his story begins in chapters 13-15.

Chapter 13	Chapter 14	Chapter 15
Jonathan's victory over the Philistines at Geba	Jonathan's victory over the Philistine garrison at Michmash	Saul's victory over the Amalekites
Saul disobeys the law by offering sacrifices	Saul makes an oath of hunger which Jonathan inadvertently disobeys	Saul disobeys God by sparing the life of Agag, king of the Amalekites.

1.   The Years of Saul's Reign.

1 Samuel 13:1 has several variant readings which have puzzled scholars over the years. This is reflected in the various English translations.

303

KJV & NKJV	*Saul reigned one year; and when he had reigned two years over Israel...*
NAS	*Saul was forty years old when he began to reign, and he reigned thirty-two years over Israel.*
NIV	*Saul was thirty years old when he became king, and he reigned over Israel forty-two years.* (Taken from a few late manuscripts of the LXX).
RSV	*Saul was...years old when he began to reign; and he reigned...and two years over Israel.*

The King James Version attempts to reflect the Hebrew numerals of the Massoretic Text. However, this phrasing seems out of character and most scholars today believe it to be in error. Indeed, a literal rendering of the Hebrew text would read: *"Saul was a year old when he began to reign; and he reigned two years over Israel."* The Septuagint omits the entire verse. The Latin Vulgate translates the Hebrew literally. Acts 13:21 says that Saul reigned for 40 years, but this might be a round number (the NAS translators viewed 32 years of Saul's reign + 7½ years of Ishbosheth).

2.   Attack on the Geba Garrison.

> *Now Saul chose for himself 3,000 men of Israel, of which 2,000 were with Saul in Michmash and in the hill country of Bethel, while 1,000 were with Jonathan at Gibeah of Benjamin. But he sent away the rest of the people, each to his tent.*
> *And Jonathan smote the garrison of the Philistines that was in Geba, and the Philistines heard of it. Then Saul blew the trumpet throughout the land, saying, "Let the Hebrews hear."*
> *And all Israel heard the news that Saul had smitten the garrison of the Philistines, and also that Israel had become odious to the Philistines. The people were then summoned to Saul at Gilgal. (1 Samuel 13:2-4).*

The Philistines had last been mentioned in chapter 7 where they had been driven from the territory of Israel and had retreated to their own cities by the sea. Now they were back. They had infiltrated east into the mountains of central Canaan, establishing a garrison at Geba.

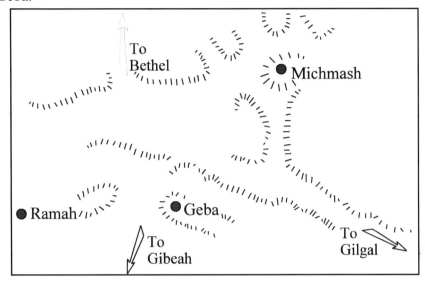

Saul had split his meager forces into two parties. There were 2000 men under his command both at Michmash and stationed in the hill country around Bethel. Another 1000 were with Jonathan to the south at Gibeah. Jonathan was able to take the initiative, capturing the garrison at Geba. This had the same effect as kicking over a hornets nest. It infuriated the Philistines and brought about an immediate retaliation.

> *Now the Philistines assembled to fight with Israel, 30,000 chariots and 6,000 horsemen, and people like the sand which is on the seashore in abundance; and they came up and camped in Michmash, east of Beth-aven.*
>
> *And when the men of Israel saw that they were in a strait (for the people were hard-pressed), then the people hid themselves in caves, in thickets, in cliffs, in cellars, and in pits.*
>
> *Also some of the Hebrews crossed the Jordan into the land of Gad and Gilead. But as for Saul, he was still in Gilgal, and all the people followed him trembling. (1 Samuel 13:5-7).*

The Philistine response to the destruction of their garrison was an all-out invasion of the Israelite territories. They boasted a thoroughly modern army against the under-equipped and untrained Israelite militia. Saul was forced to retreat to Gilgal. This was the place where the Israelites had first crossed the Jordan to enter the Promised Land under Joshua. The memorial stones still stood here. But in the face of this

> For many years, the Philistines had kept the process of smelting iron ore a closely guarded secret. This gave them a monopoly on iron weapons.

overwhelming enemy, the people were not remembering the past victories of the Lord. Instead, they were hiding. Some were going back across the Jordan to find refuge on the east bank.

3.   Decision at Gilgal.

> *Now he waited seven days, according to the appointed time set by Samuel, but Samuel did not come to Gilgal; and the people were scattering from him. (1 Samuel 13:8).*

Samuel had promised to meet Saul at Gilgal within seven days of his arrival there. But it wasn't a recent promise. He had made this promise all the way back in 1 Samuel 10:8. Saul arrives in Gilgal and waits the seven days. But there is no Samuel. And the Philistines are getting closer. And Saul's army is shrinking quickly. Finally, Saul decides that he can wait no longer and he calls for the sacrifices to be brought and he offers them himself.

What was his sin? Not in merely offering the sacrifice, for David and Solomon both did the same thing (2 Samuel 24:25; 1

> "To obey is better than sacrifice" (1 Samuel 15:22).

Kings 3:15). Saul's sin was in disobeying the command of the Lord as given through Samuel. Immediately he finds himself confronted by Samuel.

> *And it came about as soon as he finished offering the burnt offering, that behold, Samuel came; and Saul went out to meet him and to greet him. (1 Samuel 13:10).*

Samuel questions the actions of Saul (*"What have you done?"*). Saul immediately begins a process of rationalization.

Rationalization #1:   "I saw that the people were scattering from me" (13:11).
Who is at fault? It is the people. "I'm merely their representative and I have to go along with whatever they decide."

Rationalization #2:   "You did not come within the appointed days" (13:11). Samuel is also at fault.

Rationalization #3:   "The Philistines were assembling at Michmash" (13:11). Saul also blames the circumstances.

Rationalization #4:   "The Philistines will come down against me at Gilgal, and I have not asked the favor of the Lord" (13:12). Who is number 4 on Saul's fault list? God himself. "He apparently is not going to help me, so I had better buy him off."

Rationalization #5:   "I forced myself and offered the burnt offering" (13:12).
"The people, Samuel, the circumstances and you, God, twisted my arm, and I just could not help myself."

> It is ironic that Gilgal was both the scene of Saul's coronation as well as of the announcement that the kingdom would go to another.

Do you see what it missing in Saul's reasoning? There is a complete lack of repentance. He is remorseful for the results of his sin, but he does not admit his guilt.

And Samuel said to Saul, "You have acted foolishly; you have not kept the commandment of the Lord your God, which He commanded you, for now the Lord would have established your kingdom over Israel forever. 14 But now your kingdom shall not endure. The Lord has sought out for Himself a man after His own heart, and the Lord has appointed him as ruler over His people, because you have not kept what the Lord commanded you." (1 Samuel 13:13-14).

The judgment against Saul is that he will not be the founder of a dynasty. It shall not be his descendants who sit upon the throne of Israel. This distinction shall be given to another.

4.   Saul and Jonathan.

Saul's bad situation had gotten a lot worse. The Philistine threat was growing. The number of his forces had been reduced to a mere 600 (13:15). Samuel had come and gone. And the Lord was not on his side. In the midst of this bleak outlook, victory comes at the hands of Jonathan.

> *And Saul was staying in the outskirts of Gibeah under the pomegranate tree which is in Migron. And the people who were with him were about six hundred men, 3 and Ahijah, the son of Ahitub, Ichabod's brother, the son of Phinehas, the son of Eli, the priest of the Lord at Shiloh, was wearing an ephod. And the people did not know that Jonathan was gone. (1 Samuel 14:2-3).*

Saul had moved from Gilgal back to his home town of Gibeah. He still had his 600 men and he had added to his entourage the new high priest, Ahijah, the great-grandson of Eli in all of his priestly finest.

Why is Ahijah mentioned along with his ancestry? Perhaps it is to point to the company which Saul was keeping - the son of an accursed line of priests.

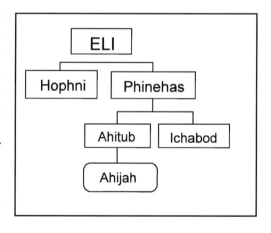

> *Then Jonathan said to the young man who was carrying his armor, "Come and let us cross over to the garrison of these uncircumcised; perhaps the Lord will work for us, for the Lord is not restrained to save by many or by few." (1 Samuel 14:6).*

The Philistines had established an outpost at the top of one of the passes leading to Michmash. This was the objective to which Jonathan now turned his attention.

> *And his armor bearer said to him, "Do all that is in your heart; turn yourself, and here I am with you according to your desire." (1 Samuel 14:7).*

Jonathan's armor bearer had no less faith. An armor bearer in those days was often a teenage boy who was not yet considered of age. The armor that he carried would consist of a giant shield nearly the size of a man. It was a two-handed job and so he would depend upon the warrior on whose behalf he was bearing the armor. They decide upon a plan. They will approach the Philistine outpost guarding Michmash and reveal their position.

- If the Philistines call for them to wait, then they will stand their ground and wait.
- If the Philistines call for them to come up, then they will go up, believing that the Lord has given the victory.

Did you notice anything about this plan? There was no plan for either retreat or defeat. There is no third option. They assume that there will be eventual victory and that it will either come now or it will come later.

> *Then Jonathan climbed up on his hands and feet, with his armor bearer behind him; and they fell before Jonathan, and his armor bearer put some of them to death after him.*
> *And that first slaughter which Jonathan and his armor bearer made was about twenty men within about half a furrow in an acre of land.*
> *And there was a trembling in the camp, in the field, and among all the people. Even the garrison and the raiders trembled, and the earth quaked so that it became a great trembling. (1 Samuel 14:13-15).*

Up to this point, the Philistines thought of the Israelites only in terms of those who came down from the mountains to have their farm implements sharpened. Nothing to fear from them. They were nothing but a band of backwoods farmers. But this farmer does some plowing that leaves 20 professional soldiers dead. There is an interesting parallel between the stories of Jonathan and Gideon, the judge of Israel.

Gideon	Jonathan
Went alone with a servant into the camp of the Midianites.	Went alone with his armor bearer against the Philistines.
Sets forth the fleece as a sign of God's victory.	Sets the invitation of the Philistines to come up as the sign of God's victory.
The Midianites are thrown into a panic by Gideon's 300.	The Philistines are thrown into a panic by Jonathan and his armor bearer.
In their panic, the Midianites fought one another.	Every man's sword was against his fellow (14:20).
Reinforcements come from Ephraim.	Reinforcements come out of hiding in Ephraim (14:22).

> *Now the men of Israel were hard-pressed on that day, for Saul had put the people under oath, saying, "Cursed be the man who eats food before evening, and until I have avenged myself on my enemies." So none of the people tasted food. (1 Samuel 14:24).*

Saul thought to motivate the Israelites to fight harder, and so he places them under an oath and a curse, forbidding them to eat. As a result, the fighting men of Israel find themselves running out of energy. The result is exactly the opposite of what Saul had desired - *"the slaughter of the Philistines has not been great"* (14:30).

Jonathan hadn't heard about the oath which his father made. And so, when he comes upon some honey dripping from a honeycomb, he partakes of it.

At the day's end, the Israelites came upon the spoil which the Philistines had left in their retreat. Since they were now famished, they *"took sheep and oxen and calves, and slew them on the ground; and the people ate them with the blood"* (14:32). To eat blood was a sin against the Mosaic Law (Leviticus 3:17; 7:26; 17:10-16).

- Saul wants to go on attacking the Philistines and taking spoil all night and "not leave a man of them."
- The priest suggests they "draw near to God." When Saul does this, there is no answer from the Lord. Saul reasons that this must be because of some sin among the Israelites.
- Saul says, "Let's cast lots and find out who the sinner is. Even if it is my own son I will kill him." Within a few minutes, he finds himself confronted with the folly of his own words.
- When they cast the lots, they find out it is indeed Saul's son, Jonathan, the hero, who had brought about this great deliverance in Israel. Saul declares his intention to have Jonathan executed. Jonathan, in a great display of faith and loyalty, agrees to give up his life.
- The Israelites intervene, demanding that Jonathan's life be spared.

5.   Saul and the Amalekites

Up to now Saul has only forfeited the right of his line to rule Israel. In Chapter 15 we will see the climax of his life and the loss of his kingship. This begins with God's Command to Strike the Amalekites.

> *Then Samuel said to Saul, "The Lord sent me to anoint you as king over His people, over Israel; now therefore, listen to the words of the Lord.*
> *"Thus says the Lord of hosts, `I will punish Amalek for what he did to Israel, how he set himself against him on the way while he was coming up from Egypt.*
> *"`Now go and strike Amalek and utterly destroy all that he has, and do not spare him; but put to death both man and woman, child and infant, ox and sheep, camel and donkey.'" (1 Samuel 15:1-3).*

The Amalekites were among the descendants of Esau. They were a nomadic desert tribe who lived in the northern Sinai. The fighting between the Amalekites and the Israelites went all the way back to the wilderness wanderings.

- The Amalekites had dogged the Israelites during their 40 years in the wilderness, picking off any who lagged behind (Deuteronomy 25:17-18).

- It was the Amalekites who had repulsed the initial attempt of Israel to enter the promised land at Kadesh-Barnea.
- In the days of the Judges, the Amalekites had joined the Moabites and the Ammonites in invading Israel and taking Jericho (Judges 3:12-14).
- The Amalekites had joined the Midianites to invade Israel in the days of Gideon (Judges 6:3).

Because of this, every living thing of Amalek's is to be put to death. If this seems cruel, remember that this is the same God who promised Abraham that if there were ten righteous men in Sodom he would spare the whole valley, the whole cesspool, not just Sodom but Gomorrah, Zeboim, Admah, and Bella, all five cities of the plain. The Amalekites were a cancer in the land of Canaan. Like a cancer, they were to be completely exterminated. It isn't wise to leave a few cancer cells behind and it isn't wise to leave a bit of sin behind.

Oftentimes we read such a passage and find difficulty with it. Our real problem is that we have too light a view of sin. The question is not why God ordered the destruction of the Amalekites, but why hasn't He also ordered our own destruction when we are completely deserving of that judgment. Jesus summed this up perfectly when He pointed to such judgments and then said, *"I tell you... unless you repent, you will all likewise perish"* (Luke 13:3).

> *So Saul defeated the Amalekites, from Havilah as you go to Shur, which is east of Egypt.*
> *And he captured Agag the king of the Amalekites alive, and utterly destroyed all the people with the edge of the sword. (1 Samuel 15:7-8).*

Saul responded in obedience to the Lord. He gathered together a huge force and moved down and conquered the Amalekites. This does not mean that each and every Amalekite was destroyed. They would continue to be a force with which to be reckoned. In David's day, they would be responsible for the destruction of the city of Ziklag and the capture of a number of Israelite prisoners (1 Samuel 30:1).

> *But Saul and the people spared Agag and the best of the sheep, the oxen, the fatlings, the lambs, and all that was good, and were not willing to destroy them utterly; but everything despised and worthless,*

that they utterly destroyed. (1 Samuel 15:9).

Agag was probably a dynastic title like "pharaoh" (see Numbers 24:7). It may have come from the Akkadian *agagum*, "to become angry." Ancient kings would sometimes keep the kings whom they captured, keeping them as a living monument to their success. Judges 1:6-7 tells of Adonai-bezek who had kept a retinue of 70 conquered kings with their thumbs and big toes amputated. Perhaps Saul rationalized that, since all of the other kings were doing this, he would act in the same way. What is ironic is how Saul had been ready to put his own son to death in the previous chapter but was now unwilling to execute a wicked king.

But this is not all. Saul and the people also took for themselves the choice pick of the flocks of the conquered Amalekites. These things had been dedicated by God for destruction, but they decided that these things were too good for God. They were committing the sin of Achan who had stolen some of the spoil from Jericho.

> *And Samuel came to Saul, and Saul said to him, "Blessed are you of the Lord! I have carried out the command of the LORD."*
>
> *But Samuel said, "What then is this bleating of the sheep in my ears, and the lowing of the oxen which I hear?"*
>
> *And Saul said, "They have brought them from the Amalekites, for the people spared the best of the sheep and oxen, to sacrifice to the Lord your God; but the rest we have utterly destroyed." (1 Samuel 15:13-15).*

Notice the pronouns. "**I** have been obedient. **They** brought the oxen and sheep. The **people** spared the best to sacrifice to the Lord **your** God." When Samuel points out his disobedience, Saul argues that the purpose of the spoil was to bring sacrifices to the Lord. It is like the little boy who was caught with his hand in the cookie jar and who exclaimed, "I was getting it for you!"

> *And Samuel said, "Has the Lord as much delight in burnt offerings and sacrifices as in obeying the voice of the Lord? Behold, to obey is better than sacrifice, and to heed than the fat of rams. 23 For*

313

rebellion is as the sin of divination, and insubordination is as iniquity and idolatry, because you have rejected the word of the Lord, He has also rejected you from being king." (1 Samuel 15:22-23).

God ordained sacrifices in the Old Testament. Sacrificing was a part of obedience to God. But it is not the mere act of killing an animal which was pleasing to God. God is not really impressed with a bunch of dead animals. What impresses God is the giving of self. When you take that which you own and for which you have worked and give it to God, that involves a real sacrifice. The best kind of sacrifice is the giving of yourself in obedience.

Saul asks Samuel for forgiveness. Samuel replies that the consequences of Saul's sin will be long-lasting. Samuel will not even travel the same path as the fallen king.

But Samuel said to Saul, "I will not return with you; for you have rejected the word of the Lord, and the Lord has rejected you from being king over Israel."

And as Samuel turned to go, Saul seized the edge of his robe, and it tore.

So Samuel said to him, "The Lord has torn the kingdom of Israel from you today, and has given it to your neighbor who is better than you.

"And also the Glory of Israel will not lie or change His mind; for He is not a man that He should change His mind." (1 Samuel 15:26-29).

Having been told that his kingdom would be taken from him, Saul instinctively did what came natural. He reach out to hold on. To hold on to his kingdom. To hold on to his status. To hold on to Samuel. In the process, he ripped a portion of Samuel's cloak, bringing a fitting illustration to the prophetic words.

Do you remember the reaction of Eli when he was told that his sons would not follow him in the priesthood? There had been an acceptance of God's will. Saul is different. He wants to hold on. The rest of the book of 1 Samuel will be the account of Saul trying to hold on.

Then Samuel went to Ramah, but Saul went up to his house at Gibeah of Saul.

And Samuel did not see Saul again until the day of his death; for Samuel grieved over Saul. And the Lord regretted that He had made Saul king over Israel. (1 Samuel 15:34-35).

Saul would see Samuel one more time. But it would take place after Samuel had died. And it would take place on the eve of his own death.

THE RISE OF DAVID

Chapter 15 of 1 Samuel ends with Saul having been rejected as the King of Israel. As he grasps Samuel's cloak and tears it, he is told that the kingdom of Israel will be torn from him and given to another. This other is a young shepherd boy named David.

Chapter 16		Chapter 17	Chapter 18
David Introduced		David on the field of battle	David in the Court of Saul
To Samuel	To Saul		
David Anointed by Samuel	David plays for Saul	David slays Goliath	David becomes the object of Saul's fear

Saul had been the people's choice for king, though he had also been sanctioned by God. Now Saul would be rejected in favor of a new king. The anointing of a boy from Bethlehem to be the new king of Israel is a reminder to us that David's greater Son was also from Bethlehem and that He was anointed, not merely with oil, but with the very Spirit of God.

Now the Spirit of the Lord departed from Saul, and an evil spirit from the Lord terrorized him. (1 Samuel 16:14).

The Spirit had departed from Saul. But the empty house which has been swept clean is now replaced by an "evil spirit." The startling thing about this evil spirit was that it was from the Lord. What was the nature of this spirit? It was not necessarily a demon. Rather, it was a messenger from God - and angel sent on an errand of trouble. This should not surprise us. The Israelites had already seen the Lord send an angel of death against the firstborn of the Egyptians.

315

Saul's servants then said to him, "Behold now, an evil spirit from God is terrorizing you. 16 Let our lord now command your servants who are before you. Let them seek a man who is a skillful player on the harp; and it shall come about when the evil spirit from God is on you, that he shall play the harp with his hand, and you will be well." (1 Samuel 16:15-16).

We are meant to see Saul and David in contrast. We can note that this contrast extends throughout their lives.

Saul	David
From the tribe of Benjamin	From the tribe of Judah
First seen looking for his father's donkeys.	First seen caring for his father's sheep.
Head and shoulders above the rest of the men of Israel.	The youngest and least impressive of eight brothers.
God's Spirit is removed from Saul.	The Spirit of the Lord comes mightily upon David.
An evil spirit from the Lord terrorizes Saul.	David's playing of the harp causes evil spirit to depart from Saul.
Anointing by Samuel followed by Saul's defeat of Nahash and the Ammonites.	Anointing by Samuel followed by David's defeat of Goliath and the Philistines.

In each case, the anointing brought about the promise of great things that were to follow, yet it was given at a time when none of the accomplishments had yet been actualized. This is significant because we also have an anointing from the Lord (1 John 2:20). It is not an anointing that is based on anything you have done. It is an anointing based on the deeds of another. Yet it is also promissary of great things to come. That was soon realized when Israel was faced with a challenge.

*Now the Philistines gathered their armies for battle;
and they were gathered at Socoh which belongs to Judah, and
they camped between Socoh and Azekah, in Ephes-dammim.*

And Saul and the men of Israel were gathered, and camped in the valley of Elah, and drew up in battle array to encounter the Philistines.

And the Philistines stood on the mountain on one side while Israel stood on the mountain on the other side, with the valley between them. (1 Samuel 17:1-3).

As you leave the coast land area of Palestine along the Mediterranean and move eastward, the first geographical feature you encounter is a range of low foothills known as the Shephelah. Over the years the streams flowing down from these hills have cut deep gorges known as Wadis. The Valley of Elah is one such Wadi.

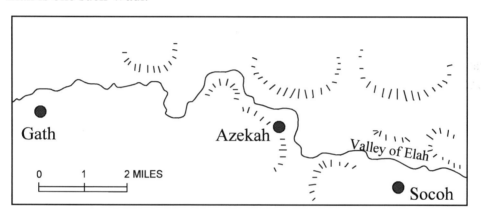

The Philistines held the seacoast plains of Canaan. The Israelites held the mountains. The Shephelah was the contested area between. This would be the scene of the confrontation. Located about fifteen miles west of Bethlehem, this Wadi served as a pass from east to west (the stream disappears entirely in the dry season leaving a riverbed of small round stones).

Then a champion came out from the armies of the Philistines named Goliath, from Gath, whose height was six cubits and a span.

And he had a bronze helmet on his head, and he was clothed in scale-armor which weighed five thousand shekels of bronze. 6 He also had bronze greaves on his legs and a bronze javelin slung between his shoulders. 7 And the shaft of his spear was like a weaver's beam, and the head of his spear weighed six hundred shekels of iron; his shield-carrier also walked before him. (1 Samuel 17:4-7).

The name "Goliath" seems to be Indo-European in origin. He is described as having the latest armaments in modern warfare. When we put these together, we are presented with the following description:

Item	Description	Equivalent
Height	*six cubits and a span*	9 feet, 8 inches
Armor	*5000 shekels of bronze*	125 pounds
Head of his Spear	*600 shekels of iron*	15 pounds

The height of Goliath has brought about considerable speculation since there has been no man in recorded history to achieve such stature. The Hebrew manuscript of Samuel found in the Dead Sea Scrolls (4QSam) contains a textual variant in this description putting him instead at four cubits and a span, making him six feet nine inches. This reading is confirmed both by the Vaticanus, a Greek translation of the Old Testament, as well as in the Antiquities of Josephus. [3]

This does not negate the fact that Goliath was the equivalent of a human tank. Standing head and shoulders over the rest of the population of both Philistines and Israelites, he would have looked indestructible. To even get to him, one would have to get past the large figure-eight shield which was held by his armor bearer. We ought to take note of how the Hebrew readers of this book would have viewed this description.

- David, the promised future King, goes out to fight the one who is at **enmity** with God's people
- The giant is described in terms of his height (6 cubits) and his armor with **scales** and the head of his spear (600 shekels)
- He kills the giant with a blow to the **head**.

Do you see it? This description is given in terms of the prophecy that was given back in Genesis 3:15. It was the promise of one who would come from the seed of the woman and who would vanquish the seed of the serpent with a blow to the head. Of course, we know that the ultimate fulfillment of that prophecy was not in David, but in the Son of David. It was fulfilled in David's greater son, Jesus Christ, who conquered our giant.

---

[3] For more on this topic, see the article by J. Daniel Hays,"Reconsidering the Height of Goliath," Journal of the Evangelical Society, December 2005. Vol 48:4.

And he stood and shouted to the ranks of Israel, and said to them, "Why do you come out to draw up in battle array? Am I not the Philistine and you servants of Saul? Choose a man for yourselves and let him come down to me.

"If he is able to fight with me and kill me, then we will become your servants; but if I prevail against him and kill him, then you shall become our servants and serve us." (1 Samuel 17:8-9).

Warfare in the ancient world was a violent and bloody affair (this is true for war in any age). It was not uncommon for 20 or 30 thousand men to fall in a single battle. Goliath was a part of a highly cultured race. He offers a relatively peaceful alternative. A representative from each of the two warring nations will fight and decide the issue. Instead of thousands falling in battle, only one man shall die. It is in this context that David volunteers to represent Israel.

And David said to Saul, "Let no man's heart fail on account of him; your servant will go and fight this Philistine." (1 Samuel 17:32).

The fact that David succeeded in actually trying on the armor of Saul indicates that it must have come close to fitting. Otherwise he would not have been able to don it in the first place. Remember that Saul was head and shoulders over all of Israel (10:23). His armor would have been sized as an extra-extra large.

David was not a little boy. But neither was he used to fighting in armor. He was untrained in its use. He was unaccustomed to moving about while carrying this additional weight. And so, David put the armor of Saul aside, content to wear the armor of God.

And he took his stick in his hand and chose for himself five smooth stones from the brook, and put them in the shepherd's bag which he had, even in his pouch, and his sling was in his hand; and he approached the Philistine. (1 Samuel 17:40).

A sling consisted of two long cords tied to a pocket at the center. The slinger would place a stone in the pocket, whirl to ends of the cord and then release one of them, letting the stone fly at its target. I've used a sling before and I admit that it takes a lot of practice. The sling was one of the accepted weapons of the Israelites. It was not dependent upon the ironworks of the

Philistines. There had been an entire brigade of 700 slingers from the tribe of Benjamin who could *"sling a stone at a hair and not miss" (Judges 20:16).*

> *Then the Philistine came on and approached David, with the shield-bearer in front of him.*
>
> *When the Philistine looked and saw David, he disdained him; for he was but a youth, and ruddy, with a handsome appearance.*
>
> *And the Philistine said to David, "Am I a dog, that you come to me with sticks?" And the Philistine cursed David by his gods.*
>
> *The Philistine also said to David, "Come to me, and I will give your flesh to the birds of the sky and the beasts of the field." (1 Samuel 17:41-44).*

Military soldiers worked in teams of two. The warrior would be preceded by his shield-bearer. This was a full-time job in itself because the shields that were then in use were large body shields. The shield-bearer was in charge of defense while the warrior was in charge of offense. This same sort of tactic was used by Jonathan in 1 Samuel 14.

This was not merely a battle between two men. At stake here was the honor of the Lord of hosts. And David was here as the representative, both of the people of God as well as of the Lord Himself. There is a parallel here between David and the last son of David.

David	Jesus Christ, Son of David
Son of Jesse	A shoot from the stem of Jesse (Isaiah 11:1).
Chastised by his older brother.	He came to His own and those who were His own did not receive Him (John 1:11).
Refused to wear the armor of Saul.	Laid aside His glory to take the form of a man.
He met Goliath as the representative of Israel.	He went to the cross as our representative, dying for our sins.
He also served as the representative of the Lord.	He served as the mediator between God and men.

He used a rock.	He is the Rock.
He won the victory through the death of Goliath.	Won the victory through His own death, burial, and resurrection.

Do you remember the incident of the Ark within the Temple of Dagon? There is an interesting similarity with the fall of Dagon and the fall of Goliath.

Ark Versus Dagon	David Versus Goliath
The Ark had been captured by the Philistines and placed in the Temple of Dagon.	Goliath saw in David an easy victory.
Dagon was found face down before the Ark.	Goliath fell on his face.
Dagon was found with his head removed which led to an enduring practice.	David cut off Goliath's head and kept it as a trophy.
Dagon was seen by all to be a dead idol of stone.	The Lord is seen to be the living God (17:26).

Chapter 18 begins with Saul's son, Jonathan, coming to love David and make a covenant with him. The chapter ends with Saul's daughter, Michal, coming to love David and marry him.

18:1	18:6	18:10	18:13	18:20
Jonathan loves David	Women sing David's praises	Saul throws spear at David	David prospers before the people	Michal loves David
Saul sets David over the men of war.	Saul looks on David with suspicion	Saul is afraid of David	Saul dreads David	Saul is even more afraid of David

Now it came about when he had finished speaking to Saul, that the soul of Jonathan was knit to the soul of David, and Jonathan loved him as himself. (1 Samuel 18:1).

Jonathan recognized in David a kindred spirit despite very different backgrounds. Jonathan was the son of a king and heir to the throne. David was a simple shepherd boy. Jonathan was a fully mature man in his prime. David was still a relatively young man, though he had gained the respect of men due to his victory over Goliath. They had both achieved overwhelming victory in a time when defeat seemed probable. They both were renown as heros. This naturally kindred spirit led to a close friendship.

> *Then Jonathan made a covenant with David because he loved him as himself. 4 And Jonathan stripped himself of the robe that was on him and gave it to David, with his armor, including his sword and his bow and his belt. (1 Samuel 18:3-4).*

It has become increasingly popular to assert that the love between Jonathan and David was a homosexual relationship. The truth is that the Hebrew word used here for love is never used of homosexual relationships in the Bible. This same word is used in 1 Kings 5:1 where we read that King Hiram of Tyre had loved David all the days of his life. This usage indicates the friendly relations between two neighboring kings.

Both Saul and Jonathan began by loving David. When David first came to the court of Saul and played the harp in his presence, we read that *"Saul loved him greatly" (16:21).* Now, as Jonathan came to know this remarkable young man, he also came to love him. The gift of his own personal weapons was made greater by the fact that weapons were not common among the Israelites. At the start of the campaigns against the Philistines, there had been only two sets of weapon in the entire army of Israel. One set had belonged to Saul. The other set was Jonathan's — now given to David. In Jonathan's attitude and actions toward David, we see a picture of Christ's love put into action for us.

Jonathan	Jesus
Loved David as himself	Loved us as Himself
Entered into a covenant with David	Established a new covenant with us
Gave his possessions to David	Blessed us with every spiritual blessing

Stripped himself of the signs of his princely prerogatives	Laid aside the prerogatives of His deity to go to the cross

> *And it happened as they were coming, when David returned from killing the Philistine, that the women came out of all the cities of Israel, singing and dancing, to meet King Saul, with tambourines, with joy and with musical instruments.*
>
> *And the women sang as they played, and said, "Saul has slain his thousands. And David his ten thousands." (1 Samuel 18:6-7).*

As the victorious Israelites made their way back to their homes, they were greeted in each Israelite town and village with singing and rejoicing, the ancient equivalent of a ticker-tape parade. At the heart of the celebration were the two heroic figures: Saul and David. The fact that Saul was held up as a heroic figure was rather gracious. He hadn't done anything heroic recently. But Saul didn't see it that way. Indeed, he saw it through the green eyes of jealousy.

> *Then Saul became very angry, for this saying displeased him; and he said, "They have ascribed to David ten thousands, but to me they have ascribed thousands. Now what more can he have but the kingdom?"*
>
> *And Saul looked at David with suspicion from that day on. (1 Samuel 18:8-9).*

In verse 5 we read that David's promotion *"was pleasing in the sight [eyes] of all the people and also in the sight [eyes] of Saul's servants."* Now we read that *Saul became very angry, for this saying displeased him* (literally, *it was displeasing in his eyes*). Saul knew from Samuel's prophecy that the kingdom had already been snatched from him by God and given to another. Saul was on the lookout for such a man. It may be that he had heard by now of Samuel coming to anoint David in Bethlehem. Even if he did not know about David's anointing, it was obvious that David was growing in popularity. Here was one whose praises the people of the land were proclaiming. There is a contrast here between David and Saul. It is a contrast that has been developing for the past three chapters.

	DAVID	**SAUL**
Chapter 16	David is given God's Spirit	God's Spirit departs from Saul and he is given an evil spirit.
Chapter 17	David faces Goliath in faith and victory.	Saul fears Goliath.
Chapter 18	David is loved by others, even those of Saul's family.	Saul tries to murder David and have him killed.

Then Saul said to David, "Here is my older daughter Merab; I will give her to you as a wife, only be a valiant man for me and fight the Lord's battle." For Saul thought, "My hand shall not be against him, but let the hand of the Philistines be against him." (1 Samuel 18:17).

Saul had originally promised that whoever killed Goliath would have the hand of his daughter in marriage. Perhaps David had been a bit too young for that. Or perhaps Saul had conveniently forgotten his promise. But now he offers his daughter to David. Unfortunately, his motives leave something to be desired.

Saul wants David dead. But he doesn't want to do the deed himself (he had already tried that and it hadn't worked). Instead, he will try to set it up so that the Philistines will kill him. Does this sound familiar? A later king would suppose, "If I put Uriah the Hittite in the forefront of the battle..."

But David said to Saul, "Who am I, and what is my life or my father's family in Israel, that I should be the king's son-in-law?"

So it came about at the time when Merab, Saul's daughter, should have been given to David, that she was given to Adriel the Meholathite for a wife. (1 Samuel 18:18-19).

David was a man of true humility. He was not seeking Saul's throne. He was not even seeking the hand of one of Saul's daughters. And so, the daughter that had originally been promised to the slayer of Goliath was given to another. Instead, David was given Michal, the younger daughter of Saul, to be his wife.

Now Michal, Saul's daughter, loved David. When they told Saul, the thing was agreeable to him.

And Saul thought, "I will give her to him that she may become a snare to him, and that the hand of the Philistines may be against him." Therefore Saul said to David, "For a second time you may be my son-in-law today." (1 Samuel 18:20-21).

Just as Jonathan had developed a love for David, so also Michal, Saul's youngest daughter, also developed a love for him. Instead of making Saul mad, it pleased him, not because his attitude had changed toward David, but because he saw this as an opportunity to entrap him. This scene is played out in the form of a chiasm:

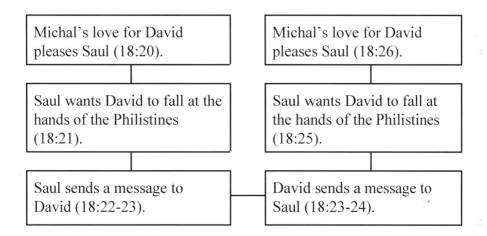

Michal's love for David pleases Saul (18:20).	Michal's love for David pleases Saul (18:26).
Saul wants David to fall at the hands of the Philistines (18:21).	Saul wants David to fall at the hands of the Philistines (18:25).
Saul sends a message to David (18:22-23).	David sends a message to Saul (18:23-24).

The offer of marriage is made again to David, who objects that he is *"a poor man and lightly esteemed" (18:23).* He is told that he will be given the king's daughter in marriage for a dowry of 100 Philistine foreskins. David responds with not 100, but 200 such trophies from the Philistines.

One of the walls in the mortuary temple of Rameses III depicts what seems to be a pile of foreskins collected as a means of determining the body count following a battle.

When Saul saw and knew that the LORD was with David, and that Michal, Saul's daughter, loved him, 29 then Saul was even more afraid of David. Thus Saul was David's enemy continually. (1 Samuel 18:28-29).

The story of David is a story of a once and future king. It is the story of one from Bethlehem who was lowly esteemed in the eyes of men, but who was a man after God's own heart. It is the story of one who was obedient to authority, even such authority that would put him in jeopardy.

The rest of 1 Samuel is taken up with Saul's various pursuits of David. Throughout these pursuits, both people and even the circumstances conspire to assist David while every hand of man and God are against Saul.

19:1	20:1	21:10	22:6	24:1	26:1
David flees the presence of Saul	David & Jonathan make a covenant	David flees to Gath	Saul Pursues David		
			1st Pursuit	2nd Pursuit	3rd Pursuit
David assisted by Michal	David assisted by Ahimelech	David assisted by the king of Moab	David encouraged by Jonathan	David cuts Saul's robe	David takes Saul's spear & jug
The Lord assists David			David assisted by situation	Abigail assists David	David flees to Gath

Throughout all of these incidents, David maintains his integrity, refusing to lift up his hand against the anointed of the Lord. The point is that David is seeking God's kingdom while Saul is seeking his own kingdom. As the section moves to its final climax, the closing chapters of the first book of Samuel constantly shift back and forth between David and Saul.

27:1	28:1	29:1	31:1
DAVID • Comes to Gath • Given Ziklag • Secretly raids the enemies of Israel	**SAUL** • Seeks of the witch of Endor. • Is condemned by Samuel.	**DAVID** • Accompanies Philistines to Battle. • Sent back home. Finds home burned. • Rescues his people.	**SAUL** • Defeated. • Commits suicide. • His body is dishonored.

Victory	Spiritual Defeat	Victory	Defeat & Death
Appears to be one with the Philistines.	Has fellowship meal with a medium.	Is delivered from Philistines & lives.	Fights Philistines & dies.

For a time, David lives in Gath with his men. But this began to be uncomfortable both for David as well as for the Philistines. After all, David had made his reputation as "David the Giant Philistine-Killer." They still remembered the old Israelite song that told how Saul had slain his thousands and David his ten thousands. They knew that those numbers referred to how many Philistines David had slain.

> While Saul is losing to the Philistines, David is being given a city from the hands of the Philistines.

David is given the city of Ziklag. This city had originally been claimed both by the tribe of Judah (Joshua 15:31) as well as by the tribe of Simeon (Joshua 19:5; 1 Chronicles 4:30). It was a border town, laying in the no-man's land between Israel and Philistia.

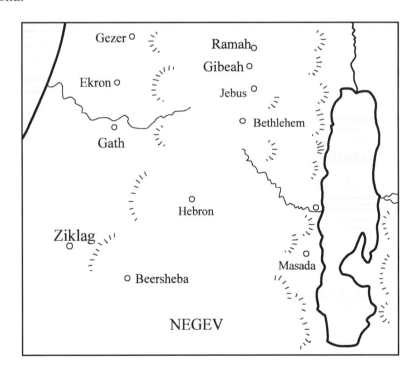

This was the time of the beginning of the Iron Age and the Philistines enjoyed a monopoly on the secret of smelting iron. But this changed radically after David became king. Could it be that he stole the secret of iron-smelting and brought it to the Israelites?

> *Now it came about in those days that the Philistines gathered their armed camps for war, to fight against Israel. And Achish said to David, "Know assuredly that you will go out with me in the camp, you and your men."*
>
> *And David said to Achish, "Very well, you shall know what your servant can do." So Achish said to David, "Very well, I will make you my bodyguard for life." (1 Samuel 28:1-2).*

As the Philistines prepared an invasion force to strike at the very heart of Israel, David found himself drawn into the service of Achish. He was appointed

> There is a touch of irony here as David who made his start cutting off the head of Goliath is now made "guardian of the head" of Achish.

bodyguard — literally, "guard of my head" (שֹׁמֵר לְרֹאשִׁי). Furthermore, this was not to be a temporary appointment. It was to be forever. It would be permanent. David's deception put him in the position of having to fight against the people of God in open warfare. There is a parallel here between the loyalty which David promises toward the Philistines and the oath by which Saul binds himself to the medium of Endor. Each is being put into a precarious position and the suspense deliberately builds to see how this will be resolved.

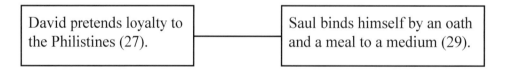

| David pretends loyalty to the Philistines (27). | Saul binds himself by an oath and a meal to a medium (29). |

> *Now Samuel was dead, and all Israel had lamented him and buried him in Ramah his own city. And Saul had removed from the land those who were mediums and spiritists. (1 Samuel 28:3).*

We read of the death of Samuel back in chapter 25. Why is it mentioned here again? It is because now Saul was feeling that loss. He desperately needed a word from the Lord and Samuel was no longer available to give it. Furthermore there was no one else to serve as a substitute for Samuel as all of the mediums and spiritists had been removed from the land. Saul could not even go to the high priest because he had murdered the high priest and his entire family.

> *So the Philistines gathered together and came and camped in Shunem; and Saul gathered all Israel together and they camped in Gilboa. (1 Samuel 28:5).*

Shunem is located in the Valley of Jezreel at the southern foot of Mount Moreh, nine miles east-northeast of Megiddo. Mount Gilboa is several miles to the south on the southeastern edge of the Valley of Jezreel. Instead of coming up the narrow mountain passes as they had in the past, the Philistines now moved across the wide open plains of Jezreel. Here they could maneuver their chariot corps to full effect. If this military operation was successful, it would result in splitting the land in two.

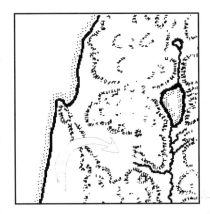

> *When Saul saw the camp of the Philistines, he was afraid and his heart trembled greatly.*
> *When Saul inquired of the Lord, the Lord did not answer him, either by dreams or by Urim or by prophets. (1 Samuel 28:6-7).*

Saul had every reason to fear. The Philistines were big and they had the best in military weaponry and there were a lot of them. His seeking was met with silence. God had already given His message to Saul. There would be nothing more forthcoming.

> *Then Saul said to his servants, "Seek for me a woman who is a medium, that I may go to her and inquire of her." And his servants said to him, "Behold, there is a woman who is a medium at En-dor." (1 Samuel 28:7).*

The Hebrew word for Medium is *'Ob* (אוֹב). This is a Hittite loan-word. It originally was used to describe a pit and spoke of the place of departed spirits. It came to be used both of the spirits of the dead as well as of those who were supposedly able to contact those spirits.

> *"Your voice shall also be like that of a SPIRIT from the ground" (Isaiah 29:4).*

"Do not turn to MEDIUMS or spiritists..." (Leviticus 19:31).

The Mosaic Law strictly forbade God's people from consulting mediums. The penalty for such actions was death. In accordance with God's law, Saul had ordered that mediums and spiritists be driven from the land. And yet, he now seeks to consult with one. He is directed by his servants to the town of En-dor, located on the northern slope of Little Hermon. He determines to make his way to this spiritual brothel in order to partake in a seance.

> *Then Saul disguised himself by putting on other clothes, and went, he and two men with him, and they came to the woman by night; and he said, "Conjure up for me, please, and bring up for me whom I shall name to you."*
> *But the woman said to him, "Behold, you know what Saul has done, how he has cut off those who are mediums and spiritists from the land. Why are you then laying a snare for my life to bring about my death?"*
> *And Saul vowed to her by the Lord, saying, "As the Lord lives, there shall no punishment come upon you for this thing." (1 Samuel 28:8-10).*

To arrive at Endor from Mount Gilboa would have involved a long 8-mile detour around the Philistine forces. Saul took this route under the cover of night. The woman of Endor at first refuses to participate. It is not until Saul takes a solemn oath invoking the name of the Lord that she agrees to participate.

> *Then the woman said, "Whom shall I bring up for you?" And he said, "Bring up Samuel for me."*
> *When the woman saw Samuel, she cried out with a loud voice; and the woman spoke to Saul, saying, "Why have you deceived me? For you are Saul."*
> *And the king said to her, "Do not be afraid; but what do you see?" And the woman said to Saul, "I see a divine being [אֱלֹהִים, Elohim] coming up out of the earth."*
> *And he said to her, "What is his form?" And she said, "An old man is coming up, and he is wrapped with a robe." And Saul knew that it was Samuel, and he bowed with his face to the ground and did homage. (1 Samuel 28:11-14).*

This passage has troubled theologians for hundreds of years. There have been three alternate interpretations offered for this passage.

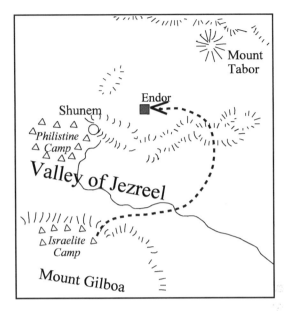

- This was truly Samuel speaking from the grave. This interpretation takes the passage naturally when it says that *"the woman saw Samuel"* (28:12).
- This was a demonic manifestation pretending to be Samuel. This view was held by Augustine.
- This was a trick of the woman. This is perhaps supported by the Septuagint which uses a term in this passage which is also used of ventriloquists.

The reason for the varied interpretation is because people do not care for the implications of what happened - that a seance was actually able to bring back Samuel from the dead. However, this need not be considered as normative. Just because Samuel actually appeared to the medium in this instance does not give credibility to all such mediums.

Evidently, only the woman saw the form of Samuel, for Saul asked in verse 14, *"What is his form?"* and did not realize that it was Samuel until she had given a description of the prophet. Notice what it was about the description which identified the visionary arrival as Samuel. It was the fact that he was an old man who was *"wrapped with a robe"* (28:14). Saul remembered that robe. He could not help but remember how Samuel had predicted the loss of the kingdom and had turned to go and how he, Saul, had grabbed the robe of Samuel and had torn it. He had been told that in just such a manner the kingdom would be torn from his grasp.

> *Then Samuel said to Saul, "Why have you disturbed me by bringing me up?" And Saul answered, "I am greatly distressed; for the Philistines are waging war against me, and God has departed from me and answers me no more, either through prophets or by dreams; therefore I have called you, that you make known to me what I should do." (1 Samuel*

28:15).

Saul wants a word from the Lord, but Saul has consistently ignored the word from the Lord that has been given to him. There is a principle here. It is that no second word from the Lord is given until the first word is heard.

> *And Samuel said, "Why then do you ask me, since the Lord has departed from you and has become your adversary?*
> *"And the Lord has done accordingly as He spoke through me; for the Lord has **torn** the kingdom out of your hand and given it to your neighbor, to David.*
> *"As you did not obey the Lord and did not execute His fierce wrath on Amalek, so the Lord has done this thing to you this day.*
> *Moreover the Lord will also give over Israel along with you into the hands of the Philistines, therefore tomorrow you and your sons will be with me. Indeed the Lord will give over the army of Israel into the hands of the Philistines!" (1 Samuel 28:16-19).*

While in the past the Lord had delivered Israel from the Philistine threat on more than one occasion, now Israel would be delivered by God into the hands of the Philistines (verse 19). This prophecy is fulfilled the next day.

> *And the Philistines overtook Saul and his sons; and the Philistines killed Jonathan and Abinadab and Malchi-shua the sons of Saul. (1 Samuel 31:2).*

The battle went against Israel and Saul began a retreat back up the mountain of Gilboa. Of the four sons of Saul, three were killed, including Jonathan. As volley after volley of Philistine arrows fell upon the hapless Israelite army, Saul was seriously wounded. The nature of the wound would prevent his escape and the Philistines were closing in. Saul knew of the reputation of the Philistines. They had captured Samson and had gouged out his eyes and had made a public spectacle of him. Saul fears the worst. He fears that he will be both tortured and humiliated. And so, he takes his own life.

The Philistines take the body of the Lord's anointed king and mutilate it, placing it on display on the walls of a nearby city.

> David had cut off the head of the Philistine champion. Now the Philistines do the same to Saul.

Now when the inhabitants of Jabesh-gilead heard what the Philistines had done to Saul, 12 all the valiant men rose and walked all night, and took the body of Saul and the bodies of his sons from the wall of Beth-shan, and they came to Jabesh, and burned them there. (1 Samuel 31:11-12).

Jabesh-gilead was the city which Saul had rescued at the very beginning of his reign (1 Samuel 11). This was a city on the east bank of the Jordan. When they had been besieged by the Ammonites and threatened with the disfigurement of having the right eye of every man gouged out, it was Saul who had led the forces of Israel to fight on their behalf. The men of Jabesh-gilead remember the debt which they owed their king and place themselves at risk by coming to rescue his mutilated corpse. Thus, the bodies of Saul and his sons which were first humiliated are now honored.

DAVID AS KING OVER JUDAH

Then the men of Judah came and there anointed David king over the house of Judah" (2 Samuel 2:4a).

David had already been anointed by Samuel. Now he is anointed by the men of Judah and becomes the king over that tribe. His first act of kingship is to commend the honorable actions of the men of Jabesh-gilead. The obvious conclusion is that David's rule over Judah was not the action of a rebel who was usurping authority, but one who had gone out of his way to honor the Lord's anointed one.

The other tribes follow Ish-bosheth, one of the surviving sons of Saul for seven years. David steers clear of the political intrigue during this period, but Ish-bosheth is ultimately killed and David's kingship is extended over all of Israel. There is an interesting parallel between how David

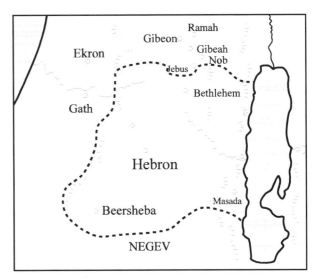

became king of Judah and how he now becomes king over all Israel.

2 Samuel 1:1 - 3:5	2 Samuel 3:6 - 5:16
Ammalekite tries to curry favor with David by bringing news of Saul's death.	Abner seeks to curry favor with David by negotiating the delivery of the kingdom.
Ammalekite is killed (1:14-16).	Abner is murdered (3:22-32).
David laments over Saul and Jonathan (1:17-21).	David laments over Abner (3:33-34).
David anointed (2:1-7).	David anointed (5:1-5).
David defeats Israel (2:8-32).	David takes Jerusalem (5:6-10).
Children born to David in Hebron (3:2-5).	Children born to David in Jerusalem (5:13-16).

The wording used in 2 Samuel 3:1 is striking. The tribes of Israel come to David and say, *We are your bone and your flesh*. This language harkens back to Genesis 2 where Adam says of his newly created bride:

This is now bone of my bones,
And flesh of my flesh (Genesis 2:23).

Something similar is happening here in this passage. Israel comes to David and they enter with him into a covenant of kingship. They bind themselves to David in the way a wife binds herself to a husband. David is not only to be Israel's king; he will also be Israel's bridegroom.

David was thirty years old when he became king, and he reigned forty years.
At Hebron he reigned over Judah seven years and six months, and in Jerusalem he reigned thirty-three years over all Israel and Judah. (2 Samuel 5:4-5).

It has been theorized by modern scholars that the 40 year reigns ascribed to Moses, to Eli, to David and to Solomon are merely to be understood as a long, undetermined number of years. But this passage gives a breakdown of what comprised those forty years.

Up to this time, David had been reigning in Hebron. Hebron was centrally located in Judah and would always be associated with that tribe. If the other tribes were to accept the concept of a unified nation, it would be necessary to have a capital city which had no former associations. Jerusalem was such a city.

Jerusalem was a city of the Jebusites. They had been living here before the days of Abraham. One of their kings had been Melchizedek, a priest of God. But now it was merely a Canaanite city. The Israelites under Joshua had been unable to drive out the Jebusites (Joshua 15:63). And even though the Israelites had captured and burned Jerusalem early in the days of the Judges (Judges 1:8), the Jebusites had returned to rebuild and refortify their city.

> *Now the king and his men went to Jerusalem against the Jebusites, the inhabitants of the land, and they said to David, "You shall not come in here, but the blind and lame shall turn you away"; thinking, "David cannot enter here."*
> *(2 Samuel 5:6).*

The old city of Jerusalem was built upon a high ridge and was surrounded on three sides by steep ravines. An approaching enemy would have to climb to the top of the ridge and then would find himself facing high fortifications with no room to maneuver. Furthermore, Jerusalem had its own internal water supply. A tunnel had been carved into the mountain leading down to a pool which was in turn fed by a natural spring. The boast of the city was that, even if these fortification were manned by blind and lame, they would be enough to keep out any enemy.

> *Nevertheless, David captured the stronghold of Zion, that is the city of David. (2 Samuel 5:7).*

The word "Zion" (צִיּוֹן) seems to refer to a "high place" or a "place of protection." The term is rare in the historical books.

And David said on that day, "Whoever would strike the Jebusites, let him reach the lame and the blind, who are hated by David's soul, through the water tunnel." (2 Samuel 5:8a).

Located on the east side of the city is the Gihon Spring. It is the city's only local source of fresh water. Unfortunately, the spring is located at the bottom of the ridge upon which the city was built. The Jebusites resolved this problem by excavating a tunnel through the bedrock which went beneath the city walls and then down a vertical shaft to the spring.

Now David had said, "Whoever strikes down a Jebusite first shall be chief and commander." And Joab the son of Zeruiah went up first, so he became chief. (1 Chronicles 11:6).

The shaft was discovered by Captain Charles Warren of the British Engineers in 1867. He and his sergeant entered the Gihon Spring, followed the narrow tunnel into the mountainside, and came upon a vertical shaft rising nearly 40 feet straight up. It was possible for the inhabitants of Jerusalem to stand at the top of the shaft and drop a bucket with a line attached and draw up water. Apparently, this was the route used to capture the city of Jerusalem. David's forces would have crept in through this route to come up inside the city gates.

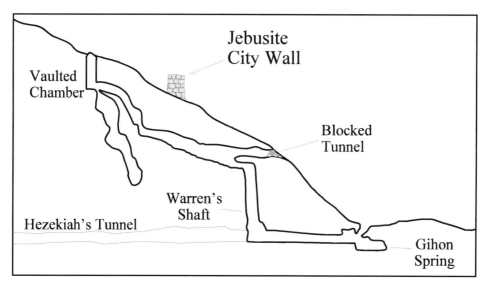

So David lived in the stronghold, and called it the city of David. And David built all around from the Millo and inward. (2 Samuel 5:9).

Jerusalem now became David's capital city. Because it was in previously unoccupied territory, it was considered to be free of any tribal associations. The "Millo" (מִלּוֹא) was the original fortification around which the city was built (the word מִלּוֹא means "to fill"). Its exact location remains uncertain.

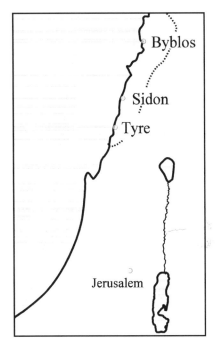

> *Then Hiram king of Tyre sent messengers to David with cedar trees and carpenters and stonemasons; and they built a house for David. (2 Samuel 5:11).*

The Phoenicians were the great sea power of that day (they were the only sea power of that day). They also had a great natural resource in forests of cedar trees - this resource of lumber had contributed to making them the sea power which they had come to be.

The major cities of Phoenicia were Byblos (from which we get our word "Bible"), Sidon, and Tyre. As powerful as the king of Tyre was, he still saw the need of an alliance with David. And yet, David was not carried away with his fame and good fortune.

> *And David realized that the Lord had established him as king over Israel, and that He had exalted his kingdom for the sake of His people Israel. (2 Samuel 5:12).*

Success and power always bring temptations which are difficult to resist. We can see time and time again the specter of a successful man who develops an over-inflated ego, leading him to sin. The key to resisting such temptation is the realization of the sovereignty of God and the fact that we owe any success to Him.

> *Now it came about when the king lived in his house, and the Lord had given him rest on every side from all his enemies, 2 that the king said to Nathan the prophet, "See now, I dwell in a house of cedar, but the ark of God dwells within tent curtains." (2 Samuel 7:1-2).*

David's next concern was a permanent dwelling in which to house the ark. Since the days of the Wilderness Wanderings, the ark had been kept within the Tabernacle - a tent designated as the "Tent of Meeting." In those early days, it was necessary for this structure to be a tent, for the Israelites were a nomadic people and they required a portable place of worship.

But that had now changed. They now had a land in which the Lord had given them rest. They had a capital city. And David felt that it was appropriate that a permanent place of worship be established - a House of God.

> *"...The Lord also declares to you that the Lord will make a house for you." (2 Samuel 7:11b).*

While David had desired to build a house for the Lord, God says that it is He who will build a house for David.

> *"When your days are complete and you lie down with your fathers, I will raise up your descendant [seed] after you, who will come forth from you, and I will establish his kingdom. 13 He shall build a house for My name, and I will establish his kingdom forever. 14 I will be a father to him and he will be a son to Me; when he commits iniquity, I will correct him with the rod of men and the strokes of the sons of men, 15 but my lovingkindness shall not depart from him, as I took it away from Saul, whom I removed from before you. 16 And your house and your kingdom shall endure before Me forever; your throne shall be established forever." (2 Samuel 7:12-16).*

The promise to David revolves around the establishment of a seed. This takes us all the way back to Genesis 3:15. It was there that the Lord had promised Adam and Eve that there would come One who would be of the seed of the woman. This Seed would crush the serpent's head. He would be the destroyer of the works of Satan. This promise is fulfilled in two parts. The immediate fulfillment will be in the person of Solomon. He will be the seed who will build a house in the name of

> Dead Sea Scroll 4Q Florilegium, a midrash scroll, shows that the Qumran scribes took the "son" in verse 14 to be a reference to Messiah.

the Lord. It will be Solomon who constructs the temple of God in Jerusalem. Solomon will found the Davidic dynasty. But the ultimate fulfillment of this prophecy is seen in Jesus.

Solomon	Jesus
Son of David.	Ultimate son of David.
Established the united monarchy of Israel.	Established the kingdom of God upon earth.
Built the temple.	He is the temple.
Established a kingdom that would continue until 586 B.C.	Established an eternal kingdom that will never end.
Chastened because of his iniquity.	Took upon Himself the sins of the world.

The first part of verse 14 (*"I will be a father to him and he will be a son to Me"*) is quoted twice in the New Testament.

- Hebrews 1:5 quotes it in a context that speaks of Jesus as the Son of God.
- 2 Corinthians 6:18 gives a partial quote as the Lord tells US that *"I will be a father to you, and you shall be sons and daughters to Me."*

The implications of this are striking. This passage refers, not only to Solomon, not only to Jesus, but also to us. We are a part of the house of God that He promises to establish.

The book of 2ⁿᵈ Samuel can be divided into two major sections corresponding to the two majors parts of David's reign. There is a rising action and then there is a falling action. What links these two parts together is the narrative of David's sin.

1:1	11:1	13:1
Rising Action ↗	David's Sin & Repentance	↘ **Falling Action**
David's Reign Prospers		David's Reign Troubled

Chapters 11-12 form the central and pivotal section of 2 Samuel. It is presented in a chiastic format. The first section will be the road of David's sin. The second section will be the road to David's repentance and

339

restoration.

David sends Joab to besiege Rabbah (11:1).

David sleeps with Bathsheba who becomes pregnant (11:2-5).

David has Uriah killed (11:6-17).

Joab sends a message about the murder (11:18-27).

The Lord sends David a messenger (12:1-14).

The Lord strikes David's son who dies (12:15-23).

David sleeps with Bathsheba who becomes pregnant (12:24-25).

Joab sends for David to come and take Rabbah (12:26-31).

This passage hardly presents David in a good light. He manages to disobey three of the ten commandments:
- Coveting
- Adultery
- Murder.

David attempts to cover up his sin with the murder of Uriah. He is brought to repentance only when the prophet Nathan comes and confronts him with his sin. Nathan does this by coming to David and telling the story of a great injustice that involves a rich man taking a poor man's little lamb. David is enraged at this story of injustice and, when he calls for justice to be done, Nathan points out that David has just declared his own judgment.

> *Nathan then said to David, "You are the man! Thus says the Lord God of Israel, 'It is I who anointed you king over Israel and it is I who delivered you from the hand of Saul. 8 I also gave you your master's house and your master's wives into your care, and I gave you the house of Israel and Judah; and if that had been too little, I would have added to you many more things like these! 9 Why have you despised the word of the Lord by doing evil in His sight? You have struck down Uriah the Hittite with the sword, have taken his wife to be your wife, and have killed him with the sword of the sons of Ammon. 10 Now therefore, the sword shall never depart from your house, because you have despised Me and have taken the wife of Uriah the Hittite to be your wife.'" (2*

340

Samuel 12:7-10).

David's anger was stopped cold by the simple pronouncement of Nathan: "You are the man!" This is a pronouncement of his sin. He has already pronounced judgment upon himself. He will suffer the consequences of his sin. Because of his sin, the sword will never depart from his house. Because of his sin, others will die.

There is a contrast here between David and David's greater descendant. A thousand years later, the Son of David would stand in this same city before a Roman governor who would proclaim, "Behold the man!" (John 19:5).

David	Jesus
He figuratively took another man's lamb and killed it.	He was the figure of the Lamb who was put to death.
He sinned against God.	He was obedient to the point of death.
Anointed to be king.	Anointed by the Holy Spirit.
Murdered a man in order to take his wife.	Gave up his own life to purchase a bride.
He sinned resulting in death to a number of his sons.	He took our sins upon Himself, resulting in life to all who believe.

Jesus is the Second David. He is the Man. He is the One who died in your place. If you will behold the Man, you will live. If you come before the Lord wanting to hear and to judge the sins of others, you will go away empty. But if you come to hear of the terrible truth of your own sins, then you will be ready to receive God's salvation.

The words of Nathan are presented in the format of a covenant lawsuit. The format of this lawsuit is such that we first read of the suzerain's past faithfulness to the vassal. David has acted the part of an unfaithful vassal to his Lord, the God of Israel.

> *"Thus says the Lord, 'Behold, I will raise up evil against you from your own household; I will even take your wives before your eyes and give them to your companion, and he will lie with your wives in broad daylight. 12 Indeed you did it secretly, but I will do this thing before all Israel, and*

under the sun.'" (2 Samuel 12:11-12).

The rest of the book of 2nd Samuel is going to be a fulfillment of this prophecy. David has succeeded in conquering all of his surrounding enemies. But God is going to raise up an enemy from his own household. One from his own family will rise against him. And in the same manner that he has taken another man's wife, one will come and will sleep with his wives. Instead of doing such a deed in secret, this will be accomplished openly and in the sight of all Israel. All shall witness the shame of David. From the same rooftop on which David had initially looked down to see Bathsheba, his son Absalom will conduct a rooftop orgy with the wives of David (2 Samuel 16:20-22). We see a growing parallel between David and his previous sin with Bathsheba versus the ongoing situations with his children.

David's Sin	David's Children
David lusts for Bathsheba, the wife of Uriah	Amnon lusts for Tamar, his half-sister.
David sends for Bathsheba and commits adultery with her.	Amnon pretends to be sick and then rapes Tamar.
David secretly plots to have Uriah put to death.	Absalom plots to murder his half-brother Amnon.
Nathan comes and tells a story that turns out to be a parable designed to bring David to repentance.	Joab has a woman of Tekoa come and tell a story that turns out to be a parable designed to bring Absalom back home.

David faces a threat similar to the threat that Saul had once thought was coming from David. Saul had thought that David was going to rebel against him and now, years later, Absalom actually did institute a rebellion against David.

Saul	David
Thought that David was going to rebel	Seems slow to see that Absalom was in rebellion
He immediately moves against David	He refuses to move against Absalom

| Consumed with protecting his own position | Focused on submission to the Lord |

Absalom's rebellion resulted in David having to flee Jerusalem. The narrative pictures David leaving the city and going to a vantage point on the Mount of Olives as he weeps over the city. We are reminded of how, a thousand years later, Jesus would leave Jerusalem and go to the Mount of Olives to weep over the city.

David escaped across the Jordan River where he was able to raise a fighting force to meet his rebellious son. Absalom pursued the forces of David but was then met with a crushing defeat in which he was killed. Absalom got what he deserved. By contrast, Jesus got what we deserved. He died in our place, paying the penalty of our sins.

Absalom	Jesus
His glorious, princely hair was caught and led to his death.	He left his glory to come to earth to die.
He was caught in a tree.	He died on a tree.
He was pierced by his enemies.	He was pierced by the Roman soldier
He got what he deserved.	He got what we deserved.

The story ends with the death of Absalom and with David's heartbreak over the loss of his son. It is in this instance that we see David as a man of sorrows. In seeing him in such a light, we are reminded of the second David. David says, "I wish I had died instead of you." The Second David says, "I did die instead of you."

CHIASTIC APPENDIX TO 2ND SAMUEL

The last four chapters of 2nd Samuel tell several different stories, most of which seem to have taken place earlier in David's reign. They are presented in a chiastic arrangement that has praise at its center and that is flanked by an intercessory prayer of David at the beginning and at the end:

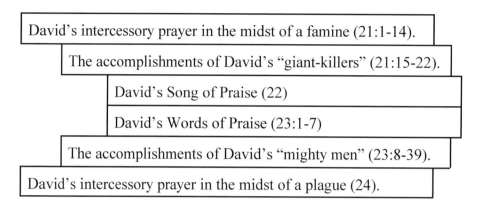

David's intercessory prayer in the midst of a famine (21:1-14).

The accomplishments of David's "giant-killers" (21:15-22).

David's Song of Praise (22)

David's Words of Praise (23:1-7)

The accomplishments of David's "mighty men" (23:8-39).

David's intercessory prayer in the midst of a plague (24).

David faces two temptations in the last chapter of this book. The first temptation will see him failing. The second temptation will see his success.

- To Count Success on the World's Scale.
- To Give to God that which is Easy to Give.

The first temptation involved David taking a census of the people. What was wrong with numbering the people? After all, there were numberings that took place both before this and after this that were allowed and even ordered by God.

We are not specifically told why it was wrong for David to engage in this numbering. We can speculate that it was because he would use this information to elevate his own status, exalting himself.

In 1 Chronicles 21:1 this temptation is ascribed to Satan. In 2 Samuel 24:1 we read that it was the anger of the Lord that moved David to number Israel. There is a lesson here. It is that even the temptations of Satan must first pass through a nail-scarred hand.

> *Now David's heart troubled him after he had numbered the people. So David said to the LORD, "I have sinned greatly in what I have done. But now, O LORD, please take away the iniquity of Thy servant, for I have acted very foolishly." (2 Samuel 24:10).*

David recognizes his sinful actions and the sinful attitudes that spurred them and he takes it to the Lord in repentance. He does not make excuses. He confesses his guilt and asks for forgiveness.

> *When David arose in the morning, the word of the LORD came to the prophet Gad, David's seer, saying, 12 "Go and speak to David, 'Thus the LORD says, "I am offering you*

three things; choose for yourself one of them, which I may do to you."'"

13 So Gad came to David and told him, and said to him, "Shall seven years of famine come to you in your land? Or will you flee three months before your foes while they pursue you? Or shall there be three days' pestilence in your land? Now consider and see what answer I shall return to Him who sent me."

14 Then David said to Gad, "I am in great distress. Let us now fall into the hand of the LORD for His mercies are great, but do not let me fall into the hand of man." (2 Samuel 24:11-14).

David throws himself upon the mercies of the Lord. That does not mean there will not be physical suffering as consequence for his actions, but it does reflect an understanding of God's forgiveness and God's goodness.

So the LORD sent a pestilence upon Israel from the morning until the appointed time; and seventy thousand men of the people from Dan to Beersheba died. (2 Samuel 24:15).

There is a contrast between David and the Son of David. David sinned and brought great destruction upon the people. The Son of David was without sin and, by His obedience, He brought life to many.

When the angel stretched out his hand toward Jerusalem to destroy it, the LORD relented from the calamity, and said to the angel who destroyed the people, "It is enough! Now relax your hand!" And the angel of the LORD was by the threshing floor of Araunah the Jebusite. (2 Samuel 24:16).

This is the second time the Lord intervened on this selfsame spot. It was here that Abraham had once prepared to slay his son, Isaac, in obedience to the command of the Lord. The angel of the Lord had been sent to provide a substitute. Now again, the wave of death is halted on this spot.

So Gad came to David that day and said to him, "Go up, erect an altar to the LORD on the threshing floor of Araunah the Jebusite." 19 And David went up according to the word of Gad, just as the LORD had commanded. (2 Samuel 24:18-19).

David was told to go and erect an altar on the site where the plague of destruction had halted. It was to serve as a testimony to what God had done in the past and also what God would do in the future in sending His Son to die on our behalf. This would also be the site of the future temple.

> *And Araunah looked down and saw the king and his servants crossing over toward him; and Araunah went out and bowed his face to the ground before the king. 21 Then Araunah said, "Why has my lord the king come to his servant?" And David said, "To buy the threshing floor from you, in order to build an altar to the LORD, that the plague may be held back from the people."*
>
> *22 And Araunah said to David, "Let my lord the king take and offer up what is good in his sight. Look, the oxen for the burnt offering, the threshing sledges and the yokes of the oxen for the wood. 23 Everything, O king, Araunah gives to the king." And Araunah said to the king, "May the LORD your God accept you."*
>
> *24 However, the king said to Araunah, "No, but I will surely buy it from you for a price, for I will not offer burnt offerings to the LORD my God which cost me nothing." So David bought the threshing floor and the oxen for fifty shekels of silver. (2 Samuel 24:20-24).*

Araunah offers to give to David both the threshing floor as well as the sacrifices and the wood on which to make the offering. David refuses. He will pay the price himself. The fact that the plague had stopped here indicates that Araunah and his cattle had been spared. In this, Araunah is a picture of us while David is a picture of Christ who has paid the price on our behalf.

David says that he will not offer that as a sacrifice which has cost him nothing. That is a fundamental principle of a sacrifice -- it imposes a cost to the giver. This echoes the sacrifice that Christ made on our behalf and underscores the corollary to this principle. It is that it cost God to forgive your sins. The cost was His only begotten Son and it was a cost that was paid in blood.

1ˢᵗ & 2ⁿᵈ KINGS
The Book of the Kings

The books that we know as First and Second Kings record the history of Israel from the death of David to the Babylonian Captivity. But they are much more than a mere history of Israel. They are primarily theological in nature in that they trace God's relationship with His Covenant people through their breaking of His covenant and their resulting punishment at the hands of their enemies. In particular, we see God's dealing with the leaders of the nation - her prophets, priests and kings.

DEVELOPING A CHRONOLOGY OF KINGS

The books of Samuel and Kings cover the historical period from Samuel to the Exile into Babylon.

1ˢᵗ Samuel	2ⁿᵈ Samuel	1ˢᵗ Kings	2ⁿᵈ Kings
Samuel & Saul	Saul & David	Solomon & Divided Kingdom	Fall of the Divided Kingdoms

The narrative runs smoothly in 1 Kings 1-11 because we are following the history of only one kingdom. But from 1 Kings 12 - 2 Kings 17 the author deals with both the Northern Kingdom of Samaria and the Southern Kingdom of Judah, shifting back and forth between these two. After 2 Kings 17 and the fall of the Northern Kingdom, the flow of history is again smooth as we read only of the Southern Kingdom.

1 Kings 1-11	1 Kings 12 - 2 Kings 17	2 Kings 18-25
United Kingdom under Solomon	Northern Kingdom	
	Southern Kingdom of Judah	

1. Old Testament writers did not use a universal reference point in establishing dates. Instead, they used various sorts of regal dating

methods ("In the 4th year of Hezekiah..."). This makes it difficult to be exact in establishing dates for Old Testament events.

2. Regal Reckoning.

The first year of a king might refer to the first year in which he served as regent or it might refer to his first year upon the throne.

3. Accession versus Non-accession Year Reckoning.

Accession Year Reckoning	Accession Year	1st Year	2nd Year
Non-Accession Year Reckoning	1st Year	2nd Year	3rd Year

Both types of reckoning were used in ancient times to determine which year it might be. Furthermore, in the Non-Accession Method, the last year of one ruler would be the same as the first official year of his successor. Such a year would count twice. Edwin Thiele suggests that these two differing systems were used at different times in Israel's history (1977).

	Accession Year Dating	Non-Accession Year Dating	Accession Year Dating
Judah	Rehoboam to Jehoshophat	Jehoram to Joash	Amaziah to Zedekiah
Israel	-	Jeroboam to Jehoahaz	Jehoash to Hoshea

4. The Assyrian Eponym List.

It was the custom in Assyria to name each year after one of the officers of the state. He would be known as the eponym. We have records of a consecutive list of Assyrian eponyms from 853 to 703 B.C. The Assyrians also included records of solar eclipses. Total eclipses were visible in Nineveh in 832, 763 and 585 B.C. By correlating the eclipses with the Eponym Lists, we have reliable dates for the years from 892 to 648 B.C.

PURPOSE OF KINGS

To understand the purpose of this book, one must first understand the date and circumstances of its writing. The last event recorded in 2 Kings 25:27-30 is the release of Jehoiachin from prison during the 37th year of his imprisonment in 560 B.C. [597 B.C. minus 37 years of captivity = 560 B.C.]. This marks the earliest date that Kings could have been completed in its present form.

Since there is no mention of a return to Jerusalem after the captivity, it seems probable that the book was written before that event in 538/539 B.C. This marks the latest date that Kings could have been written. It is written in the Captivity. The author has just seen the final remnant of the nation of Israel destroyed. He sits down to relate the account of how that took place. The purpose is two-fold:

1.   To Answer the Question: "How did we get here?"

The Northern Kingdom of Israel had long ago been taken into captivity. The Southern Kingdom of Judah is now in its own captivity. It seems as though the promises of God have failed. What went wrong? This book answers that question.

2.   To Give a Warning of the Consequences of Sin.

This book tells of the disastrous consequences of Israel's love affair with idolatry. The Jews learned their lesson from this experience. Though they struggled with other problems, overt idolatry was never again an issue among the Jews.

THE SUCCESSION OF SOLOMON

Now King David was old, advanced in age; and they covered him with clothes, but he could not keep warm. 2 So his servants said to him, "Let them seek a young virgin for my lord the king, and let her attend the king and become his nurse; and let her lie in your bosom, that my lord the king may keep warm." 3 So they searched for a beautiful girl throughout all the territory of Israel, and found Abishag the Shunammite, and brought her to the king. 4 The girl was very beautiful; and she became the king's nurse and served him, but the king did not cohabit with her. (1 Kings 1:1-4).

As the book opens, we are struck by David's feebleness and apparent inability to act decisively. This is the man who...

> Abishag is called a Shunammite. Shunem was a town to the southwest of the Sea of Galilee at the foot of Little Hermon.

- Killed Goliath with a simple sling.
- Eluded the wrath of Saul for so many years.
- United all of the Kingdom of Israel.
- Conquered all of the surrounding enemies of Israel.

At this point, David is barely 70 years of age (2 Samuel 5:4-5 says that he became king at the age of 30 and ruled for 40 years). But these years have not been kind to him. His years in exile and his years on the battlefield have taken their toll. And perhaps the worst of all have been the series of disasters which have involved his own family. It had begun with his sin with Bathsheba and his vain attempt at a coverup. The years which followed saw family tragedy.

- The rape of Tamar by her half-brother.
- The murder of Amnon at the hands of Absalom.
- The rebellion of Absalom.

There is a lesson here. It is that sin, while it can be forgiven, still carries its negative consequences. As a result, David was now a broken man. He seems to have been well past his prime, both physically as well as mentally. He has deteriorated to the point of no longer being able to keep warm in the chilly Jerusalem nights. To this end, his attendants obtain the services of a Shunammite girl who will be able to keep the old king warm.

> *Now Adonijah the son of Haggith exalted himself, saying, "I will be king." So he prepared for himself chariots and horsemen with fifty men to run before him. 6 His father had never crossed him at any time by asking, "Why have you done so?" And he was also a very handsome man, and he was born after Absalom. 7 He had conferred with Joab the son of Zeruiah and with Abiathar the priest; and following Adonijah they helped him. (1 Kings 1:5-7).*

Adonijah was one of the sons of David. Verse 6 specifies that he had been born after Absalom and, by saying this, compares his actions to those of Absalom who attempted to overthrow David. Adonijah was aided in his quest for the throne by several of David's longtime associates.

- Joab was the nephew of David (Zeruiah was David's sister) and had served for many years as the commander of David's army.
- Abiathar was the son of Ahimelech, the high priest of Nod who had been put to death by Saul when David was a fugitive.

These two leaders in the nation now throw their support behind Adonijah who is seeking to make certain that he will be the successor to the throne. There were certain men who had been specifically excluded from the plans of Adonijah.

- Zadok the priest: In 1 Chronicles 12:26-28 he is listed as a warrior of the house of Levi. He had served jointly with Abiathar as chief priest under David's rule.
- Benaiah the son of Jehoiada was the head of the 30 most valiant of David's men.
- Nathan the prophet.
- The mighty men who belonged to David.

Nathan is the man of the hour. He comes to Bathsheba with the situation and they plan how they are going to make David aware of the problem. Nathan was a good friend. He had called David to repentance when he sinned with Bathsheba. And now he comes to David's aid with Bathsheba to warn of impending danger. But he does so in a way designed to catch his attention, reminiscent of the previous time when he had captured David's attention with a story. Nathan sends Bathsheba to the King to warn him. Then he comes in himself to back up her story.

David orders immediate action to be taken in confirming Solomon as king. Solomon is to be given the mule of the king to ride and brought down to the Gihon, the main spring supplying water to the city of Jerusalem.

> *The king said to them, "Take with you the servants of your lord, and have my son Solomon ride on my own mule, and bring him down to Gihon. 34 Let Zadok the priest and Nathan the prophet anoint him there as king over Israel, and blow the trumpet and say, 'Long live King Solomon!' 35 Then you shall come up after him, and he shall come and sit on my throne and be king in my place; for I have appointed him to be ruler over Israel and Judah." (1 Kings 1:33-35).*

The Gihon Spring had been instrumental in the original conquest of Jerusalem at the beginning of David's reign. 2 Samuel 5:8 indicates that the city was taken "through the water tunnel." I have had opportunity to follow the route down the steep tunnel that is cut through Mount Ophel, the site of the original city. This tunnel allowed the inhabitants of the city to travel under the city walls to get water from a natural spring which flowed on the lower slopes of the mountain. Now David orders that Solomon is to be taken to this same spring to be anointed and proclaimed master of the city and king of the nation.

> *So Zadok the priest, Nathan the prophet, Benaiah the son of Jehoiada, the Cherethites, and the Pelethites went down and had Solomon ride on King David's mule, and brought him to Gihon.*
>
> *39 Zadok the priest then took the horn of oil from the tent and anointed Solomon. Then they blew the trumpet, and all the people said, "Long live King Solomon!"*
>
> *40 All the people went up after him, and the people were playing on flutes and rejoicing with great joy, so that the earth shook at their noise. (1 Kings 1:38-40).*

The instructions of David are carried out. Solomon is brought on David's mule to the Gihon spring, much the same way that a later Son of David will be brought to Jerusalem riding upon a donkey and receiving the same accolades. Indeed, it will be very close to this same location where Jesus shall make His own triumphal entry into the city. This was Solomon's triumphal entry. And lest there be any doubt as to David's intentions, he also bowed himself in the presence of his son.

> *Moreover, the king's servants came to bless our lord King David, saying, "May your God make the name of Solomon better than your name and his throne greater than your throne!" And the king bowed himself on the bed.*
>
> *48 The king has also said thus, "Blessed be the Lord, the God of Israel, who has granted one to sit on my throne today while my own eyes see it." (1 Kings 1:47-48).*

David viewed Solomon's ascension to the throne of Israel as a fulfillment of the covenant promise which God had made concerning the continuation of a descendant of David upon the throne of Israel. In 2 Samuel 7, God had promised that the throne of David would be established forever. This promise has been ultimately fulfilled in the person of Jesus.

Adonijah's supporters are quick to distance themselves from him and scatter to the four winds. Adonijah himself seeks refuge at the horns of the sacrificial altar which stood before the Tent of Meeting. His safety is guaranteed by Solomon as long as he acts in an appropriate manner.

> Horns were a sign of strength and potency. To hold onto the horns of the altar was to appeal to the Lord.

Evidently, Adonijah expected to be put to death as a rival claimant to the throne - an action that he himself would have taken against Solomon had he been successful. Such actions were not unknown in the ancient world.

Chapter 1 of 1st Kings closes with Adonijah being left on probation. He is allowed to live, providing he takes no further action against the king. This comes to fruition in the following chapter. In his exposition of 1st Kings, Ralph Davis points out that the first two chapters of 1 Kings form a couplet. They are given to us in something of a parallel.

1 Kings 1	1 Kings 2
Nathan approaches the king through Bathsheba.	Adonijah approaches the king through Bathsheba.
David swears an oath in response to Bathsheba (1:29-30).	Solomon swears an oath in response to Bathsheba (2:23).
Focus is upon the succession of the kingdom.	Focus is upon the security of the kingdom.

In chapter 2, Adonijah goes to Bathsheba, the mother of Solomon, and seeks her intercession to obtain as his wife the former nurse of David.

> *Then he said, "Please speak to Solomon the king, for he will not refuse you, that he may give me Abishag the Shunammite as a wife." (1 Kings 2:17).*

On the surface of things, this seems to be a harmless request. Perhaps Bathsheba thought this to be the case, for she agreed to make the request on Adonijah's behalf. Evidently she did not know what it signified. In ancient times, the king's harem would pass to the king's successor. Take a man's kingdom and you would also take his wives. When David had taken Saul's kingdom, he also took the wives of Saul into his keeping (2 Samuel 12:8). When Absalom drove David out of Jerusalem, he made it a point to go among the concubines of David in the sight of all Israel (2 Samuel 16:20-22).

Now Adonijah is requesting one of the members of the harem of David. Perhaps he is using the excuse, "She did not actually enter into sexual relations with him, she merely was there to keep him warm." But the implications would be present nonetheless. And Solomon sees through the request and even recognizes the conspirators involved.

> *King Solomon answered and said to his mother, "And why are you asking Abishag the Shunammite for Adonijah? Ask for him also the kingdom - for he is my older brother - even for him, for Abiathar the priest, and for Joab the son of Zeruiah!"*
>
> *23 Then King Solomon swore by the Lord, saying, "May God do so to me and more also, if Adonijah has not spoken this word against his own life." (2 Kings 2:22-23).*

Accordingly, both Adonijah and Joab who has evidently been partners in the conspiracy are put to death. Abiathar is banished from the priesthood and permitted to return to his own home in fulfillment of the prophecy originally made to Eli (Abiathar was the great, great grandson of Eli through Phinehas).

SOLOMON'S REIGN

The reign of Solomon saw a remarkable period of peace in that portion of the ancient world. Assyria was in a state of decline as it wrestled with internal strife and was further weakened with battles against Aram. Egypt also suffered the effects of a general decline, never again reaching her former dominance as a world power. Into this power vacuum rose the kingdom of Solomon who entered into a prosperous alliance with King Hiram of Tyre. The Phoenicians were the masters of the Mediterranean Sea.

1.   Solomon's Wisdom.

> *In Gibeon the LORD appeared to Solomon in a dream at night; and God said, "Ask what you wish me to give you." (1 Kings 3:5).*

When the Lord said to Solomon, "What do you want me to do for you?" He was probing Solomon's heart. "Solomon, what is it that is important to you? What is your goal in life? For what are you aiming?" Have you ever asked yourself that question? What is important to you? What do you want out of life? Most of us think in terms of power or wealth or long life, or some variation of those themes.

That is a great way to open a conversation in which you can share your faith. Merely ask someone, "For what are you living? What are your goals?" It is a question with which many people struggle. And when they answer it, their answer often comes out in such a materialistic way that it frightens even them. For what are you living? If you were to take a piece of paper and write down what your goal in life is, what would it be?

Someone once asked Major Ian Thomas what he was living for. His immediate response was, "To make visible the invisible Christ." Is that your goal?

> *"So give Your servant an understanding heart to judge Your people to discern between good and evil. For who is able to judge this great people of Yours?" (1 Kings 3:7-9).*

Solomon asks for "an understanding heart" — literally a "hearing heart." This is a request for discernment, the ability to look at the world and to understand it. Yet this was not a request simply for theoretical understanding. Solomon desires a wisdom which shall enable him to:

- Correctly lead the people of God.
- Discern between good and evil.

God has always desired that his people know the difference between good and evil. Adam and Eve learned that difference the hard way - by engaging in evil and learning first hand of its deadly effects.

God agrees to grant the request of Solomon. He gives him a "wise and discerning heart" - literally, a "wise and understanding heart." By this, the Lord gave Solomon the ability to judge and rule well. But that is not all. He went beyond this to give Solomon an understanding in areas beyond those having to do with rulership. We need only read through the books of Proverbs and Ecclesiastes to find that Solomon was given wisdom, the skill of living.

2.   The Extent of Solomon's Rule.

> *Now Solomon ruled over all the kingdoms from the River to the land of the Philistines and to the border of Egypt; they brought tribute and served Solomon all the days of his life. (1 Kings 4:21).*

"The River" refers to the Euphrates. It was commonplace among ancient empires that when the old king died, the subject nations would withhold tribute and challenge the new king in rebellion. This necessitated repeated punitive expeditions to reinforce the former king's terms and to prove the ability of the new king to enforce his will. Solomon did not have to do this. Instead, God gave to him a peaceful reign.

3.   The Prosperity of Solomon's Reign.

> *So Judah and Israel lived in safety, every man under his vine and his fig tree, from Dan even to Beersheba, all the days of Solomon. (1 Kings 4:25).*

It was not only Solomon who amassed riches. The people of Israel in his day also enjoyed a great amount of prosperity. The statement that "every man under his vine and his fig tree" became a favorite catch phrase used by the prophets to indicate the ideal conditions prevailing in Messiah's kingdom (Micah 4:4; Zechariah 3:10). The fact that a man could enjoy the fruit of the vine and the fig tree meant that there was a complete absence of warfare and it ensuing economic disruption.

4.   Solomon's Temple.

Construction of the Temple began on the fourth year of Solomon's reign (1 Kings 6:1). The building project took seven years and was climaxed with the dedication of the Temple.

- Location: The site for the Temple was high atop a threshing place at the top of Mount Moriah, located just north of the old Jebusite city of Jerusalem.

- Structure: The Temple was patterned after the same structure of the Tabernacle, except that it was bigger. Because it was built upon a mountain, you went up a series of stairs till you came to the highest part of the Temple -- the Holy of Holies.

The Temple was a rather small structure when compared to many of the modern churches of today. But it was not designed to hold an assembly of people. The congregation was not supposed to meet within the Temple - they were to direct their worship toward the Temple and the One whose presence was signified therein.

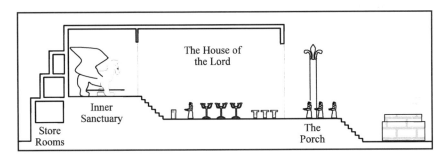

There were windows in the upper part of the Temple (6:4) as well as storerooms surrounding the Temple. The main structure was built of stone. But the stone was not shaped at the construction site. Each stone was prepared at the place of quarrying so that *there was neither hammer nor axe nor any iron tool heard in the house while it was being built (6:7)*. One can imagine this structure being raised in a reverent silence.

The Holy of Holies was in the shape of a perfect cube. The original Holy of Holies in the Tabernacle had been 10 cubits by 10 cubits by 10 cubits (a room 15 feet cubed). The Holy of Holies in the Temple was twice the size - 20 cubits by 20 cubits by 20 cubits (a room 30 feet cubed). It is interesting that these are the same proportions of the dimensions given for the New Jerusalem in Revelation 21:16.

Most Holy Place	New Jerusalem
Signified the presence of God	Signifies the Bride - the wife of the Lamb.
Overlaid with pure gold (1 Kings 6:20)	Made of pure gold (Revelation 21:18)

Filled with the glory of God (1 Kings 8:10)	Illuminated by the glory of God (Revelation 21:23)

Just as the creation of heaven and earth and the Sabbath rest that followed had taken seven days, so now the work of the building of the Temple took a corresponding seven years. There is a sense in which the Temple was to serve as a prototype of the earth that served as God's footstool.

> *And it came about when the priests came from the holy place, that the cloud filled the house of the Lord, 11 so that the priests could not stand to minister because of the cloud, for the glory of the Lord filled the house of the Lord. (1 Kings 8:10-11).*

This was the same cloud that had led the Israelites through the wilderness. It was the same cloud that had filled the Tabernacle as the time of its inauguration (Exodus 40:34-35). This was the cloud which the rabbis called "the Shekinah Glory," from the Hebrew root meaning "to dwell." It signified that God had taken up residence within the Temple, dwelling in the midst of His people.

5.   God's Covenantal Promise to Solomon.

> *Now it came about when Solomon had finished building the house of the Lord, and the king's house, and all that Solomon desired to do, 2 that the Lord appeared to Solomon a second time, as He had appeared to him at Gibeon. (1 Kings 9:1-2).*

This marks the second time that the Lord had appeared to Solomon. This was not a common occurrence. God did not do a lot of appearing to people in the Scriptures. Such appearances were very rare and special. Solomon had been greatly blessed in the fact that God had appeared to him. There is a principle here. It is that great privilege is accompanied by great responsibility. When you have been greatly blessed by God, it is also true that you have a greater responsibility to act in accordance with that blessing.

Verses 4-9 contain a repetition of the promise originally given to Solomon in 1 Kings 6:12-13. However this time there is a difference. This time the promise is accompanied by a warning:

9:4-5	Promise	IF you walk before Me as your father David walked, in integrity of heart and uprightness, doing according to all I have commanded keeping my statutes and ordinances THEN I will establish the throne of your kingdom over Israel forever
9:6-9	Warning	IF you or your sons shall turn away from following Me shall not keep My commandments & statutes go and serve other gods and worship them, THEN I will... Cut off Israel Israel will be a proverb & a byword This house will be ruined Everyone will be astonished

There is a principle here. It is that God will always be glorified in His people. He will either be glorified when they are obedient or else He will be glorified when they are disobedient. Notice that it was not mere outward obedience that was required. God is not only interested in outward actions. He is also interested in what goes on in the inside. He is interested in "integrity of heart and uprightness."

This marks a high point in the career of Solomon. The later years of his reign were to see a turning away from the Lord.

Contrasting Elements in Solomon's Career		
	His Early Years	**His Later Years**
Political Realm	Nation unified and Solomon exalted on the international scene	Tribes rebellious and loss of influence in Egypt, Edom, and Syria.
Economic Realm	People willing to donate time and money. Silver "as common as stones."	Heavy taxes and forced labor becomes burdensome.

Social Realm	Focus on building the Temple.	Focus upon other building projects of Solomon.
Spiritual Realm	Dedication to the Lord.	Other gods are worshiped.
Military Realm	Israelite military is exclusively infantry (cavalry not permitted under Mosaic Law).	Large chariot corps developed.

SOLOMON'S SINS

The Law of the Lord had given some very specific requirements for how the king of Israel was supposed to conduct himself.

> *When you enter the land which the Lord your God gives you, and you possess it and live in it, and you say, "I will set a king over me like all the nations who are around me," 15 you shall surely set a king over you whom the Lord your God chooses, one from among your countrymen you shall set as king over yourselves; you may not put a foreigner over yourselves who is not your countryman. 16 Moreover, he shall not multiply horses for himself, nor shall he cause the people to return to Egypt to multiply horses, since the Lord has said to you, "You shall never again return that way."*
>
> *17 He shall not multiply wives for himself, or else his heart will turn away; nor shall he greatly increase silver and gold for himself. (Deuteronomy 17:14-17).*

These laws were given in the days of Moses, hundreds of years before Israel ever had a king. Notice the specific prohibitions.

- Multiply horses or cause people to return to Egypt for horses (17:16).
- Multiply wives (17:17).
- Greatly increase silver and gold for himself (17:17).

We have already seen how Solomon had transgressed two of these prohibitions in the previous chapters. Now we come to the third and perhaps the most serious of the forbidden things.

1.   The Sin of Having Foreign Wives: *Now King Solomon loved many foreign women along with the daughter of Pharaoh: Moabite, Ammonite, Edomite, Sidonian, and Hittite women, 2 from the nations concerning which the Lord had said to the sons of Israel, "You shall not associate with them, nor shall they associate with you, for they will surely turn your heart away after their gods." Solomon held fast to these in love. (1 Kings 11:1-2).*

The multitude of wives which were accumulated by Solomon were the result of the many marital alliances with surrounding cities, nations, and kingdoms. But this was no excuse for breaking the explicit command of God.

There is a principle here. Expediency is never an excuse for doing wrong. Solomon might well have tried to justify his actions by saying it was a means to fulfilling God's promise to raise up the kingdom of David. But it is never right to do wrong.

Verse 2 says that Solomon held fast to these in love - his affections for them would lead to a corresponding decrease in his affections and his love for the Lord. Sin always does that. You cannot love sin and still love the Lord. They are opposites. The more you love sin, the more you will move away from the Lord.

But it is not merely outward or overt sin that pulls you away from God. There can be things which, of themselves, are merely neutral and amoral which can compete for your affections. Money is one of these things. Jesus warned that you cannot serve God and money (Luke 16:13). The more you love money, the less you will love the Lord.

2.   The Sin of a Turned Heart: *He had seven hundred wives, princesses, and three hundred concubines, and his wives turned his heart away. 4 For when Solomon was old, his wives turned his heart away after other gods; and his heart was not wholly devoted to the Lord his God, as the heart of David his father had been. (1 Kings 11:3-4).*

Verse 4 says that Solomon's heart was not "wholly devoted" (perfected). This is the same word that was used in 1 Kings 8:61 where Solomon called the people to be "wholly devoted to the Lord." There is nothing more tragic than one who started on the right path but who later turned away. In Solomon's case, it was his many wives who were instrumental in turning his heart away from the Lord.

This is why it is so important that believers marry believers. The Bible speaks explicitly against Christians marrying unbelievers.

> *Do not be bound together with unbelievers; for what partnership have righteousness and lawlessness, or what fellowship has light with darkness? 15 Or what harmony has Christ with Belial, or what has a believer in common with an unbeliever? (2 Corinthians 6:14-15).*

How many times have I heard the plaintive wail, "Perhaps I can bring him to Christ!" It rarely works that way. Usually it has the opposite effect. Usually such a relationship results in the Christian being pulled away from the Lord.

This "turning away" did not happen all at once. It was a gradual thing. We see this by the fact that it happened "when Solomon was old" (11:4). He began by merely allowing his wives to worship in their accustomed manner. But he eventually found himself joining in their idolatrous worship.

3.   The Sin of Idolatry: *For Solomon went after Ashtoreth the goddess of the Sidonians and after Milcom the detestable idol of the Ammonites. 6 Solomon did what was evil in the sight of the Lord, and did not follow the Lord fully, as David his father had done. 7 Then Solomon built a high place for Chemosh the detestable idol of Moab, on the mountain which is east of Jerusalem, and for Molech the detestable idol of the sons of Ammon. 8 Thus also he did for all his foreign wives, who burned incense and sacrificed to their gods. (1 Kings 11:5-8).*

What started as mere political expedience took Solomon to the point where he was bowing down and worshiping false gods.

Ashtoreth	Plural form of Ishtar/Astar, literally, "Goddess." In the Canaanite pantheon, Ishtar was the female consort of Baal. As such, she was a fertility goddess and her worship involved certain fertility rites.

Milcom	Also known as "Molech" - literally, "King." This was the god of the Ammonites.
Chemosh	This was the national god of Moab. The meaning of the name is uncertain ("Conqueror"?). His name is found on the Moabite stone describing him as a war god.

The mountain which is east of Jerusalem seems to be a reference to the Mount of Olives. This had formerly been a place where God was worshiped (2 Samuel 15:32). But now it was taken and made a place of apostasy.

It is not that Solomon renounced the Lord. It is that he tried to worship God and the other false gods. And in doing so, he tried to relegate God to the position of being only one god among others. God will never take second place. He wants to be first place in your life.

GOD'S JUDGMENT AGAINST SOLOMON

Now the Lord was angry with Solomon because his heart was turned away from the Lord, the God of Israel, who had appeared to him twice, 10 and had commanded him concerning this thing, that he should not go after other gods; but he did not observe what the Lord had commanded. (1 Kings 11:9-10).

The writer does not tell us that God was angry with Solomon because of the amassing of riches or because he had developed a chariot corps or even because of his many wives. The anger of God was due to his sin of idolatry.

There is a lesson here. It is that God takes worship very seriously. He has ordained how He is to be worshiped and He does not permit that worship to go to another. Solomon was all the more culpable because the Lord had appeared to him twice (11:9). Greater revelation always results in greater responsibility. We today have been given greater revelation, for we have the completed Scriptures. Because of that, we have a greater responsibility.

So the Lord said to Solomon, "Because you have done this, and you have not kept My covenant and My statutes, which I have commanded you, I will surely tear the kingdom from you, and will give it to your servant." (1 Kings 11:11).

The covenant which had been given to Solomon contained conditions. The promises which were a part of that covenant were conditional in nature. If Solomon obeyed, then the kingdom would continue. If Solomon disobeyed, then the kingdom would be taken from him and given to another.

> *"Nevertheless I will not do it in your days for the sake of your father David, but I will tear it out of the hand of your son. 13 However, I will not tear away all the kingdom, but I will give one tribe to your son for the sake of My servant David and for the sake of Jerusalem which I have chosen." (1 Kings 11:12-13).*

There is a temporary respite in this judgment. It is not carried out upon Solomon; it will be carried out upon his son. The reason for this is not because Solomon deserves the respite. The reason is because of David. Here is the principle. Our obedience sometimes results in blessings for our children. And the reverse is also true; our disobedience sometimes results in negative consequences upon our children. Sin always bears children. And our sins affect the lives of our children. The popular idea that a sin between two "consenting adults" affects no one else is a myth. It is a lie and has led to great sorrow.

THE RISE OF JEROBOAM

When Solomon was building up the fortifications in and around the city of Jerusalem, he appointed Jeroboam as the overseer for the forced labor crews over the house of Joseph - the tribes of Ephraim and Manasseh.

> *It came about at that time, when Jeroboam went out of Jerusalem, that the prophet Ahijah the Shilonite found him on the road. Now Ahijah had clothed himself with a new cloak; and both of them were alone in the field. 30 Then Ahijah took hold of the new cloak which was on him and tore it into twelve pieces. 31 He said to Jeroboam, "Take for yourself ten pieces; for thus says the Lord, the God of Israel, 'Behold, I will tear the kingdom out of the hand of Solomon and give you ten tribes 32 (but he will have one tribe, for the sake of My servant David and for the sake of Jerusalem, the*

city which I have chosen from all the tribes of Israel), 33
because they have forsaken Me, and have worshiped
Ashtoreth the goddess of the Sidonians, Chemosh the god of
Moab, and Milcom the god of the sons of Ammon; and they
have not walked in My ways, doing what is right in My sight
and observing My statutes and My ordinances, as his father
David did.'" (1 Kings 11:29-33).

God sends a prophet to Jeroboam with a message. This message is conveyed with a graphic picture. The prophet is wearing a new cloak. He takes the cloak and begins to rip it apart. He continues to rip until there are twelve pieces. The clothing is ruined. He then gives to Jeroboam ten of these pieces. It is a picture of what God is going to do to the nation of Israel. Ten tribes will be ripped from the house of David and given to Jeroboam because of the

> The tearing of this cloak is reminiscent of the time that Saul tried to hold onto Samuel and tore his cloak. Samuel used that instance to illustrate that the kingdom would be torn from Saul. There was also a tearing when Jesus died upon the cross. In His case, it was the veil of the Temple which was rent, demonstrating that the way to God had been opened for all. What Solomon lost in the dividing of the kingdom, Jesus repaired, not only in the restoring of the breach between Israel and Judah, but in restoring the breach between men and God, thus tearing down the dividing wall between all men.

idolatry which Solomon has brought into the land. The son of Solomon will be permitted to retain a single tribe (Levi doesn't count as a separate tribe as the Levites have no separate inheritance).

This is meant as a punishment against Solomon for his idolatry. But Solomon's punishment brings both privilege and responsibility to Jeroboam. He will have the privilege of being king over the northern tribes. He will also have the responsibility of following the Lord.

> *"I will take you, and you shall reign over whatever*
> *you desire, and you shall be king over Israel. 38 Then it will*
> *be, that if you listen to all that I command you and walk in My*
> *ways, and do what is right in My sight by observing My*
> *statutes and My commandments, as My servant David did,*
> *then I will be with you and build you an enduring house as I*
> *built for David, and I will give Israel to you." (1 Kings*
> *11:37-38).*

Jeroboam is given essentially the same promises and the same responsibilities which had first been given to Solomon. If he will follow the

Lord, then God will be with him and build for him "an enduring house" in the same way He built such a dynasty for David. There is a lesson which the writer of Kings is seeking to impart to his readers, those who are facing the prospect of a Babylonian Captivity. It is that God is able to take cursing and to turn it into blessing.

Historical Lesson	Immediate Lesson	Today's Application
Solomon's curse was that all but one of the tribes would be taken from his son.	Judah's curse was that the Temple was destroyed and her people carried to a foreign land.	Jesus came to His own and His own did not receive Him (John 1:11).
Jeroboam was given 10 tribes and the promise of an enduring house.	Judah was given the opportunity to return and rebuild.	As many as did receive Him have been given the right to become sons of God (John 1:12).
Jeroboam would continue to be blessed as long as he obeyed.	The restoration of worship and of relationship would only take place through obedience.	If we continue to walk in the light, we have fellowship with one another and cleansing from sin (1 John 1:7).

Romans 11 tells us that the unbelief in Israel has made it possible for the gospel to go to the Gentiles. This does not mean that we should take up an attitude of anti-Semitism or of smug self-righteousness. The church only continues to enjoy the benefits of blessing as she is obedient to the same terms of the covenant - believing and obeying the commands and the promises of God.

> *Solomon sought therefore to put Jeroboam to death;*
> *but Jeroboam arose and fled to Egypt to Shishak king of*
> *Egypt, and he was in Egypt until the death of Solomon. (1*
> *Kings 11:40).*

The inclusion of the word "therefore" makes it appear that the reason Solomon attempted to put Jeroboam to death was because he had heard about this prophecy. This is certainly possible. However the word "therefore" is absent from the Hebrew text. The Hebrew contains only a   conjunctive ("and"). It seems more likely that Jeroboam used this prophecy as an excuse to attempt to incite a revolution. Verse 27 specifically states that Jeroboam rebelled against the king. The account which follows relates how it came about that this rebellion took place.

Verse 26	Verse 27	Verses 28-39	Verse 40
Jeroboam rebelled against the king	This was the reason why he rebelled against the king...	Ahijah's Prophecy	Solomon sought to put Jeroboam to death

In this regard, Jeroboam stands in marked contrast to David who also had received a prophecy that he would be king. While David was willing to trust the Lord for His timing, Jeroboam takes matters into his own hands.

David	Jeroboam
Told by Samuel that he would replace Saul as king.	Told by Ahijah that he would be given 10 tribes from Solomon's son.
He was content to wait for the Lord to bring this about.	He determined to fulfill the prophecy by inciting a revolt.

From this, we can already see that Jeroboam will eventually take the northern tribes in a direction away from the Lord. His is the way of self-will. It leads ultimately to captivity. Note that Jesus is the One who restores the spiritual captivity of His people. He did so by being submissive to the Father's will and the Father's timing. When Satan offered to give to Jesus the kingdoms of the world, He refused the temptation. As a result, there will come a day when the Father will deliver all things over into His hand (1 Corinthians 15:23-25).

THE DIVIDED KINGDOM

The promise of kingship from the line of Judah had a long tradition, going back all the way to the prophecy of Jacob. Reuben, the firstborn of Jacob, had sinned against his father and lost the birthright. Simeon and Levi had also disqualified themselves from leadership. This promise of leadership had come to Judah.

Judah was the tribe from which David had come. Because of this, when the other tribes split off and went their own way, Judah remained faithful to the lineage of David. Even though Jerusalem was thought of as a neutral city, it still lay within the boundaries of the lands of Judah. Furthermore, Judah had been exempted from the forced labor which Solomon demanded of the rest of Israel.

The land of Judah was geographically divided from the rest of Israel by the deep valley of Sorek. It was bordered in the east by the Dead Sea, on the west by the lands of the Philistines and in the south by Edom and the Sinai Desert.

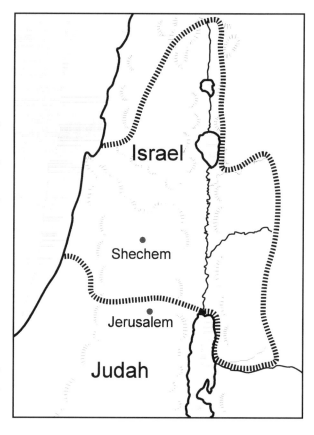

The history of the northern and southern kingdoms would run in parallel courses. Though both of these kingdoms would see periods of rebellion against the Lord, Judah's history would be marked by occasional periods of repentance and return.

REHOBOAM

Now Rehoboam the son of Solomon reigned in Judah. Rehoboam was forty one years old when he became king, and he reigned seventeen years in Jerusalem, the city which the Lord had chosen from all the tribes of Israel to put His name there. And his mother's name was Naamah the Ammonitess. (1 Kings 14:21).

Rehoboam was the son of Solomon. His mother was of the country of Ammon - presumably one of the 700 foreign wives which Solomon had married. Theirs had been a political marriage and it had produced this young man.

> Some scholars have wrestled with the idea that Rehoboam was 41 at the beginning of his reign since we read of "the young men who grew up with him" in 1 Kings 12:10. Furthermore, 2 Chronicles 13:7 speaks of the splitting of the kingdom having taken place at a time when Rehoboam "was young and timid and could not hold his own against them."

The parallel account in 2 Chronicles 11:17 tells us that the people of Judah served the Lord for three years. It was only after Rehoboam felt himself secure and established as king of Judah that he led the nation in forsaking the way of the Lord (2 Chronicles 12:1).

Rehoboam's story is one of good beginnings but poor endings. It is a pattern which we shall see repeated in a number of the kings of Judah. It began with Solomon. Now it is seen in his son. It is often seen in people today. The Christian life has been likened to a race. Paul said that we all run. But it is not a sprint; it is a marathon. We are in for the long haul. We are running for eternity. No one ever won only the first half of a race. You only win if you cross the finish line.

1.   The Sins of Judah: *Judah did evil in the sight of the Lord, and they provoked Him to jealousy more than all that their fathers had done, with the sins which they committed. 23 For they also built for themselves high places and sacred pillars and Asherim on every high hill and beneath every luxuriant tree. 24 There were also male cult prostitutes in the land. They did according to all the abominations of the nations which the Lord dispossessed before the sons of Israel. (1 Kings 14:22-24).*

Judah actually seems to have descended more readily into idolatry and the worship of false gods than did Israel. This process had begun with Solomon and the pagan practices of his foreign wives. It now returned with a vengeance.

- High Places: It was the custom throughout the entire fertile crescent to conduct worship in a "high place." The origin of this practice may go back all the way to the Tower of Babel.
- Sacred Pillars: This is an obelisk. They were used by the Canaanites as fertility symbols.
- Asherim: An Asherah was a tree which was used for worship. Asherim (plural) were an entire grove of such trees.

- Male Cult Prostitutes: A part of the pagan worship involved homosexual acts within the places of worship. It was thought that participation in such actions would incite the various gods who ruled over the wind and the rain to participate and thus bring fertility to the land.

The people of Israel had been forbidden from participating in these pagan practices. But now they entered into them with a passion. As a result, the Lord soon brought judgment upon the land.

2.   Invasion from Egypt: *Now it happened in the fifth year of King Rehoboam, that Shishak the king of Egypt came up against Jerusalem. 26 He took away the treasures of the house of the Lord and the treasures of the king's house, and he took everything, even taking all the shields of gold which Solomon had made. 27 So King Rehoboam made shields of bronze in their place, and committed them to the care of the commanders of the guard who guarded the doorway of the king's house. 28 Then it happened as often as the king entered the house of the Lord, that the guards would carry them and would bring them back into the guards' room. (1 Kings 14:25-28).*

The body of Shishak was discovered at an intact burial tomb at Tanis in 1938. The 21st Dynasty of Egypt had been friendly to Israel to the point of Pharaoh's daughter being wedded to King Solomon. However these good relations did not last past Solomon's death. Now there came a Libyan to the throne who founded a new ruling family - the 22nd Dynasty. He is known in historical records as Sheshonq (the Biblical Shishak). He was able to reunify the country which had been previously divided and brought a certain amount of stability to the crown. He then turned his attention to foreign policy, renewing an alliance with Byblos and regaining control of Nubia. It is likely this same Sheshonq who had given refuge to such enemies of Israel as Jeroboam and Hadad the Edomite. Now he marched into Judah. Archaeological records list 150 cities which he claimed to have taken in this campaign. Among the cities which were looted was Jerusalem and its temple.

> We know from Egyptian records at Karnak that this raid extended all the way into Galilee.

Egyptian records list the thousands of pounds of gold and silver that the son of Shishak offered to the Egyptian gods following his raid into Canaan. This was the plunder which he had taken from

Solomon's Temple. From this time on, the reign of Rehoboam would be only a shadow of its former glory. The golden shields of Solomon were replaced by shields of bronze, a less-valued commodity. The old forms continued, but they lost some of their luster.

JEROBOAM & THE NORTHERN KINGDOM

Then Jeroboam built Shechem in the hill country of Ephraim, and lived there. And he went out from there and built Penuel. (1 Kings 12:25).

Shechem was already an ancient city, nearly a thousand years old dating back before the days of Jacob. Jeroboam built up this city and made it his initial capital. Later he built a secondary palace at Penuel, the place where Jacob had wrestled with the angel on the Jabbok River. These two sites were located amidst the center of the Northern Kingdom and were designed to unify the people under his rule. To further cement this unity, Jeroboam determined to change the manner of worship in Israel.

Jeroboam said in his heart, "Now the kingdom will return to the house of David. 27 "If this people go up to offer sacrifices in the house of the Lord at Jerusalem, then the heart of this people will return to their lord, even to Rehoboam king of Judah; and they will kill me and return to Rehoboam king of Judah."
28 So the king consulted, and made two golden calves, and he said to them, "It is too much for you to go up to Jerusalem; behold your gods, O Israel, that brought you up from the land of Egypt." 29 He set one in Bethel, and the other he put in Dan. (1 Kings 12:26-29).

Jeroboam was now the king of the Northern Kingdom. But he was a king with a problem. The law of the Lord mandated that all Israelites make a pilgrimage three times a year to worship the Lord in His Temple. And here lay the problem. The Temple was in Jerusalem. And Jerusalem was in Judah. And this land was under the domain of Rehoboam. This state of affairs would give Rehoboam ample opportunity to wage a propaganda campaign which could ultimately result in Jeroboam being removed and the Kingdom being reunited.

Jeroboam came up with an alternative plan of worship. It was a plan

371

which appealed to convenience. The plan was for two centers of worship to be set up within the Northern Kingdom. They would be located at the extreme northern and southern borders of the kingdom.

1. Bethel ("House of God").

    This was the place where Jacob had his vision of a ladder reaching to heaven (Genesis 28:11-19). It was located a mere 12 miles north of Jerusalem and sat atop a bare mountaintop.

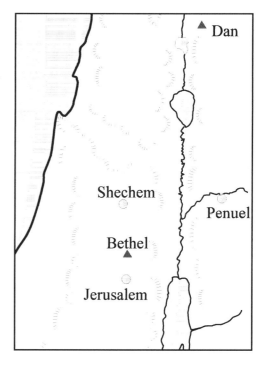

2. Dan.

    The tribe of Dan had originally been given an allotment of land between Judah, Ephraim and Benjamin. This location was uncomfortably close to the Philistines and, in the days of the judges, they migrated northward to the area north of the Sea of Galilee on the slopes of Mount Hermon (Judges 18). Capturing the Canaanite city of Laish, they renamed it Dan and made it their religious center with their own Levitical priesthood descended from Moses (Judges 18:30).

At each of these two locations there was erected a golden calf. Perhaps it was reasoned that such a means of worship had been instituted by Aaron at Mount Sinai. In actuality, both Aaron and Jeroboam had borrowed this calf worship from Egypt where the sacred cow was the symbol of the goddess Hathor.

Many of the Hebrews who remained faithful to the teachings of the Law fled to the south to where they could worship in peace. Included in this exodus were many of the Levites. As this strong core of faithful moved out, the Northern Kingdom would find itself subject to apostasy and eventual ruin.

SOUTHERN KINGDOM OF JUDAH	CATEGORY	NORTHERN KINGDOM OF ISRAEL
19 Kings, 1 Queen	Kings	19 Kings
Jerusalem	Capital	Samaria
1 Dynasty	Dynasties	5 Dynasties and several independent kings.
Judah & Benjamin	Tribes	10 Northern Tribes.
Most were unstable; some were good & some were bad.	Character of the Kings	All were bad, but only Ahab and Ahaziah were Baal worshipers.
By Babylon in 586 B.C.	Conquered	By Assyria in 721 B.C.
Returned to the land.	Afterward	No return.

THE PROPHECY AGAINST THE ALTAR OF BETHEL

Now behold, there came a man of God from Judah to Bethel by the word of the Lord, while Jeroboam was standing by the altar to burn incense. (1 Kings 13:1).

The altar against which this prophecy is pronounced is one of two altars that Jeroboam had caused to be set up. One altar was at Dan on the northern boarder of Israel. The other altar was here at Bethel on the southern boarder of Israel. His religious program seems to have been generally accepted by the people of Israel. But then a day came when a "man of God" arrived from Judah.

1.	The Pronouncement: *And he cried against the altar by the word of the Lord, and said, "O altar, altar, thus says the Lord, 'Behold, a son shall be born to the house of David, Josiah by name; and on you he shall sacrifice the priests of the high places who burn incense on you, and human bones shall be burned on you.'" 3 Then he gave a sign the same day, saying, "This is the sign which the Lord had spoken, 'Behold, the altar shall be split apart and the ashes which are on it*

373

shall be poured out.'" *(1 Kings 13:2-3).*

The man of God speaks directly to the altar. After all, the altar is the visible sign of Jeroboam's transgression. There ought not to have been an altar here. The fact that there was an altar here was a sign that Jeroboam had instituted a religious system different than that which had been established by God.

The prophecy foretells the coming of a son of David - Josiah by name. This man would offer a sacrifice where Jeroboam was now offering a sacrifice. But his sacrifice would be the lives of the false priests whom Jeroboam had established.

Jeroboam	Josiah
King of Northern Kingdom of Israel	He would be king of Judah
Took the throne via rebellion	He would be a legitimate descendant of David
Set up an altar at Bethel and offered sacrifices on it	He would slaughter the false priests upon this altar
Ruled from 931 to 910 B.C.	Ruled from 640 to 609 B.C.

This prophecy was given nearly 300 years before Josiah would come on the scene. There is a lesson here. It is that God uses a calendar, not a stopwatch. There are promises in the Scriptures which were made thousands of years ago and which still have not yet been fulfilled. But they will be. Just because Christ does not come back tomorrow does not mean that He is not coming back.

2.   Jeroboam's Response: *Now when the king heard the saying of the man of God, which he cried against the altar in Bethel, Jeroboam stretched out his hand from the altar, saying, "Seize him." But his hand which he stretched out against him dried up, so that he could not draw it back to himself. 5 The altar also was split apart and the ashes were poured out from the altar, according to the sign which the man of God had given by the word of the Lord. (1 Kings 13:4-5).*

Jeroboam was furious over this prophecy. He pointed at the man of God and ordered that he be arrested. But no sooner had he done this when the hand with which he had pointed was itself "dried up." This king who "took a hand" in establishing his own religious system found that his own hand completely impotent before the presence of the Lord.

3.   Jeroboam's Request: *The king said to the man of God, "Please entreat the Lord your God, and pray for me, that my hand may be restored to me." So the man of God entreated the Lord, and the king's hand was restored to him, and it became as it was before. (1 Kings 13:6).*

Jeroboam quickly changes his tune. He goes from threatening to pleading. But this is not true repentance. This is seen in the manner of his request. He asks the man of God to intercede on his behalf: "Please entreat the Lord **your** God, and pray for me." He seems to recognize that the God of Abraham is not his God. God is the prophet's God, but He is not the God of Jeroboam. True repentance takes place when God becomes **your** God.

4.   Jeroboam's Invitation.

Once he had been healed, Jeroboam took a different track - if you can't beat them, then join them. He invited the man of God to eat with him. But the man refused. He had been given some very specific instructions from the Lord.

- Don't eat with anyone in Israel.
- Don't drink with anyone in Israel.
- Don't even travel home the same way.

5.   The Failure of the Man of God.

Having refused Jeroboam's offer of hospitality, the man of God began making his way back to Judah. He had been told not to eat or drink or even to travel along the same path in Israel. But while he was on his way, something happened to change his resolve. It was an old prophet who lived in Bethel. He intercepted the man of God and spun a yarn about an angel having brought a change of plan.

He said to him, "I also am a prophet like you, and an angel spoke to me by the word of the LORD, saying, 'Bring him back with you to your house, that he may eat bread and drink water.'" But he lied to him. (1 Kings 13:18).

This old prophet was lying through his teeth. What was the purpose of this deception? He wished to bend the man's will to his own, so he made up a story about an angel appearing to him. There is an important lesson here. God's truth remains true. It remains true even though an angel might be claimed to have brought a contradicting message.

The Mormon church preaches such a message. They claim that an angel named Moroni appeared to Joseph Smith with some new revelation which changed that which was previously taught. Many people have unwittingly followed this message. They have followed in the tragic path of this man of God. The apostle Paul reminds us of the importance of holding to the plain truths of God even in the face of the claim of contradicting supernatural revelation.

> *But even though we, or an angel from heaven, should preach to you a gospel contrary to that which we have preached to you, let him be accursed. (Galatians 1:8).*

The man of God accepted the prophet's words at face value. And in doing so, he departed from the clear revelation of God.

> *Now it came about, as they were sitting down at the table, that the word of the Lord came to the prophet who had brought him back; 21 and he cried to the man of God who came from Judah, saying, "Thus says the Lord, 'Because you have disobeyed the command of the Lord, and have not observed the commandment which the Lord your God commanded you, 22 but have returned and eaten bread and drunk water in the place of which He said to you, "Eat no bread and drink no water"; your body shall not come to the grave of your fathers.'"(1 Kings 13:20-22).*

This time the Lord really does speak to the old prophet. The message is one of judgment against the man of God. He is judged because he disobeyed the clear command of the Lord. As he continues on his way, he is met by a lion which kills him.

Now I have to ask a question. What is the point of this story?

Why is it inserted in this narrative of kings and kingdoms? The man of God is a microcosm of the people of Israel. They had been given clear instructions from the Lord as to how He was to be worshiped and how they were to live. Jeroboam has come on the scene and has established an alternative means of worship. It is not that Jeroboam is telling people to worship a different God - he is merely telling them to worship the Lord in a different way. His is the religion of pragmatism. It is the way of convenience. Who wants to travel all the way to Jerusalem to worship when you can do it without ever leaving the comfort of your own home?

The Man of God	The People of Israel
Given specific instructions as to how he was to travel through Israel.	Given specific instructions as to how they were to worship God.
He followed the old prophet's alternate instructions.	They followed Jeroboam's alternate method of worship.
He was killed by a lion.	They would ultimately be taken into captivity by the lion of Assyria.

ABIJAM'S EVIL REIGN OVER JUDAH

Now in the eighteenth year of King Jeroboam, the son of Nebat, Abijam became king over Judah. 2 He reigned three years in Jerusalem; and his mother's name was Maacah the daughter of Abishalom. 3 He walked in all the sins of his father which he had committed before him; and his heart was not wholly devoted to the Lord his God, like the heart of his father David. (1 Kings 15:1-3).

Our story now moves from Jeroboam in the north back to the Kingdom of Judah in the south. The reader should take care not to confuse Abijah, son of Jeroboam with Abijam, son of Rehoboam.

We are specifically told that Abijam followed in the sins of Rehoboam and Solomon. There is a lesson here for fathers. It is the lesson of the harvest. You always sow what you reap, but you often reap more than what you sow. If you are setting an example of sinfulness, then your children will take that example and will often surpass it. On the other hand, if you teach your children to serve the Lord and to follow Him, they will often not only follow your example, but will surpass it.

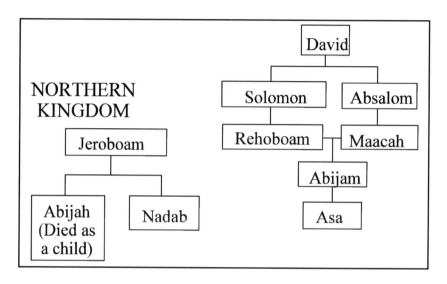

ASA'S REFORMATION IN JUDAH

> *So in the twentieth year of Jeroboam the king of Israel, Asa began to reign as king of Judah. (1 Kings 15:9).*

Asa would bring about the first of four revivals in the Kingdom of Judah. His reign of 41 years would mark a returning to the Lord.

> *Asa did what was right in the sight of the Lord, like David his father. (1 Kings 15:11).*

Throughout the rest of the book of Kings, we will read of each of the kings of Judah a summary statement of the way in which he conducted himself. This summary will say one of two things.

a.   He walked in the sins of his fathers.
              Or...
b.   He walked right in the sight of the Lord like David.

There are two ways in which you can live. You can live in sin, or you can live in the sight of the Lord, determined to obey Him and please Him.

Asa was such a man. He wished to do right in the sight of God.

> *He also put away the male cult prostitutes from the*
> *land and removed all the idols which his fathers had made.*
> *He also removed Maacah his mother from being*
> *queen mother, because she had made a horrid image as an*
> *Asherah; and Asa cut down her horrid image and burned it*
> *at the brook Kidron. (1 Kings 15:12-13).*

The writer of Kings makes no mention of the prophet Azariah (2 Chronicles 15:1-7) who was a moving influence in the life of Asa. There are times when God will use a man or a woman as an influence for good behind the scenes. 2 Chronicles 15 relates how Asa called an assembly of the people in which all were invited to renew their covenant with the Lord.

> *But the high places were not taken away; nevertheless*
> *the heart of Asa was wholly devoted to the Lord all his days.*
> *(1 Kings 15:14).*

Although Asa was *wholly devoted to the Lord*, it did not necessarily follow that all of his subjects were equally devoted to God. While it is true that you can legislate morality, you cannot legislate devotion. You can make a person to act in the appropriate manner, but you cannot make a person believe. You can govern outward actions, but you cannot govern attitudes. Only the Lord can do that.

The reforms which Asa brought about in Judah served as a beacon for the worship of the Lord to all Israelites. He gave an open invitation to members of every tribe of Israel to come and worship in the Temple.

> *And he gathered all Judah and Benjamin and those*
> *from Ephraim, Manasseh and Simeon who resided with them,*
> *for many defected to him from Israel when they saw that the*
> *Lord was with him. (2 Chronicles 15:9).*

This was seen as a threat to the continued security of the Northern Kingdom and the response was an embargo against all traffic coming from or going into Judah.

> *Now there was war between Asa and Baasha king of*
> *Israel all their days. 17 Baasha king of Israel went up against*
> *Judah and fortified Ramah in order to prevent anyone from*
> *going out or coming in to Asa king of Judah. (1 Kings 15:16-*

17).

Baasha had murdered all of the dynasty of Jeroboam (we are told that story in the latter part of this chapter). He invaded Judah and captured the city of Ramah, a scant 5 miles north of Jerusalem. There are several different cities in Palestine by this name. The name means "high place." Those towns with this name were all built on top of a mountain. The purpose of Baasha's taking of this city was *to prevent anyone from going out or coming in to Asa king of Judah.* It was not enough for Baasha to walk in the path of idolatry. He also wanted to stop others from worshiping the Lord. Evil is like that. Evil always wants company.

> *Then Asa took all the silver and the gold which were left in the treasuries of the house of the Lord and the treasuries of the king's house, and delivered them into the hand of his servants. And King Asa sent them to Ben-hadad the son of Tabrimmon, the son of Hezion, king of Aram, who lived in Damascus, saying, 19 "Let there be a treaty between you and me, as between my father and your father. Behold, I have sent you a present of silver and gold; go, break your treaty with Baasha king of Israel so that he will withdraw from me."*
>
> *20 So Ben-hadad listened to King Asa and sent the commanders of his armies against the cities of Israel, and conquered Ijon, Dan, Abel-beth-maacah and all Chinneroth, besides all the land of Naphtali. (1 Kings 15:18-20).*

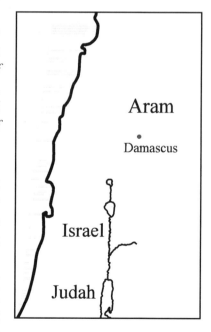

Instead of turning to the Lord for help, Asa responds to the incursion by soliciting assistance from the King of Aram (modern Syria), the country to the northeast of Israel.

The Aramaeans had been long-standing enemies of Israel. David had subdued the Aramaean tribes, occupying Damascus (2 Samuel 8:6), but in the days of Solomon, Rezon ben Eliada had retaken Damascus, being "Israel's adversary as long as Solomon lived" (1 Kings 11:23-25).

Now there was a new dynasty in Damascus headed by Ben-Hadad (there will be several kings of Damascus with this name. Hadad was the name of one of the pagan deities of that day). Asa stripped the treasures of the Temple and used them to bribe Ben-Hadad into invading Israel from the north.

> "For the eyes of the Lord move to and fro throughout the earth that He may strongly support those whose heart is completely His. You have acted foolishly in this. Indeed, from now on you will surely have wars." - Hanani the Seer to Asa (2 Chronicles 16:9).

Why would Asa turn to Aram for help instead of turning to the Lord? Perhaps he had been infected with the idea of a dichotomy between the spiritual realm versus the social and political realm. He was willing to turn to the Lord for spiritual matters but sought to handle secular matters on his own. We are often tempted to do the same thing. We trust in Christ for eternal life, but we won't trust Him to deal with a difficult situation at work.

THE HOUSE OF BAASHA'S EVIL REIGN IN THE NORTH

Once again, our scene shifts back to the northern kingdom of Israel. We have already seen Baasha as the king who was pitted against Asa, but now we are told of his origins.

> *Now Nadab the son of Jeroboam became king over Israel in the second year of Asa king of Judah, and he reigned over Israel two years. 26 He did evil in the sight of the Lord, and walked in the way of his father and in his sin which he made Israel sin.*
>
> *27 Then Baasha the son of Ahijah of the house of Issachar conspired against him, and Baasha struck him down at Gibbethon, which belonged to the Philistines, while Nadab and all Israel were laying siege to Gibbethon. 28 So Baasha killed him in the third year of Asa king of Judah and reigned in his place. (1 Kings 15:25-28).*

Baasha was a usurper to the throne, an assassin-turned king. This sets the tone for the rest of the history of the northern kingdom of Israel. There will be a number of different dynasties which rule over Israel and each will end with the assassination of a king and the murder of his progeny.

It came about as soon as he was king, he struck down all the household of Jeroboam. He did not leave to Jeroboam any persons alive, until he had destroyed them, according to the word of the Lord, which He spoke by His servant Ahijah the Shilonite, 30 and because of the sins of Jeroboam which he sinned, and which he made Israel sin, because of his provocation with which he provoked the Lord God of Israel to anger. (1 Kings 15:29-30).

The execution of the entire family of Jeroboam was a punishment for the sins of Jeroboam in leading Israel into idolatry. However Baasha proved to be no better at following the Lord than Jeroboam. He seems to have continued in following the same spiritual idolatry which had been instituted by Jeroboam. As a result, he was confronted by the prophet Jehu.

Now the word of the Lord came to Jehu the son of Hanani against Baasha, saying, 2 "Inasmuch as I exalted you from the dust and made you leader over My people Israel, and you have walked in the way of Jeroboam and have made My people Israel sin, provoking Me to anger with their sins, 3 behold, I will consume Baasha and his house, and I will make your house like the house of Jeroboam the son of Nebat. 4 Anyone of Baasha who dies in the city the dogs will eat, and anyone of his who dies in the field the birds of the heavens will eat." (1 Kings 16:1-4).

As the house of Jeroboam had been removed for its idolatry, so the house of Baasha would be removed for continuing in the same idolatry. Elah was the son of Baasha and succeeded him to the throne of Israel. It was after a reign of only two years that he was assassinated by Zimri, one of his military commanders.

House of Jeroboam	House of Baasha
Founder of the dynasty rebelled against Rehoboam and reigned for a long period - 22 years.	Founder of the dynasty murdered Nadab and reigned in his place for a long period - 24 years.
Jeroboam instituted idolatry in the land.	Baasha continued the program of idolatry.

382

Nadab, the son of Jeroboam, succeeded his father and reigned only 2 years before being assassinated.	Elah, the son of Baasha, succeeded his father and reigned only 2 years before being assassinated.

THE RISE OF THE HOUSE OF OMRI

The assassination of Elah and its resulting execution of all of the members of the house of Baasha left a power vacuum. Zimri may have thought to become king himself, but he was unable to gain a following and his reign lasted only a week. Following his untimely death, there arose two contenders for the throne of Israel.

- Tibni, the son of Ginath.
- Omri, commander of the army.

After a civil war which lasted 6 years, it was Omri who came out as the winner in this conflict - he seems to have had both the military expertise as well as the support of the army it taking the throne.

1. Samaria: *He bought the hill Samaria from Shemer for two talents of silver; and he built on the hill, and named the city which he built Samaria, after the name of Shemer, the owner of the hill. (1 Kings 16:24).*

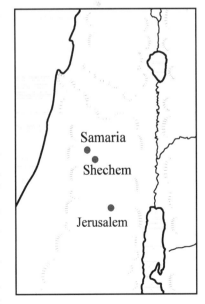

Samaria was to become the new capital city of Israel. It was located on a large oval hilltop, from the top of which the Mediterranean Sea was visible to the west. It lay 6½ miles northwest of Shechem and along the major north-south highway.

Samaria was surrounded by a double wall with towers and bastions. Its main gate faced east where a low ridge joins the hill of Samaria to the major north-south mountain range.

2.   Ahab's Marriage Alliance: *Ahab the son of Omri did evil in the sight of the Lord more than all who were before him. 31 It came about, as though it had been a trivial thing for him to walk in the sins of Jeroboam the son of Nebat, that he married Jezebel the daughter of Ethbaal king of the Sidonians, and went to serve Baal and worshiped him. 32 So he erected an altar for Baal in the house of Baal which he built in Samaria. (1 Kings 16:30-32).*

    Ahab, the son of Omri and successor to his throne, entered into an alliance with the Phoenicians, sealing it by taking a Phoenician princess to be his wife. This alliance would have long-lasting repercussions in Israel.

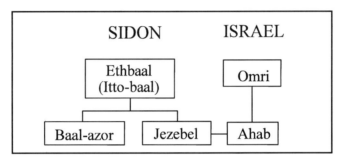

    It is because of this Phoenician influence that Ahab soon finds himself engaged, not only in idolatry, but in the worshiping of Baal, the god of the Phoenicians. Up to this time, the Israelites had been guilty of attempting to worship Yahweh in an improper manner - through the use of idols which had been established at Bethel and at Dan. But now they turned away completely from any attempt to worship the Lord and turned instead to a false god.

3.   The Rebuilding of Jericho: *In his days Hiel the Bethelite built Jericho; he laid its foundations with the loss of Abiram his firstborn, and set up its gates with the loss of his youngest son Segub, according to the word of the Lord, which He spoke by Joshua the son of Nun. (1 Kings 16:34).*

    Jericho had been destroyed in the days of Joshua. It had been the first city of Canaan to fall to the Israelites when they entered into the land. As such, it had been accursed, all its inhabitants and even the plunder of the city given over to be burned. Achan's sin had been that of attempting to take some of that plunder for himself and he had paid with his life.

Joshua had issued a decree that Jericho was not to be rebuilt. With his decree came a curse that the man who would attempt to rebuild Jericho would suffer the loss of both his firstborn son and his youngest son (Joshua 6:26).

Apparently with the full blessing of Ahab, Hiel set out to rebuild Jericho. In keeping with the ancient curse, he seems to have deliberately sacrificed both his oldest and his youngest sons. This was the sort of activity which was commonplace among Baal worshipers.

THE MINISTRY OF ELIJAH

Now Elijah the Tishbite, who was of the settlers of Gilead, said to Ahab, "As the Lord, the God of Israel lives, before whom I stand, surely there shall be neither dew nor rain these years, except by my word." (1 Kings 17:1).

Elijah comes out of the pages of obscurity and onto the scene of ministry in a single sentence. We know only that he was from *the settlers of Gilead.* Gilead was the designation for the lands of Israel on the east side of the Jordan River. These were the lands which had been taken by the two and a half tribes.

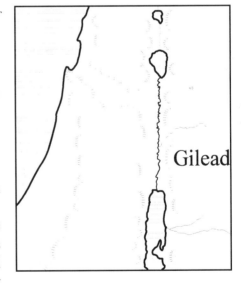

- Reuben
- Gad
- Half of the tribe of Manasseh

When Moses had led the Israelites to the Jordan, these tribes had looked at this land and they had said, "We don't need to go any further. We don't care what the promised land looks like, we will settle for this land."

Elijah now comes on the scene from Gilead. His name means "my God is Yahweh." And he is a man with a message. His message is one of the judgment of God. *"There shall be neither dew nor rain these years, except by my word" (17:1)* James tells us that this lack of rain was in answer to a prayer that was prayed by Elijah (James 5:17). Why would Elijah pray such a prayer? We normally pray for that which is good for our country. But Elijah prayed for the judgment of God to fall on his land and on his people. In doing so, he was praying in accordance with the Scriptures.

> *And it shall come about, if you listen obediently to my commandments which I am commanding you today, to love the Lord your God and to serve him with all your heart and all your soul, 14 that He will give the rain of your land in its season, the early rain and the late rain, that you may gather in your grain and your new wine and your oil.*
>
> *15 And He will give grass in your fields for your cattle,* and you shall eat and be satisfied. 16 Beware, lest your hearts be deceived and you turn away and serve other gods and worship them. 17 Or the anger of the Lord will be kindled against you, and He will shut up the heavens so that there will be no rain, and the ground will not yield its fruit; and you will perish quickly from the good land which the Lord is giving you. (Deuteronomy 11:13-17).

The covenant that God made with Israel consisted of both blessings and cursings. If they would be obedient to serve the Lord, then He would bless them with rainfall and cause their crops to grow and to prosper. If they would turn away from the Lord, then rain would be removed from the land and they would see a lack of prosperity.

Now we can understand why Elijah prayed this prayer. He was a man for his times. The glory days of Solomon had come and gone. The kingdom was now a divided kingdom. Although the southern kingdom of Judah had enjoyed an occasional good king, the northern kingdom of Israel had not. Each king had been progressively worse than the one before. Omri had been the worst of an entire line of bad kings. And now Ahab was a man after his father's heart. He had gone so far as to marry a Phoenician princess named Jezebel. Her name meant "Helper of Baal" and she was as good as her name. Under her influence, Baal had become the god of Samaria and the prophets of the Lord had been persecuted and scattered.

Now comes Elijah. His name means "My God is Yahweh." He stands before Ahab and he invokes a solemn oath in the name of the Lord. "As the Lord lives" — if this oath does not come to pass, then God will cease to live. When we were kids, we said things like, "I cross my heart and hope to die." God says the same thing, only He means it.

The promise of the Lord is that there will be *neither dew nor rain*. This is the worst weather forecast in history. But it is more than that. It is a challenge. Baal is a god of fertility, a rain god. He will be seen to be impotent before the God of Israel.

At the end of this three year period, we read of a climactic confrontation between Elijah and Ahab, the king of Israel.

> *When Ahab saw Elijah, Ahab said to him, "Is this you, you troubler of Israel?"*
> *18 He said, "I have not troubled Israel, but you and your father's house have, because you have forsaken the commandments of the Lord and you have followed the Baals. 19 Now then send and gather to me all Israel at Mount Carmel, together with 450 prophets of Baal and 400 prophets of the Asherah, who eat at Jezebel's table." 20 So Ahab sent a message among all the sons of Israel and brought the prophets together at Mount Carmel. (1 Kings 18:17-20).*

Ahab has been searching for Elijah these past three years. He has sent envoys to every surrounding kingdom and has even gone so far as to solicit oaths from surrounding kings to the effect that they have no knowledge of his whereabouts. Finally his enemy stands before him. Notice the accusation.

Ahab	*"Is this you, you troubler of Israel?"*
Elijah	*"I have not troubled Israel, but you and your father's house have"*

Ahab felt that Elijah was a troubler because his prayer had brought a drought. But the real troubler of Israel were those who had brought about a spiritual drought over the land. There is a contrast between these two men.

Ahab	Elijah
King of Israel	Prophet of God
A man of the world	A man of the Word
Walked independently of God in open rebellion	Walked dependently on the Lord in humble submission
Angry and frustrated.	Bold and effective.

Now Elijah gives certain instructions to Ahab. He who has searched far and wide for the prophet now finds himself obeying the instructions of that prophet. All of Israel is to be gathered together. They are coming to witness a challenge — a battle of the Gods.

The place of this confrontation would be Mount Carmel. This is a long ridge, rising up in a sharp promontory from the Mediterranean Sea and running twelve miles toward the southeast where it connects with the central mountain ridge that runs the length of Israel.

The Hebrew word "Carmel" means "garden." The Song of Solomon (7:5) uses the imagery of the lush trees atop Carmel to describe the beauty of the beloved's head.

Imagine the scene. A national holiday has been declared. People from all over Israel begin to gather to Mount Carmel with its commanding view of the Mediterranean Sea. They have come to see an epic battle between the God of Israel versus the gods of the Canaanites.

> *Elijah came near to all the people and said, "How long will you hesitate between two opinions? If the Lord is God, follow Him; but if Baal, follow him." But the people did not answer him a word. (1 Kings 18:21).*

The people of Israel are pictured as being at a crossroads, hesitating and pondering which path to take. Elijah calls the people to make a commitment. It wasn't that they were against God. It is that they were trying to worship both God and Baal. People often try to do the same thing today. They go to church on Sunday morning and live for the devil the rest of the week. They are like a fan that oscillates back and forth. They are the double-minded man of James 1:8. To such a one there is a warning:

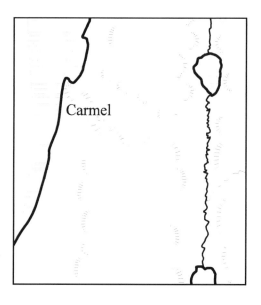

Carmel

> *"No one can serve two masters; for either he will hate the one and love the other, or he will hold to one and despise the other. You cannot serve God and mammon." (Matthew 6:24).*

Is God the complete and total Lord of your life? If not, then I ask you the same question that Elijah asked: "How long?" What are you waiting for?

> *Then Elijah said to the people, "I alone am left a prophet of the Lord, but Baal's prophets are 450 men. 23 Now let them give us two oxen; and let them choose one ox for themselves and cut it up, and place it on the wood, but put no fire under it; and I will prepare the other ox and lay it on the wood, and I will not put a fire under it. 24 Then you call on the name of your god, and I will call on the name of the Lord, and the God who answers by fire, He is God." And all the people said, "That is a good idea."*
>
> *25 So Elijah said to the prophets of Baal, "Choose one ox for yourselves and prepare it first for you are many, and call on the name of your god, but put no fire under it." (1 Kings 18:22-25).*

Here is the way in which the battle will be fought. Two altars will be erected. Two animals will be killed and placed upon the altars. Then each group will pray that fire might come down from heaven and consume the sacrifice. Whichever altar begins to burn will be considered to be the winner.

1. In the Old Testament fire was used as a sign of the presence and supply of the Lord.
    - The Burning Bush (Exodus 3:2)..
    - The Pillar of Fire (Exodus 13:21-22).

2. Fire from heaven was a sign that God had accepted the priests, their sacrifices, and their service.
    - When the first sacrifices were offered upon the Tabernacle altar in the wilderness, fire came down from heaven and consumed the burnt offering (Leviticus 9:23-24).
    - When the first sacrifices were offered in Solomon's Temple, fire came down from heaven and consumed the burnt offering (2 Chronicles 7:1).

In the same way, fire from heaven would now demonstrate the Lord's acceptance of Elijah's offering.

3. Fire was a sign of divine judgment and wrath against sin and rejection of God's plan.
    - The flaming sword at the entrance to the Garden of

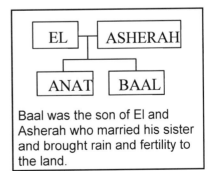

Baal was the son of El and Asherah who married his sister and brought rain and fertility to the land.

Eden (Genesis 3:24).
- The destruction of Sodom and Gomorrah by fire from heaven (Genesis 19:24).

The people are in favor of this test. They think that it is a fair test. If anything, it is possibly rigged in favor of the prophets of Baal since he was believed to be the storm god. He made the lightning and the thunder. He is the fire god. If there is anything that a fire god should be able to do, it is to make fire.

> *Then they took the ox which was given them and they prepared it and called on the name of Baal from morning until noon saying, "O Baal, answer us." But there was no voice and no one answered. And they leaped about the altar which they made.*
>
> *27 It came about at noon, that Elijah mocked them and said, "Call out with a loud voice, for he is a god; either he is occupied or gone aside, or is on a journey, or perhaps he is asleep and needs to be awakened."*
>
> *28 So they cried with a loud voice and cut themselves according to their custom with swords and lances until the blood gushed out on them.*
>
> *29 When midday was past, they raved until the time of the offering of the evening sacrifice; but there was no voice, no one answered, and no one paid attention. (1 Kings 18:26-29).*

The people watch as the 450 prophets of Baal begin to cry out to their god. An hour passes, then two and then three. The sun climbs into the sky and the shrieks of the prophets of Baal echo over the mountain. But nothing happens. Finally, in the heat of the day, Elijah decided to have some fun.

- *"Call out with a loud voice, for he is a god..."*
  Perhaps the batteries in his hearing aid need recharging and he can't hear you. Cry a little louder.
- *"Either he is occupied or gone aside."*
  He is indisposed and can't take any incoming calls at the moment.
- *"Or is on a journey."*
  Maybe he has packed his bags and taken a vacation to the Bahamas.
- *"Or perhaps he is asleep and needs to be awakened."*
  Perhaps he took a couple of sleeping pills and you will have to pray really loud if you are going to wake him up.

Elijah's words have the effect of driving these prophets into a wild religious frenzy. They begin to cut themselves with swords and spears. There is a principle here. It is that sincerity is no substitute for truth. These false prophets were completely sincere in their belief - but they were sincerely wrong. I know a lot of people who do not believe the gospel of Jesus Christ. They are very sincere in their beliefs. Some are even willing to die for their beliefs. But such sincerity is not a proof that they are right in their beliefs. It is possible to be sincerely wrong. You might be thinking, "This has no relevance to me. I have never bowed down before an idol or prayed to Baal." But there are other forms of idolatry.

- Pleasure and comfort.
- Business and the making of money and the security which comes from such activity.
- Social standing.
- Covetousness (Colossians 3:5 equates covetousness with idolatry).

The day was far spent and now it was past *time of the offering of the evening sacrifice* -- in the late afternoon with the sun heading for the horizon. The prophets of Baal have exhausted themselves with their prayers and their sun god is heading for the sea. It is now that Elijah prepares to pray.

> *Then Elijah said to all the people, "Come near to me." So all the people came near to him. And he repaired the altar of the Lord which had been torn down.*
> *31 Elijah took twelve stones according to the number of the tribes of the sons of Jacob, to whom the word of the Lord had come, saying, "Israel shall be your name."*
> *32 So with the stones he built an altar in the name of the Lord, and he made a trench around the altar, large enough to hold two measures of seed. (1 Kings 18:30-32).*

Elijah takes great care in the building of this altar. It is constructed with twelve stones. These twelve stones represent the twelve tribes of Israel. Even though the kingdom has been divided, the Lord sees all of Israel as His people.

> *Then he arranged the wood and cut the ox in pieces and laid it on the wood. And he said, "Fill four pitchers with water and pour it on the burnt offering and on the wood."*
> *34 And he said, "Do it a second time," and they did it*

*a second time. And he said, "Do it a third time," and they did
it a third time.*

*35 The water flowed around the altar and he also filled
the trench with water. (1 Kings 18:32-35).*

As Elijah gives his instructions for the soaking of the altar, I imagine the people looking at one another in amazement. Has the sun finally gotten to this old prophet of God? The contest is to be won by producing fire. The last ingredient you need to produce fire is water. In obedience to his command, they carry four pitchers of water down the mountain to the Mediterranean Sea and fill them with salt water. These are brought back up the mountain and poured onto the altar. Elijah looks at the result, shakes his head, and says, "No, it isn't wet enough. Do it again!" A second time and then a third time the process is repeated until the altar is soaked in water.

Why the water? Because Elijah wanted there to be no mistake in the people's understanding that a miracle was about to take place. He was making certain that any skeptics in the crowd would be silenced. The miraculous nature of what was about to take place would be obvious to all.

*Then the fire of the Lord fell and consumed the burnt
offering and the wood and the stones and the dust, and licked
up the water that was in the trench. (1 Kings 18:38).*

The fire that came from the Lord was special. It not only consumed the offering, it also consumed the wood and the stones and the dust and the water. It was an all-consuming fire.

*When all the people saw it, they fell on their faces;
and they said, "The Lord, He is God; the Lord, He is God."
(1 Kings 18:39).*

In verse 21, Elijah had set the proposal before the people that if Yahweh is God, then He is to be followed. They now respond to the miracle with a statement of faith. *"Yahweh, he is Elohim."* This was in direct answer to the prayer of Elijah. He had not only prayed that the Lord would send fire down from heaven, he had also prayed that the people would repent and return to the Lord.

*Then Elijah said to them, "Seize the prophets of Baal;
do not let one of them escape." So they seized them; and
Elijah brought them down to the brook Kishon, and slew them
there. (1 Kings 18:40).*

The false shepherds of Baal were taken and put to death. Why? Because they bore the responsibility of deliberately leading the people of God in the worship of idols. There is a principle here. It is that leaders are more liable. They bear a greater responsibility. James 3:1 warns, *"Let not many of you become teachers, my brethren, knowing that as such we shall incur a stricter judgment."*

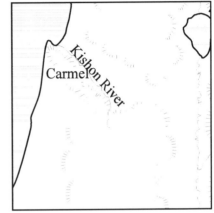

The scene of this execution is the brook Kishon. The brook Kishon flows down from the Central mountain range and then meanders along the foot of the Carmel Range as it makes its way northwest to the Mediterranean Sea. It was here that Gideon had once slaughtered the Midianites. It is here that Elijah has all of the prophets of Baal put to death. Subsequently, Elijah prays and the rains come once more.

The closing chapters of 1st Kings take us back and forth between the perspective of the king and the prophet. We see Elijah's dejection and the Lord giving promises to him and we see Ahab's sin and repentance. When we come to 2nd Kings, we come to the transition between the ministries of Elijah and Elisha. This marks a pivotal point for the entire two volumes.

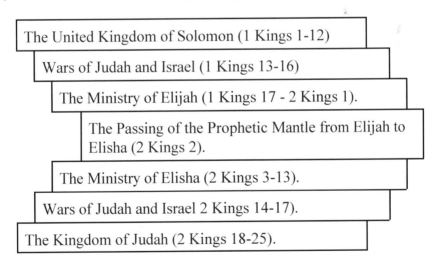

The United Kingdom of Solomon (1 Kings 1-12)

Wars of Judah and Israel (1 Kings 13-16)

The Ministry of Elijah (1 Kings 17 - 2 Kings 1).

The Passing of the Prophetic Mantle from Elijah to Elisha (2 Kings 2).

The Ministry of Elisha (2 Kings 3-13).

Wars of Judah and Israel 2 Kings 14-17).

The Kingdom of Judah (2 Kings 18-25).

Elisha asks for a double portion of the spirit of Elijah — literally a "double mouthful" (פִּי־שְׁנַיִם). The double portion was always the portion of the firstborn. It was the inheritance of the heir of the family. Elijah had no children that we know of. Elisha wished to be his spiritual heir. The good news of the gospel is that Jesus is the firstborn Son who gave us the privileges that were rightly His own. He has given us of His portion. He has given to us the fulness of His Spirit.

Elijah makes no guarantees. He does not answer the request of Elisha because he cannot answer his request. The Spirit is not Elijah's to give. Only God can give His Spirit.

> *As they were going along and talking, behold, there appeared a chariot of fire and horses of fire which separated the two of them. And Elijah went up by a whirlwind to heaven. 12 Elisha saw it and cried out, "My father, my father, the chariots of Israel and its horsemen!" And he saw Elijah no more. Then he took hold of his own clothes and tore them in two pieces. (2 Kings 2:11-12).*

The image of the chariot of the Lord is a common one among the writings of the prophets. The chariot was a symbol of strength, of protection and of judgment.

> *The chariots of God are myriads, thousands upon thousands; The Lord is among them as at Sinai, in holiness. (Psalm 68:17).*

> *For behold, the Lord will come in fire And His chariots like the whirlwind, To render His anger with fury, And His rebuke with flames of fire. (Isaiah 66:15).*

> *Behold, he goes up like clouds, And his chariots like the whirlwind; His horses are swifter than eagles. Woe to us, for we are ruined. (Jeremiah 4:13).*

> *Did the Lord rage against the rivers, Or was Thine anger against the rivers, Or was Thy wrath against the sea, That Thou didst ride on Thy horses, Or Thy chariots of salvation (Habakkuk 3:8).*

The chariot was a tool of war. It was to the ancient world what the armored tank and the jet aircraft are to the modern mechanized world. If Elijah had been caught up today, he would have been accompanied by the B-

1 Bomber.

Elisha had been promised that he would have his request for a double portion of Elijah's spirit fulfilled if he saw Elijah being taken up. The spirit of Elijah was one that was able to see past the physical world to the spiritual realities which go unseen by most. The seeing of Elijah's going was the first such use of that spirit. The ministry of Elisha is one of continued miracles. It is as though the Holy Spirit has been poured out in an overflowing manifestation.

KINGS OF ISRAEL AND JUDAH

On the political scene, there was a movement toward alliance and even unification as Ahab, king of Israel, approached Jehoshaphat, king of Judah, with the offer of an alliance. The alliance was sealed by the marriage of Ahab's daughter to Jehoshaphat's son. This was to have long reaching implications:

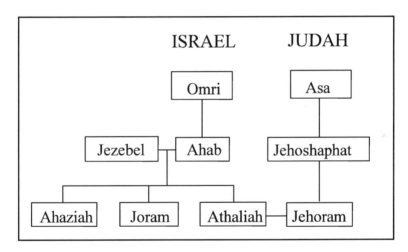

Later in the same year, Ahab and Jehoshaphat marched against Damascus and were defeated. Ahab was killed in the battle and Jehoshaphat barely escaped.

Returning to Judah, Jehoshaphat was rebuked by the prophet Jehu for having entered into the alliance with an enemy of Yahweh. Jehoshaphat repented of his sin and continued his religious reforms, establishing a judicial system invested in the Levites and priests.

Jehoshaphat had several sons. Jehoram, as the firstborn, was made co-regent for several years and then became king upon the death of his father. The first thing that Jehoram did upon coming to the throne was to murder all of his brothers and other high-ranking nobles so that none might pose a threat to his authority. Jehoram had married Athaliah, daughter to Ahab and Jezebel. He followed after his wife in the Canaanite religious system. Shrines to Baal were set up in the high places around Judah.

During his reign, Edom revolted and became an independent state. Perceiving this weakness, the Philistines and the Arabs raided Judah, murdering and pillaging. They even plundered the king's own palace and put to death most of his sons. Ultimately, the Lord judged Jehoram with a disease which caused his bowels to fall out. He died a terrible and painful death.

The young son of Jehoram came to the throne at the death of his father. Like his father and mother, Ahaziah worshiped false gods and practiced the Canaanite cultic rituals. He joined with his uncle Joram, king of Israel, in a war against Aram. The battle ended in defeat and Ahaziah was wounded. He was convalescing in Jezreel when a palace revolt broke out in Israel, led by Jehu. Ahaziah sought refuge in Samaria, but was captured, brought before Jehu, and put to death.

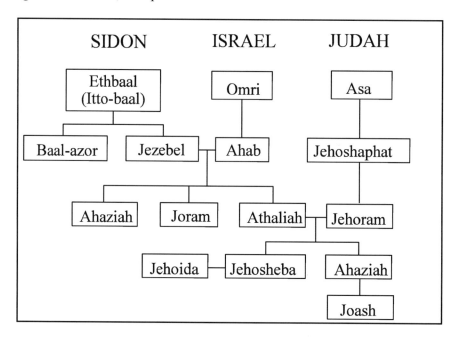

Athaliah, the queen mother used this opportunity to seize power, murdering all of her children and grandchildren. However, one of her daughters took her infant nephew and hid him in the temple, a building that had been all but deserted by the Jews. His name was Joash.

The young crown prince Joash was raised in the temple by Jehoida, a faithful priest. After six years, a coup successfully placed the young prince upon the throne. Athaliah was put to death.

Joash was only 7 years old when he came to the throne of Judah. For many years, Jehoida, the high priest who had raised him, was the ruling power of Judah. As long as Jehoida lived to guide the young king, the nation prospered. Under his direction, the Temple was cleansed and restored. The sacrifices which had been abandoned were reinstated. After the death of Jehoida, Joash was swayed by the opinion of the young liberal party and began to worship false gods. He even went so far as to have Zechariah, the son of Jehoida, stoned when he spoke out against this idolatry.

The Arameans invaded Judah and Jerusalem, pillaging the city and killing many of the king's officers. What was remarkable about this invasion is that the victorious invaders were vastly outnumbered by the military forces of Judah.

> *Indeed the army of the Arameans came with a small number of men; yet the Lord delivered a very great army into their hands, because they had forsaken the Lord, the God of their fathers. Thus they executed judgment on Joash. (2 Chronicles 24:24).*

This military defeat was a judgment from the Lord against Judah and her wayward king. Joash was finally assassinated by his own servants and his son, Amaziah, reigned in his place. Amaziah was 25 years old when he came to the throne, he was to rule Judah for the next 29 years. He was a good king, obeying all of the commands of Yahweh during the first part of his reign. But after a successful expedition into Edom, he brought back the idols of the Edomites and set them up for display. It was not long before they were being worshiped. Soon after this, Amaziah was defeated in battle against the Israelites of the Northern Kingdom. The Israelites led Amaziah in chains back to Judah. They pillaged Jerusalem, tearing down a portion of the wall and looting the gold and silver in the Temple.

When a conspiracy was uncovered, Amaziah fled to Lachish to escape assassination. The conspirators followed him there and put him to death. Apparently this was not considered to be a move against the Davidic Dynasty, but rather was designed to place a worshiper of Yahweh upon the throne (2 Chronicles 25:27).

Uzziah had already served as co-regent with his father for 23 years when he was crowned king of Judah. Like his father before him, Uzziah began his reign with a return to Yahweh. Uzziah concentrated on building up a very strong, professional military. He used this to conquer the Philistines and the Arabians. He also built up much of Jerusalem, adding towers, gates and war machines to protect the city. However, in his pride, he entered into the temple and tried to offer incense upon the altar, something that was only to be undertaken by the priests. As a result, he was stricken with leprosy.

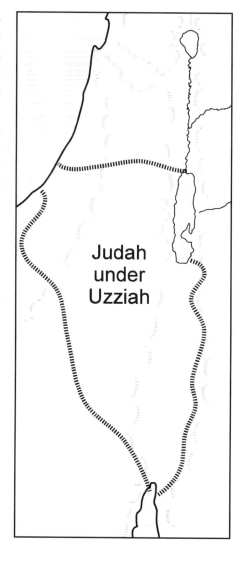

Jotham followed his father's example by obeying the Law of the Lord. However, it is notable that he never entered the Temple. There are several possible reasons for this. He may have been showing respect for his father who had been judged for his sin in the Temple. Or he may have been superstitious about entering the Temple, thinking that he might also contract leprosy.

As soon as he came to the throne, Ahaz began to follow the Canaanite religious practices, even sacrificing his own children to the false gods. Because of the sins of Ahaz, the Lord allowed the Philistines, the Edomites and the Syrians to invade and conquer the border cities of Judah. It was at this time that Judah lost the port of Elath on the Gulf of Aqaba.

Because of these military threats, Ahaz made an alliance with the Assyrians, robbing the Temple to send money to bribe Tiglath-Pileser. In return, the Assyrians offered to attack Aram and Israel (they had been planning to do so anyway). Isaiah confronted Ahaz and advised him to trust in the Lord instead of Assyria. He even offered to give Ahaz a sign from the Lord to prove the truth of his words. When Ahaz refused to choose a sign, the Lord Himself chose one, promising that a child world be born and that, before the child had reached a certain age, the kings of Aram and Israel would be overthrown. It is in the midst of this prophecy that Isaiah tells of a Child whose name would be Immanuel, literally "God with us."

Tiglath-Pileser III died in 727 B.C. and Israel took this opportunity to revolt, stopping payment of the annual tribute. Ahaz wisely continued to pay the required tribute as the Assyrians swept down from the north, laying siege to the capital city of Samaria. For three years, Samaria held out under the siege until famine and disease had decimated the population. When the city fell in 721 B.C., the surviving population was deported. The Northern Kingdom of Israel had ceased to exist.

The Jews of the Southern Kingdom were terrified as they watched the inhuman cruelties which the Assyrians inflicted upon their captives. Now the Assyrians began to eye the Southern Kingdom of Judah. It was only a matter of time before they attacked.

HEZEKIAH

Hezekiah was 25 years old when he came to the throne. The prophet Isaiah had already been ministering for 35 years. With the advent of Hezekiah, a great revival began. He began his reign by destroying all of the Canaanite idols and then repairing the Temple of God.

1.   Envoys from Merodach-baladan.

        Merodach-baladan had managed to snatch Babylon and hold it from the Assyrians. Looking for allies against Assyria, he sent envoys to Hezekiah, king of Judah. In a moment of pride, Hezekiah foolishly showed these envoys all of the treasures of the temple. As a result, the word got out of the great wealth that was stored up in Jerusalem.

2.   Solicitations to rebellion.

        Philistia, Egypt and Ethiopia sent envoys to Hezekiah, urging him to join in a rebellion. Isaiah warned him not to put his trust in Egypt.

        And the Lord said, "Even as My servant Isaiah has gone naked and barefoot three years as a sign and token against Egypt and Cush, 4 so the king of Assyria will lead away the captives of Egypt and

the exiles of Cush, young and old, naked and barefoot
with buttocks uncovered, to the shame of Egypt.
> *"Then they shall be dismayed and ashamed*
> *because of Cush their hope and Egypt their boast."*
> *(Isaiah 20:3-5).*

Hezekiah listened to the warning of Isaiah and continued to pay homage to Assyria.

3.   Revolt against Assyria.

When Assyria was drawn into an extended conflict with Merodach-baladan, Hezekiah was persuaded to join Egypt; in a revolt. The cities of Philistia also joined in, along with Tyre and Sidon. In 701 B.C. Sennacherib conducted a massive campaign against this western alliance. The Phoenician cities each submitted or were destroyed. The Egyptians were routed and Judah was left to face Sennacherib alone.

Hezekiah offered to pay any tribute in return for peace. Sennacherib set the price at 300 talents of silver and 30 talents of gold (in that day even a single talent was considered to be a fortune).

> *And Hezekiah gave him all the silver which*
> *was found in the house of the Lord, and in the*
> *treasuries of the king's house.*
> *At that time Hezekiah cut off the gold from the*
> *doors of the temple of the Lord, and from the*
> *doorposts which Hezekiah king of Judah had overlaid,*
> *and gave it to the king of Assyria. (2 Kings 18:15-*
> *16).*

Instead of keeping his agreement, Sennacherib changed his mind and decided to try to take Jerusalem.

4.   Hezekiah's Tunnel and the Siloam Inscription.

> *Now the rest of the acts of Hezekiah and all his might,*
> *and how he made the pool and the conduit, and brought*
> *water into the city, are they not written in the Book of the*
> *Chronicles of the Kings of Judah" (2 Kings 20:20).*

> *It was Hezekiah who stopped the upper outlet of the*

waters of Gihon and directed them to the west side of the city of David. And Hezekiah prospered in all that he did. (2 Chronicles 32:30).

Hezekiah ordered a tunnel to be cut through the mountain on which Jerusalem rests. This tunnel served to bring water from the Gihon Spring down into the city. The conduit, cut from solid rock in a rather circuitous route, was 1,750 feet long, with an average width of two feet, and an average height of six feet. In 1880 a boy was wading in the pool of Siloam and entered Hezekiah's Tunnel. Nineteen feet inside the entrance, he noticed marks on the wall of the tunnel. It was an inscription. It was later cut out and taken by the Turkish government to the Archaeological Museum in Istanbul where it can be seen today. It relates how a team cut through each end of the mountain to some together at a point in the middle:

Author and guide in Hezekiah's Tunnel

The boring through is completed. And this is the story of the boring through: while yet they plied the drill, each toward his fellow, and while yet there were three cubits to be bored through, there was heard the voice of one calling unto another, for there was a crevice in the rock on the right hand. And on the day of the boring through the stone cutters struck, each to meet his fellow, drill upon drill; and the water flowed from the source to the pool for a thousand and two hundred cubits, and a hundred cubits was the height of the rock above the heads of the stone cutters.

While the Biblical narrative recounts Hezekiah's part in the construction, this inscription tells the same story from the point of view of the workers who dug the tunnel.

5.   Jerusalem delivered.

This time, Hezekiah turned to the Lord for help and was promised deliverance. In a single night, the Assyrian army was overthrown.

> *Then it happened that night that the angel of the Lord went out, and struck 185,000 in the camp of the Assyrians; and when men rose early in the morning, behold, all of them were dead.*
> *So Sennacherib king of Assyria departed and returned home, and lived at Nineveh. (2 Kings 19:35-36).*

The palace of Sennacherib was discovered in 1847 by the English archaeologist Austen Henry Layard at Kuyunjik. A total of 71 rooms were uncovered. Many of the walls were lined with sculptured slabs. One of Sennacherib's campaigns is described on the Taylor Prism, a clay octagonal cylinder which today resides in the British Museum (an even better copy is on a prism at the Oriental Institute of the University of Chicago). It contains the following:

> *As for Hezekiah, the Jew, who did not submit to my yoke, 46 of his strong walled cities, as well as the small cities in their neighborhood, which were without number, by escalade and bringing up siege engines, by attacking and storming on foot, by mines, tunnels and breaches, I besieged and took 200,150 people, great and small, male and female, horses, mules, asses, camels, cattle and sheep without number, I brought away from them and counted as spoil. **Himself, like a caged bird, I shut up in Jerusalem, his royal city.** Earthworks I threw up against him. The one coming out of his city gate I turned back to his misery. The cities of his which I had despoiled, I cut off from his land and gave them to Mitinti king of Ashdod, Padi king of Ekron, and Silili-bel king of Gaza. Thus I diminished his land.*

It is interesting to note Sennacherib's description of this campaign. He brags about how he had besieged the city of Jerusalem, closing up Hezekiah as a bird in a cage, but makes no mention of the outcome of the battle. The remaining years of Hezekiah's life were peaceful and prosperous as the Lord continued to bless him.

The reformation brought about in the days of Hezekiah did not last beyond his life. His son, Manasseh, has the distinction of being one of the worst kings that Judah ever had. One of Manasseh's first acts was the arrest and execution of the prophet Isaiah. The old prophet was placed inside a hollow tree trunk and then sawn apart. Manasseh was involved in all of the practices of the Canaanite religious system.

- Worship of false gods.
- Child sacrifice.
- Sorcery.
- Idols in the Temple of God.

Because of Manasseh's sin, the Lord allowed the Assyrians to invade Judah. The Scriptures tell how Manasseh was captured and taken in chains to Babylon. At this time in history, Babylon was a part of the Assyrian Empire and Esarhaddon, the king of Assyria, used it as his southern palace.

In Babylon, Manasseh repented and turned back to God. Soon after this, he was released and allowed to return to Jerusalem. He now led Judah back to the Lord, tearing down the false idols in the land.

Amon (642-640 B.C.) was 22 years old when he came to the throne. He quickly undid much of what his father had accomplished, leading the Jews back into idolatry. He was murdered by his own servants after a short reign of only two years.

JOSIAH

Josiah was only an eight year old boy when he came to the throne. Even as a boy, he served Yahweh and began to bring a revival to Judah. As he grew older, Josiah began a program of reforms, breaking down the idols and executing the Canaanite priests. Then he began the work of rebuilding the Temple. While the Temple was being restored, a copy of the Scriptures was located. It was brought to Josiah and read to him.

> *Moreover, Shaphan the scribe told the king saying, "Hilkiah the priest has given me a book." And Shaphan read it in the presence of the king.*
> *And it came about when the king heard the words of the hook of the law, that he tore his clothes. (2 Kings 22:10-11).*

When Josiah heard the terms of the covenant of Yahweh read, he was struck with the realization that Judah had transgressed that covenant. Accordingly, he now led the nation in a prayer of repentance. For this, he was informed by the prophetess Huldah that the nation would not be judged in his lifetime.

The final years of Josiah's reign saw a great number of changes on the international scene. Nineveh, the capital of Assyria, fell to the combined assault of the Medes and the Chaldeans in 612 B.C. A remnant of Assyrians escaped to Carchemish where they allied themselves to the Egyptians in an attempt to hold off the Medes and the Chaldeans. When Pharaoh Necho, the king of Egypt, began to march through Palestine toward Carchemish, Josiah tried to intercept him at Megiddo.

> *After all this, when Josiah had set the temple in order, Neco king of Egypt came up to make war at Carchemish on the Euphrates, and Josiah went out to engage him.*
>
> *But Neco sent messengers to him, saying, "What have we to do with each other, O King of Judah? I am not coming against you today but against the house with which I am at war, and God has ordered me to hurry. Stop for your own sake from interfering with God who is with me, that He may not destroy you."*
>
> *However, Josiah would not turn away from him, but disguised himself in order to make war with him; nor did he listen to the words of Neco from the mouth of God, but came to make war on the plain of Megiddo. (2 Chronicles 35:20-22).*

In spite of the warning of Necho that he had been sent by God, Josiah met him in battle in the Valley of Megiddo. In the heat of the battle, Josiah was shot by a stray arrow and he ultimately died from his injury.

THE SONS OF JOSIAH

Josiah had left three sons and a grandson. Each one of them would sit for a time upon the throne of Judah.

With Josiah dead, the people of Judah placed Jehoahaz (also known as Joahaz) upon the throne.

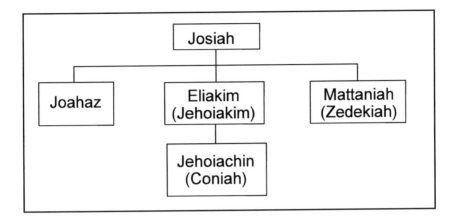

1.   Joahaz (609 B.C.).

Joahaz (also known as Jehoahaz) remained on the throne for three months. At the end of that time, Pharaoh Necho came to Jerusalem and deposed Joahaz, placing a tribute on the land of Judah of 100 talents of silver and a talent of gold. Joahaz was taken to Egypt for the remainder of his life.

2.   Jehoiakim.

Necho now placed Eliakim upon the throne of Judah and changed his name to Jehoiakim. Jehoiakim's first act was to raise a levy of taxes to pay a bribe to the Egyptians. Jeremiah had been prophesying for nearly 20 years when Jehoiakim became king. The prophet denounced the wickedness of the leadership of Judah and warned that Jehoiakim would die and, instead of a royal burial, he would be given that accorded to a beast of burden.

   a.   The Battle of Carchemish (605 B.C.).

   Pharaoh Necho met Nebuchadnezzar at Carchemish on the Euphrates in 605 B.C. The Egyptians were defeated with enormous losses. They retreated south with Nebuchadnezzar hot on their heels.

   b.   Nebuchadnezzar in Palestine.

   Prince Nebuchadnezzar pursued the Egyptian forces all the way down to Palestine, encountering no serious resistance along the way.

As Nebuchadnezzar arrived in Canaan, he called for Jehoiakim, king of Judah, to swear allegiance to him and pay a tribute. Jehoiakim complied and was permitted to retain his throne.

Nebuchadnezzar also took hostages from among the Hebrew nobility at this time. Among these hostages was Daniel and his companions, Shadrach, Meshach and Abed-nego. These were taken to Babylon to receive a Chaldean indoctrination.

c.   The Chaldean/Egyptian War.

Nebuchadnezzar mounted an invasion into Egypt in 601 B.C. The outcome of this campaign was indecisive with each side inflicting heavy casualties upon the other. As a result, Nebuchadnezzar returned to Babylon to regroup and strengthen his forces.

d.   Judah's Rebellion (597 B.C.).

Jehoiakim saw this and interpreted it as a defeat for Nebuchadnezzar. He promptly rebelled and allied himself with the Egyptians. Retribution from Babylon was quick in coming. Nebuchadnezzar captured Jerusalem and threw Jehoiakim into chains, placing his 18 year old son Jehoiachin on the throne.

3.   Jehoiachin (597 B.C.).

Jehoiachin, also known as Coniah, was only 18 years old when he became king of Judah. Nebuchadnezzar set him upon the throne and then moved down against Egypt. While he was in Egypt, young Jehoiachin foolishly rebelled, contrary to the advice of Jeremiah.

Nebuchadnezzar returned, recaptured Jerusalem, and took Jehoiachin, his family, servants and princes, threw them into chains, and marched them away to Babylon. This second deportation was made up of about 10,000 of the nobles of Judah. Among them was the prophet Ezekiel.

4.   Zedekiah (597-586 B.C.).

Having deposed Jehoiachin, Nebuchadnezzar now placed Zedekiah, uncle to Jehoiachin, upon the throne of Judah.

a.   Intrigue with Egypt.

Zedekiah was constantly vacillating between Egypt and Babylon. In 593 B.C. when Pharaoh Necho died, representatives from the city-states of Edom, Moab, Ammon and Tyre met in Jerusalem, hoping that the new Egyptian ruler would join them in a new rebellion against Babylon.

However, the new pharaoh, Psammetichus II, adopted a policy of non-interference. The plot against Babylon left Zedekiah on the spot and he had to travel to Babylon where he swore allegiance once again to Nebuchadnezzar.

b.   Rebellion.

In 588 B.C. Psammetichus II died and Pharaoh Hophra (Apries) came to the throne of Egypt. He immediately persuaded the countries in and around Palestine to join him in a revolt against Babylon.

c.   Jerusalem under siege.

Nebuchadnezzar assembled his army and invaded Palestine, setting up his headquarters at Riblah on the Orontes River. From there, he launched simultaneous invasions of Judah, Ammon, Edom and Tyre with a small reconnaissance patrol to the Egyptian border.

Zedekiah sent messengers to Jeremiah, asking for help from the Lord. Jeremiah's response was that the city of Jerusalem was doomed.

> *You shall also say to this people,*
> *"Thus says the Lord, 'Behold, I set before you*
> *the way of life and the way of death. 9 He who*
> *dwells in this city will die by the sword and by*
> *famine and by pestilence; but he who goes out*

and falls away to the Chaldeans who are besieging you will live, and he will have his own life as booty. 10 For I have set My face against this city for harm and not for good,' declares the Lord. 'It will be given into the hand of the king of Babylon, and he will burn it with fire.'" (Jeremiah 21:8-10).

Judah was quickly overrun except for the cities of Jerusalem, Lachish, and Eziekah. The siege of Jerusalem began on January 588 B.C. It would be another year and a half before the city was taken.

d.   The siege lifted.

The siege of Jerusalem was temporarily interrupted when Pharaoh Hophra led the Egyptian army up into Palestine in an attempt to relieve Tyre and Sidon. When the Chaldeans who had been besieging Jerusalem heard the report about them, they lifted the siege from Jerusalem (Jeremiah 37:5). Many of the inhabitants of the city were heartened by this, thinking that it indicated a turn in their fortunes. Instead of heeding the warnings of Jeremiah, they strengthened their resolve to hold out against Nebuchadnezzar.

As Pharaoh Hophra marched up along the Way of the Philistines, the Chaldeans who had been besieging Jerusalem pulled out and hit the Egyptians, driving them back into Egypt. Having defeated the Egyptian threat, they returned to Jerusalem.

e.   The fall of Jerusalem.

The siege continued for many long months as the food ran out and disease and starvation spread through the city. On July 10, 586 B.C. Nebuchadnezzar's forces broke through the northern wall of Jerusalem. It would be another month before the southern wall could be taken.

On the ninth day of the fourth month the famine was so severe in the city that there was no food for the people of the land. Then the city was broken into, and

408

all the men of war fled by night by way of the gate between the two walls beside the king's garden, though the Chaldeans were all around the city. And they went by way of the Arabah. But the army of the Chaldeans pursued the king and overtook him in the plains of Jericho and all his army was scattered from him. Then they captured the king and brought him to the king of Babylon at Riblah, and he passed sentence on him. During this siege, Zedekiah and the remnants of his army broke out of Jerusalem and fled east toward Jericho, only to be captured and brought to Riblah where Nebuchadnezzar still maintained his headquarters. When he was come. Nebuchadnezzar began to call him a wicked wretch and a covenant-breaker and one that had forgotten his former words, when he promised to keep the country for him. (Antiquities 10:8:2).

Zedekiah was forced to watch his sons being executed and then his eyes were put out. He was thrown into chains to be dragged back to Babylon where he would die in prison. The Jewish survivors were hauled across the Syrian Desert to Babylon, many of them perishing en route. Jerusalem was burned and the walls of the city were torn down. All military, civil, and religious leaders were either executed or carried away into captivity. The Southern Kingdom of Judah had ceased to exist.

1ˢᵗ & 2ⁿᵈ CHRONICLES
A View from the Temple

When we come to the books of 1ˢᵗ and 2ⁿᵈ Chronicles, we find ourselves in familiar territory. It is familiar because much of this same material has been covered in the pages of the books of 2ⁿᵈ Samuel and 1ˢᵗ and 2ⁿᵈ Kings. At the same time, there are some distinct differences in outlook between these books. The most distinctive difference is that the books of Chronicles have a temple outlook. Everything in Chronicles is stated from the perspective of the temple. The relationship of the books of Samuel and Kings to Chronicles is similar to the relationship of the Synoptic Gospels to the Gospel of John.

Samuel and Kings	Relates historical fact with little commentary	Synoptic Gospels
Chronicles	Tells meaning of the fact	John

If the books of Samuel and Kings have their focus upon the kings and prophets of Judah and Israel, the books of Chronicles have their focus upon the tabernacle and the temple. Kings relates the political and royal fortunes of the nation while Chronicles focuses upon the sacred and ecclesiastical aspects of the nation.

Kings	Chronicles
Prophetic Perspective: Judgments	Priestly Perspective: Hope
Wars are prominent	Temple is prominent
History of the thrones	Continuity of the Davidic line
Record of both Israel & Judah	Mostly Judah
Morality	Redemption

The books of Chronicles will give a particular perspective. It is a perspective that sees the history of the kings of Israel as seen from the temple in Jerusalem. As a rule, if something cannot be seen from the temple, it is generally not emphasized, even if it is mentioned at all. While the ministries of Elijah and Elisha occupied a position of prominence in the books of the Kings, they are barely even mentions in Chronicles.

PURPOSE OF CHRONICLES

The books of Chronicles are written to those who have returned from Babylon. The return itself is mentioned in the last two verses of the book. It begins with a series of genealogies that go all the way back to Adam and it closes with the Israelites back in their own land. We could say by inference that it begins in the Garden of Eden and it ends with the people of God back in the place where God had planted them. The following reasons can be surmised:

1.   To set forth a record of the priestly worship of God's people from David to the exile. This is seen by way of the temple perspective we mentioned earlier. The temple was the place of worship and there is a special emphasis upon worship within this book.

        God takes worship seriously. He gives an entire book of worship music in the Psalms; He gives an instruction manual of worship in the book of Leviticus; and He gives a history of worship here in the Chronicles.

2.   To show the fulfillment of the promises of the Mosaic Law regarding faithfulness and unfaithfulness to the covenant. The Law had foretold what would be the penalty for the transgressing of the covenant. It would bring travail and invasion and ultimately it would bring removal from the land. This is all described in the books of Chronicles.

OUTLINE OF THE BOOKS OF CHRONICLES

The first nine chapters of Chronicles are largely made up of genealogical lists. These genealogies begin with Adam and echo those which are found in Genesis, taking all the way to the establishment of the twelve tribes of Israel. There is a sense in which these chapters are a genealogical recapitulation of everything from Genesis to 1st Samuel.

1 Chron 1-9	1 Chron 10-29	2 Chron 1-9	2 Chron 10-28	2 Chron 29-36
Genealogies of Israel	The United Kingdom		Divided Kingdom	Reunited Kingdom
	King David	King Solomon	Kings of Judah	
Genesis to 1 Samuel	2 Samuel	1 Kings	2 Kings	

The beginning of the book is similar to the beginning of the book of Matthew and is given for the same reason. Both books establish the genealogy of the king; Matthew does this by going back to Abraham, but the Chronicles do it by showing the line of the king all the way back to Adam. We are then given a thumbnail sketch of the table of nations before Israel in particular is singled out.

The rest of these genealogical records take us through all twelve of the tribes of Israel, though there is no mention of the tribe of Dan. Instead the sons of Joseph are each laid out.

1	Adam to Abraham and his sons	Lineage of David
2	Sons of Israel down to David	
3	Sons of David and Solomon	
4	Sons of Judah and Simeon	
5	Sons of Reuben, Gad, and half the tribe of Manasseh	
6	Sons of Levi, their musicians, and their settlements	
7	Sons of Issachar, Benjamin, Naphtali, Manasseh, Ephraim, Asher	
8	Sons of Benjamin (given in greater detail)	
9	Summary of Jerusalem after the exile • Priestly families • Levitical families	

Following this long and extended genealogical record, our narrative opens with the death of King Saul. The writer assumes that you are already familiar with Saul, so he is given no extended introduction. His mention is to provide a backdrop for the introduction of the kingship of the house of David. The rest of 1st Chronicles is taken with the reign of David.

KINGS AND CHRONICLES IN PARALLEL

2nd Chronicles contains a parallel history with that which is found in 1st and 2nd Kings. Because of this, we shall not spend a great deal of time repeating an overview of that period of history except to point out the very important difference between these two accounts. It is one of perspective. As we have already noted, the perspective of the books of Chronicles is always from the vantage point of the Temple. It is this temple perspective that is the particular distinctive of this book.

			1st Chron	1 Adam (Genealogies)
		United Kingdom		10 Reign of David
1st Kings	1 Reign of Solomon		2nd Chron	1 Reign of Solomon
	12 Jeroboam	Divided Kingdom		10 Focus on the Southern Kingdom of Judah to the Captivity
	17 Elijah & Ahab			
2nd Kings	1 Elijah & Ahaziah			
	2 Elisha			No mention of the ministries of Elijah or Elisha
	17 Fall of Samaria			
	18 Hezekiah	Judah Alone		
	25 Babylonian Captivity	Exile		
				36:22 Return from Babylon

The reformations under Hezekiah and Josiah are described in terms of a reformation of both Israel as well as Judah, even though the northern kingdom of Israel had by this time been taken away into captivity.

Now Hezekiah sent to all Israel and Judah and wrote

letters also to Ephraim and Manasseh, that they should come to the house of the Lord at Jerusalem to celebrate the Passover to the Lord God of Israel. (2 Chronicles 30:1).

This indicates that a remnant had escaped the Assyrian deportation of the northern kingdom and that the ten lost tribes were not as lost as some today suppose. When Josiah calls the people to celebrate the Passover, we read that all Judah and Israel were involved in this celebration (2 Chronicles 35:18).

The writer of the Chronicles draws our attention to the importance of a right relationship with the Lord in the area of worship. The high points of the book are those times when God's people are devoting themselves to returning to a worship of the Lord. That an entire book of the Bible is concerned with the history of worship suggests how we ought to evaluate our own lives. Do we count success in terms of worship?

1 Chron 1-9	1 Chron 10-29	2 Chron 1-9	2 Chron 10-28	2 Chron 29-36
Genealogies of Israel	The United Kingdom		Divided Kingdom	Reunited Kingdom
	King David	King Solomon	Kings of Judah	
	Preparations for the temple	Construction of the temple	Temple forgotten	Temple restored & destroyed

THE PRAYER OF JABEZ

And Jabez was more honorable than his brothers, and his mother named him Jabez saying, "Because I bore him with pain." 10 Now Jabez called on the God of Israel, saying, "Oh that Thou wouldst bless me indeed, and enlarge my border, and that Thy hand might be with me, and that Thou wouldst keep me from harm, that it may not pain me!" And God granted him what he requested. (1 Chronicles 4:9-10).

There is a typical play on words with the name of Jabez. He asks that the Lord would keep him from harm that it may not pain me! Literally, that it might not *jabez* me. We are not told all that much about Jabez but we are told some rather significant things.

1.   We are told that he was an honorable man in an environment that was not honorable.

2.   We are told the meaning of his name and this is evidently meant to have significance.

3.   We are told the details of his prayer for blessing.   He asked for the blessing of God. He asks specifically for an enlarging of his territory and that God's hand would be with Him. He asked that the Lord would keep him from evil and that he would not be the cause of pain.

> Bruce Wilkinson's little book "The Prayer of Jabez" is only 90 pages and they are small pages with fairly large print. The book is about prayer and specifically uses the Prayer of Jabez as a model for prayer in much the same way that we typically use the Lord's Prayer for such a model. There is nothing in itself wrong with this as there are a lot of prayers in the Scriptures that could serve as similar models.

4.   We are told that God answered his prayer.

Why do the Scriptures give us this information? Are we to think of it as mere interesting Bible trivia or are we to do as Wilkinson has done and ponder the message found here and apply it to our own prayer life? I can not fault him for wishing to apply the Scriptures, though we ought to use due caution in not making this the only prayer that we pray.

THE REIGN OF DAVID

1st Chronicles					
1-9	10	11-12	13-16	17-27	28-29
Genealogies	Histories				
	Death of Saul	Reign of King David			
		Mighty men	Ark & worship	Covenant promises	Temple site

1.   David's Mighty Men (1st Chronicles 11-12).

This section begins with all Israel coming and recognizing

David's kingship. *Then all Israel gathered to David at Hebron and said, "Behold, we are your bone and your flesh. 2 In times past, even when Saul was king, you were the one who led out and brought in Israel; and the Lord your God said to you, 'You shall shepherd My people Israel, and you shall be prince over My people Israel.'" (1 Chronicles 11:1-2).*

Notice the reference to Israel being the "bone and flesh" of David. This is meant to remind us of the language of the first marriage in the Garden of Eden where the woman was to be bone of Adam's bone and flesh of Adam's flesh. The Israelites use that sort of marriage language to describe their relationship with David as their king.

We can understand this language to point ultimately to David's better Son, the person of Jesus who is the bridegroom of the church. What Israel says of David, we say to the Son of David — we are bone of His bone and flesh of His flesh.

From here, we are taken on a brief tour of the exploits of some of David's mighty men. Particularly heroic is the story of a time when David was campaigning against the Philistines in the area near Bethlehem. David longed for a drink of water and three of his might men fought their way through the Philistine lines to obtain for him a drink of water from the well in Bethlehem. Rather than drink it, he poured it out as an offering and a testimony to his concern for the lives of his men. The story reminds us of the One who was greater than David who also came from Bethlehem.

David	Jesus
Born in Bethlehem.	Born in Bethlehem.
His mighty men put themselves at risk.	He is the "mighty man" who gave of Himself for others.
Poured out the water they brought because of their sacrifice.	Poured out His own blood for us as the ultimate sacrifice.

2.   Ark of the Covenant and Worship of God (1st Chronicles 13-16).

We have already been introduced to the ark of the covenant. This represented the throne of God upon earth. It had been lost to the Philistines in the days of Saul, but then had been returned when the

416

Lord brought signs of judgment against those people. It was returned to the Israelites, but they kept it in Kiriath-jearim in the territory of Judah. David resolved to bring it up to Jerusalem.

> *David and all Israel went up to Baalah, that is, to Kiriath-jearim, which belongs to Judah, to bring up from there the ark of God, the Lord who is enthroned above the cherubim, where His name is called. 7 They carried the ark of God on a new cart from the house of Abinadab, and Uzza and Ahio drove the cart. 8 David and all Israel were celebrating before God with all their might, even with songs and with lyres, harps, tambourines, cymbals and with trumpets. 9 When they came to the threshing floor of Chidon, Uzza put out his hand to hold the ark, because the oxen nearly upset it. 10 The anger of the Lord burned against Uzza, so He struck him down because he put out his hand to the ark; and he died there before God. 11 Then David became angry because of the Lord's outburst against Uzza; and he called that place Perez-uzza to this day. (1 Chronicles 13:6-11).*

As the ark was being brought to Jerusalem, an unfortunate tragedy took place. Instead of transporting the ark in the manner that had been prescribed, it was placed on an ox cart like a piece of furniture. It was much more than that; it represented the throne of the Lord of heaven.

As the cart was jostled, Uzza put up his hand to steady the ark and he was struck dead by the Lord. David named the place Perez-uzza because the Lord had *perezed* against Uzza. The word *perez* means "outburst" and Uzza had suffered the affects of that outburst. The transportation of the ark is halted here and not resumed until chapter 14. In the interim, we are told of David's other activities and this forms a chiastic outline for this section.

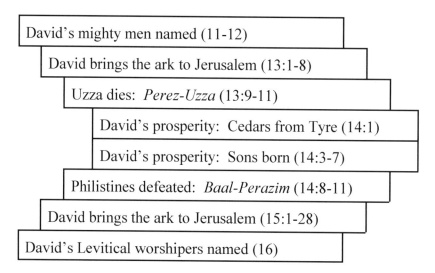

David's mighty men named (11-12)

David brings the ark to Jerusalem (13:1-8)

Uzza dies: *Perez-Uzza* (13:9-11)

David's prosperity: Cedars from Tyre (14:1)

David's prosperity: Sons born (14:3-7)

Philistines defeated: *Baal-Perazim* (14:8-11)

David brings the ark to Jerusalem (15:1-28)

David's Levitical worshipers named (16)

After relating David's overthrow of the Philistines at a place that is given the name *Baal-Perazim* ("outburst of Baal"), David moves to bring the ark the rest of the way to Jerusalem. This time he is careful to have the ark moved in the proper way: *Then David said, "No one is to carry the ark of God but the Levites; for the Lord chose them to carry the ark of God and to minister to Him forever." (1 Chronicles 15:2).* The entire section is concluded as David names the various Levitical worshipers who will care for the ark and for the temple.

3.   Covenant Promises (1st Chronicles 17-27).

This section begins with David making plans to build a house for the Lord. The Lord responds through Nathan the prophet with a message that it is the Lord who will build a house for David (17:10).

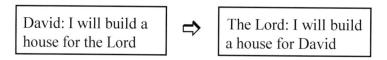

| David: I will build a house for the Lord | ⇨ | The Lord: I will build a house for David |

The Lord goes on to tell of how David will have a descendant whose kingdom will be established and whose throne will be forever

(17:11-14).   As we read the details of this prophecy, we can understand it being fulfilled in the person of Solomon, the son of David who succeeded him to the throne.   At the same time, we are given to understand that the prophecy does not conclude with Solomon.   It suggests the coming of One who will be greater than Solomon.

Solomon	Jesus
Son of David.	Ultimate Son of David.
Established united monarchy of Israel.	Established kingdom of God on earth.
He built the temple.	He is the temple.
Established a kingdom that would last until 586 B.C.	Established a kingdom that will never end.
Chastened because of his iniquity.	Chastened because of our iniquities.

4.   David's Census: *Then Satan stood up against Israel and moved David to number Israel (1 Chronicles 21:1).*

The account of David's census is repeated in 2 Samuel 24, but it is only here that we learn that Satan was the instigator of this census.   This brings up the question: why was it wrong for David to take a census of the people?   It seems to have been a matter of pride on the part of David but, more than that, the numbering of the people stands in opposition to the promise that had been given to Abraham that there would come a day when the descendants of Israel would be unable to be numbered (Genesis 15:5; 26:4).

Though he is warned by Joab, his chief of staff, against this course of action, David's will prevails and the numbering takes place. As a result, judgment is pronounced against Israel and David is given three choices as to the form that judgment will take:

- Three years of famine. [1]

---

[1]   2 Samuel 24:13 reads "seven years of famine."   This may be due to a scribal error, though we have no direct manuscript evidence that this is the case.

- Three months of military defeat.
- Three days of pestilence.

David chooses the last of these alternatives, considering it better to fall into the hands of the Lord than into the hands of his enemies. Accordingly, a pestilence comes upon Israel so that 70,000 die. It is as this destruction comes upon Jerusalem that there is a reprieve.

> *And God sent an angel to Jerusalem to destroy it; but as he was about to destroy it, the Lord saw and was sorry over the calamity, and said to the destroying angel, "It is enough; now relax your hand." And the angel of the Lord was standing by the threshing floor of Ornan the Jebusite. 16 Then David lifted up his eyes and saw the angel of the Lord standing between earth and heaven, with his drawn sword in his hand stretched out over Jerusalem. Then David and the elders, covered with sackcloth, fell on their faces. 17 David said to God, "Is it not I who commanded to count the people? Indeed, I am the one who has sinned and done very wickedly, but these sheep, what have they done? O Lord my God, please let Your hand be against me and my father's household, but not against Your people that they should be plagued." (1 Chronicles 21:15-17).*

As the angel of the Lord moves against Jerusalem and comes to the site of the future temple, there is a reprieve. David makes intercession for the nation, asking that the hand of God be against his own life instead of against the lives of the people. He offers his own life as a substitute. In this offering, we are reminded of another time when the angel of the Lord came as a messenger of death. It was the time of the Exodus when the Passover was instituted. At that time, the blood of the Passover lamb availed to cause the angel of death to pass over each house where the blood was applied. This time there is no Passover lamb. This time it is the king who is offering his own life as a substitute.

Jesus fulfills both these types. He is both our Passover lamb as well as the king who offers Himself in place of His people. He is the One whose sacrifice is prefigured in all of the sacrifices that would ever take place within the temple.

Passover	The Census	The Cross
Egypt	Jerusalem	
Angel of Death coming upon all of Egypt	Angel of Death coming upon all of Jerusalem	Penalty for sin coming upon all of the world
Blood of the Passover lamb allows the angel of death to pass over each house	David intercedes for the people of Jerusalem and offers a sacrifice to the Lord	The Better David offered Himself as the ultimate interceding sacrifice

David subsequently purchased the threshing floor of Ornan where the pestilence ceased its deadly advance and here he built an altar to the Lord. It would be on this same site that the temple would ultimately be constructed. You will recall that Abraham's offering of Isaac took place in the land of Moriah (Genesis 22:2). We learn here in 2 Chronicles 3:1 that the setting for the temple site was on Mount Moriah. Tradition has it that it was on the exact same location where Abraham had offered his son Isaac. It is fitting that the place where God initially offered a ram as a substitute for the ancestor of the Israelites should also be the location for the construction of the temple. It would be within eyesight of that temple that Jesus would hang upon a cross, serving as the ultimate substitute to pay for the sins of the world.

THE ARK BROUGHT TO JERUSALEM

The focus of Chronicles quickly turns to the Temple and its furnishings. Notable among those furnishings was the Ark of the Covenant.

And David said to all the assembly of Israel, "If it seems good to you, and if it is from the Lord our God, let us send everywhere to our kinsmen who remain in all the land of Israel, also to the priests and Levites who are with them in their cities with pasture lands, that they may meet with us; 3 and let us bring back the ark of our God to us, for we did not seek it in the days of Saul." (1 Chronicles 13:2-3).

The ark was a wooden chest overlaid with gold. It had a top of solid gold on which were mounted the figures of two cherubim - two angels perched as an honor guard. The ark represented the throne of God. It was the place where God was said to be "seated above the cherubim."

The ark had been lost at the Battle of Ebenezer (1 Samuel 4). The Philistines had taken it and had placed in one of their pagan temples. But then they found their idols falling apart and plagues breaking out in their city. They had moved the ark from city to city and had experienced this same phenomenon in each city into which they brought the ark.

Finally, the Philistines had returned to ark to Israel. But the Israelites had no better luck. Some Levites had taken in upon themselves to look inside the ark and a number of men had died. The ark had now sat in the house of Abinadab for nearly 70 years. Saul had not sought to change its place of residence. But David did. And by so doing, David demonstrated a care for the things of the Lord.

> *And they carried the ark of God on a new cart from the house of Abinadab, and Uzza and Ahio drove the cart. 8 And David and all Israel were celebrating before God with all their might, even with songs and with lyres, harps, tambourines, cymbals, and with trumpets. (1 Chronicles 13:7-8).*

David and the Israelites were doing the right thing, but they were doing it in the wrong way. In the midst of their celebration, they were sowing the seeds of disaster. God had given explicit instructions as to how the ark was to be handled. No one was to touch the ark. It was to be carried by two wooden poles which ran through rings along the side of the ark. These poles were never to be removed (Exodus 25:15). But when the Philistines had sought to return the ark to Israel, they had placed it onto a cart. The Israelites had now adopted that method of moving the ark. They even went so far as to obtain a brand new cart. But they ignored God's design.

We can fall into the same snare. We do this when we adopt the world's methods and ignore God's timeless truths concerning how we are to worship Him and how we are to do His work. A lot of people want to love God without obeying His precepts. But when God says to do something a certain way, we need to do it that way.

> *When they came to the threshing floor of Chidon, Uzza put out his hand to hold the ark, because the oxen nearly upset it. 10 And the anger of the Lord burned against Uzza, so He struck him down because he put out his hand to*

422

the ark; and he died there before God. (1 Chronicles 13:9-10).

Uzza was the son of Abinadab, the high priest. He had grown up in the house with the ark. And it seems as through he had grown a little casual about the presence of the ark. And so, it did not seem an important thing to touch the ark. After all, he didn't want to ark to go bouncing down the street.

> *Then David became angry because of the Lord's outburst against Uzza; and he called that place Perez-uzza to this day. (1 Chronicles 13:11).*

There is a play on words here. It reads literally that "David became angry because of the PEREZ of the Lord PEREZED against Uzza, and the place is now called PEREZ-Uzza to this day." David's reaction to God's outburst was anger.

People sometimes become angry with God. They forget that we do not worship a little God. He is holy. He is other than we are. The question is not why did God kill Uzza, but rather why He does not kill us, too.

There is a lesson here. It is that we can get so used to God's grace that we come to take it for granted. The disciples did that. They ate with Jesus and talked with Him and walked with Him. And then one night in the middle of a storm-tossed sea, they watched Him still the storm with a single word and they were startled with the terrifying realization that He was different.

The ark is not mentioned again until chapter 15, but when it is finally moved to Jerusalem, David gives some very explicit instructions as to how no one is to carry the ark except the Levites (1 Chronicles 15:2).

DAVID'S DESIRE FOR A TEMPLE

> *And it came about, when David dwelt in his house, that David said to Nathan the prophet, "Behold, I am dwelling in a house of cedar, but the ark of the covenant of the Lord is under curtains." (1 Chronicles 17:1).*

David's next concern was a permanent dwelling in which to house the ark. Since the days of the Wilderness Wanderings, the ark had been kept within the Tabernacle - a tent designated as the "Tent of Meeting." In those early days, it was necessary for this structure to be a tent, for the Israelites were a nomadic people and they required a portable place of worship.

That had now changed. They now had a land in which the Lord had given them rest. They had a capital city. And David felt that it was appropriate that a permanent place of worship be established - a House of God. He begins making plans to build such a house for the Lord.

The Lord comes through Nathan the prophet and says that David is not to build a house for the Lord. Rather, it is the Lord who will build a house for David.

> *"...Moreover, I tell you that the Lord will build a house for you. 11 And it shall come about when your days are fulfilled that you must go to be with your fathers, that I will set up one of your descendants after you, who shall be of your sons; and I will establish his kingdom. 12 He shall build for Me a house, and I will establish his throne forever. 13 I will be his father, and he shall be My son; and I will not take My lovingkindness away from him, as I took it from him who was before you. 14 But I will settle him in My house and in My kingdom forever, and his throne shall be established forever." (1 Chronicles 17:10b-14).*

The promise to David revolves around the establishment of a seed (the word translated "descendant" in verse 11 is literally "seed"). This takes us all the way back to Genesis 3:15. It was there that the Lord had promised Adam and Eve that there would

> Dead Sea Scroll 4Q Florilegium, a midrash scroll, shows that the Qumran scribes took the "son" in verse 13 to be a reference to Messiah.

come One who would be of the seed of the woman. This Seed would crush the serpent's head. He would be the destroyer of the works of Satan. This promise is fulfilled in two parts. The immediate fulfillment will be in the person of Solomon. He will be the seed who will build a house in the name of the Lord. It will be Solomon who constructs the temple of God in Jerusalem. Solomon will found the Davidic dynasty. But the ultimate fulfillment of this prophecy is seen in Jesus.

THE DIVISION OF THE PRIESTHOOD

In 1st Chronicles 24 we read of how David divided the priests by lot into 24 families. The priestly service would be rotated among these families so that each family would serve in the temple twice a year. All of the priests would come together at the special feast days. This system of 24 courses would continue in the days of the New Testament and is mentioned in Luke 1 where Zacharias was of the division of Abijah (Luke 1:5).

In the following chapter, there are a corresponding division of 24 groups of singers and musicians. Their duty was to accompany the daily times of worship with a symphony of praise and to prophesy with lyres, harps, and cymbals (1st Chronicles 25:1).

We see this same grouping of 24 elders in the book of Revelation where 24 elders are pictured in heaven around the throne of God as the worship and honor Him and sing praises to Him. We are called to the same service of worship. We are called today as a people who have been set apart for worship to the Lord. This involves a praise of music and of prayer.

PLANS FOR THE TEMPLE

Throughout 1st Chronicles 28, David sets forth what will be the plans of the new temple that will be built by Solomon and then he concludes in verse 19, "All this," said David, "the Lord made me understand in writing by His hand upon me, all the details of this pattern."

This is significant. Both the plans of the Tabernacle in the wilderness and now the temple in Jerusalem had a heavenly architect. They were both planned and designed by the Lord. Hebrews 8:5 says that Moses was warned by God when he was about to erect the tabernacle; for, "See," He says, "that you make all things according to the pattern which was shown you on the mountain."

Why was it so important that the tabernacle and the temple be built according to such exact specifications? It is because both the tabernacle and the temple were to serve as a picture and a type of the Messiah who was to come.

SOLOMON'S TEMPLE

At the time of the death of David, the ark of the covenant was residing in a tent in Jerusalem that had been set up for that purpose while the tabernacle was still located in Gibeon.

Then Solomon, and all the assembly with him, went to the high place which was at Gibeon; for God's tent of meeting was there, which Moses the servant of the Lord had made in the wilderness. 4 However, David had brought up the ark of God from Kiriath-jearim to the place he had prepared for it; for he had pitched a tent for it in Jerusalem. (2 Chronicles 1:3-4).

Chapters 3-7 of 2nd Chronicles is given over to the building of the Temple. We are given details of both its construction as well as the worship and celebration that takes place once it is completed.

- The construction and furnishing of the Temple (3-4).
- The ark is brought to the Temple (5).
- Solomon's prayer of dedication (6).
- The celebration of dedication (7).

Construction of the Temple began in the fourth year of Solomon's reign (1 Kings 6:1). The building project took seven years and was climaxed with the dedication of the Temple.

- Location: The site for the Temple was high atop a threshing place at the top of Mount Moriah, located just north of the old Jebusite city of Jerusalem. The name *Moriah* (מוֹרִיָּה) seems to carry the idea of "the place where it shall be seen." The name was significant because it had been here that Abraham had offered up Isaac and it had been seen that he was faithful.

Dome of the Rock in Jerusalem

And Abraham called the name of that place The Lord Will Provide, as it is said to this day, "In the mount of the Lord it will be provided." (Genesis 22:14). This is one of those cases where the King James Version has given us a more exact translation: *Abraham called the name of that place Jehovah-jireh: as it is said to this day, In the mount of the*

Lord it shall be seen. The Hebrew word רָאָה (*ra'ah*) means "to see" and the use of the Qal imperfect as found in יְהוָה יְרָאֶה is better translated, "The Lord will see."

- Structure: The Temple was patterned after the same structure of the Tabernacle, except that it was bigger. Because it was built upon a mountain, you went up a series of stairs till you came to the highest part of the Temple -- the Holy of Holies. The highest part of the mount today is that portion of the bedrock around which is built the Dome of the Rock.

- The Bronze Altar: The altar was a huge structure measuring 20 cubits square and 10 cubits in height. This would be the scene of the daily sacrifices.

- The Sea: Outside the temple was a great laver of water known to the Jews as "the Sea" measuring 10 cubits in diameter (4:2). This laver stood on the backs of 12 oxen. When Revelation 4 pictures the elders gathered around the throne of God and a great crystal sea, this is an image from the temple.

- The furniture: Instead of a single lampstand and a single table of showbread, the temple held ten lampstands and ten tables of bread.

When the work was completed, Solomon called for the ark of the covenant to be brought and housed in the temple.

> *Now when Solomon had finished praying, fire came down from heaven and consumed the burnt offering and the sacrifices; and the glory of the Lord filled the Temple.*
> *And the priests could not enter into the house of the Lord, because the glory of the Lord filled the Lord's house. (2 Chronicles 7:1-2).*

In the same way that the Lord had moved into the Tabernacle in the days of Moses, so now His presence was manifested in the Temple. Thus was fulfilled the promise that God would be with His people.

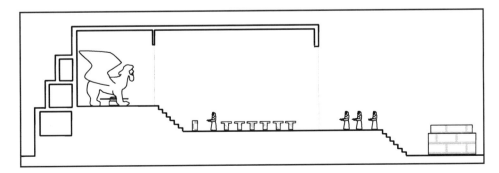

There are no remains of Solomon's Temple. It was destroyed by Babylonian King Nebuchadnezzar in 586 B.C. A second temple was rebuilt on this same spot, but that was destroyed by the Romans in A.D. 70. Today there stands on that same site the Dome of the Rock, a Muslim shrine.

THE QUEEN OF SHEBA

Now when the queen of Sheba heard of the fame of Solomon, she came to Jerusalem to test Solomon with difficult questions. She had a very large retinue, with camels carrying spices, and a large amount of gold and precious stones; and when she came to Solomon, she spoke with him about all that was on her heart. 2 And Solomon answered all her questions; nothing was hidden from Solomon which he did not explain to her. (2 Chronicles 9:1-2).

Sheba was located in the southwestern area of Arabia; in the land today known as Yemen. It is the most fertile area of Arabia and sat astride the trade routes bringing wares up and down the coasts of the Red Sea and the Indian Ocean.

The queen of this country travels to Israel because she has heard of the fabled words and wisdom of Solomon. She comes to meet him and to hear about the God he worships. At the end of her visit, she praises Solomon for his greatness and his wisdom and she blesses the Lord for the way in which He has provided.

A thousand years later, Jesus would speak of the encounter between Solomon and the Queen of Sheba and He would make an application from it. The application is to ask whether you will see what she came to see.

The Queen of the South shall rise up with this generation at the judgment and shall condemn it, because she came from the ends of the earth to hear the wisdom of Solomon; and behold, something greater than Solomon is here (Matthew 12:42).

The Queen of Sheba came to see a man of great wisdom and great wealth. But that is not all she came to see. She also came to see what God had done. Have you seen it? Have you seen what God has done in the coming of the One who was greater than Solomon? If you have not seen Him and given your life to Him, then there is coming a day when the Queen of

Sheba will rise up and condemn you because you have the opportunity to see what she saw.

REHOBOAM

The writer of the Chronicles sets forth the career of Rehoboam in a chiastic outline that begins with the same revolt of the ten northern tribes as we have already seen in 1 Kings. This event and a summary statement of the reign and wars that he had with Jeroboam serve as bookends to look at the reign of this king.

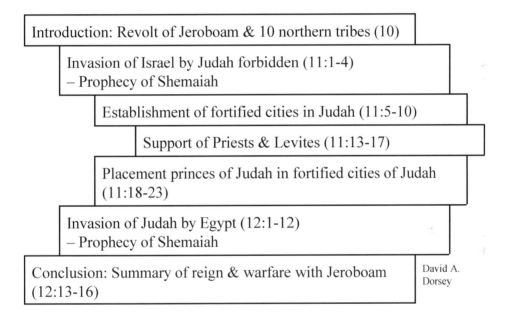

Introduction: Revolt of Jeroboam & 10 northern tribes (10)

Invasion of Israel by Judah forbidden (11:1-4)
– Prophecy of Shemaiah

Establishment of fortified cities in Judah (11:5-10)

Support of Priests & Levites (11:13-17)

Placement princes of Judah in fortified cities of Judah (11:18-23)

Invasion of Judah by Egypt (12:1-12)
– Prophecy of Shemaiah

Conclusion: Summary of reign & warfare with Jeroboam (12:13-16)

David A. Dorsey

Notice that the fulcrum of this chiastic parallel is not on Rehoboam's political career, but on his establishment of the priests and the Levites in Jerusalem as seen in contrast to Jeroboam who had excluded them from worship. This serves to remind us that the Chronicler is concerned primarily with the priestly life of the nation rather than its political or military life. To be sure, the actions of prophets and kings will be given, but it will regularly be the ministry of the Levitical priesthood that is made central and pivotal.

ABIJAH

As we saw with the life of Rehoboam, so also the life and career of

Abijah is given in a chiastic format with the priests and Levites occupying the central, pivotal place in the narrative. In this case, that central place is given to a speech of the king that has the ministry of the priests and the Levites as its focus.

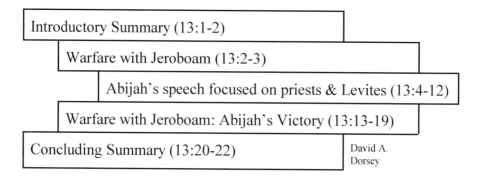

Introductory Summary (13:1-2)

Warfare with Jeroboam (13:2-3)

Abijah's speech focused on priests & Levites (13:4-12)

Warfare with Jeroboam: Abijah's Victory (13:13-19)

Concluding Summary (13:20-22)

David A. Dorsey

ASA

The reign of Asa was marked by a period of reformation and restoration as he removed the foreign altars and high places, leading the people of Judah back to the Lord. This reform was followed by an invasion from a giant army from Ethiopia.

> *Now Zerah the Ethiopian came out against them with an army of a million men and 300 chariots, and he came to Mareshah. 10 So Asa went out to meet him, and they drew up in battle formation in the valley of Zephathah at Mareshah. (2 Chronicles 14:9-10).*

Egyptologist Flinders Petrie felt this to be a reference to Osorkon I of the 22nd Dynasty of Egypt. This was the dynasty that united Egypt after the 3rd Intermediate Period. It was a dynasty made up largely of Libyans and they ruled for 200 years, running at the same time as the 23rd and 24th Dynasties and would be followed by a Dynasty from Nubia to the south.

In any case, we are given to understand that a massive Ethiopian army marched against the kingdom of Judah. Asa led his forces out and then called upon the name of the Lord for deliverance.

> *Then Asa called to the Lord his God and said, "Lord, there is no one besides You to help in the battle between the powerful and those who have no strength; so help us, O Lord our God, for we trust in You, and in Your name have come*

*against this multitude. O Lord, You are our God; let not man
prevail against You."* 12 *So the Lord routed the Ethiopians
before Asa and before Judah, and the Ethiopians fled. (2
Chronicles 14:11-12).*

Following this great victory, the revival in Judah spread to the
northern tribes to that Asa *gathered all Judah and Benjamin and those from
Ephraim, Manasseh, and Simeon who resided with them, for many defected
to him from Israel when they saw that the Lord his God was with him.* (2
Chronicles 15:9). This announcement becomes the pivotal fulcrum of the
Ada narrative:

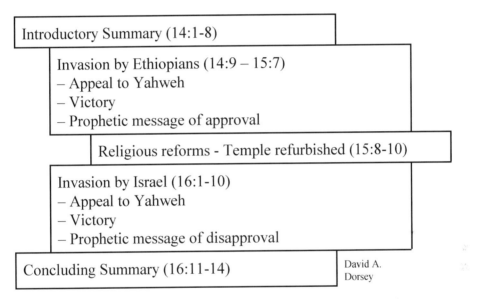

Introductory Summary (14:1-8)

Invasion by Ethiopians (14:9 – 15:7)
– Appeal to Yahweh
– Victory
– Prophetic message of approval

Religious reforms - Temple refurbished (15:8-10)

Invasion by Israel (16:1-10)
– Appeal to Yahweh
– Victory
– Prophetic message of disapproval

Concluding Summary (16:11-14)

David A.
Dorsey

The latter part of this narrative also gives a story of victory, but it is
a political victory, even as it is also a spiritual defeat. Instead of trusting in
the Lord against the attacks of Israel, Asa puts his trust in a military alliance
with Ben-Hadad of Damascus, bribing him to attack Israel. The plan is
militarily successful, but Asa is rebuked by Hanani the seer for having trusted
in men rather than in God. This legacy is followed to the end of his days.

JEHOSHAPHAT

Jehoshaphat had seen the results of his father's failures as he
wasted away with a disease that started in his feet and which eventually
took his life (2 Chronicles 16:12).

1. Jehoshaphat's Faithfulness.

> *And the Lord was with Jehoshaphat because he followed the example of his father David's earlier days and did not seek the Baals, 4 but sought the God of his father, followed His commandments, and did not act as Israel did. 5 So the Lord established the kingdom in his control, and all Judah brought tribute to Jehoshaphat, and he had great riches and honor. (2 Chronicles 17:3-5).*

Jehoshaphat did not have a good example in his own father, but he nevertheless determined to follow the godly example of his forefather, David. I have had the good fortune to have godly parents who sought to follow the Lord. Perhaps you did not have parents like that. If that is the case, you can "borrow" the heritage of your spiritual ancestors and you can pass it on to those who come after you.

2. Jehoshaphat's Training Program.

> *Then in the third year of his reign he sent his officials, Ben-hail, Obadiah, Zechariah, Nethanel, and Micaiah, to teach in the cities of Judah; 8 and with them the Levites, Shemaiah, Nethaniah, Zebadiah, Asahel, Shemiramoth, Jehonathan, Adonijah, Tobijah, and Tobadonijah, the Levites; and with them Elishama and Jehoram, the priests. 9 And they taught in Judah, having the book of the law of the Lord with them; and they went throughout all the cities of Judah and taught among the people. (2 Chronicles 17:7-9).*

Jehoshaphat began an extensive discipleship program by sending out both officials and Levites and priests to teach the book of the Law to the people of Judah. There was apparently a plan and a program to this discipleship and it involved a training program.

3. Jehoshaphat's Tribute from his Neighbors.

> *Now the dread of the Lord was on all the kingdoms of the lands which were around Judah, so that they did not make war against Jehoshaphat. 11 And some of the Philistines brought gifts and silver as tribute to Jehoshaphat; the Arabians also brought him flocks, 7,700 rams and 7,700 male goats. 12 So Jehoshaphat grew greater and greater, and he built fortresses and store cities in Judah. (2 Chronicles 17:10-12).*

When we read that *the dread of the Lord was on all the kingdoms of the lands which were around Judah*, we are inclined to think that those kingdoms were being terrorized by Judah. But that is not what the passage says. It says that *the dread of the Lord* was upon them. This same word that here is translated "dread" is often rendered "fear." The motivation behind their tribute was the fear of the Lord.

4. Jehoshaphat's Ill-advised Alliance: *Now Jehoshaphat had great riches and honor; and he allied himself by marriage with Ahab. (2 Chronicles 18:1).*

Ahab's father, Omri, had established a similar marital alliance with the king of Sidon when Ahab was married to Jezebel. This brought the worship of Baal into Israel, a situation that was faced by Elijah.

Now we read of Ahab and Jehoshaphat making an alliance. This involved the marriage of the daughter of Ahab and Jezebel to the son of Jehoshaphat and would

> 1 Kings 22:20 tells us that it was the Lord who sent a deceiving spirit to entice Ahab into this war with Ramoth-geliad and thus meet his death.

ultimately result in Baal worship being introduced in Judah.

JOASH

The marriage alliance with Israel resulted in Athaliah murdering all of the family into which she had married. Only young Joash escaped: *He was hidden with them in the house of the Lord six years while Athaliah reigned over the land (1 Chronicles 22:12).* At the end of that period, Joash comes to power. By contrast with the 1 Kings account, the Chronicler gives us all the details of this rise to power; yet in keeping with the theme of the book, these details are all seen from the perspective of the temple.

The actual reign of Joash is given to us in the typical chiastic format with the pivotal event being the death of his mentor, the high priest Jehoiada.

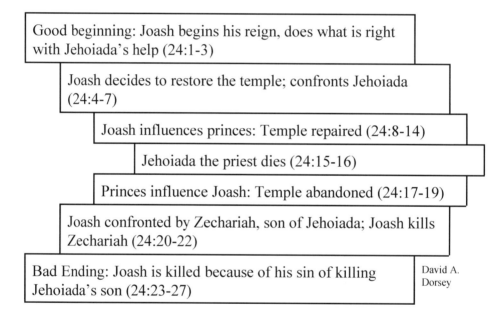

Good beginning: Joash begins his reign, does what is right with Jehoiada's help (24:1-3)

Joash decides to restore the temple; confronts Jehoiada (24:4-7)

Joash influences princes: Temple repaired (24:8-14)

Jehoiada the priest dies (24:15-16)

Princes influence Joash: Temple abandoned (24:17-19)

Joash confronted by Zechariah, son of Jehoiada; Joash kills Zechariah (24:20-22)

Bad Ending: Joash is killed because of his sin of killing Jehoiada's son (24:23-27)

David A. Dorsey

The reign of Joash is described in positive terms un puntil the death of Jehoiada. From this time, he takes a turn for the worse as he is influenced but ungodly officials so that the temple is abandoned as they turn to follow idols. Even when prophets are sent to bring them back to the Lord, Joash gives them no heed but even has the prophet Zechariah (not the same one who wrote the book by the same name) put to death.

AMAZIAH

Amaziah is the story of a king who started right in the sight of the Lord, *yet not with a whole heart*, literally, "not with a heart of shalom"

(25:2). He raised a huge army to march against the Edomites and had even hired a group of mercenaries from Ephraim until he was warned by a man of God not to do so. Accordingly, he won a great victory over Edom, but he then brought back Edomite idols, *set them up as his gods, bowed down before them and burned incense to them* (25:14).

Amaziah was warned by a prophet, but paid no heed. Judah suffered a crushing defeat at the hands of Israel and a portion of the defensive wall of Jerusalem was torn down and the temple was robbed of its gold and silver utensils. Those who were disenchanted with Amaziah's poor leadership assassinated him.

UZZIAH

Uzziah was only sixteen years old when he came to the throne and his reign would prove to be long and prosperous. It is set forth in the typically chiastic style that we have come to expect.

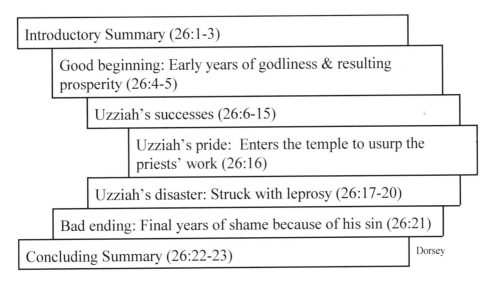

Introductory Summary (26:1-3)

Good beginning: Early years of godliness & resulting prosperity (26:4-5)

Uzziah's successes (26:6-15)

Uzziah's pride: Enters the temple to usurp the priests' work (26:16)

Uzziah's disaster: Struck with leprosy (26:17-20)

Bad ending: Final years of shame because of his sin (26:21)

Concluding Summary (26:22-23)

Dorsey

The pivotal point in the reign of Uzziah is depicted when *he entered the temple of the Lord to burn incense on the altar of incense* (26:16). Rather than an act of reverence, this was perceived as an act of pride. As a result, he was struck with leprosy and so lived with the disease to the end of his days, unable to even approach the house of God.

JOTHAM

Jotham served as regent during the days of his father's leprosy and then ruled as king after the death of his father. His rule is described as one of prosperity and obedience to the Lord, but we read that *he did not enter the temple of the Lord* (27:2), possibly as a reflection of what had happened to his father.

AHAZ

Not only did Ahaz fail to do right in the sight of the Lord, he went to the other extreme and made molten images of the Baals, sacrificing some of his male children in the fires of the Hinnom Valley on the west side of Jerusalem.

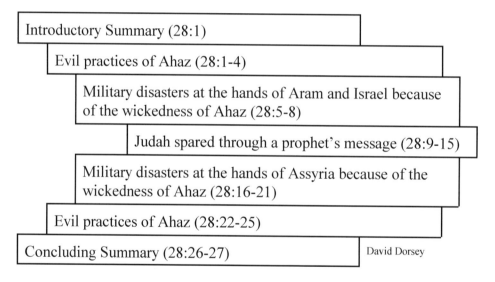

Introductory Summary (28:1)

Evil practices of Ahaz (28:1-4)

Military disasters at the hands of Aram and Israel because of the wickedness of Ahaz (28:5-8)

Judah spared through a prophet's message (28:9-15)

Military disasters at the hands of Assyria because of the wickedness of Ahaz (28:16-21)

Evil practices of Ahaz (28:22-25)

Concluding Summary (28:26-27)

David Dorsey

The pivotal point in the story of Ahaz comes when Judah has suffered a great defeat at the hands of Israel, taking a massive number into captivity. A prophet is sent to Samaria and warns that the Israelites are in danger of bringing upon themselves the judgment of God. Accordingly, the captives are released and escorted home.

Instead of trusting in the Lord, Ahaz turns to the Assyrians for help against the double-pronged threat from Edom and Philistia. The Assyrians were not much help as their invasion did not distinguish between Edom, Philisitia or Judah, but pillaged all parties before returning home. Instead of turning to the Lord, Ahaz continued in his idol worship, going so far as to close the doors of the house of the Lord (28:24).

HEZEKIAH

If Ahaz was among the worst of the kings of Judah, Hezekiah was one of the best. The beginning of his reign saw him undoing a great deal of the evil that which had been accomplished by his father.

1.   Restoration of the Temple.

     The chronicler gives us a thorough description of the cleansing of the temple, how the unclean things that had accumulated there were carried out to the Kidron Valley for disposal. The sacrifices were restored and a great celebration of worship held. So many offerings were brought that the priests were not able to keep up with them and the Levites were required to help with the priestly work, a task to which they gave themselves wholeheartedly.

2.   Passover Observance.

     Hezekiah called for a Passover celebration and sent invitations to all of Israel from Beersheba to Dan (30:5), that they should also be allowed to come and participate. While this invitation was met with scorn and rejection on the part of some, there were *some men of Asher, Manasseh, and Zebulun humbled themselves and came to Jerusalem* (30:11). Because of time constraints, the celebration was moved to the second month rather than at its normal time in the first month.

3.   Sennacherib's Invasion.

     The Assyrians had already taken the ten northern tribes of Israel into captivity in 721 B.C. Samaria had been laid waste and the kingdom was no more. Two decades later, the Assyrians were back under king Sennacherib. City after city fell before his onslaught and soon he had surrounded Jerusalem. Hezekiah turned once again to the Lord who *sent an angel who destroyed every mighty warrior, commander and officer in the camp of the king of Assyria* (32:21). The Assyrians departed, but they would return.

MANASSEH

Manasseh was only twelve years old when he came to the throne and the early years of his reign marked a falling away from the Lord. Once again, there were altars for the worship of Baal, even bringing such pagan altars into the temple of God. Tradition has it that Isaiah was put to death during this period.

Because of his sin, the Lord brought the Assyrians back, capturing Manasseh and taking him away in chains to Babylon. This proved to be a time of repentance as, only now, he turned toward the Lord. Though we are not told the details of how it took place, Manasseh was released and permitted to return to Jerusalem where he again took up the mantle of the kingship.

The rest of Manasseh's long reign was the spiritual opposite of his early years. Foreign gods and idols were removed and the repentant king sought for the rest of his life to lead his nation back to the Lord.

His son, Amon, reigned only a brief two years, but they were two years in which he turned away from the Lord to sacrifice to graven images. He was assassinated by his own servants and in his own house.

JOSIAH

The reign of Josiah is reminiscent of the days of Hezekiah. Once again, there was a turning back to the Lord. Once again, the word went out to the scattered remnants of Israel, calling for them to come and to celebrate a Passover to the Lord.

It was while the temple was being cleansed that a copy of the scroll of the law was discovered in the temple and brought to the king. When it was read in his presence, Josiah realized the magnitude of the sin of the nation and he sent an inquiry to the prophetess Huldah. The prophecy came back that the wrath of God was ordained to fall upon Judah, but because of the King's repentant spirit, that judgment would not come in his lifetime. His reign was to last for 31 years.

Meanwhile, there were world forces on a collision course that would eventually impact the tiny kingdom of Judah. A coalition of Babylon, the Medes, and the Scythians brought an end to the Assyrian Empire, destroying the city of Nineveh in 612 B.C. Into this power vacuum came Egypt as Pharaoh Necho sought to march against the forces of Babylon. To get there, it was necessary for his armies to pass through Israel, something which Josiah perceived as an act of war.

But Neco sent messengers to him, saying, "What have we to do with each other, O King of Judah? I am not coming against you today but against the house with which I am at war, and God has ordered me to hurry. Stop for your own sake from interfering with God who is with me, so that He will not destroy you." (2 Chronicles 35:21).

Was the Egyptian pharaoh telling the truth? Had God actually ordered his march? It is true that he does not use the name of Yahweh, but only refers to God (Elohim), a reference that could refer to any one of the false gods of Egypt.

Josiah marched to intercept the Egyptian forces at Megiddo since it protected a narrow pass in the steep hills and would tend to bottleneck the large Egyptian force and render their chariots useless. We are not given much in the way of details of the actual battle, but it was a crushing Jewish defeat. It would become something of a byword in the same way we speak of Napoleon's Waterloo. The book of Revelation makes reference to a great battle that culminates at Armageddon, literally, "Mount of Megiddo."

THE SONS OF JOSIAH

We have already noted the careers of the sons of Josiah in our treatment of 2 Kings. There is little that is added by the chronicler as he depicts the continuing unfaithfulness of the ensuing kings. The chronicler gives this summary:

The Lord, the God of their fathers, sent word to them again and again by His messengers, because He had compassion on His people and on His dwelling place; 16 but they continually mocked the messengers of God, despised His words and scoffed at His prophets, until the wrath of the Lord arose against His people, until there was no remedy. (2 Chronicles 36:15-16).

The end came when the Chaldean king Nebuchadnezzar came against Jerusalem and captured it, pulling down its walls and burning the temple to the ground. The people were carried off into captivity. It is here that the chronicler adds a significant detail not previously given.

Those who had escaped from the sword he carried

away to Babylon; and they were servants to him and to his sons until the rule of the kingdom of Persia, 21 to fulfill the word of the Lord by the mouth of Jeremiah, until the land had enjoyed its sabbaths. All the days of its desolation it kept sabbath until seventy years were complete. (2 Chronicles 36:20-21).

We learn here that the seventy year captivity was enforced so that the land could enjoy its sabbaths. This is a reference back to Leviticus 26:35 that warns Israelite unfaithfulness in keeping the ordinances of God which, among other things, included the command to observe a sabbatical year, would result in a captivity in which the people would be removed from the land so that the accumulated sabbatical observances could eventually be applied. It may be surmised that the Israelites had failed to observe the sabbatical years since the days of the judges.

What is interesting about this reference to seventy years and the corresponding sabbatical years that would have been involved in its calculation (70 x 7 = 490) is that these same numbers appear in Daniel 9, not to look back at a past infraction of the covenant, but to look forward to the coming of God's Messiah who would bring an end to the old covenant and institute a new and better covenant through His death on the cross. When we see this correlation, we can understand how the entire Old Testament looked forward to the coming of Jesus, the King of the Jews who would bring a lasting Sabbath rest to the people of God.

EZRA

This book in named after the person who appears in chapters 7-10 of the book. Both the Hebrew Scriptures as well as the Greek Septuagint use Ezra (or Esdras) for the title. In the Hebrew Bible, the book of Ezra was joined to the book of Nehemiah. This was done so that the number of the books of the Hebrew Bible would, correspond to the number of letters in the Hebrew alphabet, twenty-two.

Jerome divided the books into two separate books in his Latin Vulgate and our English Bibles follow this tradition. There seems to be some evidence that they were originally written as two separate books. Ezra 2 is repeated in Nehemiah 6:7-70 and this likely would not have been the case had they been written together.

The Septuagint included the books which we know as the Apocrypha. These were books which were reckoned by the Jews not to have the same authority as those which had been written by the prophets. The Septuagint contains an Apocryphal book of Esdras while the Latin Vulgate contains two such additional books.

Hebrew Bible	Septuagint	Vulgate	Apocrypha
Ezra	Esdras B	1st Esdras	–
Nehemiah	Esdras B	2nd Esdras	–
–	Esdras A	3rd Esdras	1st Esdras
–	–	4th Esdras	2nd Esdras
This is simplified chart gives only a general outline and does not take into account that parts of the Septuagint, Vulgate, and Apocrypha do not have an exact correlation with the Hebrew Bible.			

1.   Esdras A in the Septuagint seems to date to the 2nd century B.C. and is an addendum to the book of Ezra. It deals with events from Josiah to Ezra and contains portions of our book of Ezra, though they are not exact duplicates.

2.   The Apocryphal Second Esdras was written in the late first century A.D. and contains no connection with our book of Ezra (it is apocalyptic in nature, made up of seven visions and set in the days of the Persian Empire). All of our copies are in Latin and no Greek

manuscript has thus far been located.

EZRA, NEHEMIAH, AND ESTHER

DATE	LEADER	TASK	BOOK		EVENTS
537	1st Return under Zerubbabel	Return & Rebuild Jerusalem	Ezra		
			1		Proclamation by Cyrus
			2		Census of returned Exiles
			3		Worship & Rebuilding of Temple
			4		Opposition from Samaritans
520			5		Temple construction resumed
516			6		Temple completed
473	Esther	Deliver Jews	Esther	Esther is Queen of Persia	
458	2nd Return under Ezra	Return & Reform	7		Ezra Investigates Resettlement
457			8		Ezra's Return with Second Group
			9		Ezra's Prayer of Anguish
			10		Reforms on Mixed Marriage
537	Nehemiah	Rebuild the Walls of Jerusalem	Nehemiah		
			1		Nehemiah's grief
			2		Permission to Rebuild Walls
			3		Work Progressing
			4		Opposition by Outsiders
			5		Nehemiah's Provisions
			6		Completion of the City Walls
			7		Census of First Exiles
	Ezra	Revival	8		Revival through God's Word
			9		Repentance
			10		Commitment
		Reform	11		Leaders in Jerusalem
433			12		Dedication of the Wall
			13		Reforms on Foreign Marriages

The book of Ezra spans 92 years of Jewish history from the decree of Cyrus allowing the Jews to return to the land (539 B.C.) to the decree of Artaxerxes which halted the work of rebuilding the city of Jerusalem (446 B.C.).

Ezra, Nehemiah. and Esther all deal with the story of Israel following the Babylonian Captivity. Nebuchadnezzar's Babylon did not long outlive that king. It was soon replaced by the empire of the Persians. The Persians had a different method of maintaining their empire. They determined that a happy and prosperous people made better taxpayers, so they permitted dispossessed peoples to return to their homelands. Under the Persian rule, there were three specific returns of Jews to the land of Judah.

- The first was led by Zerubbabel and involved an initial rebuilding of Jerusalem.
- The second was led by Ezra who oversaw the re-institution of the sacrifices.
- The third was led by Nehemiah and involved the rebuilding of the defensive walls of Jerusalem.

The story of Esther takes place in the interim between Ezra and Nehemiah. However it is a separate narrative as its focus is not upon the land of Judah but deals with the Jews throughout the Persian Empire.

OUTLINE OF EZRA

1	First Return under Sheshbazzar and Zerubbabel	Return from Babylon	The Edict of Cyrus
2			The Exiles who returned
3		Rebuilding of the Temple	Construction begun
4			Construction opposed
5			Construction delayed
6			Construction completed
7	Second Return under Ezra	Return from Babylon	Decree of Artaxerxes
8			The Journey
9		Restoration of the People	Mixed marriages
10			Solution to the problem

RETURN TO THE LAND

Now in the first year of Cyrus king of Persia, in order to fulfill the word of the Lord by the mouth of Jeremiah, the Lord stirred up the spirit of Cyrus king of Persia, so that he sent a proclamation throughout all his kingdom, and also put it in writing (Ezra 1:1).

This book starts out with a conjunction. It is translated here as "now" but could just as easily have been translated "and." There is a point being made. This is a continuing saga. Ezra is not a "stand-alone" book. It takes up the thread of history set down by the books of Kings and Chronicles. By opening with this conjunction, the author shows that this is a continuing story.

> The first 2 or 3 verses of Ezra are nearly identical with the closing verses of Chronicles. This book is telling the rest of the story.

The nation of Israel was a nation desolate. The northern 10 tribes had been taken into captivity by Assyria in 721 B.C. and foreigners had been settled in their place. Then in three successive deportations, the southern kingdom of Judah had been taken away to Babylon and the land left a desolated waste.

With this conjunction, the story continues. Cyrus the Great comes on the scene and issues a proclamation which allows the Jews to return to their land. There is a lesson here. It is that God has a continuing story. There are times when it looks as though that story is going to end. The Babylonian Captivity seemed to be such a time. The temple was destroyed, the land desolated, the people decimated. But that isn't the end. It is only the beginning of a new chapter in God's continuing story. What is going on in your life? Problems that threaten to destroy and desolate and decimate? Situations that seem insurmountable? The tapestry of your life becoming unraveled? Take hope! There is a continuing story.

Thus says Cyrus king of Persia, "The Lord, the God of heaven, has given me all the kingdoms of the earth and He has appointed me to build Him a house in Jerusalem, which is in Judah. 3 Whoever there is among you of all His people, may his God be with him! Let him go up to Jerusalem which is in Judah and rebuild the house of the Lord, the God of Israel; He is the God who is in Jerusalem. 4 Every survivor, at whatever place he may live, let the men of that place support him with silver and gold, with goods and cattle, together with a freewill offering for the house of God which is in Jerusalem." (Ezra 1:2-4).

When we first read this, we are inclined to think that they are the words of a believer. Cyrus is attributing his victories over the Babylonian Empire to Yahweh and describes himself as an agent of the Lord is decreeing that the Temple of God be rebuilt in Jerusalem. From archaeological records, we

> The phrase "the God of heaven" tends to be used much more in the Exilic and post Exilic writings.

learn that this was the policy of Cyrus toward all religions and people groups. Cyrus had his own reasons for instituting his political policy and they were not God's reasons. Nevertheless, the actions of Cyrus were also fulfilling the plan of God for His people. The actions of the king were doing the will of God even though that king was working on his own agenda.

> *"It is I who says of Cyrus, 'He is My shepherd! And he will perform all My desire.' And he declares of Jerusalem, 'She will be built,' and of the temple, 'Your foundation will be laid.'" (Isaiah 44:28).*

Over a hundred years before the coming of Cyrus, God declared through the prophet Isaiah that this same Cyrus would perform His will by ordering the rebuilding of Jerusalem. Cyrus had not even been born when this was written.

> *"For the sake of Jacob My servant, and Israel, My chosen one, I have also called you by your name; I have given you a title of honor though you have not known Me." (Isaiah 45:40).*

The Lord states that He chose Cyrus to perform certain things even though Cyrus himself was an unbeliever who did not know the Lord. God is not restricted to using believers to carry out His plan. In the same way that He used Cyrus, so also He used the pharaoh of the Exodus.

> *"For the Scripture says to Pharaoh, 'For this very purpose I raised you up, to demonstrate My power in you, and that My name might be proclaimed throughout the whole earth.'" (Romans 9:17).*

It was the Lord who raised up the unbelieving pharaoh of the Exodus to his position of leadership over Egypt. He did this so that, by bringing him to defeat through the plagues and through the incident at the Red Sea, the name of the Lord might be proclaimed throughout the whole earth.

Are we to take these instances of Cyrus and the pharaoh of Egypt as being the exceptions rather than the rule? Does God's plan only extend to the great and the powerful while ignoring the humble and the weak? Not at all! If there were anyone who was said to have "free will," it was the king. He could point to someone and say, "Off with his head" and that head would topple. Thus, when the book of Proverbs states the principle of God's sovereignty over rulers as a general principle, the implication is that God is sovereign over all men.

> *"The king's heart is like channels of water in the hand of the Lord; He turns it wherever He wishes." (Proverbs 21:1).*

The Babylonian Empire did not last very long past the death of Nebuchadnezzar. It began a steady decline with his successors and, in the ensuing vacuum, there arose a king from the east whom we know as Cyrus.

Cyrus was the product of a union between the nobility of Media and Persia. Both the Medes and the Persians lived to the east of Mesopotamia. Cyaxeres of the Medes entered into an alliance with the Persians who lived to the south of him, having one of his daughters marry a Persian king. The resulting union brought about Cyrus, a man who was both a Mede and a Persian.

Cyrus began as a vassal to his grandfather Astyages, but soon set out on a campaign of conquest. Anatolia fell to him when he conquered Croesus (known to the Greeks as Midas) and the kingdom of Lydia. Then Gobryas, the king of Elam, revolted and came over to him. The only resistance left was at Babylon.

Over a hundred years later, the Spartan General Xenophon relates a story how that Cyrus diverted the Euphrates River and marched a force up the dried up riverbed and into Babylon (the river ran through the city). Whether or not the story is true, we do know from records that he took the city without a fight.

It has been said that man's free will flows in the channels which have been dug by the sovereignty of God. Such a concept is presented here. The Lord carries out His plans and protects His people, not merely in spite of a pagan king, but He actually uses that pagan king to work out His will. Paul takes this principle a step further to teach that the rulers themselves are placed in their positions of authority by the Lord.

> *"Let every person be in subjection to the governing authorities. For there is no authority except from God, and those which exist are established by God." (Romans 13:1).*

Paul was not speaking in the context of a Christian king or governor. It was during the reigns of the Roman Emperors that he penned these words. He did not say that only those authorities which are obedient to divine laws are established by God, but all authorities. This means that, whether a leader has taken a throne by force of arms or through inheritance or even through a national election by the vote of the "free will" of the populace, it is ultimately the Lord who places in office those whom He has chosen.

> *Then the heads of fathers' households of Judah and Benjamin and the priests and the Levites arose, even everyone whose spirit God had stirred to go up and rebuild the house of the Lord which is in Jerusalem.*
> *All those about them encouraged them with articles of silver, with gold, with goods, with cattle and with valuables, aside from all that was given as a freewill offering. (Ezra 1:5-6).*

As the call went out for people to return and rebuild the Temple, there were two responses which are mentioned in this passage. First, there were those who went. We are told specifically that God had been at work in stirring up their spirit to go and to do this work. We have already seen how God can motivate a pagan king to accomplish His will. Here we see how He also motivates His own people to do His will.

The second group is made up of people who did not make the journey, but who nevertheless supported the word with gifts and offerings. There is a lesson here. Not everyone is called to be a missionary to a foreign country. But those who do not go themselves are nevertheless able to support those who do go.

REBUILDING OF THE TEMPLE

As the Jews returned to the land, one of their early priorities was the rebuilding of the temple. This was seen as the physical place where the presence of God was to be manifested. It was not long before opposition arose to this project.

> *Then the people of the land discouraged the people of Judah, and frightened them from building, 5 and hired counselors against them to frustrate their counsel all the days of Cyrus king of Persia, even until the reign of Darius king of Persia. (Ezra*

"To discourage" is literally "to weaken the hands," a Hebrew idiom (Jeremiah 38:4). As a participle, the verb *rapah* indicates a continuing process. The opposite idiom is "to strengthen the hands" (Ezra 6:22; Nehemiah 6:9; Isaiah 35:3; Jeremiah 23:14).

4:4-5).

This is a blanket statement which covers the history of the reigns of Cyrus, Cambyses, and finally Darius. Some Bible scholars see in verse 6 a primarily a parenthetical statement regarding the rebuilding of the wall around Jerusalem, which takes place later on in time, and then picks up again with verse 24 about the rebuilding of the temple.

I don't believe this to be the case. The problem is that there were three different Persian kings as well as a governor by the name of Darius. The second problem is the use of Ahasuerus in verse 6. We are used to seeing it used in the book of Esther where it refers to Xerxes, but it is not a name, it is merely a title and can refer to any of the Persian kings. The summary statement is made in verse 5 that the Jews had construction problems from the days of Cyrus to the days of Darius. The line of kings for this period was as follows:

King	Date of Reign	Actions Taken
Cyrus	539-530	Granted permission for the Jews to return and rebuild Jerusalem and the Temple
Cambyses	530-522	Put a stop to the reconstruction
Smerdis	522	He was a pretender to the throne and quickly overturned
Darius	522-486	Granted permission for the reconstruction of the Temple to continue
Xerxes	486-464	He was the King who elevated Esther
Artaxerxes	464-423	Granted permission for Nehemiah to return and rebuild the walls of Jerusalem.

What has thrown Bible students astray is the mention of "Artaxerxes." The name translated "Artaxerxes" here in Ezra 4-6 is spelled slightly different than the Artaxerxes found in Nehemiah 7-8 (the difference is the kind of "s" used). I would suggest that the "Artaxerxes" mentioned here in Ezra is really a reference to the ruler which we know as Cambyses. Thus, it was under Cambyses that the building of the Temple was halted, contrary to the previous orders of his father, Cyrus. It remained halted for a period of close to ten years when it was taken up again, not at the behest of a king, but as a result of the preaching of two prophets.

> *When the prophets, Haggai the prophet and Zechariah the son of Iddo, prophesied to the Jews who were in Judah and Jerusalem in the name of the God of Israel, who was over them, 2 then Zerubbabel the son of Shealtiel and Jeshua the son of Jozadak arose and began to rebuild the house of God which is in Jerusalem; and the prophets of God were with them supporting them. (Ezra 5:1-2).*

As we read this, we must understand that the books of the Bible are not arranged in an exact chronological order from Genesis to Revelation. There are occasional overlaps. This is one of them. As we turn from the end of Ezra 4 to begin chapter 5, we must understand that the books of Haggai and Zechariah have been written in the interim.

> *Then the word of the Lord came by Haggai the prophet, saying, 4 "Is it time for you yourselves to dwell in your paneled houses while this house lies desolate?" (Haggai 1:3-4).*

Haggai describes the situation that existed among the people of the land. There were housing shortages, disappointing harvests, lack of clothing and jobs, and inflation had taken its toll. People were working more and more for less and less.

Haggai uses a play on words as he proclaims that because the Lord's house had remained "a ruin" (*hareb*, Haggai 1:4, 9), the Lord would bring "a drought" (*horeb*, Haggai

> Haggai is very down-to-earth and is to this era what the epistles are to the New Testament. Zechariah, by contrast, contains a great many symbols and visions and is to this era what Revelation is to the New Testament.

1:11) on the land. The reason that things were going hard for the Jews was because they were not giving their full devotion to the Lord. Ezra's account does not give us the exact dates of when this took place. But we do find that information provided in the books of Haggai and Zechariah. The following table shows the specific dates for those ministries:

Prophet	Date of his Ministry	
Haggai	2nd year of Darius, in the 6th month (Haggai 1:1).	August - December, 520 B.C.
Zechariah	2nd year of Darius, in the 8th month (Zechariah 1:1).	October, 520 B.C.

Notice what is the mechanism that the Lord uses to renew the work of construction on His Temple. It is the prophetic revelation which brings about a renewed leadership to the task at hand.

God speaks to His prophets	⇨	Prophets preach	⇨	Leaders lead	⇨	The people follow

The Lord works to move the leadership of His people to bring about His work. This is the normal pattern in which God works.

Prophets	Priest	King
Zechariah & Haggai	Jeshua	Zerubbabel, though technically not a king, was a descendant of the royal line.

Both the prophets and the priests and the descendant of the king had a role in the completion of the work of the Temple. They were working together and there is no indication of any jealousy or friction between any of them.

In obedience to the instructions of the prophets, the people resume the work, even though no permission had been given by the Persian governors. There is a principle here. It is that we ought to obey God rather than man. This is not an excuse for rebellion against authority, but it does mean that we recognize the Lord as a higher authority.

When the Persians learn of the work of rebuilding, an appeal is made on the basis of the initial decree of Cyrus. A search is made and the decree is located. As a result, the present king of Persia issues a decree that the work on the Temple is to be continued to completion.

> *Then Tattenai, the governor of the province beyond the River, Shethar-bozenai and their colleagues carried out the decree with all diligence, just as King Darius had sent.*
> *And the elders of the Jews were successful in building through the prophesying of Haggai the prophet and*

Zechariah the son of Iddo. And they finished building according to the command of the God of Israel and the decree of Cyrus, Darius, and Artaxerxes king of Persia. (Ezra 6:13-14).

Once permission has been given, the full weight of the Persian government lends itself to assist in the project. There is a symphony of effort as the elders and the prophets and the Lord and even the kings of Persia combine their mutual efforts to rebuild the Temple of God.

This temple was completed on the third day of the month Adar; it was the sixth year of the reign of King Darius. (Ezra 6:15).

Chapter 3	Chapter 4	Chapter 5	Chapter 6
The work of rebuilding is BEGUN	The work of rebuilding is HALTED	The work of rebuilding is RENEWED	The work of rebuilding is COMPLETED

And the sons of Israel, the priests, the Levites and the rest of the exiles, celebrated the dedication of this house of God with joy.
They offered for the dedication of this temple of God 100 bulls, 200 rams, 400 lambs, and as a sin offering for all Israel 12 male goats, corresponding to the number of the tribes of Israel.
Then they appointed the priests to their divisions and the Levites in their orders for the service of God in Jerusalem, as it is written in the book of Moses. (Ezra 6:16-18).

Now the Jews enter into a service of dedication as they present the results of their labors to the Lord. It is a joyous time of sacrifice and worship as the priests are appointed to their appropriate divisions. The priesthood was divided into 24 courses so that each course would officiate twice per year in the temple. All of the courses would come together at the times of the great feasts.

As they come, it is for a time of celebration to the Lord. We are told the number of sacrifices that are brought and the number is considerably less than was brought for the initial dedication of the Temple in the days of Solomon. There are significantly less worshipers gathered and the Temple may be considerably smaller. But that is okay. The issue is not the size of the offering, the number of people, or the size of the structure. The issue is the heart of worship.

One key thing that is lacking in this dedication which was observable in the previous dedications of the Tabernacle and Solomon's Temple was the visible presence of the Lord in the Shekinah Cloud. After the Tabernacle was erected, we read that the cloud of the glory of the Lord filled the Tabernacle so that even Moses was not able to enter in (Exodus 40:34-35). In the same way, when Solomon's Temple was dedicated, the cloud of God filled the Temple so that the priests were for a time unable to minister (2 Kings 8:10-11). But this time there is no mention of the cloud. There is no visible presence of the Lord. The people celebrate, but there is silence from heaven. The book of Malachi contains a promise of the coming of the Lord's presence.

> *"Behold, I am going to send My messenger, and he will clear the way before Me. And the Lord, whom you seek, will suddenly come to His temple; and the messenger of the covenant, in whom you delight, behold, He is coming," says the Lord of hosts. (Malachi 3:1).*

The promise was that the Lord would one day come to His temple. But that coming would be preceded by a messenger who would prepare the way before Him. This was literally fulfilled in the persons of John the Baptist and Jesus. John was the messenger of God who broke the prophetic silence after 400 years. And Jesus is the Lord incarnate who came suddenly to His Temple, overturning the tables of those who had defiled it and presenting Himself as the very Messiah of God.

THE MINISTRY OF EZRA

The phrase "after these things" in Ezra 7:1 moves us forward in time to the year 458 B.C. This was almost 60 years after the events of the previous chapter. The Temple had long since been rebuilt. The sacrifices had long since been underway. All of the events in the book of Esther had taken place. If we were approaching this story in chronological order, we would read Ezra 1-6 and then turn to the book of Esther and read that entire book and then we would come back to Ezra 7-10 before coming finally to the book of Nehemiah.

1st Return under Zerubbabel	Events of the book of Esther	2nd Return under Ezra	3rd Return under Nehemiah
Ezra 1-6	Book of Esther	Ezra 7-10	Book of Nehemiah
537-516 B.C.	473 B.C.	458-457 B.C.	537 B.C.

Because of this, chapter seven might seem to be anticlimactic, a bit like the cavalry that arrives only after the battle has been completed. After all, the work has been completed. The opposition has been overcome. The sacrifices have been re-instituted. What more is there to do? But I want to suggest that, rather than being anticlimactic, Ezra's ministry marks a new page in the spiritual life of Israel.

There is a principle here. It is the principle of generational spirituality. It means that each generation is responsible for developing its own spiritual relationship with the Lord. I can not rest upon the spirituality of my parents. My children cannot rest on my spirituality. To be effective, the faith of our fathers must become my faith as well.

This does not mean that we can therefore neglect the spiritual upbringing of our children. Far from it! It means that we must bring our children up, not only to worship the God which we worship, but to do so in a way that is fresh and exciting and real and relevant to them. I may experience a generation gap, but such a gap dare not enter into the spiritual lives of my children.

Are you leaving a godly heritage for your children? My parents did that for me. There were several means by which they did it.

- We had a tradition of daily Bible-reading in which our entire family would sit around the dinner table and read the Scriptures together.
- We had a regular attendance in church. It was unthinkable to skip church attendance if you were not on your sickbed and virtually at death's door.
- Any time that we were going out the door, my mother would call out a blessing upon us.

As we were raising our daughter, we also had some similar family traditions. There were regular Bible Studies in our home. There was the memorization of Scriptures. And there was the regular teaching of the doctrines of the faith.

Now that I am a grandparent, I have come to find a renewed consciousness about such a family heritage. It involves a commitment that you and your family and all of your descendants shall follow the Lord.

Joshua did that. He stood before all of the tribes of Israel and he urged them to follow his example as he said, "As for me and my house, we shall follow the Lord" (Joshua 24:15). Both of these aspects, a generational spirituality as well as a family heritage of spirituality must be held in tension. They are both important.

Generational Spirituality (Each generation must have its own personal relationship with the Lord)		Family Heritage of Spirituality (We are called to lead our families in a heritage of following the Lord)

1.   Ezra's Commission.

As chapter 7 opens, we are introduced to Ezra the scribe. He is both a scribe and a priest and receives a commission from King Artaxerxes to lead a group of Jews back to the land. The actual words of the decree are given in Ezra 7:12-26. These verses switch to the Aramaic language, it being the language in which the decree would have been originally penned.

There had already been an initial return of Jews to the Land. That had taken place 80 years earlier. Now an edict is provided to permit a second return from among the ancestors who did not elect to return with the first group. The specific mention of the priests and Levites indicates that this second return is for the purpose of reviving and reforming the Temple worship.

These returnees were not made up only of the tribes of Levi and Judah. They are said in Ezra 7:13 to include any of the people of Israel. There is a lot of talk today about the "lost tribes of Israel." But the truth is that there were was a representative remnant of all of the tribes to be found in the land in a later age.

2.   Ezra's Controversy.

When he comes to the land, Ezra encounters a problem there. Introduced in the ninth chapter, it is the problem of intermarriage with the people of Canaan.

> *Now when these things had been completed,*
> *the princes approached me, saying, "The people of*
> *Israel and the priests and the Levites have not*

separated themselves from the peoples of the lands, according to their abominations, those of the Canaanites, the Hittites, the Perizzites, the Jebusites, the Ammonites, the Moabites, the Egyptians and the Amorites. 2 For they have taken some of their daughters as wives for themselves and for their sons, so that the holy race has intermingled with the peoples of the lands; indeed, the hands of the princes and the rulers have been foremost in this unfaithfulness." (Ezra 9:1-2).

Ezra goes before the Lord and prays a prayer of repentance as he intercedes for the people of God. Meanwhile, outside the Temple, the people have gathered and are formulating a plan of action.

Shecaniah the son of Jehiel, one of the sons of Elam, said to Ezra, "We have been unfaithful to our God and have married foreign women from the peoples of the land; yet now there is hope for Israel in spite of this. 3 So now let us make a covenant with our God to put away all the wives and their children, according to the counsel of my lord and of those who tremble at the commandment of our God; and let it be done according to the law. 4 Arise! For this matter is your responsibility, but we will be with you; be courageous and act." (Ezra 10:2-4).

The situation was serious. As we have pointed out, the spiritual future of the entire nation was at stake. The drastic situation called for an equally drastic solution. The question that we must ask is whether this was the correct solution. Were the Israelites right in divorcing their pagan wives? The passage does not specifically say and there are arguments for either side.

On the one hand, it can be argued that the plan was brought about in the context of prayer and a desire to return to the Lord. On the other hand, there is no specific confirmation in the historical narrative that this plan was approved by the Lord. What we do have, albeit a generation later, is God's clear statement that He hates divorce (Malachi 2:14). A summary of the arguments are listed on the following chart:

The Plan was of God	The Plan was a Mistake
The absence of condemnation indicates approval, especially in light of the fact that Ezra closes on this note.	There is no editorial confirmation. If Nehemiah is seen as the continuation of Ezra, then it is possible that this was merely a problem along the way which was not satisfactorily resolved at the time.
Ezra agrees to the plan after a long time of prayer.	The Lord did not reveal the plan to Ezra as a prophecy; it was suggested by someone who was not a prophet.
The nation was in danger of falling into idolatry and Deuteronomy 7:2-3 specifically forbids such intermarriage.	It is never right to do wrong so that good may come of it. Malachi 2:14 contains a scathing indictment against Israel for its practice of divorce.
Nearly the entire nation agreed to the proposal.	Majority opinion is no guarantee of righteousness (an example is the case of the 10 spies who gave a report at Kadesh Barnea).
The actions of Ezra and the nation marked a return to the observance of the Law. There was already a new generation growing that would have pagan roots.	The New Testament confirms that believers are to remain married to an unbelieving spouse (1 Corinthians 7:12-14). 1 Corinthians 7:14 tell how maintaining such a mixed marriage can have a positive effect upon the children.

The book of Malachi was written only a few years following the decisions that were made within this chapter. It therefore can be considered to be a commentary upon the actions of which we read.

Judah has dealt treacherously, and an abomination has been committed in Israel and in Jerusalem; for Judah has profaned the sanctuary of the Lord which He loves and has married the daughter of a foreign god. (Malachi 2:11).

This is an indictment of the very condition that is described in this chapter. Apparently the problem did not immediately disappear following the mass divorces at the end of this chapter. Nehemiah 13:23 tells us that the same pattern of intermarriage with pagans began to be adopted by some of the Israelites in Nehemiah's day. Nehemiah's reaction was not to order the same mass divorces, but instead, to urge the people to stop entering any future marriages with pagan Gentiles. He also deposed the high priest who had become a relative through marriage to one of the pagan enemies of Israel (Nehemiah 13:28). Malachi goes on to address the particular problem of divorce.

This is another thing you do: you cover the altar of the Lord with tears, with weeping and with groaning, because He no longer regards the offering or accepts it with favor from your hand. 14 Yet you say, "For what reason?" Because the Lord has been a witness between you and the wife of your youth, against whom you have dealt treacherously, though she is your companion and your wife by covenant. 15 But no one has done so who has a remnant of the Spirit. And what did that one do while he was seeking a godly offspring? Take heed then to your spirit, and let no one deal treacherously against the wife of your youth. 16 "For I hate divorce," says the Lord, the God of Israel, "and him who covers his garment with wrong," says the Lord of hosts. "So take heed to your spirit, that you do not deal treacherously." (Malachi 2:13-16).

This passage could almost be taken as a direct indictment against the decision and decree of Ezra. Under the cover of their tears of repentance, fraught with weeping and with groaning, the Jews made a grave decision to divorce their Gentile wives, even though they had entered into those marriages by covenant (2:14).

It is in the midst of such actions that the Lord stands as a witness against them, proclaiming in no uncertain terms that He hates divorce and that one who proceeds with such a divorce is doing it quite apart from the leading of the Spirit. In conclusion, we must cite two possible interpretations:

- Interpretation #1: The decision of Ezra and the people of Israel was a correct, though difficult one. Although they did the right thing, it carried its own negative consequences as later generations used this as an excuse to casually divorce their own wives.

  Viewed in this regard, the Malachi passage would then point out a problem which the next generation saw as they used the divorces of the previous generation to participate in unwarranted divorces.

- Interpretation #2: Though they had the best of intentions in seeking to repent and return from their sinful attitudes, Ezra and the people of Israel took a bad situation and made it worse by this instigation of across-the-board divorces. As a result, they lost the opportunity to be an influence for righteousness in this lost generation.

NEHEMIAH
Rebuilding the Walls

Ezra was already in Jerusalem, but God needed someone else. He needed a politician. Imagine that! God used a politician named Nehemiah to do great things. We ought to pray for our leaders to be anointed with this Spirit of God. Nehemiah was such a man.

Under the ministry of Haggai and Zechariah, the people had rebuilt the Temple. Then Ezra had led a return to the land with a second group of returning Jews and had instituted a revival in the land. Nehemiah came on the scene about 12 or 13 years after Ezra had made his return to the land. The book of Nehemiah can be divided into two major parts:

1	2:1-10	2:11-20	3-6	7	8-12	13
Nehemiah talks to God	Nehemiah talks to the King	The work planned	The work completed	Number of the people	Covenant renewal	Further reform
Conception			Complete		Consecration	
Work				Worship		
Rebuilding the Wall				Revival of the People		

The book of Nehemiah begins and ends with prayer. The prayer at the beginning of the book takes place when Nehemiah, the cupbearer to the king of Persia, hears of the sad state of affairs back in Jerusalem.

- The Jews have returned to the land.
- The Temple has been rebuilt.
- The people in Judah are in distress and reproach (1:3).
- The wall of Jerusalem is broken down and the gates are burned with fire (1:3).

Nehemiah responds by going before the Lord with a prayer of repentance. That is striking because Nehemiah wasn't a party to the sins that had resulted in the scattering of the nation and the destruction of Jerusalem. They had taken place long before he was born. But he nevertheless realizes the truth of a national guilt.

REBUILDING THE WALL

1.   Nehemiah before the King (Chapter 2:1-10).

      Nehemiah makes his request of Artaxerxes, the king of the Persian Empire. He specifically requests letters of authorization for his travels as well as for the acquisition of the building materials he shall need to perform the task.

      When he is asked by the king how long this project would take and how long it would be before Nehemiah could return to his palace duties, we read that Nehemiah "gave him a definite time." This tells me something about Nehemiah. He was a man both of prayer as well as of planning. He was not "shooting from the hip." He had carefully thought through what would be needed.

2.   Reconnaissance by night (2:11-16).

> *So I came to Jerusalem and was there three days. 12 And I arose in the night, I and a few men with me. I did not tell anyone what my God was putting into my mind to do for Jerusalem and there was no animal with me except the animal on which I was riding. 13 So I went out at night by the Valley Gate in the direction of the Dragon's Well and on to the Refuse Gate, inspecting the walls of Jerusalem which were broken down and its gates which were consumed by fire. 14 Then I passed on to the Fountain Gate and the King's Pool, but there was no place for my mount to pass. 15 So I went up at night by the ravine and inspected the wall. Then I entered the Valley Gate again and returned. 16 And the officials did not know where I had gone or what I had done; nor had I as yet told the Jews, the priests, the nobles, the officials, or the rest who did the work. (Nehemiah 2:11-16).*

      We are given some considerable detail as to the reconnaissance. We are specifically told that Nehemiah was in the city for three days. This is striking because he has been waiting to get to Jerusalem for over four months and he gets the permission and he gets the funding and he finally arrives at the city and then, for three days, there is no apparent activity. Why?

There is a lot that goes on in ministry behind the scenes. A lot of it is planning. Nehemiah is seen to be the master planner. A part of that plan involves going through the city by night and developing a vision. He then will go on to share that vision with the people.

Here is the principle. You must have the vision yourself before you can give it to others. Don't try to infect others with your Christian faith unless you have the real disease yourself. If it is not real in your life, then don't try to export it.

3.   Delegation of Labor (Chapter 3).

Throughout chapter 3 we are given a listing of each section of the wall and the names of those to whom that portion of labor was assigned. Why is this included? I'm not certain, but I find it interesting that Nehemiah knew their names. That tells me something about leadership. It has to be personal.

4.   Opposition (Chapter 4-6).

Opposition comes in each of these three chapters. It comes both from without as well as from within.

Chapter 4	Chapter 5	Chapter 6
Opposition from Without	Opposition from Within	Opposition from Without
Sanballat and Tobiah conspire against the work with a planned attack	Jewish nobility taking financial advantage of their Jewish brothers	Sanballat and Geshem plot to assassinate Nehemiah

And it came about from that day on, that half of my servants carried on the work while half of them held the spears, the shields, the bows, and the breastplates; and the captains were behind the whole house of Judah. 17 Those who were rebuilding the wall and those who carried burdens took their load with one hand doing the work and the other holding a weapon. 18 As for the builders, each wore his sword girded at his side as he built, while the trumpeter stood near me. (Nehemiah 4:16-18).

The fact that Nehemiah and the people of Israel were trusting in the Lord did not mean that they did not make careful preparations against the attacks of their enemies. Have you ever known someone who was described as being so heavenly minded that he was of no earthly good? We ought to be Street-smart Christians.

COVENANT RENEWAL OF THE NATION

The first part of the book of Nehemiah deals with the rebuilding of the wall of the city of Jerusalem. The latter part of the book deals with the rebuilding of the spiritual life of the nation.

1.   The Place of Revival: *And all the people gathered as one man at the square which was in front of the Water Gate, and they asked Ezra the scribe to bring the book of the law of Moses which the Lord had given to Israel. 2 Then Ezra the priest brought the law before the assembly of men, women, and all who could listen with understanding, on the first day of the seventh month. 3 And he read from it before the square which was in front of the Water Gate from early morning until midday, in the presence of men and women, those who could understand; and all the people were attentive to the book of the law. (Nehemiah 8:1-3).*

Where do you go to find revival? I would expect it to be in the temple. That was the place of Jewish worship. It was the place where the sacrifices were made every morning and every evening. It had been rebuilt in the years prior to Nehemiah's arrival in Jerusalem.

Yet this revival did not begin at the temple. It started at the *Sha'ar Ha-Mayim* - the Gate of the Water. This gate faced eastward toward the Mount of Olives. Its name came from the fact that it was near to the Gihon Spring and people would go out this gate to get water.

Where do you find real revival? In the parking lot of a shopping mall? On a wilderness mountainside by a burning bush? In a lion's den of Babylon? In the belly of a whale? With a Samaritan woman by a well? Jesus said that the place is not important. What is important is that you learn to worship the Father in spirit and in truth. This revival began with:

• A hunger for the Word: *They asked Ezra the scribe to bring the book of the law of Moses (8:1).*

- An attention to the commands of God: *All the people were attentive to the book of the law (8:3).*
- An attitude of worship: *Ezra opened the book in the sight of all the people for he was standing above all the people; and when he opened it, all the people stood up. 6 Then Ezra blessed the Lord the great God. And all the people answered, "Amen, Amen!" while lifting up their hands; then they bowed low and worshiped the Lord with their faces to the ground. (8:5-6).*
- An understanding of God's truth: *They read from the book, from the law of God, translating to give the sense so that they understood the reading (8:8).* It is noteworthy that the Scriptures had to be translated for the people because many of them had grown up in a foreign land and were unfamiliar with the Hebrew language.

2. A Celebration of Revival: *And all the people went away to eat, to drink, to send portions and to celebrate a great festival, because they understood the words which had been made known to them. (Nehemiah 8:12).*

The initial reaction to the reading of the law was anything but joyful. The people heard the law and they recognized that they had fallen far short and this led them to mourn and to grieve. But then Ezra and Nehemiah called them to rejoice and to celebrate. Why? The answer is seen in verse 10: *"Do not be grieved, for the joy of the Lord is your strength."*

The bad news is that you are not good enough or strong enough or righteous enough to stand in the presence of God. But the good news of the gospel is that Jesus was good enough and strong enough and righteous enough. He was strong in your place. His strength is such that He took your sins upon Himself on the cross.

ESTHER
God's Providential Salvation

The book of Esther follows a chiastic outline with the central actions of Esther being the pivotal point of the book. As such, there is both a rising action and a descending action.

1:1 - 2:18	2:19-23	3:1-15	4:1 - 7:10	8:1 - 9:17	9:18-32	10:1-3
Esther becomes Queen	Mordecai saves the King's Life	Haman plots against Jews	Esther acts to deliver her people	Jews to defend themselves	Jews celebrate	Mordecai rewarded
Esther & Mordecai in the Persian Court		Trouble for the Jews		Victory for the Jews	Esther & Mordecai in the Persian Court	

THE CAST OF CHARACTERS

Esther is the only book of the Bible that makes no mention of God. Yet the Lord is seen behind the scenes throughout this entire narrative. There are four main characters in this narrative. Two of them are Jewish and two are Gentiles.

1.   Esther.

Esther is a Jewish orphan who is living in the kingdom of Persia. She is raised by her cousin Mordecai and finds herself at the center of events where she is able to play a key role in the delivering of her people from the threat of destruction.

The name Esther (אֶסְתֵּר) sounds similar to the Persian word for "star." Her Jewish name is *Hadassah*. It is similar to the Akkadian word *hadassatu*, meaning "bride."

2.   Ahasuerus.

This seems to be a Persian title rather than a specific name. It is also used in Ezra 4:6 and in Daniel 9:1 in contexts that refer to other Persian kings. This king has traditionally been taken to refer to the Persian King known in Greek writings as Xerxes. He is known in Greek writings because he conducted an invasion of Greece in 480 B.C. While the account in Esther makes no mention of this invasion, it is likely that the events in this book take place after the forces of Xerxes had been repulsed in Greece.

Secular writings make no mention of Esther. Herodotus and Ctesias identify the wife of Xerxes both before and after the Persian expedition into Greece as Amestris. This is presumably a reference to the Biblical Vashti. This fits in with the Biblical account that tells us Esther did not become queen until the seventh year of the reign of Ahasuerus (Esther 2:16).

3.   Mordecai & Haman are seen in contrast to one another. They serve as protagonist and antagonist.

Haman	Mordecai
A descendant of Agag (Esther 3:1), the king of the Amalekites whose life Saul spared in disobedience to the command of God	From the tribe and family of Saul (Esther 2:5).
Enemy of the people of God	Savior of the people of God
Saul did not recognize the danger that Agag posed to the people of God. He was blind to the real issues.	Mordecai was alert to the real issues and overheard that which brought salvation to the people of God and death to the evil Haman.

Was Haman a literal descendant of the king of the Amalekites, or was this a reference to some other Agag? We cannot be certain, but at the very least it seems obvious that we are to make the connection and see in him a symbol of evil and one who is to be judged by God.

THE NARRATIVE

1.　The story begins with the reigning queen coming under the king's disfavor and being deposed. To take her place, the palace holds the ancient equivalent of a beauty pageant with the winner to become the new queen. Esther wins the contest and becomes the new reigning queen, but she keeps her Jewish heritage a secret.

2.　Esther's older cousin Mordecai overhears a plot against the king and relays it to Esther who sends the warning to the king, giving credit to Mordecai. The plotters are captured and executed.

3.　Haman the Agagite is promoted to a position of authority and he becomes incensed when Mordecai does not pay to him what he considers to be appropriate homage. Haman determines to take his revenge, not only upon Mordecai, but against all of the Jews.

4.　Haman prevails upon the king to institute a policy of ethnic cleansing that will result in all Jews within the Persian Empire being put to death and their possessions going to the Persian Treasury.

5.　Mordecai sends word to Esther to go into the presence of the king to intercede for the Jews. She at first is reluctant since it is the death penalty to go uninvited into the presence of the king and her predecessor was deposed over this same issue of going and/or not going into the presence of the king. Mordecai ultimately prevails upon her to go and she does so on the condition that the Jews will fast and pray on her behalf.

6.　Esther throws a series of banquets for the king to which she also invites Haman. Haman is so pleased at being invited that he is bursting with pride and finds himself even more chaffed at what he considers Mordecai's insulting behavior. At the urging of his wife, he has a gallows constructed upon which he plans to have Mordecai executed.

7.　During a sleepless night, the king has his palace scribes read some of the historical records and is reminded of the service that was done to him by Mordecai. He decides to repay Mordecai. He asks Haman what shall be done for one who has done great service to the crown. Thinking that he is the one of whom the king is considering for this great honor, he responds that the honored one should be treated with all of the royal honors normally due to a king. Only then does he learn that it is Mordecai who is to be thus honored.

8.   Before any action can be taken, Haman is summoned to Esther's banquet. It is there she reveals that the plan to exterminate the Jews will involve both her own death as well as the death of the man whom the king had planned to honor. When it comes to light that the king has been manipulated by Haman, the king orders Haman's execution on the very gallows that were constructed for Mordecai.

9.   The Jews are given permission from the Persian crown to defend themselves against all who attempt to carry out the policy of ethnic cleansing. They do so on the appointed day and are thus delivered.

POINTS TO PONDER

- Esther is the book of God's providence. Although God is never mentioned within the book, He is behind the scenes bringing about deliverance of His people through the circumstances that are in His hand.
- The success of Haman's plot to exterminate the Jews would also exterminate the promised seed through which the Messiah was to come. At stake is not only the people of Israel but also the salvation of all mankind.
- When God wins, the person that He uses is often unexpected. You have only to read the resumes of people such as Moses, David, Peter, Paul, James, and John to see that God delights in using people that would be rejected by the world.
- When God wins, the person He uses is usually unpretentious. God raises up the humble and He brings down the proud. This does not mean that you ought to go out and try to look humble. Real humility is on the inside.

INTRODUCTION TO THE BOOKS OF POETRY

The Old Testament is arranged in our English Bibles into four major groupings. We come in our study of the Old Testament to the second of those major groupings:

Pentateuch	Historical Books	Poetical Books	Prophetical Books
Books of History		Books of Experience	Books of Hope
The historical past		The spiritual present	The prophetic future
Moral life of the people	National life of the people	Spiritual life of the people	Future life of the people

The poetical books of the Bible are made up of five books. They run the gamut of human emotions and human experiences:

Book	Problem	God Seen as...	Man seen as...	Theme
Job	Problem of Pain and Suffering	Sovereign	On his face before God	Woe
Psalms	Problem of Prayer and Worship	Holy One	Before the throne of God	Worship
Proverbs	Problem of Conduct	All-wise	Receiving instruction	Wisdom
Ecclesiastes	Problem of Meaning and Significance	Creator	Looking at life under the sun	Why?

Song of Solomon	Problem of Love	Lover of His people	In a love relationship	Wedding

More than any other books of the Bible, these five books take in all of life experiences. They reach down to where we live and breath and hurt and love. As such, they transcend the national scope of Israel and are international in their outlook. Though they are set in history, their message is timeless.

TYPES OF HEBREW POETRY

When we think of poetry, we normally think in terms of rhythm and rhyme. These are sometimes found in Semitic poetry, but it is more common to find a parallelism of thought. Whereas English poetry contains rhythm and rhyme, Hebrew poetry uses a technique known as "parallelism of thought." There are several types of parallelism in Hebrew poetry.

1.   Synonymous Parallelism.

This first line states a principle and then the second line repeats the same thought in different words.

>   *But his delight is in the law of the Lord;*
>   *And in His law he meditates day and night. (Psalm 1:2).*

This repetition serves to emphasize the importance of the truth being taught. This same format is used throughout the Proverbs (11:25; 19:29; see also Psalm 3:1).

2.   Antithetical Parallelism.

The writer gives the positive side of the doctrine in the first line, and then gives the negative side in the second line. Thus, the thought is not repeated, but reversed.

>   *For the Lord knows the way of the righteous,*
>   *But the way of the wicked will perish. (Psalm 1:6).*

See also Psalm; 11:5; 14:6; 18:18; 32:10; Proverbs 12:4; 13:1; 14:12; 16:1-2; 16:9; 16:25; 19:4; Luke 1:52.

3.   Synthetic Parallelism.

The first line expresses a truth. Then the second line expresses another truth which is related to the first truth and which builds upon it. Thus, the author develops a system of truth through a progression of thought.

> *How blessed is the man who does not walk in the*
> *counsel of the wicked,*
> *Nor stand in the path of sinners,*
> *Nor sit in the seat of scoffers! (Psalm 1:1).*

See also Exodus 14:1; Job 19:25; Psalm 49:7-8; 51:11; 95:3; 145:18; Proverbs 9:13; 22:15; Song of Solomon 5:10-16.

4.   Completive Parallelism.

The second line completes the train of thought which was begun in the first line.

> *Train up a child in the way he should go,*
> *Even when he is old he will not depart from it.*
> *(Proverbs 22:6).*

This type of parallelism is found in Psalm 63:9; 66:18; Proverbs 13:14; 19:20; 22:10; 31:15.

5.   Parabolic Parallelism.

The first line of the parallel illustrates the truth which is then expressed outright in the second line.

> *Like the legs which hang down from the lame,*
> *So is a proverb in the mouth of fools.*
> *Like one who binds a stone in a sling,*
> *So is he who gives honor to a fool.*
> *Like a thorn which falls into the hand of a drunkard,*
> *So is a proverb in the mouth of fools. (Proverbs 26:7-9).*
>
> *Like a dog that returns to its vomit,*
> *Is a fool who repeats his folly. (Proverbs 26:11).*

See also Job 5:26; 24:5; Psalms 49:14; 103:13; 127:4; Proverbs 11:22; 15:17; Song of Solomon 2:2 for other examples of this type of parallelism. Proverbs 25-26 contain an abundance of these parallels.

6.   Comparative Parallelism.

The first line of the parallel expresses something that is better than the object presented in the second line.

> *It is better to live in a desert land,*
> *Than with a contentious and vexing woman.*
> *(Proverbs 21:19).*

Also found in Psalm 37:16; 84:10; 118:8-9; Proverbs 15:16-17; 16:8; 16:19; 17:1; 19:1; 21:9; Ecclesiastes 4:6; 4:13.

7.   Chiastic Parallelism.

A chiasm is a type of parallelism where two (or more) items are mentioned and then mentioned again, but the second time they are mentioned in the opposite order.

> *Adonai,*
> *Thou hast been our dwelling place*
> *In generation and generation*
> *Before the mountains*
> *Were born*
> *Or*
> *Thou didst give birth*
> *To the earth and the world,*
> *Even from everlasting to everlasting,*
> *Thou art*
> *God. (Psalm 90:1-2).*

See further examples in Psalm 3:7-8; 6:2-3; 58:6; 135:15-18. Chiasms are not limited to poetry. They are seen in all sorts of literary genre and we have seen entire books of the Bible set forth in a chiastic arrangement.

8.   Climactic Parallelism.

The second line repeats verbatim a phrase from the first line and then adds or subtracts an idea.

> *Ascribe to the Lord, O sons of the mighty,*
> *Ascribe to the Lord glory and strength. (Psalm 29:1).*

See also Psalm 29:4,7; Ecclesiastes 1:2.

CHARACTERISTICS OF BIBLICAL POETRY

1. Parallelism of Thought.

    Parallelism is used frequently and interchangeably throughout poetic sections of both the Old and the New Testament. Occasionally a poet decides to follow a more rigid format as in Psalm 119 where we find a perfect acrostic. Each paragraph begins with a separate letter of the Hebrew alphabet and each beginning word of every line begins with the same letter of that paragraph.

2. Vividness of Expression.

    Biblical poetry uses a great deal of figurative language as well as various figures of speech in order to paint a picture in the mind of the reader. The purpose of poetry is usually not to teach doctrine, but to establish feeling. Instead of setting forth a complete systematic theology on the doctrine of God, the author attempts to make you feel the might and the power of God.

    > *The voice of the Lord is powerful,*
    > *The voice of the Lord is majestic,*
    > *The voice of the Lord breaks the cedars;*
    > *Yes, the Lord breaks in pieces the cedars of Lebanon.*
    > *And He makes Lebanon skip like a calf,*
    > *And Sirion like a young wild ox.*
    > *The voice of the Lord hews out flames of fire.*
    > *The voice of the Lord shakes the wilderness;*
    > *The Lord shakes the wilderness of Kadesh. (Psalm 29:4-8).*

    We see pictured the great power of God in such a way that is much more vivid to our minds than if I were to stand up and recite the doctrine of omnipotence from *Berkhof's Systematic Theology.*

3.   Honest Concreteness.

We rarely see vague, theoretical, or philosophical ideas presented in Biblical poetry. Instead, the author is usually very honest and exact in what he thinks and feels.

Break the arm of the wicked and the evildoer,
Seek out his wickedness until Thou dost find none.
(Psalm 10:15).

O God, shatter their teeth in their mouth;
Break out the fangs of the young lions, O Lord.
(Psalm 58:6).

This honesty is appealing to the reader and often allows us to identify with the author and with his emotions.

4.   Emotional Appeal.

Biblical poetry, as well as any other poetry, appeals primarily to the emotions rather than to the intellect. You are meant, not merely to think and reflect, but also to feel. We must keep this principle in mind when developing our theology and doctrine. It is a mistake to base a doctrinal belief solely upon a poetic passage. Rather, the poetry should be used to illustrate and amplify the doctrinal point that is presented elsewhere.

WISDOM LITERATURE

Strictly speaking, there is a difference between the genres of poetic literature versus wisdom literature. Some of the Poetical Books are specifically designated as wisdom literature, though it might be argued that all contain wisdom.

Poetic Literature	Wisdom Literature
Psalms Song of Solomon	Job Proverbs Ecclesiastes

473

With the probable exception of Job, these books were all written at about the same time period (although in the case of Psalms and Proverbs they were not completed to their present form for another 200 years).

Poetic Books	Wisdom Books
The Narrator is viewed as a normal man.	The Narrator is viewed as the wise voice of experience.
Touch the heart.	Touch the mind.
Focus upon human emotion.	Focus upon wisdom.
Love for God and for others.	Living before God and with others.

What do we mean when we speak of "Wisdom Literature?" We usually think of wisdom as the result of compiling knowledge. The Biblical view of wisdom involves a skill. The same Hebrew word that is used for "wisdom" is found in Exodus 35:25 where all the skilled women spun with their hands and again in verse 35 where God had filled certain people with skill to perform every work of an engraver and of a designer and of an embroiderer. The Biblical view of wisdom involves a learned skill. It is the skill of living and it involves an understanding of life. The Christian develops his world and life view by beginning with God:

This same format is seen in the relationship of the Law to the Wisdom Literature of the Old Testament.

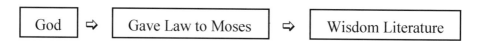

The people of the world operate in just the opposite manner. They start with how they want to live and then they look for a system of thought or even a god (or lack thereof) to support that position.

The Wisdom Literature will teach you how to live. It will not see the world through rose-colored glasses. Pain and suffering will not be whitewashed. It will be seen in all of its undiminished intensity.

JOB
The Problem of Pain

Job is one of the oldest stories in the world. It is an epic poem of man's contemplations of suffering when God is silent. It stands as one of the great works of world literature.

The book of Job is made up of a historical narrative at both the beginning and at the end of the book that serve as bookends for the extensive dialogue and discourses that make up the central body of the book.

1-2	3-31	32-37	38-41	42
Historical Prologue: Job's test	Job's three friends	Elihu's speeches	God speaks	Historical Epilogue: Job's restoration
	Dialogue and Discourses			

The prose sections at the beginning and at the end of the book contain very simple and archaic Hebrew in contrast to the central section that is highly ornate in its language.

Prose Sections	Poetry Sections
Plain language	Highly ornate
Written in pure Hebrew	Contain many expressions characteristic of Chaldaean

This is a book that deals with the problem of pain. This is not a pleasant subject, but our reflection on the topic of pain is more than a study in masochism. It is ultimately a study that brings us face to face with God. C.S. Lewis speaks to this problem of pain:

> "God whispers to us in our pleasures, speaks to us in our conscience, but shouts in our pains; it is his megaphone to arouse a deaf world. Alas man, happy, is a man without the least inkling that his actions do not "answer", that they are not in accord with the laws of the universe.... No doubt pain as God's megaphone is a terrible instrument. it may lead to final

and unrepentant rebellion. But it gives the only opportunity the bad man can have for amendment. It removes the veil, it plants the flag of truth within the fortress of a rebel soul." (*The Problem of Pain*).

Job's experience with God could not have taken place apart from Job's suffering. This is because real faith does not come to maturity until it has been through the fire of crisis.

WHAT THE BOOK OF JOB IS NOT

It is easy to use the book of Job in a wrong way. There are certain things this book is not designed to do.

- It is not a systematic treatment of the question of suffering. We do not find a theology outline when we come to this book. Instead, the problems of God and His treatment of man are hammered out on the anvil of the experience of the redeemed soul. There is a lesson here. It is that we learn theology only as we live it.
- It is not a book of simple answers to complicated questions. Suffering is complicated. There are no easy answers to the question of pain. The friends of Job are going to offer some answers, but their answers will be inadequate. When you face tragedy, there are no intellectual answers that make everything okay. That does not mean that there are no intellectual answers. But those answers will not be simplistic. They will be as profound as the God of the universe.
- It is not a brief for philosophical discussion in the midst of existential suffering. When one is in pain, it is not the mind that's broken; it is the heart. Death is something you discuss in terms of a philosophic exercise only until it is your time to die. Then it becomes ever so much more. Suffering is not merely an intellectual theory. The point of suffering is that it hurts. You can't just file it away in your notebook.
- It is not an argument for divine earthly judgment (although the book does end with Job's restoration). Divine earthly retribution and reward is an observation, not a principle. The fact is, the most godly man who ever lived, Jesus Christ, died on a cross.

THE CAST OF CHARACTERS

1. Job.

    He is the hero of the story. As you read through the narrative, you are meant to step into his sandals and to see the world through his eyes.   We are

    > We do not know the meaning of the name "Job" (אִיּוֹב). It is similar in spelling to the Hebrew word bya, meaning "enemy," but this is likely mere coincidence.

    introduced to Job at the very outset of the book: There was a man in the land of Uz, whose name was Job, and that man was blameless, upright, fearing God, and turning away from evil. (Job 1:1).

    - Job was a good man. He is described as blameless, upright, fearing God, and turning away from evil. He was a beacon of light in a dark world.

    - Job was also a rich man. This is seen in verses 2-3: *And seven sons and three daughters were born to him. 3 His possessions also were 7,000 sheep, 3,000 camels, 500 yoke of oxen, 500 female donkeys, and very many servants; and that man was the greatest of all the men of the east. (Job 1:2-3).*

    There is a teaching going around that is a reaction to today's prosperity theology. It says that you cannot be good and rich at the same time. Job contradicts that teaching. He was a good man. He was also a rich man.

2. Mrs. Job.

    She plays only a minor part in the story. When he has lost everything he has, she advises him to curse God and die (2:9). Later he laments that his breath is offensive to his wife (19:17).

3. God.

    While there are one or two exceptions, the term יְהוָה (*Yahweh*) is found in the narrative portions and not during the conversations of Job with his three friends. It is found extensively in the first two chapters of the book and beginning in chapter 38 where Job has his encounter with the Lord. Throughout the central dialog, we find God instead referred to as אֱלוֹהַ (*Eloha*) -- the singular form of אֱלֹהִים (*Elohim*) or else as אֵל (*El*).

The attribute of God that comes most to the forefront in the book of Job is His sovereign power and righteousness. He is God and He can do as He wills with His creation and any actions He takes are just and righteous.

Throughout Job's suffering, he calls God to account, insisting that he is innocent of any wrongdoing and that he is therefore undeserving of the lot that has been accorded him. This brings up the question of undeserved pain. It is a question with which theologians have often struggled. It asks, "If God is both all powerful and all righteous and good, then how can He permit suffering to continue?"

4.   Satan.

Our English name "Satan" is a transliteration of the Hebrew שָׂטָן, which means "enemy." The verbal form שָׂטַן means "to oppose." It is interesting to note that the first Biblical use of this word describes the angel of the Lord:

> *But God was angry because he was going, and the angel of the Lord took his stand in the way as an **adversary** against him. Now he was riding on his donkey and his two servants were with him. (Numbers 22:22).*

Another example of where שָׂטָן refers to someone other than Satan is in the account of those who rose up in opposition to the reign of Solomon.

> *Then the Lord raised up an **adversary** to Solomon, Hadad the Edomite; he was of the royal line in Edom. (1 Kings 11:14).*

Here in the book of Job, the designation שָׂטָן is preceded by the definite article -- he is THE Satan. He is seen accusing Job and his motives. As the narrative shows at the end of the story, the accusation turns out to be false.

5.   Job's Friends.

All three of Job's friends come to the same conclusion. They believe that God blesses good people and that He curses bad people and, since Job has had bad things happen to him, they conclude that he has some hidden sin in his life.

a.   Eliphaz ("God is victorious"). He is mentioned first among Job's three friends and he seems to have been their leader. This is seen in Job 42:7 when we read that the Lord said to Eliphaz the Temanite, *"My wrath is kindled against you and against your two friends, because you have not spoken of Me what is right as My servant Job has."*

- It should be noted that there is an Eliphaz who was the oldest son of Esau (Genesis 36:4).
- The Eliphaz of Job is called a Timanite. Tima was one of the sons of Ishmael (Genesis 25:15).

b.   Bildad.

He is described in Job as a "Shuhite." This would make him a descendant of Shuah, one of the sons of Abraham through Keturah (Genesis 25:2).

c.   Zophar.

The name Zophar comes from the Hebrew צָפִיר to describe a goat. He is described as a Naamathite (Job 2:11). The significance of this designation is unknown. Of the three friends, his condemnation of Job is the most harsh.

6.   Elihu.

His name means "he is my God." It was a common name among the Jews. He is described as a Buzite; Buz was one of the sons of Nahor, the brother of Abram (Genesis 22:21). He describes himself as younger than the other three friends of Job and he initially withholds his comments out of respect for their age (Job 32:4). When he does speak, it is to show both his impatience for the words of his elders while holding to the same misconception that Job's suffering is the result of discipline.

SETTING FOR THE STORY

The story is set in two different locations. It begins in one place and ends there as well, but there is a secondary location that has a great impact upon the first.

1.   The land of Uz.

        We do not know for certain the location of Uz. A clue is given to us in Job 1:3 when Job is described as the greatest of all the men of the east. Some of the copies of the Septuagint add a notation at the end of the book of Job that the land of Uz lay on the borders of Edom and Arabia.

        In describing his past life, Job speaks of how he sat in the gates of the city (Job 29:7). This is seen in contrast to the nomadic life of the Israelites after they came out of Egypt.

2.   The Presence of the Lord: *Now there was a day when the sons of God came to present themselves before the Lord, and Satan also came among them. (Job 1:6).*

        We are not specifically told where this takes place, but it seems evident that this is no earthly court. It was a place where the sons of God came to present themselves before the Lord (Job 1:6). There is a lesson here. It is that the events of heaven have a direct impact upon what takes place here on earth. The opposite is also true. Events on earth have a heavenly impact. That means what you do here on earth is important, for it has eternal repercussions.

THE AUTHOR OF THE BOOK

There are some Jewish traditions that point to Moses as being the author of the book.
- There are more Egyptian loan-words found in Job than in any other books of the Bible outside of the Pentateuch.
- There are some words and phrases used in Job that are normally used only by Moses (Sons of God, Almighty).
- The land of Uz seems to have been located in the proximity of Midian where Moses spent 40 years.

THE DATE OF COMPOSITION

Most evidence points to a relatively early date for the composition of the book of Job. As such, it presents to us some of the most primitive, elemental revelation of the Bible.

- There is no mention of Israel or the law.
- The term "Almighty" is regularly used as a reference to God. This was especially common in the patriarchal narrative.
- Job's longevity (he lived to be 140 years old) suggests a patriarchal era if not earlier.

Another suggestion as to the authorship of the book is that it is penned by Elihu, the young man who spends most of the book listening.

THE STORY OF JOB

Job was a man who had everything. A family. Wealth. Respect. Health. The story opens with a picture of his prosperity as well as his piety. He has not been so caught up in his wealth that he forgets God. He has been blessed by the Lord and he is thankful.

1.   The Heavenly Challenge.

> *Now there was a day when the sons of God came to present themselves before the Lord, and Satan also came among them. 7 And the Lord said to Satan, "From where do you come?" Then Satan answered the Lord and said, "From roaming about on the earth and walking around on it." 8 And the Lord said to Satan, "Have you considered My servant Job? For there is no one like him on the earth, a blameless and upright man, fearing God and turning away from evil."*
> *9 Then Satan answered the Lord, "Does Job fear God for nothing? 10 Hast Thou not made a hedge about him and his house and all that he has, on every side? Thou hast blessed the work of his hands, and his possessions have increased in the land. 11 But put forth Thy hand now and touch all that he has; he will*

surely curse Thee to Thy face."

12 Then the Lord said to Satan, "Behold, all that he has is in your power, only do not put forth your hand on him." So Satan departed from the presence of the Lord. (Job 1:6-12).

What Job could not see from his perspective is the cosmic challenge that was being issued before the throne of God. The interesting thing about this challenge is that God evidently baits Satan. It is clear who is in charge in this confrontation. Satan is able to do no more than is allowed by the Lord.

We also come away with the sense that there is more going on here that even is evident to the angelic realm. The Lord has His own reasons for allowing Satan's challenge to be considered and we are not privy to those reasons.

2. Job's Calamities.

In a single day, all that Job had was taken from him. He was sitting and watching the news at noon when there was a flash.

- A group of terrorists attacked his servants, killed them all and made off with all of his oxen and all of his donkeys.
- Fire came down from heaven and consumed all of his sheep and all of the servants that were watching them. There was nothing left but smoke on the skyline.
- Another group of terrorists attacked those servants who were watching his camels and they were all taken.
- There was a structural collapse and all of his children were killed (7 sons, 3 daughters).

What was Job's reaction? Sorrow? Grief? Certainly! But in the midst of that grief, he worshiped the Lord, saying. *"Naked I came from my mother's womb, and naked I shall return there. The Lord gave and the Lord has taken away. Blessed be the name of the Lord." (Job 1:21).*

There is a wonderful sense of Job's recognition of the fact that he owns nothing and that God owns everything. He says, "I came into this world with nothing." He recognizes that anything that has been given to him has been given from the hands of a God of grace and that Job is only a steward.

During her last semester at college, we loaned our daughter

the use of one of our cars. It made it a bit easier for her and she appreciated its use. When the semester was over, she didn't say, "Well I've been driving that car and you shouldn't take it back." She considered herself fortunate to have been able to use it for that period.

Job recognizes the same thing, not about a car, but about everything. He has a proper theology of nakedness that says, "Everything is God's. I am only given my possessions on a temporary loan from God and if He wants them back it is okay."

3.   Satan's Second Accusation.

Satan has already accused Job and the accusation has proven to be unfair. Satan once again comes into the presence of God and accuses Job. He says to God, "Job only remains faithful to you because he is in good health." And so God allows Satan permission to take away Job's health. He is afflicted with boils from head to toe. Painful. Irritating. Ugly. Full of puss.

4.   Job's Continuing Endurance.

Everything he has is gone. No family. No possessions. No health. The only thing that has not been taken is his nagging wife.

> *Then his wife said to him, "Do you still hold fast your integrity? Curse God and die!" But he said to her, "You speak as one of the foolish women speaks. Shall we indeed accept good from God and not accept adversity?" In all this Job did not sin with his lips. (Job 2:9-10).*

Once again, his reply is a wonderful reflection of his understanding of the sovereignty of God. He knows that all the good that he has ever received came from God and he knows that God has allowed this calamity to come as well.

When I was in seminary, I received a "B" on an exam when I really felt that I deserved an "A". I went and mentioned my feelings to the professor. It didn't change my grade. But I noticed that I never went and complained about getting an "A" when I might have deserved a "B," when I received a grade that was higher than what I might have deserved.

5.   Job's Three Friends.

Next Job is joined by three friends. They come and they sit with him in silence for a solid week. They suffer with him and they mourn with him and as long as they do that, they are a great help to Job. There are times when words merely get in the way and when the best thing to do is to be with someone in their grief and to be silent. These three friends do exactly that for an entire week and then they ruin it all by speaking. Their message is the complete antithesis of that which was suggested by Job's wife.

- She said, "Curse God and die."
- They say, "Curse Job and live."

Their message is that good things happen to good people and that bad things happen to bad people, so Job must have done something very bad to deserve these calamities, so he needs to repent and confess that bad sin he is hiding and return to God and then everything will be okay.

The next thirty chapters are made up of Job arguing with his three friends as he insists on his own innocence and they insist that he must be guilty of some hidden sin. In those chapters his friends give us some excellent theological reasons why bad things happen. A lot of what they say is very accurate. When we read their reflections, we ought to understand that the things they say are accurate. But their advice isn't applicable to Job. It is like the professor who gave an essay test and one of the students wrote a long, precise, and detailed answer. But when he got his paper back, the professor had written, "That is an excellent answer to the wrong question." Good advice, but it doesn't fit. A good diagnosis, but to the wrong disease. That is what takes place here in the pages of the book of Job.

Neither those friends nor Job could see the real reason for Job's troubles. As the readers of this passage, we have been permitted to "peak behind the veil" to see just a part of what was going on in heaven. The point is that there are some things that happen in this life for which we see no reason. There are other times when we might be able to see a portion of God's reason for suffering and some of the benefit it brings, but it will not be until we get to heaven that we will see the whole picture and then we will understand.

There are three cycles of discussion that ensue between Job and his three friends.

1st Cycle of Debate	2nd Cycle of Debate	3rd Cycle of Debate
Eliphaz: Suffering comes because of sin, so Job should repent **Job:** My one consolation is that I have not turned against God	**Eliphaz:** You are condemned by your own words and are in sin **Job:** Both your words and God's had have brought me down	**Eliphaz:** You cannot fool God; He sees to punish the wicked **Job:** I wish to present my case to God that He might judge me fairly
Bildad: Past generations testify that, if Job is righteous, God will restore him **Job:** I cannot presume to speak of what God does	**Bildad:** Listen to what happens to the wicked! **Job:** Both you had God have wronged me, but I yet hope to stand before my Redeemer	**Bildad:** Man is too small and weak to be right before God **Job:** Your words are no help to the small and the weak
Zophar: Remove your sin and God will remove His reproach from you **Job:** You have said nothing I did not know; I will trust in God even though He slay me	**Zophar:** The triumph of the wicked is short-lived **Job:** The wicked enjoy their wickedness while I am left to my misery	**Job:** I call upon the testimony of my past works of righteousness

Job continues to maintain his innocence. He says...

- I made a covenant with my eyes that I would not look on a woman to lust (31:1).
- I gave food and clothing to the poor and the widow and the orphan (31:16-20).
- I did not let my own prosperity get in the way of my relationship with God (31:24-28).

At the end of Job's lengthy defense, we are introduced to a fourth friend. His name is Elihu and he describes himself as having been younger than the others. Because of his youth, he has remained silent up to this time.

> *Then these three men ceased answering Job, because he was righteous in his own eyes. 2 But the anger of Elihu the son of Barachel the Buzite, of the family of Ram burned; against Job his anger burned, because he justified himself before God. 3 And his anger burned against his three friends because they had found no answer, and yet had condemned Job. 4 Now Elihu had waited to speak to Job because they were years older than he. (Job 32:1-4).*

In the chapter leading up to his confrontation with Job, Elihu describes the Lord's majesty in terms that anticipate the manner of God's manifestation

- Listen closely to the thunder of His voice, and the rumbling that goes out of His mouth. Under the whole heaven He lets it loose, and His lightning to the ends of the earth (37:2-3).
- With moisture He loads the thick cloud; He disperses the cloud of His lightning (37:11).
- Do you know how God establishes them and makes the lightning of His cloud to shine? (37:15).
- Do you know about the layers of thick clouds? (37:16).
- The wind has passed by (37:21).
- Out of the north comes golden splendor ((37:22).

Elihu is a young man with a young man's anger at what he sees: the obstinate attitude of Job, and the ineffectual condemnation of his three friends. He makes the point that because God is God He does not need man's permission to act and does not need man's judgment to be righteous.

6.   Job's Confrontation with God.

Finally in chapter 38, the Lord Himself answers Job. "Finally!" we think, "God is going to appear to Job and tell him all of the reasons for his sufferings and Job will see and hear and understand. God is going to let Job in on what we saw in chapters one and two and which has been hidden from Job in all these succeeding chapters."

It doesn't happen. God does not give Job any of the reasons. He doesn't give to him the behind-the-scenes glimpse that we have had. It isn't that there are no reasons. From our vantage point we can see all sorts of reasons. We can see the ramifications of the heavenly conflict between God and Satan. We can see how God is building up Job's character and developing a message that he will spread to future generations. But God doesn't tell Job any of that. God doesn't give Job any answers to his questions and God doesn't give Job any comfort in his situation.

He will eventually. Before the book is done, Job will have a new family and renewed possessions and renewed vigor of health. But none of that comes right now. Instead, God says to Job, "Who are you to question Me?"

> *Then the Lord answered Job out of the whirlwind and said, 2 "Who is this that darkens counsel by words without knowledge? 3 Now gird up your loins like a man, and I will ask you, and you instruct Me! 4 Where were you when I laid the foundation of the earth? Tell Me, if you have understanding, 5 who set its measurements, since you know? Or who stretched the line on it? 6 On what were its bases sunk? Or who laid its cornerstone, when the morning stars sang together, and all the sons of God shouted for joy?" (Job 38:1-7).*

> *"Have you ever in your life commanded the morning, and caused the dawn to know its place?" (Job 38:12).*

> *"Have you entered into the springs of the sea? Or have you walked in the recesses of the deep? 17 Have the gates of death been revealed to you? Or have you seen the gates of deep darkness? Have you understood the expanse of the earth? Tell Me, if you know all this." (Job 38:16-18).*

> *Then the Lord said to Job, "Will the faultfinder contend with the Almighty? Let him who reproves God answer it." (Job 40:1).*

Do you see the continuing refrain? God says to Job, "Who are you?" It is a rhetorical question. No answer is needed. When you stand in the presence of God, it is evident that we are in no position to pass judgment upon God.

Job gets the point. He understands it. He says: *"Behold, I am insignificant; what can I reply to Thee? I lay my hand on my mouth. Once I have spoken, and I will not answer; Even twice, and I will add no more." (Job 40:3-5).*

Job got the point. He has no answer for the God of the universe. He has spoken before in the presence of his friends, but he is not able to speak in the presence of God. God answers, "I'm not finished yet."

> *Then the Lord answered Job out of the storm, and said, "Now gird up your loins like a man; I will ask you, and you instruct Me. Will you really annul My judgment? Will you condemn Me that you may be justified? Or do you have an arm like God, And can you thunder with a voice like His?" (Job 40:6-9).*

And so, God continues for another two chapters in asking Job what is essentially the same question, "Who are you?" The amazing thing about this is that Job was satisfied. His reply shows a turning point in his thinking.

> *Then Job answered the Lord, and said, "I know that Thou canst do all things, And that no purpose of Thine can be thwarted." (Job 42:1-2).*

> *"I have heard of Thee by the hearing of the ear; but now my eye sees Thee; therefore I retract, and I repent in dust and ashes." (Job 42:5-6).*

He understands and he repents of his former attitude of pride and arrogance and of thinking that he has the right to question God. And God forgives Job. We know that by the conclusion of the story.

7. The Conclusion of the Story: *And it came about after the Lord had spoken these words to Job, that the Lord said to Eliphaz the Temanite, "My wrath is kindled against you and against your two friends, because you have not spoken of Me what is right as My servant Job has. Now therefore, take for yourselves seven bulls and seven rams, and go to My servant Job, and offer up a burnt offering*

for yourselves, and My servant Job will pray for you. For I will accept him so that I may not do with you according to your folly, because you have not spoken of Me what is right, as My servant Job has." (Job 42:7-8).

Do you see the continuing refrain? Four times the Lord speaks of "My servant Job." He not only rebuked the three friends of Job, but he also tells them that if they want to get right with God then they must have Job intercede on their behalf.

LESSONS FROM THE BOOK OF JOB

There are some important lessons that we learn from the book of Job.

1.   We learn that God is both all-loving as well as all-powerful.

A lot of people seem to think that God must be either one or the other. Either He must be a God of love but He isn't all-powerful, or else He must be a sovereign and all-powerful God who isn't very nice. Job teaches us that He is both powerful and good. Evil enters the world, not through the hands of God, but through Satan. And although Satan is able to perform his deeds, it is only at the permission of God and only as God has allowed him to work.

2.   There are no simple answers to complicated questions.

Systematic theologians have a fit with the book of Job. Systematic theologians try to make everything fit into nice, neat packages. This book will not fit. It resembles life. Life does not fit into nice, neat packages. It is messy. When you point to wounds, both physical and emotional, there is only one answer. It is to look at the nail scars of Jesus and to realize that they are there for you.

3.   When you face suffering and tragedy, it is good to express your grief and your trouble to God, but do not think that you are in a position to pass judgment upon God. Job himself learned that lesson.

Then Job answered the Lord, and said, "I know that Thou canst do all things, And that no purpose of Thine can be thwarted. 'Who is this that

*hides counsel without knowledge?' Therefore I have
declared that which I did not understand, things too
wonderful for me, which I did not know." (Job
42:1-3).*

There is no neutrality when it comes to judging between God
and man. Either we are in a position to judge God or else God is in a
position to judge us. Job learned the lesson that God is our judge and
he learned to allow God to be God. That is why God asked Job all
those rhetorical questions:

- Where were you when I laid the foundations of the earth?
- Did you have a hand in creating the seas and the oceans?
- Were you there when I made day and night?
- Did you set a day at 24 hours?
- Did you place the stars in the sky? Can you move them about
  by the strength of your own will?

The point is that God knows a lot more about the workings of His
universe than you do. And that brings us to our next point.

4.   God is in control, even when it doesn't seem as if He is.

When we see bad things happen, we must remember that it is
not that God somehow lost the power or insight to direct the affairs
of our little planet. Jesus warned us that we would see kingdoms rise
and we would see kingdoms fall and that would not mean that God
had lost control. God is building His own kingdom and that is the
only kingdom that shall endure forever.

5.   God has a purpose in what He allows, even if we don't know what it
is.   We look at tragedies and they appear to be meaningless and
senseless and chaotic, but God knows how to take even tragedies and
bring good out of them. He is able to cause all things to work together
for good to those who love God, to those who are called according to
His purpose (Romans 8:28). That does not mean that bad things do
not happen. As long as the Evil One is on planet earth evil things will
continue to take place. Our comfort is in knowing that God
specializes in taking such evil and bringing good out of it.

6.   Tragedy can serve as a wake-up call.

C.S. Lewis described pain as "God's megaphone to a deaf world." We live in a nation that has been increasingly deaf to the Word of God. There is a message that is being delivered to us. It is a message designed to call us to repentance.

> *Now on the same occasion there were some present who reported to Him about the Galileans, whose blood Pilate had mingled with their sacrifices. And He answered and said to them, "Do you suppose that these Galileans were greater sinners than all other Galileans, because they suffered this fate? I tell you, no, but, unless you repent, you will all likewise perish." (Luke 13:1-3).*

These were not the actions of a proper government. Pilate was not putting down a rebellion or keeping the peace. He had murdered people as they went to worship. They were in church and he sent his soldiers in and slaughtered them. Notice the response of Jesus to this terrible murder of these people. He says that there is a message there for us. It is that we need to repent.

7.   God has not remained distant from us in our pain.

This is the message of the cross. God drew near. He took on flesh and He walked our dirty streets and He went to our dirty cross and He felt the pain and the pathos as He took upon Himself the penalty for our sins. A man grieving for his lost son looked up and asked, "Where was God when my son died?" And the answer echoes back from the cross, "I was here in the same place as when My Own Son died."

> *For we do not have a high priest who cannot sympathize with our weaknesses, but One who has been tempted in all things as we are, yet without sin. Let us therefore draw near with confidence to the throne of grace, that we may receive mercy and may find grace to help in time of need. (Hebrews 4:15-16).*

PSALMS
The Book of Worship

The book of Psalms has an internal structure that divides it into five books. It has been suggested that this division can be compared to the five books of the Torah.

Book 1	Book 2	Book 3	Book 4	Book 5
Chapters 1-41	Chapters 42-72	Chapters 73-89	Chapters 90-106	Chapters 107-150
Mostly written by David		Mostly by Asaph	Mostly anonymous	Many by David
Genesis	Exodus	Leviticus	Numbers	Deuteronomy
Begins with man by a tree (1); then a picture of the raging of the nations (2); near the end of the section we see the Psalmist as a sojourner (39:12).	Begins with a thirst for God (42); and a prayer for God's salvation against an ungodly nation (43); ends with God as a rock and a refuge (71).	Begins with a promise of God's blessing to those who are pure in heart (73). Ends with the Davidic Covenant	Begins with prayer of Moses and a reminder of man's frailty (90). Ends with a confession of Israel's sins in the wilderness (106) as well as in the land.	Begins with a reminder of God's past faithfulness (107). Psalm 119 has a special emphasis upon the word of God.

More than any other book of the Bible, the Psalms give us the heart of God. It is in these chapters that we enter the very throne room of God.

1.   Titles for the Book.

      a.   Hebrew Titles.

- *Tehillim* ("praises") from the root word *halal*, to praise.
- *Tephilloth* ("prayers") from the singular *tephillah*, a prayer. This word is used in Psalm 72:20 to describe the preceding portion of the book.

b. Greek Title: Ψαλμοι (*Psalmoi*). The root meaning describes the twang of a stringed instrument. It suggests that the Psalms are meant to be accompanied by music.

2. Authors.

- David: There are 73 of the psalms that are specifically assigned to David. Most of these are in the first two books.
- Asaph: One of the leaders in music. He was a Levite. Twelve of the Psalms are assigned to him by their superscription.
- Heman (Psalm 88).
- Ethan (Psalm 89).
- Solomon (Psalm 72 and 127).
- Moses (Psalm 90).

Author	Bk 1	Bk 2	Bk 3	Bk 4	Bk 5	Total
David	37	18	1	2	15	73
Asaph	-	1	11	-	-	12
Sons of Korah	-	7	4	-	-	11
Moses	-	-	-	1	-	1
Solomon	1	-	-	-	1	2
Heman	-	1	-	-	-	1
Ethan	-	1	-	-	-	1
Anonymous	4	4	-	14	28	50

In addition to these, the superscriptions of the Septuagint also assign Psalms to three other men.

- Haggai and Zechariah (Psalm 146-149).
- Jeremiah (Psalm 137).

At least two of the Anonymous Psalms are ascribed to David in the New Testament (Acts 4:25; Hebrews 4:7).

3.   Characteristics of the Psalms.

- The writings of the Psalms cover a thousand years of history. The earliest ascription is to Moses and the last points to Ezra (according to the Septuagint).
- Psalms is the only book of the Bible that is meant to be accompanied by musical instruments. Some of these instruments are mentioned in the superscriptions while others are described in the body of the Psalms themselves.
- Psalms is quoted more in the New Testament than all of the rest of the books of the Old Testament combined.
- Most of the Bible relates God's message to us. The Psalms tell us what is to be our response back to God. While the rest of the Bible tells us that we ought to worship the Lord, the Psalms tell us how we ought to worship the Lord.
- Psalms is a very "sensory" book. You hear the singing, you feel the clapping of hands, you smell the aroma of worship, you taste and see that the Lord is good (34:8).
- The Psalms are filled with pictures of Jesus. We see His death, burial, and resurrection and we also see His coming in glory. He is described as the Son, the suffering servant, the High Priest after the order of Melchizedek, and the Lord of David.

BOOK ONE

Nearly all of this first book is written by David. Many of these Psalms are dedicated to the choir director at Jerusalem. They were to be used for worship in the tabernacle and in the temple. The term Yahweh tends to be used more than Elohim to speak of God.

Psalm 1 serves as a preamble -- an introduction to all of the Psalms. It does this, not by telling us about parallelisms or structure or authorship, but by telling us of two different types of people in the world. Everyone in the world can be categorized under one of these two general headings.

- The righteous (Verses 1-3).
- The wicked (Verses 4-5).

This is a Wisdom Psalm. As such, it almost resembles something that we would expect to read in the book of Proverbs. And this tells me something about the Psalms. It tells me that there is wisdom in worship.

When we think of the Proverbs, we think of wisdom. The Proverbs are full of pithy little sayings that speak to everyday life. They are full of practical wisdom. They appeal to the pragmatist because they work in everyday life. They speak to the mind.

When we think of the Psalms, we normally think of worship and that which touches the heart. They speak of all sorts of feelings. But what we learn in this opening Psalm is that heart and mind are not mutually exclusive. They make up the whole man and they form the difference between the wise and the foolish. This Psalm is going to contrast two types of people. Everyone in the world fits into one of these two categories:

> *How blessed is the man who does not walk in the counsel of*
> *the wicked,*
> *Nor stand in the path of sinners,*
> *Nor sit in the seat of scoffers!*
> *But his delight is in the law of the Lord,*
> *And in His law he meditates day and night. (Psalm 1:1-2a).*

This is the man who has internalized the Law. He has the law on the inside and not merely on the outside. He is a doer of the law and not merely a hearer. Notice the movement. He does not walk... nor stand... nor sit.

How blessed is the man who does not...		
Walk...	In the counsel...	Of the wicked
Stand...	In the path...	Of sinners
Sit...	In the seat...	Of scoffers

What is the point of this poetic movement? It is to demonstrate that every area of life is at question in the way we live. Walking, standing or sitting, we are to follow the Lord.

Our blessing comes from God. But it also comes with our disassociation with certain things. Christianity is both positive and negative. It involves a turning to God, but it also involves turning away from those things that are contrary to God. These two aspects are summed up in the contrast between faith versus repentance. Repentance involves turning away from that which is against God and faith involves the embracing of God.

Psalm 2 was sung at the coronation of the kings of Israel. It gives the threefold description of the chosen one of God: Messiah, King and Son of God.

> *Why are the nations in an uproar,*
> *And the peoples devising a vain thing? (Psalm 1:2).*

This Psalm begins with the nations in an uproar. They are in an uproar because the people have devised a vain thing. What is the answer to such an uproar? It is the gospel. Jesus has called us to make disciples of the nations by teaching them the good news.

> *The kings of the earth take their stand,*
> *And the rulers take counsel together*
> *Against the Lord and against His Anointed (Psalm 2:2).*

Notice the reference to God's anointed one. This is the Hebrew word Messiah. It is the same word that is translated in the Greek of the New Testament as the Christ.

> *6 But as for Me, I have installed My King upon Zion,*
> *My holy mountain.*
> *7 I will surely tell of the decree of the Lord:*
> *He said to Me, "Thou art My Son,*
> *Today I have begotten Thee.*
> *8 Ask of Me, and I will surely give the nations as Thine inheritance,*
> *And the very ends of the earth as Thy possession.*
> *9 Thou shalt break them with a rod of iron,*
> *Thou shalt shatter them like earthenware." (Psalm 2:6-9).*

There was a practice in the ancient world where a pot would be made to represent one's enemy and then it would be broken to identify the enemy with destruction. The movie, "The Quiet Man" with John Wayne shows the same sort of activity. A name is written on a pad and then one strikes through it.

The enemies of God shall be broken and the nations shall be given to the Son as His inheritance. It is for this reason that Jesus sent His apostles to make disciples of the nations.

Psalms 4-5. These two Psalms form a unit. They depict the man of God praying both night and day.

Psalm 4	Psalm 5
An evening Psalm	A morning Psalm
Meditate in your heart upon your bed (4:4). In peace I will both lie down and sleep (4:8)	In the morning, O Lord, Thou wilt hear my voice; In the morning I will order my prayer to Thee and eagerly watch (5:3).

Psalm 4 can be divided into four parts: There is a prayer, a call to trust in light of that prayer, a second prayer and then a commitment to trust in the light of that prayer.

4:1	4:3	4:6	4:8
Prayer	A call to trust in the Lord	Prayer	A commitment to trust in the Lord

The Psalm is about faith. It is about trusting the Lord when the dark shadows come. It is one thing to trust the Lord in the light, but it is often harder to trust Him in the darkness.

In Psalm 5, David speaks of those who are his enemies and asks the Lord that He might hold them guilty (5:10). How does this fit in with the New Testament idea of how we are to love our enemies? We must understand that David's "enemies" are not his enemies merely because he does not like them. They are his enemies because they are God's enemies.

> *4 For Thou art not a God who takes pleasure in wickedness;*
> *No evil dwells with Thee.*
> *5 The boastful shall not stand before Thine eyes;*
> *Thou dost hate all who do iniquity.*
> *6 Thou dost destroy those who speak falsehood;*
> *The Lord abhors the man of bloodshed and deceit. (Psalm 5:4-6).*

God is righteous and His love is righteous. Sin is by definition that which is contrary to the righteousness and the goodness of God. Therefore the Bible tells us in no uncertain terms that God hates the one who does iniquity.

Psalms 22-24 form a unit and perhaps reflect the past, present and future King.

Psalm 22:	The Suffering Servant
Psalm 23:	The Good Shepherd
Psalm 24:	The Sovereign King

Psalm 22 brings echoes of the deepest possible agony. It begins with a cry to the Lord from an abandoned soul. This Psalm can be divided into two major sections.

- A Prayer for Present Trouble (22:1-18).
- A Prayer for Future Deliverance (22:19-31).

As the Psalm begins, the writer has been abandoned by God and cries out day and night to the Lord without answer or rest. By the time the Psalm ends, the troubles are past and we look to future praise of the Lord for His past faithfulness.

Psalm 23 is the best known of all the Psalms. It is the Shepherd's Psalm and pictures the Lord as our shepherd who is with us to guide and to comfort.

The Lord is my shepherd,
I shall not want. (Psalm 23:1).

When you read Psalm 23, you need to read it through the eyes of a sheep. The life of a sheep is dependent upon the shepherd. No one was ever intimidated by a sheep. The height of foolhardiness is an independent sheep. A sheep without a shepherd is asking to be lamb chops.

My relationship with the Lord is that same that exists between a shepherd and his sheep. It is a relationship of the one in need with the one who is the protector and sustainer.

The safety of the sheep depends upon the strength of the shepherd. If a mere man is my shepherd, then my security is only as strong as that man. But if the Lord is my shepherd, then I shall have no needs.

We cannot read this without remembering that Jesus describes Himself as the "good shepherd" who gives his life for his sheep. He not only walks with us through our valley of the shadow of death, He also went through that valley on our behalf, suffering the death we would have died.

Psalm 24

> *1 A Psalm of David.*
> *The earth is the Lord's, and all it contains,*
> *The world, and those who dwell in it.*
> *2 For He has founded it upon the seas,*
> *And established it upon the rivers. (Psalm 24:1-2).*

When we come to Psalm 24, the focus has now turned to the Lord as the sovereign king and owner of all that exists. Because God is the Creator, He is sovereign over who shall and who shall not come into His presence.

> *3 Who may ascend into the hill of the Lord?*
> *And who may stand in His holy place?*
> *4 He who has clean hands and a pure heart,*
> *Who has not lifted up his soul to falsehood,*
> *And has not sworn deceitfully.*
> *5 He shall receive a blessing from the Lord*
> *And righteousness from the God of his salvation. (Psalm 24:3-5).*

Who is able to come into the presence of God? Who is able to come into His holy place? Who is able to ascend into His mountain (the word translated "hill" can also be rendered "mountain")? In one sense, the "mountain of God" is a reference to the temple in Jerusalem. On the other hand, it also echoes that which the temple represents, the very presence of God.

What is the requirement for one who would come into the presence of God? It is that he be without sin. It is that he have both clean hands and a pure heart; that he be right with God on both the outside as well as on the inside. There is only One who has perfectly fulfilled this requirement. It was fulfilled in Jesus. It is also fulfilled in those who trust in Him and who are credited with the righteousness of Christ.

BOOK TWO

This collection runs from Psalm 42 to 72. It includes many Psalms by David and also some written by the sons of Korah. In this book, the title Elohim is used much more than is the name Yahweh.

Psalm 42 pictures the one who is thirsty for the presence of the Lord.

1 As the deer pants for the water brooks,
So my soul pants for Thee, O God.
2 My soul thirsts for God, for the living God;
When shall I come and appear before God? (Psalm 42:1-2).

The opening words of the Psalm paint a vivid picture. It is a picture of a deer in the country. It is a hot day. In the heat of the day, the deer is panting. It longs for the cool, bubbling waters of the stream. This thirst is not described as a casual option. You know about casual options. You go to the refrigerator and you are not really thirsty, but you think a Pepsi or a Sprite or iced tea might be nice. This thirst is much more. It is an urgent thirst.

What does it mean to really thirst for God? Jesus said, "Blessed are those who hunger and thirst for righteousness, for they shall be satisfied" (Matthew 5:6). God promises to satisfy the longing that fills mens hearts. Our problem is that we view our relationship with the Lord as a casual option.

This Psalm pictures of a man in the midst of despair. This is the circumstance of the world today. Man today is without hope. He asks the same question which the Psalmist asks in verse 3: "Where are you, God?"

Why are you in despair, O my soul?
And why have you become disturbed within me?
Hope in God, for I shall again praise Him for the help of His
presence. (Psalm 42:5).

The Psalmist turns from talking to the Lord or to us to talk to himself. He addresses His soul. He says, "Soul, what are you doing in such a condition? Why aren't you hoping in God?" You see, he knows where the answer is. It is in God. It is in His presence.

- Not in theology.
- Not in church.
- Not in a correct doctrinal position.

There is something special about being in the presence of God. We must be careful when we talk about the presence of God. After all, God is omnipresent. He is everywhere. But it is possible to have an experience of His presence. When you are driving on the highway and someone cuts you off, are you in the presence of God? You ought to be.

Look at the experience of the early church in Acts 2. Here is an example of men who were experiencing the presence of God. They did not say, "Well, it is time for the Spirit to come and so, even though we don't feel any different, it must have happened."

Christians today want a Christianity that does not depend on the existence of God. Ask yourself how your own church would be changed this Sunday if suddenly the presence of God was taken away. Would it be noticed? Or would the service go on as usual?

There have been books written and classes taught and seminars held on what is wrong with the church. A lot of different answers have been suggested:

> Methods.
> Missions.
> Programs.
> Social needs.
> Better preaching.

But you rarely hear anyone speak of the presence of God. In the letters to the seven churches, not once did Jesus say, "Your relationship with Me is good, but you need to update your Sunday School Program." The Psalmist realizes this. In the midst of the problem, he sees the solution. It is to hope in God.

Psalm 45 is A Royal Wedding song. The Superscription sets forth the theme of the Psalm.

> *For the choir director; according to the Shoshannim.*
> *A Maskil of the sons of Korah. A Song of Love. My heart*
> *overflows with a good theme; I address my verses to the*
> *King; My tongue is the pen of a ready writer. (Psalm 45:1).*

This is a love song. But is isn't only a love song. We read that it is a Maskil - a teaching Psalm. There is something here that will touch both your heart and your head.

Verses 1-9 are a description of the King. We are not told which king is being described. Tradition has it that it is Solomon who is in view. But as we read through this Psalm, we see things said that go far beyond Solomon. The ultimate king in this Psalm is King Jesus.

> *Thou hast loved righteousness, and hated wickedness;*
> *Therefore God, Thy God, has anointed Thee with the oil of*
> *joy above Thy fellows.*
> *All Thy garments are fragrant with myrrh and aloes and*
> *cassia;*
> *Out of ivory palaces stringed instruments have made Thee*
> *glad. (Psalm 45:7-8).*

Jesus was known as the "Man of sorrows." But He was also a man who was imbued with joy. Hebrews 12:2 speaks of how He endured the cross for the joy that was set before Him. And on the night of the Last Supper, He said to His disciples, "These things I have spoken to you, that My joy may be in you, and that your joy may be made full." You have a duty and a calling. It is a calling to be filled with joy.

Psalm 51 is David's prayer for forgiveness after his sin with Bathsheba.

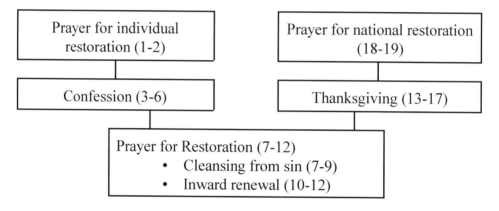

Psalms 52-59 are given in the context of David's flight from Saul.

Psalms 52-55 are described in their superscription as Maskils of David. These are thought to be instructional in nature.

Psalms 56-60 are described as Mikhtams of David. Each of them give David's prayer to the Lord during a specific historical instance.

Psalm 57 begins by telling us the historical circumstances in which it was penned.

> *For the choir director; set to Al-tashheth.*
> *A Mikhtam of David, when he fled from Saul, in the cave.*
> *Be gracious to me, O God, be gracious to me,*
> *For my soul takes refuge in Thee;*
> *And in the shadow of Thy wings I will take refuge,*
> *Until destruction passes by (Psalm 57:1).*

There is a play on words in the Hebrew that does not translate very well into the English. It is found in the word "wings." While this term can and is used of the wings of a bird or an angel, it is also used for the corner of a garment.

Psalm 72, the last Psalm of Book 2, ends with a benediction (verses 18-19) followed by the words, The prayers of David the son of Jesse are ended (72:20).

BOOK THREE

This book contains Psalms 73-89. The first ten of these Psalms are written by Asaph, one of the music directors who served during the reigns of David and Solomon. The rest are from the sons of Korah, from David, and two are from Ethan the Ezrahite. These Psalms tend to focus upon Israel, Jerusalem, and the Temple.

> *Oh, give ear, Shepherd of Israel,*
> *Thou who dost lead Joseph like a flock;*
> *Thou who art enthroned above the cherubim, shine forth!*
> *(Psalm 80:1).*

> *His foundation is in the holy mountains.*
> *The Lord loves the gates of Zion*
> *More than all the other dwelling places of Jacob.*
> *Glorious things are spoken of you, O city of God. Selah.*
> *(Psalm 87:1-3).*

Psalm 89. This Book ends with Psalm 89 which is a covenant Psalm. Take note of how many times the word "covenant" appears in this Psalm.

BOOK FOUR

This book contains Psalms 90-108. There is an exclusive use of the term Yahweh in this book. It is filled with the theme of praise and of thanksgiving.

Psalm 90 begins with the prayer of Moses.

> *A Prayer of Moses the man of God.*
> *Lord, Thou hast been our dwelling place in all generations.*
> *Before the mountains were born,*
> *Or Thou didst give birth to the earth and the world,*
> *Even from everlasting to everlasting,*

Thou art God. (Psalm 90:1-2).

Beginning with this Psalm, we see a series of songs that present the Lord's sovereign rulership over the world and over His people.

Psalm 92 was read in the temple each Sabbath day. As the people came together to worship the Lord, they would be called by these words:

> *A Psalm, a Song for the Sabbath day.*
> *It is good to give thanks to the Lord,*
> *And to sing praises to Thy name, O Most High;*
> *2 To declare Thy lovingkindness in the morning,*
> *And Thy faithfulness by night,*
> *3 With the ten-stringed lute, and with the harp;*
> *With resounding music upon the lyre.*
> *4 For Thou, O Lord, hast made me glad by what Thou hast done,*
> *I will sing for joy at the works of Thy hands. (Psalm 92:1-4).*

You can imagine the people gathered together to partake in the Sabbath worship. On this day of rest, they are called to remember what God has done for them.

Psalm 100 culminates with the rulership theme, ending upon a climactic note.

> *A Psalm for Thanksgiving.*
> *Shout joyfully to the Lord, all the earth.*
> *2 Serve the Lord with gladness;*
> *Come before Him with joyful singing.*
> *3 Know that the Lord Himself is God;*
> *It is He who has made us, and not we ourselves;*
> *We are His people and the sheep of His pasture.*
> *4 Enter His gates with thanksgiving,*
> *And His courts with praise.*
> *Give thanks to Him; bless His name.*
> *5 For the Lord is good;*
> *His lovingkindness is everlasting,*
> *And His faithfulness to all generations. (Psalm 100:1-5).*

This is a call to worship and to serve and to honor the Lord. The call goes out in the first two verses. Verse 3 answers the question of why we should worship Him. We worship Him because He made us and we are His people.

The second half of the Psalm echoes the first half. Again there is a call to worship the Lord, giving thanks to Him and praising Him. Why? Because of His lovingkindness and His faithfulness.

Psalm 103-108 gives a rehearsal of the wondrous works and deeds of the Lord. He is seen as the Creator and Sustainer of the universe. As we move through these chapters, we move from the creation to the calling of the nation of Israel, the exodus from Egypt and the coming into the promised land.

BOOK FIVE

The last book consists of Psalms 107-150. These are primarily songs of praise to the Lord. A number of them are Psalms of David.

Psalm 110 is the most quoted in the New Testament. It is the Psalm that Jesus used to challenge the religious leaders of Jerusalem. It is the Psalm of the Priest-King.

> *A Psalm of David.*
> *The Lord says to my Lord:*
> *"Sit at My right hand,*
> *Until I make Thine enemies a footstool for Thy feet." (Psalm*
> *110:1).*

When we think of a footstool, we think of a comfortable piece of furniture on which you set your feet when you kick back to watch the afternoon football game. But this is not the image that is in view in this verse. This reflects the ancient practice of a king bowing in complete submission to a master conqueror.

Jesus pointed to this Psalm as a puzzle that pointed to His own identity. It pictures Yahweh as addressing Himself to the Lord of David. This brings us to the obvious question of how David can have a lord since the Messiah was to be the son of David. A child was never the lord of the parent; it was always the parent who exercised lordship over the child. The answer is to understand that the Son of David is more than mere man. He occupies a position that makes Him the Lord of His earthly parents.

This Psalm points, not to the victory of the past, but to the eventual complete victory of the Messiah over his enemies in the future. As such, it is a song in three parts.

110:1	110:4	110:5
The Divine King	The Divine Priest	The Divine Warrior
• Reigning beside God Himself. • Reigning with absolute power. • Reigning with a mighty army (vs 3)	• Established by an immutable oath • Established for eternity	• Fiercely enacting judgment and wrath (vs 5-6). • Unceasingly pursuing the work of victory (7)
• Exalted to a position of honor, rest, and authority • Ruling with absolute omnipotence • Mercifully making enemies his friends	• Exalted to a position of intercession and mediation • Guaranteeing our eternal salvation	

To be seated at one's right hand was to be in the place of honor. Thus when Joseph brought his sons to be blessed by Jacob, he was careful to place the older son at that patriarch's right hand and was displeased when his father crossed his hands to put the hand of blessing upon the head of the younger son.

Notice the patience of God. The Father is pictured as speaking to the Son: *Sit here until...* We are in the between times today. We are awaiting a final consummation. The reason that the enemies of God do not perish today is not a reflection of the inability of God, but rather reflects the patience of God.

Psalms 113-118 are known as the *Hallel* -- the Praise Psalms. These particular Psalms were sung each year at the Passover. Near the end of these Psalms there is a Messianic Prophecy.

> *I shall give thanks to Thee, for Thou hast answered me;*
> *And Thou hast become my salvation.*
> *22 The stone which the builders rejected*
> *Has become the chief corner stone.*
> *23 This is the Lord's doing;*
> *It is marvelous in our eyes. (Psalm 118:21-23).*

It is no mistake that the final week of the ministry of Jesus prior to His crucifixion took place on the Passover as the people gathered to Jerusalem singing this Psalm. Thus when the Psalmist goes on to say…

> *This is the day which the Lord has made;*
> *Let us rejoice and be glad in it. (Psalm 118:24).*

He is referring to the day in which Messiah would come.

Psalm 119 is one of several alphabetic Psalms. It is divided into 22 parts, each of which corresponds with one of the letters of the Hebrew alphabet. Each line of the first series of stanzas begins with the first letter of the Hebrew alphabet (Aleph). The next series of stanzas each begins with the next letter of the Hebrew alphabet. Psalms 9, 25, 34, 37, 111-112 and 145 are all alphabetic Psalms.

Psalms 120-124 are termed "the Songs of Ascent." They would traditionally be sung by pilgrims as they made their way up to Jerusalem to celebrate one of the feasts.

> *A Song of Ascents, of David.*
> *I Was glad when they said to me,*
> *"Let us go to the house of the Lord."*
> *2 Our feet are standing*
> *Within your gates, O Jerusalem,*
> *3 Jerusalem, that is built*
> *As a city that is compact together;*
> *4 To which the tribes go up, even the tribes of the Lord--*
> *An ordinance for Israel--*
> *To give thanks to the name of the Lord. (Psalm 122:1-4).*

These songs would culminate with the arrival of the pilgrims in the temple. The last of the Songs of Ascent ends with a rousing praise.

> *A Song of Ascents.*
> *Behold, bless the Lord, all servants of the Lord,*
> *Who serve by night in the house of the Lord!*
> *2 Lift up your hands to the sanctuary,*
> *And bless the Lord.*
> *3 May the Lord bless you from Zion,*
> *He who made heaven and earth. (Psalm 134:1-3).*

There are 15 of these Psalms of Ascent. They are also called the Psalms of Degrees. One tradition had it that they were compiled by Hezekiah to commemorate his recovery from his illness. The king had become very sick and on the verge of death. The Lord brought healing and promised that he would have another 15 years of life. As a sign to the king, the sun's shadow moved backward 15 degrees on the sundial. These 15 "Psalms of Degrees" are said to commemorate that sign.

Psalm 136 is a liturgical Psalm. The Priest would say the first line and then the people would respond with the continuing refrain, "For His kindness is everlasting."

> *Give thanks to the Lord, for He is good;*
> *For His lovingkindness is everlasting.*
> *Give thanks to the God of gods,*
> *For His lovingkindness is everlasting.*
> *Give thanks to the Lord of lords,*
> *For His lovingkindness is everlasting. (Psalm 136:1-3).*

In light of some of the complaints against the repetition of modern praise music, one wonders whether people have noted the sort of repetition we have occasionally found within the Psalms.

Psalm 137 is one of several Psalms in this fifth book that describe the Babylonian Captivity that took place in 586 B.C.

> *By the rivers of Babylon,*
> *There we sat down and wept,*
> *When we remembered Zion.*
> *2 Upon the willows in the midst of it*
> *We hung our harps.*
> *3 For there our captors demanded of us songs,*
> *And our tormentors mirth, saying,*
> *"Sing us one of the songs of Zion."*
> *4 How can we sing the Lord's song In a foreign land? (Psalm 137:1-4).*

The captive Israelites are invited to a party at the palace. The request is that they sing one of the Temple songs. The Babylonians want to rejoice over their victory over God's people. But there is no song in the heart of these captives.

5 If I forget you, O Jerusalem,
May my right hand forget her skill.
6 May my tongue cleave to the roof of my mouth,
If I do not remember you,
If I do not exalt Jerusalem
Above my chief joy. (Psalm 137:5-6).

In verse 5 the Psalmist and his companions in exile make themselves a promise. It is a promise of loyalty. "If I ever compromise, let me lose my skill." Remember that these are musicians. Music is their whole life. But their loyalty to the Kingdom of God is such that it is greater than their music. This is not naked nationalism. This is a love for God's kingdom promises. This brings us to a question. Where is your loyalty? What is the most important thing in your life? Are you willing to put it in second place to God's kingdom?

Psalms 138-145 are all Psalms of David, given at different times and in different circumstances. Psalm 139 is a depiction of the omnipotence and the omnipresence of God, yet it is made all the more striking as David relates those qualities to his own experiences. It would be correct to say that God's presence extends everywhere; it is much more personal to say:

If I ascend to heaven, You are there;
If I make my bed in Sheol, behold, You are there. (Psalm 139:8).

Psalms 145-150 are a series of closing benedictions and praises to the Lord. Each of these ends with a call to praise the Lord. They come to a crashing crescendo of praise in the final psalm.

Praise the Lord!
Praise God in His sanctuary;
Praise Him in His mighty expanse.
Praise Him for His mighty deeds;
Praise Him according to His excellent greatness.
Praise Him with trumpet sound;
Praise Him with harp and lyre.
Praise Him with timbrel and dancing;
Praise Him with stringed instruments and pipe.
Praise Him with loud cymbals;
Praise Him with resounding cymbals.
Let everything that has breath praise the Lord.
Praise the Lord! (Psalm 150:1-6).

TYPES OF PSALMS

1.   Psalms of Lament (Psalm 22, 42).

  •   Addresses the Lord in the first person.
  •   Describes the problem to the Lord.
  •   An affirmation of trust ("as for me…") in which the Psalmist determines that he will follow the Lord in spite of the present lamentable circumstances.
  •   A plea for God's deliverance from the present crisis.
  •   A statement either of assurance of God's answer or else praise to the Lord.

2.   Imprecatory Psalms (Psalm 35, 69, 109, 137).

These psalms contain imprecations (curses) on the enemies of God. This brings us to a problem because the New Testament teaches us that we are to love our enemies and not to curse them (Matthew 5:43-44). How can we pray these prayers today in the light of the fuller revelation that we have received? I believe there are several ways in which these psalms can be applied today.

  •   We can see the curses that the enemies of God deserve and we can be reminded of the One who became a curse for us, taking upon Himself that which we deserved.
  •   We can pray that those who are the enemies of God be overcome by God, either overcome by God's grace or else overcome by His justice and righteousness.
  •   We can take to ourselves the same zeal for the glory of God that is characterized by the Psalmist.

3.   Penitential Psalms (Psalm 51).

These are prayers of repentance for sin and requests for restoration to fellowship with the Lord. These psalms remind us that God is ready and willing to forgive those who come to Him with a heart of repentance.

4.   Praise Psalms.

A great many of the psalms contain praise to the Lord for His various attributes. The Hebrew phrase "Hallelujah" (הַלְלוּ יָהּ) is found only in the Psalms and specifically only in Psalm 104-150 (Books 4-5). The Greek form of this praise is found in the book of Revelation.

5.   Prophecy in the Psalms.

Strictly speaking, there are not a lot of outright prophecies in the Psalms that say, "This or that shall take place in the future." What we often see instead is the person and work of Christ displayed in a way that goes far beyond the experiences of the Psalmist.

- A promise of resurrection: *For Thou wilt not abandon my soul to Sheol; Neither wilt Thou allow Thy Holy One to undergo decay. (Psalm 16:10).*
- The cry from the cross: *My God, my God, why hast Thou forsaken me? (Psalm 22:1).*
- Mocked by men: *All who see me sneer at me; They separate with the lip, they wag the head, saying, 8 "Commit yourself to the Lord; let Him deliver him; Let Him rescue him, because He delights in him" (Psalm 22:7-8).*
- Bones out of joint: *I am poured out like water, And all my bones are out of joint; My heart is like wax; It is melted within me. (Psalm 22:14).*
- Hands and feet pierced: *For dogs have surrounded me; A band of evildoers has encompassed me; They pierced my hands and my feet. (Psalm 22:16).*

While these Psalms suggest the shared mutual experience of the Psalmist with the Promised One, it is interesting to note that the most literal fulfillment of these experiences is not that of the Psalmist, but is that of Jesus who suffered the very literal experiences described. What the Psalmist can only experience in part or in figure, Jesus experienced completely.

THE VALUE OF THE PSALMS

1.   A Commentary on the Old Testament.

The Psalms often help us to "fill in the gaps" as they tell us the emotions behind the narratives of the Old Testament. This is especially true of those Psalms that contain historical superscriptions. These superscriptions are to be found in our earliest Hebrew texts and therefore reflect a very ancient tradition.

2.   Liturgy for Worship.

Many of the Psalms are designed for the leading of public worship. They take us beyond a mere "head knowledge" to draw us near to the heart of God. At the same time, they remind us that praise does not only take place in a "feel good" setting. Praise can also take place in time of trouble and trial and when the worshiper is dealing with a heaviness of soul.

3.   A Pattern for Prayer.

I know of no better way to learn how to pray than to pray through the Psalms. There are prayers here for every occasion.

4.   Wisdom for Living.

We don't normally think of finding wisdom in the Psalms. That is normally found in the wisdom literature. But there are some of the Psalms that are designed to teach us.

> *For the choir director.*
> *A Psalm of the sons of Korah.*
> *Hear this, all peoples;*
> *Give ear, all inhabitants of the world,*
> *2 Both low and high,*
> *Rich and poor together.*
> *3 My mouth will speak wisdom;*
> *And the meditation of my heart will be understanding.*
> *4 I will incline my ear to a proverb;*
> *I will express my riddle on the harp.*
> *5 Why should I fear in days of adversity,*
> *When the iniquity of my foes surrounds me,*
> *6 Even those who trust in their wealth,*
> *And boast in the abundance of their riches?*
> *7 No man can by any means redeem his brother,*
> *Or give to God a ransom for him--*
> *8 For the redemption of his soul is costly,*
> *And he should cease trying forever--*

9 That he should live on eternally;
That he should not undergo decay.
10 For he sees that even wise men die;
The stupid and the senseless alike perish,
And leave their wealth to others. (Psalm 49:1-10).

Verse 4 actually states that the Psalmist is going to impart wisdom through his words. The wisdom given is one of perspective with regard to money. It doesn't matter if you have a lot of money or if you only have a little money, if you are high or low, rich or poor, this Psalm has something to teach you.

The point is that you should not look for riches as an answer to the needs of life because money cannot purchase the truly important things. That does not mean money is bad, but it carries with it an inherent danger that you will begin to trust in your money.

PROVERBS
The Skill of Living

It was customary in the ancient world to use as the title of a book the first word or sentence of that book. The same thing is done in Proverbs. The title is given in the first verse of the book.

The proverbs of Solomon the son of David, king of Israel (Proverbs 1:1).

The Hebrew word translated "proverb" is *Mashal*. It comes from the root verb that describes the act of ruling, reigning, or exercising dominion. That means the Proverbs are more than mere catchy sayings. They are rules for living. They are given so that the Lord might have dominion over your life. They are concentrated truths. It is like frozen orange juice. You simply add water and it will expand.

The Proverbs are also practical truths. They do not merely say that you ought to do the right thing, they often illustrate in a very practical manner.

Differing weights are an abomination to the Lord,
And a false scale is not good. (Proverbs 20:23).

The Proverbs have no grey areas. They are black and white. They show good and evil. And they force you to pass judgment upon yourself.

THE AUTHORS OF THE BOOK

Author	Chapters	Further Information
Solomon	1-24	Attributed to Solomon
	25-29	Also attributed to Solomon but transcribed by the men of Hezekiah
Agur, son of Jakeh	30	His name is thought to be Arabic
King Lemuel	31	

There are several contributing authors to the Proverbs. They were collected over a long period of time. The early chapters are attributed to Solomon as seen in Proverbs 1:1. This gives us a great insight into the reason behind the writing of this book.

The kingdom of Israel was at its pinnacle of glory. The glory of the world in that day was Israel and the glory of Israel was Jerusalem and the glory of Jerusalem was the Temple. It was the greatest wonder in the world. Yet there were already cracks in the kingdom. The unity of the nation was already being threatened. At the death of Solomon, the northern tribes would pull out of the Union. The kings and the priests who followed would be corrupt. It is in the midst of this situation that God gives a book telling how to live godly in an ungodly world. This brings us to the purpose of the book.

THE PURPOSE OF THE BOOK

The purpose of the book of Proverbs is given to us in Proverbs 1:2-6. It is to know wisdom.

To know wisdom and instruction,
To discern the sayings of understanding,
3 To receive instruction in wise behavior,
Righteousness, justice and equity;
4 To give prudence to the naive,
To the youth knowledge and discretion,
5 A wise man will hear and increase in learning,
And a man of understanding will acquire wise counsel,
6 To understand a proverb and a figure,
The words of the wise and their riddles. (Proverbs 1:2-6).

The stated purpose of the Proverbs is that we might know wisdom. This brings us to an obvious question. What is wisdom? Webster's Dictionary might give one definition. It might define wisdom as having a high degree of knowledge or in being practical in your decision-making skills. The Bible presents quite a different picture of wisdom. It is seen in the book of Exodus. In this passage, the Lord is giving Moses instructions as to the preparation of the garments of the high priest.

"Then bring near to yourself Aaron your brother, and
his sons with him, from among the sons of Israel, to minister
as priest to Me-- Aaron, Nadab and Abihu, Eleazar and

Ithamar, Aaron's sons. 2 And you shall make holy garments for Aaron your brother, for glory and for beauty. 3 And you shall speak to all the skillful persons whom I have endowed with the spirit of wisdom, that they make Aaron's garments to consecrate him, that he may minister as priest to Me." *(Exodus 28:1-3).*

The use of "wisdom" in this passage refers specifically to the artistic skill that these people exhibited. This perhaps gives us a clue as to the meaning of wisdom. It is the art of living skillfully. The Proverbs give you guidelines on how to run your life. It is a handbook for running the Christian race. It is your life's Owner's Manual.

Once you know that you need wisdom and that wisdom is to be found in the Bible, where do you start? You start with the next verse of Proverbs.

The fear of the Lord is the beginning of knowledge;
Fools despise wisdom and instruction. (Proverbs 1:7).

This is the big idea in the book of Proverbs. It is placed right at the beginning of the book. It is also found right at the end of the book of Ecclesiastes.

The conclusion, when all has been heard, is: fear God and keep His commandments, because this applies to every person. 14 For God will bring every act to judgment, everything which is hidden, whether it is good or evil. *(Ecclesiastes 12:13-14).*

Do you see it? The fear of the Lord is both the beginning as well as the end of wisdom. What is this fear of the Lord? What does it mean to fear God? First let me say that the Hebrew word for "fear" is fear. When we speak of fear, we can refer to two types.

1.   A Fear that Drives Away.

Imagine that we are all back in the second grade. It has been a long time since I was there, but imagine that which brought fear. One of the things that might fill you with fear is the schoolyard bully. He is big and he is mean and he is out to make your life miserable. If he is big enough and if he is mean enough and if you are small enough, then his coming just might fill you with fear, mortification, and a terror that causes your knees to shake and a sinking feeling in

516

the pit of your stomach that is known as fear. You are afraid for good reason. He is stronger than you are and his intentions toward you are for evil.

2.   A Fear that Brings Wonder.

Let's say that you are still in the second grade, but now something wonderful has taken place. Your class is going on a long field trip and the bully has been left behind. This field trip is exceptionally long for 2nd graders and takes you all the way to the nation's capitol. You are taken to see the White House, the home of the President of the United States. While you are there with your group, one of the Secret Service Agents says, "We have a special surprise for you. One of you has been selected for a special privilege." He points to you and before you know it, you are being escorted into the Oval Office -- the inner sanctum of the most powerful man in the world.

You look at the desk and the leather chair. You take note of the large circular seal on the floor. As you look up, there he is. The president himself. He smiles and he welcomes you and you try to stutter a reply, but your tongue gets tangled around your eye teeth so that you can't see what you are saying. What is the emotion that fills you? It is fear. But it is a fear of a different kind. It is a fear that is full of awe and wonderment.

What kind of fear is present when we speak of the fear of the Lord? It is a little of both. Our fear of the Lord is a fear of awe and wonderment, a fear that would have us draw near. But it is also a fear that is accompanied by trembling. Those two words go together when we speak of the Lord's presence.

It is not mere respect or reverence, though it includes that. It is the realization that God is a lot bigger than I am and that He does what He wants. It includes a respect for God's authority. It means that you believe what He says is true and that you order your life accordingly. If you have not stood in the presence of God and feared Him, then you have not stood in the presence of God.

I love the depiction given to us by C.S. Lewis in his *Chronicles of Narnia* when the children first hear about Aslan, the Christ-figure in the book. They ask whether Aslan is a man.

"Aslan a man?" said Mrs. Beaver sternly. "Certainly not. I tell you he is the King of the Wood and the son of the great Emperor-Beyond-the Sea. Don't you know who is the King of Beasts? Aslan is a lion - the Lion, the great Lion."

"Ohh!" said Susan, "I'd thought he was a man. Is he - quite safe? I shall feel rather nervous about meeting a lion."

"Then he isn't safe?" said Lucy.

"Safe?" said Mr. Beaver. "Don't you hear what Mrs. Beaver tells you? Who said anything about safe? Course he isn't safe. But he's good."

It is the beginning of wisdom to realize that God is great and wondrous and majestic and that He is to be approached with awe and wonderment and with fear. This is not a fear that drives away, but a fear that draws near.

A COMPARISON WITH THE PSALMS

I believe that the books of Psalms and Proverbs are placed side by side in our Bibles for good reason. These two book compliment one another as they speak to the whole man.

Psalms	Proverbs
Books of Worship.	Books of Wisdom.
Speaks to our Spirit.	Speaks to our Intellect.
Life in the prayer closet.	Life out in the street.
Teaches us how to be holy before God.	Teaches us how to practice our holiness before men.
Teach you to love the Lord with all your heart and soul and mind.	Teach you to love your neighbor as yourself.

LITERARY FORM OF THE PROVERBS

For the most part, the Proverbs are given in the form of couplets. The clauses of these couplets are related in terms of parallelism. Most poetry in the Hebrew language was not made up of rhyming words, but of rhyming thoughts and ideas. There are four major types of parallelism used.

Type	Example	Explanation
Repetitious Parallelism	To know wisdom and instruction, To discern the sayings of understanding (Proverbs 1:2).	The 1st line makes a statement of truth. The 2nd line restates and reinforces that truth.
Contrastive Parallelism	The fear of the Lord is the beginning of knowledge; Fools despise wisdom and instruction. (Proverbs 1:7).	The 1st line makes a statement of truth. The 2nd line gives a corollary in opposite terms.
Completive Parallelism	The Lord has made everything for its own purpose, Even the wicked for the day of evil. (Proverbs 16:4).	The 1st line makes a statement of truth. The 2nd line adds and expands on the original idea.
Comparative Proverb	As the door turns on its hinges, So does the sluggard on his bed. (Proverbs 26:14).	The 2nd line compares something described in the 1st line by way of illustration.

OUTLINE OF THE PROVERBS

The book of Proverbs does not follow a specific outline. Much of it is presented in short, pithy sayings. Yet there is an overall pattern that can be seen.

1:1	1:7	10:1	21:1	30:1	31:1
Prologue	Appeal to Wisdom	One-verse maxims		Larger Couplets	Good Woman
Purpose of the Proverbs	Wisdom Personified	Proverbs of Solomon	Proverbs collected by men of Hezekiah	Words of Agur	Words of King Lemuel

519

Proverbs tells a story. It is the story of a young man. He begins by deciding which school he shall attend -- the School of Wisdom or the School of Folly. Recruiters from both schools come and make their pitch. The young man decides to enroll in the School of Wisdom. From chapters 10-29 he takes classes (graduate and post graduate level). Upon graduation, he goes out and he finds a good woman to be his wife.

THE WAY OF WISDOM

11 I have directed you in the way of wisdom;
I have led you in upright paths.
12 When you walk, your steps will not be impeded;
And if you run, you will not stumble. (Proverbs 4:11-12).

What is wisdom? It is competence with regard to the complexities of life. It is more than just having high moral values. It includes those high moral values, but it is much more than that. It also involves knowing what to do when the moral rules do not apply.

The most righteous and moral deed done at the wrong time or in the wrong order can bring disaster. Most of the situations encountered in life are not covered by the rules.

How do you get this kind of wisdom? The Proverbs tell us that living life is like walking a path. Verse 11 speaks of "upright paths." Following a path normally involves walking. Sometimes there are emergencies that make you run, but more often than not, you walk if it is a very long path. The way you make progress along a path is by walking -- one step at a time. These daily, repeated, monotonous strides are what we call walking. Your character is determined, not by the dramatic events that come your way, but by the routine, daily choices you make.

Tim Keller tells the story of a little boy who accidentally broke his father's watch. He put it back into his father's drawer and did not tell anyone. His father found the watch and called the children in, asking them who had broken it. The little boy remained silent. Years later, after the boy had grown to adulthood, he was driving down a road at night and accidentally hit and killed a little girl. Without stopping to reflect over the implications of his actions, he fled the scene. He got home and realized what he had done, but now he was too afraid to turn himself in. The authorities eventually tracked him down and arrested him and sent him to prison.

When asked about his life, he commented that what fixed his destiny was not the decision he made on the road, but rather the decision he made as a little boy and the same decision he had been making day after day for years in avoiding responsibility.

> *13 Take hold of instruction; do not let go.*
> *Guard her, for she is your life.*
> *14 Do not enter the path of the wicked,*
> *And do not proceed in the way of evil men.*
> *15 Avoid it, do not pass by it;*
> *Turn away from it and pass on.*
> *16 For they cannot sleep unless they do evil;*
> *And they are robbed of sleep unless they make someone stumble. (Proverbs 4:13-16).*

There are some who, in their effort to get others to think well of them, wish as their chief goal to bring everyone else down. They cannot stand it if someone else gets credit or affirmation.

> *17 For they eat the bread of wickedness,*
> *And drink the wine of violence.*
> *18 But the path of the righteous is like the light of dawn,*
> *That shines brighter and brighter until the full day.*
> *19 The way of the wicked is like darkness;*
> *They do not know over what they stumble. (Proverbs 4:17-19).*

How do you get to this deep darkness? It is by way of a path. That path consists of individual steps -- individual choices. You make them one step at a time. Every time you receive grace and do not recognize it as such, you are walking down a path. Every time you are wrong and do not admit it but instead try to shift the blame or rationalize your bad choices, you are walking down a path.

> *20 My son, give attention to my words;*
> *Incline your ear to my sayings.*
> *21 Do not let them depart from your sight;*
> *Keep them in the midst of your heart. (Proverbs 4:20-21).*

Notice where the sage puts the emphasis. It is not in will power. It is not in activity. It is in placing the word of God in your heart. Augustine said: "The key to changing a life is not the acts of the will, but the loves of the heart." What is the heart?

22 For they are life to those who find them,
And health to all their whole body.
23 Watch over your heart with all diligence,
For from it flow the springs of life. (Proverbs 4:22-23).

Verse 23 tells us that the heart is the source of the springs of life. A spring is an out flowing stream of water. Likewise, there are things that come out of the heart. What comes out of the heart? Life. What is in your heart determines your actions, your loves, your very perception of reality. Once you get the heart right, everything else falls into place.

1.   Your mouth gets straightened out.

> *Put away from you a deceitful mouth,*
> *And put devious lips far from you. (Proverbs 4:24).*

2.   Your eyes get straightened out.

> *Let your eyes look directly ahead,*
> *And let your gaze be fixed straight in front of you.*
> *(Proverbs 4:25).*

3.   Your feet get straightened out.

> *Watch the path of your feet,*
> *And all your ways will be established. (Proverbs 4:26).*

4.   Your path gets straightened out.

> *Do not turn to the right nor to the left;*
> *Turn your foot from evil. (Proverbs 4:27).*

In your heart, you have decided what will bring you happiness in life. You might not put it into those words, but whatever it is you are putting as your life's goal is set as the object of your heart's desire. What is the most important thing to your heart? Everything else in your life is determined by the answer to that question.

What does that have to do with wisdom? Everything. Whatever your heart has determined as its true desire will determine all of the ultimate choices you make in this life.

- If having money is your ultimate goal, then you are going to choose jobs or make lifestyle decisions that will obtain that goal. You will either burn out or else you will exploit people in an effort to make more and more money. The irony is that those tactics will actually tend to undermine your heart's goal and will end up making less money.
- If marriage or romance to Mister Right is your ultimate goal, you will either be too picky in choosing a mate or else you will be so desperate to be married that you will marry the first one who comes along. Thus if marriage is your most important thing, it will cause you to make decisions that will undermine the possibility of you having it.
- If your children are the most important thing in your life, then you will over-discipline them because everything has to be right or else you will under-correct them because you are afraid for them to dislike you. Once again, the way you make decisions will undermine the very thing that you most want.

If anything but God is the main love of your heart, then you will be a fool and you will fail to get that thing you desire. How can you change the desire of your heart? Pelagius said that you could change the heart merely through self-effort. Augustine said that it is impossible and that only God can change the heart.

This proverb began by calling for the way of wisdom. It is a common theme in the Proverbs. Wisdom is seen as having a way because life does not consist of a single step, but of many steps. There is a way to wisdom. A thousand years after Solomon, a group of men sat in an upper room and one of them said, "I am THE WAY, the truth and the light." He did not merely say...

- That he was one way among many
- That he knew the way
- That he could show others the way

He said that He is the way. A Jew who was present could hardly have failed to make the connection. God regularly spoke in the proverbs about the way of wisdom.

PRINCIPLES OF WORK

Ill-gotten gains do not profit,
But righteousness delivers from death.

3 The Lord will not allow the righteous to hunger,
But He will thrust aside the craving of the wicked.
4 Poor is he who works with a negligent hand,
But the hand of the diligent makes rich.
5 He who gathers in summer is a son who acts wisely,
But he who sleeps in harvest is a son who acts shamefully.
(Proverbs 10:2-5).

Each of these Proverbs has the common theme of work. We begin by seeing that righteousness is better than ill-gotten wealth. It brings a better and longer-lasting reward. The Christian sees life, not merely in terms of a job or a career, but in terms of eternity. Notice the chiastic parallel.

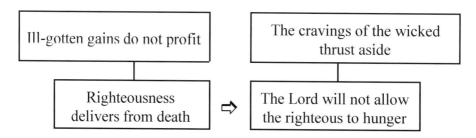

For what do you hunger? If it is what the world has to offer, then you will never be satisfied. But the Lord's gifts do bring satisfaction. It is so obvious that it almost needs not be said. But the proverb says it and so will we. Slackness leads to poverty. And the corollary is that work leads to riches.

It has been interesting to see the effect that the state lottery has had upon people. I have seen people fantasizing about what they would do if they won. They long to be rich and this is a longing that tempts of covetousness. While it is true that some do come by riches from pure happenstance, the normal way to acquire money is to work for it. Look down at verse 26:

Like vinegar to the teeth and smoke to the eyes,
So is the lazy one to those who send him. (Proverbs 10:26).

This is a note to employers. To have a sluggard working for you is like having vinegar in your teeth and smoke in your eyes.

1.   Skilled work will lead to Success.

        This is why we teach our children the importance of education. This does not necessarily mean a college education.

There is nothing more tragic than a college graduate who has no marketable skill or who has no training in an actual employable field.

> *Do you see a man skilled in his work?*
> *He will stand before kings;*
> *He will not stand before obscure men. (Proverbs 22:29).*

If you wish to be wise in the workplace, then find out what you are good at and do it. Notice the promised result. It is not a financial reward - although it undoubtedly includes that. It is the reward of recognition.

Now you might be thinking, "You can keep the recognition, just hand over the money." But the truth is that employee satisfaction is never generated solely by salary. I have in my day seen some very highly paid, yet dissatisfied workers.

Perhaps you are familiar with the Abraham Maslow's "Hierarchy of Needs." He stated that all people have five levels of need which motivate them.

- Self-actualization (creativity, growth)
- Ego Needs (Self-esteem & recognition)
- Social Needs (friendship & social acceptance)
- Safety Needs
- Physiological Needs (food & shelter)

According to Maslow, the providing of food and shelter is only a small part of the reason why you work. You work because God designed you that way. He filled you with certain needs and he has provided for them.

2.   Diligent work will lead to success.

What tasks are you most tempted to put off until tomorrow? Many of us have a "to do" list. But which things would find themselves on a "to do later" list? Let's face it, there is a little of the sluggard in most of us.

> *The way of the sluggard is as a hedge of thorns,*
> *But the path of the upright is a highway. (Proverbs 15:19).*

Can you imagine trying to walk through a hedge of thorns? That would not be an easy task. Here is the lesson. It is that the sluggard ends up working harder than a hard-working person. Why is that? Why would the sluggard work harder than anyone else? Have you ever known someone like that? Someone who worked hard at not working?

When I first started working for the Fire Department, one of the old-timers came up to me and said, "John, you don't goof off very well." While it wasn't meant to be a compliment, I took it that way.

> *Go to the ant, O sluggard,*
> *Observe her ways and be wise,*
> *7 Which, having no chief,*
> *Officer or ruler,*
> *8 Prepares her food in the summer,*
> *And gathers her provision in the harvest. (Proverbs 6:6-8).*

Our attention is directed to the example of the ant. Small yet sturdy. He is the picture of efficient preparation. He goes about his business, accomplishing his work without anyone having to stand over him and check up on him.

Perhaps there is a lesson here for supervisors. There are some employees who need to have a supervisor looking over their shoulder upon occasion. But there are others to whom this level of supervision will only be a hindrance. How efficient would our industrious ant colony be if every worker had a supervisor who was checking his every move?

The point that we are to learn is one of self-motivation. The sluggard is encouraged to put aside his sluggardness and to follow the example of the hard-working ant.

> *How long will you lie down, O sluggard?*
> *When will you arise from your sleep?*
> *10 "A little sleep, a little slumber,*
> *A little folding of the hands to rest - "*
> *11 And your poverty will come in like a vagabond,*
> *And your need like an armed man. (Proverbs 6:9-11).*

In verse 9, the sluggard is asked a rhetorical question. How long? His is the art of procrastination. He is mimicked in verse 10. He just wants to sleep a little longer. Notice the lack of definiteness.

He just wants to sleep a little bit longer. It isn't that he wants to procrastinate, it's just that he hasn't gotten around to getting out of bed. The result is seen in verse 11. It is disastrous.

The proverb appeals to your self interest. The lazy man is more interested in his present comfort than in his future security. He is a tragedy waiting to happen.

PRINCIPLES OF BUSINESS AND FINANCE

Do not withhold good from those to whom it is due,
When it is in your power to do it.
Do not say to your neighbor, "Go, and come back,
And tomorrow I will give it." (Proverbs 3:27-28).

This proverb speaks of the importance of paying your debts. We are not to withhold payment to those in whose debt we are. When we owe a debt and have the ability to pay it, then we are to do so in a timely manner.

The Hebrew of this passage contains what for us is a difficult colloquialism. אַל־תִּמְנַע־טוֹב מִבְּעָלָיו says literally, "Do not withhold good from the one of lordship (m*a ba'al*)." The idea here is that when you are indebted to someone, they exercise a level of lordship over you.

The rich rules over the poor,
And the borrower becomes the lender's slave. (Proverbs 22:7).

At the same time, there is a warning not to make money your goal in life, for it is a goal that is fleeting.

Do not weary yourself to gain wealth,
Cease from your consideration of it.
5 When you set your eyes on it, it is gone.
For wealth certainly makes itself wings,
Like an eagle that flies toward the heavens. (Proverbs 23:4-5).

If your pursuit in life is to make a lot of money, it will be a vain pursuit. It is an endeavor guaranteed to fail.

He who trusts in his riches will fall,

But the righteous will flourish like the green leaf. (Proverbs 11:28).

PRINCIPLES OF SPIRITUAL SPEECH

For lack of wood the fire goes out,
And where there is no whisperer, contention quiets down.
(Proverbs 26:20).

The Bible describes a spiritual arsonist as a gossip. Such a person is pictured here as a whisperer. Entire churches have been burned down because of such whisperings. Proverbs 22 contains a string of related ideas, each of which relates to the way in which we speak.

Drive out the scoffer, and contention will go out,
Even strife and dishonor will cease.
11 He who loves purity of heart
And whose speech is gracious, the king is his friend.
12 The eyes of the Lord preserve knowledge,
But He overthrows the words of the treacherous man.
13 The sluggard says, "There is a lion outside;
I shall be slain in the streets!"
14 The mouth of an adulteress is a deep pit;
He who is cursed of the Lord will fall into it. (Proverbs 22:10-14).

In these few verses, we are taken to the scoffer, the gracious speech of the pure, the words of the sluggard and the mouth of the adulteress. A similar string of proverbs regarding a person's speech is found in the first few verses of Proverbs 13.

A wise son accepts his father's discipline,
But a scoffer does not listen to rebuke.
2 From the fruit of a man's mouth he enjoys good,
But the desire of the treacherous is violence.
3 The one who guards his mouth preserves his life;
The one who opens wide his lips comes to ruin. (Proverbs 13:1-3).

The last of these is a common theme among the Proverbs and echoes the words of James 1:19 where we are called to be slow to speak and slow to anger.

When there are many words, transgression is unavoidable,
But he who restrains his lips is wise. (Proverbs 10:19).

He who restrains his words has knowledge,
And he who has a cool spirit is a man of understanding.
28 Even a fool, when he keeps silent, is considered wise;
When he closes his lips, he is counted prudent. (Proverbs 17:27-28).

PRINCIPLES OF LOVE AND MARRIAGE

The ideas of love and marriage form bookends in the book of Proverbs. Early in the book, we read instructions to a young man as to how he is to manage himself with regard to love and marriage. At the end of the book of Proverbs, we have a portrait of the virtuous woman.

1.   A Call to Sexual Purity.

My son, give attention to my wisdom,
Incline your ear to my understanding
That you may observe discretion,
And your lips may reserve knowledge.
For the lips of an adulteress drip honey,
And smoother than oil is her speech;
But in the end she is bitter as wormwood,
Sharp as a two-edged sword.
Her feet go down to death,
Her steps lay hold of Sheol.
She does not ponder the path of life;
Her ways are unstable, she does not know it.
(Proverbs 5:1-6).

The Proverb warns of the deceptiveness of the wayward woman. Men are too easily charmed by such a woman. She speaks in such a way as to stroke his ego - but her smooth words are really poison to his soul. The sage concludes with a call, not to abstinence, but to monogamy. It is not that sex is bad; it is that it is designed to be with your wife.

Drink water from your own cistern,
And fresh water from your own well. (Proverbs 5:15).

Sexual relations are at their best when they are pure and unpolluted. This is the picture of "fresh water."

2. A call to Promote your Spouse.

> *An excellent wife is the crown of her husband,*
> *But she who shames him is as rottenness in his bones.*
> *(Proverbs 12:4).*

Though this statement is addressed to wives, it seems to me that it is equally true of both husbands and wives. Do you want to be treated with glory and honor by your husband? Then make it known that he is the greatest thing on two feet. Build him up, both in public and in private. There is nothing more distasteful to me than to see a husband or a wife who publicly berates his/her spouse.

3. Avoid Nagging.

> *A constant dripping on a day of steady rain*
> *And a contentious woman are alike;*
> *He who would restrain her restrains the wind,*
> *And grasps oil with his right hand. (Proverbs*
> *27:15-16).*

> *It is better to live in a corner of a roof,*
> *Than in a house shared with a contentious woman.*
> (Proverbs 21:9; the same proverb is repeated verbatim in 25:24).

Nagging is not a new phenomenon. It did not start with women's rights or the sexual revolution. It is as old as Solomon. Lest we should think that the Proverbs speak only of the contentious woman, there is also a reference to the contentious man.

> *Like charcoal to hot embers and wood to fire,*
> *So is a contentious man to kindle strife. (Proverbs*
> *26:21).*

4. The Pursuit of Excellence.

An excellent wife, who can find?
For her worth is far above jewels.
11 The heart of her husband trusts in her,
And he will have no lack of gain.
12 She does him good and not evil
All the days of her life.
13 She looks for wool and flax
And works with her hands in delight.
14 She is like merchant ships;
She brings her food from afar. (Proverbs 31:10-14).

The Hebrew phrase translated "excellent woman" (the King James calls her the "virtuous woman") is related to an adjective that is often translated "valorous", "powerful", or even "wealthy." Certainly we could do an entire study of the virtues of the Proverbs 31 woman. Space will allow us only to make several observations.

- She conducts her affairs in such a way as to instill trust on the part of her husband (31:11). He is not at all worried that she will do anything to hurt him. He trusts both her love and her loyalty to him as well as her common sense.

- She is both hard-working and efficient. She is not a couch potato, but rather is industrious. But it is also an efficient industriousness which gets things accomplished.

- She is a part-time businesswoman. She is involved in the purchasing of property (31:16) and exercises a business ability in the world, yet does so under the authority of her husband. Her business activities do not cause her to neglect her primary duties to her family.

- Praise is given both to her husband as well as to her. In verse 23 her husband is said to be "known in the gates." The gates were the place of governmental and business affairs. It would be like saying, "He is known in the business community." In verse 31 she is also said to be praised "in the gates."

Do you want to be known as successful? Lift up your mate! He or she is your claim to fame.

LIFE HABIT PRINCIPLES

1.   Taking a stand with integrity.

> *Like a trampled spring and a polluted well*
> *Is a righteous man who gives way before the wicked.*
> *(Proverbs 25:26).*

2.   Self control.

> *Like a city that is broken into and without walls*
> *Is a man who has no control over his spirit. (Proverbs*
> *25:28).*

> *He who is slow to anger is better than the mighty,*
> *And he who rules his spirit, than he who captures a*
> *city. (Proverbs 16:32).*

3.   Forgiveness.

> *If your enemy is hungry, give him food to eat;*
> *And if he is thirsty, give him water to drink;*
> *22 For you will heap burning coals on his head,*
> *And the Lord will reward you. (Proverbs 25:21-22).*

This principle is cited in Romans 12:20 with the same reference to heaping burning coals upon the head. To what does it refer? It sounds like a form of revenge as though it were a bad thing, but the point of the passage in Romans 12 is that we are NOT to take revenge upon those who have wronged us (Romans 12:19).

Some have wondered whether this is not a reference to providing help in time of need -- providing warmth when your enemy is cold. The problem is that we know of no figure of speech that uses such a reference. Instead, it seems to be a picture of repentance, similar to that which is expressed in the orient when a person dons sackcloth and pours ashes upon his head (2 Samuel 13:19).

4.   Tact.

> *He who blesses his friend with a loud voice early in*
> *the morning,*

It will be reckoned a curse to him. (Proverbs 27:14).

Let your foot rarely be in your neighbor's house,
Lest he become weary of you and hate you. (Proverbs
25:17).

5.   Seriousness.

Like a madman who throws
Firebrands, arrows and death,
19 So is the man who deceives his neighbor,
And says, "Was I not joking?" (Proverbs 26:18-19).

6.   Friendship

Faithful are the wounds of a friend,
But deceitful are the kisses of an enemy. (Proverbs
27:6).

Iron sharpens iron,
So one man sharpens another. (Proverbs 27:17).

LESSONS FROM THE PROVERBS

1.   The Universal Need for Wisdom.

The underlying message of the Bible is that there are two kinds of people in the world -- God's people and those who are not God's people.

Believers	Unbelievers
Wisdom Righteous	Foolishness Unrighteous

There is no middle ground. You are in either one category or else you are in the other. Are you righteous? If you are not, then take a good look at the alternative, for it describes you. Do you live by the wisdom of God? If you do not, then the Bible describes you as a fool.

2.   The Universal Arena of Wisdom.

        You do not have to read very far into Proverbs to find that it deals with a great many topics and a great many circumstances. There is a principle here. It is that the Scriptures have something to say about every arena of life. Sometimes we get the idea that the Bible only tells us what we ought to do on Sunday morning and that the rest of the week is ours. The fact that wisdom has a universal arena means that we all must seek to apply the wisdom of the Scriptures to all areas of life. There is no distinction between the sacred and the secular. All true wisdom is God's wisdom.

        This was a common message of the Old Testament prophets. The idea of a dichotomy between the sacred and the secular, between religious ceremony and practical righteousness is nothing new. They often warned Israel that religious ritual is meaningless when divorced from righteous living.

        The New Testament gives us the same message. James tells us that true religion is not in your denominational affiliation or your doctrinal creed but in visiting orphans and widows in their distress and keeping oneself unstained by the world (James 1:27).

        A woman came to G. Campbell Morgan and asked, "Is it okay if I ask God for little things?" Morgan replied, "Madame, can you think of anything in your life that could be considered as big to the God of the universe?"

3.   Proverbs Teaches us that what is Wise is also what is Good.

        Have you ever seen the classic Hollywood movie, *The Rainmaker*, starring Burt Lancaster? The story takes place in the west where farmers are suffering a severe drought. The Rainmaker comes, promising that he will be able to bring rain for a price. While staying at a certain ranch, he meets the farmer's lonely daughter who is going through a difficult time of doubting her femininity. Feeling sorry for her, the Rainmaker makes love to her to reassure her. When her brother finds out, he is ready to take a gun and to shoot the Rainmaker. Her father, however, intervenes with the rebuke, "Noah, you're so full of what's right you can't see what's good."

        It has been quite a number of years since Situation Ethics came on the scene. These days you don't hear about Situation Ethics. It isn't that they have gone out of style - it is that they have become the only ethics of which anyone knows and it is no longer necessary to give them a specific label.

The world denies the existence of right and wrong and is only concerned with what feels good. The book of Proverbs corrects this kind of sloppy thinking.

4.   Proverbs is not a book of promises, it is a book of principles. Proverbs is not a book of laws, it is a book of lessons. You can take many of these principles and find exceptions to the rule. For example, you can probably think of cases where two Christian parents raised up a child in the way he should go and then when he was old he departed from the faith. Does that mean that the Proverbs are not true? No, but it does mean that Proverbs is a book of principles and not of promises.

Proverbs are generalizations. They point out what is generally true. There are exceptions to these generalizations. For example...

- *The fear of the Lord prolongs life, but the years of the wicked will be shortened* (Proverbs 10:27), but Abel died early.
- *When a man's ways are pleasing to the Lord, He makes even his enemies to be at peace with him* (Proverbs 16:7), but Paul's enemies never ceased their efforts to destroy him.

5.   While the Bible is all true, it does not contain all truth. And while other religious writings contain some truth, they are not all true. Scholars tell us that Proverbs 23:13 - 24:22 seem to be derived from Egyptian proverbs. They are written by people who did not know the Covenant God, but they said some wise things that are right on the mark. Proverbs 31:1-5 give us proverbs from an unknown king named Lemuel. The Septuagint tells us that he was the king of Massa (the word translated "oracle" in Proverbs 31:1). That would make him an Arab king. Yet he said some things that are true. All truth is God's truth. That means we Christian should be able to learn from others and that we should never be arrogant about our faith.

6.   The Book of Proverbs does not give us a rose-colored view of the world. It presents the world as a place where bad things really do happen. Tragedy strikes and trouble comes and Proverbs doesn't make those things go away, but it does give you wisdom on how to deal with it.

7.   Christians are called to be street-smart. We are to have common sense. We ought to know about what works and what doesn't work. On of the best ways to be street-smart is to go to the Proverbs and learn how the world works.

ECCLESIASTES
The Question of Life

Ecclesiastes was a part of five books known as the Megilloth - the "Scrolls." These five books were read at special feast days throughout the year.

Song of Solomon	Ruth	Lamentations	Ecclesiastes	Esther
Passover	Shabuot (Pentecost)	Fall of Jerusalem	Sukkot (Tabernacles)	Purim
Nisan 14	Sivan 8	Ab 9	Tishri 15	Adar 14
April 17	June 9	August 8	September 24	March 19

Note: The English equivalent dates are only close approximations.

Ecclesiastes was read by the Jews each year at the Feast of Tabernacles - that time when the Jews would gather to Jerusalem and build booths in which they would reside for that week.

A booth is a temporary shelter. And they would read this book which would remind them that life is temporary and that only those things you do for the Lord will make a lasting difference.

THE TITLE OF THE BOOK

This book has both a Hebrew title as well as a Greek rendition of that title. Both titles set forth the idea of the "Preacher."

1.   Hebrew Title: *Qoheleth.*

The title is taken from the very first sentence of the book: "The words of the *Preacher.*"

- The Qahal is the assembly, the congregation.
- The Qoheleth is the one who addresses that assembly.

The fact that the title has a feminine ending is not particularly significant. Most ancient titles and designations of office had a feminine ending. Such a use is no reflection upon the gender of the one holding the office.

2. Greek Title: Εκκλησιαστης (*Ekklesiastes*).

Our English title for this book is taken from the Greek Septuagint, the translation of the Hebrew Old Testament into Greek. It means, "Assembly-speaker, preacher." It is related to the Greek word for "church."

MESSAGE OF THE BOOK

This book is a sermon. It includes bad news and good news. The "bad news" has given the book a bad name. The reason for this is that the Preacher does not give simple pat answers to complex problems. The main question asked in this book is this: What is life all about? The Bible is not afraid to raise the hard issues. It asks, "Why should I try to be good? Does it matter? After all, sometimes things go better for me when I don't try to serve God. So why bother?"

The people in our generation are asking these same questions. This book ought to be studied by all of our young people. There is only one answer to the questions that are being asked by people today. The answer is found in the living God.

Before he died, Francis Schaeffer said that if he had an hour to talk to someone about Christ, he would talk for the first 45 minutes about how there are no answers. He would teach about the hopelessness of man. Only then would he share Jesus as the answer. That is what Ecclesiastes does.

DATE OF WRITING

Assuming that Solomon is indeed the author, the book would have been written around 945 B.C. It seems to have been written later in Solomon's life. Solomon had been one of the greatest of the Hebrew kings. His reign was one of peace and prosperity. It has been said that what David won through war, Solomon preserved through peace. And yet, there was a dark side to Solomon's reign. With all of his reputed wisdom, he found himself turning away from the Lord. It began very gradually. He entered into marital alliances with the surrounding countries. He took to be his wives the daughters of the surrounding pagan nations. As those wives came to Israel, they brought with them their pagan gods.

Ecclesiastes is a journal of a man's search for meaning in life. Much of that search takes place apart from God. The conclusion will be that life apart from God is empty.

THEMES

1.   The futility of life "under the sun" (1:2, 14).

> *The words of the Preacher, the son of David, king in Jerusalem.* 2 *"Vanity of vanities," says the Preacher, "Vanity of vanities! All is vanity."* *(Ecclesiastes 1:1-2).*

The word "vanity" is the Hebrew word *habal* and literally refers to a small breath of wind, a breeze. This is seen in Isaiah 57:13 where we read:

> *But the wind will carry all of them up,*
> *And a breath (**habal**) will take them away.*

When used figuratively, this word refers to that which is "worthless, vain or empty." This was also the name of Adam's son, Abel. When you wanted to emphasize a point in Hebrew, you repeated it. Jesus did this ("Truly, truly"). By repeating this word ("vanity of vanities"), the writer expresses the superlative. He does the same thing in the Song of Solomon ("Song of songs"). The idea here is that there is an emptiness which is above all other emptinesses. The Preacher wants to emphasize and underline and boldface this point.

ALL IS EMPTY!!!!!

Don't take it from me. Take it from Solomon. Take it from the wisest man who ever lived. Take it from the man who tried everything there was to try, who did everything there was to do. Take it from the King of the Upper Class. It is all empty.

Life without God is meaningless and empty. When we take

God out of the equation, the world makes absolutely no sense. You are born in one hospital and you die in another hospital and what happens in the "between time" doesn't change either of those facts.

Life is transient. Everything you have and everything you are will one day be forgotten. That is the message of Ecclesiastes. It portrays life "under the sun." It is a rather depressing picture. It is depressing because life without God is always depressing.

The good news is that God has not left us "under the sun." For Christians, life is not "under the sun" but rather with the Son. And that makes all the difference in the world. There is a little rhyme taught to me as a child which goes:

> Only one life, will soon be past,
> Only what's done for the Lord will last."

There is a principle here. It is the principle of permanence. The only permanent thing is our service to the Lord. It may be forgotten in this life, but it is written where it counts.

2.	The importance of serving God throughout life (11:9 12:1, 13 14).

The author shows that the meaning of life is not to be found in experiencing the things of this world. True meaning is found only in serving the Creator. There is something fulfilling about finding out what it was for which you were made and then doing that thing.

3.	Learn to Enjoy the Journey.

> *The light is pleasant, and it is good for the eyes to see the sun.* 8 *Indeed, if a man should live many years, let him rejoice in them all, and let him remember the days of darkness, for they will be many. Everything that is to come will be futility. (Ecclesiastes 11:7-8).*

Life is good. It is a gift of God that is to be treasured. The beauty of light is all the more pleasant when it is recognized that darkness eventually comes. Even if a man lives many years, the days of darkness will also be over a course of many years. You live and then you die and the days in which you will be dead far outnumber the days which you will live. The emptiness of death comes to all men. So live while you are alive.

In Ecclesiastes 3 we read that there is an appointed time for everything and a time for every event under the sun. This includes each of the seasons of life. The morning. The noon. And the twilight of life. We are called to treasure all of the seasons of life. Here is the principle. Life is meant to be enjoyed, not merely endured.

> "There are two things to aim at in life: first, to get what you want; and after that, to enjoy it. Only the wisest of mankind achieve the second." (Author unknown).

That sounds good and even has a measure of truth, but it contains a subtle trap. It is the trap of thinking that you must obtain certain things or achieve certain goals before you can begin enjoying life.

I tend to be like that. I remember one particular vacation where we were going to spend several weeks in the mountains of North Carolina. We drove north along the coast, going through Savannah and Charleston over a couple of days. By the third day, we still had not gotten to the mountains and I found myself not having much fun. Paula asked me what was wrong and I replied, "We are not there yet." It was as though I had a goal - "Get to the mountains" - and couldn't bring myself to relax until I had achieved the goal. I like to think that I am better than I used to be and I'm learning to enjoy the journey. But this applies to more than just vacations. It also applies to life.

The Westminster Catechism asks the question, "What is the chief end of man?" The answer is, "To know God and to enjoy Him forever." We are called to enjoy the life which God has given and to enjoy the God who has given it.

> *Rejoice, young man, during your childhood, and let your heart be pleasant during the days of young manhood. And follow the impulses of your heart and the desires of your eyes. Yet know that God will bring you to judgment for all these things. 10 So, remove grief and anger from your heart and put away pain from your body, because childhood and the prime of life are fleeting. (Ecclesiastes 11:9-10).*

You are only young once. Enjoy it while you can! This is a

call to the optimism of youth. There is time enough to be pessimistic in the grave. There are a series of parallel injunctions:

Rejoice, young man...	During your childhood
And...	
Let your heart be pleasant...	During the days of young manhood

The parallel continues:

> *And follow...*
> > *the impulses of your heart*
> > *and*
> > *the desires of your eyes*

This is a call to follow your dreams. What is it that you want to accomplish in life? Do it now while you are still young! I love the part that Robin Williams plays in the movie, *Dead Poets Society*. He is a teacher of poetry for an old, established all-boys school. On the first day of class, he takes his students downstairs to a hall filled with old photos of past classes. Some of those photographs are 50 and 75 years old. Most of those in the photos have lived and died.

They are nothing but worm food and daisy fertilizer. The pictures portray them in their youth and vitality, but that was in the past and now they are dead. And as they gaze on these long-forgotten portraits of youth, they hear the whisper of the Preacher. *Carpe Deum* - "Seize the Day!" Life is short. All too soon, they will be nothing more than a faded photograph on a wall. So seize the day - make each day count. Live purposefully. Meaningfully. Do great things while there is time for greatness. And yet, there is a warning. This warning serves as a balance.

Yet know that God will bring you to judgment for all these things (10:9). In your quest to live your life meaningfully, do not forget that it is God who

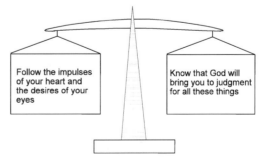

sets the standard for what is truly meaningful. In verse 10 is a third injunction. As in the previous two cases, the injunction is given, followed by its rationale.

Verse 8	Verse 9	Verse 10
Enjoy Life while you Live	Follow the pursuits of Youth	Remove anger from your heart and pain from your body
Darkness is coming	You will be judged	Youth is fleeting

So, remove anger from your heart and put away pain from your body, because childhood and the prime of life are fleeting (11:10). Life is too short to harbor anger. As to pain, put it aside while you can. There will be plenty of time to hurt when you are older.

OUTLINE OF ECCLESIASTES

In the same way that the Psalms are divided into five separate books that correspond to the five books of the Torah, so also the book of Ecclesiastes can be divided into five sermons that correspond to those same five books of the Torah.

Chapters 1-2	Chapter 3	Chapters 4-5	Chapters 6-9	Chapters 10-12
1st Sermon	2nd Sermon	3rd Sermon	4th Sermon	5th Sermon
All of creation is emptiness, but man ought to enjoy goodness because it is from God	There is profit in seeing God as the giver of all of the seasons of life	Instead of being fearful, enjoy life while it lasts because it is a gift from God	Man sees life as a struggle, but God gave life to be enjoyed	Because of the emptiness of this life, man ought to fear the Lord and follow His word

FIRST SERMON: CHAPTERS 1-2

In the first sermon, Solomon relates his grand experiment as he attempts to find significance and fulfillment through wisdom, through pleasure and though his various accomplishments.

1:12	2:1	2:4	2:12	2:18	2:24
Attempts to Find Significance through...			Frustration of...		Conclusion
Wisdom	Pleasure	Accomplishments	Death	Life	
Man trying to find significance without God					God's Gift

Solomon realizes that, no matter what he has collected or built or accomplished, he will have to leave it all behind when he dies. You will never see a hearse with a U-Haul. But that is not the worst of it. To make matters worse, you do not really know if the person to whom you leave all of your inheritance will be deserving of that inheritance.

It doesn't matter that you have acted wisely in whatever you have built and in whatever you have invested your time and effort and finances. There is no guarantee that the person to whom you leave it will act wise or whether he will squander it.

Indeed, Solomon will spend 40 years in building a united kingdom of Israel and making it into the premier nation of the world of that day. It will take his son, Rehoboam, only a few months to tear apart the nation. At Solomon's death, Rehoboam will meet with the elders of Israel and he will act so badly that 10 of the tribes of Israel will secede from the union.

Solomon's conclusion is a gloomy one for those who would find significance for life "under the sun." His conclusion is that this is as good as it gets. He concludes that "there is nothing better." It is only when the Lord enters the picture that a man can find fulfillment in any of his labors. When you place God first in your life and serve Him with all that you do, only then can you find true and lasting satisfaction.

SECOND SERMON: CHAPTER 3

The Preacher opens in verse 1 with an introduction to the principle that there is a proper time for everything. He is speaking of those things which take place "under heaven." As was true in the last chapter, so now also the Preacher is giving us a picture of life as it exists "under the sun."

It has been said that there are four seasons to a man's life:

> There is the time when he believes in Santa Claus.
> There is the time when he no longer believes in Santa Claus.
> There is the time when he is Santa Claus.
> There is the time when he looks like Santa Claus.

This chapter also presents the seasons in a man's life. It does so by way of a series of fourteen contrasts. These contrasts cover nearly every event of life.

Having stated all of the various activities of life, the Preacher then comes to a summarizing question in verse 9: What profit is there to the worker from that in which he toils? Of what profit are all of these activities? This is a rhetorical question. It expects an obvious negative answer. The Preacher has spent the last two chapters demonstrating that these various activities have no ultimate profit.

> *He has made everything appropriate in its time. He has also set eternity in their heart, yet so that man will not find out the work which God has done from the beginning even to the end (Ecclesiastes 3:11).*

He has made each one to be appropriate in its time (3:11). The word translated "appropriate" is the same word used to describe the beauty of Sarah (Genesis 12:11,14), Rachael (Genesis 29:17), Esther (Esther 2:7), and the daughters of Job (Job 42:15). It is used to describe both men and women - Joseph is said to have been beautiful of form and beautiful of face (Genesis 39:6).

There is a design to life. And it is a beautiful design. The problem is that you do not see the entire story in this life. And because you do not see the entire story, you miss the beauty.

> *I have seen that nothing is better than that man should be happy in his activities, for that is his lot. For who will bring him to see what will occur after him? (Ecclesiastes 3:22).*

The Preacher now repeats the conclusion to which he came in verse 12. He repeats that conclusion now almost word for word. It is that you should make the most of this time that you do have. Life is precious. Life is short and eternity is long, so make the most of the now.

THIRD SERMON: CHAPTERS 4-5

This sermon begins by looking at the loneliness created by a life of rivalry and competition.

4:1	4:9	5:1	5:8	5:10
Words of Wisdom in dealing with...				
Yourself	Others	The Lord	The King	Finances
For what you STRIVE	Who you NEED	What you SAY	What you THINK	What you LOVE

The Preacher concludes this section with some very practical observations that tell us how we ought to live.

1. Enjoy It While You Can: *Here is what I have seen to be good and fitting: to eat, to drink and enjoy oneself in all one's labor in which he toils under the sun during the few years of his life which God has given him; for this is his reward. (Ecclesiastes 5:18).*

   If your eyes are only on tomorrow's financial promises, then you will never learn how to enjoy today. How would you live differently if you learned that you only had six months left to live? What would you do? With whom would you spend time? To whom would you say, "I'm sorry"? Do it! You only have a few years. Enjoy the now! Live deliberately!

2. What You Have is Given by God - Be Thankful: *Furthermore, as for every man to whom God has given riches and wealth, He has also empowered him to eat from them and to receive his reward and rejoice in his labor; this is the gift of God. (Ecclesiastes 5:19).*

   If God has gifted you with riches (and if you live in the United States then you DO have a certain level of riches compared with the rest of the world), you have an obligation to thank Him for those riches and to enjoy His gift with an attitude of thanksgiving.

But even if you are penniless, God has gifted you with the wealth of life. Whether it be eyes to see or ears to hear or a mind to contemplate or any combination of these, give thanks to the Lord, for these are gifts from Him.

3.   Don't Waste Your Time Worrying about the Brevity of this Life: *For he will not often consider the years of his life, because God keeps him occupied with the gladness of his heart. (Ecclesiastes 5:20).*

There is a temptation when reading the teachings of this book concerning the brevity of life that we stop and spend our life bemoaning its brevity. That is the wrong response. A proper response in to accept this precious gift of life and to do that to which God has called us.

What has God called you to do? To be a fire fighter? Then enjoy being a fire fighter for the glory of God. To be a housewife? Be a housewife with gladness in your heart as you make your home the house of God. To be a businessman? Recognize that all business is God's business and that He has gifted you with a place in which to do His work. Enjoy your business and be thankful to the Lord for that business.

FOURTH SERMON: CHAPTERS 6-9

This section begins by looking at the unfulfilled life and the fact that neither riches, long life, appetites, wisdom, nor striving are ultimately fulfilling in this life. That is not to say that the benefits of life cannot be enjoyed or that wisdom should be rejected, but these are not an end to themselves. The sermon concludes that we ought to enjoy that which the Lord has granted to us in this life, even while we do not make more of those things than they really are.

FIFTH SERMON: CHAPTERS 10-12

This sermon begins with a series of proverbs, but then begins to build up to its conclusion in the last chapter: *Remember also your Creator in the days of your youth (Ecclesiastes 12:1a).* This verse contains a continuation of the thought that was begun in the previous chapter. The subject was the brevity of youth. The following chart captures the flow of thought:

11:9	11:10	12:1
Rejoice...during your childhood. Let your heart be pleasant during the days of young manhood.	Remove vexation from your heart and put away pain from your body...	Remember also your Creator in the days of your youth
Know that God will bring you to judgment	Childhood and the prime of life are fleeting	Before the evil days come...

Because youth is brief, we are called to utilize the days of our youth in the best possible way. This involves remembering the Lord. Christianity is a religion of remembrance. The primary feast of the Jews was the Passover. This was a feast of remembrance. It remembered two aspects concerning the Lord.

- It remembered that He is the Creator.
- It remembered that He is the Redeemer.

We also have a celebration of remembrance. It is the Lord's Supper. In partaking of this rite, we remember the same two aspects of God as the Creator of the New Creation and that He is the Redeemer. We are called to remember. I would suggest that this means more than merely remembering the fact of God's existence. This is a call to serve the Lord in one's youth.

> *Remember also your Creator in the days of your youth, before the evil days come and the years draw near when you will say, "I have no delight in them" (Ecclesiastes 12:1).*

The Preacher goes on to describe in detail the conditions of these coming "evil days." He does this by using a series of double metaphors. Each of these metaphors has two pictures.

- The first picture is that of a house that is in an escalating condition of disrepair.
- The second picture is of a person growing older.

For example, verse 2 speaks of the time *before the sun, the light, the moon, and the stars are darkened, and clouds return after the rain.* This is a general picture of dark days. We speak similarly of entering the twilight of one's life. At such a time, the lights of the mind are dimmed. Your thought processes are not what they used to be. More often than not, your mind feels as though it is in the clouds. As one person put it, "Just about the time that your face clears up, your mind begins to go." There are three things that mark the onset of old age. The first is the loss of memory... and I can't remember the other two.

Verse 3 speaks of *the day that the watchmen of the house tremble.* The "keepers of the house" are a reference to the arms and hands of the aged that begin to shake with the onset of old age. The description of how *the grinding ones stand idle because they are few* (12:3) is a humorous reference to teeth. They don't chew as much as they used to because there are not that many of them left. This was before the era of false teeth. The analogy is carried over into verse 4 where *the doors on the street are shut as the sound of the grinding mill is low.* As you lose your teeth, your face begins to sag around the mouth and, instead of the noise of chewing, there is the soft sound of gumming.

It is a grim picture. No one wants to get old. Of course, most of us aren't too excited about the alternative, either. Like the song says, "Everybody wants to go to heaven, but nobody wants to die."

Old age brings with it certain fears. There is the fear of high places due to the fact that it is easier to take a spill and it now takes longer to heal from such a fall. There is also the fear of traveling. The elderly are less inclined to take risks, for they are more aware of the adverse consequences.

It is true that modern technology has made it much easier to deal with many of these burdens of the elderly. We have eyeglasses and hearing aids and false teeth and dyed hair and all sorts of other technology to assist in dealing with the evils of aging. While these inventions are wonderful, they do not deal with the source of the problem -- the fact of a body that is wearing out from the inside out. They do not deal with the problem of eventual death.

The preacher concludes that this aging process only stops when man goes to his eternal home while mourners go about in the street (12:5). It is because of this we are called to remember the Lord while we are still alive on planet earth.

> *Remember Him before the silver cord is broken and the golden bowl is crushed, the pitcher by the well is shattered and the wheel at the cistern is crushed; 7 then the dust will return to the earth as it was, and the spirit will return to God who gave it. (Ecclesiastes 12:6-7).*

SONG OF SONGS
The Book of Love

All of the Scriptures are holy, but the Song of Songs is the holy of holies. (Rabbi Akiba ben Joseph, Mishnah Yadaim 3:5).

Like so many of the books of the Old Testament, the title for the book is taken from the first verse that appears in the book. The title of the book is itself a superlative. When you wanted to place the stress of importance upon something in the Hebrew language, you repeated it. Thus we read of the "Holy of Holies" -- that most holy place or of the "King of Kings" -- the most exalted of kings. The author does this same thing in the first verse of this book.

The Song of Songs, which is Solomon's. (Songs 1:1).

From this title, it has been traditionally concluded that Solomon is the author of the song. But it could also be that the song is about Solomon and that the author is unknown. There are within the book several Greek and Persian words. This means that if Solomon were the original author, then it is likely that a later editor updated the language and, in doing so, added the Greek and Persian words.

On the other hand, we read in 1 Kings 4:32 that Solomon authored 3000 proverbs and 1005 songs. If this is also his song, then it is the one that won the Grammy Award, for it is the "Song of Songs."

VARIOUS INTERPRETATIONS OF THE BOOK

1. The Allegorical Interpretation: The entire book is seen as an allegory dealing with the Lord's love for His people Israel. That view began among the rabbis and has passed over into the Christian Church, making it an allegorical view of Christ's love for the Church.

    The problem in this view is that an allegory typically attempts to assign meanings to all of the different parts of the story and this simply will not work in this song.

2.   The Cultic Interpretation: The poems in the book are poems that were used in the ritual of marriage and were read or sung at the ceremony. The Song of Solomon is then seen as a part of the ancient liturgy and is a reflection of the ritual of a poetic people.

3.   The Shepherd Interpretation: This view sees the Song of Solomon as a drama or a story depicting King Solomon trying to woo a Shulamite maiden to become a part of his palace harem. However, the Shulamite maiden is in love with a hometown boy, a shepherd. At the end of the story, she rejects all of the splendor of the palace and returns to the hometown boy. In this view, Solomon is the villain of the story. I hold this view to be in error for the following reasons:

- The Song itself only describes two people and not three. They speak to one another as "my beloved" and "my love." Both delight in one another and there is no hint of a secret lover hiding in the wings.

- Making Solomon out to be the villain takes all of these passages that speak of love as merely the lustful urgings of an evil and twisted man.

- To view the Shulamite as leaving her legal husband to return to her shepherd lover would make her an adulteress rather than a heroine.

4.   The Typical Interpretation: This view holds that King Solomon is a type of Christ and that the bride is a type of the Church. This interpretation is different from the allegorical view in the sense that an allegory has to have meaning in every phrase, while the typical view does not necessarily have to do that. In this way, we can see this as both a love song between two people and, at the same time, we can see illustrations of our love relationship with the Lord.

5.   The Natural or Literal Interpretation: This view simply takes the Song of Solomon at face value. It is a series of very beautiful, lyrical love poems with much to teach the people of God.

The Song of Solomon was one of the scrolls of the Megilloth, the scrolls that were read at the various feast days. Song of Solomon was traditionally read at the Passover. This tells me something of how the Jews viewed this book. It was a love story, but it also carried with it certain spiritual connotations.

The love story between this man and this woman was mirrored in the love story of God and His people.

THE CAST OF CHARACTERS

There are two primary characters:

- Solomon (the Hebrew actually reads Shelomoh): Means "peaceful."
- Shulamith: This is the feminine form of Shelomoh.

These two names are the masculine and the feminine of the same root. This is Mr. and Mrs. Solomon. In addition, there are several brothers of the Shulamite who are mentioned and a chorus which is described as "the Daughters of Jerusalem."

OUTLINE OF THE BOOK

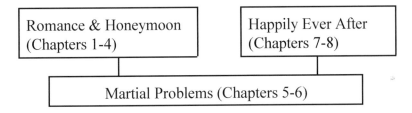

Although this is a poetic song and not a narrative, we can take the lyrics and put them together to see something of a story unfold.

- The story begins in the land of Ephraim where there lives a maiden with her brothers and mother. They work the land and she labors in the vineyard but has no time to spend on herself and her skin is deeply tanned by the sun.

  I am black but lovely,
  O daughters of Jerusalem,
  Like the tents of Kedar,
  Like the curtains of Solomon.
  6 Do not stare at me because I am swarthy,
  For the sun has burned me.
  My mother's sons were angry with me;
  They made me caretaker of the vineyards,

> *But I have not taken care of my own vineyard. (Song of*
> *Songs 1:5-6).*

She makes reference to her "mother's sons" in verse 8. This might
indicate that these are her stepbrothers. Instead of caring for her, they
have been angry with her and forced her to labor in the vineyards.

- One day as she is working in the fields, she meets a stranger and it is
love at first sight. She initially takes him for a shepherd and asks where
he keeps his flocks of sheep.

> *Tell me, O you whom my soul loves,*
> *Where do you pasture your flock,*
> *Where do you make it lie down at noon?*
> *For why should I be like one who veils herself*
> *Beside the flocks of your companions? (Song of Songs*
> *1:7).*

- They speak words of love to one another and when he departs, he
promises to return for her in the spring.

> *My beloved responded and said to me,*
> *"Arise, my darling, my beautiful one,*
> *And come along.*
> *11 For behold, the winter is past,*
> *The rain is over and gone.*
> *12 The flowers have already appeared in the land;*
> *The time has arrived for pruning the vines,*
> *And the voice of the turtledove has been heard in our land.*
> *13 The fig tree has ripened its figs,*
> *And the vines in blossom have given forth their fragrance.*
> *Arise, my darling, my beautiful one,*
> *And come along!" (Song of Songs 2:10-13).*

- She waits and she dreams for his return and then, one day, he does
return. However, it is not as a shepherd but as the reigning King.

> *What is this coming up from the wilderness*
> *Like columns of smoke,*
> *Perfumed with myrrh and frankincense,*
> *With all scented powders of the merchant?*
> *7 Behold, it is the traveling couch of Solomon;*

Sixty mighty men around it,
Of the mighty men of Israel.
8 All of them are wielders of the sword,
Expert in war;
Each man has his sword at his side,
Guarding against the terrors of the night.
9 King Solomon has made for himself a sedan chair
From the timber of Lebanon.
10 He made its posts of silver,
Its back of gold
And its seat of purple fabric,
With its interior lovingly fitted out
By the daughters of Jerusalem.
11 Go forth, O daughters of Zion,
And gaze on King Solomon with the crown
With which his mother has crowned him
On the day of his wedding,
And on the day of his gladness of heart." (Song of Songs
3:6-11).

- Solomon comes and takes his bride and they return to the city of Jerusalem. This is a wonderful story and, for the Christian, it is our story. The Good Shepherd has come and won our hearts and has promised to return for us one day and take us to be His bride.

- A temporary separation takes place in chapters 5-6 as the bride awakens to find that her husband is gone. She searches for him. Meanwhile, he is taking a walk though the orchard and thinking of his bride and contemplating her beauty. Finally the couple is reunited and they live happily ever after.

Put me like a seal over your heart,
Like a seal on your arm.
For love is as strong as death,
Jealousy is as severe as Sheol;
Its flashes are flashes of fire,
The very flame of the Lord.
7 Many waters cannot quench love,
Nor will rivers overflow it;
If a man were to give all the riches of his house for love,
It would be utterly despised. (Song of Songs 8:6-7).

OBSERVATIONS REGARDING THE BOOK

- There are no references to God. [1]
- The book is never quoted in the New Testament.
- Both Jerome and Origen tell us that the Jews would not permit their young people to read this book until they were 30 years of age.

LESSONS FROM THE SONG OF SONGS

1. God is concerned with all of life, not merely that which takes place in church on Sunday morning. He is the God of all of life. All of life is all of God's. He is with you on the golf course and in the movie theater and is involved with every realm of human endeavor. The Song of Solomon shows God's concern with all of life. This speaks against the heresy of Dualism that says the body is bad and only the spirit is good. God is concerned with all things. He is the redeemer of the commonplace.

2. God is concerned with our sexuality. He created sex both for reproduction as well as for enjoyment within the proper bounds of marriage. Some people tend to define sin by how much they enjoyed it. But sex was created by God and meant to be enjoyed, albeit within the bounds of marriage.

3. All of life reflects our relationship with God. Therefore we should not be surprised to find parallels between this love story and our relationship with Christ. The New Testament likens the marriage union to that which exists between Christ and His church. As you read of the depth of love that exists between Solomon and his bride, you remember that this is an illustration of how much God loves you.

4. The Scriptures contain love songs. You come to the Bible looking for doctrine and instead you find this love song. There is a warning here. It is possible to have all of the right doctrines and still miss the love.

---

[1] Song of Solomon 8:6 speaks of jealousy as "the flame of *Ya*" and the NAS renders this "the flame of the Lord." The NIV renders this same phrase as "a mighty flame" and this sort of rendering is attested in the LXX, the NET, KJV, RSV, and the NKJV.

INTRODUCTION TO THE PROPHETS

For far too long, the Old Testament prophets have been considered only in terms of their ministry of foretelling the future. While they did have such a ministry, this ignores much of their practical value. The prophets are to the Old Testament what the epistles are to the New Testament.

- The prophets contain the "so what?" of the Old Testament.
- The prophets take the teachings of the law and the wisdom of the poetical books and they put it into practice in everyday life.
- While the poetical books touch the heart and the mind, the prophets take that truth and put it to work in everyday life.

The Torah was foundational to the message of the prophets. They were people of the covenant and they called to Israel using covenant language. The covenant stipulations set forth certain blessings for those who kept the covenant and it set forth cursings for those who broke the covenant. Leviticus 26 presents an entire cycle of disciplines and punishments that God threatens to bring upon His people if they continue in disobedience. In verses 1-13 there are promises of blessings that will come "if you walk in My statutes and keep My commandments so as to carry them out" (Leviticus 26:3).

- God will send the rain for their crops
- The people will eat well and live securely in the land
- Their enemies will fall before them: *Five of you will chase a hundred, and a hundred of you will chase ten thousand (26:8).*
- God will be with His people and will bless them with His presence.

Beginning in verse 14, we see a promise of the curses that will come upon the people if they reject the Lord.

- They will experience diseases and lack of health
- Their enemies will invade and partake of their crops
- They shall suffer defeat: *You shall flee when no one is pursuing you (26:17).*
- If these things do not bring them back, then God will bring an even harsher cycle of discipline: *"If also after these things, you do not obey Me, then I will punish you seven times more for your sins"*

(26:18).

- Beginning in verse 27, we read of an even harsher cycle: *"Yet if in spite of this, you do not obey Me, but act with hostility against Me, 28 then I will act with wrathful hostility against you; and I, even I, will punish you seven times for your sins" (26:27-28).*
- These cycles continue to get worse and worse until finally the Lord says that He will remove the people from the land.

Throughout this chapter we see a great amount of patience on the part of God. Five times throughout this chapter we see the repeated refrain: *"If you will not listen to me..."* At the same time, the people are warned against taking this patience for granted. Therefore the Lord brings judgment in cycles of increasing severity, culminating finally in exile from the land.

The Greatest Possible Curse	The Greatest Possible Blessing
To be removed from the land	To be returned to the land

This means there was a conditional nature to the promises of the prophets which is not always immediately apparent. This is seen in the case of the prophet Jonah who was sent to Nineveh to announce its impending destruction. It was to take place within forty days. The forty days came and went and there was no destruction. What went wrong? The inhabitants of the city repented and the judgment was not executed. We are given to understand that this was a conditional prophecy, even though the words of the prophecy do not in themselves cite a conditionality.

Prediction	Contingency	Fulfillment
Nineveh will be destroyed in 40 days	They turned to the Lord in repentance	God relented concerning the calamity

This process is described in Jeremiah 18 where the prophet has been observing a potter at his wheel. Jeremiah notes that the potter was able to do with the clay as he wished and could not be faulted over the uses that he chose. The Lord goes on to set forth this principle:

> *At one moment I might speak concerning a nation or concerning a kingdom to uproot, to pull down, or to destroy it; 8 if that nation against which I have spoken turns from its evil, I will relent concerning the calamity I planned to bring*

on it. 9 Or at another moment I might speak concerning a nation or concerning a kingdom to build up or to plant it; 10 if it does evil in My sight by not obeying My voice, then I will think better of the good with which I had promised to bless it. (Jeremiah 18:7-10).

Prediction	Contingency	Fulfillment
If I speak concerning a nation to destroy it...	If they turn from their evil...	I will relent of the calamity
If I speak concerning a nation plant it...	If they do evil and do not obey...	I will think better of the good

This naturally brings up the question: How can we determine whether a prophecy is conditional or unconditional? It is a simple matter when the prophecy is given with a specific conditional modifier, but what about those situations, like the prophecy of Jonah regarding Nineveh, when no condition is set forth? There are certain assurances that are made in prophecy that are given so that we may have a high degree of certainty of their fulfillment.

1.   Statements of Certainty.

An example of this is seen in the first two chapters of Amos as God repeats again and again the phrase, "I will not turn back my wrath." Yet even in these situations, Amos 5:4 calls for sincere and extensive repentance to "Seek Me and live."

2.   The use of Signs.

Signs and symbolic actions were given as guarantees that the Lord had a high degree of determination to bring the prophecy about. Isaiah 7:11-14 gives this sort of sign so that Ahaz would know it was to be fulfilled.

3.   Sworn Predictions.

In certain cases, the Lord takes a divine oath to show that His promise shall indeed come to pass.

• Amos 4:2. *The Lord God has sworn by His holiness, "Behold, the days are coming upon you When they will take you away with meat hooks, And the last of you with fish hooks."*

- Ezekiel 5:11. *"So as I live," declares the Lord God, "surely, because you have defiled My sanctuary with all your detestable idols and with all your abominations, therefore I will also withdraw, and My eye shall have no pity and I will not spare."*
- Isaiah 62:8. *The LORD has sworn by His right hand and by His strong arm, "I will never again give your grain as food for your enemies; Nor will foreigners drink your new wine, for which you have labored."*

ISAIAH
The Fifth Gospel

No prophet says so much about the coming of the Messiah as Isaiah. For this reason, his book has been called the fifth gospel. Indeed, the book of Isaiah has a curious likeness to the Bible in brief.

The Bible	Isaiah
Old Testament: 39 books New Testament: 27 books	Judgment: 39 Chapters Comfort: 27 Chapters
Total: 66 Books	Total: 66 Chapters

- Isaiah begins where the book of Genesis begins; with man in sin and in rebellion against God.
- Isaiah ends where the book of Revelation ends; with the creation of the new heavens and the new earth, the righteous enjoying the glory of the Lord and the wicked being delivered to everlasting punishment.

THE AUTHOR

Both the author and the date during which he wrote are identified in the very beginning of the book that bears his name.

> *The vision of Isaiah the son of Amoz, concerning Judah and Jerusalem which he saw during the reigns of Uzziah, Jotham, Ahaz, and Hezekiah, kings of Judah. (Isaiah 1:1).*

The name Isaiah (יְשַׁעְיָהוּ) means "salvation from Yahweh." These are the same two words that make up the name "Joshua" and "Jesus" (יְהוֹשֻׁעַ), but their order is reversed.

Over the last 150 years, liberal scholars have proclaimed that the book of Isaiah was the product of several different authors. There are several reasons that are given

- The first half of the book deals with judgment while the second half of the book deals with the glory of God's future hope.
- The latter portion of the book has events during the Persian Empire as its focus. The prophets of the Old Testament normally wrote about events and countries that existed within their own day. The mention of the name of Cyrus serves as proof to liberal critics that Isaiah could not have written the latter part of this book. However, a similar situation is seen in 1 Kings 13:2 where Josiah is mentioned by name hundreds of years before he was born.
- There is no mention of Isaiah in this portion of the book. The only personal name found within the book apart from characters in the past like Abraham is that of Cyrus the Great who died in 530 B.C.

The unity of the book of Isaiah was not brought into serious question until the rise of liberalism in the 19th century. A full copy of the scroll of Isaiah was discovered among the initial Dead Sea Scrolls. The Isaiah scroll was intact and showed no distinction between the first half and the second half of the book.

Josephus speaks of how Cyrus the Great became aware of the prophecies about himself that were contained in the book of Isaiah (Antiquities 11:1:2). Whether or not Cyrus did indeed have interaction with the book of Isaiah, the statement of Josephus at least reflects the popular Jewish opinion that the latter half of Isaiah was written prior to the days of Cyrus.

It is noteworthy that Isaiah's special title for God is "the Holy One of Israel." He uses it 12 times in the first half of the book and another 13 times in the latter part of the book. Outside of Isaiah, this title is used only six other times in the entire Bible.

1.   Isaiah the Man.

- Isaiah moved in the circles of the wealthy, the influential and the elite. The Hebrew of the book of Isaiah is the best of the entire Bible. This was a man who was evidently highly educated.

- He was a friend and a confidant of King Hezekiah. He had ready access to the palace at Jerusalem.

- We read in Isaiah 6 of a vision with its setting in the Temple. Because only priests were permitted into the Temple, this suggests that Isaiah might have been from the ranks of the priesthood.

2.   His Family.

Isaiah was married to a prophetess (Isaiah 8:3). We have Mr. Prophet marrying Mrs. Prophet. When two prophets have children, what do they name their kids? They name them after prophetic themes.

- Maher-shalal-hash-baz (Isaiah 8:3). His name literally means "speedy is the prey." His name is prophetic. It is a promise. The promise is that there is coming a judgment against those who refuse to turn away from their idolatry and their sin. The picture is of a wild animal that is about to pounce upon its prey. In just such an unexpected manner, the judgment of God would come.

- Shear-jashub (Isaiah 7:3). This name means, "a remnant shall return." His name reflects the promise that, though the nations of Israel and Judah would be carried off into captivity, there would remain a remnant that would return.

OUTLINE OF ISAIAH

We said that the book of Isaiah has a curious and coincidental likeness to the Bible in that Isaiah has 66 chapters just as the Bible has 66 books. Furthermore, the main division of Isaiah takes place at the close of the first 39 chapters of Isaiah in the same way that the Old Testament ends after the 39th book of the Bible.

Chapters 1-35	Chapters 36-39	Chapters 40-66
Judgments in the Present	Historical Interlude	Glory in the Future
The Judgment of God		The Comfort of God
Messiah the Judge		Messiah the Servant
Groan		Glory
God's Government "A throne" (6:6)		God's Grace "A Lamb" (53:7)

The first section begins and ends the same way. It begins with the woe of judgment and it ends with the woes of judgment. Sandwiched between these judgments are a long list of woes.

```
┌─────────────────────────────────────────────┐
│ Woes of Judgment against Judah (1-5)         │
├─────────────────────────────────────────────┤
│ A Son and A Song of Salvation (6-12)         │
├───────────────────────────────────────────────┐
│   Woes to the Nations.                         │
│      •  Babylon (13:1 - 14:23).                │
│      •  Assyria (14:24-27).                    │
│      •  Philistia (14:28-32).                  │
│      •  Moab (15-16).                          │
│      •  Damascus (17).                         │
│      •  Cush (18).                             │
│      •  Egypt and Cush (19-20).               │
│      •  Babylon (21:1-10).                     │
│      •  Edom (21:11-12).                       │
│      •  Arabia (21:13-17)                      │
│      •  Jerusalem (22).                        │
│      •  Tyre (23).                             │
│      •  A warning (24).                        │
├───────────────────────────────────────────────┘
│ A Song of Salvation (25-27)                   │
├─────────────────────────────────────────────┤
│ Woes of Judgment (28-35)                      │
└─────────────────────────────────────────────┘
```

THE WORLD OF ISAIAH'S DAY

The vision of Isaiah the son of Amoz, concerning Judah and Jerusalem which he saw during the reigns of Uzziah, Jotham, Ahaz, and Hezekiah, kings of Judah. (Isaiah 1:1).

Isaiah's ministry spanned the reigns of five kings of Judah since Isaiah later spoke during the reign of Manassah. It was a time for the rise and the fall of kingdoms. It saw the fall of the Northern Kingdom of Israel to the Assyrians and it saw the invasion of Jerusalem by those same Assyrians.

ISAIAH 1 - A MICROCOSM OF THE BOOK

The first chapter of Isaiah has been described as a microcosm of the entire book.

- It begins with judgment.
- It moves to salvation.
- It closes with a promise of the future.

The visionary message begins with words that are reminiscent of both the beginning and the end of the Pentateuch. Consider the following...

Isaiah 1:1	Genesis 1:1	Deuteronomy 32:1
Listen, O heavens, and hear, O earth	*In the beginning God created the heavens and the earth*	*Give ear, O heavens, and let me speak; and let the earth hear the words of my mouth*

> *Listen, O heavens, and hear, O earth;*
> *For the LORD speaks,*
> *"Sons I have reared and brought up,*
> *But they have revolted against Me.*
> *3 An ox knows its owner,*
> *And a donkey its master's manger,*
> *But Israel does not know,*
> *My people do not understand." (Isaiah 1:2-3).*

Notice that verses 2-3 does not address the nation of Israel. Instead, it addresses the heavens and the earth. They are called as witnesses in a legal court. Serving as both Prosecutor and Judge is the Lord. And in the dock stands Israel.

> *Alas, sinful nation,*
> *People weighed down with iniquity,*
> *Offspring of evildoers,*
> *Sons who act corruptly!*
> *They have abandoned the Lord,*
> *They have despised the Holy One of Israel,*
> *They have turned away from Him. (Isaiah 1:4).*

The phrase "offspring of evildoers" is translated from the Hebrew *Zera' Merayim*, literally "Seed of Evil Ones." This is not a reflection upon their earthly parents. It is a reflection of their spiritual parentage. It calls to mind the seed of the serpent as seen in Genesis 3:15.

How the faithful city has become a harlot,
She who was full of justice!
Righteousness once lodged in her,
But now murderers. (Isaiah 1:21).

God has become angry with His wife over her unfaithfulness. His wife has turned away. His bride has committed spiritual adultery. He has every right to divorce this unfaithful wife.

The Faithful City	A Harlot
Was once a lodging place for righteousness.	Is now a lodging place for murderers.

These same two pictures of God's city and its people are seen in the book of Revelation. In Revelation 12 we see the picture of a woman giving birth to a child. We recognize the child as Israel and the woman as Israel. Later in the book we see another vision. Again it is a woman, but this time we see her as a prostitute. She has become drunk with the blood of the saints and she has prostituted herself with the dragon that manifests itself in the Roman Empire.

The same picture is seen here in Isaiah. The once-faithful city has become a prostitute. But the good news is that He is a forgiving husband. The city that was once called "faithful" shall again be made into a "city of righteousness" and a "faithful city" (1:26).

Then I will restore your judges as at the first,
And your counselors as at the beginning;
After that you will be called the city of righteousness,
A faithful city.
27 Zion will be redeemed with justice
And her repentant ones with righteousness. (Isaiah 1:26-27).

The movement here is similar to that which is seen in the book of Revelation. There we are given the image of a prostitute clothed in scarlet and drunk with the blood of the saints. She is seen in Revelation 17-18. But then we turn the page to Revelation 19 and we see instead a virgin bride.

We can see our own story within these pages. The Bible teaches that we have all sinned and have been unfaithful to the Lord, but He has redeemed us and made us into a spotless bride.

ISAIAH'S INAUGURAL VISION

Isaiah's vision took place *in the year of King Uzziah's death* (Isaiah 6:1). Uzziah was one of the good kings of Israel (he is also called Azariah). He reigned for a very long time, but he became prideful and fell into sin. As a result, God struck him with leprosy.

> *And King Uzziah was a leper to the day of his death; and he lived in a separate house, being a leper, for he was cut off from the house of the LORD. And Jotham his son was over the king's house judging the people of the land. 22 Now the rest of the acts of Uzziah, first to last, the prophet Isaiah, the son of Amoz, has written. (2 Chronicles 26:21-22).*

The official royal historian for the reign of King Uzziah was none other than Isaiah the son of Amoz. The same year that King Uzziah died marked the beginning of a special ministry. It began with a heavenly vision.

> *In the year of King Uzziah's death, I saw the Lord sitting on a throne, lofty and exalted, with the train of His robe filling the temple.*
> *Seraphim stood above Him, each having six wings; with two he covered his face, and with two he covered his feet, and with two he flew. 3 And one called out to another and said, "Holy, Holy, Holy, is the LORD of hosts, The whole earth is full of His glory." 4 And the foundations of the thresholds trembled at the voice of him who called out, while the temple was filling with smoke. (Isaiah 6:1-4).*

Isaiah sees a tremendous vision. It takes place within the setting of the Temple. It is a holy vision of the presence of God. God is not seen here as "the man upstairs." He is the Sovereign Lord of the Universe. The awesomeness of God is seen in Isaiah's response to this vision.

> *Then I said, "Woe is me, for I am ruined! Because I am a man of unclean lips, And I live among a people of unclean lips; For my eyes have seen the King, the LORD of hosts." (Isaiah 6:5).*

A proper view of God will result in a proper view of yourself. Isaiah does not look at God and say, "I'm okay, you're okay." He says, "I am undone!" The man who thinks it is easy to stand before a holy and righteous God has never stood before the Holy and Righteous God.

> *Then one of the seraphim flew to me, with a burning coal in his hand which he had taken from the altar with tongs. 7 And he touched my mouth with it and said, "Behold, this has touched your lips; and your iniquity is taken away, and your sin is forgiven." (Isaiah 6:6-7).*

Isaiah had a problem. It was called sin. It was a problem that disqualified him from the ministry. Indeed, it was a problem that disqualified him from heaven. But now his sin is removed. Notice what it was that took away the sin of Isaiah. It was something from the altar. It is that which represents the sacrifice. When Isaiah can do nothing to save himself, something is done on his behalf that brings salvation to him.

> *Then I heard the voice of the Lord, saying, "Whom shall I send, and who will go for Us?" Then I said, "Here am I. Send me!" (Isaiah 6:8).*

God saved us, not merely as an end unto itself, but for a reason. God saved us that we might serve Him. Isaiah is called to service. His service will be such that he will represent the Lord.

AHAZ AND THE SIGN FROM HEAVEN

> *Now it came about in the days of Ahaz, the son of Jotham, the son of Uzziah, king of Judah, that Rezin the king of Aram and Pekah the son of Remaliah, king of Israel, went up to Jerusalem to wage war against it, but could not conquer it.*
> *When it was reported to the house of David, saying, "The Arameans have camped in Ephraim," his heart and the hearts of his people shook as the trees of the forest shake with the wind. (Isaiah 7:1-2).*

Ahaz found his tiny kingdom threatened with enemies from the north, especially the kingdoms of Israel and Aram. The Assyrian Empire was at its zenith and the fierce Assyrian warriors had spread their reign of terror throughout most of the known world, plundering and burning wherever they went. The small kingdoms that lay along the shores of the Mediterranean were no match for these hoards and they decided that the only way they could resist the onslaught was to band together into a single alliance. Accordingly, Egypt, Aram (Syria) and the Northern Kingdom of Israel formed an alliance and asked Judah to join with them. Ahaz, the king of Judah, refused.

Tensions mounted as the confederation threatened to invade Judah and install a puppet king of their own choosing. Ahaz found himself surrounded by enemies on all sides. It was into this scene that Isaiah came with a message from the Lord. The message was one of hope in the midst of what had all the appearances of an eventual collision of forces.

It was into this scene that Isaiah came. He was a man with a message. The message was from God. The message was that the enemies of God would fail.

> Approximately 20 years had passed since the close of chapter 6 to the beginning of chapter 7. During that time had been the reign of King Jotham, but Isaiah makes no mention of him.

> *Thus says the Lord God, "It shall not stand nor shall it come to pass. 8 For the head of Aram is Damascus and the head of Damascus is Rezin (now within another 65 years Ephraim will be shattered, so that it is no longer a people), 9 and the head of Ephraim is Samaria and the head of Samaria is the son of Remaliah. If you will not believe, you surely shall not last."'" (Isaiah 7:7-9).*

God gives a prophecy to Ahaz. He tells Ahaz what will take place in the future. The threat of Israel and Aram will be short-lived. There is salvation at hand and it will not come by anything that Ahaz can do. The only part that he must play is to believe.

> *Then the LORD spoke again to Ahaz, saying, 11 "Ask a sign for yourself from the LORD your God; make it deep as Sheol or high as heaven." 12 But Ahaz said, "I will not ask, nor will I test the LORD!" (Isaiah 7:10-12).*

The Lord does not call for a "blind faith." Faith is required, but it is a faith that is accompanied by a sign. God offers to put His signature to the promise that He has given. In the case of Ahaz, God even permits Ahaz to choose what the sign shall be. He says, "Ask anything you want. Make it as great a sign as you desire. Make it something whereby the greatness of My strength will be seen." But Ahaz refuses to ask for such a sign. *But Ahaz said, "I will not ask, nor will I test the LORD!"* (Isaiah 7:12).

At first glance, Ahaz seems to be doing a very noble and pious thing. He gives the excuse that he does not want to test the Lord. But that is not a correct response. It is like the man who says, "I do not pray because I do not want to bother God with my problems." Such a stance is the result of a heart of unbelief.

> Then he said, "Listen now, O house of David! Is it too slight a thing for you to try the patience of men, that you will try the patience of my God as well? 14 Therefore the Lord Himself will give you a sign: Behold, a virgin will be with child and bear a son, and she will call His name Immanuel. 15 He will eat curds and honey at the time He knows enough to refuse evil and choose good. 16 For before the boy will know enough to refuse evil and choose good, the land whose two kings you dread will be forsaken. (Isaiah 7:13-14).

There is a "child motif" that runs through this section of Isaiah from chapter 7 to chapter 9 and includes the mention of five different children.

- Shear-jashub (Isaiah 7:3).
- Immanu-el (Isaiah 7:14; 8:8).
- Maher-shalal-hash-baz (Isaiah 8:3).
- Isaiah's children (Isaiah 8:18).
- The Royal Child (Isaiah 9:6-7).

This motif serves as an organizing principle within these chapters. The chapters can be taken and understood as a single unit:

1. The first two stanzas in this unit begin with a historical prologue. The first of these is seen in the beginning of chapter 7; the second is seen in the beginning of chapter 8.

2. The flow of movement takes us on a cycle that begins with a historical prologue and ends in the shadow of the Lord and/or His judgment upon men.

3. The connecting links between the historical sections and the promise of judgments are a series of "child signs." Each child that is mentioned has a special meaning attached to his name that forms a part of the prophecy.

This is a symphony in three parts. The person of Immanu-el

dominates the first two parts, leading to the climactic conclusion that introduces the Royal Son.

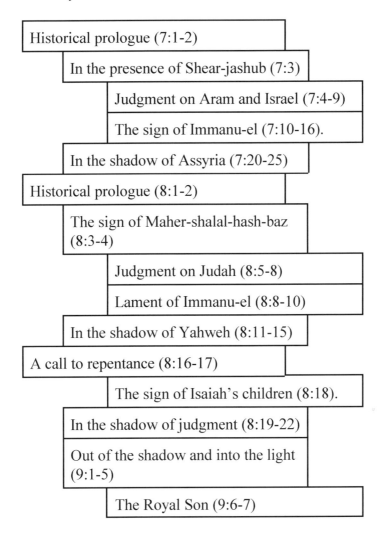

Historical prologue (7:1-2)

In the presence of Shear-jashub (7:3)

Judgment on Aram and Israel (7:4-9)

The sign of Immanu-el (7:10-16).

In the shadow of Assyria (7:20-25)

Historical prologue (8:1-2)

The sign of Maher-shalal-hash-baz (8:3-4)

Judgment on Judah (8:5-8)

Lament of Immanu-el (8:8-10)

In the shadow of Yahweh (8:11-15)

A call to repentance (8:16-17)

The sign of Isaiah's children (8:18).

In the shadow of judgment (8:19-22)

Out of the shadow and into the light (9:1-5)

The Royal Son (9:6-7)

Immanu-el stands out in contrast to the other children in that there is no father mentioned. Even the mother is not named except to refer to her as "the virgin." In this regard, Immanu-el and the Royal Child of chapter 9 are seen to be similar. This same "child motif" is seen in the book of Hosea. This is notable because Hosea is commonly thought to have been a contemporary of Isaiah.

The sign is that a young maiden shall be with child. She shall have a son. He will be called Immanuel. But the prophecy does not end here. It goes on to tell what the sign will signify. The sign has been given for a specific localized reason.

> *He will eat curds and honey at the time He knows*
> *enough to refuse evil and choose good. 16 For before the boy*
> *will know enough to refuse evil and choose good, the land*
> *whose two kings you dread will be forsaken. (Isaiah 7:15-16).*

The sign was not to end with the birth of Immanuel. It was only to begin there. The rest of the sign was that the child would grow and develop into a young boy. Before that boy had reached the age of being able to tell the difference between right and wrong, the kings of both Aram and Israel would die. It would have been a happy story if it could have ended on this note. But that is not the case. Isaiah goes on to give Ahaz a glimpse of things to come.

> *The LORD will bring on you, on your people, and on*
> *your father's house such days as have never come since the*
> *day that Ephraim separated from Judah, the king of Assyria.*
> *18 And it will come about in that day, that the LORD will*
> *whistle for the fly that is in the remotest part of the rivers of*
> *Egypt, and for the bee that is in the land of Assyria. 19 And*
> *they will all come and settle on the steep ravines, on the*
> *ledges of the cliffs, on all the thorn bushes, and on all the*
> *watering places. (Isaiah 7:17-19).*

Because of the sin of Ahaz, both in worshiping the false gods of the Canaanites as well as in demonstrating his unbelief of Yahweh, he is told that the Lord will bring enemies from both Egypt and Assyria who will come and make life miserable for the kingdom of Judah.

I believe that the sign of Immanuel was given as a partial fulfillment in the days of Ahaz. This is seen in the following chapter where Immanuel himself is addressed (Isaiah 8:8). But that is not the end of the story. Even though his name was Immanuel and expressed the truth that God was working in the lives of His people, there remained a further and more complete fulfillment. That fulfillment is seen in the person of Jesus. Matthew 1:22-23 presents to us the truth that Jesus is the ultimate fulfillment of the Immanuel. He is God with us.

It is no mistake that Isaiah used the specific word that he did. The Hebrew word *Almah* (translated "virgin") technically means a "young maiden." Every time it is used in the Old Testament, it describes a young unmarried damsel. What is it about the virgin birth of Christ that is so important?

- Because sin is passed down from the father?

- Because of the supernatural origin of Jesus?
- Because Jesus is God?

No! It is because this was the promised sign. This sign points to the fulfillment of the promise that God would be with us. Jesus is the virgin-born Son who is "God with us." We partake in the presence of God when we receive Him in faith, trusting Him as our Lord and Savior. We apply the message of this passage when we apply the Gospel to our hearts.

ISAIAH 36-39: THE HISTORICAL INTERLUDE

The historical section of Isaiah, found in chapters 36-39, are repeated almost verbatim in 2 Kings 18-20. It may be that the writer of Kings has taken and used the record made by Isaiah.

1 35	36 37	38 39	40 66
Series of messages under the Assyrian struggle	Invasion of Sennacherib of Assyria	Hezekiah without an heir interacts with Babylon	Series of messages looking ahead to the Babylon & Persia
Prophetic Messages	**Historical Section**		Prophetic Visions
Messages of Judgment		Messages of Comfort	

The chronology of the Historical Section is reversed. The events of chapter 38-39 took place before the events of chapter 36-37. Why did Isaiah do this? It was because he wanted to link the historical sections to the two corresponding messages of judgment and of comfort.

ISAIAH 40-66: THE PROMISE OF SALVATION

The latter portion of Isaiah takes on a very different message from that of the first half of this book. The focus moves from God's judgment to God's salvation. It is such a strong contrast that some scholars have theorized that this was penned by a different author, but such a view is not supported within the actual text. This section can be divided into three parts.

They can generally be categorized as follows:

40 48	49 59	60 66
Under the Shadow of Mesopotamia	The Servant of the Lord	Future Glory
Focus on Israel returning to the Land	Focus on Messiah as Suffering Servant	Focus on new Heaven and Earth
Redemption Promised	Redemption Provided	Redemption Realized

These divisions are not clear-cut. The themes found therein are often interrelated as the major themes of comfort and the good news of the coming of the Lord are presented.

THE LIFE OF CHRIST AS SEEN IN ISAIAH

Isaiah presents an extensive portrait of the Messiah. Only the book of Psalms gives us more in the way of prophecy and Isaiah is unsurpassed for its rich details.

- Virgin Birth: *Therefore the Lord Himself will give you a sign: Behold, a virgin will be with child and bear a son, and she will call His name Immanuel* (Isaiah 7:14).
- His titles of deity and kingship: *For a child will be born to us, a son will be given to us; And the government will rest on His shoulders; And His name will be called Wonderful Counselor, Mighty God, Eternal Father, Prince of Peace* (Isaiah 9:6).
- His ministry in Galilee: *But there will be no more gloom for her who was in anguish; in earlier times He treated the land of Zebulun and the land of Naphtali with contempt, but later on He shall make it glorious, by the way of the sea, on the other side of Jordan, Galilee of the Gentiles. 2 The people who walk in darkness will see a great light; those who live in a dark land, the light will shine on them.* (Isaiah 9:1-2).
- He shall be a descendant of Jesse: *Then a shoot will spring from the stem of Jesse, And a branch from his roots will bear fruit* (Isaiah 11:1).
- He will be anointed by the Holy Spirit: *And the Spirit of the Lord will rest on Him, The spirit of wisdom and understanding, The spirit of*

counsel and strength, The spirit of knowledge and the fear of the Lord (Isaiah 11:2).

- He will bring a message of salvation: *The Spirit of the Lord God is upon me, because the Lord has anointed me to bring good news to the afflicted; He has sent me to bind up the brokenhearted, to proclaim liberty to captives, and freedom to prisoners; 2 to proclaim the favorable year of the Lord, and the day of vengeance of our God; to comfort all who mourn* (Isaiah 61:1-2).

- He shall be a teacher of grace whose message shall go to the nations: *Behold, My Servant, whom I uphold; My chosen one in whom My soul delights. I have put My Spirit upon Him; He will bring forth justice to the nations. 2 He will not cry out or raise His voice, nor make His voice heard in the street. 3 A bruised reed He will not break, and a dimly burning wick He will not extinguish; He will faithfully bring forth justice. 4 He will not be disheartened or crushed, until He has established justice in the earth; And the coastlands will wait expectantly for His law.* (Isaiah 42:1-4).

- The physical beating that would be given Him: *Just as many were astonished at you, My people, so His appearance was marred more than any man, and His form more than the sons of men* (Isaiah 52:14).

- He would be pierced for our sins: *But He was pierced through for our transgressions, He was crushed for our iniquities; The chastening for our well-being fell upon Him, And by His scourging we are healed* (Isaiah 53:5).

- He would take our sins upon Himself: *All of us like sheep have gone astray, each of us has turned to his own way; but the Lord has caused the iniquity of us all To fall on Him* (Isaiah 53:6).

- He would remain silent throughout His sufferings rather than speaking out in His own defense: *He was oppressed and He was afflicted, yet He did not open His mouth; like a lamb that is led to slaughter, and like a sheep that is silent before its shearers, so He did not open His mouth* (Isaiah 53:7).

- His death would be associated both with wicked men and with a rich man: *His grave was assigned with wicked men, yet He was with a rich man in His death, because He had done no violence, nor was there any deceit in His mouth* (Isaiah 53:9).

JEREMIAH
The Weeping Prophet

Jeremiah has been known as the "weeping prophet." It isn't that he was a crybaby. It is that he loved his countrymen and saw what they were going through and it brought him to tears. We also read in the Bible that Jesus wept (John 11:35). There is a lesson here. It is that God calls us to be involved in the lives of people. That implies an emotional involvement.

Jeremiah is the largest book of the Bible. Though the Psalms have more chapters, they are not generally as long as those found within the book of Jeremiah.

Jeremiah lived at the time of the fall of Jerusalem and this is his primary topic. His book is arranged in a chiastic format that places the fall of Jerusalem at the very center and then gives a second account of that same fall of the city as its conclusion.

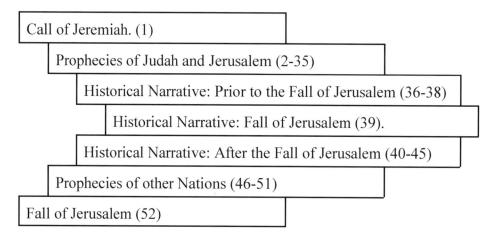

Call of Jeremiah. (1)

Prophecies of Judah and Jerusalem (2-35)

Historical Narrative: Prior to the Fall of Jerusalem (36-38)

Historical Narrative: Fall of Jerusalem (39).

Historical Narrative: After the Fall of Jerusalem (40-45)

Prophecies of other Nations (46-51)

Fall of Jerusalem (52)

The Author

Jeremiah introduces himself as the author of this book at the very outset.

> *The words of Jeremiah, the son of Hilkiah, of the priests who were in Anathoth in the land of Benjamin, 2 to whom the word of the Lord came in the days of Josiah, the son of Amon, king of Judah, in the thirteenth year of his reign. (Jeremiah 1:1-2).*

From this introduction we can see that Jeremiah was "of the priests." We have already noted the difference between the office of the priests versus that of prophet. A prophet went to the people about God. A priest went to God about the people. Jeremiah did both.

JEREMIAH CONTRASTED WITH ISAIAH

Isaiah	Jeremiah
Saw the Northern Kingdom of Israel taken into Captivity at the hands of Assyria	Saw the Southern Kingdom of Judah taken into Captivity at the hands of Babylon
Isaiah foretold of the judgments that would come in the future	Jeremiah explained the reasons for the judgments that Judah was experiencing
Looks primarily to the future	Looks primarily to the present
Bold and fearless	Gentle and compassionate
Was married to a prophetess and had children with prophetic names	Was commanded not to take a wife or have any children

HISTORICAL SETTING

Jeremiah was a man of his times. You cannot understand the message of Jeremiah apart from an understanding of the world in which he lived. This setting is described in the first three verses of the book.

> *The words of Jeremiah, the son of Hilkiah, of the priests who were in Anathoth in the land of Benjamin, 2 to whom the word of the Lord came in the days of Josiah, the son of Amon, king of Judah, in the thirteenth year of his reign. 3 It came also in the days of Jehoiakim, the son of Josiah, king of Judah, until the end of the eleventh year of Zedekiah, the son of Josiah, king of Judah, until the exile of Jerusalem in the fifth month. (Jeremiah 1:1-3).*

These were tumultuous times for the tiny kingdom of Judah. It was a time of clashing empires and of world unrest as nations rose and fell. For those in Judah, it was a period that began with a bright beacon of hope as Josiah came on the scene.

1.   Josiah's Reforms.

Jeremiah's ministry began during the days of good king Josiah. Josiah was the last of the good kings of Judah. When he came to the throne as an 8-year old child, the worship of Yahweh had been all but forgotten. The Temple lay in disarray. The sacrifices were no longer offered. He ordered that they begin again and that the Temple be reopened.

As the Temple was put back in order, a copy of the Scriptures were found. It may well have been the book of Deuteronomy. These writings were brought to the king and he read them. He read the blessings and the curses of the law that were promised to those who obeyed and to those who broke the covenant. He quickly recognized what had taken place in Judah.

Josiah led the nation back to the Lord in repentance. He ordered that the temples to pagan gods be destroyed and he put a stop to the popular ritual prostitution cult and the child sacrifices. Because of his faithfulness, the Lord promised that He would withhold the destruction of Judah until after Josiah had died.

2.   The Fall of Assyria.

There was a new power growing in the east. It came from Babylon. The new Chaldean king Nabopolassar and his son Nebuchadnezzar formed a coalition of nations that banded together to attack Assyria.

- The Chaldeans
- The Medes
- The Scythians

In 612 B.C. this coalition sacked Nineveh, the capital city of Assyria. The remnants of the Assyrian army fled westward.

3.   Pharaoh Necho and the Battle of Megiddo.

With Nineveh fallen, the neighboring kingdoms surged forward to fill the power vacuum that was left. One such kingdom was Egypt. Pharaoh Necho II was the leading monarch of the 26th dynasty and he set forth to claim his share of the spoils. While en route, he sent for permission from Josiah to pass through the land of Israel.

> *After all this, when Josiah had set the temple in order, Neco king of Egypt came up to make war at Carchemish on the Euphrates, and Josiah went out to engage him. 21 But Neco sent messengers to him, saying, "What have we to do with each other, O King of Judah? I am not coming against you today but against the house with which I am at war, and God has ordered me to hurry. Stop for your own sake from interfering with God who is with me, that He may not destroy you."*
>
> *However, Josiah would not turn away from him, but disguised himself in order to make war with him; nor did he listen to the words of Neco from the mouth of God, but came to make war on the plain of Megiddo. 23 And the archers shot King Josiah, and the king said to his servants, "Take me away, for I am badly wounded." 24 So his servants took him out of the chariot and carried him in the second chariot which he had, and brought him to Jerusalem where he died and was buried in the tombs of his fathers. And all Judah and Jerusalem mourned for Josiah. (2 Chronicles 35:20-24).*

Josiah refused permission to Pharaoh Necho to pass through the land. Their armies met on the plain of Megiddo. There was in that day a narrow mountain pass that ran into this valley. The valley is known today by its more popular name of Armageddon. It was there that Josiah met his end.

It may well be that it is this event that gave rise to the later symbolism used by John in the book of Revelation. It is a symbol for a great and decisive conflict.

4.   The Descendants of Josiah.

Following the death of Josiah, the people of Israel placed Jehoahaz on the throne of Judah. His reign was to be short-lived, for Necho of Egypt moved in to place a king of his own choosing in

577

Judah. For this position he selected another of Josiah's sons.

Jehoahaz	Installed by the Israelites after Josiah's death	Removed by Pharaoh Necho after only 3 months
Eliakim (Jehoiakim)	Set on the throne by Necho	Reigned for 11 years and deposed by Nebuchadnezzar
Jehoiachin (Coniah)	Son of Jehoiakim set on throne by Jews	Nebuchadnezzar removed him after only 3 months
Zedekiah	Youngest son of Josiah put on throne by Nebuchadnezzar	Reigned 11 years before being taken by Nebuchadnezzar

5.   The Battle of Carchemish.

Pharaoh Necho had insisted that is that it was the Lord who had called him to go to war. We learn from Jeremiah that there may have been some truth to these words:

> *The Lord of hosts, the God of Israel, says, "Behold, I am going to punish Amon of Thebes, and Pharaoh, and Egypt along with her gods and her kings, even Pharaoh and those who trust in him. 26 And I shall give them over to the power of those who are seeking their lives, even into the hand of Nebuchadnezzar king of Babylon and into the hand of his officers. Afterwards, however, it will be inhabited as in the days of old," declares the Lord. (Jeremiah 46:25-26).*

The Lord had indeed called Egypt to come up and fight against Nebuchadnezzar. This calling was given in order to punish Egypt. The two armies met at a place called Carchemish. In one of the most famous land battles of the ancient world, Nebuchadnezzar defeated the Egyptian armies.

6.   Nebuchadnezzar's First Deportation.

Nebuchadnezzar's conquests eventually brought him southward to Judah. He took Jerusalem in the third year of Jehoiakim. Jehoiakim was permitted to remain upon the throne of Jerusalem as a vassal to Nebuchadnezzar, but as a guarantee of his good behavior, a number of the young Jewish nobility were taken as royal hostages to Babylon. Among their number were Daniel and his three friends, Shadrach, Meshach and Abed-nego.

7. Jehoiakim and Jeremiah (Jeremiah 36).

> *And it came about in the fourth year of Jehoiakim the son of Josiah, king of Judah, that this word came to Jeremiah from the Lord, saying, 2 "Take a scroll and write on it all the words which I have spoken to you concerning Israel, and concerning Judah, and concerning all the nations, from the day I first spoke to you, from the days of Josiah, even to this day. 3 Perhaps the house of Judah will hear all the calamity which I plan to bring on them, in order that every man will turn from his evil way; then I will forgive their iniquity and their sin." (Jeremiah 36:1-3).*

The Lord speaks to Jeremiah and instructs that a scroll is to be prepared that documents all of the prophecies that God has given against Judah. The reason for this is that the nation might be brought to repentance.

> *Then Jeremiah called Baruch the son of Neriah, and Baruch wrote at the dictation of Jeremiah all the words of the Lord, which He had spoken to him, on a scroll. (Jeremiah 36:4).*

The use of a scribe was normal for that day. Jeremiah uses a scribe named Baruch the son of Neriah. One of the significant finds that archaeologists have unearthed is a clay signet seal belonging to Baruch the son of Neriah dating to this period. It could well be that this is the same man who served as the scribe to Jeremiah. Once the scroll is written, Jeremiah instructs Barach to go and read the scroll to those who have gathered in the Temple.

> *Now it came about in the fifth year of*

Jehoiakim the son of Josiah, king of Judah, in the ninth month, that all the people in Jerusalem and all the people who came from the cities of Judah to Jerusalem proclaimed a fast before the Lord. 10 Then Baruch read from the book the words of Jeremiah in the house of the Lord in the chamber of Gemariah the son of Shaphan the scribe, in the upper court, at the entry of the New Gate of the Lord's house, to all the people. (Jeremiah 36:9-10).

Word of the scroll soon gets back to King Jehoiakim and the scroll is brought to him to be read in his presence.

Now the king was sitting in the winter house in the ninth month, with a fire burning in the brazier before him. 23 And it came about, when Jehudi had read three or four columns, the king cut it with a scribe's knife and threw it into the fire that was in the brazier, until all the scroll was consumed in the fire that was in the brazier. 24 Yet the king and all his servants who heard all these words were not afraid, nor did they rend their garments. (Jeremiah 36:22-24).

Instead of repentance, the king responded with an act of open defiance and contempt for the prophetic warning.

Then the word of the Lord came to Jeremiah after the king had burned the scroll and the words which Baruch had written at the dictation of Jeremiah, saying, 28 "Take again another scroll and write on it all the former words that were on the first scroll which Jehoiakim the king of Judah burned. 29 And concerning Jehoiakim king of Judah you shall say, 'Thus says the Lord, "You have burned this scroll, saying, 'Why have you written on it that the king of Babylon shall certainly come and destroy this land, and shall make man and beast to cease from it? 30 Therefore thus says the Lord concerning Jehoiakim king of Judah, "He shall have no one to sit on the throne of David, and his dead body shall be cast out to the heat of the day and the frost of the night. 31 I shall also punish him and his descendants and his servants for their iniquity, and I shall bring on them and the inhabitants of Jerusalem and the men of Judah all the calamity that I have declared to them-- but they did not listen."'" (Jeremiah 36:27-31).

Because of the continued rebellion of Jehoiakim, not only would Jerusalem be destroyed, but also Jehoiakim himself would be punished so that his descendants would not be permitted to sit upon the throne of David.

7.   Jehoiakim's End.

> *Jehoiakim was twenty-five years old when he became king, and he reigned eleven years in Jerusalem; and he did evil in the sight of the Lord his God. 6 Nebuchadnezzar king of Babylon came up against him and bound him with bronze chains to take him to Babylon. 7 Nebuchadnezzar also brought some of the articles of the house of the Lord to Babylon and put them in his temple at Babylon. (2 Chronicles 36:5-7).*

The Bible is not specific to tell us how Jehoiakim died. Josephus relates the Jewish tradition that he was put to death in Babylon and that his corpse was cast out upon the fields to be picked over by scavengers.

8.   Jehoiachin and the Second Deportation (2 Kings 24:8-16).

With Jehoiakim taken away by Nebuchadnezzar, his son Jehoiachin now came to the throne. He is known by several different names:

- Jehoiachin
- Jeconiah
- Coniah

His reign was to be a brief one. He reigned for three months and 10 days. Apparently his ascension to the throne was in itself an act of rebellion against Nebuchadnezzar, for it brought a quick siege against the city of Jerusalem.

Jehoiachin was eighteen years old when he became king, and he reigned three months in Jerusalem; and his mother's name was Nehushta the daughter of Elnathan of Jerusalem. 9 And he did evil in the sight of the Lord, according to all that his father had done.

10 At that time the servants of Nebuchadnezzar king of Babylon went up to Jerusalem, and the city came under siege. 11 And Nebuchadnezzar the king of Babylon came to the city, while his servants were besieging it. 12 And Jehoiachin the king of Judah went out to the king of Babylon, he and his mother and his servants and his captains and his officials. So the king of Babylon took him captive in the eighth year of his reign. 13 And he carried out from there all the treasures of the house of the Lord, and the treasures of the king's house, and cut in pieces all the vessels of gold which Solomon king of Israel had made in the temple of the Lord, just as the Lord had said.

14 Then he led away into exile all Jerusalem and all the captains and all the mighty men of valor, ten thousand captives, and all the craftsmen and the smiths. None remained except the poorest people of the land. 15 So he led Jehoiachin away into exile to Babylon; also the king's mother and the king's wives and his officials and the leading men of the land, he led away into exile from Jerusalem to Babylon. 16 And all the men of valor, seven thousand, and the craftsmen and the smiths, one thousand, all strong and fit for war, and these the king of Babylon brought into exile to Babylon. (2 Kings 24:8-16).

Jerusalem fell in 597 B.C. and Jehoiachin as well as all of the nobility and the warriors and the craftsmen of Judah were taken into captivity. Among these captives was the prophet Ezekiel. Only the poorest of the poor were left in the land.

9.   Zedekiah and Jeremiah (Jeremiah 27:1-11).

Before leaving Jerusalem, Nebuchadnezzar placed the youngest son of Josiah upon the throne of Judah to rule over those who had been left behind. His name was Mattaniah, but Nebuchadnezzar changed it to Zedekiah. At the very outset of his reign, Jeremiah prophesies and warns Zedekiah against attempting rebellion.

In the beginning of the reign of Zedekiah the son of Josiah, king of Judah, this word came to Jeremiah from the Lord, saying-- 2 thus says the Lord to me-- "Make for yourself bonds and yokes and put them on your neck, 3 and send word to the king of Edom, to the king of Moab, to the king of the sons of Ammon, to the king of Tyre, and to the king of Sidon by the messengers who come to Jerusalem to Zedekiah king of Judah. 4 And command them to go to their masters, saying, 'Thus says the Lord of hosts, the God of Israel, thus you shall say to your masters, 5 "I have made the earth, the men and the beasts which are on the face of the earth by My great power and by My outstretched arm, and I will give it to the one who is pleasing in My sight. 6 And now I have given all these lands into the hand of Nebuchadnezzar king of Babylon, My servant, and I have given him also the wild animals of the field to serve him. 7 And all the nations shall serve him, and his son, and his grandson, until the time of his own land comes; then many nations and great kings will make him their servant. 8 And it will be, that the nation or the kingdom which will not serve him, Nebuchadnezzar king of Babylon, and which will not put its neck under the yoke of the king of Babylon, I will punish that nation with the sword, with famine, and with pestilence," declares the Lord, "until I have destroyed it by his hand.

9 "But as for you, do not listen to your prophets, your diviners, your dreamers, your soothsayers, or your sorcerers, who speak to you, saying, 'You shall not serve the king of Babylon.' 10 For they prophesy a lie to you, in order to remove you far from your land; and I will drive you out, and you will perish. 11 But the nation which will bring its neck under the yoke of the king of Babylon and serve him, I will let remain on its land," declares the Lord, "and they will till it and dwell in it." "' (Jeremiah 27:1-11).

Instead of heeding the warning of Jeremiah, Zedekiah allows himself to be swayed into entering a rebellious treaty with Egypt against Babylon. Nebuchadnezzar was furious. He marched back to Jerusalem and beseiged the city.

> *Meanwhile, Pharaoh's army had set out from Egypt; and when the Chaldeans who had been besieging Jerusalem heard the report about them, they lifted the siege from Jerusalem.*
> *Then the word of the Lord came to Jeremiah the prophet, saying, 7 "Thus says the Lord God of Israel, 'Thus you are to say to the king of Judah, who sent you to Me to inquire of Me: "Behold, Pharaoh's army which has come out for your assistance is going to return to its own land of Egypt. 8 The Chaldeans will also return and fight against this city, and they will capture it and burn it with fire."'" (Jeremiah 37:5-8).*

Because of the unpopularity of this message, Jeremiah was arrested as a traitor to the Jews and thrown into prison. Meanwhile Nebuchadnezzar quickly set the Egyptians to route and was soon back to surrounding the city of Jerusalem. Jeremiah advised surrender and for this he was taken and thrown down into a cistern, a deep pit full of mud.

> *Then they took Jeremiah and cast him into the cistern of Malchijah the king's son, which was in the court of the guardhouse; and they let Jeremiah down with ropes. Now in the cistern there was no water but only mud, and Jeremiah sank into the mud. (Jeremiah 38:6).*

A eunuch intercedes on Jeremiah's behalf and once more he is brought before the king. Again he advises Zedekiah to surrender and again Zedekiah refuses.

10.　　The Third Deportation to Babylon (Jeremiah 39).

> *Now it came about when Jerusalem was captured in the ninth year of Zedekiah king of Judah, in the tenth month, Nebuchadnezzar king of Babylon*

and all his army came to Jerusalem and laid siege to it; 2 in the eleventh year of Zedekiah, in the fourth month, in the ninth day of the month, the city wall was breached. (Jeremiah 39:1-2).

Jerusalem was taken after an extensive siege -- that seems to be the period described in verses 1-2.

Then all the officials of the king of Babylon came in and sat down at the Middle Gate: Nergal-sar-ezer, Samgar-nebu, Sar-sekim the Rab-saris, Nergal-sar-ezer the Rab-mag, and all the rest of the officials of the king of Babylon.

4 And it came about, when Zedekiah the king of Judah and all the men of war saw them, that they fled and went out of the city at night by way of the king's garden through the gate between the two walls; and he went out toward the Arabah.

5 But the army of the Chaldeans pursued them and overtook Zedekiah in the plains of Jericho; and they seized him and brought him up to Nebuchadnezzar king of Babylon at Riblah in the land of Hamath, and he passed sentence on him. 6 Then the king of Babylon slew the sons of Zedekiah before his eyes at Riblah; the king of Babylon also slew all the nobles of Judah. 7 He then blinded Zedekiah's eyes and bound him in fetters of bronze to bring him to Babylon. (Jeremiah 39:3-7).

The last thing that Zedekiah ever saw was the sight of his own sons being put to death. Then he was blinded and taken in chains back to Babylon.

The Chaldeans also burned with fire the king's palace and the houses of the people, and they broke down the walls of Jerusalem. 9 And as for the rest of the people who were left in the city, the deserters who had gone over to him and the rest of the people who remained, Nebuzaradan the captain of the bodyguard carried them into exile in Babylon. (Jeremiah 39:8-9).

The Temple was burned to the ground along with the palace of the king. The walls of the city were pulled down and the city of Jerusalem effectively ceased to exist. The survivors were rounded up and hauled away to Babylon. Jeremiah was set free and offered a place to stay in Babylon. He instead chose to remain in Judah.

11.   Gedeliah and the Final Rebellion.

Now that all claimants to the throne of Judah had been effectively removed, Nebuchadnezzar appointed Gedaliah to be the governor of that land. Since Jerusalem was now only a ruin, Gedaliah set up his government at Mizpah. This government was short-lived, for it was not long before still another insurrection had sprung up. Gedeliah was murdered along with the rest of his officers.

Fearing the wrath of Babylon, the inhabitants of the land determine to flee to Egypt. Jeremiah warns against this decision and urges them to remain in the land. Ultimately they flee to Egypt, taking Jeremiah with them.

OUTLINE OF THE BOOK

Chpt 1	Chpt 2-20	Chpt 21-45	Chpt 46-51	Chpt 52
Prologue	From Josiah to the first year of Nebuchadnezzar	From Josiah's sons to the Captivity	Oracles for the Nations	Epilogue
Call of Jeremiah				Fall of Jerusalem
	Judgment against Judah		Nations	

The book of Jeremiah can be divided into two major portions. The first part deals primarily with judgments against Judah. The second part gives oracles against the other nations.

THE CALL OF JEREMIAH

Now the word of the Lord came to me saying, 5 "Before I formed you in the womb I knew you, And before you were born I consecrated you; I have appointed you a prophet to the nations."

6 Then I said, "Alas, Lord God! Behold, I do not know

how to speak, Because I am a youth."

7 But the Lord said to me, "Do not say, 'I am a youth,' Because everywhere I send you, you shall go, and all that I command you, you shall speak. 8 Do not be afraid of them, for I am with you to deliver you," declares the Lord. (Jeremiah 1:4-8).

Jeremiah's call did not begin with Jeremiah. It began with the Lord. Jeremiah was set apart by the Lord for a special purpose and a special ministry. He was appointed as a prophet to the nations. The scope of his prophecies would be directed, not only toward Judah, but also to the rest of the nations.

Jeremiah has been known as "the weeping prophet," but at the outset, he was also a timid prophet. His ministry started when he was a young man and he thought himself too young. The Lord responds by saying, "Your ministry started when you were even younger than you think -- it started before you were even born."

9 Then the Lord stretched out His hand and touched my mouth, and the Lord said to me, "Behold, I have put My words in your mouth. 10 See, I have appointed you this day over the nations and over the kingdoms, to pluck up and to break down, to destroy and to overthrow, to build and to plant." (Jeremiah 1:9-10).

Jeremiah is thus given the authority and the ability to speak God's words. His message will not merely be his own opinion, but rather will come from God. To confirm his calling, Jeremiah is given two brief visions:

1.   Vision of the Almond Rod.

And the word of the Lord came to me saying, "What do you see, Jeremiah?" And I said, "I see a rod of an almond tree." 12 Then the Lord said to me, "You have seen well, for I am watching over My word to perform it." (Jeremiah 1:11-12).

The first vision that Jeremiah sees is a rod. The rod is from the wood of an almond tree. There is a play on words here, for the word for almond tree (שָׁקֵד) is a homonym for the word translated "I am watching" (שֹׁקֵד) in verse 12.

The point is that the events taking place in the days of

Jeremiah are not an indication that God has gone on vacation. He is watching and He is involved in history and He is bringing His word to fulfillment.

2.   Vision of the Boiling Pot.

> *And the word of the Lord came to me a second time saying, "What do you see?" And I said, "I see a boiling pot, facing away from the north."* 14 *Then the Lord said to me, "Out of the north the evil will break forth on all the inhabitants of the land." (Jeremiah 1:13-14).*

The judgments of God had been simmering for a long time, but now they were coming to a boil. Jeremiah sees a boiling pot. It is from the north. It is about to boil over everyone living in the land.

REASON FOR THE JUDGMENT

> *"Has a nation changed gods,*
> *When they were not gods?*
> *But My people have changed their glory*
> *For that which does not profit.*
> 12 *Be appalled, O heavens, at this,*
> *And shudder, be very desolate," declares the Lord.*
> 13 *"For My people have committed two evils:*
> *They have forsaken Me,*
> *The fountain of living waters,*
> *To hew for themselves cisterns,*
> *Broken cisterns,*
> *That can hold no water." (Jeremiah 2:11-13).*

Here is the basis for judgment against Judah. It is because the people of God had done something that was unheard of, even among pagans. They had departed from the God of their fathers.

This is described in the symbolic terms of a cistern. A cistern was a large opening normally carved out of rock. It was designed to catch water to see people through the dry season. Some of these rock-hewn cisterns could be huge. The problem would come if the cistern cracked. All of the water would leak out. This is contrasted with the concept of "living waters." This was a reference to moving waters that would flow in the form of a stream.

The departure of the Jews from the Lord was tantamount to leaving a never-ending source of flowing water to obtain broken cisterns from which all the water had long since leaked out.

In chapter 5, the Lord instructs Jeremiah to go on a quest. He is to go up and down the streets of Jerusalem in search of a righteous man.

> *Roam to and fro through the streets of Jerusalem,*
> *And look now, and take note.*
> *And seek in her open squares,*
> *If you can find a man,*
> *If there is one who does justice, who seeks truth,*
> *Then I will pardon her. (Jeremiah 5:1).*

In the book of Genesis, Abraham had asked God to spare Sodom and Gomorrah if there were ten righteous people in the cities. Jeremiah is told that Jerusalem will be spared if there is a single righteous man. The fact that Jerusalem is ultimately destroyed is in itself an indictment against the sinfulness of the city.

> *"Behold, I am bringing a nation against you from afar,*
> *O house of Israel," declares the Lord.*
> *"It is an enduring nation,*
> *It is an ancient nation,*
> *A nation whose language you do not know,*
> *Nor can you understand what they say.*
> *16 Their quiver is like an open grave,*
> *All of them are mighty men.*
> *17 And they will devour your harvest and your food;*
> *They will devour your sons and your daughters;*
> *They will devour your flocks and your herds;*
> *They will devour your vines and your fig trees;*
> *They will demolish with the sword your fortified cities in*
> *which you trust." (Jeremiah 5:15-17).*

The nation which is destined to come up against Judah is Babylon. The Babylonians are described here as those who devour. Over the next few years, the armies of Babylon would come and gobble up the kingdom of Judah, taking its people away into captivity. Jeremiah goes on to foretell that this captivity would last for a period of seventy years.

PROPHECY OF SEVENTY YEARS

For thus says the Lord,
"When seventy years have been completed for Babylon,
I will visit you and fulfill
My good word to you, to bring you back to this place.
11 For I know the plans that I have for you," declares the
Lord, "plans for welfare and not for calamity to give you a
future and a hope. 12 Then you will call upon Me and come
and pray to Me, and I will listen to you. 13 And you will seek
Me and find Me, when you search for Me with all your
heart." (Jeremiah 29:10-13).

The themes of deportation and restoration had been a familiar one in the prophets prior to the exile. But now for the first time, the Lord sets forth what is to be the duration of the deportation. It is to be a period of 70 years.

This period is explained briefly in a passage from 2 Chronicles that alludes to the prophecy of Jeremiah. In chapter 36 of that book, we read of Nebuchadnezzar's taking of Jerusalem into captivity *to fulfill the word of the Lord by the mouth of Jeremiah, until the land had enjoyed its Sabbaths. All the days of its desolation it kept Sabbath until seventy years were complete (2 Chronicles 36:21).*

Under the terms of the Mosaic Law, every seventh year, the Jews were required to allow the land a time of rest. A part of their rebellion had been to ignore the Sabbatical Law, so the Lord says in effect, "I am going to impose a rest upon the land by taking you out of the land."

The following chart indicates how this 70 year Captivity can be seen to have two separate applications:

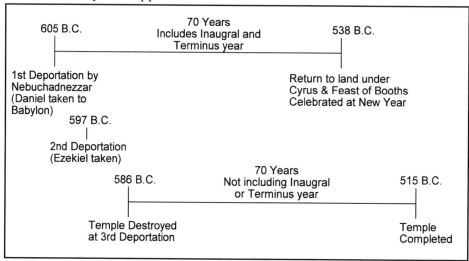

THE FIELD OF HANAMEL

> *And Jeremiah said, "The word of the Lord came to me, saying, 7 'Behold, Hanamel the son of Shallum your uncle is coming to you, saying, "Buy for yourself my field which is at Anathoth, for you have the right of redemption to buy it."'"* (Jeremiah 32:6-7).

What is so unusual about this purchase is that it is made at a time when Nebuchadnezzar was besieging Jerusalem. That is not a time when you are normally looking at rising real estate costs. But the Lord tells Jeremiah to take the deed to the property and to seal it up in an earthenware jar for safekeeping, for there will come a time when this land will again have value and prosperity. The Dead Sea Scrolls were discovered in these sorts of earthenware jars. They remind us of the promise of God for a day of restoration.

THE NEW COVENANT

> *"Behold, days are coming," declares the Lord, "when I will make a new covenant with the house of Israel and with the house of Judah, 32 not like the covenant which I made with their fathers in the day I took them by the hand to bring them out of the land of Egypt, My covenant which they broke, although I was a husband to them," declares the Lord. 33 "But this is the covenant which I will make with the house of Israel after those days," declares the Lord, "I will put My law within them, and on their heart I will write it; and I will be their God, and they shall be My people. 34 And they shall not teach again, each man his neighbor and each man his brother, saying, 'Know the Lord,' for they shall all know Me, from the least of them to the greatest of them," declares the Lord, "for I will forgive their iniquity, and their sin I will remember no more." (Jeremiah 31:31-34).*

We have already seen the concept of a covenant introduced in other writings of the prophets. The truth of the Scriptures is that God has entered into a covenant relationship with men. Throughout the book of Jeremiah, the prophet has continually charged the people with being a nation of covenant-breakers. They have transgressed the covenant and have therefore brought the curses of the covenant upon themselves. They are called to repent, but they continue to refuse. Why? Because of an internal problem. Jeremiah has already pointed out this problem:

> *9 The heart is more deceitful than all else*
> *And is desperately sick; Who can understand it?*
> *10 I, the Lord, search the heart, I test the mind,*
> *Even to give to each man according to his ways,*
> *According to the results of his deeds. (Jeremiah 17:9-10).*

Hebrews 8 quotes this passage to show that the New Covenant is better than the Old Covenant. There are four specific reasons why this is so.

> Notice with whom the New Covenant is made. It is made with the same people with whom the Old Covenant was made. It is made with the House of Israel and with the House of Judah. How then are we a part of that covenant? We are a part of that covenant through faith. It is through faith that we become a part of "spiritual Israel."

1.   The New Covenant is Better because it is an Internal Covenant: *I will put My law within them, and on their heart I will write it (31:33).*

The participant in the New Covenant has something that the believer of past ages never had. He has the Holy Spirit living within him. He has the Keeper of the Covenant indwelling him. And that makes a big difference. It means that God has gifted His people in a special way, working from the inside out.

2.   The New Covenant is Better because it in All-Inclusive: *And they shall not teach again, each man his neighbor and each man his brother, saying, 'Know the Lord,' for they shall all know Me, from the least of them to the greatest of them," declares the Lord (31:34).*

The Old Covenant was primarily Jewish in scope. It was focused upon the land of Israel and upon the sacrifices that took place in Jerusalem. If you wanted to enter the Old Covenant and were not Jewish, you had to proselyte to Judaism. This called for circumcision and an adherence to the Law. But this changes with the New Covenant. Even though it is made with the House of Judah and with the House of Israel, it looks outward to the world to invite all men to enter the Kingdom.

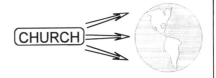

Old Covenant	New Covenant
Jerusalem	CHURCH
Let us go unto the House of the Lord	Go unto all the world and make disciples of all the nations

3.   The New Covenant is Better because it Forgives Sins: *For I will forgive their iniquity, and their sin I will remember no more (31:34).*

The Israelites broke the Old Covenant. God wrote His commands on tablets of stone and when the Israelites disobeyed, Moses took the tablets and shattered them. But the New Covenant is not written upon tablets of stone. It is written in men's hearts. And because it is written in men's hearts, it brings with it the means of fulfilling its obligations. How can you possibly fulfill the obligations of the New Covenant? It is only by trusting in the One who fulfilled them on your behalf. That is what verse 34 says: *For I will forgive their iniquity, and their sin I will remember no more.*

This was the greatest failure of the Old Covenant. It could not forgive sins. It could temporarily cover sins with animal sacrifices that looked forward to a future fulfillment. But the blood of sheep and goats can never take away sin. For this there needed to be a New Covenant relationship.

4.   The New Covenant is Better because is does not become Obsolete.

When He said, "A new covenant," He has made the first obsolete. But whatever is becoming obsolete and growing old is ready to disappear (Hebrews 8:13).

All other things being equal, new is better than old. A new dress versus an old dress. A new loaf of bread is better than an old crusty one. People naturally gravitate to that which is new. The fact that a New Covenant was promised indicates that the Old Covenant would be rendered obsolete.

Notice the tense which the writer uses. It is the present tense.

It denotes continuing action in the present time. As he was writing these words, something was taking place on the horizon that was making the Old Covenant obsolete and which would eventually cause it to disappear. What is this things that was going to happen? It would be the destruction of Jerusalem and its temple. Within a few short years, the Roman legions under General Titus would besiege the city and take it. The temple would be burnt to the ground. And the sacrifices and all of its ceremony and ritual would cease.

The days of the Old Covenant are gone. We are to live by the Spirit, trusting in His power and walking in the light of His teaching. Jesus is the fulfillment of the Law and has brought us into a New Covenant relationship with Himself. Therefore we are called to hold onto Jesus.

LESSONS FROM JEREMIAH

1.   The Lesson of God's Sovereignty.

> *The word which came to Jeremiah from the Lord saying, 2 "Arise and go down to the potter's house, and there I shall announce My words to you." 3 Then I went down to the potter's house, and there he was, making something on the wheel. 4 But the vessel that he was making of clay was spoiled in the hand of the potter; so he remade it into another vessel, as it pleased the potter to make.*
> *5 Then the word of the Lord came to me saying, 6 "Can I not, O house of Israel, deal with you as this potter does?" declares the Lord. "Behold, like the clay in the potter's hand, so are you in My hand, O house of Israel." (Jeremiah 18:1-6).*

The point is made that God as the Creator has every right to do with His creation as He sees fit. He is able to forgive those who repent and He is able to condemn those who do not and nobody can pass judgment on His decisions. He goes on to say that if a nation or a people will repent of their evil, then God will relent of the calamity that He has prophesied to bring upon them.

> *At one moment I might speak concerning a*

> *nation or concerning a kingdom to uproot, to pull down, or to destroy it; 8 if that nation against which I have spoken turns from its evil, I will relent concerning the calamity I planned to bring on it. 9 Or at another moment I might speak concerning a nation or concerning a kingdom to build up or to plant it; 10 if it does evil in My sight by not obeying My voice, then I will think better of the good with which I had promised to bless it. (Jeremiah 18:7-10).*

We have already examined this sort of language under the heading of conditional prophecies. The point is that there is always hope in light of repentance.

2.   The Lesson of God's Justice.

> *Thus says the Lord, "Let not a wise man boast of his wisdom, and let not the mighty man boast of his might, let not a rich man boast of his riches; 24 but let him who boasts boast of this, that he understands and knows Me, that I am the Lord who exercises lovingkindness, justice, and righteousness on earth; for I delight in these things," declares the Lord. (Jeremiah 9:23-24).*

God delights in kindness and in justice and in righteousness. He hates sin. That message comes through loud and clear throughout the book of Jeremiah. God hates sin so much that He sent His own Son to die so that sin and death might be defeated.

3.   The Lesson of God's Grace.

Though Judah had sinned greatly as a covenant-breaker, God repeatedly gave her people opportunities to repent and return to Him. In spite of all their continued rebellion, there remains a promise of hope for the future.

> *"In those days and at that time," declares the Lord, "search will be made for the iniquity of Israel, but there will be none; and for the sins of Judah, but they will not be found; for I shall pardon those whom I leave as a remnant." (Jeremiah 50:20).*

4.   The Lesson of Leadership.

As go the leaders, so also goes the nation. The corollary of this is that nations sometimes are given the leaders that they deserve as a part of His judgment against sin.

> *The prophets prophesy falsely,*
> *And the priests rule on their own authority;*
> *And My people love it so!*
> *But what will you do at the end of it? (Jeremiah 5:31).*

The point is that we should pray for our leaders; both our ecclesiastical leaders as well as the leaders of our nation.

LAMENTATIONS
The Sorrow of Repentance

This is not the most popular book in the Bible. We normally prefer books with happy endings. This is not one of them. It is a book about deep sorrow.

There are five chapters to the book, just as there are five books to the Torah. Unlike most chapter divisions in our English Bible, these chapter divisions find their origin in the Hebrew text. They are evidenced by the fact that each chapter except the last forms an alphabetized acrostic. Thus in chapter 1, the first word of the first verse begins with the Hebrew letter א and then the next verse begins with the letter ב until you have gone through the entire Hebrew alphabet.

Chapter 1	Chapter 2	Chapter 3	Chapter 4	Chapter 5
3rd person plural ("they")		1st person singular ("I")	1st person plural ("we")	
Each verse begins with an acrostic		Each line begins with an acrostic	Each verse begins with an acrostic	No acrostic
Writer addresses himself to his readers				Writer prays to God
Jerusalem is a weeping widow	The Lord's anger has burned against the city	The writer is a man afflicted, yet a man with hope	The plight of the enslaved citizens of the city	A prayer for restoration

AUTHORSHIP

The author of this book is not named. Jewish tradition has it that it was Jeremiah. There is no reason to doubt that this was the case. He is one who weeps over the plight of Jerusalem, yet there is also hope of a future relationship with the Lord.

The author never says, "I told you so." He is not berating the people; instead, he is hurting with the people. One of the marks of a Christian is his compassion. The author of Lamentations demonstrates that kind of compassion. He is not gleeful of the destruction that comes on Jerusalem.

If the author is Jeremiah, and I think that it is, he had every right to say, "I told you so." They ignored everything he told them and they treated him harshly. But instead, we see in this book that he has identified himself with the people of the Captivity. He does not look down his nose at them. Instead he associates himself with the sins of the people.

> *Let us examine and probe our ways,*
> *And let us return to the Lord.*
> *We lift up our heart and hands*
> *Toward God in heaven;*
> *We have transgressed and rebelled,*
> *Thou hast not pardoned (Lamentations 3:40-42).*

Jeremiah was a pastor with a pastor's heart. Even though he was faithful and obedient, he associated himself with the people of God.

It has been noted by scholars that the language of Lamentations is deliberately reflective of the 28th chapter of Deuteronomy.

Lamentations	Deuteronomy 28
She dwells among the nations, But she has found no rest (1:3).	*Among those nations you shall find no rest, and there shall be no resting place for the sole of your foot* (28:65)
Her adversaries have become her masters (literally, "her head" - 1:5).	*He shall be the head, and you shall be the tail* (28:44)
Her little ones have gone away As captives before the adversary (1:5b).	*Your sons and your daughters shall be given to another people* (28:32).
My virgins and my young men Have gone into captivity (1:18).	*You shall have sons and daughters but they shall not be yours, for they shall go into captivity* (28:41).

Should women eat their offspring, The little ones who were born healthy? (2:20).	*You shall eat the offspring of your own body, the flesh of your sons and of your daughters* (28:53).
On the ground in the streets Lie young and old (2:21).	*...a nation of fierce countenance who shall have no respect for the old, nor show favor to the young* (28:50).
We are worn out, There is no rest for us (5:5).	*And among those nations you shall find no rest* (28:65).

LESSONS FROM LAMENTATIONS

1.   God is Sovereign over the Events of Men.

> *Who is there who speaks and it comes to pass,*
> *Unless the Lord has commanded it?*
> *38 Is it not from the mouth of the Most High*
> *That both good and ill go forth? (Lamentations 3:37-38).*

The writer realizes that, even as bad things have taken place and they face great tragedy, God is still in control.

2.   Sin brings forth Tragic Consequences.

> *The joy of our hearts has ceased;*
> *Our dancing has been turned into mourning.*
> *16 The crown has fallen from our head;*
> *Woe to us, for we have sinned! (Lamentations 5:15-16).*

The writer recognizes that the reason for the sorrow, the heartache, and the lament is because of sin. The lie of the devil echoes from Eden: "You shall surely not die. Sin will not bear fruit. It has no lasting consequences. It doesn't matter as long as it is between two consenting adults." But the truth is that sin always bears fruit.

3.   There is Hope in the Darkness.

Remember my affliction and my wandering, the wormwood and bitterness.
20 Surely my soul remembers
And is bowed down within me.
21 This I recall to my mind,
Therefore I have hope.
22 The Lord's lovingkindnesses indeed never cease,
For His compassions never fail.
23 They are new every morning;
Great is Thy faithfulness. (Lamentations 3:19-23).

The writer of this book sees the most bitter afflictions, yet he is able to remember the compassion and the lovingkindness of God. This gives him hope. What is hope? It is faith in the future. It is faith that the God of the past will continue to be faithful in the future.

EZEKIEL
The Prophet-Priest

In the year 622 B.C., the same year that a copy of the Scriptures were found in the temple and brought to King Josiah, a baby was born to a priest named Buzi. He named his son Ezekiel, meaning "God is mighty." The boy grew up in the shadow of the Temple. His father was a priest and it is likely that he was expected to carry on the family tradition.

HISTORICAL BACKGROUND

For a number of years the Assyrian Empire had been in a state of decline. Revolts had sprung up throughout the land, most notably in Babylon and Persia. At the head of these revolts was an aggressive Chaldean prince named Nabopolassar. Finally in 612 B.C. his coalition of Chaldeans, Medes and Scythians took the Assyrian capital city of Nineveh and burned it to the ground.

It was not long before Nabopolassar's armies, led by his son Prince Nebuchadnezzar, turned westward to the lands along the Mediterranean. Challenging his authority was Pharaoh Necho of Egypt. In the middle of these two opposing forces lay the tiny kingdom of Judah.

Against the advice of Jeremiah, King Josiah of Judah marched out to fight against Pharaoh of Necho of Egypt. They met at Megiddo and Josiah was killed in the ensuing battle (2 Chronicles 35:20-24). The death of Josiah left three sons and a grandson to succeed him.

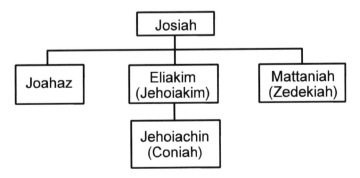

Joahaz was initially made king of Jerusalem, but his reign was short-lived as Pharaoh Necho came into Jerusalem, deposed Joahaz and put his brother Eliakim on the throne in his stead, changing his name to Jehoiakim.

The Egyptians met the army of Nebuchadnezzar at the epic battle of Carchemish and the Egyptians were routed. Nebuchadnezzar came down into Palestine and took Jerusalem, instituting what would be the first of three successive deportations.

First Deportation	603 B.C.	Jehoiakim left in power by Nebuchadnezzar	Sons of nobility including Daniel taken hostage
Second Deportation	597 B.C.	Jehoiakim and Jeconiah both deposed and Zedekiah placed on throne	Nobility, warriors and craftsmen taken
Third Deportation	586 B.C.	Zedekiah deposed and Gedaliah left as governor	All the inhabitants of Jerusalem and the surrounding areas taken

Ezekiel was a part of this second group. They were taken to Mesopotamia and relocated by the River Chebar. This was one of the many canals that crisscross southern Mesopotamia. It is here that our story opens.

COMPARISON WITH OTHER BOOKS OF THE BIBLE

There were three prophets who were all ministering the Word of God during this period.

Jeremiah	Ezekiel	Daniel
His ministry began in the reign of Josiah	His ministry began with the Second Deportation	His ministry began with the First Deportation
The Weeping Prophet	Prophet of Hope	Prophet of the Nations

Main focus upon the land	Main focus upon the land	Main focus on the nations
Prophesied to the Jews of Jerusalem	Prophesied to the Jews by the River Chebar	Prophesied to the Chaldeans in Babylon
Writes from Jerusalem	Writes from Mesopotamia	
-	Mentions Daniel three times	Mentions Jeremiah
Ends with the fall of Jerusalem	Ends with a vision of a future temple	Ends with a promise of future resurrection

Neither Ezekiel nor Daniel began their ministries until after they were deported from Palestine.

Ezekiel	Revelation
Begins with a vision of the chariot-throne of God	Begins with a vision of Christ amidst the lampstands
Four living creatures	Four living creatures
Battle of Gog and Magog	Battle of Gog and Magog
Ends with a vision of the rebuilt Temple	Ends with a vision of the New Jerusalem

When we come to the last few chapters of Ezekiel, we shall see that there is no small correlation between the description of Ezekiel's temple and the description of the New Jerusalem of Revelation 21-22.

Ezekiel has a great deal of drama. Symbolism and drama are given of God. Ezekiel acts out the truths of God in a very vivid and symbolic way. He acts out the realities of what is happening. We are called to do the same thing. We are called to act out the realities of the gospel in our lives. Always witness and when necessary use words. We are living in a post-modern world. The means of communication has changed greatly in my lifetime. It is in such a world that Ezekiel communicates a great deal. Here is the principle. In this day, more than any other time since Biblical times, what we do is more important than what we say.

OVERVIEW OF EZEKIEL

The Book of Ezekiel can be divided into two major parts.
- Message of Judgment (1-32)
- Message of Restoration (33-48)

1:1	25:1	33:1
God's Judgment on Judah	Oracles against the Nations	Oracles of Salvation
Message of Judgment		Message of Restoration

The entire first part of Ezekiel deals with the subject of the judgment of God. This section is divided into two parts:

- Chapters 1-24 deal with the judgment of God against His own people.
- Chapters 25-32 turn to God's judgment against the enemies of His people.

There is a lesson here. It is that when judgment first comes, it begins with the people of God. He judges His own people first. Why is this? It is because His people represent Him on earth and God takes very seriously how He is represented.

> *But I acted for the sake of My name, that it should not be profaned in the sight of the nations among whom they lived, in whose sight I made Myself known to them by bringing them out of the land of Egypt. (Ezekiel 20:9).*

> *But I acted for the sake of My name, that it should not be profaned in the sight of the nations, before whose sight I had brought them out. (Ezekiel 20:14).*

> *But I withdrew My hand and acted for the sake of My name, that it should not be profaned in the sight of the nations in whose sight I had brought them out. (Ezekiel 20:22).*

Three times in this chapter God says that the reason He brings judgment against His people is because He will not allow His name to be profaned in the sight of the nations. He will not allow His name to be associated with sin.

He will not allow pagans to look at the sins of His people and say, "If that is what it means to be a Christian, then I want no part of it."

This is important. When you become a Christian, you take on the official position of an ambassador of Christ. You represent the God of the universe on planet earth. He will not allow you to misrepresent Him.

1:1	God's Judgment on Judah	Ezekiel's Call
3:1		Oracles of Judgment
8:1		Vision of the Temple
12:1		Oracles of Judgment
15:1		Parables and Pictures
20:1		Oracles of Judgment
24:1		Parables and Pictures
25:1	Oracles against the Nations	• Ammon • Moab • Edom • Philistia • Tyre • Sidon • Egypt
33:1	Oracles of Salvation	Ezekiel's call to be a watchman
34:1		Oracles of Restoration
38:1		Gog and Magog
40:1		Vision of the Temple

KEY WORDS AND PHRASES

1.   Son of Man.

        This phrase is found over 90 times in Ezekiel. He uses the phrase to describe himself. By so doing, he is identifying himself with the people to whom he is ministering. You will remember that someone else was also fond of using this title. It was Jesus. He called Himself "Son of Man" almost 90 times in the gospels. He did so for the same reason that Ezekiel did -- to identify himself with mankind.

2.   The Glory of the God of Israel.

This phrase appears 11 times in the first 11 chapters. It tells me something about God. He is interested in His own glory.

CHRONOLOGY OF EZEKIEL

For the most part, the book of Ezekiel is arranged in chronological order. He gives 12 specific chronological references.

Ezekiel's References	Year from Deportation	Modern Date
Ezekiel 1:2	The 5th year	July 593 B.C.
Ezekiel 8:1	The 6th year	September 592 B.C.
Ezekiel 20:1	The 7th year	August 591 B.C.
Ezekiel 24:1	The 9th year	December 588 B.C.
Ezekiel 26:1	The 11th year	February 586 B.C.
Ezekiel 29:1	The 10th year	January 587 B.C.
Ezekiel 29:17	The 27th year	April 571 B.C.
Ezekiel 30:20	The 11th year	April 587 B.C.
Ezekiel 31:1	The 11th year	June 587 B.C.
Ezekiel 32:1	The 12th year	March 585 B.C.
Ezekiel 32:17	The 12th year	March 585 B.C.
Ezekiel 33:21	The 12th year	January 585 B.C.
Ezekiel 40:1	The 25th year	April 573 B.C.

Note: The months are close approximates

EZEKIEL'S CALL

Now it came about in the thirtieth year, on the fifth day of the fourth month, while I was by the river Chebar among the exiles, the heavens were opened and I saw visions of God. (Ezekiel 1:1).

Shortly after Ezekiel's 30th birthday, something happened to him that was to change the course of his life. What follows is the first of many visions. People have come up with all sorts of "space ship" theories regarding the vision of this chapter. It is thought to have served as the impetus for Steven Spielberg's *Close Encounters of the Third Kind* as it portrayed creatures and burning fire and wheels within wheels. Let me set the record straight. This is not a U.F.O. Instead it presents the throne of God in specific temple language.

In reading the description of the artifacts that were located within Solomon's temple, we read of *the altar of incense refined gold by weight; and gold for the model of the **chariot**, even the cherubim, that spread out their wings, and covered the ark of the covenant of the Lord (1 Chronicles 28:18)*.

Similarly, 1 Kings 7:27-33 describes within the Temple *ten stands of bronze*. These stands had on their boarders the images of lions, oxen and cherubim (7:29) as well as *four bronze wheels with bronze axles* (7:30). In verse 33 we are told that *the workmanship of the wheels was like the workmanship of a chariot wheel*. We also remember the vision that Elisha had in 2 Kings 2 of Elijah being caught up in a chariot of fire.

Furthermore, Daniel's vision of the Ancient of Days also speaks of a throne with wheels: *I kept looking until thrones were set up, and the Ancient of Days took His seat; His vesture was like white snow, and the hair of His head like pure wool. His throne was ablaze with flames, its **wheels** were a burning fire (Daniel 7:9)*. What we see in Ezekiel 1 is the chariot throne of God.

> *And as I looked, behold, a storm wind was coming from the north, a great cloud with fire flashing forth continually and a bright light around it, and in its midst something like glowing metal in the midst of the fire. 5 And within it there were figures resembling four living beings. And this was their appearance: they had human form. 6 Each of them had four faces and four wings. 7 And their legs were straight and their feet were like a calf's hoof, and they gleamed like burnished bronze. 8 Under their wings on their four sides were human hands. As for the faces and wings of the four of them, 9 their wings touched one another; their faces did not turn when they moved, each went straight forward. 10 As for the form of their faces, each had the face of a man, all four had the face of a lion on the right and the face of a bull on the left, and all four had the face of an eagle. (Ezekiel 1:4-10).*

If we are at all familiar with the book of Revelation, we shall find the description of this vision to be somewhat familiar.

Ezekiel	Revelation
A storm wind was coming from the north, a great cloud with fire flashing forth continually and a bright light around it, and in its midst something like glowing metal in the midst of the fire (1:4)	And from the throne proceed flashes of lightning and sounds and peals of thunder. And there were seven lamps of fire burning before the throne, which are the seven Spirits of God (4:5).
Figures resembling four living beings • Face of a man • Face of a lion • Face of a bull • Face of an eagle (1:8-10)	Four living creatures full of eyes in front and behind • Like a lion • Like a calf • Face like a man • Flying eagle (4:6-7)
Their wings were spread out above; each had two touching another being, and two covering their bodies (1:11)	Four living creatures, each one of them having six wings (4:8)
In the midst of the living beings there was something that looked like burning coals of fire, like torches darting back and forth among the living beings. The fire was bright, and lightning was flashing from the fire (1:13)	And from the throne proceed flashes of lightning and sounds and peals of thunder. And there were seven lamps of fire burning before the throne, which are the seven Spirits of God (4:5)
Now over the heads of the living beings there was something like an expanse, like the awesome gleam of crystal, extended over their heads (1:22)	Before the throne there was, as it were, a sea of glass like crystal (4:6)

Above the expanse that was over their heads there was something resembling a throne, like lapis lazuli in appearance; and on that which resembled a throne, high up, was a figure with the appearance of a man (1:26)	A throne was standing in heaven, and One sitting on the throne. 3 And He who was sitting was like a jasper stone and a sardius in appearance; and there was a rainbow around the throne, like an emerald in appearance (4:2-3)

There is a very obvious correlation between the visions of Ezekiel and John. They give a mutual testimony to the holiness and the majesty of God. What does it all mean?

- The images of the lion, the calf/bull, the eagle, and the man reflect the truth that God is the God over all life, whether wild animals or domesticated animals or birds or men. When we come to Ezekiel 10:14, we again see this same sight of four distinct images. But this time, there is a difference: *And each one had four faces. The first face was the face of a cherub, the second face was the face of a man, the third the face of a lion, and the fourth the face of an eagle (Ezekiel 10:14)*. This time there is a change. This time we read of a cherub in place of the calf/bull. But the point is still the same. It is that God is the sovereign of all life, whether animals or birds or angels or men.

- The wheels are a picture of the mighty power of God. Remember that the symbol of a chariot was a powerful one. Chariots to that era were what thermonuclear power would be today.

THE COMMISSION OF EZEKIEL

The vision of the glory of God was followed immediately by the commission of Ezekiel to the prophetic ministry.

> *Then He said to me, "Son of man, stand on your feet that I may speak with you!" 2 And as He spoke to me the Spirit entered me and set me on my feet; and I heard Him speaking to me. 3 Then He said to me, "Son of man, I am sending you to the sons of Israel, to a rebellious people who have rebelled against Me; they and their fathers have*

transgressed against Me to this very day." (Ezekiel 2:1-3).

Ezekiel did not have an easy commission. He was being sent to a people who were by nature a rebellious people.

> *As for them, whether they listen or not-- for they are a rebellious house-- they will know that a prophet has been among them. 6 And you, son of man, neither fear them nor fear their words, though thistles and thorns are with you and you sit on scorpions; neither fear their words nor be dismayed at their presence, for they are a rebellious house. 7 But you shall speak My words to them whether they listen or not, for they are rebellious. (Ezekiel 2:5-7).*

There is a lesson that we can learn from this passage. It is the lesson of the sovereignty of success in ministry. We usually think that if we do the right thing and say the right thing that we will have a successful ministry. We think that if our church has the right kind of worship music and if the pastor's sermon isn't too long and if we have a lot of programs, then people will flock to our church. That isn't necessarily so. Jesus said to His disciples, "I will build My church."

He does. He delights in taking a man whom the world considers unqualified and doing a great work through such a man. He says to Ezekiel, "You go out and preach the words that I am going to give you and the result will be that a prophet will have gone out and spoken My words."

It was not Ezekiel's job to build a big church or to convert the people. He is merely called to be faithful in preaching the Word of God. As such, he is likened to a watchman.

> *Son of man, I have appointed you a watchman to the house of Israel; whenever you hear a word from My mouth, warn them from Me. 18 When I say to the wicked, "You shall surely die"; and you do not warn him or speak out to warn the wicked from his wicked way that he may live, that wicked man shall die in his iniquity, but his blood I will require at your hand. 19 Yet if you have warned the wicked, and he does not turn from his wickedness or from his wicked way, he shall die in his iniquity; but you have delivered yourself.*
>
> *20 Again, when a righteous man turns away from his righteousness and commits iniquity, and I place an obstacle before him, he shall die; since you have not warned him, he shall die in his sin, and his righteous deeds which he has done*

shall not be remembered; but his blood I will require at your hand. 21 However, if you have warned the righteous man that the righteous should not sin, and he does not sin, he shall surely live because he took warning; and you have delivered yourself. (Ezekiel 3:17-21).

The responsibility of Ezekiel was not to make people repent. His responsibility was to speak the truth -- to give the warning.

> *"Now you, son of man, listen to what I am speaking to you; do not be rebellious like that rebellious house. Open your mouth and eat what I am giving you."*
> *9 Then I looked, behold, a hand was extended to me; and lo, a scroll was in it. 10 When He spread it out before me, it was written on the front and back; and written on it were lamentations, mourning and woe.*
> *1 Then He said to me, "Son of man, eat what you find; eat this scroll, and go, speak to the house of Israel." 2 So I opened my mouth, and He fed me this scroll. 3 And He said to me, "Son of man, feed your stomach, and fill your body with this scroll which I am giving you." Then I ate it, and it was sweet as honey in my mouth. (Ezekiel 2:8 - 3:3).*

Just as the workings of God in the book of Revelation were represented by a scroll, so also the judgments of God and its resulting lamentations and mournings and woes are represented by a scroll. Just as the scroll of Revelation was written on the inside and on the back, so this one is also written on the front and back.

Ezekiel is given the scroll and told to eat it. What does this represent? It pictures how the word is to become part of his life. Only then will he be able to pass it on to others. There is a lesson here. If the spiritual truths that you teach to others are not a part of your own life, then you have no business trying to pass them on to others.

Ezekiel eats the scroll. It doesn't sound very tasty. After all, it is full of lamentations, mourning and woe. Yet in spite of that, we read that it was sweet as honey in his mouth. There is a sweetness to the word of God, even when it involves those portions of the Scripture that contain the harshest judgments. Why it this the case? Perhaps it is because, after the judgment comes the restoration. There is going to be a lot of judgment in the book of Ezekiel, but at the end will be a message of hope.

ILLUSTRATIONS OF JUDGMENT

Ezekiel is given a number of instructions from the Lord. He is to engage in various activities that will serve as visual object lessons of the Lord and His relationship with His people.

1. Illustration of the Brick: *Now you son of man, get yourself a brick, place it before you, and inscribe a city on it, Jerusalem. 2 Then lay siege against it, build a siege wall, raise up a ramp, pitch camps, and place battering rams against it all around. 3 Then get yourself an iron plate and set it up as an iron wall between you and the city, and set your face toward it so that it is under siege, and besiege it. This is a sign to the house of Israel. (Ezekiel 4:1-3).*

   Ezekiel is instructed to take a brick that shall represent Jerusalem and then to play out the actions of a siege around the city. This is to serve as a sign of the judgment that is about to fall upon the city.

2. Illustration of Lying on his Side: *As for you, lie down on your left side, and lay the iniquity of the house of Israel on it; you shall bear their iniquity for the number of days that you lie on it. 5 For I have assigned you a number of days corresponding to the years of their iniquity, three hundred and ninety days; thus you shall bear the iniquity of the house of Israel. 6 When you have completed these, you shall lie down a second time, but on your right side, and bear the iniquity of the house of Judah; I have assigned it to you for forty days, a day for each year. (Ezekiel 4:4-6).*

   The next object lesson involves Ezekiel lying on first his left side and then later on his right side for a series of days. Once again, we are told what this is to represent. This points to the iniquity of Israel and of Judah. The days specified are representative of years; a day for each year.

   Bible scholars have wrestled with these numbers to see how they fit in with the events of Biblical chronology. A number of solutions have been suggested. Compounding the problem is the fact that the Septuagint replaces the number 390 with 190. Some have thought this to be a friendly assist to help make the text fit into a more obvious timetable. What is the significance of these numbers? They can be understood on the following chart:

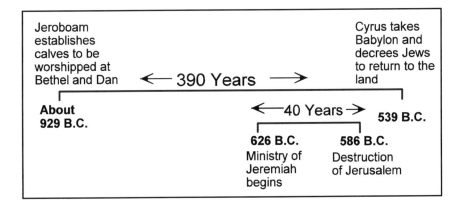

The first number seems to be a reference to the beginning of Jeroboam's establishment of Bethel and Dan as alternate places of worship. Jeroboam came to rule the 10 tribes in 931 B.C. and this action took place in the first few years of his reign.

How then are we to see the 40 year judgment of Judah? On the one hand, the number 40 regularly appears as a number representing judgment (Noah's rain for 40 days and 40 nights; Moses on Mount Sinai for 40 days receiving the Law; the Israelites wandered in the wilderness for 40 years). On the other hand, we see the reigns of several of the godly kings of Judah being of 40 years duration.

- David (1 Kings 2:11).
- Solomon (1 Kings 11:42).
- Jehoash (2 Kings 12:1).
- Joash (2 Chronicles 24:1).

The testing of Judah can be seen in the warnings of the prophets who saw the coming exile. It is perhaps no coincidence that there are 40 years from the beginning of the ministry of Jeremiah to the destruction of Jerusalem in 586 B.C.

3.   Ezekiel's Diet.

The Lord goes on to instruct Ezekiel on how he is to eat a regimented diet that includes barley cakes cooked over dung. The point was to show the awfulness of the judgment that was soon to come upon Jerusalem for her sins.

We read this and we go, "Ughhh." Ezekiel had the same reaction. We are supposed to have this reaction. The point is that God has this reaction to sin.

4.   Ezekiel's Wife.

Later in the book of Ezekiel, we read of where his wife dies. Ezekiel is warned ahead of time of her impending death and is told not to make an outward display of mourning.

> *And the word of the Lord came to me saying,* *16* *"Son of man, behold, I am about to take from you the desire of your eyes with a blow; but you shall not mourn, and you shall not weep, and your tears shall not come.* *17* *Groan silently; make no mourning for the dead. Bind on your turban, and put your shoes on your feet, and do not cover your mustache, and do not eat the bread of men."* *18* *So I spoke to the people in the morning, and in the evening my wife died. And in the morning I did as I was commanded. (Ezekiel 24:15-18).*

The point being made was that, as terrible as it is to lose a beloved wife, it is even more terrible to lose one's relationship with the Lord. When the people ask about the absence of mourning, Ezekiel replies that they will soon be doing the same thing when they see their beloved Jerusalem destroyed. Instead of mourning, the news of that destruction will be such that no amount of mourning will suffice.

THOUGHTS ON SIN'S EFFECTS

> *Then the word of the Lord came to me saying,* *2* *"What do you mean by using this proverb concerning the land of Israel saying, 'The fathers eat the sour grapes, But the children's teeth are set on edge'?* *3* *As I live," declares the Lord God, "you are surely not going to use this proverb in Israel anymore.* *4* *Behold, all souls are Mine; the soul of the father as well as the soul of the son is Mine. The soul who sins will die." (Ezekiel 18:1-4).*

There was a truism in ancient Israel of that day that children often reap the results of the sins of their parents. The idea here was that a parent could escape the effects of sin, but they would eventually catch up with his children. The time for such postponements had reached an end in Ezekiel's day. The judgment that was due the nation was now soon to fall. This does not mean that God takes any particular pleasure or delight in punishing sin.

> *"Do I have any pleasure in the death of the wicked," declares the Lord God, "rather than that he should turn from his ways and live?" (Ezekiel 18:23).*

God does not get His kicks by judging sin. His Spirit grieves over sin. His Son wept openly over the sin of Jerusalem. In the same way, the Lord pleads with His people to repent.

> *"Cast away from you all your transgressions which you have committed, and make yourselves a new heart and a new spirit! For why will you die, O house of Israel? 32 For I have no pleasure in the death of anyone who dies," declares the Lord God. "Therefore, repent and live." (Ezekiel 18:31-32).*

Ezekiel brings a message of repentance and life. This brings us to our next point. It is that Ezekiel is a book about salvation.

EZEKIEL AND THE PROMISE OF SALVATION

The 34th chapter of Ezekiel takes up a "shepherd motif." It begins with a biting indictment against the shepherds of Israel -- those who held positions of responsibility and yet had failed to lead the people in the ways of righteousness.

> *Then the word of the Lord came to me saying, 2 "Son of man, prophesy against the shepherds of Israel. Prophesy and say to those shepherds, 'Thus says the Lord God, "Woe, shepherds of Israel who have been feeding themselves! Should not the shepherds feed the flock? 3 You eat the fat and clothe yourselves with the wool, you slaughter the fat sheep without feeding the flock. 4 Those who are sickly you have not strengthened, the diseased you have not healed, the broken*

you have not bound up, the scattered you have not brought back, nor have you sought for the lost; but with force and with severity you have dominated them. 5 And they were scattered for lack of a shepherd, and they became food for every beast of the field and were scattered." '" (Ezekiel 34:1-5).

The problem is that the shepherds of Israel were fleecing the flock instead of feeding the flock. In the midst of this indictment there is a promise. It is a promise that the Lord Himself shall one day take on the role of a shepherd in order to care for His sheep.

For thus says the Lord God, "Behold, I Myself will search for My sheep and seek them out. 12 As a shepherd cares for his herd in the day when he is among his scattered sheep, so I will care for My sheep and will deliver them from all the places to which they were scattered on a cloudy and gloomy day. 13 And I will bring them out from the peoples and gather them from the countries and bring them to their own land; and I will feed them on the mountains of Israel, by the streams, and in all the inhabited places of the land. 14 I will feed them in a good pasture, and their grazing ground will be on the mountain heights of Israel. There they will lie down in good grazing ground, and they will feed in rich pasture on the mountains of Israel. 15 I will feed My flock and I will lead them to rest," declares the Lord God. 16 "I will seek the lost, bring back the scattered, bind up the broken, and strengthen the sick; but the fat and the strong I will destroy. I will feed them with judgment." (Ezekiel 34:11-16).

Notice that the Lord as Shepherd does not come to save the fat and the strong. Those who are self sufficient are destroyed and become partakers of judgment. It is those who recognize their own brokenness and sickness who shall be saved.

This promise is fulfilled in Jesus Christ. He is the Good Shepherd who came to give His life for the sheep. In verse 15 we see the essence of His ministry:

"I will feed My flock and I will lead them to rest," declares the Lord God. (Ezekiel 34:15).

Jesus said this of Himself. He is the One who said, "Come to me, all you who labor, and I will give you rest (Matthew 11:28). But that is not all. Ezekiel goes on to describe the eventual judgment of His flock.

> *And as for you, My flock, thus says the Lord God,*
> *"Behold, I will judge between one sheep and another,*
> *between the rams and the male goats." (Ezekiel 34:17).*

Jesus foretold this same judgment. But there was a difference. He said that He would be the one who judged between the sheep and the goats. A contradiction? Not at all. When we read of Jesus doing anything, we understand that this is a reference to the actions of the Lord.

When we come to Ezekiel 36:26-27 we have a vivid description of the salvation promise of the Lord. It is a promise to save, not only on the surface, but from the inside out.

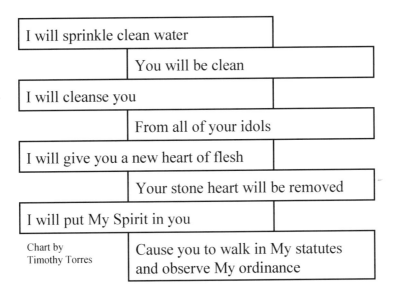

| I will sprinkle clean water |
| You will be clean |
| I will cleanse you |
| From all of your idols |
| I will give you a new heart of flesh |
| Your stone heart will be removed |
| I will put My Spirit in you |
| Cause you to walk in My statutes and observe My ordinance |

Chart by
Timothy Torres

Is the work of salvation monergistic or synergistic? Does God initiate and accomplish the work of salvation or does He function in cooperation with unregenerate man to bring about this regenerating work? The answer is seen in these verses. It is God who is seen doing the work of salvation. He is even the One causing us to walk in His statutes and to observe His ordinances.

ORACLE AGAINST TYRE

> *Son of man, because Tyre has said concerning*
> *Jerusalem, "Aha, the gateway of the peoples is broken; it has*

opened to me. I shall be filled, now that she is laid waste," 3 therefore, thus says the Lord God, "Behold, I am against you, O Tyre, and I will bring up many nations against you, as the sea brings up its waves." (Ezekiel 26:2-3).

This prophecy is striking in the literal manner in which it was fulfilled. Early in January 332 B.C. Alexander the Great came to Tyre, the most powerful naval port in the Mediterranean at that time. The city of Tyre stood on a rocky island about a half mile off the coast. It was surrounded by massive walls that rose to a height of 150 feet. The city was considered invincible.

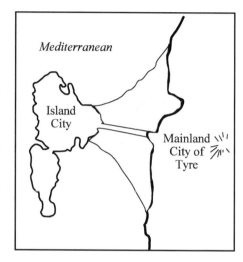

Nebuchadnezzar had attacked Tyre in Ezekiel's day and had finally destroyed the mainland city. Even after a 13 year siege he had not been able to capture the island city.

Alexander sent envoys asking that the city come to terms with him. The envoys were murdered and their bodies thrown into the sea. Alexander settled down in what was to be the longest siege of his career.

Alexander had no navy and so he decided to bring the island to him. He began by demolishing the ruins of the mainland city and using the rubble to construct a causeway across the water which separated the island from the coast. It was grueling work and further hampered by constant raids that the people of Tyre made in their swift warships.

Alexander went to Sidon and Byblos and confiscated a fleet of ships which could bottle up the fleet of Tyre. The causeway was finally completed and Alexander launched a three-pronged simultaneous attack.

- His infantry attacked across the causeway.
- A portion of his new fleet assaulted the harbor on the north side of the island, bottling the enemy fleet inside.
- The rest of his fleet breached a weakened portion of the southern wall of Tyre.

The city of Tyre fell to Alexander on July 29, 332 B.C. The siege had taken 7 long months. Thousands of the inhabitants were slaughtered. The 30, 000 remaining survivors were sold into slavery while 2000 captured troops were crucified. Writing at some time between 592 and 570 B.C., the prophet Ezekiel gave the following predictions concerning the overthrow and eventual destruction of the city of Tyre.

> *Behold, thus says the Lord God, "Behold, I am against you, O Tyre, and I will bring many nations against you, as the sea brings up its waves.*
>
> *"And they will destroy the walls of Tyre and break down her towers; and I will scrape her debris from her and make her a bare rock.*
>
> *"She will be a place for the spreading of nets in the midst of the sea, for I have spoken," declares the Lord God, "And she will become spoil for the nations." (Ezekiel 26:3-5).*

Beginning in verse 7, we are given a more detailed picture of the destruction that will come against Tyre in the person of Nebuchadnezzar. However, in verse 12, there is a change as Ezekiel turns from what "he" will do to those whom he simply refers to as "they."

> *"Also they will make a spoil of your riches and a prey of your merchandise, break down your walls and destroy your pleasant houses, and throw your stones and your timbers into the water.*
>
> *"So I will silence the sound of your songs, and the sound of your harps will be heard no more. 14 And I will make you a bare rock; you will be a place for the spreading of nets. You will he built no more, for I the Lord have spoken," declares the Lord God. (Ezekiel 26:12-14).*

There are a number of points to this prophecy. Let's list them:
- Many nations will come against Tyre (26:3).
- Her walls and towers will be broken down (26:4).
- The debris of the city will be removed (26:4).
- Nebuchadnezzar will attack (26:7).
- Stones and timbers thrown into the water (26:12).
- Tyre will be a bare rock and a place for spreading of nets (26:14).
- The city will not be rebuilt (26:14).

The fulfillment of this prophecy was not the product of blind chance. There is not another city in all of the ancient world that had the same kind of destruction which Alexander brought against Tyre. Alexander was the unwitting servant of the Lord, bringing Divine judgment against the pagan city.

If you go to site of ancient Tyre today, you will find a place for the spreading of nets. A small fishing village occupies the site while, several miles down the coast, a modern city has taken for itself the name Tyre.

ORACLE AGAINST THE KING OF TYRE

Son of man, take up a lamentation over the king of Tyre, and
say to him, "Thus says the Lord God,
'You had the seal of perfection,
Full of wisdom and perfect in beauty.
13 You were in Eden, the garden of God;
Every precious stone was your covering:
The ruby, the topaz, and the diamond;
The beryl, the onyx, and the jasper;
The lapis lazuli, the turquoise, and the emerald;
And the gold, the workmanship of your settings and sockets,
Was in you.
On the day that you were created
They were prepared.
14 You were the anointed cherub who covers,
And I placed you there.
You were on the holy mountain of God;
You walked in the midst of the stones of fire.
15 You were blameless in your ways
From the day you were created,
Until unrighteousness was found in you.
16 By the abundance of your trade
You were internally filled with violence,
And you sinned;
Therefore I have cast you as profane
From the mountain of God.
And I have destroyed you, O covering cherub,
From the midst of the stones of fire.
17 Your heart was lifted up because of your beauty;
You corrupted your wisdom by reason of your splendor.
I cast you to the ground; I put you before kings,
That they may see you.
18 By the multitude of your iniquities,
In the unrighteousness of your trade,
You profaned your sanctuaries.
Therefore I have brought fire from the midst of you;

It has consumed you,
And I have turned you to ashes on the earth In the eyes of all
who see you.
19 All who know you among the peoples
Are appalled at you;
You have become terrified,
And you will be no more.""" (Ezekiel 28:12-19).

This is part of a larger oracle against the city of Tyre. The earlier part of this chapter speaks out against the "Prince of Tyre." Now the address changes. These verses are directed against the "King" of Tyre. He is the real power behind the throne. There are some things said of this person that lead some Bible scholars to believe that this is a reference to Satan.

- He was in Eden, the garden of God (28:13).
- He was created (28:13).
- He was the anointed cherub (28:14).
- He was on the holy mountain of God (28:14).

This description seems to go beyond the realm of mortal man. Though some scholars would see this description as mere Semitic poetry describing an exalted monarch, it seems to me that there is meant to be a greater understanding that we are to see Satan in this description.

DRY BONES

The hand of the Lord was upon me, and He brought
me out by the Spirit of the Lord and set me down in the
middle of the valley; and it was full of bones. 2 And He caused
me to pass among them round about, and behold, there were
very many on the surface of the valley; and lo, they were very
dry. (Ezekiel 37:1-2).

This is a picture of deadness and decay. It is not that Israel is merely in need of CPR. This is a picture of complete hopelessness. The nation has been uprooted. It is a picture of death. There is nothing but a pile of bones.

And He said to me, "Son of man, can these bones
live?" And I answered, "O Lord God, Thou knowest."
4 Again He said to me, "Prophesy over these bones,

*and say to them, 'O dry bones, hear the word of the Lord.' 5
Thus says the Lord God to these bones, 'Behold, I will cause
breath to enter you that you may come to life. 6 And I will put
sinews on you, make flesh grow back on you, cover you with
skin, and put breath in you that you may come alive; and you
will know that I am the Lord.'" (Ezekiel 37:3-4).*

This is a startling prophecy. It is the prophecy of a resurrection. This
is all the more startling as there as of yet had been no clear prophecy of a
future resurrection. As we continue to read, we learn that it is Israel that was
to be resurrected.

*Then He said to me, "Son of man, these bones are the
whole house of Israel; behold, they say, 'Our bones are dried
up, and our hope has perished. We are completely cut off.' 12
Therefore prophesy, and say to them, 'Thus says the Lord
God, "Behold, I will open your graves and cause you to come
up out of your graves, My people; and I will bring you into
the land of Israel. 13 Then you will know that I am the Lord,
when I have opened your graves and caused you to come up
out of your graves, My people. 14 And I will put My Spirit
within you, and you will come to life, and I will place you on
your own land. Then you will know that I, the Lord, have
spoken and done it," declares the Lord.'" (Ezekiel 37:11-14).*

Now we see what sort of resurrection is envisioned in this passage.
It is the resurrection of the nation of Israel. What brings about this
"resurrection"? It is when the Lord puts His Spirit into them. We might be
tempted to look at the return of the Israelites under Zerubbabel or the revival
under Ezra, but those accounts make no mention of the Spirit being placed
within the people of God. To the contrary, the presence of God was notably
lacking from the temple during these times. When did the Spirit of God
come? He came at Pentecost. That was the fulfillment of this prophecy.

GOG & MAGOG

*Son of man, set your face toward Gog of the land of
Magog, the prince of Rosh, Meshech, and Tubal, and
prophesy against him (Ezekiel 38:2).*

The word *rosh* is simply the Hebrew word for "head" or "chief." The most natural translation would be to follow that of the King James Version: *Son of man, set thy face against Gog, the land of Magog, the CHIEF PRINCE of Meshech and Tubal, and prophesy against him*

Trying to translate this as a proper noun and make it refer to Russia has little Scriptural merit. Such a country was unknown in Biblical times. The term "Russia" did not come into use until nearly a thousand years after Christ.

Meshech and Tubal seem to refer to locations on the east and northeast sides of the Black Sea. Herodotus spoke of the tribes of Tibareni and Moschi, the former of which was located east of the Thermodon River which flows into the Sea of Asov on the northeast portion of the Black Sea and the latter of which lay between the sources of the Phasis and the Cyrus Rivers, located on the east side of the Black Sea. These were lands belonging to the people group known as the Scythians.

Scythian invaders moved down into the Levant during the days of the collapse of Nineveh and destroyed Ashkelon and Ashdod before being bribed to depart by Pharaoh Psammetichus (663-609 B.C.). Ezekiel is now saying that it will happen again. In what ways have the prophecies of these two chapters been fulfilled? There seem to be several possibilities:

The Maccabean Revolt	In 168 B.C. the Jews revolted against their Seleucid oppressors and saw wave after wave of expeditionary forces come against them. The Jews were ultimately victorious and won their independence.	This interpretation has the advantage in seeing the conquest of the invaders; something that is promised in Ezekiel's prophecy.
The Roman Conquest of Jerusalem	In 66 A.D. the Jews rebelled against Rome and the response was a Roman invasion of Israel and the destruction of Jerusalem and the Temple.	The problem is that Ezekiel describes the destruction of the invaders and this did not take place in the Roman War.
Futurist	This view sees this prophecy as still yet to be fulfilled at some time in the future.	

Symbolic	This view sees the prophecy as using the image of a past invasion to describe God's eventual victory over evil.	A number of minor details are given that would be meaningless or ambiguous.

Notice that these views are not necessarily mutually exclusive to one another. It is entirely possible that there was an immediate fulfillment as well as a symbolic application that can be appropriately taken for all time.

THE GLORIOUS TEMPLE

Early during the ministry of Ezekiel (chapter 8), he is given a vision of the Temple in Jerusalem. He sees the idolatry that is taking place within the very house of God.

- At the beginning of the vision, Ezekiel sees the glory of the presence of the Lord within His temple (8:4).
- Then the glory of God is seen at the doorway to the temple (9:3).
- It next leaves the doorway and moves out to the Eastern Gate (10:18).
- From there it moves completely out of the city of Jerusalem: *And the glory of the Lord went up from the midst of the city, and stood over the mountain which is east of the city* (Ezekiel 11:23).

Do you know which mountain is to the east of the city? It is the Mount of Olives. This was a sign of judgment against the Jews. The Temple was the place where you went to meet God. But God left the Temple.

There is a principle here. The way God destroys His Temple is by leaving it. For a number of years the physical structure of the Temple was to remain in Jerusalem, but for all intents and purposes, it had already been destroyed. In light of this passage, it is almost anticlimactic when Ezekiel hears in chapter 33 that Jerusalem has been destroyed. The Temple is not even mentioned. Why? Because it had already ceased to function as a Temple when God left it.

We say that Nebuchadnezzar destroyed the Temple, but we are only partially correct. God had already destroyed the Temple by leaving it. Remember the principle: The way God destroys His Temple is by leaving it.

Do you remember the Triumphal entry of Jesus into Jerusalem? Where did He go? To the palace of Herod Antipas? To the Fortress of Antonia? No. He went to the Temple. And when the religious leaders of the

Temple rejected Him, He left the Temple and went out to the Mount of Olives where he foretold the eventual destruction of the Temple. It is no coincidence that the last place we see Jesus before His ascension into heaven is on the Mount of Olives, the same place where we last see the presence of God in Ezekiel's vision. This brings us to a question. Where is God's Temple today? It is here. It is the church. It is the corporate body of believers that come together to meet the Lord.

There is a warning here. It is that God is still in the Temple-destroying business. God destroys His Temple by leaving it. And God destroys churches in the same way. He does not bring a bulldozer or a stick of dynamite. He just leaves. The building and the services and the people might all remain. But it is no longer a church.

This is why it is so important that we have a repentant attitude when we come together to worship the Lord. We come together to meet Him. He will only be there as we have put aside the world's idols, those things that draw our attention from Him.

The book of Ezekiel ends with a glorious vision of a New Temple. The prophet is taken on a guided tour through the structure -- a structure that is tantalizingly familiar if we have read the book of Revelation.

Ezekiel's Vision	John's Revelation
A Temple within the city (40-48)	The New Jerusalem (21-22)
Ezekiel is taken in this vision to a very high mountain (40:2)	John is carried in the Spirit to a great and high mountain (21:10)
A man uses a rod to measure the dimensions of the temple (40:5-ff)	An angel measures the city with a rod (21:15-17)
The entire temple area is measured as a perfect square (42:15-20)	The entire city is measured as a perfect cube (21:16)
The presence of the glory of the Lord enters the temple (43:3-4)	There is no need of sun or moon because the Lord illumines His city (22:5)
No foreigner is admitted into the temple (44:9)	Nothing unclean and no unbeliever is allowed into the city (21:8, 27)
A river of water flows out of the temple (47:1)	A river of the water of life comes from the throne of God (22:1)

There are a total of 12 gates around the city (48:30-34)	There are 12 gates to the city (21:21)
The name of the city shall be: "The Lord is there" (48:35).	The throne of God shall be there (22:3)

Just as Ezekiel had previously seen the glory of the Lord leave the Temple in Jerusalem, now he sees the glory of the Lord come into this house.

> *And the glory of the Lord came into the house by the way of the gate facing toward the east. 5 And the Spirit lifted me up and brought me into the inner court; and behold, the glory of the Lord filled the house. (Ezekiel 43:4-5).*

DANIEL
Prophecies of the Nations

The book of Daniel has been alternately placed within the Hebrew books of history as well as among the prophets. The truth is that this book is both historic as well as prophetic.

HISTORICAL BACKGROUND

We have already noted there were three separate deportations of Judah to Babylon. The book of Daniel begins with the first of these deportations.

> *In the third year of the reign of Jehoiakim king of Judah, Nebuchadnezzar king of Babylon came to Jerusalem and besieged it. 2 And the Lord gave Jehoiakim king of Judah into his hand, along with some of the vessels of the house of God; and he brought them to the land of Shinar, to the house of his god, and he brought the vessels into the treasury of his god. (Daniel 1:1-2).*

Nebuchadnezzar met and defeated the forces of Egypt at Carchemish in northern Syria in 606 B.C. It was an epic battle and changed the balance of world power for the next fifty years. Moving southward, Nebuchadnezzar came to Jerusalem and took it after a short siege. It was during this time that Nebuchadnezzar received word from Babylon that his father had died. It was necessary for him to return home immediately lest some contender for the throne rise up in his absence. To make sure that the Jews would not revolt against him, he gave orders that hostages be taken from among the nobility of Judah. The criteria and purpose of these hostages is given in verses 3-4.

> *Then the king ordered Ashpenaz, the chief of his officials, to bring in some of the sons of Israel, including some of the royal family and of the nobles, 4 youths in whom was no defect, who were good-looking, showing intelligence in every branch of wisdom, endowed with understanding, and discerning knowledge, and who had ability for serving in the king's court; and he ordered him to teach them the literature and language of the Chaldeans. (Daniel 1:3-4).*

Nebuchadnezzar's plan for these hostages went far beyond mere intimidation. His plan was nothing less than the indoctrination of these young noblemen so that they would become good Babylonian citizens, faithful to his empire. Among these hostages was a young man named Daniel. The book of Daniel goes on to deal with events taking place in Mesopotamia during the Babylonian Captivity. As such, it fills in the gap between the end of Kings and Chronicles and the beginning of Ezra.

OUTSTANDING FEATURES OF THE BOOK

1.   Partially Written in Aramaic.

The first chapter of Daniel is written in Hebrew. When we come to Daniel 2:4 there is a change:

Then the Chaldeans spoke to the king in Aramaic...

From this point until the end of chapter 7, the book is written in Aramaic. Then from chapter 8 to the end of the book is written in Hebrew. Aramaic was the lingua franca -- the common language of that day. It is similar to Hebrew. Indeed, our Hebrew Bible generally uses the Aramaic alphabet. As we look at this section, we find that it is primarily concerned with narratives and prophecies that relate to Gentiles. Because of this language division, we can suggest an outline of the book of Daniel.

1:1	2:4 7:28	8:1 12:13
Written in the Third Person		Written in the First Person	
Seven Historical Narratives		Four Prophetic Visions	
Hebrew	Written in Aramaic	Written in Hebrew	
Prologue	Prophetic History relating to the Gentiles	Prophetic History relating primarily to the Jews	

2.   Emphasis on the Kingdom.

The word "kingdom" is found 55 times within the book of Daniel. This is a book about the kingdoms of this world in contrast with the

Kingdom that God promises to establish. This concept is set forth in Daniel 2:44.

> *And in the days of those kings the God of heaven will set up a kingdom which will never be destroyed, and that kingdom will not be left for another people; it will crush and put an end to all these kingdoms, but it will itself endure forever. (Daniel 2:44).*

What is this kingdom of which Daniel spoke? It is God's kingdom. It is the church.

3.   Emphasis on Prayer.

Throughout the book we see Daniel and his companions involved in a life of prayer. Daniel is seen both with regular prayer times as well as praying in times of crisis.

4.   The Spiritual Battle.

In the book of Daniel we are given insights into the spiritual battle that surrounds us. We learn that there are events that occur which only mask the real conflicts taking place in the heavenlies.

DANIEL COMPARED TO EZEKIEL

Daniel was a contemporary with Ezekiel, but their messages were very different. While Ezekiel looked to God's dealings with Israel, Daniel expanded that view to include God's dealings with the nations.

Ezekiel	Daniel
A priest who spoke of matters of spirit	A statesman who spoke of matters of state
Emphasizes times of Israel's glory	Emphasizes times of Gentile's glory
Residence as a prisoner	Residence in a palace

Focused his attention on Israel and the Jews	Focused his attention on Gentiles and the world

THE NARRATIVE/ARAMAIC PORTION OF DANIEL

That portion of Daniel that is written in Aramaic is given in the form of a chiastic parallel. It begins with a dream of four kingdoms and it ends with a night vision of four beasts.

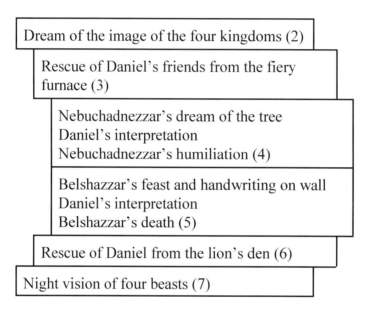

Dream of the image of the four kingdoms (2)

Rescue of Daniel's friends from the fiery furnace (3)

Nebuchadnezzar's dream of the tree
Daniel's interpretation
Nebuchadnezzar's humiliation (4)

Belshazzar's feast and handwriting on wall
Daniel's interpretation
Belshazzar's death (5)

Rescue of Daniel from the lion's den (6)

Night vision of four beasts (7)

This section of Daniel begins and ends with visions and dreams that set forth a scheme of prophetic history. Chapters 3 and 6 each give an account in which the reigning king mandated a form of worship that was unacceptable to the Jews.

- In both cases, the heroes of the narrative engaged in civil disobedience in order to remain faithful to the Lord.
- In both cases they were sentenced to death.
- In both cases there was a supernatural deliverance.

> The use of a fiery furnace has an Assyrian counterpart in the days of Ashurbanipal, whose brother, Shamash-shumukin, was put to death in such a furnace.

Chapters 4-5 also give parallel accounts.

- In both cases there is an example of unwarranted pride on the part of the Gentile ruler.
- In both cases, a supernatural message is sent that can only be interpreted by Daniel.
- In both cases, the fulfillment of the prophecy comes very soon after it is given.
- In both cases, the Gentile king to whom the prophecy is given suffers a grievous setback.

NEBUCHADNEZZAR'S BABYLON

The city of Babylon now became the center of the ancient world. Not only was it the center of government, but it was the center of trade and culture as well.

1.   Physical Description of the City.

Herodotus, writing 150 years after Nebuchadnezzar, tells us that the city of Babylon was a vast square in design, each side having a length of 14 miles and making a complete circuit of 56 miles. He adds that the walls of the city were 300 feet high and were so wide that three chariots could race along the top side by side.

The Euphrates River ran straight through the center of the city. The banks of the river were lined with brick and large gates crossed the river where it entered and exited from the city. A large part of the city was given over to farmland. With both a food and water supply, Babylon could withstand a siege indefinitely.

2.   The Defenses of the City.

Herodotus states that the outer wall of the city was 300 feet high and 80 feet thick. Surrounding this outer wall was a huge moat which was fed through canals from both the Euphrates and the Tigris Rivers. Around the center of the city was a second double-wall. If an invader managed to pass the outer wall and then also passed through the first inner wall, he would find himself within a narrow space between the first and second inner wall which could be flooded in times of emergency.

3.   The Hanging Gardens.

The Hanging Gardens of Babylon were considered by the Greeks to be one of the seven wonders of the world. They were 400 feet square and were raised on terraces one above the other to the height of the city wall. Viewed from a distance, they had the appearance of a forest-covered mountain, standing in marked contrast to the level plains of the Mesopotamian Valley.

It is said that Nebuchadnezzar built the Gardens for his wife, Amyhia, the daughter of Cyaxeres, the king of the Medes. The Gardens were said to relieve her homesickness for the mountains of her native Media.

In order to maintain the exotic plants of the Gardens under the blazing sun of the Babylonian plains, a powerful pump was built inside the terraced wall which kept a steady flow of water, insuring that the soil was always moist.

4.   Temples.

Under Nebuchadnezzar, every temple in Babylon was rebuilt. He lists eight which were built within the city itself. The greatest of all was the Temple of Bal-Merodach. It stood in a square enclosure with each side measuring 1200 feet and entered by 12 gates. In the middle rose a tower of solid brick, like a pyramid. The sanctuary on the top rose in eight stories and was 300 feet high.

BELSHAZZAR AND THE FALL OF BABYLON

Daniel 5 tells the story of Belshazzar, the last king of Babylon. The problem is that historical records tells us that Nabonidus was the last king of Babylon and that he was allowed to live on a pension following the Persian conquest of Babylon.

In 1854 Sir Henry Rawlinson found an inscription of Nabonidus in which his eldest son was mentioned, but no name was given. Records indicated that Nabonidus had given this son the power of regency while he traveled south to excavate in the ruins around Ur. More recent inscriptions have shown this son to be Belshazzar.

Babylonian records tell us that the city of Babylon fell to the Persians without a fight. Writing 150 years after the event, the Spartan General Xenophon tells a story of how the Persians dammed up and diverted the waters of the Euphrates River and then moved a small force up the exposed riverbed into the city to open the gates to the invaders.

THE VISIONS OF DANIEL 2 AND 7

Chapters 2 and 7 give a series of corresponding visions. As the vision of chapter 7 opens, Daniel sees the four winds of heaven that are driving the sea. Remember that the word for "wind" and the word for "spirit" are the same. Daniel would be reminded of a time when *the Spirit of God was moving over the surface of the waters* (Genesis 1:2). Now God is again moving the waters. There is a correlation we can understand between the dream of chapter 2 and the vision of chapter 7.

Vision of Daniel 2	Interpretation	Vision of Daniel 7
Vision of a Great Statue	Kings and their Kingdoms	Vision of Beasts coming out of the Sea
Head of fine Gold	Babylon	Lion with 2 wings of an Eagle
Breast and Arms of Silver	Media-Persia	Bear with three ribs in its teeth
Belly and Thighs of Bronze	Greece	Leopard with 4 wings of a bird and 4 heads
Legs of Iron and Clay and 10 toes	Rome? Antiochus?	Beast with iron teeth and 10 horns
All destroyed by Stone cut without hands	Coming of the Lord and His Kingdom	Ancient of Days takes His seat and passes judgment
A kingdom which will never be destroyed (2:44)		*His kingdom will be an everlasting kingdom* (7:27)

The four in the series is characterized by the number ten. There are ten toes in the image and there are ten horns on the fourth beast. The number ten goes back to the ten commandments. It carried the idea of a number of completeness.

We have a tendency to read this and think of these kingdoms as being "on the earth" instead of "in the land" (בְּאַרְעָא, *BeAretz* – note that this is Aramaic and not Hebrew). Its focus is upon Israel. That means Antiochus best fits this prophecy if we do not identify the fourth beast as Rome. No matter which interpretation is assigned, there are several lessons that can be drawn from this chapter.

- Earthly power in and of itself degenerates into brutality. This is seen in the image of beasts that arise from the ocean.
- It is the tendency of brutality to increase. Each of these seems to be more terrible than the last.
- Restoration is an act of God, not of man. It is the Lord who in the end is seen to overcome these beasts.
- Jesus quoted from Daniel 7:13 at His trial before Caiaphas.

Caiaphas asked Jesus: Are you the son of God? (Matthew 26:63). Jesus answered Caiaphas: You shall see the Son of Man (Matthew 26:64). At that point Jesus had not yet been given all authority. But He has today. That is what He told His disciples in Matthew 28:18. Today He has been given all authority. And one of these days, Caiaphas will see Him returning on the clouds of the sky with great glory.

VISION OF THE RAM AND THE GOAT

Daniel 8 starts a new section of the book, yet there is a distinct connection between this chapter and the previous chapter.

Daniel 7	Daniel 8
Dream comes in the first year of Belshazzar king of Babylon	Vision given in the third year of the reign of Belshazzar the king
Successive beasts rise up out of the ocean • Babylon • Medea-Persia • Greece • Other Kingdom	A ram is standing by the canal; a goat comes from the west • Medea-Persia • Greece
Terrible beast has ten horns	Large horn broken gives way to 4 smaller horns

Out comes a small horn...	Out comes a small horn that...
• Three previous horns pulled up • Eyes of a man and a mouth uttering great boasts • Intends to make alterations in times and in law • Wages war against the saints and overpowers them • Saints are given into this hand for a time, times and half a time • Then sovereignty, dominion, and greatness are given to the people of the saints of the Highest One	• Grows exceedingly • Magnifies itself against the host of heaven • Removes the regular sacrifice and the sanctuary is thrown down • Flings truth to the ground and performs his will • Endures for 2300 mornings and evenings • Then the holy place will be properly restored

A comparison of these two chapters suggests that they are two different visions of essentially the same thing. We will see even more of this when we come to Daniel 11, but before going any further, a history lesson is in order.

ANTIOCHUS IV EPIPHANES

When Alexander the Great lay on his deathbed, his general gathered around and asked, "To whom do you bequeath your kingdom?" He replied, "To the strongest." With those words, he plunged his empire into civil war as each of his generals attempted to carve up a piece of the kingdom. After a hundred years of fighting, two main powers emerged from this.

- Ptolemy took Egypt
- Seleucus and his descendants eventually gained possession over Syria, Mesopotamia and Anatolia.

In 190 B.C. the Seleucid king Antiochus III lost the Battle of Magnesia to the Romans. His son, Antiochus IV, was sent as a hostage to Rome where he spent 12 years. Antiochus IV was treated well in Rome and sent to Latin schools where he roomed with a young Roman named Popilius. While he was here, he learned to respect the power and the endurance of the Romans.

Antiochus IV eventually escaped from Rome and returned to Syria so that, at the death of his father and his brother, he was able to take the throne for himself. He fancied himself as another Alexander and he set out on a mission of conquest.

He had heard that Egypt was making offers to Judah to turn against him, so he decided to make sure that his hold there remained undisturbed. In order to stabilize his position in Judah, he appointed men whom he could trust to positions of responsibility. One of these positions was that of high priest.

In doing this, he touched the Jews at their most sensitive spot — their religion. He created the very explosive situation which he had sought to avoid. Judah became a powder keg, waiting for a spark to set it off.

1.   First Invasion of Egypt (170 B.C.).

        Antiochus invaded Egypt in 170 B. C. Although he failed to capture the capital city of Alexandria, he succeeded in gaining possession of almost all of Upper Egypt. He even marched south to Memphis where he had himself crowned as Pharaoh.

2.   First Revolt in Judah.

        While Antiochus was in Egypt, a rumor reached Jerusalem to the effect that he had been killed. To celebrate the news, the Jews took all of the Seleucid officials and threw them off the walls of the city. Antiochus, still very much alive, heard the news of the rebellion while he was still back in Egypt. He promptly left Egypt and marched into the city of Jerusalem. In three days he killed 80,000 people and led an equal number away as slaves. He also entered the Holy of Holies in the Temple and set up pagan idols there and sacrificed pigs upon the altar. Before returning to Syria, Antiochus established the following laws in Jerusalem.

        - Jews could not assemble for prayer.
        - Observance of the Sabbath was forbidden.
        - Possession of the Scriptures was illegal.
        - Circumcision was illegal.
        - It was illegal to refuse to eat hogs or any other food that was prohibited by the Mosaic Law.
        - It was illegal not to participate in the monthly sacrifice honoring Antiochus. This involved eating of the meat that had been offered in sacrifice.

These laws were designed to extinguish the religious faith of the

Jews. The penalty for breaking any of these laws was death.

3.   Second Invasion of Egypt (168 B.C.).

      The Seleucid control over Egypt did not last long once Antiochus left. He returned to Egypt in 168 B.C. to complete the job. Once again, he was victorious. Only the capital city of Alexandria stood against him. As Antiochus marched on Alexandria, who should come out of the city to meet him but his old friend Popilius at the head of a small embassy.

> *On their first approach he [Antiochus] saluted them and held out his right hand to Popilius; but Popilius put into his hand a written tablet containing the decree of the Senate and desired him first to read that. (Livy).*

      The Senate's message was a crisp order to Antiochus to put an end to his Egyptian campaign and retreat. Antiochus replied that he would call his advisors together and consult them on what was to be done. Popilius responded by taking a swagger stick that he had been carrying and using it to draw a circle around Antiochus on the sand. He told Antiochus not to step out of the circle until he had given his decision concerning the contents of the letter. Antiochus hesitated for a few moments, astonished at the authoritative attitude of Popilius. Then he agreed to leave.

4.   Second Revolt in Judah.

      As Antiochus left Egypt, he received news that the Jews had rebelled again. He was furious. To let out his frustrations, he sent an army under his general Apollonius to Jerusalem. Apollonius entered Jerusalem under the guise of peace and was therefore unopposed. On the Sabbath day when the Orthodox Jews would not fight, the Seleucid army fell upon the Jews, killing thousands and carrying off the women and children as slaves.

      Antiochus now began an intense persecution of the Jews. He set up a statue of Zeus in the Temple and forced the Jews to worship it. The statue had an uncanny resemblance to Anitiochus.

- Two women were brought in for circumcising their children and they led them publicly about the city with their babies hanging at their breasts, and then threw them down from the top of the wall. (2 Maccabees 6:10).

- There is another story told of one woman and her seven sons who were dragged before the king. They were commanded to reject their faith and to worship Antiochus. They refused and were killed one by one in agonizing torture.

The spark had been set to the powder keg. It was only a matter of time before the explosion was set off.

5.   The Maccabean Revolt.

The Maccabean Revolt started in 166 B.C. in the small, village of Modi'in, 17 miles to the northwest of Jerusalem. A Seleucid officer arrived in the village early one morning with a few soldiers. They proceeded to erect an altar in the middle of the town square. Assembling the villagers, the Seleucid official ordered that Mattathias, a Jewish priest, slaughter a pig upon the altar and offer it to Zeus. The villagers would then eat of the pig's flesh, signifying their acceptance of the Greek religion. When Mattathias did not respond, the old man was offered wealth and honor if he would obey. Mattathias refused.

Suddenly one of the villagers stepped out of the crowd and walked up to the altar, announcing that he was willing to make the sacrifice. Mattathias was enraged. Grabbing the sacrificial knife from the villager, he slit the villager's throat and then turn and killed the Seleucid official. Before the astonished soldiers could take in what was happening, the five sons of Mattathias attacked them and slaughtered them.

The villagers banded together under the leadership of Mattathias and his five sons, stripping the soldiers of their weapons and uniforms and hiding the bodies. The handful of rebels moved out into the hills. The revolt had begun.

In the following years, the sons of Mattathias and specifically his son Judas organized the resistance movement. Judas was given the nickname of *Maccabee*, meaning "Hammer" because of his hammer strikes against the Seleucids. After three and a half years of fighting, the Jews liberated the Temple Mount and were able to purify the Temple and restore the sacrifices. To this day, the Jews celebrate this time in the Feast of Chanukah.

The parallels between the prophecies of Daniel 7-8 with the career of Antiochus Epiphanes are striking.

- He comes on the heels of the wars among Alexanders generals
- He is known in history for his uttering of great boasts
- Magnifies himself against the Jews and against their God
- He puts a stop to the sacrificial system and makes alterations to the Law
- He attempts to overturn the truth of the Scriptures
- For a time he has power over the nation of Israel
- His sway over the Temple endures for approximately 3 and a half years (2300 mornings and evenings).
- Then the holy place is ultimately properly restored

I have to conclude that Antiochus did indeed fulfill these prophecies. On the other hand, Jesus indicated that there would come "an abomination of desolation which was spoken of through Daniel the prophet" that would come in the future who would again stand in the holy place (Matthew 24:15). The implications of this are obvious. Jesus said that it would happen again.

It did. Within 40 years from the time that Jesus spoke these words, the Romans landed three legions in Palestine while a fourth marched up from Egypt. They converged upon Jerusalem and the city fell in August of A.D. 70. The Roman General Titus entered the Temple and burned it to the ground. It has never been rebuilt and to this day there remains upon the site an abomination that renders it desolate to Jewish worshipers.

Will there be a third fulfillment of this prophecy in the future? I don't believe that the Scriptures mandate such a fulfillment, but I would not presume to tell God what He can and cannot do. What we can do is to point out the fulfillments that have already taken place.

DANIEL'S SEVENTY WEEKS

"Seventy weeks have been decreed for your people and your holy city, to finish the transgression, to make an end of sin, to make atonement for iniquity, to bring in everlasting righteousness, to seal up vision and prophecy and to anoint the most holy place." (Daniel 9:24).

This prophecy has to do with the restoration of the city of Jerusalem. It is a prophecy of *the holy city* and *the most holy place*. But that is not all.

The scope of this prophecy transcends the mere rebuilding of Jerusalem when it speaks of:

- Finishing the transgression.
- Making an end of sin.
- Making atonement for iniquity.
- Bringing in everlasting righteousness.
- Sealing up vision and prophecy.

From our perspective, we can see that each of these aspects were ultimately fulfilled in the person of Jesus Christ. By His death upon the cross, He finished transgression and made an end of sin and made atonement for iniquity. It is through that atonement that he brought in everlasting righteousness. As a result of this completed redemptive work, there is no further need for vision or for further prophecy as we have the completed Scriptures today.

All of these things are to take place within the scope of "seventy weeks" - literally, "seventy sevens." Just as Daniel had been reading of 70 years of captivity, so now he is told that 70 weeks remain. This reckoning of time seems very foreign to us since we count time by tens, adding up either decades or centuries. The Jews, on the other hand, were Sabbath oriented. It is for this reason that they counted time by parts of seven. Every seven years they had a year-long holiday. Every 49th year all of their debts were forgiven.

Such groups of sevens are not unusual in the Scriptures. A similar wording is used in Leviticus 25:6 where *seven weeks of years* is said to refer to the 49 years between Jubilees. In Numbers 14:34, the Israelites were told that the 40 years they would spend in the Wilderness would correspond to the 40 days that the spies spent in the land of Canaan. Ezekiel was instructed to lie on his left side for 390 days and on his right side for 40 days. This was to be understood as *a day for each year* (Ezekiel 4:6).

I want to suggest that these 70 weeks are to be understood by each day of these "weeks" representing a single year. This means that we are dealing with a period of 70 weeks of years – a total of 490 years.

7 Weeks		49 Years
62 Weeks	=	434 Years
+ 1 Week		+ 7 Years
70 Weeks		490 Years

So you are to know and discern that from the issuing

of a decree to restore and rebuild Jerusalem... (Daniel 9:25).

This period begins with a very specific event. The event is the issuing of a decree to restore and to rebuild Jerusalem. The Hebrew word translated "decree" is simply *dabar*, the normal Hebrew word for "saying" or "word." The problem that we have is that the Bible records several different decrees concerning rebuilding within Jerusalem.

Author	Passage	Date	Specifics of the Decree
Cyrus	Ezra 1:1-4	539 B.C.	Permitted Jews to return to the land and rebuild their Temple. This work was discontinued because of false accusations (Ezra 4:6-13).
Darius	Ezra 6:8-12	520 B.C.	Permitted Jews to complete the rebuilding of the Temple
Artaxerxes	Ezra 7:11-28	457 B.C.	Allowed Ezra authority to lead the nation in the Laws of God
Artaxerxes	Nehemiah 1	445 B.C.	Nehemiah given permission to rebuild the walls of Jerusalem

One interpretation of this decree views the seven weeks and the subsequent mention of the 62 weeks as not necessarily taking place concurrently. This would allow for Cyrus to be understood to be the one who gives the decree to restore and rebuild Jerusalem and for the High Priest to be the "anointed one" whose untimely death would signal the soon desecration of the Temple.

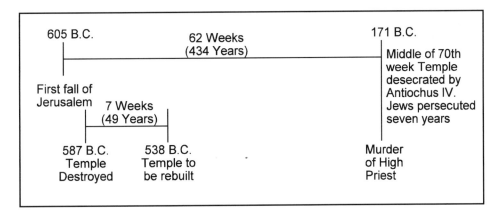

641

While this view does fit within the historical framework, I believe it is at best a type of the complete fulfillment that was to follow. Sir Robert Anderson taught that this prophecy was to be reckoned in "prophetic years" of only 360 days, measured by twelve months of thirty days each. He used this complicated formula to add up an exact number of days from the final decree of Artaxerxes to the Triumphal Entry of Jesus in A.D. 33.

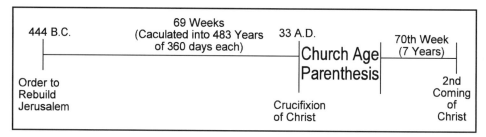

This is the view that has been traditionally adopted by those holding to Dispensationalism. It postulates a giant parenthesis between the 69th and 70th weeks into which the age of the church is to take place. It seems evident that the theory is contrived, having been born out of a supposed necessity. There is no hint that we are to expect there to be a great gap or an intervening age between the 69th and 70th week. The Jews knew exactly how many days ought to be in a year and even added an "intercalary month" upon occasion to correct their calendar. Furthermore, it seems that Daniel himself understood the years of Jeremiah in the usual sense.

A third option best fits the facts of history as well as the demands of the prophecy. It is to see the decree as one given to Ezra in the 7th year of Artaxerxes. That Persian king began his reign in 464 B.C. This would place his decree to Ezra around 457 B.C. Later, in Ezra's priestly prayer, he alludes to possibly having been given permission, not only to build up the Temple, but also to build the walls of Judah and Jerusalem.

> *For we are slaves; yet in our bondage our God has not forsaken us, but has extended lovingkindness to us in the sight of the kings of Persia, to give us reviving to raise up the house of our God, to restore its ruins and to give us a **wall** in Judah and Jerusalem. (Ezra 9:9).*

Nehemiah comes along twenty years later and goes into mourning when he hears that the walls still have not been repaired, but that is because the people had not acted upon the decree that had been given.

> *"So you are to know and discern that from the issuing of a decree to restore and rebuild Jerusalem until Messiah the*

*Prince there will be seven weeks and sixty-two weeks...
(Daniel 9:25).*

The culmination of the first 69 weeks is the advent of "Messiah the Prince." It is universally agreed among Christians that this *Anointed Prince* is a reference to Jesus. In hindsight, it is a simple matter for us to trace back to the four decrees to see which one of them aligned with the coming of Jesus.

Date for the giving of the Decree			Plus 483 Years
Cyrus	Ezra 1:1-4	539 B.C.	56 B.C.
Darius	Ezra 6:8-12	520 B.C.	37 B.C.
7th Year of Artaxerxes	Ezra 7:11-28	457 B.C.	27 A.D.
20th Year of Artaxerxes	Nehemiah 1	445 B.C.	39 A.D.

It is evident from this chart that the first decree of Artaxerxes given to Ezra in 457 B.C. is the one that matches the prophecy of Daniel. The date of 27 A.D. is within the realm of the beginning of the ministry of Jesus.

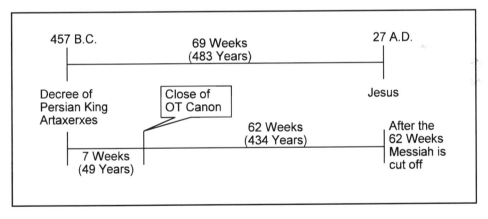

This view does not mandate any particular action that had to take place at the end of the 70th week. What it does say is that *after the sixty-two weeks the Messiah will be cut off and have nothing (Daniel 9:26).* This was fulfilled in Jesus going to the cross.

It has been pointed out that verses 25-27 are given in a chiastic arrangement which entails a series of constructions and deconstructions and an anointed one. What is not so clear is whether verse 26 describes a second person or whether it is still speaking of Messiah the Prince when we read of "the people of the prince." The same Hebrew term is used in each case. The outline is as follows:

> (Construction) *So you are to know and discern that from the issuing of a decree to restore and rebuild Jerusalem*
>
> (Messiah) *...until Messiah the Prince there will be seven weeks and sixty-two weeks*
>
> (Construction) *...it will be built again, with plaza and moat*
>
> (Messiah) *Then after the sixty-two weeks the Messiah will be cut off*
>
> (Anti-Messiah) *...and the people of the prince who is to come*
>
> (Destruction) *...will destroy the city and the sanctuary. And its end will come with a flood*
>
> (Messiah) *He will make a firm covenant with the many for one week...*
>
> (Destruction) *...but in the middle of the week he will put a stop to sacrifice and grain offering; and on the wing of abominations will come one who makes desolate, even until a complete destruction, one that is decreed, is poured out on the one who makes desolate.*

It is notable that the description changes from "Messiah the Prince" or even from "the Messiah" to "the prince." This suggests to us the possibility of two different people instead of one. Prophecy is always easier to understand after it has been fulfilled. It is because of the factor of this hindsight that we are able to distinguish between the coming of Messiah the Prince in the person of Jesus of Nazareth versus the people of the prince who is to come in the capacity of the soldiers of the Roman General Titus who came and destroyed the city and the sanctuary in A.D. 70. It is in light of this hindsight that we can see that "the prince who is to come" stands in contrast to Messiah the Prince.

> "...*the people of the prince who is to come will destroy the city and the sanctuary. And its end will come with a flood; even to the end there will be war; desolations are determined.*(Daniel 9:26).

Notice the actions of this one who is "the prince who is to come." It is he who will destroy the city and the sanctuary. It must be remembered that, at the time Daniel received this prophecy, there was no city or sanctuary. It had been destroyed by Nebuchadnezzar of Babylon. But Daniel says that it is going to happen again.

This was dramatically fulfilled in A.D. 70 when the Roman General Titus marched against Jerusalem and took the city after a siege of eight months. Since that time, the site of the Temple has been the site of desolation and a complete destruction. Today archaeologists even debate as to exactly where the original Temple was located.

> *"And he will make a firm covenant with the many for one week, but in the middle of the week he will put a stop to sacrifice and grain offering; and on the wing of abominations will come one who makes desolate, even until a complete destruction, one that is decreed, is poured out on the one who makes desolate." (Daniel 9:27).*

At first glance, verse 27 seems to be speaking of the same "prince who is to come" that was introduced in verse 26. Or is it? One is hard-pressed to find such a "firm covenant" that Titus made for a particular period, though it is noteworthy that the Jewish War lasted a total of seven years before all resistance was overcome. On the other hand, we can certainly say that Christ's death on the cross "made a firm covenant with the many" and that the rejection of His kingship is seen in the Scriptures as resulting in the fall of Jerusalem in A.D. 70.

THE ABOMINATION OF DESOLATION

The prophecy of Daniel 11 provides a vast panorama, the fulfillments of which span the period from Alexander the Great in 333 B.C. to the Maccabean Wars of 166 B.C. and the years that followed. These fulfillments are so exact that most critics of the Bible are forced to attempt to assign to the book of Daniel a date that is later than the Maccabean period.

Date	Daniel 11	Historical Fulfillment

539	*And in the first year of Darius the Mede, I arose to be an encouragement and a protection for him. (Daniel 11:1).*	There is some disagreement as to the identity of Darius the Mede. Some think it to be another name for Cyrus the Great who was both a Mede as well as a Persian. Others feel it to be a reference to a Mede governor who ruled under Cyrus.
530-465	*And now I will tell you the truth. Behold, three more kings are going to arise in Persia. Then a fourth will gain far more riches than all of them; as soon as he becomes strong through his riches, he will arouse the whole empire against the realm of Greece. (Daniel 11:2).*	Cyrus the Great captured Babylon in 539 B.C. • Cambyses II, Cyrus' son (530-522) • Smerdis, Cambyses alleged brother (522) • Darius I the Great (521-486) The fourth king was Xerxes (486-465). He brought the strength of the Persian Empire against Greece, burning Athens to the ground and attempting to push into the southern peninsula before suffering the defeat at Salamis.
333-323	*And a mighty king will arise, and he will rule with great authority and do as he pleases. 4 But as soon as he has arisen, his kingdom will be broken up and parceled out toward the four points of the compass, though not to his own descendants, nor according to his authority which he wielded; for his sovereignty will be uprooted and given to others besides them. (Daniel 11:3-4).*	The prophecy now jumps forward to the rise of a great king who would accomplish all within his will. This is the story of Alexander the Great, the young king of Macedon who conquered all the Persian Empire and marched his armies all the way to the borders of India before turning back. Alexander died in Babylon in the summer of 323 B.C., a mere month before his 33rd birthday. His death plunged the newly founded empire into war as one and then another of his former generals attempted to take a portion for himself.

323-283	*Then the king of the South will grow strong, along with one of his princes who will gain ascendancy over him and obtain dominion; his domain will be a great dominion indeed. (Daniel 11:5).*	Ptolemy I Soter was one of Alexander's generals who took control of Egypt. One of his own generals was Seleucus who eventually rose to ascendancy over Mesopotamia and Syria.
252	*And after some years they will form an alliance, and the daughter of the king of the South will come to the king of the North to carry out a peaceful arrangement. But she will not retain her position of power, nor will he remain with his power, but she will be given up, along with those who brought her in, and the one who sired her, as well as he who supported her in those times. (Daniel 11:6).*	Ptolemy I died in 285 and his son, Ptolemy II Philadelphus eventually arranged an alliance with the Seleucid king Antiochus II Theos in which Antiochus II was to marry Bernice, the daughter of Ptolemy II. However, Antiochus II already had a wife named Laodice and she did not take kindly to being divorced. She conspired to have both Bernice and her infant son assassinated. Antiochus II was subsequently poisoned. Laodice ruled as regent until her own son, Seleucus II Callinicus, was old enough to assume the throne of the Seleucid Empire.
246-241	*But one of the descendants of her line will arise in his place, and he will come against their army and enter the fortress of the king of the North, and he will deal with them and display great strength. (Daniel 11:7).*	Ptolemy III Euergetes organized a campaign to avenge the murder of his sister. He captured Antioch and marched all the way to Bactria and also defeated the Seleucid navy in the Aegean, recapturing the former conquests of his father in Asia Minor.

240	*And also their gods with their metal images and their precious vessels of silver and gold he will take into captivity to Egypt, and he on his part will refrain from attacking the king of the North for some years. 9 Then the latter will enter the realm of the king of the South, but will return to his own land. (Daniel 11:8-9).*	Ptolemy III went on to recapture the treasures that had been looted from Egypt in the days of Cambyses. Ptolemy III and Seleucus II eventually made a treaty in 240 B.C. and Ptolemy III returned home to Egypt where he was given the title by the Egyptians of Euergetes – "Good worker."
226-223	*And his sons will mobilize and assemble a multitude of great forces; and one of them will keep on coming and overflow and pass through, that he may again wage war up to his very fortress. (Daniel 11:10).*	Seleucus II was succeeded by his son Seleucus III who only lived three years before being followed by his younger brother, Antiochus III (the Great). Antiochus III set out on a battle of conquest, marching to the borders of Egypt where he was met by Ptolemy IV.
218	*And the king of the South will be enraged and go forth and fight with the king of the North. Then the latter will raise a great multitude, but that multitude will be given into the hand of the former. 12 When the multitude is carried away, his heart will be lifted up, and he will cause tens of thousands to fall; yet he will not prevail. (Daniel 11:11-12).*	Antiochus III was defeated by Ptolemy IV at the Battle of Raphia in 218 B.C. Antiochus III had to give up Palestine and Phoenicia to Egypt. Over the next 15 years, Antioch III was busy fighting elsewhere and his conquests took him all the way to the Caspian Sea in the north and to the Indus River in the east.

202-201	*For the king of the North will again raise a greater multitude than the former, and after an interval of some years he will press on with a great army and much equipment. (Daniel 11:13).*	Antiochus III returned to take up arms once more against Egypt, taking Gaza in 201 B.C.
201	*Now in those times many will rise up against the king of the South; the violent ones among your people will also lift themselves up in order to fulfill the vision, but they will fall down. (Daniel 11:14).*	A pro-Seleucid party rose up in Jerusalem, but it was put down by the Egyptian general Scopas who pushed up to the area north of Israel that would be known as Caesarea Philippi.
200	*Then the king of the North will come, cast up a siege mound, and capture a well-fortified city; and the forces of the South will not stand their ground, not even their choicest troops, for there will be no strength to make a stand. (Daniel 11:15).*	As Antiochus III counterattacked, Scopas retreated to Sidon and found himself under siege at that city by the Seleucid King, finally losing the city to him.
198	*But he who comes against him will do as he pleases, and no one will be able to withstand him; he will also stay for a time in the Beautiful Land, with destruction in his hand. (Daniel 11:16).*	Antiochus III moved southward into Palestine, taking Jerusalem in 198.

195	*And he will set his face to come with the power of his whole kingdom, bringing with him a proposal of peace which he will put into effect; he will also give him the daughter of women to ruin it. But she will not take a stand for him or be on his side. (Daniel 11:17).*	Antiochus III entered into an alliance with the young Ptolemy V who was still a boy. The alliance was sealed by Ptolemy V marrying Cleopatra, the daughter of Antiochus III. Rather than being an influence on behalf of her father, Cleopatra became an ardent supporter of Egypt, even reigning a regent after the death of her husband in 181.
192	*Then he will turn his face to the coastlands and capture many. But a commander will put a stop to his scorn against him; moreover, he will repay him for his scorn. (Daniel 11:18).*	Antiochus III had invaded Thrace and was now asked by a league of city states in central Greece to aid them in their fight against Macedonia and the Peloponnesians. Meanwhile, the Romans threw in their weight against Antiochus III and he was forced to withdraw from Greece.
189-188	*So he will turn his face toward the fortresses of his own land, but he will stumble and fall and be found no more. (Daniel 11:19).*	The Romans under Lucius Cornelius Scipio Asiaticus, the brother of Scipio Africanus, followed Antiochus III into Anatolia and met him in battle. Though the Romans were greatly outnumbered, they won a victory. Antiochus III had to give up all of Anatolia as well as his son, Antiochus IV who went as a hostage to Rome.

187	*Then in his place one will arise who will send an oppressor through the Jewel of his kingdom; yet within a few days he will be shattered, though neither in anger nor in battle. (Daniel 11:20).*	Antiochus III was killed by an enraged mob when he attempted to rob the temple of Bel in Elymais to pay the Roman demands. Seleucus IV Philopator succeeded to the throne and sought to take funds from the temple in Jerusalem (2 Maccabees 3:7-40). Seleucus IV was eventually poisoned.
	Verses 21-35 are to be understood as describing the career of Antiochus IV Epiphanes.	
175	*And in his place a despicable person will arise, on whom the honor of kingship has not been conferred, but he will come in a time of tranquility and seize the kingdom by intrigue. (Daniel 11:21).*	When Seleucus IV was murdered, his son Demetrius was the next in line for the throne, but the realm was instead taken by Antiochus IV, the second son of Antiochus III. He took for himself the title Epiphanes Theos—God Manifest—and therefore becomes a type of antichrist.
170	*And the overflowing forces will be flooded away before him and shattered, and also the prince of the covenant. (Daniel 11:22).*	Ptolemy VII Philometor became of age and attempted to regain the lands of Palestine from the Seleucids, but was eventually defeated and captured by Antiochus IV.
170	*And after an alliance is made with him he will practice deception, and he will go up and gain power with a small force of people (Daniel 11:23).*	The Egyptians responded by taking Physcon, the brother of Ptolemy VII and making him king of Egypt. Antiochus IV invaded Egypt with the stated purpose of reinstating Ptolemy VII.

	In a time of tranquility he will enter the richest parts of the realm, and he will accomplish what his fathers never did, nor his ancestors; he will distribute plunder, booty, and possessions among them, and he will devise his schemes against strongholds, but only for a time. (Daniel 11:24).	This is a summary of the accomplishments of Antiochus IV. By this time, he had gained control of everything from the Mediterranean to India.
170	*And he will stir up his strength and courage against the king of the South with a large army; so the king of the South will mobilize an extremely large and mighty army for war; but he will not stand, for schemes will be devised against him. (Daniel 11:25).*	Ptolemy VII eventually worked out an agreement with his brother, Physcon, in which they would split the kingdom of Egypt into two parts and reign jointly. They now unified themselves against Antiochus IV, but he entered Egypt and laid siege to Alexandria.
	And those who eat his choice food will destroy him, and his army will overflow, but many will fall down slain. (Daniel 11:26).	Ptolemy VII had supposedly been under the protection of Antiochus IV, but now they found themselves at odds.
170	*As for both kings, their hearts will be intent on evil, and they will speak lies to each other at the same table; but it will not succeed... (Daniel 11:27).*	Negotiations continued and Ptolemy VII and his brother, Physcon, seemed to come to an agreement, though the intrigues between them would continue for some time.
	...for the end is still to come at the appointed time. (Daniel 11:27).	It was only a matter of time before hostilities broke out again.

169	*Then he will return to his land with much plunder; but his heart will be set against the holy covenant, and he will take action and then return to his own land. (Daniel 11:28).*	Antiochus IV returned from Egypt with great plunder. Several years earlier, he had accepted a bribe from a Jewish priest named Jason to remove the current high priest and put Jason in his place. Jason was eventually removed when another priest, Menelaus, offered a still higher bribe. When Jewish representatives came before the king with their complaint, Antiochus IV put them to death.
168	*At the appointed time he will return and come into the South, but this last time it will not turn out the way it did before. (Daniel 11:29).*	Antiochus IV invaded Egypt again, trapping the two Ptolemaic kings in Alexandria.
168	*For ships of Kittim will come against him; therefore he will be disheartened, and will return and become enraged at the holy covenant and take action; so he will come back and show regard for those who forsake the holy covenant. (Daniel 11:30).*	Popillius Laenas, a representative of Rome, met with Antiochus IV and ordered him out of Egypt on the authority of Rome. Antiochus IV agreed. Coming to Jerusalem, he found the Jews in revolt where Jason, acting on the rumor that Antiochus IV had been killed in Egypt, had raised a force to remove Menelaus from the priesthood.
168	*And forces from him will arise, desecrate the sanctuary fortress, and do away with the regular sacrifice. And they will set up the abomination of desolation (Daniel 11:31).*	Antiochus IV desecrated the temple, stopped the regular temple sacrifices, and set up a statue of Zeus in the temple whose features were made to resemble Antiochus IV.

167	*And by smooth words he will turn to godlessness those who act wickedly toward the covenant... (Daniel 11:32a).*	1 Maccabees 1:11-15 describe how certain of the Jews accepted the changes of Antiochus IV and went so far as to build a gymnasium in Jerusalem and to seek to have their circumcisions reversed. Verse 43 goes on to say that "many even from Israel gladly adopted his religion; they sacrificed to idols and profaned the Sabbath."
167	*...but the people who know their God will display strength and take action (Daniel 11:32b).*	There were those Jews who refused to turn from their observance of the Law. This turned into open revolt when the Maccabees took up arms against the Seleucids.
167	*And those who have insight among the people will give understanding to the many; yet they will fall by sword and by flame, by captivity and by plunder, for many days (Daniel 11:33).*	Since they were fighting in order to retain their Torah observances, the Maccabees initially took a stance of not fighting on the Sabbath day. The Seleucids took advantage of this by attacking on the Sabbath and slaughtering many. After this, the priest Mattathias (father of the Maccabees) explained to the people that it would be permissible to defend themselves on the Sabbath.
167	*Now when they fall they will be granted a little help, and many will join with them in hypocrisy (Daniel 11:34).*	The Maccabees were joined by "a company of Hasideans, mighty warriors of Israel, all who offered themselves willingly for the law" (1 Maccabees 2:42). As a result, many who had previously gone along with the changes imposed by Antiochus IV now joined the revolt.

166	*And some of those who have insight will fall, in order to refine, purge, and make them pure, until the end time; because it is still to come at the appointed time (Daniel 11:35).*	The priest Mattathias died shortly thereafter. Eventually, the Maccabees managed to retake the temple and to purify it and restore the worship. This is celebrated today by Hanukkah.

The attention of the prophecy now returns to Antiochus IV and summarizes his career without regard to a chronological sequence.

Then the king will do as he pleases, and he will exalt and magnify himself above every god, and will speak monstrous things against the God of gods; and he will prosper until the indignation is finished, for that which is decreed will be done. (Daniel 11:36).	"So Antiochus carried off eighteen hundred talents from the temple, and hurried away to Antioch, thinking in his arrogance that he could sail on the land and walk on the sea, because his mind was elated" (2 Maccabees 5:21). Furthermore, he eventually adopted the title, "King Antiochus, God Manifest."
And he will show no regard for the gods of his fathers or for the desire of women, nor will he show regard for any other god; for he will magnify himself above them all (Daniel 11:37).	Speaking of Antiochus IV, we read the following report in 2 Maccabees 9:2. "He had entered the city called Persepolis and attempted to rob the temples and control the city. Therefore the people rushed to the rescue with arms, and Antiochus and his army were defeated, with the result that Antiochus was put to flight by the inhabitants and beat a shameful retreat."
But instead he will honor a god of fortresses, a god whom his fathers did not know; he will honor him with gold, silver, costly stones, and treasures (Daniel 11:38).	It is noteworthy that the coins of his era have the image of Zeus rather than the more customary Apollos.

And he will take action against the strongest of fortresses with the help of a foreign god; he will give great honor to those who acknowledge him, and he will cause them to rule over the many, and will parcel out land for a price (Daniel 11:39).	Antiochus IV sold the priesthood to the highest bidder, first to Jason, and later to Menelaus. The "strongest of fortresses" seems to be a reference to the Temple Mount in Jerusalem which Antiochus IV determined to convert to a temple to Zeus.
And at the end time the king of the South will collide with him, and the king of the North will storm against him with chariots, with horsemen, and with many ships; and he will enter countries, overflow them, and pass through. (Daniel 11:40).	We have no records of any final war with Egypt, though Jerome quotes Porphyry as stating that this took place in the eleventh year of the reign of Antiochus IV (*Commentary on the Book of Daniel*, Moses Stuart, 1850, Boston: Crocker & Brewster, page 355).
He will also enter the Beautiful Land, and many countries will fall; but these will be rescued out of his hand: Edom, Moab and the foremost of the sons of Ammon (Daniel 11:41).	It is more likely that we are to understand this as a summarization of the career of Antiochus IV and his invasions of Egypt and Israel.
Then he will stretch out his hand against other countries, and the land of Egypt will not escape (Daniel 11:42).	A summary of the conquests of Antiochus IV in Egypt.
But he will gain control over the hidden treasures of gold and silver, and over all the precious things of Egypt; and Libyans and Ethiopians will follow at his heels (Daniel 11:43).	Prior to his departure from Egypt, Antiochus IV had thoroughly looted the country.
But rumors from the East and from the North will disturb him, and he will go forth with great wrath to destroy and annihilate many (Daniel 11:44).	Antiochus IV left Israel upon hearing the news of revolts in Parthia and Anatolia.

And he will pitch the tents of his royal pavilion between the seas and the beautiful Holy Mountain; yet he will come to his end, and no one will help him (Daniel 11:45).	Though he had successfully conquered Jerusalem and the Holy Mountain, Antiochus IV eventually met his defeat and death.

We have already described the career of Antiochus IV who eventually entered the Temple and erected a statue of himself for worship. Daniel describes him as the despicable king and traces his career from verse 21 to the end of the chapter.

- He is described as one on whom the honor of kingship has not been conferred (11:21). The son of his older brother was actually in line for the throne, but Antiochus IV took it for himself.

- He captures one of the Ptolemies and makes an alliance with him with a view to placing him back on the throne of Egypt as a puppet king under his vassalage (11:23).

- He sets his heart against the holy covenant (11:29), coming to Jerusalem and insisting that a process of Hellenization be instituted.

- He finally comes against Egypt, only to find that the ships of Kittim (Rome) have come against him (11:30). He is disheartened and returns to Jerusalem to take out his anger and frustration upon the Jews.

- He desecrates the Temple: *And forces from him will arise, desecrate the sanctuary fortress, and do away with the regular sacrifice. And they will set up the abomination of desolation. (Daniel 11:31).*

What are we to make of the fact that Jesus described the abomination of desolation as spoken of by Daniel the prophet as an event that was still in the future? Matthew 24:15 could not be more clear – it was going to happen again.

It did. In A.D. 70 the Roman general Titus broke through the defenses of the city of Jerusalem and eventually broke through to the temple. It was desecrated and destroyed. To this day, there remains an abomination that effectively renders it desolate -- an abomination known as the Dome of the Rock.

PROPHECY OF MICHAEL

> *Now at that time Michael, the great prince who stands guard over the sons of your people, will arise. And there will be a time of distress such as never occurred since there was a nation until that time; and at that time your people, everyone who is found written in the book, will be rescued. 2 And many of those who sleep in the dust of the ground will awake, these to everlasting life, but the others to disgrace and everlasting contempt. (Daniel 12:1-2).*

With these words, Daniel seems to take us on a trip to the future as he pictures the final resurrection and judgment. This is introduced with the rise of a new prince. He is described as Michael, the great prince. Some have suggested that Michael is another name for Jesus, the Son of God.

- He is the "great prince" (Daniel 12:1).
- His coming is a sign of the final judgment and the resurrection (Daniel 12:1-2).
- When Gabriel faced an insurmountable foe, it was Michael who was able to arrive and provide assistance (Daniel 10:13). He alone is able to stand up against those spiritual forces (Daniel 10:21).
- Michael is the one who is pictured in Revelation 12:7 as defeating Satan.

There are several problems with this identification:

- Michael is only one among a number of "chief princes" (Daniel 10:13).
- Michael is described in Jude 1:9 as an archangel. That passage goes on to say that Michael did not dare pronounce against him a railing judgment, but said, "The Lord rebuke you."
- There is no hint in any of these passages that we are to equate Michael with Jesus.

Daniel's prophecy deals with a time of distress such as never occurred since there was a nation until that time (12:1). Certainly this is foreshadowed by the troubles at Jerusalem that we have seen in history -- the two abominations of desolation that took place at the Temple.

Yet there is coming an even greater trouble. It is a trouble of the final judgment. It is mentioned in these two verses. It is the time of the resurrection. Notice that this general resurrection is described in its two aspects. Many who sleep in the dust of the ground shall arise...

- Some to everlasting life.
- Others to everlasting contempt.

THE SEALING OF THE BOOK

But as for you, Daniel, conceal these words and seal up the book until the end of time; many will go back and forth, and knowledge will increase. (Daniel 12:4).

This stands in contrast to the instructions that would be given to the Apostle John at the close of the book of Revelation. John is told, "Do not seal up the words of the prophecy of this book, for the time is near" (Revelation 22:10).

- In Daniel's case, the fulfillment of the prophecy was a long way off.
- In the case of the book of Revelation, much of John's prophecy was at their very doorstep.

How are we to understand this prophecy that "knowledge will increase"? Many people like to point to the technological explosion that has taken place in the last 30 or 40 years. We are today living in the information age.

While that is true, something else also comes to mind. It is the promise of further revelation. This promise is fulfilled in the pages of the New Testament. It is in the greater and understanding of salvation that our knowledge has increased in a day when the truths of prophecy are no longer such a sealed book to us. It is not that we have all of the prophetic details of the future, but rather that now we can see the fulfilled promises of Messiah and salvation and we can understand and believe.

HOSEA
Prophecies of the Nations

There are four similar names found in the Bible that must not be confused with one another:
- Joshua: Brought Israel into the Promised Land.
- Hoshea: Last king of Israel.
- Hosea: Prophet who ministered prior to the reign of Hoshea.
- Jesus: Fulfills the type seen by Hosea.

Over the years, I have heard quite a number of well-known scholars and Bible teachers. There are a few whom I have personally gotten to know. In nearly every case, this further level of acquaintance took place outside of the classroom. You can't get to know a person very well in a classroom. Hosea must have known that lesson, for he takes us out of the classroom and into the privacy of his home. We get a glimpse of his home life and it is not necessarily a happy life. Hosea comes down from behind the pulpit and bares his soul.

When you learn how to do that, not for its shock value, but for its incarnational necessity, then you will learn how to be a pastor and a minister to real people. Hosea writes from the heart. His book is full of passion and emotion. As you read his words, you hear the sobs of a broken heart. While Jeremiah tells us that he is weeping, Hosea reflects this attitude in short, broken sentences. As a result, there is a distinct absence of the normal rhythm and parallelism that is common to Hebrew writing. This makes it a bit harder for us to understand his message. This is a book about the love of God and how Israel has rebuffed and ignored that love.

DATE OF AUTHORSHIP

> *The word of the Lord which came to Hosea the son of Beeri, during the days of Uzziah, Jotham, Ahaz, and Hezekiah, kings of Judah, and during the days of Jeroboam the son of Joash, king of Israel. (Hosea 1:1).*

The opening verse of Hosea states the date of its composition. This is a very long period stretching over a period of more than 50 years. Jeroboam came to the throne a few years prior to the accession of Uzziah. In

Hosea 1:4, Hosea prophesies that the Lord will punish the house of Jehu for the bloodshed of Jezreel. Jehu had taken the throne through assassination. Jeroboam II was Jehu's great grandson. Jeroboam would be succeeded by his son Zechariah who would reign only six months before ending the line of Jehu.

> 743 B.C. - Death of Jeroboam II
> 721 B.C. - Fall of Samaria and the Northern Kingdom

Hosea was one of the prophets to the Northern Kingdom of Israel. His day saw a great deal of prosperity in the land. What could not be readily seen apart from the prophetic message were the storm clouds on the horizon.

The reign of Jeroboam II (782-753 B.C.) saw the high water mark of the Northern Kingdom of Israel. Jeroboam II extended his influence northward all the way to the borders of Hamath, making Israel almost as big as she

> The jasper seal of "Shema, servant of Jeroboam", discovered by Schumacher at Megiddo, is to be identified with Jeroboam II, as is now epigraphically certain. The lifelike and magnificently executed lion, which appears on it, furnishes evidence of the state of art during this era.

had been in the days of Solomon (2nd Kings 14:25). With this vast military victory came a period of great economic prosperity. This period of prosperity brought with it a corresponding social corruption. At the root of the issue was apostasy. The nation had long since abandoned the Lord to follow after idolatry.

Hosea and Amos both prophesied during this period. Their writings reflect the moral and religious decay of the Israelites during this time.

- Hosea was called upon to act out the relationship between Yahweh and the nation by marrying an unfaithful prostitute.
- Amos, a shepherd from the eastern regions of Israel, spoke out against the social injustices of the day. He warned that the prosperity of the nation was fleeting. Within 30 years of the death of Jeroboam, the Northern Kingdom would cease to exist.

While the emphasis of Amos is upon social injustice, the emphasis of Hosea is upon spiritual unfaithfulness.

OUTLINE OF THE BOOK

Hosea is divided into two major parts. The first three chapters contain a living parable as Hosea is told to go and marry a wife of harlotry - a prostitute. He has children by her and then she is unfaithful to the marriage. This relationship illustrates the similar unfaithfulness of Israel in her relationship with the Lord.

Hosea 1-3	Hosea 4-13	Hosea 14
Hosea's Marriage	Hosea's Message	
• Gomer's Unfaithfulness • Gomer's Discipline • Gomer's Restoration		Ultimate restoration

The first three chapters utilize Hosea's marriage as a living parable of God's relationship with Israel. The remainder of the book consists of a large circuit that begins and ends with a Covenant Lawsuit. Both at the outset and at the close of this section the Covenant is specifically mentioned (compare Hosea 6:1, 7 with Hosea 12:1).

It has been suggested that Hosea can be outlined in the same way as the book of Deuteronomy. Both of these books follow the Suzerain Treaty Format:

1.   Preamble (Chapter 1).
2.   Historical Prologue (Chapters 2-3).
3.   Ethical Stipulations (Chapters 4-7).
4.   Sanctions (Chapters 8-9).
5.   Succession Arrangements (Chapters 10-14).

HOSEA'S FAMILY - A PROPHETIC PORTRAIT

When the Lord first spoke through Hosea, the Lord said to Hosea, "Go, take to yourself a wife of harlotry, and have children of harlotry; for the land commits flagrant harlotry, forsaking the Lord." 3 *So he went and took Gomer*

the daughter of Diblaim, and she conceived and bore him a
son. (Hosea 1:2-3).

Hosea was told to do something that would have shocked him even as it shocks us. He was to go and marry a "wife of harlotry" (literally - a "woman of fornication"). Let me say for the record that Christians are not normally called to such a marriage. In Hosea's case, he was called to play out the role of the Lord and His relationship to Israel. Hosea was to be like the Lord and his wife would demonstrate the same unfaithfulness that Israel had demonstrated.

There is a lesson here for us. It is that our marriages today are also to reflect the relationship of the Lord with His people. Husbands are called to love their wives as Christ loved the church and gave Himself for her (Ephesians 5:25). Wives, you are to show the same submissive and respectful and loyal nature to your husbands that the church is to show toward the Lord (Ephesians 5:22).

Hosea was told to marry a woman who would reflect the same level of purity and devotion that Israel demonstrated toward God. He was to marry a prostitute as a picture of the people of the promise land who had prostituted their spiritual lives. Hosea's marriage would become a paradigm for God's relationship with His people. By looking at Hosea's unfaithful wife, they would see themselves.

Yahweh	&	Israel
Hosea	&	Gomer
Christ	&	The Church
Husband	&	Wife

Hosea's portrayal did not end with his relationship with his wife. He was also to give names to his children that would reflect spiritual truths.

- Jezreel: *And the Lord said to him, "Name him Jezreel; for yet a little while, and I will punish the house of Jehu for the bloodshed of Jezreel, and I will put an end to the kingdom of the house of Israel. 5 And it will come about on that day, that I will break the bow of Israel in the valley of Jezreel" (Hosea 1:4-5).*

> The Hebrew word "Jezreel" means "God sows" or "God scatters" and is taken from the word זֶרַע, (*zera*) "to scatter seed."

The name of this first child was to be a reminder of a great evil that had taken place in Israel's political history. That evil took place at Jezreel. This is a bit like naming your child Alamo if you are a Texan or Dachau if you are from Germany. I had the opportunity to visit Dachau a number of years ago and to preach in a church that was just a few miles from that historic concentration camp where so many thousands of Jews were literally worked and starved to death.

Here was a child named Jezreel. What happened at Jezreel? That was where Jehu assassinated both Ahaziah, the king of Judah and Joram, the king of Israel. Neither was a great loss, but Jehu also went on to have all 70 of the children of Jehu put to death.

This Valley of Jezreel thus becomes a symbol for the place where God balances His books. It is the place of judgment. We know it today by the name of one of its key cities - Megiddo. It is this city that has given rise to the popular name "Armageddon."

- Lo-Ruhamah: *Then she conceived again and gave birth to a daughter. And the Lord said to him, "Name her Lo-ruhamah, for I will no longer have compassion on the house of Israel, that I should ever forgive them. 7 But I will have compassion on the house of Judah and deliver them by the Lord their God, and will not deliver them by bow, sword, battle, horses, or horsemen." (Hosea 1:6-7).*

The Hebrew word לֹא (*lo*) mere means "no." Thus Lo-ruhamah means "no compassion." By this, the Lord was giving testimony that the Northern Kingdom would be given no respite, but that it would be destroyed. On the other hand, future hope is offered to the Southern Kingdom of Judah.

- Lo-Ammi: *When she had weaned Lo-ruhamah, she conceived and gave birth to a son. 9 And the Lord said, "Name him Lo-ammi, for you are not My people and I am not your God." (Hosea 1:8-9).*

The Hebrew word *am* refers to "people." Hosea names this child, "Not mine." This is a stunning rebuke. The people of Israel had rightly thought of themselves as the people of God. But they had lost the right to consider themselves by such a name.

By these three names, the Lord is telling the Northern Kingdom of Israel that judgment is on the horizon and that they will soon be judged for their sins. At the same time, there is given a promise of future hope.

Yet the number of the sons of Israel
Will be like the sand of the sea,
Which cannot be measured or numbered;
And it will come about that, in the place
Where it is said to them, "You are not My people,"
It will be said to them, "You are the sons of the living God."
11 And the sons of Judah and the sons of Israel will be
gathered together,
And they will appoint for themselves one leader,
And they will go up from the land,
For great will be the day of Jezreel. (Hosea 1:10-11).

There is a promise given for future hope. It is that there will in the future be a restoration of the people of God. Paul gives us a New Testament commentary on this passage:

> *What if God, although willing to demonstrate His wrath and to make His power known, endured with much patience vessels of wrath prepared for destruction? 23 And He did so in order that He might make known the riches of His glory upon vessels of mercy, which He prepared beforehand for glory, 24 even us, whom He also called, not from among Jews only, but also from among Gentiles.*
> *As He says also in Hosea, "I will call those who were not My people, 'My people,' And her who was not beloved, 'beloved.' 26 And it shall be that in the place where it was said to them, 'you are not My people,' There they shall be called sons of the living God." (Romans 9:22-26).*

Notice how Paul interprets the passage from Hosea. He points to the fulfillment in those whom God has called not from among Jews only, but also from among Gentiles. Do you see it? The ultimate fulfillment of God's promise to Hosea is seen in the church. We have been given the title of "sons of the living God." At the same time, there is in Hosea's writings a call for the recipients of his day to repent. This is seen as we enter into the dialogue of chapter 2.

Say to your brothers, "Ammi," and to your sisters,
"Ruhamah."
2 Contend with your mother, contend,
For she is not my wife, and I am not her husband;
And let her put away her harlotry from her face,

And her adultery from between her breasts,
3 Lest I strip her naked
And expose her as on the day when she was born.
I will also make her like a wilderness,
Make her like desert land, And slay her with thirst.
4 Also, I will have no compassion on her children,
Because they are children of harlotry.
5 For their mother has played the harlot;
She who conceived them has acted shamefully.
For she said, 'I will go after my lovers,
Who give me my bread and my water,
My wool and my flax, my oil and my drink.'
6 Therefore, behold, I will hedge up her way with thorns,
And I will build a wall against her so that she cannot find her
paths.
7 And she will pursue her lovers, but she will not overtake
them;
And she will seek them, but will not find them.
Then she will say, "I will go back to my first husband,
For it was better for me then than now!" (Hosea 2:1-7).

In verse 6 the Lord proposes to put a hedge of thorns around His unfaithful wife. That doesn't sound very nice. Thorns are sharp. They stick and they hurt. But this is for her own good. It is to build a wall so that the people will have no choice but to return to the Lord. There is a lesson here. It is that God sometimes brings difficulties into our lives to drive us back to Himself.

For she does not know that it was I who gave her the grain,
the new wine, and the oil,
And lavished on her silver and gold,
Which they used for Baal.
9 Therefore, I will take back My grain at harvest time
And My new wine in its season. I will also take away My wool
and My flax
Given to cover her nakedness.
10 And then I will uncover her lewdness
In the sight of her lovers,
And no one will rescue her out of My hand.
11 I will also put an end to all her gaiety,
Her feasts, her new moons, her sabbaths,
And all her festal assemblies.

12 And I will destroy her vines and fig trees,
Of which she said, 'These are my wages which my lovers have
given me.'
And I will make them a forest,
And the beasts of the field will devour them.
13 And I will punish her for the days of the Baals
When she used to offer sacrifices to them
And adorn herself with her earrings and jewelry,
And follow her lovers, so that she forgot Me," declares the
Lord. (Hosea 2:8-13).

One of the sins of Israel was that of ingratitude. Somewhere along the line, the people had forgotten that it is the Lord who had provided the prosperity of the land. As a result, He would begin to bring about economic hardships.

After the terrorist attacks of September 11, 2001, televangelist Jerry Falwell came under a great deal of criticism when he publicly suggested that these events might be God's wake up call to Americans for the way they had ignored His teachings. Hosea's message would have received the same sorts of criticisms.

In Hosea 3 we see the final chapter in Hosea's family life. It is here that we see Hosea being told by the Lord to go and get back his wife.

> *Then the Lord said to me, "Go again, love a woman*
> *who is loved by her husband, yet an adulteress, even as the*
> *Lord loves the sons of Israel, though they turn to other gods*
> *and love raisin cakes." 2 So I bought her for myself for fifteen*
> *shekels of silver and a homer and a half of barley. 3 Then I*
> *said to her, "You shall stay with me for many days. You shall*
> *not play the harlot, nor shall you have a man; so I will also*
> *be toward you." (Hosea 3:1-3).*

Hosea goes out to find his faithless bride. He finds her as a slave and purchases her for himself from the slave market. He brings her home where he can command her future faithfulness. This is a picture of what the Lord will do with His people.

> *For the sons of Israel will remain for many days*
> *without king or prince, without sacrifice or sacred pillar, and*
> *without ephod or household idols. 5 Afterward the sons of*
> *Israel will return and seek the Lord their God and David their*
> *king; and they will come trembling to the Lord and to His*

goodness in the last days. (Hosea 3:4-5).

We know from history what took place in the days after Hosea. First Israel and then Judah were taken into captivity. When the final return took place in the days of Zerubbabel and Ezra, the Jews never again went aside to worship the false gods of the Canaanites.

Notice finally in verse 5 that the promise is that the people would return to David their king. This is especially significant when we consider that this is addressed to the Northern Ten Tribes who had rejected the kingship of the descendants of David. It is a prophecy that is ultimately fulfilled in Jesus, the son of David.

THE COVENANT LAWSUIT

A closer examination of the central chapters of Hosea suggest the possibility of a chiastic order to those central chapters.

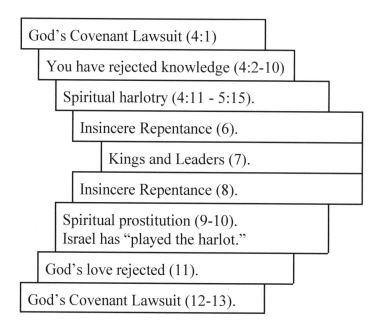

God's Covenant Lawsuit (4:1)

You have rejected knowledge (4:2-10)

Spiritual harlotry (4:11 - 5:15).

Insincere Repentance (6).

Kings and Leaders (7).

Insincere Repentance (8).

Spiritual prostitution (9-10).
Israel has "played the harlot."

God's love rejected (11).

God's Covenant Lawsuit (12-13).

Both the beginning and the close of this section contain phrasing that is reminiscent of a covenant lawsuit. You did not sign a covenant in those days. Instead you "cut" a covenant. This practice was so widespread that in later times, one could speak of entering into a covenant merely by speaking of how he "cut" with someone. Other examples of this same phenomena is seen in the following passages:

- Hosea 2:18 - *In that day I will also make [כָּרַתִּי, literally, "cut"] a covenant for them...*
- Haggai 2:5 says literally, "as for the word which I cut with you..."
- Psalm 105:9 ("...that which He cut with Abraham").
- I Kings 8:9 is literally, "where the Lord cut with the sons of Israel..."

The word translated "covenant" is בְּרִית (*beryth*). The origin of the word is uncertain. It is thought by some to have come from the Akkadian *birit*, which relates to the Hebrew בֵּין (*biyn*) -- "between." Another suggestion points to the Akkadian root *baru*, "to bind or fetter." Both ideas are present in the covenant. It is a binding action and its initiatory rite also mandated an agreement made between the two pieces of animals.

This practice of "covenant-cutting" involved taking one or more sacrificial animals and putting them to death and then cutting the animal into two parts and walking between the pieces of the animals.

> *And I will give the men who have transgressed My covenant, who have not fulfilled the words of the covenant which they made before Me, when they cut the calf in two and passed between its parts -- 19 the officials of Judah, and the officials of Jerusalem, the court officers, and the priests, and all the people of the land, who passed between the parts of the calf -- 20 and I will give them into the hand of their enemies and into the hand of those who seek their life. And their dead bodies shall be food for the birds of the sky and the beasts of the earth. (Jeremiah 34:18-20).*

As the makers of the covenant passed between the divided parts of the dead animal, they would recite the terms of the covenant. The implication was that if they broke the terms of the covenant, then may they also be killed and divided asunder as had been these animals.

The act of entering into a covenant involved in itself the symbolic death of the covenant maker. When the animals were cut, they represented the covenant-maker himself being cut and put to death. Now we can better understand the words of Hosea when he tells Israel that they have transgressed the covenant.

> *Listen to the word of the Lord, O sons of Israel,*
> *For the Lord has a case against the inhabitants of the land,*
> *Because there is no faithfulness or kindness*
> *Or knowledge of God in the land. (Hosea 4:1).*

This is covenant language. The Lord brings His legal dispute against Israel for having broken their covenant obligations.

> *For I delight in loyalty rather than sacrifice,*
> *And in the knowledge of God rather than burnt offerings.*
> *7 But like Adam they have transgressed the covenant;*
> *There they have dealt treacherously against Me. (Hosea 6:6-7).*

We have all gone the way of Adam. We have all sinned and have become covenant-breakers. The good news of the gospel is that God has made a New Covenant with men in which Christ Himself paid the penalty of a covenant-breaker on our behalf. We enter into this New Covenant through faith in Him so that His righteousness is credited to us.

It is exactly for this reason that Hosea is able to close his book upon a note of hope for the future. He calls for his readers to repent and to turn to the Lord.

> *Return, O Israel, to the Lord your God,*
> *For you have stumbled because of your iniquity.*
> *2 Take words with you and return to the Lord.*
> *Say to Him, "Take away all iniquity,*
> *And receive us graciously,*
> *That we may present the fruit of our lips." (Hosea 14:1-2).*

What is the result of such repentance? It is a restoration and a redemption.

> *I will heal their apostasy,*
> *I will love them freely,*
> *For My anger has turned away from them.*
> *5 I will be like the dew to Israel;*
> *He will blossom like the lily,*
> *And he will take root like the cedars of Lebanon.*
> *6 His shoots will sprout,*
> *And his beauty will be like the olive tree,*
> *And his fragrance like the cedars of Lebanon.*
> *7 Those who live in his shadow*
> *Will again raise grain,*
> *And they will blossom like the vine.*
> *His renown will be like the wine of Lebanon. (Hosea 14:4-7).*

LESSONS FROM HOSEA

1.   The Problem of Insincere Repentance.

> *What shall I do with you, O Ephraim?*
> *What shall I do with you, O Judah?*
> *For your loyalty is like a morning cloud,*
> *And like the dew which goes away early. (Hosea 6:4).*

One of the qualities of true repentance is that it lasts. It has been said that the problem with a living sacrifice is that it keeps crawling off the altar. Our problem is that today's repentance is often forgotten by tomorrow. The Lord presents this problem with the illustration of dew and a morning fog. They do not survive the heat of day.

Jesus also spoke about the necessity of enduring to the end. Endurance is the stuff of real faith. Saving faith is enduring faith. For this reason you are called to endure.

> *And this I pray, that your love may abound still more and more in real knowledge and all discernment, so that you may approve the things that are excellent, in order to be sincere and blameless until the day of Christ (Philippians 1:9-10).*

2.   The Problem of Social Injustice.

While the major problem that Hosea points out is that of spiritual unfaithfulness, this problem gives birth to social injustice. Hosea brings this to light when he describes...

> *A merchant, in whose hands are false balances,*
> *He loves to oppress. (Hosea 12:7).*

There is a lesson here. It is that bad theology will inevitably lead to bad living. When people are spiritually unfaithful to the Lord, it will not be long before that unfaithfulness begins to manifest itself in how they treat others.

The reverse is also true. One of the outward signs of repentance toward God is a change in the way you treat others. That was the sign that was seen in the life of the little tax collector named

671

Zaccheus. He determined to give half his possessions to the poor and to return fourfold to any whom he had defrauded (Luke 19:8). Jesus could look at him and say, "Here is a man who has received salvation."

JOEL
The Day of the Lord

The book contains no historical narrative. Because of this, we know virtually nothing of Joel or his readers. We do not even know when it was written. There are two major theories as to the date of its writing:

Date of Joel's Prophecy	
Before the Babylonian Captivity	**After the Babylonian Captivity**
• Though Jerusalem is mentioned several times, there is no hint of it having been previously destroyed and rebuilt. • The mention of the "northern army" seems to point to Assyria and/or Babylon as a present threat (2:20). • There are several references to the Temple (1:14).	• He speaks of Israel having been scattered among the nations (3:2). • He makes reference to the inhabitants of Judah having been sold to the "sons of Javin" - Greeks (3:6). • Edom is described as having done "violence to the sons of Judah" (3:19). • No mention is made of any kings. Priests and elders are seen as the leaders of the nation (2:16-17).

Several other observations can be made regarding this book.

- Joel makes no mention of the northern kingdom of Israel as a separate entity.
- When he does speak of Israel, he uses it in a sense where it seems to refer to a united covenant people of God.

The truth is that we do not know when the book of Joel is written. The Bible is not specific to tell us when it was written and that means it is not really important for us to know the date of writing. The message of the book looks past the immediate problems to see a future Day of the Lord.

Joel does not say anything about God reaching out to the Gentiles. You can read about God's program toward the Gentiles in some of the other prophetical books, but not in Joel. He is speaking to those who are family.

There are times when the Lord does this. He turns to those who are family and He conducts a family time and speaks to those who are family.

1:1	2:1	2:12	2:28	3:1	3:17
Locusts	Lord's Army	Call to Repentance	Lord's Spirit	Judgment	Promise
Judah			Nations		
Present	Imminent		Future	Ultimate	
B.C.			A.D.		

As can be seen from this chart, the center point of Joel's book it the call to repentance.

Book Begins: Mourning over Present Desolation	⇨	Book Ends: Rejoicing over Future Deliverance

THE AUTHOR

The word of the Lord that came to Joel, the son of Pethuel. (Joel 1:1).

This verse tells us virtually everything that we know about Joel. It isn't much. We don't know who Joel was and we don't know who Pethuel was. His name means "Jehovah God" and he was a prophet of God. This means the man is not going to be nearly so important to us as will be his message. Joel had something important to say because God had spoken to him and because God speaks to us through him. This is a message, not about a man's theories or a man's ideas, but from the throne of heaven.

THE LOCUST PLAGUE

This book begins with some bad things happening. It begins with a graphic description of a locust plague. That probably does not mean much to you if you do not live in an agricultural economy, but it was devastating to those to whom Joel addressed himself. C. S. Lewis described pain as God's megaphone. That is true on the personal level and sometimes it is also true on the national level.

We have seen that the story of the Old Testament is a story of the people of God falling away and then being judged for their sins and then coming back in repentance. It happened again and again in a repeating cycle. If you are a parent, then you understand this process. We went through it when we were raising our daughter. She would be warned of the consequences of disobedience. Then she would disobey. Then would come "the Day of the Father." The church experiences the same thing. God warns and sends His prophets and eventually He says, "Enough is enough."

Judah went through her period of prosperity where stocks were up and everything was prosperous and when pride built up to new levels. And then God took a little bug and demonstrated His power.

> *Hear this, O elders,*
> *And listen, all inhabitants of the land.*
> *Has anything like this happened in your days*
> *Or in your fathers' days?*
> *3 Tell your sons about it,*
> *And let your sons tell their sons,*
> *And their sons the next generation.*
> *4 What the gnawing locust has left, the swarming locust has eaten;*
> *And what the swarming locust has left, the creeping locust has eaten;*
> *And what the creeping locust has left, the stripping locust has eaten. (Joel 1:2-4).*

If you do not read this chapter through the eyes of faith, then you will only see bugs. On the other hand, if you look to see what is really happening here, you will learn that these locusts are really the army of God. They are to be a lesson to future generations.

I did not live through the Great Depression. But my wife's grandparents did and they told me what it was like. Joel tells people to do the same thing. They are to ask whether there has ever been a time as bad as this.

> *The field is ruined,*
> *The land mourns,*
> *For the grain is ruined,*
> *The new wine dries up,*
> *Fresh oil fails. (Joel 1:10).*

In describing the plight of the people, Joel breaks into a poetic alliteration. We can see the effect by a slight altering of the translation as follows:

The field fails,
The land loses,
The grain is gone,
The wine withers,
Fresh oil fails.

This is the chant of a funeral dirge. It brings the same picture of the successive waves of plagues that we saw at the outset of this prophecy. The point is that bad things happen and they keep on happening.

CALL TO REPENTANCE

"Yet even now," declares the Lord,
"Return to Me with all your heart,
And with fasting, weeping, and mourning;
13 And rend your heart and not your garments." (Joel 2:12-
13).

The rending of ones garments was the culturally accepted method of demonstrating deep emotional grief. As such, it was an appropriate method of showing repentance. The problem was that the people had made these sort of outward signs without any real repentance on the inside. We do the same thing when we go to church and engage in all of the rituals of worship while never letting it touch our hearts or our lives.

Blow a trumpet in Zion,
Consecrate a fast, proclaim a solemn assembly (Joel 2:15).

This is a call, not only for personal repentance, but also for national repentance. God comes in a mighty way when the congregation of His people turn to Him. Jesus said *if two of you agree on earth about anything that they may ask, it shall be done for them by My Father who is in heaven* (Matthew 18:19). There is a lesson here. It is that my spirituality affects you and your spirituality affects me. Living in a nation in which individuality is held forth as a desirable value, we often miss the importance of a corporate spiritual life. How often do you hear people say that they have a relationship with God and yet have nothing to do with a local church? It isn't possible. The Lord has called us to be one and, if we are not one, then we have not listened to His call.

PROMISE OF THE SPIRIT

The center point of Joel's prophecy takes place in Joel 2:28-32. It is a prophecy of the pouring forth of the Spirit of God upon all mankind.

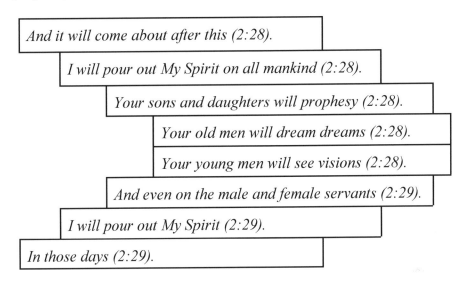

And it will come about after this (2:28).

I will pour out My Spirit on all mankind (2:28).

Your sons and daughters will prophesy (2:28).

Your old men will dream dreams (2:28).

Your young men will see visions (2:28).

And even on the male and female servants (2:29).

I will pour out My Spirit (2:29).

In those days (2:29).

This was a striking promise. It was striking, not because the Spirit of God had never come among His people, but because it had never come in a universal manner. It had come here a little and there a little. There would come a day when it would be on all mankind: Sons and daughters, old and young, even upon male and female servants. The passage continues following the close of the chiasm:

> *And I will display wonders in the sky and on the earth,*
> *Blood, fire, and columns of smoke.*
> *31 The sun will be turned into darkness,*
> *And the moon into blood,*
> *Before the great and awesome day of the Lord comes. (Joel 2:30-31).*

Many hundreds of years later, Peter quoted this passage on the day of Pentecost. He concluded that what was taking place in his day was that which Joel had promised. Notice the elements of the prophecy.

- God's Spirit to be poured out.
- Sons and daughters to prophesy.
- Dreams and visions.
- Blood and fire, and vapor of smoke.
- The sun will be turned into darkness and the moon into blood.

How are we to understand this prophecy? How much of this was fulfilled in Peter's day? I want to suggest that all of it was fulfilled in Peter's day.

- God's Spirit was poured out.
- Sons and daughters - Jewish men and women - prophesied.
- Dreams and visions were given.
- The blood of the Son of God had just been shed and now tongues of fire appeared over the heads of the followers of Christ.
- The sun had been darkened at His crucifixion.

Peter identified the details of this prophecy with the events of the death, the burial and the ascension of Jesus. In a very real way, the cross was the center point of all human history.

THE DAY OF THE LORD

The point of these prophecies is that they were given as signs. They would take place *before the great and glorious day of the Lord shall come (2:20)*. What is the "Day of the Lord?" The phrase is used throughout the Old Testament to describe a day of judgment.

> *Wail ye; for the day of the Lord is near;*
> *It will come as destruction from the Almighty. (Isaiah 13:6).*

> *Behold, the day of the Lord is coming,*
> *Cruel, with fury and burning anger,*
> *To make the land a desolation;*
> *And He will exterminate its sinners from it. (Isaiah 13:9).*

> *Alas for the day!*
> *For the day of the Lord is near,*
> *And it will come as destruction from the Almighty. (Joel 1:15).*

The Day of the Lord is not always in the future. Jeremiah, the writer of the book of Lamentations, describes the fall of Jerusalem in 586 B.C. as being a fulfillment of the Day of the Lord.

Thou didst call as in the day of an appointed feast
My terrors on every side;
And there was no one who escaped or survived
In the day of the Lord's anger.
Those whom I bore and reared,
My enemy annihilated them. (Lamentations 2:22).

Does the fact that the Day of the Lord was fulfilled in 586 B.C. mean that there are no other fulfillments? No, it does not. Peter saw a fulfillment in his day. He elsewhere describes another fulfillment which is still to come.

But the day of the Lord will come like a thief, in which
the heavens will pass away with a roar and the elements will
be destroyed with intense heat, and the earth and its works
will be burned up. (2 Peter 3:10).

The Day of the Lord is that time when God's hand enters history in judgment. It came in Peter's day. And it will come again in the future. That means we can read the prophecy of Joel and see applications in our own lives today. This is the reason the prophecy has been given to us. It is so that we will hear, respond, repent, and follow the Lord.

THE VALLEY OF JUDGMENT

For behold, in those days and at that time,
When I restore the fortunes of Judah and Jerusalem,
2 I will gather all the nations,
And bring them down to the valley of Jehoshaphat.
Then I will enter into judgment with them there
On behalf of My people and My inheritance, Israel,
Whom they have scattered among the nations;
And they have divided up My land. (Joel 3:1-2).

Joel looks forward to a time of the judgment of the nations. It is a time when Judah and Jerusalem are restored and when the Gentile nations are gathered for judgment.

The reference to the Valley of Jehoshaphat hails back to an event from Judah's history. The story is found in 2 Chronicles 20. It tells of an invasion of an alliance of all of the enemies of Judah.

> *Now it came about after this that the sons of Moab and the sons of Ammon, together with some of the Meunites, came to make war against Jehoshaphat. 2 Then some came and reported to Jehoshaphat, saying, "A great multitude is coming against you from beyond the sea, out of Aram and behold, they are in Hazazon-tamar (that is Engedi)." (2 Chronicles 20:1-2).*

Jehoshaphat did that which Joel was instructing the people to do. He called for a national time of fasting and prayer. As they were praying, the Lord sent His Spirit upon one of the leaders with a prophesy. They were to march out toward the enemy, but it would be the Lord who would fight the battle.

Trusting in the word of the Lord, Jehoshaphat marches out, placing in his front ranks neither infantry or archers, but rather the temple musicians and singers. They come to the place of the battle and they find that it has begun without them.

> *For the sons of Ammon and Moab rose up against the inhabitants of Mount Seir destroying them completely, and when they had finished with the inhabitants of Seir, they helped to destroy one another. 24 When Judah came to the lookout of the wilderness, they looked toward the multitude; and behold, they were corpses lying on the ground, and no one had escaped. (2 Chronicles 20:23-24).*

The alliance had fallen apart and those who came to fight against Judah had fallen to fighting amongst themselves. As a result, the enemies of Judah literally destroyed themselves and when Jehoshaphat and his army came upon the scene, it was to look out upon a valley full of corpses.

The name of Jehoshaphat took on a special significance that day, for it means, "Yahweh who judges." This valley of judgment along the shores of the Dead Sea was renamed the Valley of Berachah by the people of Judah, because it became a place of "blessing" the Lord.

That story became a meta-narrative and a paradigm for describing God's future work of judgment and protection for His people. He says, "I'm going to do it again. I will again arrange the affairs of men so as to cancel out the threats of nations and to bring about my Kingdom."

There is another place that has also become both a place of cursing and a place of blessing. When Jesus went to the cross, it was to become a curse for us so that we might receive the blessing of God. It was there that God entered into judgment with mankind, judging His own Son in our place and inflicting upon Him the death we deserved.

As a result, we also have an inheritance that has been offered to the nations. It is the inheritance of the children of the King and it is given freely to all who come to Him.

AMOS
The Prophet of Social Injustice

The name "Amos" means "burden." He was given a burden from God. Amos was from the area of Tekoa, located to the south of Jerusalem. However most of his prophecy is directed toward the Northern Kingdom of Israel. He tells us that he was not originally a prophet (1:1; 7:14).

> Then Amos answered and said to Amaziah, "I am not a prophet, nor am I the son of a prophet; for I am a herdsman and a grower of sycamore figs. 15 But the Lord took me from following the flock and the Lord said to me, "Go prophesy to My people Israel." 16 And now hear the word of the Lord: you are saying, 'You shall not prophesy against Israel nor shall you speak against the house of Isaac.'" (Amos 7:14-16).

Amos wasn't a professional prophet. He had no string of degrees behind his name. He had not been to propheteering school. He had not graduated from seminary. Amos wasn't even a preacher's kid. He had a real job. He wasn't paid to be good, he was good for nothing. There is a principle here. It is that God delights in using unqualified people to do His work.

- He uses a handful of Galilean fishermen.
- He uses a greedy tax-collector.
- He uses a shepherd boy with a sling, a farmer with a piece of fleece and a Samaritan woman with a jug of water.

The fact that God uses unqualified people is a sign of His grace. It also means that He can use me and He can use you.

DATE OF WRITING

> The words of Amos, who was among the sheepherders from Tekoa, which he envisioned in visions concerning Israel in the days of Uzziah king of Judah, and in the days of Jeroboam son of Joash, king of Israel, two years before the

earthquake (Amos 1:1).

Amos tells us when this book was written. It was two years before the earthquake. This would give us an exact date if only we knew when the earthquake took place. We don't. What we do know is that the Northern Kingdom of Israel had not yet been taken into captivity.

Amos tells us that he wrote during the reign of Jeroboam, son of Joash, king of Israel (1:1). This was Jeroboam II. His reign was one of great prosperity in Israel. During his reign, the borders of Israel were extended to their very greatest size since the days of Solomon. This means that when Amos preached of the coming judgment of God, the circumstances of the made it appear as though such a prophecy was unwarranted.

MESSAGE OF THE BOOK

For three transgressions and for four...	Judgments against Israel	Signs of Judgment	Promise of Restoration
1-2	3-6	7-9:10	9:11-ff
• Damascus • Gaza • Tyre • Edom • Ammon • Moab • Judah • Israel	• You were God's chosen people (3) • Against the Women (4) • Seek me that you may live (5) • Against the Men(6)	• Locusts (7:1-3) • Fire (7:4-6) • Plumbline (7:7-17) • Ripe Fruit (8) • Lord by the Altar (9:1-10)	Remnant of Israel and a promise of restoration

And he said, "The Lord roars from Zion,
And from Jerusalem He utters His voice;
And the shepherds' pasture grounds mourn,
And the summit of Carmel dries up." (Amos 1:2).

The message of Amos begins on a loud note. It begins with the "roar" of the Lord. The Hebrew word used here is usually used in the context of a lion. This stands in contrast to the way in which God has been pictured elsewhere. The same God of whom David could say, "The Lord is my shepherd," is now seen to be playing the part of a hungry lion who is going to come and gobble up the nation.

Interestingly, the book of Amos begins with the words with which the book of Joel ends. It is with this same reference to the roaring of the Lord from Zion.

Joel 3:16	Amos 1:2
And the Lord roars from Zion and utters His voice from Jerusalem....	*And he said, "The Lord roars from Zion, and from Jerusalem He utters His voice..."*

We are not entirely sure when the book of Joel was written, but it is possible that Amos picks up where Joel left off. It is for this reason that the books have this arrangement in our Bibles.

HISTORICAL SETTING

Even though Amos was from the Southern Kingdom of Judah, he was sent to prophesy to the Northern Kingdom of Israel.

1.   Political Setting.

Israel in this day was at the height of her prosperity. There were several factors that contributed to this prosperity.

• Defeat of Judah.

Jehoash, Jeroboam's father, had defeated Judah in battle, torn down a portion of the wall of Jerusalem and plundered the riches of the king's palace as well as the utensils of the Temple (2 Kings 14:13-14).

• Fall of Aram.

Aram (also known as Syria) and its capital city of Damascus, the ancient enemy of Israel, was invaded by the Assyrian army. When the Assyrians were done, they gathered up their plunder and returned to their mountain homeland on the other side of the Euphrates, leaving Israel to mop up the subdued lands.

- Decline of Egypt.

Egypt during this period was led by a dynasty of very weak rulers. They posed no threat to the countries outside of their domain. At the height of his power, Jeroboam II exercised nominal rule northward extending all the way to the Euphrates River.

2.   Economic Setting.

With all enemies subdued, a time of great economic prosperity ensued. This was especially seen in the rise of a rich merchant class. This financial prosperity brought with it a corresponding social corruption.

Although there were many rich, there were also many poor. Instead of this great wealth being utilized to relieve their distress, the rich set about using their riches to buy up the lands of the poor and to dispossess them.

3.   The Religious Setting.

The Israelites continued to be a very religious people. They built up places of worship throughout their land and they held religious festivals and they gave offerings to the Lord. But there were two problems with their practice of religion.

- It was a Pluralistic Religion.

Back in the days of Jeroboam I, places of worship had been established for Israel at Dan and Bethel. Golden calves had been erected at these locations. While it was argued that there was a precedent for this in Aaron's use of a golden calf, the obvious truth was that this led the Israelites into idolatry. It was not that they stopped worshiping the Lord, but that they stopped worshiping only the Lord. He became one God among several.

- It was a Religion without Reality.

Even when the Israelites did worship the Lord, they did not allow their religion to affect their secular lives.

I hate, I reject your festivals,
Nor do I delight in your solemn assemblies.

22 Even though you offer up to Me burnt offerings and your grain offerings,
I will not accept them;
And I will not even look at the peace offerings of your fatlings.
23 Take away from Me the noise of your songs;
I will not even listen to the sound of your harps.
24 But let justice roll down like waters
And righteousness like an ever-flowing stream. (Amos 5:21-24).

There is a lesson here. It is that church attendance makes no points with God if it is not accompanied with personal justice and righteousness. The Israelites had not abandoned their religious practices. They had merely watered them down. They said, "We want to follow God, but we don't want to be fanatical about it."

This was the world to which Amos preached. It was a world that was enamored with financial success; a world that was intent on climbing the ladder of success. In fifty years it would all be gone. The Assyrians had gone home for the time being, but within a few short years they would be back and they would completely obliterate the Northern Kingdom of Israel.

JUDGMENTS AGAINST THE NATIONS

On eight consecutive occasions throughout the first two chapters, we read the refrain: *"For three transgressions and for four..."* One by one we see each of the enemy nations around Israel being condemned by the Lord. We can imagine the people of Israel nodding their heads in agreement over these various judgments.

Nations	Relation to Israel
• Damascus • Gaza • Tyre	Pagan nations with no relation to Israel
• Edom • Ammon • Moab	Cousins to the Israelites through Esau and the children of Lot

• Judah	Part of the former nation
• Israel	The ten northern tribes

The judgments begin with those nations surrounding Israel and then they point to those nations that are related to Israel and finally they come to center upon Israel herself.

ISRAEL'S UNIQUE RELATIONSHIP

> *Hear this word which the Lord has spoken against you, sons of Israel, against the entire family which He brought up from the land of Egypt, 2 you only have I chosen among all the families of the earth; therefore, I will punish you for all your iniquities. (Amos 3:1-2).*

One might be tempted to think that Israel would be able to get away with more because of her special position. Amos tells us that Israel's special position makes her more accountable before God. It is because Israel has been chosen by God that she will be punished.

There is a principle here. It is the principle that to whom much is given, much is required. I didn't say it -- Jesus did: *And from everyone who has been given much shall much be required; and to whom they entrusted much, of him they will ask all the more (Luke 12:48).*

We live in a country where much has been given. There is a church on every street corner. You can walk into almost any bookstore and buy a Bible. Much has been given to us and we shall be judged accordingly.

Amos 3 contains a covenant lawsuit against the entire nation. It is presented in five points.

1. The Parties of the Covenant are Introduced: *Hear this word which the Lord has spoken against you, sons of Israel, against the entire family which He brought up from the land of Egypt (3:1).*
2. Covenant Indictment: *I will punish you for all your iniquities (3:2).*
3. The Sovereignty of the Sovereign (3:3-8).
4. Summons of the Guilty: *Proclaim on the citadels in Ashdod and on the citadels in the land of Egypt and say, "Assemble yourselves on the mountains of Samaria and see the great tumults within her and the oppressions in her midst" (3:9).*
5. Judgment (3:10-15).

The judgment for Israel's sins will be seen in the form of an invader who will loot her citadels and snatch away her inhabitants.

Note that verse 15 that speaks of how the houses of ivory will also perish. When we come to Amos 6:4 there is a reference to those who recline on beds of ivory. Ivory was a precious commodity in that day. You don't mine ivory from the ground or grow it in a field. It comes from the tusks of elephants. It takes a lot of elephants to build a house of ivory.

Archaeological digs in the ruins of ancient Samaria have found a number of ivory relics. This pointed to the great wealth of the city and its inhabitants. But the city that had become enamored with its collection of wealth would lose it all in the coming judgment.

CHARGE AGAINST THE WIVES OF ISRAEL

As we begin Amos 4, the prophet addresses himself to a new group: They are the cows of Bashan.

> *Hear this word, you cows of Bashan who are on the mountains of Samaria,*
> *Who oppress the poor, who crush the needy,*
> *Who say to your husbands, "Bring now, that we may drink?"*
> *(Amos 4:1).*

Bashan was that portion of Israel's land that lay on the eastern banks of the Jordan River. When the Israelites had first approached the land under Joshua, two and a half of the tribes decided that they would take for their inheritance the land on the east of the Jordan. By doing so, they were accepting God's second-best.

This land was known for its cattle. But God is not actually addressing cattle. These cows are of the human kind. It is a reference to the women of Israel. They are pictured like cows, interested only in grazing.

They are charged with oppressing the poor and crushing the needy. It is not that they were out actively doing these things. But in feeding their appetites, they were encouraging their husbands to go to any lengths to get ahead.

American culture caters to this sort of thinking. Women are taught to idolize the man who has a well-paying job, who drives a fancy car, and who is able to own a nice home. So what if his aggressive business dealings put his competition out of business. That is what capitalism is all about, isn't it?

I'm not saying that capitalism is bad, but I want to point out that it often feeds the love of money and we are told in the New Testament that the love of money is at the root of all sorts of evils (1 Timothy 6:10).

> *The Lord God has sworn by His holiness,*
> *"Behold, the days are coming upon you*
> *When they will take you away with meat hooks,*
> *And the last of you with fish hooks." (Amos 4:2).*

God swears an oath. This is more than a promise. This is a binding decree. When an oath was sworn, the implication was that the thing by which you swore would be forfeit for destruction if the oath did not come to pass. God swore by His holiness. He was saying in effect, "If My promise in this matter does not come to pass, then may My very holiness be destroyed."

What is the subject of the oath? It is a promise of Israel's coming captivity. It is described in graphic terms.

> *They will take you away with meat hooks,*
> *And the last of you with fish hooks. (Amos 4:2b).*

That this promise was literally fulfilled is graphically portrayed in the Assyrian inscriptions that show the Assyrian conquerors placing hooks through the lips of their conquered enemies.

> *"But I gave you also cleanness of teeth in all your cities*
> *And lack of bread in all your places,*
> *Yet you have not returned to Me," declares the Lord. (Amos 4:6).*

The refrain, "Yet you have not returned to Me," is found five times in this chapter (4:6, 8, 9, 10, 11). The ever-increasing cycles of discipline are reminiscent of Leviticus 26 with its similar promise of increasing disciple. There is a lesson here. When crops fail and when companies go out of business and when the stock market comes crashing down, God is in control. Why does He allow these sorts of things to take place? It is to turn the hearts of His people back to Himself.

CALL TO RETURN

Amos 5 calls to mind a funeral. It does this by announcing a funeral dirge. Someone has died and there is sorrow and mourning.

> *Hear this word which I take up for you as a dirge,*
> *O house of Israel.*
> *2 She has fallen, she will not rise again--*
> *The virgin Israel. She lies neglected on her land;*
> *There is none to raise her up. (Amos 5:1-2).*

This is not a dirge of how Israel was in the days of Amos, but rather a dirge of what she would become. At the same time, there is a promise of restoration if they will only repent.

- Seek Me that you may live (5:4).
- Seek the Lord that you may live (5:6).
- Seek good and not evil, that you may live (5:14).

In each of these calls, there is the implied warning that, if you will not seek the Lord, then you will not continue to live. There is judgment on the horizon and that judgment is bringing death.

Again the charge is given that the rich have unfairly oppressed the poor. They have done it through heavy rents and heavy taxation. They have done it by not giving to the poor.

> *Therefore, because you impose heavy rent on the poor*
> *And exact a tribute of grain from them,*
> *Though you have built houses of well-hewn stone,*
> *Yet you will not live in them;*
> *You have planted pleasant vineyards, yet you will not drink*
> *their wine.*
> *12 For I know your transgressions are many and your sins are*
> *great,*
> *You who distress the righteous and accept bribes,*
> *And turn aside the poor in the gate. (Amos 5:11-12).*

In today's society, we do not label such things as "bribes." Instead they are called "campaign contributions" and are even tax deductible, but the effect is often the same. We give money to people who already have money and we neglect those who have none.

FIVE SIGNS OF JUDGMENT

In the last three chapters of his book, Amos is given five graphic representations of God's coming judgment against Israel.

1.   Vision of Locusts.

> *Thus the Lord God showed me, and behold, He was forming a locust-swarm when the spring crop began to sprout. And behold, the spring crop was after the king's mowing. 2 And it came about, when it had finished eating the vegetation of the land, that I said, "Lord God, please pardon! How can Jacob stand, for he is small?" 3 The Lord changed His mind about this. "It shall not be," said the Lord. (Amos 7:1-3).*

There were few things more catastrophic in the economy of the ancient world than a locust swarm. You could fight an invading army, but you were helpless when a sea of locusts descended upon the crops eating everything in sight.

In view of such a vision, Amos intercedes with the Lord and, as a result, the Lord shows patience and forgiveness to Israel so that the plague does not come to pass.

2.   Vision of Fire.

> *Thus the Lord God showed me, and behold, the Lord God was calling to contend with them by fire, and it consumed the great deep and began to consume the farm land. 5 Then I said, "Lord God, please stop! How can Jacob stand, for he is small?" 6 The Lord changed His mind about this. "This too shall not be," said the Lord God. (Amos 7:4-6).*

This time, the vision is one of a fire that consumes the farm lands. Again, Amos intercedes on behalf of Israel and again there is a promise of patience and mercy from the Lord.

The point that God is making in these first two visions is that Israel has for a long time been committing deeds that were worthy of punishment, but God has been graciously patient in waiting for a repentance that has not been forthcoming.

3.   Vision of the Plumbline.

> *Thus He showed me, and behold, the Lord was standing by a vertical wall, with a plumb line in His hand. 8 And the Lord said to me, "What do you see, Amos?" And I said, "A plumb line." Then the Lord said,*
> *"Behold I am about to put a plumb line*
> *In the midst of My people Israel.*
> *I will spare them no longer.*
> *9 The high places of Isaac will be desolated*
> *And the sanctuaries of Israel laid waste.*
> *Then shall I rise up against the house of Jeroboam*
> *with the sword." (Amos 7:7-9).*

A plumbline is a measuring device. It uses a weighted line to measure how straight is a vertical wall. The Lord is pictured holding a plumb line that He uses to measure His people.

Whereas in the previous two visions, we see God's patient withholding of the punishments that were deserved, this time the Lord says that they will no longer be spared the coming judgment.

4.   Vision of Ripe Fruit.

> *Thus the Lord God showed me, and behold, there was a basket of summer fruit. 2 And He said, "What do you see, Amos?" And I said, "A basket of summer fruit." Then the Lord said to me, "The end has come for My people Israel. I will spare them no longer. 3 The songs of the palace will turn to wailing in that day," declares the Lord God. "Many will be the corpses; in every place they will cast them forth in silence." (Amos 8:1-3).*

This time, Israel is pictured as a basket of summer fruit. The point of the vision is that Israel is overly ripe for the plucking and that the end is closer than they think.

5.   Vision of the Lord by the Altar.

I saw the Lord standing beside the altar, and He said,
"Smite the capitals so that the thresholds will shake,
And break them on the heads of them all!
Then I will slay the rest of them with the sword;
They will not have a fugitive who will flee,
Or a refugee who will escape. (Amos 9:1).

The altar is a place of sacrifice and forgiveness. But it is also a place of judgment. The altar is a place where a life is taken as a judgment against sin. Where there is no repentance and faith, there is no forgiveness.

A CONCLUDING PROMISE OF HOPE

"In that day I will raise up the fallen booth of David,
And wall up its breaches;
I will also raise up its ruins,
And rebuild it as in the days of old;
12 That they may possess the remnant of Edom
And all the nations who are called by My name,"
Declares the Lord who does this.
13 "Behold, days are coming," declares the Lord,
"When the plowman will overtake the reaper
And the treader of grapes him who sows seed;
When the mountains will drip sweet wine,
And all the hills will be dissolved.
14 "Also I will restore the captivity of My people Israel,
And they will rebuild the ruined cities and live in them,
They will also plant vineyards and drink their wine,
And make gardens and eat their fruit.
15 I will also plant them on their land,
And they will not again be rooted out from their land
Which I have given them," Says the Lord your God. (Amos
9:11-15).

Who is the "booth and tabernacle of David"? It is the same One who became flesh and "tabernacled" among us (John 1:14). It is a reference to Jesus. It is through His coming that we have a rebuilding of the tabernacle of David and a restoration of the people of God.

OBADIAH
Prophecy Against Edom

Obadiah writes to the nation of Edom in the same way that Jonah and Nahum prophesied against Assyria. Edom would be tempted to gloat over the defeat of Jerusalem by Nebuchadnezzar and the ensuing Babylonian Captivity. This book is a warning against such gloating.

DATE: Written around the time of the fall of Jerusalem to Nebuchadnezzar (587/6 B.C.). Edom would be tempted to gloat over the defeat of Jerusalem and the plight of the Jews. This book is a warning against such gloating.

1:1	1:12	1:15
Vision against Edom	**Warning against Edom**	**Israel's Victory**
• Edom defeated despite her present strength and security (1-4) • Edom will be thoroughly plundered (5-7) • Edom will be cut off forever (8-10)	Do not... • Gloat over your brother's day • Rejoice over the sons of Judah • Enter the gate of My people • Gloat over their calamity • Loot their wealth • Stand at the fork of the road to cut down their fugitives • Imprison their survivors	• Day of the Lord coming against the nations (15-16) • Israel will retake their own land (17) • Victorious Israel will rule over the surrounding nations (18-21)

Like the book of Habakkuk, the book of Obadiah addresses the issue of divine justice. In this case, the focus is specifically upon the kingdom of Edom and their mistreatment of Judah during the Babylonian conquest of Jerusalem.

Here is the question: Why has God allowed Edom to prosper and to mock Judah with impunity? The answer is that God will indeed bring judgment upon Edom.

The arrogance of your heart has deceived you,
You who live in the clefts of the rock,
In the loftiness of your dwelling place,
Who say in your heart, 'Who will bring me down to earth?'
"Though you build high like the eagle,
Though you set your nest among the stars,
From there I will bring you down," declares the Lord. (Obadiah
1:3-4).

This language calls to mind the ancient city of Petra. By the end of the 4th century B.C., Petra would become the capital of Edom. It characterized the words of this prophecy as a city "in the cleft of the rock."

This prophecy was fulfilled quite literally in the days of the Maccabees and the Hasmonean kings. The tables were turned and Judah eventually conquered Edom. You can go today to the ancient capital city of Petra -- a great fortress built into solid rock. But you will be hard-pressed to find the Edomite.

However, if you read this short book and see only the tiny kingdom of Edom, you miss the point of the book. It is that God will judge the nations. In this regard, Edom is seen as a mere representative of all of the nations. What is true of Edom is true of all nations. This is taught in verse 15 where we read: *For the day of the Lord draws near on all the nations. As you have done, it will be done to you. Your dealings will return on your own head.*

The purpose of this prophecy is not merely to chastise Edom. It is so that men will repent of their wrongdoing and return to the Lord. It is so that men repent and thereby stop this prophecy from coming to pass. Prophecy always has that purpose. It is not meant for you to use to draw a futuristic timeline. It is given for you to change your life.

KEY LESSONS

- God cares for his people when they suffer.
- God warns but will eventually judge those who persecute his people.
- God will give victory to his people.
- God's faithful people will inherit the kingdom of God in its fullness: The kingdom will be the Lord's (Obadiah 1:21).

JONAH
Story of Compassion

The story of Jonah is quite different from the rest of the prophets. Instead of being a book filled with prophecies and visions, this is a narrative telling the story of Jonah and his own experiences with the Lord. The story is given in two major parts:

Jonah commissioned to go to Nineveh (1:1-3) • Jonah arose to flee		Jonah commissioned to go to Nineveh (3:1-3) • Jonah arose and went	
Jonah and the pagan sailors (1:4-16)	• Yahweh threatens judgment • Sailors respond immediately • Sailors cry out to God for mercy • Captain participates in effort • The Lord spares their lives	Jonah and the pagan Ninevites (3:3-10)	• Yahweh threatens judgment • Ninevites respond immediately • People cry out to God for mercy • King participates in effort • The Lord spares their lives
Jonah's prayer of repentance (1:17-2:10)	• Speaks of the Lord's love • Thanks God that his life and soul have been spared	Jonah's prayer of complaint (4:1-5)	• Complains of the Lord's love • Resentful and wishes that his life and soul would be taken
	The Lord's Lesson for Jonah (4:5-11)		

Some have tried to suggest that the book of Jonah is either an allegory or a parable and that we are not meant to understand it as a report of actual historical events. But Jonah was an actual historical figure. He is mentioned by name in 2 Kings 14:25 as having lived in or before the days of Jeroboam II of Israel.

Speaking of Jeroboam II, the Bible says that he *restored the border of Israel from the entrance of Hamath as far as the Sea of the Arabah, according to the word of the Lord, the God of Israel, which He spoke through His servant Jonah the son of Amittai, the prophet, who was of Gath-hepher* (2 Kings 14:25).

Jonah is a book about God. Everyone and everything that God touches obeys...

- The Storm
- The Sailors
- The Fish
- Nineveh
- The Plant
- The Worm
- The East Wind

"The Jonah narrative is given in the form of a comedy. We are meant to laugh at Jonah. Because of this playfulness, it is a story that disarms us. It flies under the radar of our personal defenses and it drops its thought-provoking bomb upon us when we least expect it." – TJ Campo

Everyone obeyed except for the preacher. Have you ever told God, "No"? Perhaps you didn't do it on the outside, but if you were honest, you were saying, "No" on the inside.

The story of Jonah is a living parable. We are told of his experiences traveling to Nineveh because there will come a day when the Israelites will also find themselves "rubbing shoulders" with the Assyrians and the people of Nineveh.

If you ask most people what is the topic of the book of Jonah, they will say something regarding his being swallowed by a great fish. This is the portion of the story that is most memorable, but it is hardly the climax of the narrative. To the contrary, it merely sets the stage so that we can approach what turns out to be the climactic event.

The second half of the book of Jonah tells of his travel to Nineveh and the repentant response to his preaching. Jonah's reaction to this tremendous repentance is anger. He is angry because he does not want Nineveh's repentance; he wants Nineveh's destruction.

This brings us to the big idea of the book. It is focused upon God's compassion, not only for the people of Nineveh, but for all the peoples of the world. The book ends with a question and that question is meant to be asked by the reader as well as by Jonah. Is it right for God and for God's people to seek vengeance or to seek compassion? What is to be our attitude toward the people of the world?

The counterpart to Jonah is Jesus Christ who spent three days, not in the belly of a fish, but in the heart of the earth. This was God's great act of compassion, not only for Nineveh, but for all the world.

JONAH 1: RUNNING FROM GOD

The word of the Lord came to Jonah the son of Amittai saying, 2 "Arise, go to Nineveh the great city, and cry against it, for their wickedness has come up before Me." (Jonah 1:1).

Nineveh was the capital city of the Assyrian Empire. The Assyrians lived along the banks of the Tigris River as it flowed down from Upper Mesopotamia in the land that today is known as Iraq. Theirs was an ancient empire. But the Assyrians had not remained within the borders of their homeland. They were an aggressive, warrior race and they had often conducted raids southward to the very borders of Israel.

> God's calling is a quest in the Tolkein sense of the word. It catches you and it changes your life forever. -- TJ Campo

Jonah's mission was like a modern Jew being sent to Adolph Hitler or to Saddam Hussein. The Assyrians were the Nazis of the ancient world. They were known for their terror-tactics. They could conquer a city and gouge out eyes and cut off arms and legs and then they would get down to serious torture.

The Assyrians were a bad people. Even God said that. He said that *"their wickedness has come up before Me."* This was the people to whom Jonah was sent. He was to speak to them about the Lord. This is a book with a missionary theme. It tells us that God has a heart for missions. He had one Son and He was a missionary. Jesus was the most cross-cultural missionary of all time. He crossed from heaven to earth.

The word of the Lord came to Jonah the son of Amittai saying, 2 "Arise, go to Nineveh the great city, and cry against it, for their wickedness has come up before Me."
But Jonah rose up to flee to Tarshish from the presence of the Lord. So he went down to Joppa, found a ship which was going to Tarshish, paid the fare, and went down into it to go with them to Tarshish from the presence of the Lord. (Jonah 1:1-3).

Jonah was told to go. He went, but he went in the wrong direction. Instead of heading to Nineveh, he got on a boat heading for Tarshish. He was told to get up and go and instead he got up to flee. Jonah knew God's will. But he did not obey it. There is a lesson here. It is that knowing God's will is not enough. Having the correct theology is not enough. Knowing requires doing. Here is the principle. Obey the obvious; trust the Lord for the obscure.

Jonah does the opposite. He goes down to Joppa and gets on a ship going to Tarshish. We aren't exactly sure where Tarshish was, but we do know that it was in the opposite direction. The Jews were landlubbers. For a Jew to get on a ship for any reason was serious business. There was only one people who avoided the ocean more than the Jews. It was the Assyrians. The Assyrian Empire crossed mountains and deserts, but they never crossed an ocean.

> Notice the repetition in verse 3 of the phrase, "The Presence of the Lord." It will be seen again in verse 10. The Hebrew way of speaking is more concrete than this. It literally speaks of being "before the face of the Lord."
>
> Jonah tries to run from the face of God. He is contrasted with Jesus who, rather than fleeing from the face of God, had the face of God flee from Him when He was on the cross.

> *And the Lord hurled a great wind on the sea and there was a great storm on the sea so that the ship was about to break up. 5 Then the sailors became afraid, and every man cried to his god, and they threw the cargo which was in the ship into the sea to lighten it for them. But Jonah had gone below into the hold of the ship, lain down, and fallen sound asleep. 6 So the captain approached him and said, "How is it that you are sleeping? Get up, call on your god. Perhaps your god will be concerned about us so that we will not perish."* (Jonah 1:4-6).

The severity of the storm is seen in the actions of the sailors, not only crying out the their various gods, but in throwing the cargo overboard. The cargo was the reason for the trip. Without the cargo, there would be no profit. That did not matter to them because they valued their lives more highly than the cargo. The stuff of life is not so important when life is on the line. There is something about a storm that helps us to realign our priorities.

Did you ever notice how pagans get spiritual when they face troubled times? These sailors did that. They recognized that this storm was not normal. It had come about as a direct result of Noah's sin.

> Here is a pagan telling a Christian to pray.

There is a lesson here. It is that sin affects more than merely the sinner. A believer who is in sin brings grief to others. These sailors were in the midst of a storm only because of their association with a sinning believer named Jonah. This was illustrated in the case of Joshua and the Israelites at Ai. They suffered a great defeat because of the sin of one man.

And each man said to his mate, "Come, let us cast lots so we may learn on whose account this calamity has struck us." So they cast lots and the lot fell on Jonah. (Jonah 1:7).

Proverbs 16:33 tells us that *the lot is cast into the lap, but its every decision is from the Lord.* This is not to say that God always honors such a method, but He did in this case.

Then they said to him, "Tell us, now! On whose account has this calamity struck us? What is your occupation? And where do you come from? What is your country? From what people are you?"
And he said to them, "I am a Hebrew, and I fear the Lord God of heaven who made the sea and the dry land."
Then the men became extremely frightened and they said to him, "How could you do this?" For the men knew that he was fleeing from the presence of the Lord, because he had told them. (Jonah 1:8-10).

Notice that the men knew of the fact that Jonah was *was fleeing from the presence of the Lord.* Didn't he know about God's omnipresence? Did he not know that it was impossible to escape from the presence of God? I think he did. But he was in a state of rebellion against God.

So they said to him, "What should we do to you that the sea may become calm for us?"-- for the sea was becoming increasingly stormy.
And he said to them, "Pick me up and throw me into the sea. Then the sea will become calm for you, for I know that on account of me this great storm has come upon you." (Jonah 1:11-12).

It is doubtful that Jonah knew how to swim. He was planning to drown. He was prepared to die so that these men in the boat could live. In this, he is a picture of Christ who died in our place. As Jonah was three days and three nights in the fish, so also Christ was three days and three nights in the heart of the earth.

Jonah	**Jesus**

The prophet who was sent to Nineveh	The One who is greater than Jonah was sent to the world
He attempted to flee from the face of God	When He was on the cross, the face of God fled from Him
He served as a substitute for the sailors	He served as a substitute for the nations
The wrath of the storm was sent because of his sin	He took upon Himself the wrath of God on our behalf

The Bible teaches us of a cosmic storm. It was caused by sin. The good news of the gospel is that God offers Himself to be given to the storm so that we might find peace.

> *And the Lord appointed a great fish to swallow Jonah, and Jonah was in the stomach of the fish three days and three nights. (Jonah 1:17).*

Some have found this fish story a bit hard to swallow. But the God of the universe is able to do things much more difficult than that. Which is harder?

Deliver Jonah from the belly of a fish	or	Deliver Jesus from the grave

We should make note that the Hebrew term used here to describe the "great fish" is simply that -- גָּדוֹל דָּג -- a big fish. It is translated in the Greek Septuagint with the term -- κητει μεγαλω -- a "big sea creature." What kind of marine life was this? The passage is not that specific. Such ambiguity is not too surprising when we remember that the Hebrews were not an ocean going people. The descriptions that we have of various forms of ocean life are very basic.

JONAH 2: IN THE BELLY OF THE FISH

The entire first chapter pictures Jonah going down. He goes down to Joppa (1:3), then he goes down into the ship (1:3), then he went down into the hold to go to sleep (1:5) and finally he finds himself in the depths of Sheol (2:2), into the heart of the seas (2:3) and down to the bottoms of the mountains (2:6). It is from here that he begins to look up as he prays.

The prayer of Jonah was not original. Most of it is taken from the Psalms. This tells me something about Jonah. He had learned the Psalms in the past. Now he learns to experience the Psalms. There are some lessons that we can learn from this prayer.

1.   What you learn in the light will be valuable in the darkness. Jonah did not start reading these Psalms while in the belly of the fish. He didn't have any copies of the Scriptures with him and certainly no reading lamp was available. Jonah remembered the prayers from the Scriptures and he put them to good use.

2.   You can pray anywhere. God was able to hear the prayer of Jonah, even from the belly of a great fish.

3.   This is not a prayer of deliverance, but a prayer of thanksgiving and of worship. Jonah thanks the Lord for his salvation. He knows that he has tried to escape the presence of God and, in so doing, has been expelled from that presence, but that does not stop him from looking to the Lord in thankfulness.

The psalm presented in this chapter is one of the most humorous in the Scriptures. The humor comes from the fact that the standardized (even clicheic) language of Hebrew psalmody is now given a literal meaning.

*   In 2:1 where Jonah says, *"I cried for help from the depth of Sheol,"* the phrase is literally "belly of sheol" and recalls that he is actually in something's belly.
*   Jonah 2:4 has him complaining that he is driven from God's sight (*I have been expelled from Thy sight*), which is exactly what he had tried--and failed--to do. When he finally is expelled, it will be as he is vomited onto dry land by the fish.

There is a sense in which Jonah is not only a type of Christ, but also a type of Israel. Like Israel, he had been sent by God on a very particular mission. He was to represent God and His message to the world. Like Israel, Jonah's reaction was one of rebellion. He sought to run away from the Lord. As a result, Jonah went into a watery captivity and this was followed by a restoration in which he was given a second chance to fulfill the command of the Lord. Throughout the prophets, we have seen this same theme of a coming captivity because of Israel's rebellion. In each case, there follows a promise of eventual restoration, but that is not the end of the story. The question that is put to Israel is whether or not she will utilize this restoration to follow the Lord.

JONAH 3: THE REPENTANCE OF NINEVEH

1.　Nineveh: *Now Nineveh was an exceedingly great city, a three days' walk. (Jonah 3:3).*

This literally reads: "Nineveh was a great city to Elohim from a walk of three days." It was suggested many years ago that the "walk of three days" was an indication of how long it took to walk around the city.

> ...when the book of Jonah speaks of Nineveh as a city of three days' journey, or when Ctesias in Diodorus ii. 3 describes its circuit as 480 stadia, it is plain that these conceptions imply an extension of the name to the whole group of cities between the Tigris and the Zab (Encyclopaedia Britannica 1902).

More recently, Dr. Donald Wiseman suggested that it is a reference to the time usually taken for an official delegation to visit an important city. Likewise, the reference to *Elohim* is not referring to its relationship with God, but rather to the fact that it was "titan" in its strength. For this reason, the NIV has translated this passage: *...Nineveh was a very important city - a visit required three days.*

Jonah 3:3	Nineveh was a city of three days
Jonah 3:4	Jonah went into the city one day's walk
Jonah 3:4	"In 40 days Nineveh will be overthrown"

2.　The Preaching of Jonah: *Then Jonah began to go through the city one day's walk; and he cried out and said, "Yet forty days and Nineveh will be overthrown." (Jonah 3:4).*

Can you imagine the scene? The morning sun breaks over the Zagros Mountains to the east and casts its fiery light on the hundreds of great towers that line the city walls of Nineveh. The city gates are open to the morning traffic as soldiers and war chariots parade the streets that are already alive with merchants proclaiming the worth of their wares.

Amid the hustle and bustle, a stranger arrives, passing between the colossal winged bulls whose graven images impose a symbolic guard over the city gates. His clothes are worn and faded from the sea and from the land. Perhaps his hair and his beard and his skin bear the bleached marks of untold travel. He raises his voice and begins to call out a warning:

"Yet forty days and Nineveh will be overthrown."

3.   The Response of Repentance: *Then the people of Nineveh believed in God; and they called a fast and put on sackcloth from the greatest to the least of them (Jonah 3:5).*

I cannot help but to wonder whether Jonah related to them the account of how he had witnessed the power of God in the storm and his experiences in the belly of the fish. Perhaps it is a mere coincidence that the name "Nineveh" is a transliteration of the Assyrian name *Ninua*, the Assyrian version of the goddess Ishtar whose name was written with the cuneiform sign of a fish within an enclosure. The people of Nineveh call for a fast and outward actions to demonstrate their inward attitude of repentance.

4.   The Edict of the King: *When the word reached the king of Nineveh, he arose from his throne, laid aside his robe from him, covered himself with sackcloth, and sat on the ashes (Jonah 3:6).*

This was the greatest mass-conversion in history. Never before or after do we read of an entire city turning to the Lord in fasting and prayer. How did it start? It has started with the repentance of a rebellious prophet. It was only when God's prophet repented that the people to whom he was to preach also repented. There is an interesting chain of events presented in this chapter.

The Biblical account does not tell us which king this was. Archaeology may give us some interesting hints. The Assyrian Empire was in a state of decline at the end of the 9th century. Her foreign possessions were slipping from her grasp and revolt was in the air. The reign of Adad-Nirari III (810-782 B.C.) is noted for the introduction of monotheism into Assyrian religion. It is notable that this king went on to attack the surrounding enemies of Israel (Damascus and Philistia).

> *"Who knows, God may turn and relent, and withdraw*
> *His burning anger so that we shall not perish?"*
> *(Jonah 3:9).*

The phrase translated "burning anger" (*meharon apu*) is literally, "the snorting of his nostrils." God is pictured with all of the anger of a snorting bull which paws the ground and prepares to vent its wrath. One of our problems is that we tend to lose sight of the holy anger of God against sin.

JONAH 4: THE COMPASSION OF GOD

In the last chapter, Jonah had just seen the biggest revival in history. You would think that he would be ecstatic. But his experience is another reaction entirely.

> *But it greatly displeased Jonah, and he became angry. (Jonah*
> *4:1).*

Jonah was displeased. He wasn't merely displeased, he was greatly displeased. Why? Because he wanted to see the judgment of God upon the city. The last thing he wanted to see was salvation in Nineveh.

> *But it greatly displeased Jonah, and he became angry.*
> *2 And he prayed to the Lord and said, "Please Lord, was not*
> *this what I said while I was still in my own country?*
> *Therefore, in order to forestall this I fled to Tarshish, for I*
> *knew that Thou art a gracious and compassionate God, slow*
> *to anger and abundant in lovingkindness, and one who*
> *relents concerning calamity. 3 Therefore now, O Lord, please*
> *take my life from me, for death is better to me than life."*
> *And the Lord said, "Do you have good reason to be*
> *angry?" (Jonah 4:1-4).*

Now we see the real reason that Jonah ran away to Tarshish. It wasn't that he was afraid of the Assyrians or of hardship or of failure on the mission field. It was to short-circuit the mercy of God from being offered to Nineveh. Jonah was prejudiced. He was afraid of success. He was afraid that the Assyrians would repent and become a part of God's people. He wanted the judgment of God to fall upon the Assyrians. His attitude was representative of all of Israel. This is why this book was written. It is to show that God is *a gracious and compassionate God, slow to anger and abundant in lovingkindness, and one who relents concerning calamity* (4:2).

In verse 4, the Lord asks, *"Do you have good reason to be angry?" (Jonah 4:1-4)*. The Lord is going to ask this same question of Jonah in verse 9.

> *Then Jonah went out from the city and sat east of it. There he made a shelter for himself and sat under it in the shade until he could see what would happen in the city. 6 So the Lord God appointed a plant and it grew up over Jonah to be a shade over his head to deliver him from his discomfort. And Jonah was extremely happy about the plant. 7 But God appointed a worm when dawn came the next day, and it attacked the plant and it withered. (Jonah 4:5-7).*

God gives Jonah an object lesson. You may have gotten some of those from the Lord. They are the circumstances that are given to you to teach something.

We read in verse 6 that God appointed this plant. We see that three times in verses 6-8 the Lord appointed various things.

> It is noteworthy that the vine is sometimes used in the Bible as a symbol for Israel. The nation of Israel would eventually be eaten up by the worm of Assyria.
>
> On the other hand, the One who described Himself as the true vine, the One who was greater than Jonah, was Himself scortched and put to death for us.

- God appointed a plant (4:6).
- God appointed a worm (4:7).
- God appointed the east wind (4:8).

There is a lesson here. It is that God appoints the good things and He also appoints those things that seem to be anything but good. Why? In order to teach you a lesson. In this case, the lesson that God was teaching Jonah was one of compassion.

Then the Lord said, "You had compassion on the

706

plant for which you did not work, and which you did not cause to grow, which came up overnight and perished overnight. 11 And should I not have compassion on Nineveh, the great city in which there are more than 120,000 persons who do not know the difference between their right and left hand, as well as many animals?" (Jonah 4:10-11).

The book of Jonah ends with a question. Why does the book end the way it does? It is because God asks you the same question that He asks of Jonah. Have you identified with the compassion of God? What is your attitude toward people who are not like you?

- Who have a different theology
- Who have a different color
- Who have a different social status

The story doesn't end with Jonah. It ends with Jesus. As Jonah was three days and three nights in the belly of the fish, so also Jesus was three days and three nights in the earth. The reason was the same -- it was a sign of the compassion of God.

LESSONS FROM JONAH

1. God is the first cause of all things. He is the one who brought the storm, the fish, the plant, the worm, and the east wind. He is the Sovereign Lord of this earth.

2. God is a Saving God. He is seen in this book as the Savior...
   - Of the sailors
   - Of Jonah
   - Of Nineveh.

3. God wants repentance. He looked for repentance in the city of Nineveh and He looked for repentance in the life of Jonah.

4. God is a God of compassion and His compassion extends both to pagan cities as well as to stubborn prophets.

MICAH
Judgment and Restoration

The name Micah means, "Who is like Ya?" *Ya* is a shortened form of Yahweh and serves as the name of God. The first verse of this book describes the prophet as *Micah of Moresheth*. We read of this same Moresheth in verse 14 where it is called *Moresheth-Gath*. This was evidently a place close to the ancient Philistine city of Gath, near to the coastlands.

> *The word of the Lord which came to Micah of Moresheth in the days of Jotham, Ahaz, and Hezekiah, kings of Judah, which he saw concerning Samaria and Jerusalem. (Micah 1:1).*

Micah was a contemporary of Isaiah. The ministry of Micah began at a time when the spiritual life of both Israel and Judah was at an all-time low. The eventual revival in the days of Hezekiah may well have been at least in part the result of Micah's ministry.

These were some troubled times from the kingdom of Judah. It was a time that saw the threat of a terrible invader from the north. The Assyrian Empire was preparing to come down upon the nation of Israel. The northern kingdom of Israel would shortly be taken into a captivity from which she would never return. The southern kingdom of Judah would also be surrounded and threatened. A great many of her cities would be carried off until only a small remnant remained.

OUTLINE OF MICAH

The book of Micah consists of a series of three oracles. Each of these oracles follows the same general pattern. Each begins with the judgment of God and each culminates in future hope:

1:1	**First Oracle:** Promise of Judgment and Eventual Regathering	God coming to judge Israel and Judah because of idolatry

2:12		The Lord will eventually regather His people and be their Shepherd
3:1	**Second Oracle:** Judgment against leaders and Israel's future glory	Judgment against Rulers and False Prophets in the Land
4:1		Future glory of the Mountain of the House of the Lord
6:1	**Third Oracle:** God's Covenant Lawsuit against Israel and the Ultimate Triumph of the Kingdom	The Lord charges the nation with disloyalty to the Covenant
7:8		The Lord will restore the nation, judge the earth and forgive past iniquities

FIRST ORACLE

Micah begins his prophecy with a thundering proclamation. God is coming and His coming will shake the earth.

Hear, O peoples, all of you;
Listen, O earth and all it contains,
And let the Lord God be a witness against you,
The Lord from His holy temple.
3 For behold, the Lord is coming forth from His place.
He will come down and tread on the high places of the earth.
4 The mountains will melt under Him,
And the valleys will be split,
Like wax before the fire,
Like water poured down a steep place. (Micah 1:2-4).

The call to the people is inclusive. It is a call to "all of you;" to all the earth and to all contained therein. At the same time, this call is given in terms of the covenant. God Himself is called as a witness and He is a witness for the prosecution. He is called to be a witness "against you."

God's coming is described in terms of the cataclysmic. His coming melts mountains and splits valleys and melts that which it hardened. It comes like a rolling avalanche and like a thundering flood. Why? Why is the coming of the Lord seen in such destructive terms? It is because of the rebellion and the sin of God's people.

All this is for the rebellion of Jacob
And for the sins of the house of Israel.
What is the rebellion of Jacob? Is it not Samaria?
What is the high place of Judah? Is it not Jerusalem?
6 For I will make Samaria a heap of ruins in the open country,
Planting places for a vineyard.
I will pour her stones down into the valley,
And will lay bare her foundations.
7 All of her idols will be smashed,
All of her earnings will be burned with fire,
And all of her images I will make desolate,
For she collected them from a harlot's earnings,
And to the earnings of a harlot they will return. (Micah 1:5-7).

Both Israel and Judah come under condemnation. He begins with the northern kingdom of Israel and its capital city of Samaria. You can go to Jerusalem today and you will find a thriving, bustling city. But if you go to Samaria, you will only find a ruined heap of scattered stones.

Beginning in verse 9, Micah turns his attention to Judah. Verses 10-16 mention a number of specific cities throughout the land of Judah. Each of these is a play on words. The first is a reference to the ancient city of Gath.

Tell it not in Gath,
Weep not at all (Micah 1:10a).

The play on words is seen in the fact that the word for Gath sounds very much like the verb, "to tell." This initial call hearkens back to the funeral dirge that David composed at the death of Saul and Jonathan.

Your beauty, O Israel, is slain on your high places!
How have the mighty fallen!
20 Tell it not in Gath,
Proclaim it not in the streets of Ashkelon;
Lest the daughters of the Philistines rejoice,
Lest the daughters of the uncircumcised exult. (2 Samuel 1:19-20).

Now again we see a lament. This time, the lament is not just for a king and his son, but for all of Judah.

10 Tell it not in Gath,

Weep not at all.
At Beth-le-aphrah [literally, "house of dust"] *roll yourself in the dust*
[Hebrew: *Aphar*].
11 Go on your way, inhabitant of Shaphir [literally, "beauty"],
in shameful nakedness.
The inhabitant of Zaanan does not escape [Hebrew: *Yatzah*] .
The lamentation of Bethezel: "He will take from you its
support."
12 For the inhabitant of Maroth
Becomes weak waiting for good,
Because a calamity has come down from the Lord
To the gate of Jerusalem.
13 Harness the chariot to the team of horses,
O inhabitant of Lachish--
She was the beginning of sin
To the daughter of Zion--
Because in you were found
The rebellious acts of Israel.
14 Therefore, you will give parting gifts
On behalf of Moresheth-gath;
The houses of Achzib will become a deception
To the kings of Israel.
15 Moreover, I will bring on you
The one who takes possession,
O inhabitant of Mareshah.
The glory of Israel will enter Adullam. (Micah 1:10-15).

Dillard and Longman's book, *Introduction to the Old Testament*, relates Moffatt's paraphrase of this passage to capture some of the word plays:

Tell it not in Tellington!
Wail not in Wailing!
Dust Manor will eat dirt,
Dressy Town will flee naked.
Safefold will not save,
Allchester's walls are down,
A bitter dose drinks Bitterton.
Toward Jerusalem, City of Peace,
The Lord sends war.
Harness the war-steeds,
O men of Barstead!

Zion's beginning of sinning,
Equal to Israel's crimes.
To Welfare a last farewell!
For Trapping trapped Israel's kings.

Is there a point to this literary device? I tend to think there is. Israel was a place that had all the right names, but they had not lived up to their names. They had the labels, but there was no life behind the labels. Do you ever feel like that? Do you ever feel as though you call yourself a Christian, yet you have somehow found yourself relegating your Christianity to a back shelf? Do you ever feel as though you get dressed up on Sunday morning to come to church and go through all the motions, yet there is something of a divorce in your life from the reality of Christ?

I want you to know that, while Micah is the prophet of judgment, there is in the midst of Micah's prophecy of judgment, a ray of hope. It begins in the next chapter.

12 I will surely assemble all of you, Jacob,
I will surely gather the remnant of Israel.
I will put them together like sheep in the fold;
Like a flock in the midst of its pasture
They will be noisy with men.
13 The breaker goes up before them;
They break out, pass through the gate, and go out by it.
So their king goes on before them,
And the Lord at their head. (Micah 2:12-13).

There is always a remnant. That is a common theme throughout the Old Testament. No matter how bad things turn, there is always the promise of a remnant. Throughout the first 200 years of the history of the United States, Christians in this country got used to being a majority. That has changed over the last generation. Christians are losing their majority status. But there is still a remnant and God can work through a remnant.

SECOND ORACLE

And I said, "Hear now, heads of Jacob
And rulers of the house of Israel.
Is it not for you to know justice?
2 You who hate good and love evil,

Who tear off their skin from them
And their flesh from their bones,
3 And who eat the flesh of my people,
Strip off their skin from them,
Break their bones,
And chop them up as for the pot
And as meat in a kettle." (Micah 3:1-3).

Instead of protecting their flock from the invading wolf pack, these leaders were worse than the wolves -- they were eating their flocks alive. Leaders are more liable. That is what James 3:1 tells us. Leaders incur a more stricter judgment. Why? Because as go the leaders, so goes the nation. This is true of the church, too. As go the leaders, so will go the church. You are hard-pressed to find anything that ever moved the church that did not first move her leaders.

Her leaders pronounce judgment for a bribe,
Her priests instruct for a price,
And her prophets divine for money.
Yet they lean on the Lord saying,
"Is not the Lord in our midst?
Calamity will not come upon us."
12 Therefore, on account of you,
Zion will be plowed as a field,
Jerusalem will become a heap of ruins,
And the mountain of the temple will become high places of a
forest. (Micah 3:11-12).

The indictment is made against the political leaders, the priests, and even the prophets. The problem was that they had come to assume that God was on their side, even when they were disobedient to the commands of God. As a result of this, there would be a coming judgment. The judgment would take place against Jerusalem and the Temple. Jerusalem would become a heap of ruins and the Temple would become a place where trees grew wild. Yet when things had gotten as bad as they could possibly be, there would still remain the promise of a future hope.

And it will come about in the last days
That the mountain of the house of the Lord
Will be established as the chief of the mountains.
It will be raised above the hills,
And the peoples will stream to it.

2 And many nations will come and say,
"Come and let us go up to the mountain of the Lord
And to the house of the God of Jacob,
That He may teach us about His ways
And that we may walk in His paths."
For from Zion will go forth the law,
Even the word of the Lord from Jerusalem.
3 And He will judge between many peoples
And render decisions for mighty, distant nations.
Then they will hammer their swords into plowshares
And their spears into pruning hooks;
Nation will not lift up sword against nation,
And never again will they train for war. (Micah 4:1-3).

This passage is repeated nearly word for word in Isaiah 2:2-4. Did Micah quote from Isaiah or the other way around? We do not know and it is not really important. Micah has just said at the end of the previous chapter that *the mountain of the temple will become high places of a forest* (3:12). Notice that he calls it the "mountain of the house of the Lord" and says that it will be established.

This is a familiar theme in the Old Testament. The Scriptures speak often about the Mountain of the house of the Lord. We hear those words and we naturally think of the temple in Jerusalem. That is where the house of the Lord was located. Yet the idea of the Mountain of the Lord was present long before the building of Solomon's temple.

- The mountain on which God appeared to Moses in the burning bush was described as "the mountain of God" (Exodus 3:1).

- The song of Moses gives a promise of how the Lord would plant His people upon the mountain of His inheritance.

    Thou wilt bring them and plant them in the mountain
    of Thine inheritance,
    The place, O Lord, which Thou hast made for Thy
    dwelling,
    The sanctuary, O Lord, which Thy hands have
    established. (Exodus 15:17).

- The mountain of God is the place from which the covering cherub was cast down in Ezekiel 28. This was said to be in Eden. Just as Eden was the place of the presence of God on the original earth, so the mountain of God is descriptive of the idea where God's presence comes to meet mankind.

The promise that is given here has to be seen against the backdrop of the darkness of the judgments of the previous chapters. Seeing them in such a light is like seeing a diamond against the backdrop of black velvet.

The previous chapters warned of a coming judgment in which the people would be scattered and the temple destroyed. First the temple would be destroyed and become a place of barrenness, but in the last days the temple would be restored as a place of blessing. There is coming a day when, not only the children of Israel, but many nations will come to the mountain of the house of the Lord.

The city of Jerusalem is surrounded upon all sides by mountains. Although it is itself upon a mountain ridge, it is not the highest. There are several surrounding mountains which are higher. But the picture here is of the mountain of the house of the Lord - the Temple Mount - being raised up above the surrounding mountains.

What does it all mean? How are we to understand this prophecy? There are some who would predict future geological changes to take place in the land of Palestine. But this is not geological language. It is figurative language.

When did the nations begin to come to the Temple? It was seen at the Pentecost incident when we are given in the Scriptures a listing of all of the nations that were gathered. But that is not all. This is a Messianic prophecy. Christ is the House of God. He is the Temple which was destroyed and which was raised up again in three days. He is the One who said, "If I be lifted up from the earth, I will draw all men to Myself" (John 12:32). This passage tells us that there is coming a day when all men will turn to God; when the throne of God will be recognized by all.

But that is not all. This also has a more immediate fulfillment. It is seen in the identity of the House of God as mentioned in verse 2. What is the house of God today? It is the church. *For it is time for judgment to begin with **the household** (του οίκου του Θεου) of God; and if it begins with us first, what will be the outcome for those who do not obey the gospel of God? (1 Peter 4:17).* Just in case there are some who would not wish to recognize Peter's words as having reference to the church, Paul says in 1 Timothy 3:15, *I write so that you may know how one ought to conduct himself in **the household** of God, which is the church of the living God, the pillar and support of the truth.*

What is the house of God today? It is the church. This means that the exhortation that is given to believers in the Old Testament will also apply to the church today.

> *And each of them will sit under his vine*
> *And under his fig tree,*
> *With no one to make them afraid,*
> *For the mouth of the Lord of hosts has spoken. (Micah 4:4).*

The reference to sitting under one's own vine and under one's own fig tree is a picture of peace and prosperity. It pictures a return to the golden age under Solomon.

> *So Judah and Israel lived in safety, every man under*
> *his vine and his fig tree, from Dan even to Beersheba, all the*
> *days of Solomon. (1 Kings 4:25).*

However, before the future time of restoration could come, there would first come a time of judgment. It is pictured in terms of a woman's labor pains.

> *Now, why do you cry out loudly?*
> *Is there no king among you,*
> *Or has your counselor perished,*
> *That agony has gripped you like a woman in childbirth?*
> *10 Writhe and labor to give birth,*
> *Daughter of Zion,*
> *Like a woman in childbirth,*
> *For now you will go out of the city,*
> *Dwell in the field,*
> *And go to Babylon.*
> *There you will be rescued;*
> *There the Lord will redeem you*
> *From the hand of your enemies. (Micah 4:9-10).*

The exile to Babylon would be painful in the extreme. But it was a necessary part of the redemption, for it would be from there that the people of God would be rescued and redeemed. It is in the context of this promise of exile and restoration that the coming of a future Davidic king is given.

> *Now muster yourselves in troops, daughter of troops;*
> *They have laid siege against us;*
> *With a rod they will smite the judge of Israel on the cheek.*
> *2 But as for you, Bethlehem Ephrathah,*

Too little to be among the clans of Judah,
From you One will go forth for Me to be ruler in Israel.
His goings forth are from long ago,
From the days of eternity. (Micah 5:1-2).

The most insulting thing that one could do in the ancient world was to strike someone on the cheek. The description of a king being struck in such a fashion is tantamount to military defeat and subjugation. Here is the point. Judah will be invaded and will suffer the ultimate insult and subjugation, but there will come from Bethlehem a promised redeemer who will return as the ruler of God's people.

Bethlehem was the city from which David had come. This was its primary claim to fame, as it was really only a small village. Ephrathah was the place name of the general area, a name that went all the way back to the days of the judges (Ruth 4:11). Just as David

> The use of the term Ephrathah distinguishes this town from another Bethlehem that was located near Mount Carmel in the territory of Zebulun (Joshua 19:15).

had come from Bethlehem, so also the future ruler of Israel would also come from Bethlehem. He would be the One whose coming had been promised and described from ages past.

THIRD ORACLE

In the third Oracle, the prophet rails against the problem of religion without reality.

With what shall I come to the Lord
And bow myself before the God on high?
Shall I come to Him with burnt offerings,
With yearling calves?
7 Does the Lord take delight in thousands of rams,
In ten thousand rivers of oil?
Shall I present my first-born for my rebellious acts,
The fruit of my body for the sin of my soul?
8 He has told you, O man, what is good;
And what does the Lord require of you
But to do justice, to love kindness,
And to walk humbly with your God? (Micah 6:6-8).

The multiplication of religious ordinances is no substitute for these qualities of justice, kindness and humility. Sometimes we get the idea that our involvement in church activities is the sum and scope of our spiritual service. Nothing could be further from the truth. Without taking anything away from the supreme importance and centrality of worship, if your Christian life is only what takes place when you come to worship, then you have no Christian life.

> *Who is a God like Thee, who pardons iniquity*
> *And passes over the rebellious act of the remnant of His possession?*
> *He does not retain His anger forever,*
> *Because He delights in unchanging love.*
> *19 He will again have compassion on us;*
> *He will tread our iniquities under foot.*
> *Yes, Thou wilt cast all their sins*
> *Into the depths of the sea.*
> *20 Thou wilt give truth to Jacob*
> *And unchanging love to Abraham,*
> *Which Thou didst swear to our forefathers*
> *From the days of old. (Micah 7:18-20).*

The closing verses of Micah give hope for the future. They picture a God who pardons iniquity and who passes over rebellious acts. That is the message of the cross. It is that God sent His Son to pardon iniquity and to be our Passover Lamb so that God might forgive our rebellious acts. This is seen in Micah 7:20 where Micah says, "Thou wilt give truth to Jacob and **unchanging love** to Abraham." The fascinating part is the play on words found in the term "unchanging." It is a play on words with the name "Jacob" which literally means "heel-grabber" but carries the idea of "supplanter, switcher, trickster or changer." Literally, the prophet says, "You will give truth to Jacob and non-Jacob mercy to Abraham."

That is what the gospel is all about. It is the story of how God sent His Son to give to us the same sort of mercy that we had not shown to others. It is the story of God saving those who did not deserve salvation. It is the story of grace.

NAHUM
The Prophet of Consolation

The book of Nahum is a prophecy directed at Nineveh, the capital city of Assyria. It is the sort of book that we can imagine Jonah to have penned. Indeed, the similarities between these two books are striking.

> We know virtually nothing of Nahum. Because the name Capernaum means "village of Nahum," some have supposed that he came from this Galilean village.

- Both Nahum and Jonah focus upon Assyria and their capital city of Nineveh.
- Both Nahum and Jonah contain prophecies of Nineveh's destruction.
- Both Nahum and Jonah close their books with a question. The question at the end of the book of Jonah points to God's compassion. The question at the end of the book of Nahum points to Nineveh's continued lack of compassion for others.

The name "Nahum" means "consolation" or "comfort." One form of this word is used in Nahum 3:7 where we read: *And it will come about that all who see you will shrink from you and say, "Nineveh is devastated! Who will grieve for her?" Where will I seek* **comforters** (מְנַחֲמִים) *for you?*

This gives us a clue as to the purpose of the book. It is a book of judgment against the city of Nineveh, but it is also a book of comfort for God's people as they see the judgment of God fall upon their enemies.

How do you handle it when bad people do bad things? And how do you handle it when bad people do bad things to you? It is one thing to ask this question from the comfort of an armchair or within the confines of a church pew. It is quite another thing to ask this question when you are suffering because someone is treating you badly.

Suffering is not fun at the best of times. But the worst sort of suffering is the suffering that is intentionally inflicted upon you by those who want to deliberately hurt you. It is easier to take a hurt that was accidentally given than it is to take a hurt that was intentionally delivered.

How do you handle such hurts? It is by recognizing God's sovereignty. It is by recognizing that nothing comes into your life without first passing through a nail-scarred hand. And it is by understanding that the Lord will eventually balance the books. The Judge of the earth will do what is right.

OUTLINE OF THE BOOK

The Lord takes vengeance against Nineveh (1:1-9)
- His anger poured out like fire (1:6)
- Mountains quake before Him (1:5)
- He pursues His enemies into darkness (1:8)

The Lord will destroy Nineveh (1:10-15)
- Assyrians are like drunks in their drink (1:10)
- They are consumed like stubble (1:10)
- The Lord will tear off the shackles (1:13)

Vivid description of attack on Nineveh (2:1-10)
- Chariots rushing back and forth (2:3-4)
- Chariots appear as lightning flashes (2:4)
- They stumble in their march (2:5)

Lament over fall of Nineveh, the Lion's Den (2:11-13)

Vivid description of attack on Nineveh (3:1-7)
- Bounding chariots (3:2-3)
- Swords flashing, spears gleaming (3:3)
- They stumble over the dead bodies (3:3)

Nineveh will be destroyed (3:8-13)
- Assyrians will become drunk (3:11)
- Fire consumes their gates (3:13)
- Her great men bound with fetters (3:10)

Nineveh consumed
- They are consumed with fire (3:15)
- They are scattered on the mountains (3:18)
- The sun rises and her armies flee (3:17)

Note that some sub-points are deliberately out of sequence.

The Book of Nahum is organized in a large chiasm. The centerpoint of this chiasm is the lament in which Nineveh is likened to a den of lions that had formerly gobbled up the nations and was now herself devoured.

The fall of Nineveh took place in 612 B.C. when a coalition of Chaldeans, Medes and Scythians attacked the city. Nahum's prophecy is vivid in its language and he utilizes a number of word pictures to describe the destruction of the city.

THE ANGER OF GOD

2 A jealous and avenging God is the Lord;
The Lord is avenging and wrathful.
The Lord takes vengeance on His adversaries,
And He reserves wrath for His enemies.
3 The Lord is slow to anger and great in power,
And the Lord will by no means leave the guilty unpunished.
In whirlwind and storm is His way,
And clouds are the dust beneath His feet. (Nahum 1:2-3).

There were a series of billboards that cropped up in the South Florida area in the late 1990's. They all had reference to the Lord and one of them boldly proclaimed, "Don't make Me come down there." -- God.

We have displayed in these verses a picture of the anger of God. It is an anger that is so terrible that it comes like a whirlwind and a storm and stirs up clouds and dust. We don't normally think of anger as a good thing. When we get angry, it is often not a righteous anger, but rather an anger that is inappropriate.

God is described as being angry, but a part of this description is that He is "slow to anger." This is the opposite of being quick-tempered. It takes a lot to get God angry. There are three possibilities when it comes to anger and only one of them is appropriate.

- It is possible to be quick to anger. There are some who try to justify being quick tempered by says, "I erupt with anger, but then it is over and done with." A nuclear bomb is like that. We are warned in the Bible against being quick to anger.

- It is also possible and equally bad to have no anger. There are times when the only appropriate response is to be angry. When we see people in rebellion against God and recognize that these actions and attitudes carry eternal repercussions, the only appropriate reaction is to be angry against sin and against evil and against the works of Satan.

- If it is bad to be quick to anger and it is also bad to have no anger, then what is the proper response for the Christian? We are to be like God and we are to be slow to anger. It should take a lot for us to become angry.

HOPE IN THE BOOK OF NAHUM

The Lord is good,
A stronghold in the day of trouble,
And He knows those who take refuge in Him. (Nahum 1:7).

In the midst of Nahum's pronouncement of anger upon the city of Nineveh, he pauses and gives these words of hope. These words are not in contradiction to what precedes or follows this verse. They are the flip side of the same truth. The same God who is a Judge and an Avenger of unrighteousness is a stronghold and a refuge for those who trust in Him.

It is the anger of God that gives us hope. If God did not get angry, then sin would be allowed to continue. If God did not get angry, there would be no deliverance from the hands of evil men. If God did not get angry, there would be no salvation.

The cross was the place where God demonstrated His anger against sin. The anger of God was poured out upon Jesus as He hung suspended between heaven and earth. It was there that the anger of God was satisfied. There is a theological word for this. It is called propitiation.

> *In this is love, not that we loved God, but that He*
> *loved us and sent His Son to be the **propitiation** for our sins.*
> *(1 John 4:10).*

This same word was used to describe something in the original temple in Jerusalem. The temple was a holy place and only the priests were permitted to enter within. Yet there was a part of the temple from which even the priests were excluded. It was the Holy of Holies. This was the innermost part of the temple. Within was only one article of furniture. It was the Ark of the Covenant -- a wooden box overlaid with gold. Sitting atop the Ark was a cover of solid gold. It had mounted on it the images of two cherubim with their wings spread over the Ark. They were there as guardians, for this lid served as the throne of God.

Only one person was permitted into the presence of the Ark and then only once a year on the Day of Atonement. The high priest could come here on that day and he would sprinkle blood upon the lid of the Ark. When he did this, that seat of judgment would become a propitiation -- a place of satisfaction. That is what Jesus is for us. He is our place of satisfaction. He is our stronghold and our refuge, our strength, and our place of safety.

The presence of a stronghold points to the fact that there is danger in the world. The need of a refuge assumes that there are things in this world from which you need to take refuge. Just as Israel was under the threat of attack from the hands of the Assyrians, so also we are under a threat of attack. Our war is not necessarily a physical war. It is primarily a spiritual war and it is fought with spiritual weapons.

The good news is that we have a stronghold. We have One in whom we can take refuge. We have a Savior who is able to save in the day of trouble.

LESSONS FROM NAHUM

1.   God is concerned with politics and political happenings.

One must be careful when applying the political statements that are addressed to Judah and to Israel to countries and nations today. We are not a theocracy. We are not a "Christian nation" in the same way that Israel was.

At the same time, we must also recognize that God is concerned with politics and with the moving of nations. We may try to separate church and state, but God will not remain separate from anything in His creation.

2.   God takes it seriously when anyone hurts His people.

I'm not much of a woodsman and my idea of camping is a Holiday Inn with air conditioning and a hot tub. But I do know enough about the outdoors to know that one thing you do not disturb is a bear cub when his mother is anywhere in the neighborhood. In the same way, you do a dangerous thing when you hurt the people of God. On two different occasions, the Lord says that He is against the people of Nineveh.

- Nahum 2:13. *"Behold, I am against you," declares the Lord of hosts. "I will burn up her chariots in smoke, a sword will devour your young lions, I will cut off your prey from the land, and no longer will the voice of your messengers be heard."*

- Nahum 3:5. *"Behold, I am against you," declares the Lord of hosts; "And I will lift up your skirts over your face, and show to the nations your nakedness and to the kingdoms your disgrace."*

By way of contrast, Paul asks us in Romans 8, *"If God is for us, who is against us?"* If we are in Christ and seeking to follow Him, then God is not against us; He is for us. When God is for you, then He is against everything that is against you because nothing can separate you from His love.

3.   When God shows compassion (as He did toward the city of Nineveh in the days of Jonah), He demands that compassion be shown to others. Jesus said the same thing. When He taught His disciples to pray, He told them to say, "Forgive us our debts, as we also have forgiven our debtors" (Matthew 6:12).

Can you think of anyone against whom you are holding a grudge? Is there an instance where someone had done wrong against you and who you need to forgive? Is there someone who needs your compassion?

If you are having a hard time letting go of a grievance that has been committed against you, perhaps it is time for you to go to the cross and to look anew upon the One who died for your sins. He suffered because of you and, at that very time, He prayed for you: "Father, forgive them, for they do not know what they are doing." He calls you to do the same thing.

Here is the principle: Forgiven people forgive. Have you been forgiven of your sins? Then you need to forgive with the same forgiveness with which the Lord has forgiven you. There is an "or else" to that statement. What happens if you refuse to forgive?

> *For if you forgive men for their transgressions, your heavenly Father will also forgive you. 15 But if you do not forgive men, then your Father will not forgive your transgressions. (Matthew 6:14-15).*

I didn't say that. Jesus did. He pointed out that if you do not forgive, it is because you have not yourself completely entered into the forgiveness of God.

4.   Grace is able to reign, even after judgment.

Though it is not mentioned in the book of Acts, we know

from church history that one of the places where the early church took root and flourished was among the Assyrians. Though they had long ceased to be a political power, they did become a spiritual power as they come to Christ and began a Christian heritage that continues even to the present.

HABAKKUK
Prayer and Praise

Habakkuk was a prophet with a problem. It was a problem faced by a lot of preachers in 21st century America. It was the problem of "business as usual." From a strictly naturalistic point of view, things were going well.

- The economy was doing okay.
- Workers were working.
- Peace was prosperous.
- Business was busy.
- The rich were becoming richer.
- And the poor didn't have press coverage, so everyone seemed to be happy.

But in all of this busy-ness and prosperity, the people had forgotten God. He just didn't fit into their busy schedules. And this spiritual forgetfulness led to other problems. "Business as usual" took on a seamier side. There was oppression and a cut-throat attitude at work. Lawyers were making a bundle by lining their pockets with legal loopholes. People were out to get what they could get while the getting was good. Justice was awarded to the one who had the deepest pockets.

Habakkuk looked out at the nation of Judah and he saw all of this and it drove him to his knees. He set out to pray. The three chapters that make up the book of Habakkuk consist of his prayer diary. Habakkuk's prayer begins with a question: Why does God allow evil to continue?

The oracle which Habakkuk the prophet saw.
How long, O Lord, will I call for help,
And You will not hear?
I cry out to You, "Violence!"
Yet You do not save.
3 Why do You make me see iniquity,
And cause me to look on wickedness?
Yes, destruction and violence are before me;
Strife exists and contention arises.
4 Therefore the law is ignored
And justice is never upheld.
For the wicked surround the righteous;

Therefore justice comes out perverted. (Habakkuk 1:1-4).

Habakkuk looks at the shape of the judicial system of his day and he asks, "Lord, how long can it go on like this? Why do you allow such things to happen?"

- Why do bad things happen to relatively good people? And...
- Why do good things happen to bad people?

I can empathize with Habakkuk. There are few things more frustrating than to see bad people "get away with it." I have a confession to make. I like to watch those old-time movies where the villain gets his come-uppance and where the hero wins the day and rides off into the sunset to live happily ever after. But life is not always like that. All too often, we see...

- Bad things happening to relatively good people. And...
- Good things happening to bad people.

Habakkuk looks at it and asks, "Lord, how can You let this go on? When will you do something? Have you gone on an extended vacation? If You are a good God, then why do You allow evil to continue? We can outline the book as follows:

1:1	1:12	3:1
Habakkuk's Problem		Habakkuk's Praise
Problem #1: Why does God allow wicked practices to continue in the land?	Problem #2: Why will God use wicked people to punish others?	Praise for the Person of God (3:1-3) Praise for the Power of God (3:4-7)
God's Answer: I will eventually bring judgment (1:5-11)	God's Answer: I will judge even those whom I use for judgment (2:2-20)	Praise for the Purpose of God (3:8-16) Praise because of Faith in God (3:17-19)

Habakkuk's prayer begins with a question: Why does God allow evil to continue? God's reply is that judgment will eventually come at the hands of invading Babylon.

"For behold, I am raising up the Chaldeans,
That fierce and impetuous people
Who march throughout the earth
To seize dwelling places which are not theirs.
They are dreaded and feared;
Their justice and authority originate with themselves.
Their horses are swifter than leopards
And keener than wolves in the evening.
Their horsemen come galloping,
Their horsemen come from afar;
They fly like an eagle swooping down to devour.
All of them come for violence.
Their horde of faces moves forward.
They collect captives like sand." (Habakkuk 1:6-9).

We read this passage and it comes as no surprise. After all, we have the perspective of history. We know that in 605 B.C. a young Babylonian prince by the name of Nebuchadnezzar entered into a coalition with the Medes and the Scythians to attack the Assyrian Empire and bring it to its knees. His forces swept over Assyria and her Egyptian allies at the Battle of Carchemish and then swept down the Levant to Israel.

You have to know and understand that the capital city of the Chaldeans was Babylon and every time you see Babylon in the Bible from the Tower of Babel in Genesis 11 to the Harlot that is called Babylon in Revelation 17-18, the name "Babylon" is vilified and serves as an image of all that is bad with the world. Now we read that it is Babylon that comes and takes the people of God into captivity. God says to Habakkuk, "I am not merely allowing this to take place, I am the one *raising up the Chaldeans* (1:6). This is a picture of the sovereignty of God. He is in control, not only when good things happen, but when bad things happen, too.

This brings Habakkuk to a new question: How can God use evil people to do His work? It is true, the people of Israel had turned away from God. But the Babylonians were even worse.

> *Are You not from everlasting, O Lord, my God, my*
> *Holy One? We will not die. You, O Lord, have appointed them*
> *to judge; and You, O Rock, have established them to correct.*
>
> *Your eyes are too pure to approve evil, and You can*
> *not look on wickedness with favor. Why do You look with*
> *favor on those who deal treacherously? Why are You silent*
> *when the wicked swallow up those more righteous than they?*
> *(Habakkuk 1:12-13).*

Habakkuk questions the actions of God. He doesn't deny them. He doesn't say, "God, you can't do that." After all, Habakkuk knows that God is God and that He can do however He pleases.

God is Sovereign: *Are You not from everlasting... You, O Lord, have appointed them to judge... You, O Rock...*	**God is Just:** *Your eyes are too pure to approve evil, and You can not look on wickedness with favor*

Habakkuk looks at these two qualities of God, that He is completely sovereign and that He is completely just and righteous, and he scratches his head and he says, "I don't get it!" Here is the question: How can God use evil people to do His work? It is true, the people of Israel had turned away from God. But the Babylonians were even worse.

> *The Chaldeans bring all of them up with a hook,*
> *Drag them away with their net,*
> *And gather them together in their fishing net.*
> *Therefore they rejoice and are glad.*
> *Therefore they offer a sacrifice to their net and burn incense*
> *to their fishing net;*
> *Because through these things their catch is large,*
> *And their food is plentiful. (Habakkuk 1:15-16).*

This imagery of a hook and a net was not completely symbolic. Some of it was quite literal. Archaeologists have uncovered wall paintings that depict the Babylonian conquerors shoving a literal hook through the lips of conquered people in order to lead them about like fish on a line. Habakkuk sums up his question in verse 17: *Will they therefore empty their net and continually slay nations without sparing?* Here is his question: You are a holy and a just God and You are going to use these people to accomplish Your will?

The answer to this question is introduced in chapter 2. It begins with a command for Habakkuk to make a permanent record of this answer.

> *Then the Lord answered me and said, "Record the vision and inscribe it on tablets, that the one who reads it may run. (Habakkuk 2:2).*

The Lord is going to give Habakkuk an answer, and it is such an important answer that Habakkuk is told to take notes. These notes were are not just for Habakkuk; they are to be preserved in writing for others to read, too. It is to be inscribed on tablets. This was not the usual method of writing. Tablets were expensive and labor-intensive. Much more commonplace was the medium of ostrica; broken pieces of pottery. Most of the archaeological finds from this period consist of such pottery. It would be used for day-to-day writing. But this message is so important that it is to be put onto tablets. It is to be written so that its message can be passed on.

> *"For the vision is yet for the appointed time; It hastens toward the goal and it will not fail. Though it tarries, wait for it; for it will certainly come, it will not delay. (Habakkuk 2:3).*

God answers Habakkuk's question by assuring him that He will ultimately bring judgment upon Babylon. Five woes or curses are pronounced against Babylon. These woes serve as a reminder that the people of Judah had become just as guilty as the people of Babylon.

There are five woes proclaimed...	
2:6	*Woe to him who increases what is not his*
2:9	*Woe to him who gets evil gain for his house, to put his nest on high*
2:12	*Woe to him who builds a city with bloodshed, And founds a town with violence!*
2:15	*Woe to you who make your neighbors drink, Who mix in your venom even to make them drunk so as to look on their nakedness!*
2:19	*Woe to him who says to a piece of wood, "Awake!" To a mute stone, "Arise!"*

These woes are directed against the coming Babylonian Empire. God is saying, "I am going to judge the coming kingdom of Babylon because of these sins." But as you heard the listing of those sins, you might have been uncomfortably aware that our own nation is guilty of those very things. The people to whom Habakkuk wrote had the same reaction. He is writing to Jews - Israelites who are living in and around Jerusalem. He is writing to the chosen people. He is writing to God's people and they are beginning to shift in their seats uncomfortably as they realize that they are also guilty of these same sins.

> *For the vision is yet for the appointed time;*
> *It hastens toward the goal and it will not fail.*
> *Though it tarries, wait for it;*
> *For it will certainly come, it will not delay.*
> *4 Behold, as for the proud one,*
> *His soul is not right within him;*
> *But the righteous will live by his faith. (Habakkuk 2:3-4).*

Look again at verse 4. Do you see what it is that is contrasted to faith? What it is that is the opposite of faith? The proud one! Pride is the opposite of faith. The just do not live because of the goodness of their works. They do not live because of their arrogant pride in thinking that they are worthy of God's acceptance. The just shall live by faith. The just shall live by confessing their inadequacy before a holy God and trusting in His Son for our salvation.

A SONG OF PRAISE

The third chapter of Habakkuk is a song of praise about the wonders of a God who is so great that He moves in history, not only to balance the books in history, but to balance them on our behalf as He saves us from our sins and sets our feet upon firm ground.

And that tells me about what is to be my reaction to this message. What do I do when I come to understand the salvation that God has wrought in a world filled with violence and suffering? I am to believe. And I am to be glad. And I am to sing. Theology is not to remain in the pages of our notebooks. It must sing! And so should we.

The song presented in this chapter is a song of praise. God is pictured in thundering majesty as He comes to act in the affairs of men.

> *God comes from Teman,*
> *And the Holy One from Mount Paran. Selah.*
> *His splendor covers the heavens,*
> *And the earth is full of His praise.*
> *4 His radiance is like the sunlight;*
> *He has rays flashing from His hand,*
> *And there is the hiding of His power (Habakkuk 3:3-4).*

The Almighty is pictured in the most graphic of terms. He is the conquering King who comes with power and radiance and majesty.

> *Thou didst go forth for the salvation of Thy people,*
> *For the salvation of Thine anointed.*
> *Thou didst strike the head of the house of the evil*
> *To lay him open from thigh to neck. Selah. (Habakkuk 3:13).*

The picture of the raging Lord of the universe is a terrifying one until we realize that He is raging on our behalf.

> *Though the fig tree should not blossom,*
> *And there be no fruit on the vines,*
> *Though the yield of the olive should fail,*
> *And the fields produce no food,*
> *Though the flock should be cut off from the fold,*
> *And there be no cattle in the stalls,*
> *18 Yet I will exult in the Lord,*
> *I will rejoice in the God of my salvation. (Habakkuk 3:17-18).*

Habakkuk says, "I will continue to praise the Lord, even in those times when I do not see His obvious blessings in my life." We are quick to praise the Lord in the good times, but do we praise Him and pronounce His goodness just as adamantly in the difficult times?

> *The Lord God is my strength,*
> *And He has made my feet like hinds' feet,*
> *And makes me walk on my high places.*
> *For the choir director, on my stringed instruments.*
> *(Habakkuk 3:19).*

The reference to a "hind" is merely Old English for a "deer." This is a quote from Psalm 18:34. It pictures a deer in a high place. The impact of this passage did not come home to me until some years ago when I had the opportunity to visit the Grand Canyon. I was gazing out at that vast expanse when I noted that on a ledge a portion of the way down that yawning precipice stood a deer. She had not fallen. She was not in trouble. She was secure and she had no problem traversing those dizzying heights.

In those times when it looks as though we are going to fall, we can take comfort. It is God who has set us in place. He has directed our paths. He makes a way for our feet. He sets us in a high place and He keeps us safe.

ZEPHANIAH
Judgment and Restoration

The word of the Lord which came to Zephaniah son of Cushi, son of Gedaliah, son of Amariah, son of Hezekiah, in the days of Josiah son of Amon, king of Judah (Zephaniah 1:1).

Normally people in the ancient world identified themselves by their name and by the name of their father. Zephaniah is unusual in that he goes back four generations. Why is this? Because his great, great grandfather was King Hezekiah.

DATE OF WRITING

This same verse gives us the date of writing. It was in the days of Josiah son of Amon, king of Judah (Zephaniah 1:1). Josiah was the king who led the Israelites back to the worship of the Lord. It was during his reign that a copy of the Scriptures was found in the temple and taken to the king. He called for fasting and prayer and national repentance.

Zephaniah came on the scene only slightly before Jeremiah. While Jeremiah prophesied over a space of many years, the book of Zephaniah is only three chapters. Both books speak of the judgment that is soon to befall Jerusalem.

Zephaniah foretells the destruction of Nineveh. That event took place in 612 B.C. This means that event had not yet taken place at the writing of this book.

MESSAGE OF THE BOOK

The book of Zephaniah is a call to repentance, yet delivered in a chiastic style. Zephaniah begins with judgment and then moves us to the centerpoint of the book where he calls for repentance.

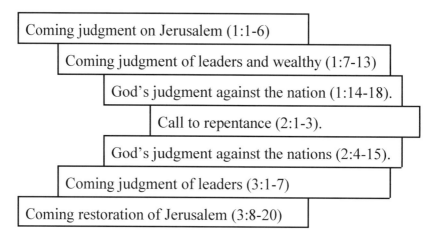

COMING JUDGMENT

> *"I will completely remove all things*
> *From the face of the earth," declares the Lord.*
> *3 "I will remove man and beast;*
> *I will remove the birds of the sky*
> *And the fish of the sea,*
> *And the ruins along with the wicked;*
> *And I will cut off man from the face of the earth," declares*
> *the Lord.*
> *4 So I will stretch out My hand against Judah*
> *And against all the inhabitants of Jerusalem.*
> *And I will cut off the remnant of Baal from this place,*
> *And the names of the idolatrous priests along with the priests.*
> *(Zephaniah 1:2-4).*

This is a prophecy of judgment. But notice the terms in which it is couched. It contains certain "buzz-words" that are designed to echo with a reminder of something with which you are familiar.

- The face of the earth.
- Man and beast.
- Birds of the sky.
- Fish of the sea.

All of these take us back to Genesis 1 and the work of creation. God's judgment is described in terms of a de-creation. It is a removal of all that has once been created and which has now been contaminated by sin and rebellion. The Lord is going to remove all things from the face of the earth -- פְּנֵי הָאֲדָמָה (*Penei haAdamah*). In poetic fashion, He then lists those things upon the face of the earth that shall be removed. His list calls to mind a reverse listing of that which was described in the six days of creation. What are the charges? What had brought about such rebuke and such punishment?

1. Religious Pluralism: *So I will stretch out My hand against Judah And against all the inhabitants of Jerusalem. And I will cut off the remnant of Baal from this place, and the names of the idolatrous priests along with the priests. 5 And those who bow down on the housetops to the host of heaven, and those who bow down and swear to the Lord and yet swear by Milcom, (Zephaniah 1:4-5).*

    Notice there were two categories of those against whom this judgment was pronounced. There were the idolatrous priests as well as the priests (these are two separate words in the Hebrew text). There are those who were not worshiping the Lord at all and there were those who, at least in name and at least in part, saw themselves in the camp of those who worshiped the Lord, but they were also swearing by the name of a false god.

    We live in a pluralistic age in which Christians and even Christian ministers are being pressured to compromise their faith. When a popular television preacher was asked in an interview whether Jesus is the only way to God, he hemmed and hawed and sidestepped the gospel because he did not want to appear narrow-minded.

    Not only do we face this sort of doctrinal pluralism, but we are also tempted by a pluralism in our affections. James speaks of *pleasures that wage war in your members* (James 4:1). Each of us is involved in a great conflict over this sort of spiritual pluralism. Who will you love? Whose kingdom will you build?

    It is very easy for us to fool ourselves into thinking that we are doing God's work and building His kingdom when, in our heart of hearts, it is really our own little domains and fiefdoms with which we are concerned.

2. Neglect of Prayer: *And those who have turned back from following the Lord, and those who have not sought the Lord or inquired of Him." (Zephaniah 1:6).*

    Notice how the prophet defines those who *have turned back from following the Lord*. They are identified as those who *have not sought the Lord or inquired of Him.* How often to we go to the Lord merely to rubber stamp our own plans, agendas, and desires instead of seeking Him and His will and inquiring what He would have us to do?

Jesus likened the moving of the Spirit to the wind. You don't tell the wind in which direction to blow. It blows where it wishes. You hear it and you see the results and, if you want to be moved by it, then you raise your sails of faith and allow yourself to be moved in that direction.

3.   Spiritual Stagnation: *And it will come about at that time that I will search Jerusalem with lamps, And I will punish the men who are stagnant in spirit, who say in their hearts, 'The Lord will not do good or evil!' (Zephaniah 1:12).*

Stagnation. The word conjures up images of a dirty, tepid, foul-smelling sludge. That is what we resemble when we are not actively allowing the Spirit of God to cleanse our hearts and our lives. You say, "That certainly does not describe me! I am involved as I can be in the life of my church." But physical action is no guarantee of spiritual movement. It is entirely possible to have a life full of "busy-ness" and if your activity is not a spiritual activity that involves loving God with all your mind and heart and soul, then you have entered the realm of spiritual stagnation.

What is the cure for religious pluralism, for neglect of prayer, and for spiritual stagnation? It is found in Zephaniah's call to repentance.

CALL FOR REPENTANCE

Gather yourselves together, yes, gather,
O nation without shame,
2 Before the decree takes effect--
The day passes like the chaff--
Before the burning anger of the Lord comes upon you,
Before the day of the Lord's anger comes upon you.
3 Seek the Lord,
All you humble of the earth
Who have carried out His ordinances;
Seek righteousness, seek humility.

Perhaps you will be hidden
In the day of the Lord's anger. (Zephaniah 2:1-3).

Notice the title that is used for the nation of Judah. She is called the "nation without shame." This is the language of non-repentance. It is a description of those who are still in their sin and who are proud of it. This is the pivotal and central point in the book. It is the "so what?" of the passage. It is a call to repentance. It is expressed in the three commands of verse 3:

- Seek the Lord
- Seek righteousness
- Seek humility

FUTURE RESTORATION

The book of Zephaniah closes with a song. It is a song of hope and a song of victory, sung by the Lord Himself. It is a song of restoration. When you restore something or someone, that assumes there was a certain standing from which there has been a fall and to which restoration is required. Zephaniah started with a reference to the judgment and the fallen condition of all creation. Now he looks for a day when it will all be restored.

1.   This Restoration involves a Marked Change.

> *For then I will give to the peoples purified lips,*
> *That all of them may call on the name of the Lord,*
> *To serve Him shoulder to shoulder. (Zephaniah 3:9).*

These words call to mind the experience of Isaiah. The book of Isaiah would have already been a part of Zephaniah's Bible—including the narrative of how Isaiah had been given a grand and glorious vision of the throne of God in which the train of God's glory filled the temple. He had seen in his vision the seraphim singing, "Holy, Holy, Holy," and Isaiah's response had been to see himself as a man of unclean lips living among a people of unclean lips.

Then one of the seraphim had taken a burning coal from the altar of incense and put it to the prophet's lips, signifying a cleansing work in which his sin was taken away and preparing him for ministry.

Here in Zephaniah, the Lord says, "What I did for Isaiah, I am going to do for all the peoples. They will all have their sins taken away. They will all have purified lips. They will all call upon the name of the Lord."

I think it no accident that, at the birth of the New Testament church in Acts 2, the event was marked with a supernatural manifestation of tongues as people spoke languages they had not previously learned as a demonstrate of purified lips and that it was followed by Peter standing and quoting the prophets of the Old Testament to show that they were calling on the name of the Lord. Verse 10 goes on to tell of the extent of this work:

From beyond the rivers of Ethiopia
My worshipers, My dispersed ones,
Will bring My offerings. (Zephaniah 3:10).

It is not just those living in Israel. It is not just Jews. The prophet says that this wonderfully inclusive change would spread to the farthest corner of the earth. In that day, beyond the rivers of Ethiopia was as far as you could possibly travel. Who are these peoples beyond the rivers of Ethiopia? They are you! They are me. They are the peoples at the uttermost parts of the earth who have heard the gospel and who have believed.

2.   This Restoration involves a Removal of our Shame

In that day you will feel no shame
Because of all your deeds
By which you have rebelled against Me;
For then I will remove from your midst
Your proud, exulting ones,
And you will never again be haughty
On My holy mountain.
12 But I will leave among you
A humble and lowly people,
And they will take refuge in the name of the Lord.
(Zephaniah 3:11-12).

Shame had its advent in the fall. The first man and the first woman had originally been unashamed in the Garden, but that changed when they fell into sin. They heard the sound of the Lord God in the garden and they were ashamed and afraid and they sought to hide themselves. The world today wrestles with its shame in a variety of ways.

- It seeks to cover the shame with the fig leaves of religion.
- It seeks to deny the shame by denying the existence of a righteous Judge. One of the indictments given against the disobedient nation was that it was a nation without shame (2:1). That is an indictment because there are times when we ought to feel shame.

These methods ultimately fail, for our own heart condemns us and shames us. But the prophet looks to a day when the shame is removed, not by pride or arrogance, but through the humility of faith. How does this take place? It takes place at the end of verse 12 when we *take refuge in the name of the Lord (3:12)*.

Back in the days when I was still with the Fire Department, my wife was driving at a speed that was a bit over the speed limit and a pair of blue lights appeared behind her and she was pulled over. The police officer came up and asked to see her driver's license. As she handed it over, she commented to the officer, "My husband, the Battalion Chief is going to be upset with me!" Do you see what she was doing? She was seeking to find refuge in the name.

We are called to do the same thing, not with a traffic ticket, but with our entire lives. Our shame is replaced by true humility when we find our refuge in Him, trusting, not in our own goodness, but in His perfect righteousness.

3.   This Restoration involves the Lord in our Midst

> *Shout for joy,*
> *O daughter of Zion!*
> *Shout in triumph, O Israel!*
> *Rejoice and exult with all your heart,*
> *O daughter of Jerusalem!*
> *15 The Lord has taken away His judgments against you,*
> *He has cleared away your enemies.*
> *The King of Israel, the Lord, is in your midst;*
> *You will fear disaster no more. (Zephaniah 3:14-15).*

There is a scene in the Disney movie, "The Lion King," when the little lion cub has been cornered by the big, mean, snarling hyenas. They are going to have him for lunch and he summons up all his strength and he roars. Because he has only a little lion cub's voice, the roar doesn't sound too impressive. But the hyenas back away and turn tail and run. The little lion cub watches with surprise, thinking that he has put these enemies to route, but then the camera angle widens and you see that behind him stands Father Lion in all of his strength and splendor. That is the picture we have here. It is a picture of the King—the Lord Himself—who is in our midst. And because He is with us, we never need fear again.

4.   This Restoration involves Salvation to the Outcast.

> *"Behold, I am going to deal at that time*
> *With all your oppressors,*
> *I will save the lame*
> *And gather the outcast,*
> *And I will turn their shame into praise and renown*
> *In all the earth.*
> *20 At that time I will bring you in,*
> *Even at the time when I gather you together;*
> *Indeed, I will give you renown and praise*
> *Among all the peoples of the earth,*
> *When I restore your fortunes before your eyes,"*
> *Says the Lord. (Zephaniah 3:19-20).*

The Lord did not come to save the strong or the noble or the wise; for in His presence there are no strong or noble or wise and those who see themselves as strong and noble and wise are those who have not seen their need for a Savior.

He came to save the lame. To gather the outcast. To take those who stood in shame for their lost condition and to turn that shame to praise. He took our shame upon Himself. Hebrews 12:2 speaks of how He *endured the cross, despising the shame*. And because He endured that shame for us, we can *abide in Him, so that when He appears, we may have confidence and not shrink away from Him in shame at His coming (1 John 2:28).*

HAGGAI
Call to Rebuild the Temple

Haggai is one of the post-exilic prophets. His book contains three discourses, all of which were written during the second year of Darius the Great. Darius was the third of the rulers of the Medo-Persia Empire. What Cyrus the Great had won and what his son Cambyses had extended, Darius took and secured and administered.

King	Dates	Biblical References
Cyrus the Great	550-530 B.C.	2 Chronicles 36:22-23; Ezra 1:1-8; Daniel 1:21
Cambyses	530-522 B.C.	Not mentioned in Scripture
Darius the Great	522-486 B.C.	Ezra 4-6; Daniel 9:1; 11:1
Xerxes	486-465 B.C.	Ahasueras of Esther
Artaxerxes	465-424 B.C.	Ezra 7; Nehemiah 2:1

Haggai and Zechariah were contemporaries. They are both post-exilic prophets. That means they prophesied after the return from the Babylonian Captivity. They prophesied in that period when the people of God who had been forcibly removed from the Promised Land had been allowed to return and rebuild their homes. The majority of Jews had elected to remain in the foreign lands to which they had been scattered, but there were some who did go back. They went to a desolated and poverty stricken land and they began to rebuild their homes and to rebuild their temple.

But then arose opposition. It came through political channels and it came in the form of a royal edict ordering the halting of the reconstruction of the temple. The work stopped and the temple stood abandoned and unfinished. Life went on. A year passed. Then another. Ten years came and went. Life was tough and the people focused on making a living. Then God spoke. He spoke through two prophets -- two witnesses to the Word and Message of God.

When the prophets, Haggai the prophet and Zechariah the son of Iddo, prophesied to the Jews who were in Judah and Jerusalem, in the name of the God of Israel, who was over them, 2 then Zerubbabel the son of Shealtiel and Jeshua the son of Jozadak arose and began to rebuild the house of God which is in Jerusalem; and the prophets of God were with them supporting them. (Ezra 5:1-2).

The book of Haggai can be divided into three sections. Each of these three sections begins with a question and in each case, the question introduces a sermon that is given to answer the question.

1:1-15	2:1-9	2:10-19	2:20-23
First Sermon	Second Sermon	Third Sermon	Closing words to Zerubbabel
People's Work Prominent	God's Work Prominent		
Question: *Should the house of God continue to be desolate?* Twofold Response: • Reverence • Work	Question: *How does this temple compare with the former temple?* Twofold Response: • Nations will come • The glory will come	Question: *Is holiness contagious?* Twofold Response: • People are unclean • Blessings will come	
People reluctant to restore covenant fellowship	People unconvinced of restoration possibilities	People unfit to take part in restoration	Zerubbabel as symbol of the people
Charge to begin Building	Encouragement to Finish		

These three sermons are given over a period of two months. As the first sermon is given, the work of rebuilding has been delayed for years. This first sermon comprises a call to action. The action involves the completion of the work of rebuilding the Temple. The next two sermons are calls to continue the action that was begun as a result of the first sermon.

FIRST SERMON: A KINGDOM PRIORITY

Priorities are important. They help us to determine what we need to do and when we need to do it. There is nothing so useless as doing well that which does not have to be done at all.

First Sermon 1:1-15		
Question:	Twofold Response:	
Is it time for you to dwell in paneled homes while the House of the Lord is desolate?	The people showed reverence for the Lord.	They came and worked on the house of the Lord of hosts, their God

Twice in this section Haggai calls for the people to *consider your ways* -- literally, "Set your heart" (1:5, 7).

1. The people had a problem with priorities: *Is it time for you yourselves to dwell in your paneled houses while this house lies desolate?* (1:4).

    It is easy to understand how they could fall into this sort of thinking. We do it all the time. That means Haggai's message can be applied to us today. Where are your priorities? Is the building of the Lord's house and the Lord's kingdom first place in your life?

    The story is told of a teacher who was speaking to a group of business students. As he stood in front of the group, he pulled out a one-gallon jar and set it on the table in front of him. He also produced about a dozen fist-sized rocks and carefully placed them, one at a time, into the jar. When the jar was filled to the top and no more rocks would fit inside, he asked, "Is this jar full?"

    Everyone in the class yelled, "Yes." The teacher replied, "Really?" He reached under the table and pulled out a bucket of gravel. He dumped some gravel in and shook the jar causing pieces of gravel to work themselves down into the spaces between the big rocks. He then asked the group once more, "Is the jar full?"

    By this time the class was on to him. "Probably not," one of them answered. "Good!" he replied. He reached under the table and brought out a bucket of sand. He started dumping the sand in the jar and it went into all of the spaces left between the rocks and the gravel. Once more he asked the question, "Is this jar full?"

"No!" the class shouted. Once again he said, "Good." Then he grabbed a pitcher of water and began to pour it in until the jar was filled to the brim. Then he looked at the class and asked, "What is the point of this illustration?" One eager beaver raised his hand and said, "The point is, no matter how full your schedule is, if you try really hard you can always fit some more things in it!"

"No," the speaker replied, "that's not the point. The truth this illustration teaches us is: If you don't put the big rocks in first, you'll never get them in at all."

It is a good story, but it still misses the point. Developing priorities must begin with recognizing that there is one real priority. If the big rock in your life is not the One who is the Rock, then you have bought into an imbalanced sense of priorities and your life will not be what it should.

2.   The people were experiencing a dissatisfaction: *You have sown much, but harvest little; you eat, but there is not enough to be satisfied; you drink, but there is not enough to become drunk; you put on clothing, but no one is warm enough; and he who earns, earns wages to put into a purse with holes* (1:6).

There is a corollary between what you give to God and what you enjoy from God. When John Rockefeller was asked how much money he needed to be happy, his reply was, "Just a little bit more." The quest for happiness through the obtaining of wealth is a vain effort. Someone said, "I know that money cannot buy happiness, but I would not mind being miserable in style." However, misery is miserable, no matter how much money one has.

When I say that there is a corollary between what you give to God and what you enjoy from God, I am not speaking only of the giving of money, though this also applies to how you utilize money. There are many different ways you can give to the Lord and I have found that the Lord will press you on exactly that point where you want to hold back from Him. Why is that? It is because the Lord wants you to enjoy Him to the fullest.

God is most pleased with you when you are most pleased in Him. He wants you to enjoy Him to the uttermost. One of the means of accomplishing that is when you give of yourself to Him.

3.   The people were more concerned with their own comforts than with

the glory of the Lord: *"Go up to the mountains, bring wood and rebuild the temple, that I may be pleased with it and be glorified," says the Lord (1:8).*

What you do with your resources is a reflection of your concern with God's glory. I didn't say that; Jesus did. He said, "Where your treasure is, there will your heart be also" (Matthew 6:21).

This is a call to get out of your comfort zone and into God's worship zone. I say it that way because the two are mutually exclusive. By contrast, man's natural tendency is to sit down and stay seated. We gravitate by nature to that which is comfortable. To put it another way, we tend to avoid the extremes of hot or cold and to move to the lukewarm. What is the answer to such a situation? It is given in verse 12. It is the fear of the Lord: *And the people showed reverence for the Lord* (1:12b). How do you get that kind of reverence for the Lord? You get it by first repenting and confessing that you do not have it and then by asking God to give it to you. And then there is one more step. You show the reverence that you want to have.

Jesus gave this same formula in Revelation 2:4-5 when He spoke to the church that had left their first love. He said...

- Remember therefore from where you have fallen.
- Repent
- Do the deeds you did at first

That is not the same as pretending. I am not talking about an act of hypocrisy. I am talking about repenting and telling God about your lack of faith and your lack of love and then stepping out in an act of faith and love as you look for the Lord to give you on the inside what you are doing on the outside.

SECOND SERMON: ENCOURAGEMENT

Have you ever had the experience of returning as an adult to the elementary school you attended as a child? The first thing you noticed is that the building seemed so much smaller. As we come to Haggai's second sermon, he addresses those readers who remembered the former temple being so much larger.

Second Sermon 2:1-9		
Question:	Twofold Response:	
How does this Temple compare with the Former Temple?	The nations will come and I will fill this House with glory	The latter glory of this House will be greater than the former

Haggai lived in a day of past glory. The Temple was being rebuilt, but it fell far short of the glory of the former Temple. The people who were working on its rebuilding could not help but to compare it to Solomon's Temple and note that it did not measure up to the original. It is hard to continue in faithfulness when you can't see the results. This chapter is written to combat that kind of discouragement.

1.   You can be encouraged by the Presence of God: *"But now take courage, Zerubbabel," declares the Lord, "take courage also, Joshua son of Jehozadak, the high priest, and all you people of the land take courage," declares the Lord, "and work; for I am with you," says the Lord of hosts.* 5 *As for the promise which I made you when you came out of Egypt, My Spirit is abiding in your midst; do not fear!* (2:4-5).

This is covenant language. The covenant that God made with His people when He brought them out of Egypt is that He would be with them. His presence was seen in the cloud by day and in the pillar of fire by night. The Pentecost event took place when, instead of a cloud and a pillar of fire over the Tabernacle, the Spirit of God came upon man and woman alike and was manifested in flaming tongues of fire over each person.

There is a lesson here. It is that the same Spirit that led the Israelites through the wilderness is with you personally today. This truth has several ramifications:

- If God's Spirit is with you, then you do not have to be afraid of anything. The Lord is bigger than any of your problems and, as Paul asks in Romans 8, "If God is for us, then who can possibly be against us?"

- If God's Spirit is with you, then you can attempt great things with confidence that the One who is with you can see you through.

I must insert a cautionary disclaimer here. When I speak of doing great things, I am not speaking of greatness in the way the world sees greatness. God's presence is no guarantee that you are going to receive a financial raise or a job promotion. It doesn't mean you are going to marry the prom queen or the millionaire. It does not say that you are going to drive an expensive car or live in a luxurious home.

I am speaking of doing great things for God and for His kingdom and that often has a quality of greatness that is exactly the opposite of the way the world sees greatness.

At the same time, Jesus said: *Truly, truly, I say to you, he who believes in Me, the works that I do shall he do also; and greater works than these shall he do; because I go to the Father* (John 14:12).

2.   You can be encouraged by the Power of God: *For thus says the Lord of hosts, 'Once more in a little while, I am going to shake the heavens and the earth, the sea also and the dry land. 7 And I will shake all the nations* (2:6-7).

God shook the heavens and the earth...

- At creation
- At the flood
- At Sinai
- When Jesus came, there was a star in the sky, the sun turned black, there was an earthquake.

But the greatest shaking of all was not physical. It was spiritual. At Pentecost there was a shaking of the nations. They were shaken so that they might enter an unshakable kingdom. The shaking of the heavens and the earth was done in the same way that the wind might shake a tree that is full of ripened fruit. The wind blows and it shakes the tree and its branches and the fruit literally falls to the ground. The writer of the Epistle to the Hebrews quotes this passage to speak of the eternal kingdom to which we are called.

> *See to it that you do not refuse Him who is speaking. For if those did not escape when they refused him who warned them on earth, much less shall we escape who turn away from Him who warns from heaven. 26 And His voice shook the earth then, but now He has promised, saying, "Yet once more I*

will shake not only the earth, but also the heaven."

And this expression, "Yet once more," denotes the removing of those things which can be shaken, as of created things, in order that those things which cannot be shaken may remain.

Therefore, since we receive a kingdom which cannot be shaken, let us show gratitude, by which we may offer to God an acceptable service with reverence and awe (Hebrews 12:25-28).

God has "shaken things up" so that you might enter into something that is unshakable. This is a promise of security. It means that you have something that all the forces of darkness cannot take from you.

Is God shaking things up in your life? Have you found yourself recently removed from your comfort zone? Do you find the ongoing changes in the world and maybe even in the church to be distressing? There is a message of hope here. It is that God is shaking things up so that He might bring about that which is unshakeable.

3. You can be encouraged by the Possessions of God: *"And I will shake all the nations; and they will come with the wealth of all nations; and I will fill this house with glory," says the Lord of hosts. 8 The silver is Mine, and the gold is Mine," declares the Lord of hosts* (2:7-8).

Are you having problems with your finances? Have you been wishing that you had a rich uncle? You do have a rich Father -- all of the gold and silver belongs to Him. He has blessed you with everything that you need.

Notice how that silver and gold and wealth are described as coming to Him. They are brought by the nations. This was very literally fulfilled in Haggai's day. The very people who had opposed the rebuilding of the Temple were ordered by the Persian King Darius to pay the full cost of the rebuilding of the Temple from the royal revenues in their own taxation district.

Moreover, I issue a decree concerning what you are to do for these elders of Judah in the rebuilding of this house of God: the full cost is to be paid to these people from the royal treasury out of the taxes of the provinces beyond the River, and that without delay (Ezra 6:8).

I believe this verse also to have a long range application. God has shaken the nations and they have come with their gold and their silver. That is us. We are not only the recipients of the wealth of the Lord, we are also the means by which that wealth is distributed. The church in the United States is a wealthy church. But we are not called to come and hoard our wealth. We are mere stewards. We are called to be the means by which the Lord blesses His church universal.

4.	You can be encouraged by the Peace of God: *"The latter glory of this house will be greater than the former," says the Lord of hosts, "and in this place I shall give peace," declares the Lord of hosts* (2:9).

It is true that the Temple became more glorious in the days of Herod the Great. But I do not believe this to be a prophecy only of Herod's Temple. It is a prophecy of Christ. He is the Prince of Peace and the manifestation of the real glory of God.

What made the Temple glorious? It was not the gold or the silver. It was the presence of God. God's presence was manifested in a baby. Jesus came to manifest the presence of God to men. He is the Immanuel -- the One who is God with us.

He is the One who came to be the Prince of Peace. Islam often presents itself as though it were a religion of peace. But the story of Mohammed is not a story of peace. On the other hand, when Peter whacked off the ear of the high priest's servant, Jesus told him to put his sword away. Jesus came to bring peace. He brought peace by dying.

THIRD SERMON: GOD'S CLEANSING

I spent a large part of my life as a career fire fighter and I can attest that fire fighting is often dirty work. The soot and the grease and the grime seem to permeate everything. Many a time I have taken a shower, only to find that the smoke odor continues to exude from the pores of my skin. The Bible teaches us that we have a cleansing problem. It is called sin. There are some today who do not like to use that word, but it is a perfectly legitimate word. To ignore it would be like a fire fighter coming out of a working fire and ignoring the fact that he was contaminated by the scene in which he had been working. You may choose to ignore the sin in your life, but it will not ignore you. The third sermon of Haggai deals with this issue of being clean from sin. It introduces the subject with a question.

Third Sermon 2:10-19		
Question:	Twofold Response:	
Does the Unclean produce that which is Clean?	Consider from this day: I have brought economic sanctions against you	Consider from this day: I will bless you

Haggai begins this sermon with a riddle. The riddle asks the question: "How does something that is unclean produce that which is clean?" The answer is obvious. It isn't possible. This had direct application to that day when it came to the rebuilding of the Temple. The people were seeking to build an outward edifice of holiness, but they had not yet dealt with the inner sin in their own lives.

We often do the same thing. We work at the obvious outward problems in our lives and we pick away at those things that are not socially acceptable while ignoring that they are only indicators of a problem within.

How does something unclean produce something that is clean? And how can that which is clean come into contact with that which is unclean and not be contaminated by it? This question points us to the gospel. It is in Christ that we find the answer to the riddle. God has produced in Him the means by which we can be made clean. This worked out in a very practical way in that day. It was the discipline of God upon His people that drove them back to Himself. Because of their repentance, they are now left with a promise. It is a promise of present and future blessing. There is coming One who will be able to touch the leper and the unclean and who will not be polluted by it, for He will cleanse the leper.

CLOSING WORDS TO ZERUBBABEL

Then the word of the Lord came a second time to Haggai on the twenty-fourth day of the month saying, 21 "Speak to Zerubbabel governor of Judah saying, 'I am going to shake the heavens and the earth. 22 And I will overthrow the thrones of kingdoms and destroy the power of the kingdoms of the nations; and I will overthrow the chariots and their riders, and the horses and their riders will go down, everyone by the sword of another. 23 On that day,' declares the Lord of hosts, 'I will take you, Zerubbabel, son of Shealtiel, My servant,' declares the Lord, 'and I will make you like a signet ring, for I have chosen you,'" declares the Lord of hosts. (Haggai 2:20-23).

Notice the closing promise of this book. It is that Zerubbabel would be made like a signet ring. A signet ring had a special use:

> There is a possible play on words with the previous verses. Verse 19 closed with the question: "Is the seed yet in the barn?" The name Zerubbabel literally means "seed of Babylon."

- It served as a person's legal signature
- It validated royal authority when used to seal a document
- It was a guarantee of a future promise.

This is a significant promise, for it is the overturning of a curse that had been made back in the book of Jeremiah.

"As I live," declares the Lord, "even though Coniah the son of Jehoiakim king of Judah were a signet ring on My right hand, yet I would pull you off; 25 and I shall give you over into the hand of those who are seeking your life, yes, into the hand of those whom you dread, even into the hand of Nebuchadnezzar king of Babylon, and into the hand of the Chaldeans." (Jeremiah 22:24-25).

The blessings of God had been taken away in the days of Coniah, but now there is a promise of their restoration under Zerubbabel. The promise is that Zerubbabel would be "like a signet ring." Where do you put a signet ring? On your right hand (see Jeremiah 22:24). That is where we find Jesus -- He is seated at the right hand of God. He is the fulfillment of this promise. He is the descendant of Zerubbabel who would be the signet ring of God.

ZECHARIAH
Visions of Victory

The book of Zechariah is paralleled in the New Testament by the book of Revelation. There are a number of things that are introduced in Zechariah that are echoed in the book of Revelation.

Zechariah	Revelation
Four horsemen/chariots (1 & 6)	Four horsemen (6)
Man with a measuring line measures Jerusalem (2:1-2)	Man with a rod measures the Temple Mount (11:1-2)
Picture of Satan ready to accuse Joshua the high priest (3:1)	Satan described as accusing the brethren (12:10)
Lampstand and two olive trees said to represent the two anointed ones (4:1-14)	Lampstand and two olive trees said to represent the two witnesses (11:3-12)
Flying scroll signifies the curse that is going over the land (5:1-3)	Seals of the book bring forth judgments upon the land (6:1-17).

We have already noted that Zechariah and Haggai were contemporaries. In both cases, we are told exactly when they received their messages from the Lord.

- Haggai 1:1. *In the second year of Darius the king, on the first day of the sixth month, the word of the Lord came by the prophet Haggai to Zerubbabel*
- Zechariah 1:1. *In the eighth month of the second year of Darius, the word of the Lord came to Zechariah the prophet.*

Zechariah started preaching only two months after Haggai started preaching. They spoke at the same time and to the same people. In spite of this, the two books are very different. Haggai is conversational and prophetic while Zechariah is apocalyptic and contains visions and oracles, especially in its first 6 chapters.

Haggai's ministry called the people back to complete the rebuilding of the Temple. Zechariah's message must be seen in that context as he encourages them in that work of rebuilding, letting them know that they will succeed in this effort.

OUTLINE OF ZECHARIAH

The book of Zechariah can be seen in three major parts

- First there are a series of eight Visions that are given (Chapters 1-6).
- Then come two Sermons (Chapters 7-8).
- Finally we have two Burdens (Chapters 9-14).

1:1	**Eight**	Four Horsemen		
1:18	**Visions**		Horns and smiths: Judgment goes forth	
2:1			Measuring Line: Flee from Babylon	
3:1				Joshua the Priest
4:1				Zerubbabel and the Lampstand
5:1			Flying Scroll: Judgment goes forth	
5:5			Woman and Basket: Build in Shinar	
6:1		Four Chariots		
7:1	**Two**	A Call for True Justice		
8:1	**Sermons**	A Promise of Future Restoration in Jerusalem		
9:1	**Two**	Judgment on the Enemies of Israel		
12:1	**Burdens**	The Coming of the Lord		

The name Zechariah means, "The Lord Remembers." This is an appropriate name for the giver of this prophecy, for he tells us of how the Lord will remember His people.

> 8 *I will whistle for them to gather them together,*
> *For I have redeemed them;*

And they will be as numerous as they were before.
9 When I scatter them among the peoples,
*They will **remember** Me in far countries,*
And they with their children will live and come back.
10 I will bring them back from the land of Egypt,
And gather them from Assyria;
And I will bring them into the land of Gilead and Lebanon,
Until no room can be found for them. (Zechariah 10:8-10).

Do you ever feel as though you have been forgotten in the tedious tension of daily living? There is good news here. It is that there is One who has not forgotten. There is One who remembers, even when you feel scattered and confused. He is waiting to bring you home.

A PAST LEGACY

"The Lord was very angry with your fathers. 3 Therefore say to them, 'Thus says the Lord of hosts, "Return to Me," declares the Lord of hosts, "that I may return to you," says the Lord of hosts. 4 "Do not be like your fathers, to whom the former prophets proclaimed, saying, 'Thus says the Lord of hosts, "Return now from your evil ways and from your evil deeds."' But they did not listen or give heed to Me," declares the Lord. 5 Your fathers, where are they? And the prophets, do they live forever? 6 But did not My words and My statutes, which I commanded My servants the prophets, overtake your fathers? Then they repented and said, 'As the Lord of hosts purposed to do to us in accordance with our ways and our deeds, so He has dealt with us.'" (Zechariah 1:2-6).

Zechariah writes in a day of return. Since the days of Cyrus the Great, the Jews who lived in Captivity had been permitted to return to the land. But only a very small percentage had chosen to do so. It had gotten comfortable in Babylon. I can see how that can happen. We tend to get comfortable where we are and, before long, it is harder and harder to get out of our "comfort zone."

But the problem of which Zechariah speaks is not a matter of physical location as much as it is one of spiritual location. He does not chastise them for not having returned to the land -- he chastises them for not having returned to the Lord.

This is a call to repentance. It is a call to return to the Lord. Such a call presupposes something about the one being called. A call to return presupposes that the one being called has departed. Zechariah sets forth the past departures of Israel in this section. Zechariah points to the past ancestors of his present recipients and he says, "Don't you be like them!"

1.   They heard a warning but did not listen: *Do not be like your fathers, to whom the former prophets proclaimed, saying, 'Thus says the Lord of hosts, "Return now from your evil ways and from your evil deeds." But they did not listen or give heed to Me,' declares the Lord (1:4).*

I have seen some tragic accidents during my career as a fire fighter. One of the most senseless took place on the dock where there were two huge gantry cranes being moved. These cranes are the size of a small skyscraper and they move along on a rail at less than one mile per hour. Whenever they are moving, a loud siren goes off so that you cannot help but to hear.

That was why it was so surprising to get called out on the fatal injury of a dockworker. It was one of the stevedores who had been writing notes on his clipboard. He saw the movement of the cranes. He heard the alarms, but he did not move because he considered himself to have plenty of time to get out of the way.

2.   They built up something that did not last: *Your fathers, where are they? And the prophets, do they live forever? (1:5).*

Jesus likens life to a building project. He tells the story of two houses being built. One is constructed on a solid foundation of rock; the other is built upon shifting sands. Which one is going to last? Only the one upon the certain foundation will remain.

On what are you building your life? Is it upon that which lasts? This mortal life will not last. Beauty will fade, money will be taxed and inflated away to nothingness. Possessions will rust and rot. Only those things that are imperishable will remain.

There is nothing so empty as doing well that which needs not be done at all. And there is nothing so foolish as spending your time building that which is guaranteed to eventually fall down to dust and decay. Does that mean you should never seek a career or buy a car or build a house? No, it doesn't. Remember that Zechariah writes these words in the context of building a temple. But the building of the temple will not be an end unto itself. Its construction serves a larger and a lasting purpose. It serves to focus the builders' attention upon the One to whom the temple points.

If you are working at a career or buying car or building a house, you make sure you are doing it for the right reason. The right reason is not to have the career or the car or even the house, but that these might be used to bring you and your family to worship and honor the Lord because, in the end, that is what will last.

3.   They were promised a judgment that they did not escape: *But did not My words and My statutes, which I commanded My servants the prophets, overtake your fathers? Then they repented and said, 'As the Lord of hosts purposed to do to us in accordance with our ways and our deeds, so He has dealt with us.' (1:6).*

We worship a God who always keeps His promises. That can be a good thing and it can also be a bad thing. It is a good thing when the promise is for your good and for your blessing. It is a bad thing when the promise is for your judgment, but even then, that does not mean that God is doing a bad thing by keeping His promises.

When a fire fighter comes into a burning building and yells, "Everyone get out; this building is on fire," no one accuses him of being negative or of doing a bad thing. He comes in the guise of a rescuer. The Lord comes the same way, even when He is warning of judgment that is to come.

THE VISION OF THE HORSEMEN

On the twenty-fourth day of the eleventh month, which is the month Shebat, in the second year of Darius, the word of the Lord came to Zechariah the prophet, the son of Berechiah, the son of Iddo, as follows (Zechariah 1:7).

This vision begins several months after the opening prophecy of this book. The Spirit of the Lord had already come to Zechariah as He had also come to Haggai earlier that same year. In both cases, the purpose was the same. It was a call to action.

The Jews were once more living in their land. The Babylonian Captivity had ended with the coming of the Persians and the Jews had been given permission to return to the land. A number of them had done so and they had begun to rebuild their temple, but then politics reared its ugly head and this rebuilding project was halted. The temple still lay in ruins. The legacy of the Babylonian destruction remained. It is in this situation that Zechariah is given a vision. It is a vision of horsemen.

> *I saw at night, and behold, a man was riding on a red horse, and he was standing among the myrtle trees which were in the ravine, with red, sorrel, and white horses behind him. (Zechariah 1:8).*

Zechariah sees a night vision. I am not sure that this has any special significance except to add to the drama of the vision. This vision is of four horsemen. We know from our New Testament perspective that this is not the only time that such a vision has been seen.

Zechariah 1	Zechariah 6	Revelation 6
Red horse Red horse Sorrel horse (speckled?) White horse	Red Black White Dappled (Spotted)	White Red Black Ashen (Pale green?)
Sent out by God to patrol the earth	Four spirits of heaven going out to patrol the earth	Called by the four living creatures around the throne

Translators have struggled with the color of the third horse. The NAS translates this as a "sorrel" horse. The NIV renders this color as "brown" while the KJV described it as "speckled." The same Hebrew word is used to describe a "lucious vine" (Isaiah 5:2; 16:8; Jeremiah 2:21) and there was even a valley by the same name -- the Valley of Sorek from which Delilah came (Judges 16:4). As we look at all three of these passages, we see that the horses have similar, but not identical colors. There is enough of a similarity to suggest a commonality between them.

1.   The Identity of the Horsemen: *Then I said, "My lord, what are these?" And the angel who was speaking with me said to me, "I will show you what these are." 10 And the man who was standing among the myrtle trees answered and said, "These are those whom the Lord has sent to patrol the earth." (Zechariah 1:9-10).*

If we are puzzled as to the identity of these horsemen, Zechariah was no less puzzled. He asks the question as to their identity and the answer he is given is that they are *those whom the Lord has sent to patrol the earth*. The translation makes this sound quite official, but the Hebrew term used (Hithpael infinitive of הָלַךְ) merely means "to walk" or "to go." These horsemen are sent to go across the earth.

Notice that these horsemen have been sent by the Lord. He is their Master and He is the one who has sent them. When they report their findings, they report to the Lord. When they do their work, they are doing His work. They ride at His bidding.

This is important because, when we see these horsemen in Revelation 6, there are some bad things that accompany them. There is war and there is famine and there is death and taxes and poverty. These are not good, but we should recognize that the presence of these things is not a sign that the Lord has lost control of history. He continues to reign as the King of the universe, even when bad things take place.

2.   The Report of the Horsemen: *So they answered the angel of the Lord who was standing among the myrtle trees, and said, "We have patrolled the earth, and behold, all the earth is peaceful and quiet." (Zechariah 1:11).*

The report of the horsemen is that *all the earth is peaceful and quiet*. The conquests of the past were past. This was now a time of peace. The angel says in effect, "Wait a minute, Lord! These nations that are at peace and rest are the same ones that gloried and delighted in the fall of Jerusalem. Aren't you going to do anything about that?" The angel of the Lord responds with a prayer of intercession.

> *How long wilt Thou have no compassion for*
> *Jerusalem and the cities of Judah, with which Thou*
> *hast been indignant these seventy years? (1:12)*

This is a striking prayer, for it is a prayer from the angel of the Lord. It reminds us of the promise found in the epistle to the Hebrews that Jesus serves as our high priest to always make intercession for us (Hebrews 7:25).

This intercession involved the rebuilding of the temple. The rest of the world is in peace and safety while the temple remained unrestored. It was still in ruins. Indeed, the entire city of Jerusalem remained in ruins. It had been in ruins since the days of the Babylonian king Nebuchadnezzar. In answer, the Lord promises to *return to Jerusalem with compassion* and to rebuild His house in it (1:16).

FOUR HORNS AND FOUR CRAFTSMEN

> *18 Then I lifted up my eyes and looked, and behold, there were four horns. 19 So I said to the angel who was speaking with me, "What are these?" And he answered me, "These are the horns which have scattered Judah, Israel, and Jerusalem."*
>
> *20 Then the Lord showed me four craftsmen. 21 And I said, "What are these coming to do?" And he said, "These are the horns which have scattered Judah, so that no man lifts up his head; but these craftsmen have come to terrify them, to throw down the horns of the nations who have lifted up their horns against the land of Judah in order to scatter it." (Zechariah 1:18-21).*

On the heels of the vision of the four horsemen, Zechariah now sees two other groups of four. They are not identical with the horsemen but, like the horsemen, they also come from the hand of the Lord.

A horn in both the ancient world and in the Biblical world was a sign of power. It is for this reason that Hannah could sing her hymn of praise:

> *My heart exults in the Lord;*
> *My **horn** is exalted in the Lord,*
> *My mouth speaks boldly against my enemies,*
> *Because I rejoice in Thy salvation. (1 Samuel 2:1).*

The four horns are the powers *which have scattered Judah, Israel, and Jerusalem (1:19).* It is not needful to become specific in identifying which horn is represented by which power. We are not given enough details to set out on such an undertaking. It is sufficient to know that the horns represent the political powers of the world. These powers have recently been lifted up *against the land of Judah in order to scatter it* (1:21).

MAN WITH THE MEASURING LINE

> *Then I lifted up my eyes and looked, and behold, there*

was a man with a measuring line in his hand. 2 So I said, "Where are you going?" And he said to me, "To measure Jerusalem, to see how wide it is and how long it is."

3 And behold, the angel who was speaking with me was going out, and another angel was coming out to meet him, 4 and said to him, "Run, speak to that young man, saying, 'Jerusalem will be inhabited without walls, because of the multitude of men and cattle within it. 5 For I,' declares the Lord, 'will be a wall of fire around her, and I will be the glory in her midst.'" (Zechariah 2:1-5).

This is reminiscent of the vision of Amos who saw a plumb line that was set against the city as a sign of judgment. This time, a man is out to measure the city of Jerusalem to see its dimensions. He is told that Jerusalem is going to be so big that walls will not be able to contain her.

This is a promise, not so much of the literal city, but of the heavenly city. God is our wall and our fortress and our deliverer. This truth had some practical ramifications for Zechariah's day.

For thus says the Lord of hosts, "After glory He has sent me against the nations which plunder you, for he who touches you, touches the apple of His eye. 9 For behold, I will wave My hand over them, so that they will be plunder for their slaves. Then you will know that the Lord of hosts has sent Me." (Zechariah 2:8-9).

Zechariah is told that those nations who had been involved in the plundering of Judah in the Babylonian Captivity would themselves be plundered. The reason for this is because the Lord has a special covenant relationship with Israel -- she is the apple (literally the pupil) of His eye.

"Sing for joy and be glad, O daughter of Zion; for behold I am coming and I will dwell in your midst," declares the Lord. 11 "And many nations will join themselves to the Lord in that day and will become My people. Then I will dwell in your midst, and you will know that the Lord of hosts has sent Me to you." (Zechariah 2:10-11).

The Lord says that there is coming a day when He shall come and will dwell with His people. Not only that, but also many of the surrounding nations shall also come and will join themselves to the Lord. This was fulfilled in the coming of Jesus. He is the One in whom the Lord came to

Israel to dwell in the midst of His people. It was following His death and burial and resurrection and ascension that the nations were gathered to join themselves to the Lord.

VISION OF JOSHUA THE PRIEST

Then he showed me Joshua the high priest standing before the angel of the Lord, and Satan [הַשָּׂטָן] standing at his right hand to accuse him [לְשִׂטְנוֹ, literally, "to satan him"]. 2 And the Lord said to Satan, "The Lord rebuke you, Satan! Indeed, the Lord who has chosen Jerusalem rebuke you! Is this not a brand plucked from the fire?" 3 Now Joshua was clothed with filthy garments and standing before the angel. 4 And he spoke and said to those who were standing before him saying, "Remove the filthy garments from him." Again he said to him, "See, I have taken your iniquity away from you and will clothe you with festal robes." (Zechariah 3:1-4).

What a wonderful symbol is presented here! All of the elements are present. There is the guilty priest, clothed in his filthy garments with nothing to commend himself. There is Satan, the accuser. There is the Judge of the earth. The good news is pronounced that iniquity is to be removed and that the once guilty priest will be re-clothed with festal robes.

Now listen, Joshua the high priest, you and your friends who are sitting in front of you-- indeed they are men who are a symbol, for behold, I am going to bring in My servant the Branch. (Zechariah 3:8).

Joshua is a symbol for the people of God. Like them, he is pictured as having been accused by Satan, but then God moves in and takes away his dirty robes and replaces them with clean, white robes.

"For behold, the stone that I have set before Joshua; on one stone are seven eyes. Behold, I will engrave [literally, 'inscribe'] an inscription on it," declares the Lord of hosts, "and I will remove the iniquity of that land in one day. 10 In that day," declares the Lord of hosts, "every one of you will invite his neighbor to sit under his vine and under his fig

tree." (Zechariah 3:9-10).

We are confronted by a stone on which there are seven eyes. The seven eyes points to the sevenfold manifestation of the Spirit of God (Revelation 5:6 and Isaiah 11:2). But what is the stone? I think it is the same stone that was introduced earlier in the Scriptures. It is the Stone that the builders rejected (Psalm 118:22). It is the tested stone of Isaiah 28:16. It is a reference to the One on whom would be the Spirit of the Lord.

That brings us to the inscription. I'm not absolutely certain what is the inscription. But I'm reminded of something the Lord said to Isaiah, "Behold, I have inscribed you on the palms of My hands" (Isaiah 49:16). What are the marks on the palms of the hands of Jesus? They are the marks of His love for us. There was another inscription that was brought to mind whenever you spoke of the priesthood.

- Exodus 28:36 - *You shall also make a plate of pure gold and shall engrave on it, like the engravings of a seal, 'Holy to the Lord.'*
- Exodus 39:30 - *And they made the plate of the holy crown of pure gold, and inscribed it like the engravings of a signet, "Holy to the Lord."*
- Zechariah 14:20 - *In that day there will be inscribed on the bells of the horses, "HOLY TO THE LORD." And the cooking pots in the Lord's house will be like the bowls before the altar.*

The Exodus passages seem relevant considering these were articles worn by the priests who were mediators at that time between God and Israel.

It is at the cross that these two concepts of God's holiness and God's love find their meeting. God so loved the world that He gave His only begotten Son that we might be made holy.

TWO WITNESSES

Then the angel who was speaking with me returned, and roused me as a man who is awakened from his sleep. 2 And he said to me, "What do you see?" And I said, "I see, and behold, a lampstand all of gold with its bowl on the top of it, and its seven lamps on it with seven spouts belonging to each of the lamps which are on the top of it; 3 also two olive trees by it, one on the right side of the bowl and the other on its left side." (Zechariah 4:1-3).

The next vision involves a lampstand of gold. This was as familiar a sight to Zechariah as a vision of stars and stripes would be to an American. It is Temple-language. There was in the original Tabernacle a golden lampstand with seven spouts, each holding a lamp.

In addition to the lampstand, Zechariah sees two olive trees. One is on either side of the lampstand. If he recognizes the lampstand as a familiar figure, he does not recognize the meaning of the olive trees. How do we know this? Because he says so.

> *4 Then I answered and said to the angel who was speaking with me saying, "What are these, my lord?"*
>
> *5 So the angel who was speaking with me answered and said to me, "Do you not know what these are?" And I said, "No, my lord."*
>
> *6 Then he answered and said to me, "This is the word of the Lord to Zerubbabel saying, 'Not by might nor by power, but by My Spirit,' says the Lord of hosts. 7 'What are you, O great mountain? Before Zerubbabel you will become a plain; and he will bring forth the top stone with shouts of "Grace, grace to it!"'"* (Zechariah 4:4-7).

Notice the answer. It is an answer that points initially to Zerubbabel. Who is Zerubbabel? He is the leader and representative of those who have returned to the land. However, we are not to take this to mean that it was Zerubbabel's power or prestige that is in view here, for it is "not by might nor by power, but by My Spirit," says the Lord of hosts (4:6) Zechariah hears the reply, but he still is not entirely certain what is meant by the reply. So he repeats the question:

> *And I answered the second time and said to him, "What are the two olive branches which are beside the two golden pipes, which empty the golden oil from themselves?"*
>
> *13 So he answered me saying, "Do you not know what these are?" And I said, "No, my lord." 14 Then he said, "These are the two anointed ones, who are standing by the Lord of the whole earth."* (Zechariah 4:12-14).

Who are the two olive branches of the vision? They are the two anointed ones. Which two anointed ones are mentioned in Zechariah's prophecy?

- Zerubbabel the civil leader
- Joshua the high priest

These two symbols represent the leaders who represent the people of God. I believe this gives us a clue who the same two symbols represent when we come to see them in the book of Revelation -- they represent the people of God.

VISION OF THE FOUR CHARIOTS

> *Now I lifted up my eyes again and looked, and behold, four chariots were coming forth from between the two mountains; and the mountains were bronze mountains.*
>
> *2 With the first chariot were red horses, with the second chariot black horses, 3 with the third chariot white horses, and with the fourth chariot strong dappled horses.*
>
> *4 Then I spoke and said to the angel who was speaking with me, "What are these, my lord?" 5 And the angel answered and said to me, "These are the four spirits of heaven, going forth after standing before the Lord of all the earth, 6 with one of which the black horses are going forth to the north country; and the white ones go forth after them, while the dappled ones go forth to the south country. 7 When the strong ones went out, they were eager to go to patrol the earth." And He said, "Go, patrol the earth." So they patrolled the earth. 8 Then He cried out to me and spoke to me saying, "See, those who are going to the land of the north have appeased My wrath in the land of the north." (Zechariah 6:1-8).*

Here was a vision of four chariots. The chariot was an instrument of war. It was to the ancient world what the tank is to the modern world. These chariots are described as coming *from between the two mountains*. This was not any two mountains. The definite article is used. These are two very specific mountains. The problem is that the Bible never elsewhere speaks of two bronze mountains.

What the Bible does describe are the two pillars of bronze that stood on either side of the door to Solomon's Temple (1 Kings 7:15-16). If there is a correlation between the two, then this might be a hint to take us back to the Temple. These four chariots are seen as going out from the presence of the Lord. This is not too much of a stretch, for verse 5 tells us that *"these are the four spirits of heaven, going forth after standing before the Lord of all the earth."*

Zechariah 1:7-11describes these same horses. In that chapter, Zechariah goes on to tell us of four horns representing four powers that had been used to scatter Judah, Israel and Jerusalem. Following these are four craftsmen that throw down the four horns.

- Four horses
- Four horns
- Four craftsmen
- Four chariots

In each case, there is a picture of judgment. The four horsemen are seen again in Revelation 6:2-8 where each is identified with a specific judgment. Who are these four chariots? They are identified in verse 5: *And the angel answered and said to me, "These are the four spirits of heaven, going forth after standing before the Lord of all the earth."* They are four spirits / winds. The Hebrew word for wind and spirit is the same. They stand before the Lord. They are awaiting His command.

PROMISE OF A PRIEST-KING

> *The word of the Lord also came to me saying,* 10 *"Take an offering from the exiles, from Heldai, Tobijah, and Jedaiah; and you go the same day and enter the house of Josiah the son of Zephaniah, where they have arrived from Babylon.* 11 *And take silver and gold, make an ornate crown, and set it on the head of Joshua the son of Jehozadak, the high priest.* 12 *Then say to him, 'Thus says the Lord of hosts, "Behold, a man whose name is Branch, for He will branch out from where He is; and He will build the temple of the Lord.* 13 *Yes, it is He who will build the temple of the Lord, and He who will bear the honor and sit and rule on His throne. Thus, He will be a priest on His throne, and the counsel of peace will be between the two offices."'"* (Zechariah 6:9-13).

An offering of silver and gold was to be taken and used to make a crown. This crown was to be set upon the head of Joshua, the high priest. The high priest was to have a crown (נֵזֶר, *nezer*) that was a part of a turban. That is not what is described here. What we have here is a different Hebrew word for crown. The crown here is usually used of a king's crown (עֲטָרָה,

atarah).

What is a high priest doing wearing the crown of a king? This is a prophecy. There will come one who is from the priestly family yet who will reign as the king. This was initially fulfilled in the Hasmonean rulers that followed the Maccabean Revolt in 168 B.C. They were all from the tribe of Levi and of a priestly family.

The ultimate fulfillment of this prophecy is seen in the man whose name is Branch. This is the One who would build the Temple of the Lord. It is a Messianic prophecy. We are told a number of things about Him.

- His name is Branch. This is the same word used in Isaiah 4:2; Jeremiah 23:5; 33:15 and Zechariah 3:8 for the Messianic promises of the Branch of the Lord.
- He will branch out. There is a play on words here when we read that *a man whose name is Branch... will branch out from where He is* (6:12).
- He will build the Temple: *Yes, it is He who will build the temple of the Lord* (6:13). What is a temple? It is the place where God manifests His presence. It is where God meets man. That took place in the person of Jesus.
- He will rule: *It is He who will bear the honor and sit and rule on His throne* (6:13).
- He will be both priest and king: *He will be a priest on His throne* (6:13).
- Those who are far off will come: *Those who are far off will come and build the temple of the Lord* (6:15). This is ultimately fulfilled in the coming of the Gentiles into the church. They who were once far off have now come to be one in Christ.

RITUAL VERSUS REALITY

There is a two year gap between the end of chapter 6 and the beginning of chapter 7. There is a new issue with which Zechariah is dealing. It is the issue of ritual versus reality. It is seen in the practice of fasting.

> *Now the town of Bethel had sent Sharezer and Regemmelech and their men to seek the favor of the Lord, 3 speaking to the priests who belong to the house of the Lord of hosts, and to the prophets saying, "Shall I weep in the fifth month and abstain, as I have done these many years?"*

(Zechariah 7:2-3).

The question that is asked here introduces a topic that takes up the rest of chapter 7 and all of chapter 8. The Jews had one fast a year that God had ordained. It took place upon the Day of Atonement. But over the years, the Jews had taken up other days for fasting. Now they want to know whether they have to keep on doing this.

- Chapter 7 gives the answer in its negative aspects.
- Chapter 8 gives the answer in positive terms.

It is not that fasting is commanded or forbidden. The issue is not whether or not you need to fast. The issue revolves around the right heart to accompany fasting.

> *Then the word of the Lord of hosts came to me saying,*
> *5 "Say to all the people of the land and to the priests, 'When you fasted and mourned in the fifth and seventh months these seventy years, was it actually for Me that you fasted? 6 And when you eat and drink, do you not eat for yourselves and do you not drink for yourselves?'" (Zechariah 7:4-6).*

The Lord points out that they had been fasting for the wrong reasons. They were guilty of observing the outward actions of fasting without having manifested a true inward repentance.

> *Are not these the words which the Lord proclaimed by the former prophets, when Jerusalem was inhabited and prosperous with its cities around it, and the Negev and the foothills were inhabited? (Zechariah 7:7).*

Zechariah says, "The message that I am preaching to you today is the same message that the former prophets proclaimed to the Jews prior to the Babylonian Captivity. The reason that we are preaching the same message is because you are committing the same sin." Notice the progression that is described:

- They refused to pay attention (7:11).
- They turned a stubborn shoulder (7:11).
- They stopped their ears from hearing (7:11).
- They made their hearts like flint (7:12).

Because they would not listen to God, He stopped listening to them: *"And it came about that just as He called and they would not listen, so they called and I would not listen," says the Lord of hosts* (7:13).

> *Then the word of the Lord of hosts came saying, 2 "Thus says the Lord of hosts, 'I am exceedingly jealous for Zion, yes, with great wrath I am jealous for her.' 3 Thus says the Lord, 'I will return to Zion and will dwell in the midst of Jerusalem. Then Jerusalem will be called the City of Truth, and the mountain of the Lord of hosts will be called the Holy Mountain.'" (Zechariah 8:1-3).*

Thus begins the turn from the negative to the positive. There is a lesson here. It is not enough to say, "Don't do this!" There must also come a positive with the negative. The Jews are about to be given some amazing prophecies. Can these be believed? Yes! They come from the One who is the Lord of Hosts and who therefore has the power and the might to accomplish that which He has promised.

MESSIANIC PROPHECIES IN ZECHARIAH

There are several striking Messianic prophecies to be found within the latter chapters of the book of Zechariah.

1. The Triumphal Entry: *Rejoice greatly, O daughter of Zion! Shout in triumph, O daughter of Jerusalem! Behold, your king is coming to you; He is just and endowed with salvation, humble, and mounted on a donkey, even on a colt, the foal of a donkey (Zechariah 9:9).*

    The picture of a king coming on a donkey seems an unusual one. We normally don't think of kings riding donkeys any more than we think of presidents driving motorbikes. But the Bible gives us quite a different picture. When David wanted to make certain that the throne went to Solomon, he ordered that Solomon be placed upon the king's mule (1 Kings 1:33).

    This is at the same time both a picture of kingship as well as a picture of humility. A king who comes on a donkey; and not only a donkey, but more specifically, on a colt. Jesus came riding on a young donkey that had never before been ridden. I've tried that before and it doesn't work very well. But Jesus did not need to break in this unbroken colt. The One who calmed the storm also was able to calm a donkey.

2. Silver and the Potter's House: *And I said to them, "If it is good in your sight, give me my wages; but if not, never mind!" So they weighed out thirty shekels of silver as my wages. 13 Then the Lord said to me, "Throw it to the potter, that magnificent price at which I was valued by them." So I took the thirty shekels of silver and threw them to the potter in the house of the Lord (Zechariah 11:12-13).*

This prophecy is given in the context of wages being given to Zechariah rather than to some future personage. What we have is a parallel of contrast between the actions of Zechariah and the actions of a future person to whom was paid 30 shekels of silver.

3. The One who was Pierced: *And I will pour out on the house of David and on the inhabitants of Jerusalem, the Spirit of grace and of supplication, so that they will look on Me whom they have pierced; and they will mourn for Him, as one mourns for an only son, and they will weep bitterly over Him, like the bitter weeping over a first-born (Zechariah 12:10).*

In this case, we have a prophecy given in the context of what the Lord is promising to do. It begins back in verse 1 where the Lord is first introduced.

- I am going to make Jerusalem a cup that causes reeling to all the peoples around (12:2).
- In that day that I will make Jerusalem a heavy stone for all the peoples (12:3).
- "In that day," declares the Lord, "I will strike every horse with bewilderment" (12:4).
- In that day I will make the clans of Judah like a firepot (12:6).
- In that day that I will set about to destroy all the nations that come against Jerusalem (12:9).

Finally in verse 10 we see the same person saying, *I will pour out on the house of David and on the inhabitants of Jerusalem, the Spirit of grace and of supplication.* Do you see the point? It is still the Lord who is speaking. He has been speaking since verse 1 and He is still speaking. It is He who says that they shall see Him whom they pierced.

4.   The Striking of the Shepherd: *"Awake, O sword, against My Shepherd, and against the man, My Associate,"* declares the Lord of hosts. *"Strike the Shepherd that the sheep may be scattered; and I will turn My hand against the little ones."* (Zechariah 13:7).

Jesus cited this passage as something that would be experienced by His disciples at His betrayal, arrest, and crucifixion (Matthew 26:31; Mark 14:27).

VICTORY AT THE MOUNT OF OLIVES

Behold, a day is coming for the Lord when the spoil taken from you will be divided among you. 2 For I will gather all the nations against Jerusalem to battle, and the city will be captured, the houses plundered, the women ravished, and half of the city exiled, but the rest of the people will not be cut off from the city.

3 Then the Lord will go forth and fight against those nations, as when He fights on a day of battle. 4 And in that day His feet will stand on the Mount of Olives, which is in front of Jerusalem on the east; and the Mount of Olives will be split in its middle from east to west by a very large valley, so that half of the mountain will move toward the north and the other half toward the south. (Zechariah 14:1-4).

There have been several different interpretations given to this passage, depending upon which millennial view is held.

1.   The Historic View.

Zechariah is written at the height of the Persian Empire. Israel is no more and Judah is a tiny vassal under the sway of that Empire. But there is coming a day when Jerusalem will again be "on the map." It will be a time when the nations come against Jerusalem. It will be a time of great devastation. And yet, amazingly enough, Judah will be saved by the hand of the Lord.

There is a partial fulfillment of these events in the Maccabee Revolt of 168 B.C. Judah lay between two warring superpowers - the Seleucid Empire to the North and Egypt to the south (Daniel's King of the North and King of the South). Jerusalem underwent a terrible time of persecution. But a deliverer arose. All recognized that the hand of the Lord was present (if you doubt this, then read the books of Maccabees). The result of that time of war was that Israel again became independent and that the Temple was again made holy.

It should be noted that the Jews were not completely united during this war. Indeed, not all of the Jews were living in the land. There were a great many who had remained in Mesopotamia and there was also a large colony living within Egypt. The Jewish community in Egypt had built their own Temple in Elephantine. This might help to explain the special emphasis which Zechariah has in the "family of Egypt" making the pilgrimage to the Temple in Jerusalem (14:17, 18).

2.   A View to the Church.

From an apocalyptic point of view, the world as it had been throughout history ended when Jesus Christ died and rose again and ascended into heaven. The cross is the center-point of history. Nothing has ever been the same since then.

Within 40 years of the Messiah taking His stand on the Mount of Olives, Jerusalem was destroyed. But the destruction of the nation of Israel did not mean the destruction of God's people - for a new Kingdom had arisen -one made up of the Holy Ones of the Lord.

This Kingdom began with "living waters" which flowed from Jerusalem and through Judea and Samaria and to the uttermost ends of the earth until men of every nation proclaimed Jesus as their Lord and King (Zechariah 14:8, 9).

This bride of Christ has a special security which no man or emperor can take away (Zechariah 14:11; Revelation 21:2). In the end, those who belong to the bridegroom shall be saved and those who do not choose to honor Him shall be cursed.

3.   The Futurist View.

This view pictures the return of Jesus to the Mount of Olives, conquering His enemies and establishing His complete kingship over all the earth (note that it is possible to hold this future view with either the Premillennial or the Amillennial - and perhaps even the Postmillennial Positions).

MALACHI
The Last Message

The Hebrew word Malachi literally means, "My messenger." It is not entirely clear from the context of the book if this was to be taken as a title or the name of a prophet.

Many of the prophets give an exact dating of their prophecies. Malachi does not. We can see, however, that the concerns raised by Malachi are those which were issues during the ministries of Ezra and Nehemiah. Neither Ezra nor Nehemiah make reference to Malachi even though Malachi was likely a contemporary with them. That is normally taken as an indication that Malachi came a bit after them.

Temple Completed	Return under Ezra in the 4th year of Artaxerxes I	Return under Nehemiah	Nehemiah returns to Persia for a time	Darius II comes to the throne of Persia
516 B.C.	458 B.C.	444 B.C.	432 B.C.	423 B.C.
			Book of Malachi Written?	

That tells us a little of the setting for this book.

- After the Babylonian Captivity
- Temple had been rebuilt
- Walls of Jerusalem had been restored
- People are back in the land.

The fact that all of these events had taken place should have made Malachi a very positive and a very upbeat book. It isn't. There are some real problems with which this book deals.

The book of Malachi can be outlined in two major points:

- God's love for Israel and her unfaithful response (1-2).
- The Day of the Lord and the purging of Israel (3-4).

The book is made up of a series of statements and corresponding questions between God and the people of Israel.

1:1	God says: "I have loved you"	People answer: "How have You loved us?"	God has blessed Israel above other nations
1:6	God says: "If I am a father, where is My honor?"	People answer: "How have we despised Your name?"	The people have not offered their best to the Lord
2:10	People ask: "If we are brothers, why do we deal treacherously with one another?"		The people have defrauded one another, especially in the area of divorce
2:17	God says: "You have wearied the Lord with your words"	People answer: "How have we wearied Him?"	The people have asked for justice, but have not acted justly. God is a God of justice.
3:1	Promise of a Coming Messenger.		
3:6	God says: "Return to Me and I will return to you"	People answer: "How shall we return?"	The people are to bring the whole tithe into the storehouse
3:13	God says: "Your words have been arrogant against Me"	People answer: "What have we spoken against You?"	They have taken the attitude that it is vain to serve the Lord ("What's in it for me?")
3:16	Epilogue: Promise of Coming Judgment and Restoration		

GOD'S UNDESERVED LOVE FOR ISRAEL

"I have loved you," says the Lord. But you say, "How hast Thou loved us?" "Was not Esau Jacob's brother?" declares the Lord. "Yet I have loved Jacob; 3 but I have hated Esau, and I have made his mountains a desolation, and appointed his inheritance for the jackals of the wilderness." (Malachi 1:2-3).

The Lord illustrates His love for Israel by contrasting it with His treatment of Esau, the brother of Israel. Here were two brothers. They were from the same mother and the same father. They were twins. Yet the Lord showed His love to one and not to the other.

It is not that Jacob was a better man than Esau. Jacob was actually something of a scoundrel. He was a cheat and a trickster. His name literally meant "heel-grabber" and translated to something akin to our colloquial phrase when we describe one who is pulling my leg. Jacob was shown the favor of God, not because he earned or deserved that favor, but merely as a manifestation of the unmerited grace of God.

God says, "I loved you when you were unlovable. You therefore ought to respond in gratitude and thanksgiving."

There is a lesson here about the grace of God. Grace properly understood does not lead to licentious living. A true understanding and application of God's grace is a motivation for godly living.

THE PROBLEM OF MEDIOCRITY

> *"A son honors his father, and a servant his master. Then if I am a father, where is My honor? And if I am a master, where is My respect?" says the Lord of hosts to you, O priests who despise My name. But you say, "How have we despised Thy name?"*
>
> *7 You are presenting defiled food upon My altar. But you say, "How have we defiled Thee?" In that you say, "The table of the Lord is to be despised."*
>
> *8 "But when you present the blind for sacrifice, is it not evil? And when you present the lame and sick, is it not evil? Why not offer it to your governor? Would he be pleased with you? Or would he receive you kindly?" says the Lord of hosts.*
>
> *9 "But now will you not entreat God's favor, that He may be gracious to us? With such an offering on your part, will He receive any of you kindly?" says the Lord of hosts. (Malachi 1:6-9).*

The Lord brings forth a charge against His people. It is a charge of mediocrity. They are coming to the Lord with their offerings, but they use only the lame and the sick for those offerings. They are like the rancher who said, "I have a herd of cattle and I've decided to donate one to the Lord's work this Sunday." But that Saturday evening, one of the cows kicked through the fence, got out of the pasture and was hit and killed by a passing truck. When the rancher heard of it, he shook his head and muttered, "It sure is a shame that the Lord's cow was killed!"

C. S. Lewis pointed out that the worship of the Lord and the understanding of His truths are either the most important endeavor to which the human soul can aspire or else they are completely worthless. The only thing they cannot be is mildly important. If your worship is mediocre, there is a corresponding problem with your faith. You are like the one that James describes as a double-minded man, unstable in all his ways.

Steve Brown used to be the Senior Pastor of Key Biscayne Presbyterian Church. He tells of what happened when it was reported that President Richard Nixon was going to show up at the worship service. Everyone showed up to church that Sunday and the Sanctuary was packed. When it became apparent that Nixon wasn't going to show up, some of the people started to leave. Brown quipped, "The president may not be here, but there is someone here who is a lot more important and a lot more powerful."

What would be your reaction if you found out that the President of the United States was coming to dinner? The red carpet would be rolled out. The best china would be brought out to the table. No expense would be too great. How does your worship match up to such a standard?

THE PROBLEM OF DIVORCE

> *"For I hate divorce," says the Lord, the God of Israel, "and him who covers his garment with wrong," says the Lord of hosts. "So take heed to your spirit, that you do not deal treacherously." (Malachi 2:16).*

To understand the issue of divorce and how it had come about, we have to go back to the book of Ezra to see the first two migrations back to the land. Because of the long, hard journey, there had evidently been more young men to make the journey than there had been young women. Many more of the Jews remained in Mesopotamia and still other Jewish communities were growing up in Egypt and in other parts of the world.

If you are a young man who has returned to the land and you desire to take a wife and there is a distinct shortage of marriageable women to be found among the Jews, then where do you turn? They began to take wives from among the non-Jewish peoples.

Alarmed at this situation, Ezra goes to pray to the Lord. He prays a prayer of repentance. While he is praying, someone makes a suggestion.

"So now let us make a covenant with our God to put away all the wives and their children, according to the counsel of my lord and of those who tremble at the commandment of our God; and let it be done according to the law." (Ezra 10:3).

Ezra comes out from the house of prayer, hears the decision and agrees with it. As bad as divorce was, Ezra concluded that it was much worse to bring a curse on the covenant community. The motion had been made, it was seconded and put to a vote.

Only Jonathan the son of Asahel and Jahzeiah the son of Tikvah opposed this, with Meshullam and Shabbethai the Levite supporting them. (Ezra 10:15).

There was a very small dissenting vote. Were the minority right or wrong? The Bible does not say. It is uncommon to see a dissenting vote in the Bible. Do you remember the last one previous to this? It was in the days of Joshua and Caleb. Everyone else wanted to abandon the proposal to enter the Promised Land. Only two people disagreed.

There is a lesson here. There are times when the minority vote is correct. They might not be seen to be correct until much later. That is okay. You be sure to be faithful, even if you are in the minority.

We are not told here who was right and who was wrong. But we are told that this issue had lasting repercussions. It is entirely possible that people now were using the issue of past practice as an excuse to dissolve their marriages.

The same thing is taking place in the church today. If statistics are correct, the church in America has reached the point where divorce statistics have nearly caught up with those of the pagans. We need to model holy marriages before the world.

- Are you presently married? Make a commitment today (especially if you are married to a Christian) that the two of you are going to remain married, no matter what. Make a commitment to remove the word "divorce" from your vocabulary as it relates to your marriage.

- Are you presently separated or divorced? It may be that reconciliation is possible. But if it is not, note that there is hope that is going to be presented before the end of this book. The hope of forgiveness and comfort.

But having said that, we need to point out that divorce is always the result of sin on someone's part and sin always has lasting repercussions. For better or for worse, the divorces that had taken place in Ezra's day were still resounding with echos upon the failed marriages that are addressed here by Malachi. Husbands and wives, you are leaving a legacy to those who will come after you. Make it a legacy of loyalty and commitment and love.

THE COMING OF THE LORD

> *"Behold, I am going to send My messenger, and he will clear the way before Me. And the Lord, whom you seek, will suddenly come to His temple; and the messenger of the covenant, in whom you delight, behold, He is coming," says the Lord of hosts. (Malachi 3:1).*

Throughout the prophets, we have seen promise after promise that the Lord is going to come. But here we are told of the coming of one who would precede the coming of the Lord. It is the *messenger* - the "Malachi" of God.

The duty of this messenger would be to clear the way before the Lord. He would be a forerunner. He would get the people ready to meet the Lord. They would meet Him when He comes suddenly to His temple. We can recall the vividness of the description with which the Gospels describe the entrance of Jesus into the Temple. Coins clatter. Tables are overturned. A whiplash cracks. The Lord has come suddenly to His Temple.

The warning here is evident. It is that when the Lord comes, He is to come in judgment. His judgment is against those whose relationship with Him has been characterized by mediocrity. And yet, in the midst of this warning, there is a promise of hope.

HEALING IN HIS WINGS

> *But for you who fear My name the sun of righteousness will rise with healing in its wings; and you will go forth and skip about like calves from the stall. (Malachi 4:2).*

What does this mean when it says that the Lord has wings? The phrase translated "in his wings" also carries the idea of "corners" or an "outer edge." It is often used this way to speak of literal wings (Genesis 1:21; 7:14;

777

Exodus 19:4; 25:20; 37:9; Leviticus 1:17). But it can also be used to speak of the "corners" of a person's robe. These outer corners of the robe came to be known as a person's "wings."

- In 1 Samuel 24:4 we read *that David arose and cut off the **edge** of Saul's robe secretly*
- Deuteronomy 22:12 *"You shall make yourself tassels on the four **corners** of your garment with which you cover yourself.*
- Deuteronomy 22:30 *"A man shall not take his father's wife so that he shall not uncover his father's **skirt**."*
- Ruth 3:9 - *And he said, "Who are you?" And she answered, "I am Ruth your maid. So spread your **covering** over your maid, for you are a close relative."*

In what way is there healing in the Lord's wings? One significant fulfillment of this prophecy is to be found in Matthew 9:20 where a woman who had been suffering from a hemorrhage for twelve years, came up behind Jesus and touched the **fringe** of His cloak. Do you see it? She touched His wings and in them she found healing. This language is reminiscent of something Jesus said during his last week before his crucifixion. He looked over the city of Jerusalem and He wept.

> *"O Jerusalem, Jerusalem, who kills the prophets and stones those who are sent to her! How often I wanted to gather your children together, the way a hen gathers her chicks under her wings, and you were unwilling. (Matthew 23:37).*

There is an invitation here. The offer that was made that day to Jerusalem is also made to you. You can come to Jesus today and find healing and mercy and forgiveness under His wings. Is there a place of hurt in your life today? A place of dislocation? A place of need? The answer is found the One who came with healing in His wings.

Bibliography

Aharoni, Yohanan & Avi-Yonah, Michael,
1978   *The MacMillan Bible Atlas Revised Edition*, New York, NY: MacMillan

Allison, Dale C., Jr.
1997   *The New Moses: A Matthean Typology*. Minneapolis, MN: Fortress

Arnold, Bill T. & Beyer, Bryan E.
2002   *Readings from the Ancient Near East*. Grand Rapid, MI: Baker Academic.

Boice, James Montgomery
1983   *The Minor Prophets: An Expositional Commentary: Hosea-Jonah, Volume 1*, Zondervan Publishing House, Grand Rapids, MI
1986   *Minor Prophets: An Expositional Commentary: Micah-Malachi, Volume 2*, Zondervan Publishing House, Grand Rapids, MI

Chisholm, Robert B. Jr.
1998   *From Exegesis to Exposition: A Practical Guide to Using Biblical Hebrew*; Baker Books, Grand Rapids, MI
2003   *Handbook on the Prophets*. Grand Rapids, MI: Baker Academic

Constable, Thomas L.
2007   *Notes on Zechariah*. Garland, TX: Sonic Light

Dillard, Raymond B. & Tremper Longman III
1994   *An Introduction to the Old Testament*. Grand Rapids, MI: Zondervan

Edersheim, Alfred
1979   *The Temple*. Grand Rapids, MI: Eerdmans

Fields, Weston W.
1976   *Unformed and Unfilled*. Nutley, NJ: Presbyterian & Reformed

Gaebelein, Frank E., Ed
1992   *The Expositor's Bible Commentary: Old Testament Set, 7 Volumes*. Grand Rapids, MI: Zondervan

Harris, R. Laird & Archer, Gleason L. Jr. & Waltke, Bruce K.
1980   *Theological Wordbook of the Old Testament*. Chicago, IL: Moody

Hays, J. Daniel
2005   "Reconsidering the Height of Goliath." *Journal of the Evangelical Theological Society.* Vol 48:4.

Jensen, Irving
1978   *Jensen's Survey of the Old Testament*. Chicago, IL: Moody

Josephus, Flavius
2008   *The Works of Flavius Josephus*. Translated by William Whitson. Wesley Center Online: http://wesley.nnu.edu/biblical_studies/josephus/

Keil, C. F. & F. Diltzsch
1975   *Commentary on the Old Testament*, translated from the German, Grand Rapids, MI: Eerdmans

Klein, Meredith
1968   *By Oath Consigned: A Reinterpretation of the Covenant Signs of Circumcision and Baptism*. Grand Rapids, MI: Eerdmans
2001   *Glory in Our Midst: A Bibilical-Theological understanding of Zechariah*. Eugene, OR: Wipf & Stock Publishers

Merrill, Eugene H.
1987   *Kingdom of Priests: A History of Old Testament Israel*. Grand Rapids, MI: Baker

Morris, Henry
1976   *The Genesis Record: A Scientific and Devotional Commentary on the Book of Beginnings*. Grand Rapids, MI: Baker

Pratt, Richard L., Jr.
1990   *He Gave Us Stories: The Bible Student's Guide to Interpreting Old Testament Narratives*. Brentwood, TN: Holgemuth & Hyatt

Pritchard, James B. (Editor)
1987   *The Harper Atlas of the Bible*, New York, NY: Harper & Row

Rendsburg, Gary
1986   *The Redaction of Genesis.* Winona Lake, IN: Eisenbrauns
2006a *The Book of Genesis, Volumes 1-2.* Cantilly, VA: The Teaching Company

Robertson, O. Palmer
1980   *Christ of the Covenants.* Phillipsburg, NJ: Presbyterian & Reformed
2004   *The Christ of the Prophets*; P&R Publishing, Philipsburg, NJ

Schmidt, Dan
2002   *Unexpected Wisdom: Major Insights from the Minor Prophets.* Baker Books, Grand Rapids, MI

Tenney, Merrill C., Ed.
1975   *The Zondervan Pictorial Encyclopedia of the Bible, 5 Volumes.* Grand Rapids, MI: Zondervan

Thiele, Edwin R.
1977   *A Chronology of the Hebrew Kings.* Grand Rapids, MI: Zondervan

Waltke, Bruce K. & Fredricks, Cathi J.
2001   *Genesis.* Grand Rapids, MI: Zondervan

Whitcomb, John C. Jr. & Morris, Henry M.
1961   *The Genesis Flood: The Biblical Record and Its Scientific Implications.* Grand Rapids, MI: Baker

Made in the USA
Columbia, SC
08 December 2020